ISBN 978-1-5279-8489-9
PIBN 10926702

English
Français
Deutsche
Italiano
Español
Português

www.forgottenbooks.com

Mythology Photography **Fiction**
Fishing Christianity **Art** Cooking
Essays Buddhism Freemasonry
Medicine **Biology** Music **Ancient
Egypt** Evolution Carpentry Physics
Dance Geology **Mathematics** Fitness
Shakespeare **Folklore** Yoga Marketing
Confidence Immortality Biographies
Poetry **Psychology** Witchcraft
Electronics Chemistry History **Law**
Accounting **Philosophy** Anthropology
Alchemy Drama Quantum Mechanics
Atheism Sexual Health **Ancient History**
Entrepreneurship Languages Sport
Paleontology Needlework Islam
Metaphysics Investment Archaeology
Parenting Statistics Criminology
Motivational

No. 10404

United States
Circuit Court of Appeals
For the Ninth Circuit.

Vol

2347

UNITED STATES OF AMERICA,

Appellant,

vs.

PHILIP GREY SMITH, as Administrator with
will annexed of the Estate of Olive Wills Wigmore, Deceased, and J. A. WIGMORE,

Appellees.

Transcript of Record

Upon Appeal from the District Court of the United States
for the Southern District of California,
Central Division

FILED

MAY 2 5 1943

PAUL P. O'BRIEN,
CLERK

Rotary Colorprint, 590 Folsom St., San Francisco   60-5-19-43

INDEX

[Clerk's Note: When deemed likely to be of an important nature, errors or doubtful matters appearing in the original certified record are printed literally in italic; and, likewise, cancelled matter appearing in the original certified record is printed and cancelled herein accordingly. When possible, an omission from the text is indicated by printing in italic the two words between which the omission seems to occur.]

NAMES AND ADDRESSES OF ATTORNEYS:

For Appellant:

LEO V. SILVERSTEIN,

United States Attorney,

E. H. MITCHELL,

Asst. U. S. Attorney,

EUGENE HARPOLE,

Special Attorney, Bureau of Internal Revenue, 600 U. S. Post Office & Court House Bldg., Los Angeles, Calif.

For Appellees:

CLYDE R. BURR,

310 Security Title Insurance Building
530 West Sixth St.
Los Angeles, Calif. [1*]

---

*Page numbering appearing at foot of page of original certified Transcript of Record.

In the District Court of the United States in and for the Southern District of California

No. 2499-B.H.

UNITED STATES OF AMERICA,
a corporate body politic,

Plaintiff,

vs.

THE ESTATE OF OLIVE WILLS WIG-MORE, Deceased; PHILIP GREY SMITH, as Administrator with will annexed of the ESTATE OF OLIVE WILLS WIGMORE, Deceased, and J. A. WIGMORE,

Defendants.

COMPLAINT

COMPLAINT FOR RECOVERY OF INCOME TAXES

Plaintiff complains of the defendants and alleges:

I.

That the plaintiff is a corporate and sovereign body politic.

II.

That Plaintiff alleges upon information and belief that the defendants, J. A. Wigmore and Philip Grey Smith, as Administrator with the will annexed of the Estate of Olive Wills Wigmore are now and at all times herein mentioned have been [2] residents of the State of California, and within this judicial District.

III.

That Olive Wills Wigmore died on March 1, 1941, a resident of the City of Pasadena, County of Los Angeles, State of California. That letters of administration of her estate were issued by the Probate Division of the Superior Court of the State of California in and for the County of Los Angeles in the probate proceeding entitled In the Matter of the Estate of Olive Wills Wigmore, Deceased, Number 203,316.

IV.

That the defendant, Philip Grey Smith, is the duly appointed, qualified and acting Administrator with will annexed of the Estate of Olive Wills Wigmore.

V.

That the decedent, Olive Wills Wigmore, and J. A. Wigmore filed a joint Federal income tax return for the taxable year 1933. That on the 16th day of October, 1936, the Commissioner of Internal Revenue, on his October 1936 number 3 assessment list, page 1, line 7, for the 18th Collection District of Ohio, assessed 1933 income taxes, together with interest thereon, against Olive Wills Wigmore and J. A. Wigmore, jointly in the aggregate amount of $2,981.27. That notice and demand for the payment of said tax and interest thereon was issued to said taxpayers, Olive Wills Wigmore and J. A. Wigmore, by the Collector of Internal Revenue for the 18th Collection District of Ohio on October 22, 1936 and November 9, 1936. [3]

VI.

: That notwithstanding said notice and demand for payment the taxpayers, Olive Wills Wigmore and J. A. Wigmore and Philip Grey Smith, as administrator with the will annexed of the Estate of Olive Wills Wigmore, have wholly failed, neglected and refused to pay said 1933 income tax or the interest thereon or any part thereof and that the whole thereof is now unpaid.

VII.

That on March 15, 1937, the Collector of Internal Revenue for the Sixth Collection District at Los Angeles recorded a notice of lien securing the payment of said 1933 income tax in the office of the County Recorder of Los Angeles County, California, and with the clerk of the United States District Court in and for the Southern District of California.

FOR A SECOND CAUSE OF ACTION PLAINTIFF ALLEGES

I.

' Plaintiff realleges and repeats the contents of Paragraphs I, II, III and IV above.

II.

That on the 12th day of April, 1941, the Commissioner of Internal Revenue, on his March 1941 assessment list for the 18th Collection District of Ohio, Account #202878, assessed income taxes against Olive Wills Wigmore for the taxable year 1940 in the sum of $2,321.89, of which tax there was paid the sum of $580.48 on March 14, 1941, and that there now remains unpaid of said tax a balance of $1,741.41, together with interest thereon as provided by law. That notice and demand for the payment of said tax was issued to the taxpayer by the Collector of Internal Revenue at Los Angeles, California, on July 21, 1941.

[4]

III.

Notwithstanding said notice and demand, the balance of said 1940 income tax in the sum of $1,741.41 has not been paid, and that the whole of said balance, together with interest thereon as provided by law, remains assessed and unpaid.

IV.

That the commencement of this action is requested and sanctioned by the United States Commissioner of Internal Revenue and authorized by the Attorney General of the United States.

Wherefore, Plaintiff prays for Judgment against the defendants as follows:

I.

For the sum of $2,981.27, together with interest as provided by law, on account of the unpaid income taxes of Olive Wills Wigmore and J. A. Wigmore for the taxable year 1933.

II.

For the sum of $1,741.41 against the defendants, Estate of Olive Wills Wigmore, Deceased, and Philip Grey Smith, as administrator with the will annexed of the Estate of Olive Wills Wigmore, Deceased, together with interest thereon as provided by law, on account of the unpaid income taxes of Olive Wills Wigmore for the taxable year 1940.

III.

For Plaintiff's costs.

> LEO V. SILVERSTEIN,
> United States Attorney.
> E. M. MITCHELL,
> Asst. U. S. Attorney.
> EUGENE HARPOLE,
> Special Attorney, Bureau of
> Internal Revenue.
> By EUGENE HARPOLE,
> Attorneys for Plaintiff.

[Endorsed]: Filed Oct. 15, 1942. [5]

[Title of District Court and Cause]

ANSWER OF PHILIP GREY SMITH, AS ADMINISTRATOR WITH-WILL-ANNEXED OF THE ESTATE OF OLIVE WILLS WIGMORE, DECEASED, TO THE COMPLAINT

Comes now Philip Grey Smith, as Administrator with-will-annexed of the Estate of Olive Wills Wigmore, deceased, and, for answer to the complaint herein, admits, denies and alleges as follows:

FIRST DEFENSE TO THE FIRST CAUSE OF ACTION:

I.

Said defendant admits the allegations contained

in paragraphs I, II, III and IV of said cause of action; alleges that he is without knowledge or information sufficient to form a belief as to the truth of any of the allegations contained in paragraph V of the first cause of action, except that said defendant admits that decedent, Olive Wills Wigmore, and J. A. Wigmore filed [6] a joint Federal income tax return for the taxable year 1933; alleges that he is without knowledge or information sufficient to form a belief as to the truth of any of the allegations contained in paragraph VI of the first cause of action; alleges that he is without knowledge or information sufficient to form a belief as to the truth of any of the allegations contained in paragraph VII of said cause of action.

SECOND DEFENSE TO THE FIRST CAUSE OF ACTION:

I.

That the said Olive Wills Wigmore, deceased, duly and regularly filed her income tax return for the taxable year 1933 on March 13, 1934, in the office of the Collector of Internal Revenue in Cleveland, Ohio. That no assessment in connection with any of the taxes of the said Olive Wills Wigmore for the said taxable year of 1933 was entered by the Commissioner of Internal Revenue prior to the 16th day of March, 1936.

THIRD DEFENSE TO THE FIRST CAUSE OF ACTION:

I.

The right of action set forth in the first cause

of action in the complaint did not accrue within six years next before the commencement of this action.

FIRST DEFENSE TO THE SECOND CAUSE OF ACTION:

I.

Defendant admits all of the allegations in paragraphs I, II and III of said cause of action.

II.

Said defendant alleges that he is without knowledge or information sufficient to form a belief as to the truth of the allegations contained in paragraph IV of said cause of action. [7]

Wherefore said defendant prays that plaintiff take nothing by this complaint herein; that said defendant have his costs herein and whatever other relief is proper.

CLYDE R. BURR,
> Attorney for Philip Grey Smith, Administrator with-will-annexed of the Estate of Olive Wills Wigmore, Deceased.

(Duly Verified.)

Received copy of the within Answer this 9th day of November, 1942.

EUGENE HARPOLE,
Attorney for Plaintiff.

[Endorsed]: Filed Nov. 9, 1942. [8]

INDIVIDUAL INCOME TAX RETURN

FOR NET INCOMES FROM SALARIES OR WAGES OF MORE THAN $5,000
AND INCOMES FROM BUSINESS, PROFESSION, RENTS, OR SALE OF PROPERTY

For Calendar Year 1933

File This Return With the Collector of Internal Revenue for Your District on or Before March 15, 1934

PRINT NAME AND ADDRESS PLAINLY BELOW

J. A. Wigmore and Olive Wills Wigmore,
(Name)

36
(Street and number, or rural route)

Chesterland, Geauga County, Ohio
(Post office) (County) (State)

citizens

Cleveland

joint

yes

cash

INCOME

J. A. Wigmore Land Company,	1,000.00		
J. A. Wigmore Company,	3,000.00		
1927 Euclid Realty Company (commission)	500.00	4,500 00	
Interest on Bank Deposits, Notes, Corporation Bonds, etc.		450 00	
Rents and Royalties		78 55	
(b) Profit or Loss from Sale of Other Assets held two years or less		500 00	
Dividends on Stock of: (a) Domestic Corporations subject to taxation under Title I of 1932 Act		1,308 64	
Other Income (See schedule)		22,686 12	

DEDUCTIONS

Interest Paid	3,613 86	
Legal Fees	11,004 00	
Other Deductions Authorized by Law See schedule	22,457 55	

Net Income (Item 12 minus Item 19) Loss

COMPUTATION OF TAX

Net Income Subject to Tax	Loss	
Dividends	1,308 64	
Personal Exemption	2,500 00	
Total of Items	808 64	

CONSENT FIXING PERIOD OF LIMITATION UPON
ASSESSMENT OF INCOME AND PROFITS TAX

BUREAU OF INTERNAL REVENUE
1936 FEB 3   AM 11 42
MAILING DIV.

REC

JAN 1

REVENUE A
CLEVE!

Cleveland, Ohio, January 17, 1936

In pursuance of the provisions of existing Internal Revenue Laws

_____ J. A. Wigmore _____, a taxpayer

or taxpayers) of _Chesterland, Geauga County, Ohio_____, and
the Commissioner of Internal Revenue hereby consent and agree as follows:

That the amount of any income, excess-profits, or war-profits taxes
due under any return (or returns) made by or on behalf of the above-named

taxpayer (or taxpayers) for the taxable year (or years) _____1935_____,
under existing acts, or under prior revenue acts, may be assessed at any
time on or before June 30, 1937, except that, if a notice of a deficiency
in tax is sent to said taxpayer (or taxpayers) by registered mail on or
before said date, then the time for making any assessment as aforesaid
shall be extended beyond the said date by the number of days during which
the Commissioner is prohibited from making an assessment and for sixty
days thereafter.

J. A. Wigmore
_____ Taxpayer*.

_____ Taxpayer*.

[SEAL**]   By _____

Guy T. Helvering
_____ Commissioner of Internal Revenue

By _EGC_   _January 31, 19_
_____ (Date)

*If this consent is executed with respect to a year for which a joint return of a
husband and wife was filed, it must be signed by both spouses, except that one spouse
may sign as the agent for the other. Whenever a consent is executed by an agent, such
action must be specifically authorized by a power of attorney, which, if not previously
filed, must accompany the consent.
**If this consent is executed on behalf of a corporation, it shall be signed with the
corporate name, followed by the signature and title of such officer or officers of the
corporation as are empowered under the laws of the State in which the corporation is
located to sign for the corporation, in addition to which the seal of the corporation
must be affixed   Where the corporation has no seal, the consent must be accompanied
by a certified copy of the resolution passed by the board of directors, giving the
officer authority to sign the consent

U S GOVERNMENT PRINTING OFFICE   D—12780

J

[Endorsed]: _Filed Dec. 21, '_

PLAINTIFF'S EXHIBIT No. 3

Form 23C-1
Treasury Department
Internal Revenue Service
Form approved by Comptroller General U. S.,
Aug. 21, 1928

Assessment Certificate
Commissioner's Assessment List

18th District of Ohio   Month—October #3   Year—1936

Additional Assessments made by Commissioner:........Personal $19592.05
                                                    ....Corporation ....$ 557.83

Total Assessments $20149.88

I hereby certify that I have made inquiries, determinations, and assessments of taxes, penalties, etc., of the above classification specified in these lists, and find that the amounts of taxes, penalties, etc., stated as corrected and as specified in the supplementary pages of this list made by me are due from the individuals, firms, and corporations opposite whose names such amounts are placed, and that the amount chargeable to the collector is as above.

Dated at Washington, D. C.

Office of Commissioner of Internal Revenue, October 16, 1936.

CHAS. T. RUSSELL,
Commissioner of Internal Revenue.

[Endorsed with illegible initials.]

[18]

District—1 Ohio   Income Tax   , List   October #3 1936   Page No. 1

(Classification.)

	Old Balance	Date	Debit	Credit	New Balance	Remarks
J. A. Wigmore & Mrs. Olive		Int to 10-16-36	2580.82		2981.27	1933 656397
Wills Wigmore			400.45			272C WVR RAR
Husband and Wife						OL 7-9-36
956 S Orange Grove Ave						
Pasadena Calif						
Oct 17 P#3						

[Endorsed]:   Filed Dec. 21, 1942.

[Title of District Court and Cause.]

OPINION

In this action the government seeks to recover income taxes for the years 1933 and 1940, from the Estate of Olive Wills Wigmore. The Administrator with will annexed admits the liability of the estate for the year 1940 but alleges that the recovery for the year 1933 is [19] barred by the statute of limitations. The government contends that while the income tax was not assessed until 1936, the taxpayer, Olive Wills Wigmore, had executed a waiver the pertinent part of which is as follows:

"Consent Fixing Period of Limitations Upon Assessment of Income and Profit Tax.

Cleveland, Ohio, January 17, 1936.

"In pursuance of the provisions of existing Internal Revenue Laws J. A. Wigmore, a taxpayer (or taxpayers) of Chesterland, Coauga County, Ohio, and the Commissioner of Internal Revenue hereby *consent agree* as follows:

"That the amount of any income, excess-profits, or war-profits taxes due under any return (or returns) made by or on behalf of the above-named taxpayer (or taxpayers) for the taxable year (or years) 1933 under existing acts, or under prior revenue acts, may be assessed at any time on or before June 30, 1937, except that, if a notice of a deficiency in tax is sent to said taxpayer (or taxpayers) by registered mail on or before said date, then the time for making any assessment as aforesaid shall be extended be-

yond the said date by the number of days during which the Commissioner is prohibited from
making an assessment and for sixty days thereafter.

[Seal]   J. A. WIGMORE
                    Taxpayer
           OLIVE W. WIGMORE
                    Taxpayer
           By _____
           GUY T. HELVERING
                    Commissioner of Internal
                    Revenue
           By A. C. C.—January 31, 1936
                                              [20]

"If this consent is executed with respect to
a year for which a joint return of a husband and
wife was filed, it must be signed by both spouses,
except that one spouse may sign as the agent for
the other.   *   *   *"

The sole question for determination in this action
is whether or not the Estate of Olive Wills Wigmore
is bound by the above waiver. The administrator contends that inasmuch as Mrs. Wigmore is not named
in the document she is not bound by the same, on the
other hand, the government claims that as there was
but one return filed in 1933 by the Wigmores, it was
undoubtedly her intent in signing said waiver to be
bound thereby.

The evidence discloses that a joint return was filed
in the year 1933 by Mr. and Mrs. Wigmore and each
signed the same.

While such waiver or consent is not a contract but

essentially a voluntary, unilateral waiver of a defense by the taxpayer, (Florsheim Bros., etc. v. United States, 280 U. S. 453) at the same time, I see no reason why the rules applicable to the construction of a contract should not apply to the construction and affect of a waiver, (Stange v. U. S. 282 U. S. 270 at page 275).

There appears to be a pausity of authorities dealing with the effect of an agreement signed by a party not named therein as a party, but in 6 R. C. L. page 875, I find the following language used:

"* * * If a contract states distinctly that it is between two designated parties, the fact that another person's name appears at the end of the contract with that of the parties does not make it his contract. * * *"

Citing as authority for such statement the case of Shriner v. Craft, 166 Ala. 146, 51 So. 884, wherein the court made the following statement:

"The first assignments of error insisted on (numbered 1 and 2) are to the sustaining of the demurrer of Mary R. Shriner, on the ground that the complaint shows on its face that Mary R. Shriner was not a party to the contract sued on, and the third, fourth, and fifth assignments relate to the same subject, to wit, to the refusal of the [21] court to grant the motion for the discontinuance of the case, because of the amendment of the complaint, by striking out the name of said Mary R. Shriner.

"There was no error in either action of the

court. The contract sued on is set out in the complaint, and it states distinctly that it is between
W. A. Shriner and John Craft. The fact that
Mary R. Shriner's name appears at the end of
the contract with W. A. Shriner does not make
it her contract. * * *"

(See also 17 C.J.S. p. 803).

If the above rule is to prevail the estate of Mrs.
Wigmore is not liable.

The only analogous federal case called to my attention is the case of Commissioner v. Bryson, 79 Fed.
(2d) 397, wherein Judge Denman in his concurring
opinion said:

> "I concur in the decision. The body of the
> waiver produced by the Commissioner purports
> to be an agreement between the Bryson-Robin-
> son Corporation and the Commissioner. It is
> on a printed form, furnished by the Commis-
> sioner, and the only insertions possibly to be
> attributed to the taxpayer to whom it is tendered
> are its name in the body of the instrument and
> the signature. It was not signed in the corpo-
> rate name. The signer Bryson described himself
> to be a "former secretary". In an accompanying
> letter he disclaims authority to act for the cor-
> poration. The wording of document contains no
> agreement on the part of Bryson individually.

(Underscoring supplied)

Whether the omission of the name of Mrs. Wigmore from the body of the waiver was due to care-

lessness, or the liability for taxes rested primarily upon the husband and originally there was no intention to bind the wife by said waiver or consent, (Cole v. Commissioner, 81 Fed. (2d) 485) is mere surmise.

In Crowe v. Commissioner, 86 Fed. (2d) 796, the following statement is made:

"* * * It is clear that if respondent's contention is correct, it must be by reason of implications arising from the language of the statute and not by any clear expression of the lawmakers. Under such circumstances, the doubt must be construed in favor of the taxpayer." [22]

Judge Denman in Erskine v. U. S. 84 Fed. (2d) 690-1 said:

"Such revenue acts must be construed strictly in favor of the appellant sought to be charged as importer. He is 'entitled to the benefit of even a doubt'. Tariff Act 1897, 30 Stat. 151; United States v. Riggs, 203 U. S. 136, 139, 27 S. Ct. 39, 40, 51 L. Ed. 127; Hartranft v. Wiegmann, 121 U. S. 609, 616, 7 S. Ct. 1240, 30 L. Ed. 1012; Miller v. Standard Nut Margarine Co. 284 U. S. 498, 508, 52 S. Ct. 260, 76 L. Ed. 422."

(See also Miller, Collector v. Standard Nut Margarine Co. 284 U. S. 498-508 and Commissioner v. Bryson, 79 Fed. (2d) 397-403).

It appears to me that there is a serious doubt whether Mrs. Wigmore's Estate is bound by said waiver, and under the foregoing authorities said doubt should be resolved in favor of her estate.

The burden is upon the plaintiff, by a preponderance of the evidence, to establish that the statute of limitations has been waived. This the plaintiff has failed to do.

Plaintiff is entitled to judgment on its second cause of action as prayed for, but will take nothing on its first cause of action.

Plaintiff is directed to submit without delay proposed findings and judgment in accordance with this opinion.

Dated: Los Angeles, California, January 5, 1943.

BEN HARRISON,

Judge.

[Endorsed]: Filed Jan. 5, 1943. [23]

————

[Title of District Court and Cause.]

FINDINGS OF FACT AND CONCLUSIONS OF LAW

The above-entitled action came on for trial before the Court, sitting without a jury, at Los Angeles, California, on December 21, 1942. Plaintiff appeared by Leo V. Silverstein, United States Attorney for the Southern Division of California, Edward H. Mitchell and Edward J. O'Connor, Assistant United States Attorneys for said District, and Eugene Harpole, Special Attorney, Bureau of Internal Revenue. The defendants, The Estate of Olive Wills Wigmore and Philip Grey Smith, as Administrator of the Estate of Olive Wills Wigmore, Deceased, appeared by Burr & Smith, their attorneys. The defendant J. A. Wigmore, never having been served with process, made no appearance. Documentary evidence was introduced and thereafter the matter submitted to the Court upon briefs, and the Court having considered the evidence and the briefs submitted on behalf of the respective [24] parties, makes the following—

FINDINGS OF FACT

I.

That the plaintiff is a corporate **and** sovereign body politic.

II.

That the defendants, The Estate of Olive Wills Wigmore, Deceased, and Philip Grey Smith, as Administrator with the will annexed of the Estate of Olive Wills Wigmore, Deceased, are and at all times herein mentioned have been residents of the State of California and of this judicial district.

III.

That the commencement of the above-entitled action was requested and sanctioned by the United States Commissioner of Internal Revenue and was authorized by the Attorney General of the United States.

IV.

That Olive Wills Wigmore died on March 1, 1941, a resident of the City of Pasadena, County of Los Angeles, State of California; that letters of administration of her estate were issued by the Probate Division of the Superior Court of the State of

California in and for the County of Los Angeles
in the probate proceeding entitled "In the Matter
of the Estate of Olive Wills Wigmore, Deceased,
No. 203,316."

V.

That the defendant Philip Grey Smith is the
duly appointed, qualified and acting Administrator
with Will Annexed of the Estate of Olive Wills
Wigmore.

VI.

That the decedent Olive Wills Wigmore and her
husband, J. A. Wigmore, filed a joint Federal income tax return for the taxable year 1933 on March
13, 1934, disclosing no tax.

VII.

That thereafter, and on the 17th day of January, 1936, J. A. Wigmore and Olive Wills Wigmore
signed a consent fixing the period of limitations on
assessment of income and profits tax, which consent was in the words and figures following: [25]

"Consent Fixing Period of Limitations Upon
Assessment of Income and Profits Tax
Cleveland, Ohio, January 17, 1936

"In pursuance of the provisions of existing
Internal Revenue Laws J. A. Wigmore, a taxpayer (or taxpayers) of Chesterland, Coauga
County, Ohio, and the Commissioner of Internal Revenue hereby consent and agree as follows:

"That the amount of any income, excess-
profits, or war-profits taxes due under any re-

turn (or returns) made by or on behalf of the above-named taxpayer (or taxpayers) for the taxable year (or years) 1933 under existing acts, or under prior revenue acts, may be assessed at any time on or before June 30, 1937, except that, if a notice of a deficiency in tax is sent to said taxpayer (or taxpayers) by registered mail on or before said date, then the time for making any assessment as aforesaid shall be extended beyond the said date by the number of days during which the Commissioner is prohibited from making an assessment and for sixty days thereafter.

J. A. WIGMORE
Taxpayer
OLIVE W. WIGMORE
Taxpayer
By ....
[Seal]   GUY T. HELVERING
Commissioner of Internal
Revenue
By A. C. C.
January 31, 1936

"If this consent is executed with respect to a year for which a joint return of a husband and wife was filed, it must be signed by both spouses, except that one spouse may sign as the agent for the other. * * * "

VIII.

That on the 16th day of October, 1936, the Commissioner of Internal Revenue, on his October, 1936,

No. 3 Assessment List, page 1, line 7, for the Eighteenth Collection District of Ohio, assessed 1933
income taxes, together with interest thereon against
said Olive Wills Wigmore and J. A. Wigmore,
jointly, in the aggregate amount of $2,981.27. [26]

IX.

That no part of the Federal income taxes assessed against Olive Wills Wigmore and J. A.
Wigmore, jointly, for the year 1933, or interest
thereon, has been paid.

X.

That on the 12th day of April, 1941, the Commissioner of Internal Revenue, on his March, 1941,
Assessment List for the Eighteenth Collection District of Ohio, Account No. 202,878, assessed income
taxes against Olive Wills Wigmore for the taxable
year 1940 in the sum of $2,321.89, of which tax
there was paid the sum of $580.48 on March 14,
1941, and that there now remains unpaid of said
tax a balance of $1,741.41, together with interest
thereon as provided by law.

XI.

That Olive W. Wigmore did not consent that the
said income taxes for the taxable year 1933 could
be assessed on or before June 30, 1937, or at any
time after the 15th day of March, 1936.

From the foregoing Findings of Fact, the Court
draws the following—

CONCLUSIONS OF LAW

I.

That the consent or waiver of the statute of limitations signed by J. A. Wigmore and Olive W. Wigmore on January 17, 1936, was ineffective as to Olive Wills Wigmore and her estate and did not extend the time within which the Commissioner of Internal Revenue might assess income taxes against said Olive Wills Wigmore for the taxable year 1933.

II.

That the Commissioner of Internal Revenue was barred by the applicable statute of limitations from making any assessment of income taxes against Olive Wills Wigmore after the 15th day of March, 1936.

III.

That neither Olive Wills Wigmore, her estate nor the defendant, Philip Grey Smith, as Administrator with the Will Annexed of the Estate of Olive Wills [27] Wigmore, Deceased, is indebted to the plaintiff for any sum whatsoever on account of income taxes for the taxable year 1933.

IV.

That the defendants, The Estate of Olive Wills Wigmore, Deceased, and Philip Grey Smith, as Administrator with the Will Annexed of the Estate of Olive Wills Wigmore, Deceased, are indebted to the plaintiff for the sum of $1,741.41, together with interest provided by law, on account of the unpaid income taxes of said Olive Wills Wigmore for the taxable year 1940.

V.

That the plaintiff is entitled to judgment against the defendants, The Estate of Olive Wills Wigmore, Deceased, and Philip Grey Smith, as Administrator with the Will Annexed of the Estate of Olive Wills Wigmore, Deceased, in the sum of $1,741.41, together with interest thereon as provided by law, and for the plaintiff's costs to be taxed.

Dated: January 8, 1943.

BEN HARRISON
Judge.

Approved as to Form:

CLYDE R. BURR
Attorney for Defendants.

[Endorsed]: Filed Jan. 8, 1943. [28]

In the District Court of the United States in and
for the Southern District of California
Central Division

No. 2499-BH

UNITED STATES OF AMERICA, a corporate
body politic,

Plaintiff,

v.

THE ESTATE OF OLIVE WILLS WIGMORE,
DECEASED, PHILIP GREY SMITH, as
Administrator with the will annexed of the
Estate of OLIVE WILLS WIGMORE, De-
ceased, and J. A. WIGMORE,

Defendants.

JUDGMENT

The above-entitled case came on for trial before
the Court, sitting without a jury, at Los Angeles,
on the 21st day of December, 1942. Plaintiff appeared by Leo V. Silverstein, United States Attorney for the Southern Division of California, Edward H. Mitchell and Edward J. O'Connor, Assistant United States Attorneys for said District, and
Eugene Harpole, Special Attorney, Bureau of Internal Revenue. The defendants, The Estate of Olive
Wills Wigmore, Deceased, and Philip Grey Smith,
as Administrator of the Estate of Olive Wills Wigmore, Deceased, appeared by Burr & Smith, their
attorneys. The defendant J. A. Wigmore, never
having been served with process, made no appear-

ance. Documentary evidence was introduced and thereafter the matter submitted to the Court upon briefs, and the Court having rendered its opinion and entered its findings of fact and conclusions of law— [29]

Now, Therefore, It Is Ordered and Adjudged that the plaintiff have and recover judgment against the defendants, The Estate of Olive Wills Wigmore, Deceased, and Philip Grey Smith, as Administrator with the Will Annexed of the Estate of Olive Wills Wigmore, Deceased, for the sum of $1,741.41, principal, and $156.64, interest up to January 8, 1943, aggregating the total amount of $1,898.05, together with interest on the latter amount at the rate of 7% per annum from that date, on account of the unpaid income taxes of Olive Wills Wigmore for the taxable year 1940, and for plaintiff's costs, taxed in the sum of $...........

BEN HARRISON
Judge.

Approved as to Form:

CLYDE R. BURR
Attorney for Defendants.

Judgment entered Jan. 8, 1943. Docketed Jan. 8, 1943. Book C. O. # 13 Page 219. Edmund L. Smith, Clerk. By Murray E. Wire, Deputy.

[Endorsed]: Filed Jan. 8, 1943. [30]

[Title of District Court and Cause.]

NOTICE OF APPEAL.

Notice Is Hereby Given that the United States of America, the plaintiff above named, hereby appeals to the United States Circuit Court of Appeals for the Ninth Circuit from the final judgment entered in this action on January 8, 1943.

Dated: March 30, 1943.

> LEO V. SILVERSTEIN,
> U. S. Attorney,
> E. H. MITCHELL,
> Asst. U. S. Attorney,
> EUGENE HARPOLE,
> Special Attorney,
> Bureau of Internal Revenue.
> By EUGENE HARPOLE
> Attorneys for Plaintiff.

[Endorsed]: Filed and Mailed Copy to Philip Grey Smith, Atty. for Defts. Mar. 31, 1943. Edmund L. Smith, Clerk. By John A. Childress, Deputy Clerk. [31]

[Title of District Court and Cause.]

STATEMENT OF POINTS UPON WHICH PLAINTIFF INTENDS TO RELY UPON APPEAL.

The plaintiff, United States of America, designates the following as the points upon which it intends to rely upon appeal:

1. The District Court erred in its Finding of Fact numbered XI in that said Finding of Fact is not supported by the evidence before the Court and is contrary to the evidence before the Court and conflicts with the Court's Findings of Fact numbered VI and VII, which correctly embodied the evidence introduced. [32]

2. The District Court erred in its Conclusion of Law numbered I, for the reason that said Conclusion of Law is not supported by the Court's Findings of Fact and is repugnant to the Court's Findings of Fact numbered VI and VII.

3. The District Court erred in its Conclusion of Law numbered II for the reason that said Conelusion of Law is not supported by the Court's Findings of Fact and is repugnant to the Court's Findings of Fact numbered VI and VII.

4. The District Court erred in its Conclusion of Law numbered III for the reason that said Conclusion of Law is not supported by the Court's Findings of Fact and is repugnant to the Court's Findings of Fact numbered VI and VII.

5. The District Court erred in its Conclusions of Law numbered V for the reason that said Conclusion of Law is not supported by the Court's Findings of Fact and is repugnant to the Court's Findings of Fact numbered VI and VII.

6. The District Court erred in failing to conclude as a matter of law that the consent signed by Olive Wills Wigmore on the 17th day of January, 1936, and fully set forth in the Court's Finding of Fact numbered VII, was valid and binding upon

Olive Wills Wigmore and her estate and extended the time within which the Commissioner of Internal Revenue might assess income and excess profits taxes against her for the taxable year 1933 to and including June 30, 1937.

7. The District Court erred in entering Judgment in favor of the defendants and against the plaintiff for the reason that the evidence introduced and the Court's Findings of Fact numbered VI and VII require that as a matter of law Judgment should be entered for the plaintiff.

Dated: March 30, 1943.

LEO V. SILVERSTEIN,
U. S. Attorney,
E. H. MITCHELL,
Asst. U. S. Attorney,
EUGENE HARPOLE,
Special Attorney,
Bureau of Internal Revenue.
By EUGENE HARPOLE,
Attorneys for **Plaintiff.**

[Endorsed]: Filed Mar. 31, 1943. [33]

———

[Title of District Court and Cause.]

PLAINTIFF-APPELLANT'S DESIGNATION
OF RECORD ON APPEAL.

The Appellant, the **Plaintiff** in the above entitled action, hereby designates the following portions of the record, proceedings and evidence to be contained in the record on appeal in the above entitled action:

1. Complaint;
2. Answer:
3. Plaintiff's Exhibit 1, the 1933 income tax return of Olive Wills Wigmore;
4. Plaintiff's Exhibit 2, the waiver of Statute of Limitations; [34]
5. Plaintiff's Exhibit 3, the Commissioner's October No. 3, 1936 assessment list;
6. Opinion of District Court;
7. Findings of Fact and Conclusions of Law;
8. Judgment;
9. Notice of Appeal;
10. Statement of Points upon which plaintiff intends to rely upon appeal;
11. This designation;
12. Certificate of Clerk of the District Court.

Dated: March 30, 1943.

> LEO V. SILVERSTEIN,
> U. S. Attorney,
> E. H. MITCHELL,
> Asst. U. S. Attorney,
> EUGENE HARPOLE,
> Special Attorney,
> Bureau of Internal Revenue.
> By EUGENE HARPOLE,
> Attorneys for Plaintiff.

[Endorsed]: Filed Mar. 31, 1943. [35]

[Title of District Court and Cause.]

CERTIFICATE OF CLERK

I, Edmund L. Smith, Clerk of the District Court of the United States for the Southern District of California, do hereby certify that the foregoing pages numbered from 1 to 35 inclusive contain full, true and correct copies of: Complaint; Answer of Philip Grey Smith, as Administrator etc.; Plaintiff's Exhibits Nos. 1, 2 and 3; Opinion; Findings of Fact and Conclusions of Law; Judgment; Notice of Appeal; Statement of Points upon which Plaintiff Intends to Rely upon Appeal and Designation of Record on Appeal which constitutes the record on appeal to the United States Circuit Court of Appeals for the Ninth Circuit.

Witness my hand and the seal of said District Court this 14 day of April, A. D., 1943.

[Seal]   EDMUND L. SMITH
Clerk
By THEODORE HOCKE
Deputy Clerk.

[Endorsed]: No. 10404. United States Circuit Court of Appeals for the Ninth Circuit. United States of America, Appellant, vs. Philip Grey Smith, as Administrator with will annexed of the Estate of Olive Wills Wigmore, Deceased, and J. A. Wigmore, Appellees. Transcript of Record. Upon Appeal from the District Court of the United States for the Southern District of California, Central Division.

Filed April 15, 1943.

PAUL P. O'BRIEN,

Clerk of the United States Circuit Court of Appeals for the Ninth Circuit.

In the United States Circuit Court of Appeals
For the Ninth Circuit

No. 10404

UNITED STATES OF AMERICA, A CORPORATE BODY POLITIC,

Plaintiff,

vs.

THE ESTATE OF OLIVE WILLS WIGMORE, PHILIP GREY SMITH, as Administrator with will annexed of the Estate of Olive Wills Wigmore, deceased, and J. A. WIGMORE,

Defendants.

APPELLANT'S STATEMENT OF POINTS TO BE URGED UPON APPEAL.

1.   That the District Court erred in its Finding

of Fact numbered XI in that said Finding of Fact is not supported by the evidence before the Court and is contrary to the evidence before the Court and conflicts with the Court's Findings of Fact numbered VI and VII, which correctly embodied the evidence introduced.

2. That the District Court erred in its Conclusion of Law numbered I, for the reason that said Conclusion of Law is not supported by the Court's Findings of Fact and is repugnant to the Court's Findings of Fact numbered VI and VII.

3. That the District Court erred in its Conclusion of Law numbered II, for the reason that said Conclusion of Law is not supported by the Court's Findings of Fact and is repugnant to the Court's Findings of Fact numbered VI and VII.

4. That the District Court erred in its Conclusion of Law numbered III, for the reason that said Conclusion of Law is not supported by the Court's Findings of Fact and is repugnant to the Court's Findings of Fact numbered VI and VII.

5. That the District Court erred in its Conclusions of Law numbered V, for the reason that said Conclusion of Law is not supported by the Court's Findings of Fact and is repugnant to the Court's Findings of Fact numbered VI and VII.

6. That the District Court erred in failing to conclude as a matter of law that the consent signed by Olive Wills Wigmore on the 17th day of January, 1936, and fully set forth in the Court's Finding of Fact numbered VII, was valid and binding upon Olive Wills Wigmore and her estate and extended

the time within which the Commissioner of Internal Revenue might assess income and excess profits taxes against her for the taxable year 1933 to and including June 30, 1937.

7.   That the District Court erred in entering Judgment in favor of the defendants and against the plaintiff for the reason that the evidence introduced and the Court's Findings of Fact numbered VI and VII require that as a matter of law Judgment should be entered for the plaintiff.

Dated: This 14th day of April, 1943.

LEO V. SILVERSTEIN,
U. S. Attorney,
E. H. MITCHELL,
Asst. U. S. Atty.,
EUGENE HARPOLE,
Special Attorney,
Bureau of Internal Revenue.
By EUGENE HARPOLE
Attorneys for Appellant-
Plaintiff

Received copy of the within Appellant's Statement of Points to be urged upon Appeal this 14th day of April, 1943.

CLYDE R. BURR
Attorney for Philip Grey
Smith, Administrator

[Endorsed]: Filed Apr 15, 1943. Paul P. O'Brien, Clerk.

TOPICAL INDEX.

TABLE OF AUTHORITIES CITED.

iv.

STATUTES.

MISCELLANEOUS.

No. 10404.

IN THE

United States Circuit Court of Appeals
FOR THE NINTH CIRCUIT

UNITED STATES OF AMERICA,

Appellant,

vs.

PHILIP GREY SMITH, as Administrator with will annexed
of the Estate of Olive Wills Wigmore, Deceased, and
J. A. WIGMORE,

Appellees.

**Upon Appeal from the District Court of the United States for the
Southern District of California.**

BRIEF FOR THE UNITED STATES.

Opinion Below.

The opinion of the District Court [R. 13-18] is reported
at 48 F. Supp. 250.

Jurisdiction.

This is a suit to collect income taxes for the calendar
year 1933 in the amount of $2,981.27, together with in-
terest thereon as provided by law. The taxes were assessed
against Olive Wills Wigmore and J. A. Wigmore jointly
on October 16, 1936. [R. 21-22.] Taxpayers having
failed, after notice and demand, to pay the taxes assessed,

the United States instituted suit on October 15, 1942, against the estate of Olive Wills Wigmore, deceased, and J. A. Wigmore in the District Court to collect the taxes pursuant to Section 276(c) of the Revenue Act of 1932. [R. 2-6.] The answer of Philip Grey Smith, adminis· trator with will annexed of the estate of Olive Wills Wigmore, was filed on November 9, 1942. [R. 6-8.] J. A. Wigmore was not served with process and entered no appearance. [R. 25-26.] On January 8, 1943, the District Court entered judgment against the United States.[1] [R. 25-26.] Notice of appeal was filed on March 30, 1943. [R. 27.] Jurisdiction of this Court is invoked under Section 128(a) of the Judicial Code, as amended by the Act of February 13, 1925.

Question Presented.

Whether a joint taxpayer who signed an assessment waiver intended to extend the time for assessment of tax as against herself, even though her name did not appear in the body of the waiver.

Statute Involved.

Revenue Act of 1932, c. 209, 47 Stat. 169:

"Sec. 275. Period of Limitation Upon Assessment and Collection.

Except as provided in section 276—

(a) *General Rule.*—The amount of income taxes imposed by this title shall be assessed within two years

---

[1]This suit was also one to collect income taxes assessed against Olive Wills Wigmore for the year 1940. [R. 2-6.] Collection of these taxes was not opposed by the administrator of her estate. The judgment of the District Court, therefore, was in favor of the United States as to the unpaid income taxes for the year 1940. [R. 26.] That part of the District Court's judgment is not before this Court on appeal.

after the return was filed, and no proceeding in court
without assessment for the collection of such taxes
shall be begun after the expiration of such period.

* * * * * * * *

SEC. 276. SAME—EXCEPTIONS.

* * * * * * * *

(b) *Waivers*.—Where before the expiration of the
time prescribed in section 276 for the assessment of
the tax, both the Commissioner and the taxpayer
have consented in writing to its assessment after such
time, the tax may be assessed at any time prior to the
expiration of the period agreed upon. The period so
agreed upon may be extended by subsequent agreements in writing made before the expiration of the
period previously agreed upon.

(c) *Collection After Assessment*.—Where the assessment of any income tax imposed by this title has
been made within the period of limitation properly
applicable thereto, such tax may be collected by distraint or by a proceeding in court, but only if begun
(1) within six years after the assessment of the tax,
or (2) prior to the expiration of any period for collection agreed upon in writing by the Commissioner
and the taxpayer before the expiration of such six-
year period. The period so agreed upon may be
extended by subsequent agreements in writing made
before the expiration of the period previously agreed
upon."

Statement.

The facts found by the District Court which are material to the question on appeal are as follows [R. 18-22]:

Olive Wills Wigmore and her husband, J. A. Wigmore, filed a joint federal income tax return for the year 1933 on March 13, 1934. The return disclosed no tax liability. [R. 20.]

On January 17, 1936, J. A. Wigmore and Olive Wills Wigmore signed a consent in form as follows [R. 20-21]:

"Consent Fixing Period of Limitations Upon Assessment of Income and Profits Tax.

Cleveland, Ohio, January 17, 1936

In pursuance of the provisions of existing Internal Revenue Laws J. A. Wigmore, a taxpayer (or taxpayers) of Chesterland, Coauga County, Ohio, and the Commissioner of Internal Revenue hereby consent and agree as follows:

That the amount of any income, excess-profits or war-profits taxes due under any return (or returns) made by or on behalf of the above-named taxpayer (or taxpayers) for the taxable year (or years) 1933 under existing acts, or under prior revenue acts, may be assessed at any time on or before June 30, 1937, except that, if a notice of a deficiency in tax is sent to said taxpayer (or taxpayers) by registered mail on or before said date, then the time for making any assessment as aforesaid shall be extended beyond the said date by the number of days during which the

Commissioner is prohibited from making an assessment and for sixty days thereafter.

> J. A. WIGMORE
> Taxpayer
> OLIVE W. WIGMORE
> Taxpayer

> By...

[Seal]

> GUY T. HELVERING
> Commissioner of Internal
> Revenue

> By A. C. C.

> January 31, 1936

If this consent is executed with respect to a year for which a joint return of a husband and wife was filed, it must be signed by both spouses, except that one spouse may sign as the agent for the other. * * *"

On October 16, 1936, the Commissioner of Internal Revenue assessed income taxes for the year 1933 in the amount of $2,981.27, together with interest thereon, against Olive Wills Wigmore and J. A. Wigmore jointly. [R. 21-22.] No part of the tax and interest so assessed has been paid. [R. 22.]

Olive Wills Wigmore died on March 1, 1941, a resident of Pasadena, California. [R. 19.] Philip Grey Smith is the duly appointed, qualified, and acting administrator with will annexed of her estate. [R. 20.]

Olive Wills Wigmore did not consent that income taxes for 1933 would be assessed on or before June 30, 1937, or at any time after March 15, 1936.[2] [R. 22.]

The District Court concluded as a matter of law that the consent or waiver of the statute of limitations signed by J. A. Wigmore and Olive W. Wigmore on January 17, 1936, was ineffective as to Olive Wills Wigmore and her estate; that it did not extend the time within which the Commissioner of Internal Revenue might assess income taxes for 1933 against her; and that the statute of limitations barred assessment of income taxes for 1933 against Olive Wills Wigmore after March 15, 1936. [R. 23.]

Statement of Points to Be Urged.

The Government's statement of points, all of which are relied on here, is set out at pages 32-34 of the record. They may be condensed into one principal point, which will form the basis for the argument:

The consent signed by Olive W. Wigmore on January 17, 1936, was effective to extend the period of limitations for assessment against her of income taxes for 1933.

---

[2]Although labeled a finding of fact, this obviously is a conclusion of law, based on the District Court's conclusion as to the validity of the consent or waiver.

Summary of Argument.

Whether a consent is effective to extend the period of limitations for assessment of taxes depends upon whether the person who signed it intended to consent to such extension. Olive Wills Wigmore and J. A. Wigmore filed a joint income tax return for 1933 and both signed the consent extending the time for assessment of 1933 taxes of "J. A. Wigmore." Despite the inapt wording of the consent, Olive W. Wigmore obviously signed the consent with the purpose of extending the time for assessment on the joint return as against herself. Her consent was not required to extend the time as to J. A. Wigmore. The law will not presume that she intended to do only an unnecessary and futile thing in signing, but will ascribe the obvious purpose to her act, that of consenting to extend the time on her own behalf. This is in accord with the rule generally employed in construing suretyship and other contracts. This *prima facie* showing that the waiver was operative against Olive Wills Wigmore was not rebutted by evidence and because a statute of limitation is involved no doubt may be resolved in her favor. Neither is it open to the administrator of her estate to deny validity to a consent upon which the Commissioner has relied.

ARGUMENT.

The Consent Signed by Olive Wills Wigmore on January 17, 1936, Was Effective to Extend the Period of Limitations for Assessment Against Her of Income Taxes for 1933.

The only question presented is whether an assessment of 1933 income taxes against J. A. Wigmore and Olive Wills Wigmore (hereinafter referred to as decedent) made on October 16, 1936, was barred by the statute of limitations. [R. 11-12.] This in turn depends on the validity of a consent executed on January 17, 1936, which purported to extend the time for assessment until June 30, 1937, [R. 10.] Unless this consent was operative, the assessment was not timely made under Section 275(a) of the Revenue Act of 1932, *supra,* which required that the assessment be made within two years from March 13, 1934, the date of filing the return.

The District Court held that the consent was invalid as against decedent[3] because her name did not appear in the body of the consent. [R. 13-18.] We contend that decedent clearly intended the consent to be operative against herself and that the District Court erred in holding that it was ineffective as to her.

The practice of executing consents or waivers extending the statutory period for assessment and collection of taxes

---

[3]The validity of the consent as against J. A. Wigmore is not in question. Although he was named as a defendant in the instant suit, he was not served with process and the District Court rendered no judgment as against him.

has long existed[4] and the principles with respect to the nature of such consents have become settled.

The purpose of a consent extending the time for assessment of taxes, of course, is to give further time in which to ascertain the correct tax liability. *Stange v. United States,* 282 U. S. 270. It benefits the taxpayer, in that he is given an opportunity to protest and negotiate in an effort to effect a reduction of a proposed additional assessment. *United States v. Krueger,* 121 F. (2d) 842 (C. C. A. 3d), certiorari denied, 314 U. S. 677.

A consent is not a contract but is a volutary unilateral waiver of a defense by a taxpayer. *Florsheim Bros. Co. v. United States,* 280 U. S. 453; *Stange v. United States, supra.* No consideration is required to support it. *Loewer Realty Co. v. Anderson,* 31 F. (2d) 268 (C. C. A. 2d), certiorari denied, 280 U. S. 558; *Stern Bros. & Co. v. Burnet,* 51 F. (2d) 1042 (C. C. A. 8th). The general rules applied to determine the validity of contracts are not applicable to determine the validity of a consent. *American Feature Film Co. v. Commissioner,* 11 B. T. A. 1271; *Republic Insurance Co. v. Commissioner,* 13 B. T. A. 568.

The effectiveness of a waiver depends on intent. If the parties who signed the consent intended to be bound by it, the consent will be enforced even though it may be imperfect or defective in form. *Crown Willamette Paper*

---

[4]There was no specific statutory authority for waivers prior to Section 250(d) of the Revenue Act of 1921, c. 136, 42 Stat 227. However, the Commissioner had authority to take waivers prior to that time under the broad administrative provisions of the earlier acts. *Aiken v. Burnett,* 282 U. S. 277.

Co. v. McLaughlin, 81 F. (2d) 365 (C. C. A. 9th); *Mulford v. Commissioner,* 66 F. (2d) 296 (C. C. A. 3d); *United States v. Southern Lumber Co.,* 51 F. (2d) 956 (C. C. A. 8th), certiorari denied, 284 U. S. 680; *Heiman Grocery Co. v. Crooks,* 44 F. (2d) 854 (W. D. Mo.), appeal dismissed, 50 F. (2d) 1077 (C. C. A. 8th); *Constitution Publishing Co. v. Commissioner,* 22 B. T. A. 426.

The facts in the case at bar clearly show that decedent intended to extend the time for assessment of 1933 taxes as against herself. A joint income tax return for the year 1933 was filed and signed by both decedent and her husband. [R. 9.] Then, as the stamp in the upper left-hand corner of the return indicates, a revenue agent in report dated January 10, 1936, recommended a deficiency in tax for that year of $2,580.82, together with interest of $400.45. [R. 9.] Thereupon, on January 17, 1936, J. A. Wigmore and decedent executed the consent in question [R. 10], obviously for the purpose of securing time to protest the proposed deficiency in tax.

The body of the consent purports to extend the time for assessment of taxes due on the 1933 return filed by J. A. Wigmore. However, the only return filed by him for that year was the joint return, which was also the return of decedent. Since no other return was filed for that year, the consent manifestly was intended to refer to the joint return. *Cf. Mulford v. Commissioner, supra.*

Decedent must have intended something by her signature. If her only purpose was to extend the time for assessment as to J. A. Wigmore, it was pointless for her to sign, for her signature added nothing. His signature alone would have accomplished that. It can not be presumed that her signature was for no purpose. On the contrary, it "must be assumed that an effective and not a futile act was intended." *Stange v. United States,* 282 U. S. 270, 277. No reason appears for her signature except that of extending the time in which an assessment could be made against her. The intent to extend the time necessarily follows.[5] Although the language of the consent was not as apt as it might have been, there is no basis for denying its obvious purpose. *Burnet v. Railway Equipment Co.,* 282 U. S. 295, 302; *Mulford v. Commissioner, supra.*

No case has been found in which the question involved here was presented.[6] The District Court [R. 16] relied upon the decision of this Court in *Commissioner v. Bryson,* 79 F. (2d) 397, as analogous. However, we think that case is not in any way comparable. There a waiver, purporting to be a consent by a corporation, was signed by

---

[5]As indicated above, the District Court found that decedent "did not consent" to the assessment of income taxes for 1933 on or before June 30, 1937. [R. 22.] We think it clear that this was a conclusion of law and not of fact. Footnote 2, *supra.* But even if it be regarded as an ultimate finding of fact, it is merely an interpretation of the written consent which she signed. There was no other evidence except for the income tax return and the assessment list. Accordingly, this Court is free to construe the consent for itself. *Commissioner v. Buck,* 120 F. (2d) 775, 779 (C. C. A. 2d); *Commissioner v. Wilson,* 125 F. (2d) 307, 309 (C. C A. 7th).

[6]*United States v. Hammerstein,* 20 F. Supp. 744 (S.D. N.Y.), involved a suit against husband and wife to collect a deficiency assessed against the husband only pursuant to a waiver signed only by him. The court refused to hold the wife liable in the absence of an assessment against her, even though a joint return had been filed. *Cf.* also *Ekdahl v. Commissioner,* 18 B. T. A. 1230; *Weinstein v. Commissioner,* 33 B. T. A. 105.

Bryson as former secretary. In a letter accompanying the consent Bryson disclaimed any authority to act for the corporation. This Court held that the waiver did not extend the time for assessment of taxes against the corporation because it was not executed by any officer with authority to act; and that it did not extend the time as to Bryson individually because he signed as former secretary and not individually. If the case applies here at all, it is to show that the intent of the parties is determinative. Decedent in the instant case signed on her own behalf and not as agent for another or as former secretary, as did Bryson; and she did not accompany her consent with a letter limiting the scope of her signature in any way, as did Bryson. Not having qualified her signature in any respect, decedent's intention to be bound individually clearly appears. The District Court erred in not holding her consent to be effective.

Although the District Court recognized that a waiver was not a contract [R. 14-15], it thought that the rules for construction of contracts should be used in construing a waiver.[7] It then applied in favor of decedent a principle that when a contract states distinctly that it is between two designated parties, the fact that another person signed the contract does not make it his contract. We do not think the principle relied on by the District Court applies when the intention to be bound on the contract exists. The

---

[7]Other cases have so held. *Cf. H & B American Mach. Co. v. United States,* 11 F. Supp. 48 (C. Cls), certiorari dismissed, 297 U. S. 726; *Constitution Publishing Co. v. Commissioner,* 22 B. T. A. 426.

great weight of authority supports the rule that the intention of the parties determines whether one whose name is signed but who is not named in the body of the contract is bound thereby. See *Gloucester Mutual Fishing Ins. Co. v. Boyer,* 294 Mass. 35, 200 N. E. 557; *Schonberger v. Culbertson,* 231 App. Div. 257, 247 N. Y. S. 180; *Stouts v. Wilson Motor Co.,* 176 Okla. 316, 55 P. (2d) 990. One who signs a bond will be regarded as a surety, although his name is not mentioned in the body of the bond. In such case it is presumed that he had some purpose in signing and that his intention was to be bound. *Wheeler v. Paterson,* 64 Minn. 231, 66 N. W. 964; *Sanders v. Keller,* 18 Idaho 590, 111 Pac. 350; *Smith v. Easter,* 101 Kan. 245, 166 Pac. 510; *Campbell v. Rotering,* 42 Minn. 115, 43 N. W. 795; *Stewart v. Carter,* 4 Neb. 564; *Affeld v. The People,* 12 Ill. App. 502; *Holden v. Tanner,* 6 La. An. 74.

Thus, in construing contracts the question of intent is of primary importance in ascertaining whether one who signed a contract is bound thereon. And as in the case of waivers, the fact that a person signs a contract creates a presumption that he intended to be bound thereon. But even if all contracts were required to be construed as the District Court thought, that rule of interpretation would not apply in the case of a waiver. It is established that the test to be applied in determining whether a consent is operative is whether the person signing intended to consent in fact. *Commissioner v. Bryson,* 79 F. (2d) 397 (C. C. A. 9th); and cases cited above.

Although it is not clear to what extent its decision was influenced, the District Court surmised that the omission of decedent's name from the body of the waiver may have been because liability for the 1933 taxes rested primarily upon the husband.[8] [R. 17.] That inference is not permissible. If it were true that the decedent was not liable for the taxes, that fact would assuredly have been asserted as a defense. The answer of decedent's administrator, however, raised no question with respect to decedent's liability for the 1933 taxes [R. 6-8], and consequently her liability was in effect conceded. The sole question before the District Court and this Court is whether the consent signed by decedent is operative as to her.

The District Court also held that there was doubt as to whether decedent was bound on her waiver and that this doubt should be resolved in favor of her estate. [R. 17.] But in the case of statutes of limitations preventing col-

---

[8]In *Cole v. Commissioner*, 81 F. (2d) 485, this Court held that spouses are not jointly and severally liable for the entire amount of tax assessed upon a joint return. The decision was followed in *Crowe v Commissioner*, 86 F (2d) 796 (C. A. 7th), and *Commissioner v Rabenold*, 108 F. (2d) 639 (C. C A. 2d). Subsequently, the Supreme Court decided *Helvering v. Janney*, 311 U. S. 189, and *Taft v. Helvering*, 311 U. S. 195, in which it approved the principle that a joint return is the return of a single "taxable unit." In view of these decisions the Court of Claims and the Board of Tax Appeals now hold that the liability on a joint return is both joint and several. See *Moore v. United States*, 37 F. Supp 136 (C Cls.), certiorari denied, 314 U S. 619, rehearing denied, 314 U. S. 709; *Schoenhut v Commissioner*, 45 B. T. A. 812; *Gillette v. Commissioner*, 46 B T. A 573; *Levy v Commissioner*, 46 B. T. A. 1145. But the Circuit Court of Appeals for the Second Circuit has adhered to its former position. *Commissioner v. Uniacke*, 132 F. (2d) 781. See also *United States v. Rosebush*, 45 F. Supp. 664 (E D Wis.).

Section 51(b) of the Revenue Act of 1938, c. 289, 52 Stat 447, expressly provides that spouses, who exercise the privilege of filing a joint return, are jointly and severally liable for the tax upon their aggregate income This provision was inserted to quell any doubt as to the existence of such liability. H. Rep. No. 1860, 75th Cong., 3d Sess, pp. 29-30 (1939-1 Cum. Bull (Part 2) 728, 749).

Thus we think that if the question of the decedent's liability for the tax were involved in this case, the present state of the authorities would indicate a holding that she was both jointly and severally liable.

lection of taxes which are clearly owed, the doubts are resolved in favor of the Government. Such statutes are to be strictly construed in its favor. *Dupont de Nemours & Co. v. Davis,* 264 U. S. 456; *Bowers v. N. Y. & Albany Co.,* 273 U. S. 346; *McCarthy Co. v. Commissioner,* 80 F. (2d) 618 (C. C. A. 9th). Where a waiver is regular in form, every presumption is to be taken in favor of its validity and binding effect, and the burden is on the taxpayer to show any invalidity or ineffectiveness. *Stern Bros. & Co. v. Burnet,* 51 F. (2d) 1042 (C. C. A. 8th); *Trustees for Ohio & Big Sandy Coal Co. v. Commissioner,* 43 F. (2d) 782 (C. C. A. 4th).

In the instant case, the Government introduced the 1933 joint return, the consent signed by decedent, and the assessment list. [R. 9-12.] From these the assumption must be made, as we have shown, that decedent's intent was to extend the time for assessment as against herself. *Stange v. United States,* 282 U. S. 270; *Mulford v. Commissioner,* 66 F. (2d) 296 (C. C. A. 3d); *Wheeler v. Paterson,* 64 Minn. 231, 66 N. W. 964. This made a *prima facie* case for the Government. The burden was then upon decedent's administrator to show by evidence that the waiver was inoperative as to her. He offered no proof of any kind and the case was submitted on the Government's documentary evidence. [R. 19.] There was, therefore, no conflict in the evidence and no doubt as to decedent's intention and as to the validity of the waiver in this case. But if any doubt had existed, it should have been resolved in favor of the Government in this type of case.

Lastly, the evidence shows that the Commissioner of Internal Revenue relied on the reality of the consent executed by the decedent. He deferred assessment of the proposed additional taxes for 1933 until after the statutory period for assessment had expired. In such circumstances decedent's administrator is not permitted to say that decedent did not intend that which her signature indicated or that her consent did not have the effect of extending the period for assessment of taxes against her. *Liberty Baking Co. v. Heiner,* 37 F. (2d) 703 (C. C. A. 3d); *Trustees for Ohio & Big Sandy Coal Co. v. Commissioner, supra; Lucas v. Hunt,* 45 F. (2d) 781 (C. C. A. 5th); *Philip Carey Mfg. Co. v. Dean,* 58 F. (2d) 737 (C. C. A. 6th), certiorari denied, 287 U. S. 623; *Mulford v. Commissioner, supra; cf. Commissioner v. Bryson,* 79 F. (2d) 397 (C. C. A. 9th).

Conclusion.

The judgment of the District Court should be reversed.

Samuel O. Clark, Jr.,
Assistant Attorney General.
Sewall Key,
Samuel H. Levy,
Helen Goodner,
*Special Assistants to the
Attorney General.*

Charles H. Carr,
United States Attorney.

E. H. Mitchell,
Assistant United States Attorney.

Eugene Harpole,
*Special Attorney,
Bureau of Internal Revenue.*

June, 1943.

'No. 10404.

IN THE

United States Circuit Court of Appeals

FOR THE NINTH CIRCUIT

UNITED STATES OF AMERICA,

Appellant,

vs.

PHILIP GREY SMITH, as Administrator with-Will-annexed of the Estate of Olive Wills Wigmore, Deceased, and J. A. WIGMORE,

Appellees.

Upon Appeal from the District Court of the United States for the Southern District of California, Central Division.

BRIEF FOR THE APPELLEE PHILIP GREY SMITH, AS ADMINISTRATOR WITH-WILL-ANNEXED OF THE ESTATE OF OLIVE WILLS WIGMORE, DECEASED.

CLYDE R. BURR,

310 Security Title Insurance Building, Los Angeles,

Attorney for Philip Grey Smith, Administrator with-will-annexed of the Estate of Olive Wills Wigmore, Deceased.

FILED

JUL 20 1943

PAUL P. O'BRIEN,
CLERK

Parker & Baird Company, Law Printers, Los Angeles

TOPICAL INDEX.

TABLE OF AUTHORITIES CITED.

TEXTBOOKS.

UNITED STATES OF AMERICA,

Appellant,

vs.

PHILIP GREY SMITH, as Administrator with-Will-annexed of the Estate of Olive Wills Wigmore, Deceased, and J. A. WIGMORE,

Appellees.

Upon Appeal from the District Court of the United States for the Southern District of California, Central Division.

BRIEF FOR THE APPELLEE PHILIP GREY SMITH, AS ADMINISTRATOR WITH-WILL-ANNEXED OF THE ESTATE OF OLIVE WILLS WIGMORE, DECEASED.

Opinion Below.

The opinion of the District Court [R. 13-18] is reported at 48 F. Supp. 250.

Question Presented.

Whether both the Commissioner and the taxpayer, Olive Wills Wigmore, consented in writing to assessment of the tax against Olive Wills Wigmore for the taxable year 1933, at any time on or before June 30, 1937.

Statement.

Appellee Philip Grey Smith, as administrator with-will-annexed of the Estate of Olive Wills Wigmore, deceased, agrees with the statement presented by appellant in its opening brief, pages 4, 5 and 6, inclusive, except that appellee controverts the word "would" on page 6, first paragraph, line 2 of appellant's opening brief.

By an inadvertent printing of the transcript of record on page 22 in the eleventh Finding of Fact, the word "could" was printed to read "would." Counsel for appellant and appellee thereupon entered into a written stipulation that the transcript of record on appeal herein be corrected by interlineation of the clerk of the above entitled court. As finally corrected by interlineation, Finding No. XI set forth on page 22 of the printed transcript of record reads as follows:

"XI.

"That Olive W. Wigmore did not consent that the said income taxes for the taxable year 1933 could be assessed on or before June 30, 1937, or at any time after the 15th day of March, 1936."

Summary of Argument.

Whether the "consent in writing" is applicable to the assessment against the taxpayer who signs but is not mentioned therein depends upon whether it is clearly apparent from the face of the "consent" that both the Commissioner and such taxpayer intended it to be operative on the Commissioner and such taxpayer, although she was not named therein. If an agreement states distinctly that it is between two designated parties, the fact that another person's name appears at the end of the agreement with that of the parties does not make it the agreement of such other person. Moreover, and more specifically, the agreement in question here is a "Consent Fixing Period of Limitation Upon Assessment of Income and Profit Tax." Had the Commissioner of Internal Revenue intended that the consent apply to Olive Wills Wigmore individually, it would have been simple enough to make plain that intention. Olive Wills Wigmore might readily have been named in the body of the instrument. A designation of her there as "taxpayer" would have been amply sufficient.

Furthermore, the presumption is against the appellant, the Government. If there be any doubt as to the interpretation of the terms of the "consent in writing," that doubt certainly should be resolved against the Government, the party furnishing the printed form.

The opinion of the District Court should also be affirmed on the ground that the complaint is defective on its face in that it shows that more than two years had elapsed from the filing of the return on March, 1934, until the time of assessment, October 16, 1936.

ARGUMENT.

1. The Evidence Does Not Show a "Consent in Writing" by Both the Commissioner and Olive Wills Wigmore to Assessment Against Her After the Two Year Period, Under Par. (b) of Sec. 276 of the Revenue Act of 1932.

On March 13, 1934, decedent, Olive Wills Wigmore, and her husband, J. A. Wigmore, filed a joint Federal income tax return for the taxable year 1933 [R. 9, 20]. The return disclosed no tax liability [R. 9, 20]. On October 16, 1936, the Commissioner of Internal Revenue assessed income taxes for the year 1933 in the amount of $2,981.27, together with interest thereon, against Olive Wills Wigmore and J. O. Wigmore jointly [R. 11, 12, 21, 22]. The assessment was not timely made as to Olive Wills Wigmore under section 275(a) of the Revenue Act of 1932, c. 209, 47 Stat. 169, which requires that the assessment be made within two years from the date of filing the return. Since the return for the year 1933 was filed on March 13, 1934, the assessment to be valid must have been made before March 15, 1936 [R. 23]. However, before the two year period for the assessment had elapsed, more specifically on the 17th day of January, 1936, Olive Wills Wigmore and J. A. Wigmore signed a prepared form entitled "Consent Fixing the Period of Limitations on Assessment of Income and Profits Tax" [R. 20]. A photostatic copy of this original purported consent appears on page 10 of the transcript of record. The sole question is: did this consent operate to extend the time for assessment of 1933 income taxes against Olive Wills Wigmore until June 30, 1937, the time set therein [R. 23]?

No question is raised as to its effectiveness against J. W. Wigmore. The District Court upheld the contention of appellee (defendant below) that the consent was inoperative as to Olive Wills Wigmore and her estate, and did not extend the time within which the Commissioner of Internal Revenue might assess income taxes against Olive Wills Wigmore for the taxable year 1933 [R. 23]. Consequently the court held that neither Olive Wills Wigmore, her estate nor the defendant Philip Grey Smith, as administrator with-will-annexed of the Estate of Olive Wills Wigmore, deceased, is indebted to the plaintiff for any sum whatsoever on account of income taxes for the taxable year 1933 [R. 23].*

Appellant states, and appellee agrees, that the effectiveness of "the consent in writing" depends on intent. This was the question before the District Court [R. 14]. Appellant argues that since there was a joint income tax return filed for the year 1933 [R. 9], and since both taxpayers signed the consent in question [R. 10], it was obviously with the intent to do something in connection with the 1933 income taxes. Appellant's entire argument is a concentration on the signature of Olive Wills Wigmore affixed to the consent, with a conclusion that it must be there for some purpose. However, appellant looks beyond allotted territory in its attempt to uncover the intention of the parties interested in the purported waiver. Under the law the test to be applied in an attempt to answer the

---

*Defendants, Estate of Olive Wills Wigmore, Deceased, and Philip Grey Smith as administrator with-will-annexed of the Estate of Olive Wills Wigmore, Deceased, did not deny [R. 8] their liability for taxes assessed against Olive Wills Wigmore for the year 1940. Consequently the District Court concluded [R. 23] that they were indebted to the plaintiff on account of the admittedly unpaid income taxes of said Olive Wills Wigmore for the taxable year 1940 [R. 23, 24].

question before this court is: whether the intent of the parties is disclosed by an examination of the face of the entire instrument. If there were any reasonable attempt to arrive at any agreement or consent, it should be determined by a close scrutiny of the instrument in question. (*Campbell v. Rotering,* 42 Minn. 115, 43 N. W. 795; *Wheeler v. Patterson,* 64 Minn. 231, 66 N. W. 964; *Stoutz v. Wilson Motor Co.,* 176 Okla. 316, 55 P. (2d) 990.) This is undoubtedly the test to be applied in this particular case. Olive Wills Wigmore is dead.

. Appellee likewise calls the attention of the respected court to the consent in question [R. 10]. In an analysis of this instrument some consideration should be given to the signature of Olive Wills Wigmore affixed thereto and its effect, if any. In the subject of contracts the presumption raised by appellant from the presence of her signature has been answered in at least one court. While a waiver or consent is not a contract but essentially a voluntary unilateral waiver of a defense by the taxpayer (*Florsheim Bros. etc. v. United States,* 280 U. S. 453), the District Court, in reliance on *Stange v. United States,* 282 U. S. 270, at p. 275, logically could see no reason why the rules applicable to the construction of a contract should not apply to the construction and effect of a waiver [R. 15]. In 6 R. C. L., page 875, the following language is found:

> "* * * If a contract states distinctly that it is between two designated parties, the fact that another person's name appears at the end of the contract with that of the parties does not make it his contract. * * *"

Shriner v. Croft, 166 Ala. 146, 51 So. 884, 139 A. S. R. 19, 28 L. R. A. (N. S.) 450, is the case on which the editors of Ruling Case Law rely. In that case the following statement is made by the court:

> "The first assignments of error insisted on (numbered 1 and 2) are to the sustaining of the demurrer of Mary R. Shriner, on the ground that the complaint shows on its face that Mary R. Shriner was not a party to the contract sued on, and the third, fourth, and fifth assignments relate to the same subject, to-wit, to the refusal of the (21) court to grant the motion for the discontinuance of the case, because of the amendment of the complaint, by striking out the name of said Mary R. Shriner.

> "There was no error in either action of the court. The contract sued on is set out in the complaint, and it states distinctly that it is between W. A. Shriner and John Craft. The fact that Mary R. Shriner's name appears at the end of the contract with W. A. Shriner does not make it her contract. * * *"

Appellant apparently realizes the damaging effect this precedent has on his argument. In an attempted reinforcement, appellant, on page 13, line 8, *et seq.,* in his opening brief states the proposition that one who signs a surety *bond* will be regarded as a surety, although his name is not mentioned in the body of the bond. In such a situation, appellant urges that it is therein presumed that the surety had some purpose in signing and that his intention was to be bound. Not wishing to indulge in tangents, appellee, however, desires to point out that at least two of the authorities cited by appellant also stand for appellee's contention that a subscriber not named in the body of an instrument is liable thereon only if it can be determined from the face of the instrument that he *intended* to be bound by its conditions. For example, in *Wheeler v. Patterson*, 66 N. W. 964, at page 965, the court found this intention present and said,

> "The wording of the face of the bond shows that the person who signed, though not named in the body of the agreement, expressly declared over his signature that in witness of his obligation to perform the conditions of the bond, he signs and seals it."

And in *Campbell v. Rotering, et al.*, 43 N. W. 795, the court also found this intent present and, after explaining the rule, said at page 796:

> "For instance, where, as in this case, it reads 'We,' then stating the obligation or understanding, it is, if there be nothing else to show the contrary, the contract of the parties who execute it."

However, appellee now states his belief that the position of the parties in Principal-Surety instruments is of little similarity to those inherent in the matter now before this court. As to the instrument here involved, there is a different evidentiary burden on the parties than exists in the analogy suggested by appellant; here appellee, by showing the presence or absence of certain factors, invokes the application of presumptions and constructions totally lacking in the Principal-Surety situations.

This appeal is to be decided by determining whether or not it is disclosed on the face of the instrument that the parties intended the agreement to be operative as to Olive Wills Wigmore [R. 10]. Parties who intend to perpetuate their agreement in a written memorandum usually spell it out in the body of that instrument. The document here is on a printed form furnished by appellant through its Bureau of Internal Revenue; there is a space left for the insertion of the name or names of taxpayers who are to consent and agree with the Commissioner of Internal Revenue. A close reading of the instrument shows that here only two people agree and consent on the terms set forth therein; nowhere does the name of Olive Wills Wigmore appear in the body of the consent, and nowhere does she agree with the Commissioner or the Commissioner agree with her.

The method of agreeing that an assessment may be made within a period extending beyond the two years after the date the return was filed is clearly set forth in the statute governing the matter.

The Revenue Act of 1932, c. 209, 47 Stat. 169, states as follows in section 276(b): "Where before the expiration of time prescribed in section 275 for the assessment of the tax, both the Commissioner and the taxpayer have consented in writing to its assessment after such time, the tax may be assessed at any time prior to the expiration of the period agreed upon. The period so agreed upon may be extended by subsequent agreements in writing made before the expiration of the period previously agreed upon." Under this statute, the *taxpayer* must consent with the Commissioner of Internal Revenue in writing to put a period of limitation upon the assessment of income tax.

See, 5 *Paul & Mertens,* section 5049, p. 555, where the following is given:

"However, both the Commissioner and the taxpayer must 'consent' to the extension of time . . ."

In *U. S. v. Hammerstein* (D. C. N. Y.), 20 Fed. Supp. 744, involving a suit by the government against husband and wife, who had filed a joint income tax return to collect a deficiency claimed to be due from the wife, the court dismissed the complaint as to the wife because no timely assessment had been made against her.

The Government contended that where a joint return is made, there is only one taxpayer, an entity composed of two spouses and therefore an assessment against the member of the entity in whose name the return is filed, is an assessment against both members. The court rejected this contention and pointed out that where a husband and wife filed a joint return, each of them remains a separate and distinct taxpayer and, therefore, an assessment against the husband cannot be considered an assessment against the wife.

In *Cole v. Commissioner,* 81 Fed. (2d) 485, the question was, since deceased husband and wife filed a joint return, whether the husband's estate was liable for deficiency assessment where the deficiency was attributable to wife's income rather than the husband's. It was held that the spouses were *not* jointly and severally liable for a deficiency arising out of the separate income of one of them.

To reach this conclusion, the court made inquiry into the status of husband and wife and the filing of joint income returns. The court, at page 486, quotes from *Gummy v. Commissioner,* 26 B. T. A. 894, where the Commissioner advanced the theory that, having elected to file a joint return, the husband and wife became a single taxing entity, and, as such, "the taxpayer." The Board rejected this theory and, in speaking of an allowance of losses to individuals, quotes the word "taxpayer" from the statute. (Sec. 118 of the 1928 Act, 26 U. S. C. A., Sec. 23.) The Board decided: " 'Taxpayer' means any person subject to a tax imposed by the act, and the term 'person' includes an individual." The Board further held "Had Petitioner and his wife filed separate returns, there would be no question about the deductibility of the losses sustained by each. In filing a single joint return, they lost none of such rights; each remained an individual, and, as such, a taxpayer, within the meaning of section 118 of the statute."

In *Cole v. Commissioner, supra,* the court also quotes from *Fawcett v. Commissioner,* 31 B. T. A. 139, where the Commissioner had contended that by reason of electing to report their income for 1929 in a joint return, the husband and wife must, for all purposes of the revenue act, be treated as one. The Board there held:

> ". . . While there may be some logic in his view, we find no authority for it in the revenue acts, and it is a cardinal rule of construction of taxing statutes that there can be no tax imposed by implication or construction, and in case of doubt or ambiguity, either as to the fact of the imposition or as to the amount thereof, it must be resloved in favor of the taxpayer."

Appellee does not intend to inject into this appeal the problem of whether Olive Wills Wigmore and J. A. Wigmore were individually liable or jointly and severally liable for 1933 taxes [R. 17]; but he does contend that at the time the purported waiver was agreed upon, at least, neither the statutes (Revenue Act of 1932, c. 209, 47 Stat. 169) nor the court decisions on the subject considered persons filing a joint tax return as losing their identity of separate taxpayers. (*Commissioner v. Uniacke,* 132 F. (2d) 781, 782.) Hence, though J. A. Wigmore and Olive Wills Wigmore filed a joint 1933 tax return, yet they were separate and distinct taxpayers under the cases interpreting the word "taxpayer" as given in section 276(b), *supra.*

In *Commissioner of Internal Revenue v. Uniacke,* 132 F. (2d) 781, the Circuit Court of Appeals, second circuit, declared that while Congress in 1938 expressly imposed joint and several liability as a condition upon exercise of the privilege of filing a joint return (52 Stat. 476, 26 U. S. C. A. Int. Rev. Code, sec. 51(b)), yet it points out that this provision was not made retroactive, and disagrees with the Commissioner's contention that it was merely declaratory of the law under earlier revenue acts. In this case the Commissioner further urged that there was no injustice in treating both spouses as a "taxable unit" and holding them jointly and severally liable for the tax computed on their combined incomes, since they had voluntarily elected to obtain such tax advantages as a joint return permits. The court, at page 782, replied:

"Arguments of what is fair have little to do with the construction of tax statutes."

Therefore to be operative as against the Estate of Olive Wills Wigmore, the consent [R. 10] must have expressly mentioned Olive Wills Wigmore, *a taxpayer,* in the body thereof.

From section 276(b) of the Revenue Act of 1932, *supra,* it is also apparent that *both* the Commissioner and the taxpayer must consent in writing to any assessment after the two year period. There is thus a "period so agreed upon," which may be extended by "subsequent agreements in writing."

An examination of Plaintiff's Exhibit No. 2 discloses that the Commissioner consented only to an extension of the period as to J. A. Wigmore and not as to Mrs. Olive Wills Wigmore. J. A. Wigmore's name alone is inserted in the body of the form, and the exhibit states [R. 10] that the agreement is between the Commissioner and J. A. Wigmore. The consent of the Commissioner extends only to J. A. Wigmore, the "above named taxpayer," and since there could be no extension without the consent or "agreement" of *both* the Commissioner and the taxpayer, it would be immaterial whether Mrs. Wigmore intended to consent to an extension as to an assessment against her when she affixed her signature.

To put the matter another way, suppose that Mrs. Olive Wills Wigmore had insisted that the Commissioner had given his written consent as to her. She could not show that merely because she affixed her signature to the agreement the provisions thereof applied to her, and that the Commissioner had given his written consent as to her. The Commissioner's argument under such circumstances would undoubtedly have been that the name of J. A. Wigmore was the only name inserted in the agreement and that all references in the agreement were to Mr. Wigmore as the taxpayer, and that he did not intend to give any consent with reference to Mrs. Wigmore, who was not a party to the instrument but who merely affixed her signature. It is submitted that under such circumstances the contentions of the Commissioner would be irrefutable.

This situation is not altered by the fact that at a date later than that upon which the agreement was executed the Commissioner chose to assert, or does now assert, that he did give his written consent to an extension of the period for assessment as to the taxpayer Olive Wills Wigmore. The writing must be construed as of the time it was executed.

While appellee has found no federal case square with the facts of this case now on appeal, yet research revealed the following opinions so close on the facts as to be of persuasive influence.

In *American Loan Co. of Camden v. Helvering, Commissioner* (Ct. Ap. Dist. Col.), 70 Fed. (2d) 290, the question was who was bound by a waiver of the statute of limitations extending the period of assessment of the taxes involved therein. The court said on page 291:

"The petitioner presents also a question relating to the statute of limitations. It appears that petitioner executed and delivered to respondent a waiver of the statute of limitations dated March 7, 1930, extending the period for assessment of the taxes involved herein to December 31, 1930. The notice of deficiency was dated April 23, 1930, and the appeal was taken June 16, 1930.

"It appears that the name of the parent corporation of the affiliated group appears at the top of the printed form upon which the waiver was written but not in the caption or body of the written consent. It is argued that because of these facts the waiver should be confined to the affiliated period for which a consolidated return was filed, and should not apply to the separate return filed by petitioner. We think, however, that the petitioner and not the parent company was the party bound by the agreement, and consequently that petitioner effectually waived the statute of limitations thereby."

Commissioner of Internal Revenue v. Bryson (C. C. A. 9th Cir.), 79 Fed. (2d) 397, is more in point. In this se one of the problems was whether a waiver signed by Elmer D. Bryson, as former secretary of the corporation med in the body of the waiver, was sufficient to bind the secretary individually as transferee of the corpora- to a waiver of limitation of period for tax assess- e . The secretary was not named in the body of the waiver. The court at page 401 said:

"This contention can be disposed of briefly. The text of the document purports to bind the corporation. It is signed by the respondent as 'former secretary' of the corporation, which is described as 'taxpayer' . . . Without distorting plain words from their ordinary meaning, a transferee's waiver cannot be spelled out of the inchoate paper we are here considering."

And in a concurring opinion, Judge Denman, at page 402, discusses the waiver at length. He says:

"I concur in the decision. The body of the waiver produced by the Commissioner purports to be an agreement between the Bryson-Robinson Corporation and the Commissioner. It is on a printed form, furnished by the Commissioner, and the only insertions possibly to be attributed to the taxpayer to whom it is tendered are its name in the body of the instrument and the signature. It was not signed in the corporate name. The signer, Bryson, described himself to be a 'former secretary.' In an accompanying letter, he disclaims authority to act for the corporation. *The wording of the document contains no agreement on the part of Bryson individually.*" (Emphasis added.)

". . . *Had the Commissioner of Internal Revenue sought a waiver of the statute of limitations by Bryson individually, it would have been simple enough to make plain that intention without varying from the general form of 'Income and profits tax waiver' which has been in customary use in the Internal Revenue Department since the Revenue Act of 1921 (42 Stat. 227), and which was the form utilized in the instant case.* Bryson might have been named in the body of the instrument as 'transferee.' A description of him there as 'taxpayer' would have been amply sufficient. It is a persuasive factor negativing the Commissioner's intent to hold Bryson personally, that instead of taking such elementary steps to cause the waiver to speak thus clearly, he affixed his signature to a document which on its face bound no one, and from which can be read a transferee's liability only by an ultra refined metaphysical construction animated by a strong presumption in favor of the government and against the taxpayer." (Emphasis added.)

Although we cannot agree with appellant that a purpose must be ascribed to Olive Wills Wigmore in the affixing of her signature to the agreement, and although we contend that the agreement is clear that neither she nor the Commissioner consented to any extension of the period for assessment as to her tax, we call to the court's attention the circumstances suggested by the notation appended to the end of the agreement, which is as follows [R. 10, 14]:

> "If this consent is executed with respect to a year for which a joint return of a husband and wife was filed, it must be signed by both spouses, except that one spouse may sign as the agent for the other. * * *"

When the form was presented to Olive Wills Wigmore she had not yet signed, and in reading what preceded the place for her signature she would see a consent as to an extension with respect to the taxpayer, J. A. Wigmore. She would then read that such consent (referred to as "this consent") must be signed by both spouses to make it effective, since the return was joint.

The appellee then has effectively performed his task; he has shown that under the applicable test it was the intent of Olive Wills Wigmore not to be bound by the terms of the consent when she affixed her signature thereto, and that it was the intent of the Commissioner not to have the consent operative as to her. Since the intent of the parties was not to have the consent apply to Olive Wills Wigmore, her contention that the assessment of October 16, 1936, was invalid as to her, must be sustained.

If, despite the logic of appellee's contention, it be assumed that the intent of the parties is doubtful, still the presumption is against the government. The Commissioner supplied the consent. He originated whatever doubt may be argued to exist, and he had the burden of establishing the construction he contends should be given the consent—especially when that construction is so favorable to himself. This the plaintiff has failed to do.

As said in the *Bryson* case, *supra,* at page 402:

> "It is familiar doctrine that 'taxing acts, including provisions of limitation embodied therein (are) to be construed liberally in favor of the taxpayer.' *United States v. Updike, supra,* 281 U. S. 489, at page 496, 50 S. Ct. 367, 369, 74 L. Ed. 984."

And at page 403 of the *Bryson* case, Judge Denman stated in his concurring opinion:

> "In addition to the proper presumption which is against the government, it may be said that if there were doubt as to the interpretation of the terms of the writing, that doubt certainly should not be resolved with any presumption in favor of the party furnishing the printed form. *Commissioner v. Leasing & Building Co.* (C. C. A.), 46 F. (2d) 2, 4."

In *Erskine v. U. S.,* 84 Fed. (2d) 690-1, it was said:

> "Such revenue acts must be construed strictly in favor of the appellant sought to be charged as importer. He is 'entitled to the benefit of even a doubt.' Tariff Act 1897, 30 Stat. 151; United States v. Riggs, 203 U. S. 136, 139, 27 S. Ct. 39, 40, 51 L. Ed. 127; Hartranft v. Wiegmann, 121 U. S. 609, 616, 7 S. Ct. 1240, 30 L. Ed. 1012; Miller v. Standard Nut Margarine Co., 284 U. S. 498, 508, 52 S. Ct. 260, 76 L. Ed. 422."

Hopefully the appellant now urges that statutes of limitation should be resolved in its favor. Logically and realistically it is, of course, optional with the taxpayer whether he will waive or take advantage of the benefit of the statute of limitation. In L. O. 1095, C. B. June,

1922, page 313, the Solicitor of Internal Revenue very fairly said:

> "The Government itself insists on the benefit of the statute of limitations and holds that a refund due a taxpayer cannot be applied on a later tax when the amount refundable is barred by the statute. It is believed that both in good conscience and by legal right the same rule must apply when it works to the advantage of the taxpayer."

Lastly, as usual, appellant resorts to the plea of estoppel as against appellee. Judge Denman, at page 403 of the *Bryson* case, *supra*, once before answered appellant's contention when he said:

> "I know of no doctrine of estoppel to deny that a written instrument is something other than what its terms necessarily import, except as based on some fraud or misrepresentation. None is shown here."

2. **The Decision of the District Court Should Also Be Affirmed on the Ground That the Complaint Is Defective on Its Face in That It Shows That More Than Two Years Had Elapsed From the Filing of the Return on March 15, 1934, Until the Time of Assessment, October 16, 1936 [R. 3].**

Under the Revenue Act of 1932, c. 209, 47 Stat. 169, section 275(a), the assessment must have been made within two years after the return was filed. Under 276(c) the tax may be collected by distraint or by a proceeding in court "where the assessment of any income tax imposed by this title has been made within the period of ̣m properly applicable thereto . . .". Since this is a taxing statute, provisions therein are to be construed liberally in favor of the taxpayer. (*U. S. v. Updike.* 281 U. S. 489, 496, 50 S. Ct. 367, 74 L. Ed. 984.) Since the tax may be collected either by distraint or by proceeding in court if it has been assessed within time, it is difficult to see how a proceeding in court may be brought if not assessed within time, as required by the statute (Sec. 276(c), *supra*).

As is said in *Jenkins v. Smith,* 21 Fed. Supp. 433, at page 437:

> "Where assessments are made, or required to be made, there are two methods of compelling payment, one by suit, a judicial proceeding; the other by distraint, an executive proceeding. In either case, compliance with statutory conditions precedent, including initiation of proceedings within the time specified, is necessary. *Bowers v. New York & Albany Lighterage Co.* (1927), 273 U. S. 346, 47 S. Ct. 389, 71 L. Ed. 676."

While the lower court in the *Jenkins* case was reversed in (C. C. A. (2d) 1938), 99 Fed. (2d) 827, on the question of whether notice by the "Collector" was an inevitable constitutive factor to his right to collect, still the court in reversing did not disagree with or overrule the above quotation of the District Court.

The reasonable interpretation of section 276(c), *supra,* is that the Congress intended the assessment within time as necessary to the right to commence proceedings in court. It adds nothing to the power of the Government to sue, but places a necessary limitation upon its right to sue. Congress intended that when the period of limitation for assessment had run, the taxpayer should no longer be subject to uncertainty as to his liability to the Government.

In *U. S. v. Updike*, 281 U. S. 489, 50 S. Ct. 367, 74 L. Ed. 984, at page 990, the court held:

". . . it seems reasonably clear that the saving clause 'within the statutory period of limitation properly applicable thereto,' was inserted solely for the protection of the taxpayer; that is to say, in order to preclude collection of the tax even within 6 years after the assessment if that assessment, when made, was barred by the applicable statutory limitation."

Since the complaint herein on its face discloses a lapse of more than two years before the assessment was made [R. 3], it shows that the plaintiff had lost its right to bring a proceeding in court. Plaintiff has failed to state the *prima facie* elements of a claim. While the complaint need not plead matter anticipatory of a possible defense, still under Rule 8(a) of the Federal Rules of Civil Procedure, a pleading which sets forth a claim for relief "shall contain . . . (2) a short and plain statement of the claim showing that the pleader is entitled to relief." Rule 9(c) of the Federal Rules of Civil Procedure allows the general averment that all conditions precedent have been performed. The implication is that in the absence of this general allegation, facts must be pleaded with particularity, showing such performance or occurrence. By plaintiff's omission of both, there was no duty on defendant to deny specifically and with particularity before the District Court.

While this ground was not raised below and therefore not assigned by the District Court, still the Circuit Court of Appeals can affirm the decision of the District Court, though on another ground. As said by the court in *Mc-Brine Co., Ltd. v. Silverman,* (C. C. A. 9th) (1941), 121 Fed. (2d) 181, at page 182:

"That we may affirm on a ground not assigned by the trial court is well settled. *Collier v. Stanbrough,* 6 How. 14, 21, 12 L. Ed. 324; *Frey & Son v. Cudahy Packing Co.,* 256 U. S. 208, 210, 415 Ct. 451, 65 L. Ed. 892; 3 Am. Jur., Appeal & Error, sec. 1163, 674; 5 C. J. 5, Appeal & Error, sec. 1849, pp. 1334, 1335."

See, also:

Pevely Dairy Co. v. Borden Printing Co. (C. C. A. 9th, 1941), 123 Fed. (2d) 17.

In *Van Buskirk v. Kuhns,* 164 Cal. 472, 129 Pac. 587, the defendant appealed from a judgment against him, and from an order denying his motion for a new trial. Plaintiff sued to foreclose a mortgage on land, and defendant raised the bar of the statute of limitations. The plaintiff contended that the statute of limitations did not bar an action on defendant's promise to pay "when able," since such a promise was conditional and no cause of action accrues until the condition is performed, that is to say, until the debtor is able to pay.

The court agreed with the plaintiff, and on page 475 said:

"But if the views above expressed are sound, the very fact that prevents the statute from running (i. e., the lack of ability, on Reynold's part, to pay his debt), operates also to prevent the plaintiff from maintaining his action. The reason that the statute does not run is that the promise is conditional upon the debtor's ability to pay, and that a cause of action does not accrue until such ability exists. If the promise conditional upon such ability, it is, as is said in *Rodgers v. Byers,* 127 Cal. 528 (60 Pac. 42), incumbent upon the plaintiff to allege and prove that the condition has been complied with. This is not, like the plea of the statute of limitations, matter of defense. It is a substantive part of the cause of action, and the burden of proof with respect to it, is upon the plaintiff. (*Bidwell v. Rogers,* 10 Allen, 438; *Boynton v. Moulton,* 159 Mass. 248 (34 N. E. 361); *Veasey v. Reeves,* 6 Ind. 406; *Halladay v. Weeks,* 127 Mich. 363 (89 Am. St. Rep. 478, 86 N. W. 799); *Parker v. Butterworth,* 46 N. J. L. 244 (50 Am. Rep. 407). The complaint contains no allegation of such ability, and the court does not find it. There is, therefore, a want of averment and finding of facts establishing the existence of a cause of action. The plaintiff alleges a promise to pay in a certain event. He does not allege, and the court does not find, that the event upon which the obligation depends, has occurred. Neither the complaint, therefore, nor the findings, support the judgment. This defect is one that may be reviewed on an appeal from the judgment."

Conclusion.

The judgment of the District Court should be affirmed.

Respectfully submitted,

CLYDE R. BURR,

Attorney for Philip Grey Smith, Administrator with-will-annexed of the Estate of Olive Wills Wigmore, Deceased.

United States
Circuit Court of Appeals
For the Ninth Circuit. *see Vol*

2348

NATIONAL LABOR RELATIONS BOARD,

Petitioner,

vs.

THOMPSON PRODUCTS, INC., a corporation,

Respondent.

Transcript of Record
In Three Volumes
VOLUME I
Pages 1 to 484

Upon Petition for Enforcement of an Order of the National Labor Relations Board

FILED

MAY 14 1943

United States
Circuit Court of Appeals
For the Ninth Circuit.

NATIONAL LABOR RELATIONS BOARD,

Petitioner,

vs.

THOMPSON PRODUCTS, INC., a corporation,

Respondent.

Transcript of Record
In Three Volumes
VOLUME I
Pages 1 to 484

**Upon Petition for Enforcement of an Order of the National
Labor Relations Board**

Rotary Colorprint, 590 Folsom St., San Francisco   60-5-12-43

INDEX

[Clerk's Note: When deemed likely to be of an important nature, errors or doubtful matters appearing in the original certified record are printed literally in italic; and, likewise, cancelled matter appearing in the original certified record is printed and cancelled herein accordingly. When possible, an omission from the text is indicated by printing in italic the two words between which the omission seems to occur.]

Index   Page

Index **Page**

Index   **Page**

Index   Page

Exhibits for Respondent:

Index **Page**

Index   **Page**

Index **Page**

Index   Page

Index   Page

Index Page

United States of America
Before The National Labor Relations Board
21st Region

Case No. XXI   C2088
Date Filed 7/18, 1942

In the Matter of—

THOMPSON PRODUCTS, INC. (West Coast Plant)

and

UNITED AUTOMOBILE, AIRCRAFT & AGRI-CULTURAL IMPLEMENT WORKERS OF AMERICA (UAW-CIO)

SECOND AMENDED CHARGE

Pursuant to Section 10 (b) of the National Labor Relations Act, the undersigned hereby charges that Thompson Products, Inc. (West Coast Plant) at Bell, California employing 350 workers in manufacture of valves and bolts for aircraft industry has engaged in and is engaging in unfair labor practices within the meaning of Section 8 subsections (1) and (2) of said Act, in that in 1937 said Company, by its officers, agents and employees, formed among its employees a labor organization known as Pacific Motor Parts Workers Association, and at all times since said date has dominated and interfered with the operation and administration of the said Pacific Motor Parts Workers Association, in violation of Section 8, subsection (2) of said Act.

By the acts set forth in the paragraph above, the Company, by its officers, agents and employees interfered with, restrained and coerced its employees in the exercise of the rights guaranteed in Section 7 of the said Act, in violation of Section 8, subsection (1) of said Act.

The undersigned further charges that said unfair labor practices are unfair labor practices affecting commerce within the meaning of said Act.

Name and address of person or labor organization making the charge. (If made by a labor organization, give also the full name, local number and affiliation of organization, and name and official position of the person acting for the organization.)

> UNITED AUTOMOBILE, AIR-
> CRAFT & AGRICULTURAL
> IMPLEMENT WORKERS OF
> AMERICA (UAW-CIO)
>> By Clarence L. Johnson, Intl.
>> Representative, 5851 Ava-
>> lon Blvd., Los Angeles,
>> Calif. (ADams 8196)

Subscribed and sworn to before me this 18 day of July, 1942. At Los Angeles, California.

E. M. ENGLISH

Field Examiner National Labor Relations Board, 21st Region, Los Angeles, Calif.

2 copies to Bd. 7/20/42 M. A.

BOARD'S EXHIBIT No. 1-B

[Title of Board and Cause.]

COMPLAINT

It having been heretofore charged by United Automobile, Aircraft and Agricultural Implement Workers of America, (UAW-CIO), herein called the United, that Thompson Products, Inc., a corporation, herein called the Respondent, has engaged in and is now engaging in certain unfair labor practices affecting commerce, as set forth and defined in the National Labor Relations Act, 49 Stat. 449, herein called the Act, the National Labor Relations Board, by the Regional Director for the Twenty-first Region as agent for the National Labor Relations Board, designated by the National Labor Relations Board Rules and Regulations, Series 2, as amended, hereby alleges:

1. The Respondent is and has been at all times herein mentioned a corporation organized under and existing by virtue of the laws of the State of Ohio, having its principal offices at 2196 Clarkwood Road, Cleveland, Ohio.

2. The Respondent is and has been at all times herein mentioned licensed to do business in the State of California. The Respondent owns and operates a plant and place of business located at 8354 Wilcox Avenue, Bell, California, herein called the West Coast Plant, and the Respondent is now, and has been at all times herein mentioned, engaged at the West Coast Plant in the manufacture, sale and dis-

tribution of aircraft engine bolts, assembly bolts and miscellaneous aircraft engine and fuselage parts.

3. The Respondent, in the course and conduct of its business and in the operation of its West Coast Plant, causes and has continuously caused large quantities of raw materials, consisting principally of steel, to be purchased and transported in interstate commerce from, into and through various and several states of the United States other than the State of California to the Respondent's West Coast Plant in the State of California. The aforesaid materials so purchased and transported in interstate commerce constitute approximately 85% of the total value of the materials purchased or used by the Respondent in the course and conduct of its business and in the operation of said West Coast Plant. Respondent annually purchases steel valued at not less than $350,000.

4. The Respondent, in the course and conduct of its business and in the operation of its West Coast Plant, causes and has continuously caused large quantities of the products manufactured by it to be sold and transported in interstate commerce from said West Coast Plant in California to, through and into states of the United States other than the State of California. The aforesaid products so sold and transported in interstate commerce constitute approximately 65 per cent of the total value of the products sold or distributed by the Respondent from said West Coast Plant. The total value of the products sold or distributed by the Respondent, in the course and conduct of its business and in the opera-

tion of said West Coast Plant, is approximately $1,500,000 annually.

5. The United is a labor organization as defined in Section 2 subdivision (5) of the Act.

Pacific Motor Parts Workers Alliance, herein called the Alliance, is a labor organization as defined in Section 2 subdivision (5) of the Act.

6. The Respondent, through its officers and agents, in the course and conduct of its business at its West Coast Plant, on or about July 1937 instigated the formation of the Alliance among its employees; and has at all times since that date, down to and including the date of the filing of this complaint, dominated and interfered with the formation and administration of the Alliance, made statements to its employees favoring the Alliance, permitted the Alliance to solicit members, collect dues and engage in other activities in the West Coast Plant during working hours, while at the same time denying such privileges to the United, assisted the Alliance in soliciting members, collecting dues and engaging in other activities in the plant during working hours and otherwise actively fostered, promoted and encouraged the formation and growth of the Alliance and contributed assistance and support to the Alliance.

7. The Respondent, on or about August 12, 1937 entered into a written agreement with the Alliance covering wages, hours, and working conditions and recognizing it as the exclusive collective bargaining agent of all the employees at Respondent's West Coast Plant. Said agreement, together with cer-

tain amendments thereto and renewals thereof, has remained in full force and effect from on or about August 12, 1937, to and including the date of issuance of this Complaint.

8. By the acts described in paragraphs 6 and 7 above, the Respondent has engaged in and is engaging in unfair labor practices within the meaning of Section 8 subdivision (2) of the Act. Further, the agreement described in paragraph 7 above, together with any amendments thereto and any modification, extension or renewal thereof, is invalid and void.

9. The Respondent, through its officers, supervisory employees and agents, in the course and conduct of its business at its West Coast Plant has, from on or about July 1937 down to and including the date of filing of this complaint, interrogated employees with respect to the United and its activities, warned its employees that if the United were organized among them the West Coast Plant would be closed and its equipment moved to another location, refused to permit employees to engage in activities in behalf of the United on the company's premises or during working hours, while at the same time permitting members of the Alliance to engage in such activities on behalf of the Alliance on the plant premises during work hours, and has attempted to persuade employees not to join the United, for the purpose of inducing the employees to forego the exercise of rights guaranteed them under Section 7 of the Act, and for the further purpose of undermining the United as a representative of the employees.

10. By the acts set forth in paragraphs 6, 7 and 9 above the Respondent has interfered with, restrained and coerced and is interfering with, restraining and coercing its employees in the exercise of the rights guaranteed to them in Section 7 of the Act, and has thereby engaged in and is thereby engaging in unfair labor practices within the meaning of Section 8, subdivision (1) of the Act.

11. The acts of the Respondent set forth in paragraphs 6, 7 and 9 above occurring in connection with the operations of the Respondent, described in paragraphs 1, 2, 3 and 4 above, have a close, intimate and substantial relation to trade, traffic and commerce among and between the several states of the United States and tend to lead to labor disputes burdening and obstructing commerce and the free flow of commerce.

12. The aforesaid acts of the Respondent set forth in paragraphs 6, 7 and 9 above constitute unfair labor practices affecting commerce within the meaning of Section 8 subdivisions (1) and (2), and Section 2 subdivisions (6) and (7) of the Act.

Wherefore, the National Labor Relations Board on this 28th day of August, 1942, issues its Complaint against Thompson Products, Inc., the Respondent herein.

[Seal]   WM. R. WALSH

        Regional Director, National Labor Relations Board, Twenty-first Region, 808 U. S. Post Office and Courthouse, Los Angeles, California.

BOARD'S EXHIBIT No. 1-C

[Title of Board and Cause.]

NOTICE OF HEARING

Please Take Notice that on the 14th day of September, 1942, at 10:00 o'clock in the forenoon in Room 808, U. S. Post Office and Court House, Los Angeles, California, a hearing will be conducted before a duly designated Trial Examiner of the National Labor Relations Board on the allegations set forth in the Complaint attached hereto, at which time and place you will have the right to appear in person, or otherwise, and give testimony.

A copy of the Second Amended Charge upon which the Complaint is based is attached hereto.

You are further notified that you have the right to file with the Regional Director for the 21st Region, with offices at Room 808, U. S. Post Office and Court House, Los Angeles, California, acting in this matter as agent of the National Labor Relations Board, an answer to the said Complaint, within ten (10) days from the service thereof.

Please Take Notice that duplicates of all exhibits which are offered in evidence will be required unless, pursuant to request or motion, the Trial Examiner in the exercise of his discretion and for good cause shown, directs that a given exhibit need not be duplicated.

In Witness Whereof the National Labor Relations Board has caused this, its Complaint and Notice of Hearing, to be signed by the Regional Director for the 21st Region on this 28th day of August, 1942.

[Seal]   WM. R. WALSH

Regional Director, National Labor Relations Board, Twenty-first Region, U. S. Post Office & Court House, Los Angeles, California

---

BOARD'S EXHIBIT No. 1-D

[Title of Board and Cause.]

AFFIDAVIT AS TO SERVICE

State of California,
County of Los Angeles—ss.

I, Marion Riemer, being duly sworn, depose and say that I am an employee of the National Labor Relations Board, in the 21st Region at Los Angeles, California, on the 29th day of August, 1942, I served by postpaid registered mail, bearing Government frank, a copy of Complaint, Notice of Hearing, and Second Amended Charge to the following named persons, addressed to them at the following addresses:

Thompson Products, Inc.
2196 Clarkwood Road
Cleveland, Ohio

Thompson Products, Inc.
8354 Wilcox Avenue
Bell, California

United Automobile Aircraft & Agricultural Implement Workers of America (UAW-CIO)
5851 Avalon Boulevard
Los Angeles, California

Pacific Motor Parts Workers Alliance
Howard Curtis Baldwin, President
7727 Wilcox Avenue
Bell, California

MARION RIEMER

Subscribed and sworn to before me this 29th day of August, 1942.

[Seal]   (Illegible) LYONS

Notary Public in and for the County of Los Angeles, State of California.

My Commission Expires Nov. 24, 1943.

BOARD'S EXHIBIT 1-*D*

Form 3806 (Rev. Jan. 21, 1935)   (Postmark of)
Receipt for Registered Article No. 399380.

Registered at the Post Office indicated in the Postmark.

Fee paid 15 cents. Class postage . . . . .

Declared value. . . . . . Surcharge paid, $. . . . . .

Return Receipt fee. . . . . . Spl. Del'y fee. . . . . .

Delivery restricted to addressee: in person. . . . . . , or order. . . . . . Fee paid. . . . . .

Accepting employee will place his initials in space indicating restricted delivery.

Postmaster, per. . . . . (Mailing Office)

(Stamped)—Los Angeles, Calif. Registered. Aug. 29 1942. Return Receipt Requested. Fee Paid. No Value.

(Receipt for Registered Article No. 399381 identical with above except for number.)

(Receipt for Registered Article No. 399382 identical with above except for number.)

(Receipt for Registered Article No. 399383 identical with above except for number.)

(Post Card)

C 2088 (Illegible)

Penalty for Private Use to Avoid Payment of
Postage, $300
Postmark of Delivering Office
Post Office Department
Official Business

Return to National Labor Relations Board.

(Street and Number, or Post Office Box)—U. S. Post Office & Court House Bldg., Los Angeles, California.

Registered Article.

No. 399380.

Insured Parcel.

No..........

Los Angeles, California.

(Stamped)—Cleveland, Ohio 8 Sep 2 8:30 PM 1942.

Return Receipt

Received from the Postmaster the Registered or Insured Article, the original number of which appears on the face of this Card.

1—(Signature or name of addressee)—Thompson Products.

2 — (Signature of addressee's agent — Agent should enter addressee's name on line One above)— L. Smetana.

Date of delivery 9/2, 1942.

(Stamped)—Received Sep 7 1942. National Labor-Relations Board, Twenty-first Region, Los Angeles.

[3 additional cards identical with above except as follows:

No. 399381 bears post office stamp of Bell, Calif., Aug. 31, 1942, and is signed as follows: 1—Thompson Products Inc. 2—Leonard Stampfll. Date of delivery Aug 31 1942.

No. 399382 bears post office stamp of Los Angeles, Calif., Sept. 2, 1942, and is signed as follows: 1— UAW-CIO. 2—A. Gilbert. Date of Delivery 8/31- 1942.

No. 399383 bears post office stamp of Bell, Calif., Aug. 31, 1942, and is signed as follows: 1—Howard Curtis Baldwin. 2—Vera M. Baldwin. Date of delivery Aug 31 1942.]

BOARD'S EXHIBIT No. 1-F

[Title of Board and Cause.]

MOTION FOR CONTINUANCE

To the Regional Director, Twenty-First Region, National Labor Relations Board, Los Angeles, California:

Thompson Products, Inc., respondent in the above entitled action, hereby moves that the trial of the above case be continued to a date on or after September 28, 1942, on the following grounds:

(1) That Mr. Paul Hileman is the officer in charge of the Los Angeles Division of respondent, and is in charge of and familiar with matters occurring at the Los Angeles Division set forth in the Complaint.

(2) That respondent feels that Mr. Hileman should be present at the hearing and participate therein, and that no one else in the organization can take his place.

(3) Said Mr. Hileman has now made train reservations to leave Los Angeles Sunday, September 6th, for Cleveland, Ohio, and return reservations which will permit him to arrive in Los Angeles on September 23rd.

(4) That in addition to the possible difficulty of obtaining additional reservations, the prospective trip should not be postponed because its purpose is to make plans for expansion of the facilities of respondent herein in Los Angeles at the earliest possible moment, and no one else can make the trip for said purposes except Mr. Hileman.

(5) That the request for a continuance of at least two weeks is based on the fact that Mr. Hileman might be detained for a few days in his return, and upon his return will have to familiarize himself with the matters involved in the hearing.

Wherefore, respondent prays that the above entitled case now set for hearing on September 14, 1942, be continued to a date not earlier than September 28, 1942.

> Respectfully submitted,
> LATHAM & WATKINS
> By RICHARD W. LUND
> Attorneys for Respondent

BOARD'S EXHIBIT No. 1-G

[Title of Board and Cause.]

ORDER AND NOTICE OF CONTINUANCE

This matter having come before William R. Walsh, Regional Director for the Twenty-first Region, National Labor Relations Board, upon motion of Latham and Watkins, attorneys for Thompson Products, Inc., requesting a continuance of the hearing in this matter;

And said motion being duly considered and a continuance of the hearing herein appearing to be necessary and proper;

It Is Hereby Ordered that the hearing herein, heretofore scheduled to begin on the 14th day of September, 1942, shall be, and it hereby is, continued to September 28, 1942, on which date the hearing shall be held at 10:00 a.m. at the place stated in the Notice of Hearing heretofore issued herein.

Dated: At Los Angeles, California, this 2nd day of September, 1942.

[Seal] WM. R. WALSH

Regional Director, 21st Region National Labor Relations Board U. S. Post Office & Court House Los Angeles, California

----

[Title of Board and Cause.]

AFFIDAVIT AS TO SERVICE

State of California
County of Los Angeles—ss.

I, Marion Riemer, being duly sworn, depose and say that I am an employee of the National Labor Relations Board, in the 21st Region at Los Angeles, California, on the 2nd day of September, 1942, I served by postpaid registered mail, bearing Government frank, a copy of Order and Notice of Continuance to the following named persons, addressed to them at the following addresses:

Thompson Products, Inc.
2196 Clarkwood Road
Cleveland, Ohio

Thompson Products, Inc.
8354 Wilcox Avenue
Bell, California

United Automobile Aircraft & Agricultural Implement Workers of America (UAW-CIO)
5851 Avalon Boulevard
Los Angeles, California

Pacific Motor Parts Workers Alliance
Howard Curtis Baldwin, President
7727 Wilcox Avenue
Bell, California

MARION RIEMER

Subscribed and sworn to before me this 2nd day of September, 1942.

(Illegible) LYONS

Notary Public in and for the County of Los Angeles, State of California.

My Commission Expires Nov. 24, 1943.

BOARD'S EXHIBIT No. 1-I

Form 3806 (Rev. Jan. 21, 1935)   (Postmark of)
Receipt for Registered Article No. 380396.

Registered at the Post Office indicated in the Postmark.

Fee paid 15 cents. Class postage .....

Declared value...... Surcharge paid, $......

Return Receipt fee...... Spl. Del'y fee......

Delivery restricted to addressee: in person......, or order...... Fee paid......

Accepting employee will place his initials in space indicating restricted delivery.

Postmaster, per............. (Mailing Office)

(Stamped)—Los Angeles, Calif. Registered. Sep 2 1942. Return Receipt Requested. Fee Paid. No Value.

(Receipt for Registered Article No. 380397 identical with above except for number.)

(Receipt for Registered Article No. 380398 identical with above except for number.)

(Receipt for Registered Article No. 380399 identical with above except for number.)

(Post Card)

C 2088 (Illegible)

Penalty for Private Use to Avoid Payment of Postage, $300

Postmark of Delivering Office
Post Office Department
Official Business

Return to National Labor Relations Board.

(Street and Number, or Post Office Box)—U. S. Post Office & Court House Bldg., Los Angeles, California.

Registered Article.

No. 380396.

Insured Parcel.

No..........

Los Angeles, California.

Return Receipt

Received from the Postmaster the Registered or Insured Article, the original number of which appears on the face of this Card.

1 (Signature or name of addressee)—T P Inc.

2 (Signature of addressee's agent—Agent should enter addressee's name on line One above)—(Illegible).

Date of delivery—9-9, 1942. (Stamped also "Sep 8 1942")

[3 additional cards identical with above except as follows:

No. 380397 bears post office stamp of Bell, Calif., Sept. 3, 1942, and is signed as follows: 1—Thompson Products, Inc. 2—Leonard Stampfli. Date of delivery 9/3/1942.

No. 380398 bears post office stamp of Los Angeles, Calif., Sept. 3, 1942, and is signed as follows: 1—UAWA. 2—Sherry Wallace. Date of delivery 9/3/1942.

No. 380399 bears post office stamp of Bell, Calif., Sept. 4, 1942, and is signed as follows: 1—Howard Curtis Baldwin. 2—Vera M. Baldwin. Date of delivery Sept 3/1942]

BOARD'S EXHIBIT No. 1-J

[Title of Board and Cause.]

MOTION FOR CONTINUANCE

To the Regional Director, Twenty-first Region, National Labor Relations Board, Los Angeles, California:

Thompson Products, Inc., respondent in the above entitled action, hereby moves that the trial of the above case be continued to a date on or after October 1, 1942, on the following grounds:

That the date of September 28, 1942 to which the hearing has now been continued will not enable Mr. Ray Livingstone to be here until the trial starts. Mr. Ray Livingstone is the only person in the company familiar with the events which occurred back in 1937 and it is essential that he be here at least two (2) days before the trial starts. Mr. Livingstone has a meeting of some importance in New York on September 24, 1942 at which he is to make an address and the meeting has been scheduled for quite some time.

Wherefore, respondent prays that the above entitled case now set for hearing on September 28, 1942, be continued to a date not earlier than October 1, 1942.

Respectfully submitted,
LATHAM & WATKINS
By RICHARD W. LUND
Attorneys for Respondent

(AFFIDAVIT OF SERVICE BY MAIL— 1013a, C. C. P.)

[Title of Board and Cause.]

AFFIDAVIT OF SERVICE OF MOTION FOR CONTINUANCE.

State of California,
County of Los Angeles—ss.

C. D. Zuppann, being first duly sworn, says: That affiant is a citizen of the United States and a resident of the County of Los Angeles; that affiant is over the age of eighteen years and is not a party to the within and above entitled action; that affiant's business address is: 1112 Title Guarantee

Bldg., 5 & Hill, that on the 4th day of September, 1942, affiant served the within Motion for Continuance on the Union in said action, by placing a true copy thereof in an envelope addressed to said Union, at the office address of said Union, as follows: (Here quote from envelope name and address of addressee.) "United Automobile, Aircraft & Agricultural Implement Workers of America (UAW-CIO) 5851 Avalon Blvd., Los Angeles, Calif. Attention: Clarence L. Johnson"; and by then sealing said envelope and depositing the same, with postage thereon fully prepaid, in the United States Post Office at Los Angeles, California, where is located the office of said Union.

That there is delivery service by United States mail at the place so addressed, or there is a regular communication by mail between the place of mailing and the place so addressed.

C. D. ZUPPANN

Subscribed and sworn to before me this 4th day of September, 1942.

[Seal]   ISOBEL V. HUGHES

Notary Public in and for the County of Los Angeles, State of California.

BOARD'S EXHIBIT No. 1-K

[Title of Board and Cause.]

ORDER AND NOTICE OF CONTINUANCE

This matter having come before William R. Walsh, Regional Director for the Twenty-first Region, National Labor Relations Board, upon motion of Latham and Watkins, attorneys for Thompson Products, Inc., requesting a continuance of the hearing in this matter;

And said motion being duly considered and a continuance of the hearing herein appearing to be necessary and proper;

It Is Hereby Ordered that the hearing herein, heretofore scheduled to begin on the 28th day of September, 1942, shall be, and it hereby is, continued to October 1, 1942, on which date the hearing shall be held at 10:00 a.m., at the place stated in the Notice of Hearing heretofore issued herein.

Dated: At Los Angeles, California, this 9th day of September, 1942.

[Seal] WM. R. WALSH

Regional Director, 21st Region National Labor Relations Board, U. S. Post Office & Court House, Los Angeles, California.

BOARD'S EXHIBIT No. 1-L

[Title of Board and Cause.]

AFFIDAVIT AS TO SERVICE

State of California,

County of Los Angeles—ss:

I, Marion Riemer, being duly sworn, depose and say that I am an employee of the National Labor Relations Board, in the 21st Region at Los Angeles, California, on the 9th day of September 1942, I served by postpaid registered mail, bearing Government frank, a copy of Order and Notice of Continuance, dated September 9, 1942, to the following named persons, addressed to them at the following addresses:

Thompson Products, Inc.
2196 Clarkwood Road
Cleveland, Ohio

Thompson Products, Inc.
8354 Wilcox Avenue
Bell, California

United Automobile Aircraft & Agricultural Implement Workers of America (UAW-CIO)
5851 Avalon Boulevard
Los Angeles, California

Pacific Motor Parts Workers Alliance
Howard Curtis Baldwin, President
7727 Wilcox Avenue
Bell, California

MARION RIEMER

Subscribed and sworn to before me this 9th day of September, 1942.

[Seal]   (Illegible) LYONS

Notary Public in and for the County of Los Angeles, State of California. My commission expires Nov. 24, 1943.

————

Form 3806 (Rev. Jan. 21, 1935)   (Postmark of)
Receipt for Registered Article No. 381037.

Registered at the Post Office indicated in the Postmark.

Fee paid 15 cents. Class postage .....

Declared value...... Surcharge paid, $......

Return Receipt fee...... Spl. Del'y fee......

Delivery restricted to addressee: in person......,
or order...... Fee paid......

Accepting employee will place his initials in
space indicating restricted delivery.

Postmaster, per.............. (Mailing Office)

(Stamped)—Los Angeles, Calif. Sep 9 1942. Registered.

(Stamped)—Return Receipt Requested. Fee
Paid.

[Receipt for Registered Article No. 381038 identical with above except for Number.

Receipt for Registered Article No. 381039 identical with above except for Number.

Receipt for Registered Article No. 381040 identical with above except for Number.]

(Post Card)

C 2088 (Illegible)

Post Office Department

Official Business

Penalty for Private Use to Avoid Payment of
Postage, $300

Postmark of Delivering Office

Bell, Calif., Sep. 10, 1942. 6 p.m.

Return to National Labor Relations Board.

(Street and Number, or Post Office Box)—U. S.
Post Office & Court House Bldg., Los Angeles,
California.

Registered Article.

No. 381037.

Insured Parcel.

No.........

Los Angeles, California.

Return Receipt

Received from the Postmaster the Registered or Insured Article, the original number of which appears on the face of this Card.

1—(Signature or name of addressee)—Thompson Products Inc.

2—(Signature of addressee's agent — Agent should enter addressee's name on line One above)— Leonard Stampfli.

Date of delivery—9-10, 1942.

3 additional cards identical with above except as follows:

No. 381038 bears postoffice stamp of Cleveland, Ohio, Sept. 14, 1942, and is signed as follows:

1—T. P. Inc.

2—J. G. Pishaw

Date of delivery Sep 12 1942

No. 381039 bears postoffice stamp of Bell, Calif., Sept. 10, 1942, and is signed as follows:

1—Howard Curtis Baldwin

2—Vera M. Baldwin

Date of delivery Sep 10 1942

No. 381040 bears postoffice stamp of Los Angeles, Calif., Sept. 10, 1942, and is signed as follows:

1—UAW-CIO

2—Dorothy Eckert

Date 9/9/1942

BOARD'S EXHIBIT No. 1-M

[Title of Board and Cause.]

MOTION TO STRIKE OR IN THE ALTERNATIVE FOR A BILL OF PARTICULARS

Thompson Products, Inc., respondent in the above-entitled action hereby moves:

I.

That the following be stricken from the complaint on file herein, the basis for the motion to strike being that the matters hereinafter referred to are conclusions and not statements of fact:

1. In paragraph 6, the following:

(a) In line 3 the word "instigated."

(b) In line 5 the words "dominated and interfered."

(c) In lines 6 and 7 the words "made statements to its employees favoring the Alliance."

(d) In line 7 the words "permitted the Alliance to solicit members."

(e) In line 8 the words "engage in other activities.'"

(f) In lines 9 and 10 the words "assisted the Alliance in soliciting members, collecting dues and engaging in other activities."

(g) In lines 10 and 11 the following words "otherwise actively fostered, promoted and encouraged the formation and growth."

2. In paragraph 8 the following appearing in lines 3 to 6, inclusive: "Further, the agreement described in paragraph 7 above, together with any

amendments thereto and any modification, extension or renewal thereof, is invalid and void."

3. In paragraph 9, the following:

(a) In lines 4 and 5 the words "interrogated
employees with respect to the union and its activities."

(b) In line 5 the words "warned its employees."

(c) In lines 7 and 8 the words "refused to
permit employees to engage in activities in behalf
of the United."

(d) In lines 9 and 10 the words "while at the
same time permitting members of the Alliance to
engage in such activities."

(e) In line 11 the words "and has attempted
to persuade employees."

(f) In line 12 the words "for the purpose of
inducing the employees."

(g) In line 14 the words "and for the further
purpose of undermining the United."

II.

Or in the alternative as to any of the foregoing
not stricken that the particular facts, in concise
form, be set forth in a bill of particulars with respect to each of the foregoing matters. This alternative portion of the motion is based on the prem-
ise that respondent is unable to prepare for the
defense of this action because of the conclusions
and generalities contained in the complaint and
hereinabove moved to be stricken.

Wherefore, respondent prays that the foregoing

motion to strike or in the alternative motion for a bill of particulars be granted as to each of the matters hereinabove set forth.

Respectfully submitted,
LATHAM & WATKINS
By PAUL N. WATKINS
Attorneys for Respondent.

———

BOARD'S EXHIBIT No. 1-N

[Title of Board and Cause.]

MOTION TO DISMISS

Thompson Products, Inc., respondent in the above-entitled action hereby moves that the complaint on file herein be dismissed on the following grounds:

1. That the activities complained of took place some five and one-half years ago; that during all of said period, the alleged facts were known by the charging union; that while public policy is allegedly involved, it is of greater importance that the National Labor Relations Act be administered in a manner fair to respondent; and that this delay results in an unfairness to respondent in that it is unable at this late date to adequately defend itself with respect to matters occurring that long ago.

2. That the charges upon which the complaint is based are insufficient and do not conform with the Rules and Regulations, Series 2, as amended, particularly subdivision c, Section 4 of Article II.

Wherefore, respondent prays that the complaint on file herein be dismissed forthwith.

Respectfully submitted,

LATHAM & WATKINS

By PAUL N. WATKINS

Attorneys for Respondent

BOARD'S EXHIBIT No. 1-O

[Title of Board and Cause.]

ANSWER OF RESPONDENT

Thompson Products, Inc., respondent in the above-entitled action for answer to the complaint on file herein admits, denies, alleges and explains as follows:

1. Admits the allegations contained in paragraph 1.

2. Admits the allegations contained in paragraph 2.

3. Admits the allegations contained in paragraph 3, except with respect to the purchase and transportation of materials in interstate commerce, and in this connection alleges that a substantial portion of such materials comes indirectly and not directly to respondent from the several states.

4. Admits the allegations contained in paragraph 4, except that in connection with the sale of the products of respondent, a very substantial amount thereof is actually sold within the State of California and is not shipped by respondent through and into states of the United States other than the State of California.

5. Admits the allegations contained in paragraph 5.

6. Denies each and every allegation, matter and fact contained in paragraph 6. In this connection, respondent alleges that it or its predecessor has had a valid collective bargaining agreement with the Alliance for a long period of time, and that the Alliance has done only such things on company time or property as are permitted of a bargaining agency under such circumstances.

7. Admits the allegations contained in paragraph 7, except the allegation that respondent entered into an agreement on or about August 12, 1937 and renewed it from time to time. In this connection, respondent alleges that its first contract with the Alliance occurred after July 1, 1940.

8. Denies each and every allegation, matter and fact contained in paragraph 8.

9. Denies each and every allegation, matter and fact contained on paragraph 9.

10. Denies each and every allegation, matter and fact contained in paragraph 10.

11. Denies each and every allegation, matter and fact contained in paragraph 11. In this connection, respondent alleges that its relationships with its employees and the Alliance during the period described in the complaint have tended to lessen labor disputes burdening and obstructing commerce and the free flow of commerce, and will continue in the future so to do, and further that should the relief requested in the complaint be

granted, the result of that action will be that it will lead to labor disputes burdening and obstructing commerce and the free flow of commerce.

12. Denies each and every allegation, matter and fact contained in paragraph 12.

Wherefore, respondent prays that the complaint on file herein be dismissed with prejudice.

Respectfully submitted,

LATHAM & WATKINS

By PAUL N. WATKINS

Attorneys for Respondent whose Post Office address is 8354 Wilcox Avenue, Bell, California.

State of California,
County of Los Angeles—ss.

Paul D. Hileman, being first sworn, says: That he is the Plant Manager of respondent's Los Angeles County operations; that there are no officers of respondent in the State of California and for that reason affiant makes this verification on respondent's behalf and as its attorney in fact; that he has read the foregoing answer and knows the contents thereof and the same is true of his own knowledge, except as to those matters which are therein stated on his information or belief; and as to those matters he believes it to be true.

PAUL D. HILEMAN

Subscribed and sworn to before me this 4th day of September, 1942.

[Seal]   NEVA V. JOCKISCH

Notary Public in and for said County and State.

My commission expires November 4, 1945.

BOARD'S EXHIBIT No. 1-P

[Title of Board and Cause.]

THIRD AMENDED CHARGE

Pursuant to Section 10 (b) of the National Labor Relations Act, the undersigned hereby charges that Thompson Products, Inc. (West Coast Plant) at Bell, California, employing 350 workers in manufacture of valves and bolts for aircraft industry has engaged in and is engaging in unfair labor practices within the meaning of Section 8 subsections (1) and (2) of said Act, in that in 1937 said Company, by its officers, agents and employees, formed among its employees a labor organization known as Pacific Motor Parts Workers Alliance, and at all times since said date has dominated and interfered with the operation and administration of the said Pacific Motor Parts Workers Alliance, in violation of Section 8, subsection (2) of said Act. By the acts set forth in the paragraph above, and by other acts and statements, the Company, by its officers, agents and employees interfered with, restrained and coerced, and is interfering with, restraining and coercing, its employees in the exercise of the rights guaranteed in Section 7 of the said Act, in violation of Section 8, subsection (1) of said Act.

The undersigned further charges that said unfair labor practices are unfair labor practices affecting commerce within the meaning of said Act.

Name and address of person or labor organization making the charge. (If made by a labor organization, give also the full name, local number and affiliation of organization, and name and official position of the person acting for the organization.)

UNITED AUTOMOBILE, AIR-
CRAFT & AGRICULTURAL
IMPLEMENT WORKERS OF
AMERICA (UAW-CIO)

By CLARENCE L. JOHNSON

Intl. Representative, 5851
Avalon Blvd., Los Angeles,
Calif. Phone: ADams 8196.

Subscribed and sworn to before me this 16 day of Sept., 1942, at Los Angeles, California.

ROBERT C. MOORE

Attorney, National Labor Relations Board, 21st Region,
Los Angeles, Calif.

2 copies to Bd. 9-16-42. Mc.

———

BOARD'S EXHIBIT No. 1-Q

[Title of Board and Cause.]

AMENDED COMPLAINT

It having been heretofore charged by United Automobile, Aircraft and Agricultural Implement Workers of America, (UAW-CIO), herein called the United, that Thompson Products, Inc., a corporation, herein called the Respondent, has engaged in and is now engaging in certain unfair labor practices affecting commerce, as set forth and defined in the National Labor Relations Act,

49 Stat. 449, herein called the Act, the National Labor Relations Board, by the Regional Director for the Twenty-first Region as agent for the National Labor Relations Board, designated by the National Labor Relations Board Rules and Regulations, Series 2, as amended, hereby alleges:

1. The Respondent is and has been at all times herein mentioned a corporation organized under and existing by virtue of the laws of the State of Ohio, having its principal offices at 2196 Clarkwood Road, Cleveland, Ohio.

2. The Respondent is and has been at all times herein mentioned licensed to do business in the State of California. The Respondent owns and operates a plant and place of business located at 8354 Wilcox Avenue, Bell, California, herein called the West Coast Plant, and the Respondent is now, and has been at all times herein mentioned, engaged at the West Coast Plant in the manufacture, sale and distribution of aircraft engine bolts, assembly bolts and miscellaneous aircraft engine and fuselage parts.

3. The Respondent, in the course and conduct of its business and in the operation of its West Coast Plant, causes and has continuously caused large quantities of raw materials, consisting principally of steel, to be purchased and transported in interstate commerce from, into and through various and several states of the United States other than the State of California to the Respondent's West Coast Plant in the State of California. The aforesaid materials so purchased and transported in inter-

state commerce constitute approximately 85 per cent of the total value of the materials purchased or used by the Respondent in the course and conduct of its business and in the operation of said West Coast Plant. Respondent annually purchases steel for said West Coast Plant valued at not less than $350,000.

4. The Respondent, in the course and conduct of the business and in the operation of its West Coast Plant, causes and has continuously caused large quantities of the products manufactured by it to be sold and transported in interstate commerce from said West Coast Plant in California to, through and into states of the United States other than the State of California. The aforesaid products so sold and transported in interstate commerce constitute approximately 65 percent of the total value of the products sold or distributed by the Respondent from said West Coast Plant. The total value of the products sold or distributed by the Respondent, in the course and conduct of its business and in the operation of said West Coast Plant, is approximately $1,500,000 annually.

5. The United is a labor organization as defined in Section 2 subdivision (5) of the Act.

Pacific Motor Parts Workers Alliance, herein called the Alliance, is a labor organization as defined in Section 2 subdivision (5) of the Act.

6. The Respondent, through its officers and agents, in the course and conduct of its business at its West Coast Plant, on or about July 1937 instigated the formation of the Alliance among its em-

ployees; and has at all times since that date, down to and including the date of the filing of this Amended Complaint, dominated and interfered with the formation and administration of the Alliance, made statements to its employees favoring the Alliance, permitted the Alliance to solicit members, collect dues and engage in other activities in the West Coast Plant during working hours, while at the same time denying such privileges to the United, assisted the Alliance in soliciting members, collecting dues and engaging in other activities in the plant during working hours, permitted employees to leave their work during regularly scheduled working hours to attend meetings of the Alliance, and otherwise actively fostered, promoted and encouraged the formation and growth of the Alliance and contributed assistance and support to the Alliance.

7. The Respondent, on or about August 12, 1937, entered into a written agreement with the Alliance covering wages, hours, and working conditions and recognizing it as the exclusive collective bargaining agent of all the employees at Respondent's West Coast, Plant. Said agreement, together with, certain amendments thereto and renewals thereof, by its terms remained in full force and effect from on or about August 12, 1937, to and including November 10, 1941. On or about November 10, 1941, Respondent entered into a further written agreement with the Alliance recognizing it as the exclusive collective bargaining agent for all employees at the West

Coast Plant and covering wages, hours and working conditions. Said agreement by its terms has remained in full force and effect from on or about November 10, 1941, to and including the date of issuance of this Amended Complaint.

8. By the acts described in paragraphs 6 and 7, above, the Respondent has engaged in and is engaging in unfair labor practices within the meaning of Section 8 subdivision (2) of the Act. Further, the agreements described in paragraph 7 above, together with any amendments thereto and any modifications, extensions, or renewals thereof, are invalid and void.

. 9. The Respondent, through its officers, supervisory employees and agents, in the course and conduct of its business at it West Coast Plant has, from on or about April 1937 down to and including the date of filing of this Amended Complaint, caused one of its employees to join the United for the purpose of observing and reporting to Respondent the activities of the United and solicited and received reports of the activities of the United from said employee, interrogated employees with respect to the United and its activities, warned its employees that if the United were organized among them the West Coast Plant would be closed and its equipment moved to another location, and has attempted to persuade employees not to join the United, for the purpose of inducing the employees to forego the exercise of rights guaranteed them under Section 7 of the Act, and for the further purpose of undermining the United as a representative of the employees.

10. By the acts set forth in paragraphs 6, 7 and 9 above the Respondent has interfered with, restrained and coerced and is interfering with, restraining and coercing its employees in the exercise of the rights guaranteed to them in Section 7 of the Act, and has thereby engaged in and is thereby engaging in unfair labor practices within the meaning of Section 8 subdivision (1) of the Act.

11. The acts of the Respondent set forth in paragraphs 6, 7 and 9 above, occurring in connection with the operations of the Respondent, described in paragraphs 1, 2, 3 and 4 above, have a close, intimate and substantial relation to trade, traffic and commerce among and between the several states of the United States and tend to lead to labor disputes burdening and obstructing commerce and the free flow of commerce.

12. The aforesaid acts of the Respondent set forth in paragraphs 6, 7, and 9 above constitute unfair labor practices affecting commerce within the meaning of Section 8 subdivisions (1) and (2), and Section 2 subdivisions (6) and (7) of the Act.

Wherefore, the National Labor Relations Board on this 17th day of September, 1942, issues its

Amended Complaint against Thompson Products, Inc., the Respondent herein.

WM. R. WALSH

Regional Director, National Labor Relations Board, Twenty-first Region

[Seal]

808 U. S. Post Office and Court House, Los Angeles, California.

BOARD'S EXHIBIT No. 1-R

[Title of Board and Cause.]

NOTICE OF HEARING ON AMENDED COMPLAINT

Please Take Notice that on the 1st day of October, 1942, at 10:00 o'clock in the forenoon in Room 808, U. S. Post Office and Court House, Los Angeles, California a hearing will be conducted before a duly designated Trial Examiner of the National Labor Relations Board on the allegations set forth in the Complaint attached hereto, at which time and place you will have the right to appear in person, or otherwise, and give testimony.

A copy of the Third Amended Charge upon which the Complaint is based is attached hereto.

You are further notified that you have the right to file with the Regional Director for the 21st Region, with offices at Room 808, U. S. Post Office and Court House, Los Angeles, California, acting in this matter as agent of the National Labor Relations Board, an answer to the said Complaint, within ten (10) days from the service thereof.

Please Take Notice that duplicates of all exhibits which are offered in evidence will be required unless, pursuant to request or motion, the Trial Examiner in the exercise of his discretion and for good cause shown, directs that a given exhibit need not be duplicated.

In Witness Whereof the National Labor Relations Board has caused this, its Complaint and Notice of Hearing, to be signed by the Regional Director for the 21st Region on this 17th day of September, 1942.

[Seal]   WM. R. WALSH

Regional Director. National Labor Relations Board. Twenty-first Region, U. S. Post Office & Court House, Los Angeles, California.

BOARD'S EXHIBIT No. 1-S

Case No. XXI-C-2088

[Title of Board and Cause.]

AFFIDAVIT AS TO SERVICE

State of California,

County of Los Angeles—ss.

I, Ida N. Myers, being duly sworn, depose and say that I am an employee of the National Labor Relations Board, in the 21st Region at Los Angeles, California; on the 17th day of September, 1942, I served by postpaid registered mail, bearing Government frank, a copy of Notice of Hearing on Amended Complaint, Amended Complaint, and Third Amended Charge to the following named persons, addressed to them at the following addresses:

Thompson Products, Inc.
2196 Clarkwood Road
Cleveland, Ohio

United Automobile Aircraft & Agricultural Implement Workers of America (UAW-CIO)
5851 Avalon Boulevard
Los Angeles, California

Pacific Motor Parts Workers Alliance
Howard Curtis Baldwin, President
7727 Wilcox Avenue
Bell, California

Thompson Products, Inc.
8354 Wilcox Avenue
Bell, California

IDA N. MYERS

Subscribed and sworn to before me this 17th day of September, 1942.

[Seal]   (Illegible) LYONS

My commission expires Nov. 24, 1943.

Receipt for Registered Article No. 382069

Registered at the Post Office indicated in the Postmark.

Fee paid 15 cents. Class postage_____

Declared value...... Surcharge paid, $......

Return Receipt fee...... Spl. Del'y fee......

Delivery restricted to addressee: in person......, or order...... Fee paid......

Accepting employee will place his initials in space indicating restricted delivery.

(Stamped)—Los Angeles, Calif. Registered. Sept. 17, 1942.

(Stamped)—Los Angeles, Calif. Registered.

(Stamped)—Return Receipt Requested. Fee Paid. No Value.

Form 3806 (Rev. Jan. 21, 1935)   (Postmark of)

(Receipt for Registered Article No. 382070 identical with above except for Number.)

(Receipt for Registered Article No. 382071 identical with above except for number.)

(Receipt for Registered Article No. 382072 identical with above except for number.)

(Post Card)

C 2088 (Illegible)

Post Office Department

Official Business

Penalty for Private Use to Avoid Payment of Postage, $300

Postmark of Delivering Office

Bell, Calif., Sep. 10, 1942. 6 p.m.

Return to National Labor Relations Board.

(Street and Number, or Post Office Box)—U. S. Post Office & Court House Bldg., Los Angeles, California.

Registered Article No. 382069.

Insured Parcel.

No.........

Los Angeles, California.

Return Receipt

Received from the Postmaster the Registered or Insured Article, the original number of which appears on the face of this Card.

1. Howard Curtis Baldwin

2. Vera M. Baldwin

Date of delivery Sep. 18, 1942.

[3 additional cards identical with above except as follows:

No. 382070 bears post office stamp of Bell, Calif., Sept. 18, 1942, and is signed as follows: Thompson Products Co., Leonard Stampfli. Date of delivery 9/18 1942.

No. 382071 bears post office stamp of Los Angeles, Calif., Sept. 18, 1942, and is signed as follows: U. A. W., A. Gilbert. Date of delivery 9/18 1942.

No. 382072 bears post office stamp of Cleveland, Ohio, Sept. 21, 1942, and is signed as follows: T. P. Inc., J. G. Pishaw. Date of delivery 9/19, 1942.]

BOARD'S EXHIBIT No. 1-T

UNITED STATES OF AMERICA

National Labor Relations Board

I, Beatrice M. Stern, Executive Secretary of the National Labor Relations Board, and official custodian of its records, do hereby certify that attached is a full, true, and complete copy of:

Order Designating Trial Examiner in the Matter of Thompson Products, Inc. and United Automobile, Aircraft and Agricultural Implement Workers of America (UAW-CIO) Case No. XXI-C-2088.

In Witness Whereof, I have hereunto subscribed my name and caused the seal of the National Labor Relations Board to be affixed this 22nd day of September A. D. 1942, at Washington, D. C.

[Seal]   BEATRICE M. STERN

Executive Secretary

[Title of Board and Cause.]

ORDER DESIGNATING TRIAL EXAMINER

A charge having been filed in this matter, and it having appeared to the Regional Director of the 21st Region that a proceeding in respect thereto should be instituted, and the Board having considered the matter and being advised in the premises,

It Is Hereby Ordered that Gustaf B. Erickson act as Trial Examiner in the above case and perform all the duties and exercise all the powers granted to trial examiners under the Rules and Regulations—Series 2 as amended of the National Labor Relations Board.

Dated, Washington, D. C., September 22, 1942.

[Seal]   FRANK BLOOM

Acting Chief Trial Examiner

BOARD'S EXHIBIT No. 1-U

UNITED STATES OF AMERICA

National Labor Relations Board

I, Beatrice M. Stern, Executive Secretary of the National Labor Relations Board, and official custodian of its records, do hereby certify that attached is a full, true, and complete copy of:

Order Designating Trial Examiner in the Matter of Thompson Products, Inc. and United Automobile, Aircraft and Agricultural Implement Workers of America (UAW-CIO) Case No. XXI-C-2088.

In Witness Whereof, I have hereunto subscribed my name and caused the seal of the National Labor Relations Board to be affixed this 24th day of September A. D. 1942, at Washington, D. C.

[Seal]   BEATRICE M. STERN
Executive Secretary

[Title of Board and Cause.]

ORDER DESIGNATING TRIAL EXAMINER

A charge having been filed in this matter, and it having appeared to the Regional Director of the 21st Region that a proceeding in respect thereto should be instituted and the Board having considered the matter and being advised in the premises,

It Is Hereby Ordered that C. W. Whittemore act as Trial Examiner in the above case in place and stead of Gustaf B. Erickson and perform all the duties and exercise all the powers granted to Trial Examiners under the Rules and Regulations—Series 2 as amended of the National Labor Relations Board.

Dated, Washington, D. C., September 24, 1942.

[Seal]　　　　FRANK BLOOM

　　　　　　　Acting Chief Trial Examiner

BOARD'S EXHIBIT NO. 1-V

[Title of Board and Cause.]

Case No. XXI-C-2088

ORDER

The respondent Thompson Products, Inc. having heretofore on September 19, 1942, filed its written motions (1) to strike certain allegations from the complaint or in the alternative to be allowed a bill of particulars as to matters not stricken, and (2) that the complaint herein be dismissed forthwith.

And the said motions having been referred to the undersigned Trial Examiner for consideration and ruling.

It is ordered, upon due consideration of said motions, that they be and are now denied.

Dated September 22, 1942.

[Seal]　　　　GUSTAF B. ERICKSON

　　　　　　　Trial Examiner

United States of America

Before the National Labor Relations Board

Case No. C-2392

In the Matter of

THOMPSON PRODUCTS, INC.

and

UNITED AUTOMOBILE, AIRCRAFT AND
AGRICULTURAL IMPLEMENT WORK-
ERS OF AMERICA, affiliated with Congress
of Industrial Organizations

DECISION AND ORDER

On October 28, 1942, the Trial Examiner issued
his Intermediate Report in the above-entitled proceeding, finding that the respondent had engaged in
and was engaging in certain unfair labor practices
and recommending that it cease and desist therefrom and take certain affirmative action as set out
in the copy of the Intermediate Report attached
hereto. Thereafter the respondent filed exceptions
to the Intermediate Report and a brief in support
of the exceptions. The Board has considered the
rulings of the Trial Examiner at the hearing and
finds that no prejudicial error was committed. The
rulings are hereby affirmed. The Board has considered the Intermediate Report, the exceptions
and brief, and the entire record in the case, and
hereby adopts the findings, conclusions, and recommendations of the Trial Examiner except in the
following respect:

The Trial Examiner found that Charles Little occupied a supervisory position, and, accordingly, that certain anti-union statements and pro-Alliance activities engaged in by Little were attributable to the respondent. We do not agree with this conclusion. The record does not establish that Little's duties were of such nature that the employees would have just cause to believe that Little was acting in behalf of the management.

ORDER

Upon the entire record in the case, and pursuant to Section 10 (c) of the National Labor Relations Act, the National Labor Relations Board hereby orders that the respondent, Thompson Products, Inc., Bell, California, its officers, agents, successors, and assigns shall:

1. Cease and desist from:

(a) In any manner dominating or interfering with the administration of Pacific Motor Parts Workers Alliance or with the formation or administration of any other labor organization of its employees, and from contributing financial or other support to Pacific Motor Parts Workers Alliance or to any other labor organization of its employees;

(b) Recognizing Pacific Motor Parts Workers Alliance as the representative of any of its employees for the purpose of dealing with the respondent concerning grievances, labor disputes, wages, rates of pay, hours of employment, or any other conditions of employment;

(c) Giving effect to the agreement dated November 10, 1941, between the respondent and Pacific Motor Parts Workers Alliance, or any extension, renewal, modification or supplement thereof, or any other contract or agreement between the respondent and said labor organization which may now be in force;

(d) In any other manner interfering with, restraining, or coercing its employees in the exercise of the right to self-organization, to form, join, or assist labor organizations, to bargain collectively through representatives of their own choosing, and to engage in concerted activities for the purposes of collective bargaining or other mutual aid or protection, as guaranteed in Section 7 of the Act.

2. Take the following affirmative action which the Board finds will effectuate the policies of the Act:

(a) Withdraw all recognition from and completely disestablish Pacific Motor Parts Workers Alliance as the representative of any of its employees for the purpose of dealing with the respondent concerning grievances, labor disputes, rates of pay, wages, hours of employment, or other conditions of employment;

(b) Post immediately in conspicuous places throughout its plant in Bell, California, and maintain for a period of at least sixty (60) consecutive days from the date of posting, notices to its employees stating: (1) that the respondent will not engage in the conduct from which it is ordered to cease and desist in paragraphs 1 (a), (b), (c), and (d) of this Order; and (2) that it will take the affirmative action set forth in paragraph 2 (a) of this Order;

(c) Notify the Regional Director for the Twenty-first Region in writing within ten (10) days from the date of the receipt of this Order what steps the respondent has taken to comply herewith.

Signed at Washington, D. C., this 31 day of December, 1942.

[Seal]   HARRY A. MILLIS
               Chairman
     WM. M. LEISERSON
               Member
                     National Labor Relations
                     Board

United States of America

Before the National Labor Relations Board
Washington, D. C.

Trial Examining Division
Case No. XXI-C-2088

In the Matter of

THOMPSON PRODUCTS, Inc.

and

UNITED AUTOMOBILE, AIRCRAFT and
AGRICULTURAL IMPLEMENT WORK-
ERS OF AMERICA, affiliated with Congress of
Industrial Organizations[1]

Messrs. Robert C. Moore and Bartlett Breed,
for the Board.

Latham & Watkins, by Mr. Paul R. Watkins,
of Los Angeles, Calif.,
for the respondent.

Mr. Howard Baldwin,
of Los Angeles, Calif.,
for the Alliance.

INTERMEDIATE REPORT

Statement of the Case

Upon a third amended charge[2] duly filed on September 16, 1942, by United Automobile, Aircraft and
Agricultural Implement Workers of America, affiliated with Congress of Industrial Organizations,

herein called the Union, the National Labor Relations Board, herein called the Board, by the Regional Director for the Twenty-first Region (Los Angeles, California), issued its amended complaint[3] dated September 17, 1942, against Thompson Products, Inc., herein called the respondent, alleging that the respondent had engaged in and was engaging in unfair labor practices within the meaning of Section 8 (1) and (2) and Sections 2 (6) and (7) of the National Labor Relations Act, 49 Stat. 449, herein called the Act.

With respect to the unfair labor practices the amended complaint alleged in substance: (1) that the respondent, in July 1937, instigated the formation of Pacific Motor Parts Workers Alliance, herein called the Alliance, and since then dominated and interfered with the formation and administration

----

(1) At the hearing a motion was granted, without objection, to amend the title of the case and all formal papers, by striking "(U.A.W.-C.I.O.)" and substituting "affiliated with Congress of Industrial Organizations," wherever "United Automobile, Aircraft and Agricultural Implement Workers of America" appeared.

(2) The original, first and second amended charges were filed, respectively, on May 1, May 21, and July 19, 1942.

(3) The original complaint, issued on August 28, 1942, and notice of hearing, were duly served upon the respondent, the Union, and the Alliance. By motion received on August 31, the respondent moved for continuance of the hearing; said motion was granted on September 2 by the Regional Director, and the hearing was continued to September 28. Upon a subsequent motion by the respondent, the hearing was further continued until October 1, 1942.

of the Alliance, and contributed assistance and support to it; (2) that on August 12, 1937, and at specified dates thereafter, the respondent has entered into written agreements with the Alliance, recognizing it as the exclusive collective bargaining agent of all its employees at its Bell plant, more fully described hereinafter, and covering wages, hours, and working conditions; (3) that the respondent caused one of its employees, in April 1937, to join the Union for the purpose of observing and reporting to the respondent the activities of the Union; (4) that the respondent interrogated its employees with respect to the Union and warned them that if the Union were organized among them the Bell Plant would be closed and its equipment moved to another location; and (5) that by said activities the respondent has interfered with, restrained, and coerced its employees in the exercise of rights guaranteed in Section 7 of the Act. The amended complaint and accompanying notice of hearing were duly served upon the respondent, the Union, and the Alliance.

As found in footnote 3 above, the original complaint was issued on August 28. By motion received on September 11, the respondent moved to strike certain portions of the original complaint or, in the alternative, to be allowed a bill of particulars. By another motion, also received on September 11, the respondent moved that the complaint be dismissed. Said motions were denied on September 22 by Gustaf B. Erickson, the Trial Examiner duly designated by the Acting Chief Trial Examiner.

The respondent, by its answer verified on September 4, denied that it had engaged in the unfair labor practices alleged in the original complaint. At the opening of the hearing it was stipulated by counsel for the Board and counsel for the respondent that the denials set forth in the answer should be deemed to apply to all allegations of unfair labor practices in the amended complaint.

Pursuant to notice, a hearing was held at Los Angeles, California, between October 1 and 8, 1942, before the undersigned, the Trial Examiner duly designated by the Acting Chief Trial Examiner in place and stead of Gustaf B. Erickson. The Board and the respondent were represented by counsel and the Alliance by its president. All parties participated in the hearing and were afforded full opportunity to be heard, to examine and cross examine witnesses, and to introduce evidence bearing upon the issues. At the close of the hearing the Trial Examiner granted a motion, in which all parties joined, to conform the pleadings to the proof. Also at the close of the hearing, counsel for the Board, counsel for the respondent, and the representative of the Alliance argued orally before the undersigned. All parties waived the proffered opportunity to file a brief with the Trial Examiner.

Upon the record thus made, and from his observation of the witnesses, the Trial Examiner makes, in addition to the above, the following

FINDINGS OF FACT

I. The business of the respondent

The respondent, an Ohio corporation with its principal office in the city of Cleveland, Ohio, operates industrial plants in Cleveland, Ohio; Detroit, Michigan; and Bell, California, and, through a subsidiary corporation, Thompson Products, Ltd., operates a plant in Canada. This proceeding is concerned primarily with employees at the respondent's plant at Bell, California.

The respondent's Bell plant was purchased as a going concern by the respondent on April 8, 1937, from Jadson Motor Products Company, and thereafter was operated by the respondent under the name "Jadson Motor Products Company" until about July 1, 1940, at which time the latter name was discontinued. Thereafter and until the time of the hearing the respondent has continued to operate this plant under the name "Thompson Products, Inc., West Coast Plant." At this plant the respondent is engaging to producing and selling aircraft engine bolts, assembly bolts, and miscellaneous engine and aircraft fuselage parts.

Steel is the principal raw material used by the respondent at its Bell plant. In 1941 it purchased steel valued at not less than $350,000, of which about 85 percent was purchased and transported from sources of supply located outside the State of California. During the same year the respondent at its Bell plant manufactured and sold products valued at not less than $1,500,000. About 65 percent of such sales were made to customers outside the State of California.

The respondent employs about 400 workers at its Bell plant.[4]

II. The organizations involved

United Automobile, Aircraft and Agricultural Implement Workers of America, affiliated with Congress of Industrial Organizations, and Pacific Motor Parts Workers Alliance, unaffiliated, are labor organizations admitting to membership employees of the respondent at its Bell plant.

III. The unfair labor practices

A. The respondent's domination and interference with the formation and administration of the Alliance; other acts of interference, restraint, and coercion

1. Interference with the formation of the Alliance

When the respondent took possession of the Bell plant in April 1937, its production employees, then numbering about 86, were represented by no labor organization. Much unrest existed in the factory because of low wages and because of fear that the respondent might discontinue its operations here. At about this time many of the employees applied for membership in the Union, while some of the workers discussed the possibility of an inside or-

---

(4) The above findings of fact as to the respondent's business are based upon stipulations entered into between counsel for the Board and for the respondent.

ganization. No steps, however, were taken to form an inside union until late in the following July.

In June, Raymond S. Livingstone, the respondent's director of personnel, whose headquarters then were, and now are, at Cleveland, visited the Bell plant for a few days to investigate a controversy over the discharge of certain employees, and to acquaint himself as to personnel conditions generally. He learned of the existing unrest and, upon inquiry, was informed by Assistant Works Manager Victor Kangas that most of the men were "C.I.O."[5]

Also during June, Acting General Manager C. V. Dachtler asked Kangas to have some employee join the Union and report upon its membership, stating that the company would pay the dues.[6] Kangas assigned his friend, employee Lewis A. Porter, to this task. Lyman Hodges, then in charge of shipping and acting as the local personnel manager, gave Porter the money for his dues. Porter joined the Union, thereafter reported the number of employees attending union meetings to Kangas, and the latter transmitted the information to Dachtler.[7]

---

(5) The findings as to Livingstone's visit in June are based upon his own testimony, which is corroborated, in the main, by Kangas, now not employed by the respondent.

(6) The record does not disclose accurately whether this incident occurred before or after Livingstone's visit of the same month.

(7) Dachtler, now not employed by the respondent, was not called as a witness. The testimony of Porter and Kangas as to this assignment is uncontradicted. The respondent and the Alliance, how-

Livingstone returned to the Bell plant on July 23. On the same day, he asked Kangas if he could trust any employee to start an inside organization,

---

ever, adduced much testimony in attack upon the general credibility of both Porter and Kangas, each of whom was called as a witness by the Board. As to the latter, employee McIntire testified that, in May 1937, Kangas asked him to join the C.I.O. because (1) he feared that in the change of management the respondent would discharge him and (2) if the C.I.O. were organized it would stand behind him and strike in the event he were fired. Although Kangas was not recalled to testify on this point, genuine doubt that the incident occurred is raised by the testimony of Livingstone that he came to the plant at about this time to investigate charges that Kangas has discriminatorily discharged several C. I.O. members. The respondent adduced evidence tending to show that Kangas, several months after leaving the respondent's employ in 1940, sent a telegram to Livingstone charging misconduct on the part of an employee, an act which Plant Manager Hileman construed as an attempt to discredit the local management with the Cleveland office. The Trial Examiner considers it unnecessary to determine (1) whether or not Kangas actually solicited McIntire for union membership, or (2) whether or not he sent the wire. The sole issue, as discussed more fully hereinafter, is whether or not Kangas, as a representative of management, engaged in illegal conduct under the Act. Furthermore, even if the respondent's argument be accepted as valid,—that Kangas by character was inclined to serve his own interests, it adds support to findings, made above and hereinafter, that he engaged in unfair labor practices at the behest of Dachtler and Livingstone when it appeared to be to his best interest to do so. The respondent also adduced testimony in an effort to impeach Porter, with respect to a report concerning certain conditions in the plant allegedly and thereby correct unrest among the employees. Dachtler also recommended that such an organization be started. Arrangements were then made for department heads and foremen to meet at dinner that night. Following the dinner, Livingstone stated to those present that Crawford, the respondent's president, would not stand for an outside labor organization, and that the plant would be closed if either the C.I.O. or the A. F. of L. succeeded in organizing the employees. He also asked the supervisors what they thought of an inside organization, stating that management itself would prefer this type of organization. No one voiced any objection, and Livingstone urged all to keep the discussion confidential. After the meeting, Livingstone again asked Kangas if he had anyone yet in mind who would start an inside union. Kangas agreed to "sleep on it," and let him know the next day.[8]

---

made by Porter to the F.B.I. in July 1942, and an ensuing investigation. Since Plant Manager Hileman, at the hearing, admitted that he was not at liberty to disclose whatever he may have been told by the F.B.I. representative, the Trial Examiner is unable to make any findings as to what may, or may not, have happened. It is clear that Porter was not discharged as a result of any investigation, and the Trial Examiner is unable to find that such testimony in any way reflects upon the credibility of Porter.

(8) The findings as to this meeting of supervisors rests largely upon the testimony of Kangas and Drake, the latter a foreman in 1937. Livingstone admitted that the dinner occurred, but testified that, after he had learned that some of the foremen wanted to attend the "independent union" meeting, he called

The next morning, July 24, Kangas suggested to Livingstone that Porter could be entrusted with the task, explaining that Porter was older[9] and had done police work. Kangas then approached Porter, told him briefly what Livingstone wanted him to do and, when the employee expressed willingness, instructed him to meet Livingstone that evening at the Jonathan Club, where the personnel director was staying in Los Angeles.[10]

As instructed, Porter went to the Jonathan Club, where he met Livingstone and Dachtler.. There he was asked to persuade 12 or 15 employees to come into the office, tell management that they wanted to be represented by a union of their own, and request more pay and better working conditions. In reward

---

the supervisors together to warn them "specifically to keep out of the picture." Livingstone further admitted that he told the foremen that the respondent had "satisfactory" relations with an independent union in Cleveland, but had suffered "one headache after another" in dealing with the C.I.O. at its Detroit plant. He denied having made the statements about closing the plant attributed to him by Kangas. The Trial Examiner does not credit Livingstone's denial, nor his explanation of why the meeting was called. Credible evidence establishes that the meeting was held several days before actual organization of the Alliance began, and before any meeting was scheduled. No occasion existed, therefore, for foremen to ask if they might attend the meeting.

(9) Porter, at the time of the hearing, was 62.

(10) Livingstone denied that Porter was assigned to this task by Kangas at his request. The undersigned does not accept Livingstone's denial as true.

for this assignment, Livingstone promised Porter a life-time job, some money, and a vacation with pay.[11]

On the following Monday, during working hours, Porter approached several of his fellow employees, recommended that an inside union be formed, and urged that they get others to go with them into the office and ask for recognition and better working conditions. During the same day, upon learning from Kangas that the Union planned to hold a meeting the next night to consider a contract for submission to management, Livingstone advised Kangas to hurry Porter in his efforts, and have the group bring in its "demands" before the C. I. O. meeting.[12] The same evening Kangas, in the presence of Porter, received over the telephone, from Livingstone, the text for application cards in the

---

(11) The finding as to this meeting rests upon the credible testimony of Porter. Dachtler was not called as a witness. Livingstone testified that Porter visited him voluntarily, offered to go to C.I.O. meetings and report to him, and then asked permission to bring some of the employees into the office to talk to him. It has already been established, by unrefuted testimony, that Porter was already reporting C.I.O. meetings to Kangas and Dachtler. There existed no reason why he should visit Livingstone and Dachtler with an offer to do what he was already engaged in doing. Upon Livingstone's testimony on this point the Trial Examiner places no reliance.

(12) This finding rests upon Kangas' testimony. Livingstone denied the incident. As found heretofore, Livingstone's unsupported testimony is unreliable.

Association.[13] Kangas immediately gave the copy to a printer. During working hours on Tuesday morning, without checking out, Porter left the plant, as instructed by Kangas, obtained the cards from the printer, and gave them to Hodges. That afternoon Porter led a group of from 15 to 20 employees into the office, where he, as spokesman, asked Livingstone and Dachtler if the company would recognize an inside union if organized. Dachtler stated that he was in favor of such an

---

(13) Livingstone denied having given Kangas the text for these cards, which read as follows:

Pacific Parts Workers Alliance

I the undersigned employee of the Jadson Motor Products Company, do hereby apply for membership in the Pacific Parts Workers Alliance with the understanding that upon acceptance of the application for membership that the Pacific Parts Workers Alliance will be my exclusive representative in bargaining with my employer with reference to wages, hours and working conditions, and that I will abide by the constitution of the Pacific Parts Workers Alliance when drafted and approved by the elected representative.

This membership to be effective until one year from the date of signing.

Unrefuted evidence establishes that these cards were printed and received by Porter before the meeting of employees with Livingstone on July 27, at which meeting the employees first broached their request to form an inside union. Although former Alliance officials were questioned as to their knowledge with respect to these cards, all of them testified that they were without recollection as to the origin of the cards, or of the text appearing upon them. The surrounding circumstances fully support the testimony of Kangas and Porter, and the Trial Examiner does not accept Livingstone's denial.

organization. The employees were then told that they must obtain membership among a majority.[14] At the close of the shift that afternoon, several of the group passed out application cards at the plant gate, and at the same time announced that an organizational meeting would be held.

Formal organization of the Alliance began that evening, July 27.[15] A constitution and bylaws com-

---

(14) The respondent introduced in evidence a document which Livingstone identified as having been dictated by himself on July 26, purportedly describing the visit of the employees to his. office. The first sentence of the document read: "Minutes of a meeting held between a group of employees and the Management . . ." Livingstone gave no reasonable explanation as to why he used the term "minutes" to characterize an informal interview. Credible evidence refutes the statement also contained in the document that the meeting was held on July 26. The stenographer who testified that Livingstone dictated to her the text of the "minutes" admitted that she could not recall when the dictation was made. Under the circumstances, the Trial Examiner is convinced that the document was not prepared, as Livingstone testified, immediately after the meeting, and places no reliance upon it.

(15) At the hearing Bebb, who was chairman of this meeting, identified a document bearing the date of July 29 as being the minutes of this first meeting. The Trial Examiner, however, places no reliance upon the date appearing on the document. Porter, Bebb, and Creek, the latter the Alliance's first president, all testified that the first meeting was held on the same day that the group went to management, which was on July 27. As in the case of the "minutes" produced by Livingstone, described above, the record does not clearly establish when the minutes of the first Alliance meeting were prepared.

mittee was appointed. Porter took no further active part in the organization. A day or two later, however, at the request of Livingstone, Porter delivered a paper, which he testified he believed to contain items for a proposed agreement, to a local attorney. After the attorney read the paper, he advised Porter that he did not think much of it, that he should so tell management, and that someone else should be sent over to consult him. Porter told Kangas what the attorney had said. Thereafter the Alliance committee retained the same attorney to draw its constitution and bylaws.[16]

During the latter part of the same week Kangas, Hodges, and Porter were guests of Livingstone at the Jonathan Club. Livingstone complimented the others upon the successful launching of the Alliance, and told them they would not have to worry about their jobs in the future.[17] Porter was there-

---

(16)   Livingstone denied having sent Porter to see the attorney, who was not called as a witness. The respondent stipulated, however, that were the attorney called, he would testify that Porter made the first contact with him for the Alliance. Porter was not on any of the Alliance committees. The record reveals no reason, other than that contained in his own testimony, upon which the finding rests, as to why he should have visited the attorney. The Trial Examiner does not accept Livingstone's denial. Porter's testimony is also supported by that of Kangas, who testified that Livingstone asked him regarding an attorney and that he informed the personnel director that Porter doubtless could suggest one.

(17)   The findings as to this meeting are based upon the credible testimony of Kangas and Porter.

after rewarded by being given a 2-weeks' vacation with pay.[18]

2. Set-up of the Alliance

The Alliance constitution, adopted on August 3 at a membership meeting, provided for an executive

---

Hodges was not called as a witness. Livingstone testified that he did not recall the meeting, but admitted that it might have taken place. He denied, however, having discussed the subject of the Alliance. The Trial Examiner does not credit his denial.

(18) Porter's testimony that he alone, among employees, received a vacation with pay that year, is unrefuted. There is also considerable testimony in the record about the payment to Porter of a sum of money by the respondent as a reward for special services. Both Kangas and Porter testified that the latter received $50, and Kangas stated that this money was received by him, for delivery to Porter, from Hileman. Porter placed the incident in 1937, Kangas about a year later. The respondent adduced evidence to show that, in 1938, it paid Porter $40 for another confidential assignment,—that of investigating thefts of certain materials. Porter admitted the assignment but denied having been paid especially for it. Kangas testified that he gave Porter money on but one occasion, and that Hileman told him it was for organizing the Alliance. Hileman flatly denied having made this statement to Kangas. However, since the issue to be determined is whether the respondent used Porter as its agent in starting the formation of the Alliance, and not whether it thereafter paid Porter for his services in this respect, the Trial Examiner finds it unnecessary to resolve the conflicting testimony as to the payment of monies. It is clear that the employee received a vacation, and it is found that in this respect he was rewarded for his efforts in organizing the Alliance.

council of five members. To serve on this council it was necessary that an employee be an American citizen, 21 years or more of age, and an employee of the respondent for not less than one year. The executive council, elected annually by the membership, chose its president and vice president.

Paragraph 1 of the constitution reads, in part, as follows:

Pursuant to the authority granted by the National Labor Relations Act, commonly known as the Wagner Act, there is hereby organized and the undersigned do hereby associate themselves in an organization to be known as Pacific Motor Parts Workers Alliance, for the purposes and upon the conditions as set forth herein . . .

About 70 employees signed the document on or about August 3. Dues in the organization were 25 cents a month.

3. Written agreements between the respondent and the Alliance

Sometime between August 3 and August 12, Livingstone and Hodges checked a number of the Alliance membership cards against the pay-roll list. According to Livingstone's testimony, he found that the Alliance represented a majority of the employees at the Bell plant.

On August 12 the respondent entered into a written agreement with the Alliance, recognizing it as the exclusive bargaining agent for all its employees at this plant, and covering wages and other working conditions. By the terms of the contract, wages were increased.

Thereafter the contract was periodically renewed. At the time of the hearing, there existed between the parties an agreement dated November 10, 1941, to run for one year, with an automatic renewal clause therein.

4. The respondents interference with the administration of the Alliance, and support rendered to it

Since 1937 the Alliance executive council has met at intervals of from 1 to 3 months with management officials. Minutes of the first two meetings were prepared by Livingstone. Thereafter and until the time of the hearing, minutes of these meetings have first been submitted to management before being posted on a bulletin board for information of the employees.[19]

Executive council meetings were held in the welding room of the plant, during working hours. This fact was known to General Superintendent Kearns and, according to his own testimony, met with no remonstrance from him until the fall of 1941. At least until July 1942, Alliance dues were collected and memberships solicited openly and without objection by management, during working hours. President Baldwin of the Association admitted at the hearing that he has continued to conduct Alliance business during working hours despite warnings by management, but that he has never been disciplined for such conduct. General membership

---

(19) The findings as to the respondent's control over these minutes are based upon the testimony of Livingstone and a stipulation entered into between counsel for the Board and for the respondent.

meetings are held on Sundays. Prior to the declaration of war, on Sundays when an Alliance meeting was scheduled the plant would be shut down for 2 hours during the morning, so that shift workers might attend. Employees were permitted to make up lost time later in the day.

When applying for a job in December 1940, employee Overlander was asked by Personnel Manager Millman[20] if he belonged to any union and was told that they had an inside organization there, with which friendly relations existed.[21] Overlander thereafter joined the Alliance, having been solicited, during working hours, by Little, who had charge of the tool crib in which Overlander was an attendant.[22]

In the fall of 1941, Baldwin and Smith, the latter a member of the executive council, consulted Millman concerning the action of certain supervisors in an election then being conducted by the Alliance.

---

(20)   Millman has been personnel manager at the plant Bell since September 1940. The record does not reveal when Hodges left the respondent's employ.

(21)   Overlander's testimony as to this incident is uncontradicted.

(22)   Little was not called as a witness, and Overlander's testimony with respect to this occurrence is unrefuted. Millman denied that Little had supervisory powers. Overlander's testimony is undisputed, however, that Little gave him instructions, left instructions for employees on following shifts, and recommended to Superintendent Kearns that Overlander be given a raise. As a result of this recommendation he received an increase. Under the circumstances, the Trial Examiner finds that Little had supervisory powers over Overlander.

Baldwin testified that he inquired of Millman what classification management considered these individuals to be in, because he had read some "interpretation of the Boards' Act," which raised doubt in his mind as to whether or not they should be in the Alliance. Millman thereupon posted the following notice:

Recent National Labor Relations Board rulings hold that it is not necessary for a supervisory employee to have the power to hire and fire in order to be considered a part of the Management. An employee who supervises and directs the work of others or exercises any of the functions of Management is considered an agent of the employer and is, therefore, according to the contract between the Management and the Pacific Motor Parts Workers Alliance, ineligible to belong to the Pacific Motor Parts Workers Alliance.

Accordingly, the following named men have been asked, or will be asked, to resign their membership in the Pacific Motor Parts Workers Alliance at once:

| G. C. Beach | C. E. Weisser | Julius Olsen |
| J. E. Morse | H. E. McIntire | E. T. Fickle |

E. T. Fickle had been on the executive council of the Alliance since its inception, and Weisser for the preceding year. Fickle's duties had not been altered since 1938, and Weisser's since 1939. During part of his service on the council Fickle had been president. Millman's action in the above respect was taken without further consultation with Baldwin, and the question was never submitted to the Alliauce's membership.

James Creek, first president of the Alliance, was promoted to a supervisory position, as head of the maintenance department, 3 or 4 months before his term of office expired. He continued, however, to serve as president of the organization.

5. Conclusions as to the respondent's domination of and interference with the formation and administration of the Alliance

The foregoing findings plainly establish that the Alliance came into being at the instigation and insistence of Livingstone, as a means of defeating organization of an outside union.[23] Active support and interference were also engaged in by Kangas, Dachtler, and Hodges. It is clear that Porter served as an agent of the employer in the compaign to arouse an interest in an inside organization, as

---

(23) In its Decision and Order, In the Matter of Thompson Products, Inc. and United Automobile Workers of America, Local 300 (C.I.O.), Case No. C-1848, subsequently enforced, with modification, by the United States Circuit Court of Appeals (C.C.A. 6), the Board found that, at the respondent's Cleveland plant in April 1937, Livingstone advised the chairman of the "employees representatives," of the "Thompson Products, Inc., Employees Association," a labor organization determined by the Board to have been company-dominated, as to its reorganization into the "Automotive and Aircraft Workers Alliance, Inc.," a labor organization also found by the Board to be company-dominated. The Board further found that Livingstone advised a committee of employees as to revision of the constitution of the latter organization.

opposed to the Union, and to lead, as bell-weather, a group of his fellow employees into monagement's office with the request that the respondent recognize an inside organization when formed. Porter was rewarded for his part in forming the organization.

It has been found that a number of the respondent's supervisors, Creek, Fickle, and Weisser, served for varying periods as officers and executive councilmen of the Alliance. Personnel Manager Millman, foremen, and supervisors, since 1937, have advised employees to join the Alliance. And, as found above, the respondent has given financial and other support to the Alliance by permitting the holding of council meetings on company time and property.

Therefore the Trial Examiner concludes and finds that the respondent has dominated and interfered with the formation and administration of the Alliance, and has contributed financial and other support thereto, and that the respondent has thereby interfered with, restrained, and coerced its employees in the exercise of the rights guaranteed in Section 7 of the Act.

The Trial Examiner further finds that the agreements entered into between the respondent and the Alliance and the contractual relationship existing thereunder, have been and are a means of utilizing an employer-dominated organization to frustrate the exercise by the respondent's employees of the rights guaranteed in Section 7 of the Act.

1. Threats to move operations to Cleveland; anti-union remarks by supervisors

Soon after Livingstone asked Porter to take action resulting in formation of the Alliance, Hodges informed Porter that if the Union were not kept out of the plant, and the inside organization put in, the factory would close.[24]

In November or December 1941, Millman told employee Smith that the respondent could easily absorb the Bell plant in its Eastern operations, and would do so rather than deal with the C.I.O.[25]

When employee Crank informed Millman in April 1942, of his having joined the Union, the personnel manager told him that while he could make up his own mind, he was taking the "wrong attitude." Soon thereafter General Foreman Long approached Crank and asked him why he had joined the Union.[26]

---

(24) As found above, Hodges is no longer employed by the respondent. He was not called as a witness.

(25) The finding rests upon Smith's credible testimony. Millman's denial of making the statement is not credited by the Trial Examiner. It has previously been found that Livingstone, in 1937, had made a similar statement to all foremen, and it is reasonable to believe that the local personnel manager would accurately reflect the attitude of his superior.

(26) Crank's testimony as to both of these incidents is uncontradicted.

In the fall of 1941, employee Overlander was told by Little, his supervisor in the tool crib, that Hileman had said that the plant would close if the C.I.O. got in.[27]

2. Issuance and distribution of anti-union literature

The respondent has caused to be distributed to its employees at its Bell plant copies of "Friendly Forum," its own publication,[28] containing editorials and articles hostile to outside labor organizations, particularly the C.I.O. The following excerpt is from an editorial appearing in the May 29, 1941, issue:

> The C.I.O. has shown more contempt for Defense Efforts than it has shown desire to cooperate, while the A. F. of L. has stated a desire to cooperate, but both have been militant in their efforts to prevent even the slightest curtailment of labor's rights, especially labor's right to strike.

------

(27) Overlander's testimony as to this occurrence is unrefuted.

(28) In April 1940, the respondent issued and distributed to all employees in its Bell plant copies of "Employees Handbook" which, according to President Crawford's foreword, defined it as "a ready reference of company policies,—an understanding of what employees may expect of management and what management expects of employees . . ." This handbook describes the "Friendly Forum" as follows: "Each four weeks the company publishes a paper, Friendly Forum, which contains news of the company and of employees . . . Em-

In its issue of September 19, 1941, the respondent reprinted for distribution to its employees an address by Earl Harding, which is replete with expressions of hostility toward union organizations. A single excerpt is quoted:

> . . . we permitted labor organizers to be trained in Communist "labor colleges," not by educators, but by agitators. We even paid expenses of such "students" to Russia for post-graduate courses in revolutionary technique . .
> Then we let Communists impregnate, in many instances dominate, the American labor movement. And, in the name of "academic freedom," we let their poison filter into our schools.

3. Conclusions

By management's threats to close the plant if the Union were organized in the plant, by making inquiries as to union membership among employees, by the employment of Porter to report upon union meetings, and by anti-union articles distributed to its employees in "Friendly Forum," the respondent has interfered with, restrained, and coerced its employees in the exercise of rights guaranteed in Section 7 of the Act.

IV. The effect of the unfair labor practices upon commerce

The activities of the respondent, set forth in Section III above, occurring in connection with the op-

---

ployees are responsible for knowledge of information published either on bulletin boards or in Friendly Forum." (underlining supplied)

erations of the respondent, described in Section I above, have a close, intimate, and substantial relation to trade, traffic, and commerce among the several States, and tend to lead to labor disputes burdening and obstructing commerce and the free flow of commerce.

V. The remedy

Having found that the respondent has engaged in certain unfair labor practices, the Trial Examiner will recommend that it cease and desist therefrom and take certain affirmative action designed to effectuate the policies of the Act.

It has been found that the respondent has dominated and interfered with the formation and administration of the Alliance, and has contributed financial and other support thereto. The effect and consequences of the respondent's domination of, interference with, and support of the Alliance, as well as the continued recognition of the Alliance as the bargaining representative of its employees, constitute a continuing obstacle to the free exercise by its employees of the rights guaranteed in the Act. Because of the respondent's illegal conduct with regard to it, the Alliance is incapable of serving the respondent's employees as the genuine collective bargaining agency. Accordingly, the Trial Examiner will recommend that the respondent disestablish and withdraw all recognition from the Alliance as the representative of any of its employees for the purposes of dealing with it concerning grievances, labor disputes, wages, rates of pay, hours of employment, or other conditions of employment.[29]

It has also been found that the agreements entered into between the respondent and the Alliance have been a means whereby the respondent has utilized an employer-dominated labor organization to frustrate self-organization and defeat genuine collective bargaining by its employees. Under these circumstances any continuation, renewal, or modification of the current agreement would perpetuate the conditions which have deprived employees of the rights guaranteed to them by the Act and would render ineffectual other portions of these remedial recommendations. It will therefore be recommended that the respondent cease giving effect to any agreement between it and the Alliance, or to any modification or extension thereof. Nothing in these recommendations should be taken, however, to require the respondent to vary those wage, hour, and other substantive features of its relations with the employees themselves, if any, which the respondent established in performance of the agreement as extended, renewed, modified, supplemented, or superseded.[30]

Upon the basis of the foregoing findings of fact

---

(29)   See N.L.R.B. v. Newport News Shipbuilding and Drydock Company, 308 U.S. 241; N.L.R.B. v. The Falk Corporation, 308 U.S. 453; N.L.R.B. v. Pennsylvania Greyhound Lines, 303 U.S. 261.

(30)   See National Licorice Co. v. N.L.R.B., 309 U.S. 350, aff'g as mod. 104 F. (2d) 655 (C.C.A. 2), enf'g as mod. 7 N.L.R.B. 537; National Labor Relations Board v. J. Greenebaum Tanning Co., 110 F. (2d) 984 (C.C.A. 7), enf'g as mod. 11 N.L.R.B. 300, cert. den. 311 U.S. 662.

and upon the entire record in the case, the Trial Examiner makes the following:

CONCLUSIONS OF LAW

1. United Automobile, Aircraft and Agricultural Implement Workers of America, affiliated with Congress of Industrial Organizations, and Pacific Motor Parts Workers Alliance, unaffiliated, are labor organizations within the meaning of Section 2 (5) of the Act.

2. By dominating and interfering with the formation and administration of the Pacific Motor Parts Workers Alliance, and by contributing support to it, the respondent has engaged in unfair labor practices within the meaning of Section 8 (2) of the Act.

3. By interfering with, restraining, and coercing its employees in the exercise of the rights guaranteed in Section 7 of the Act, the respondent has engaged in and is engaging in unfair labor practices within the meaning of Section 8 (1) of the Act.

4. The aforesaid unfair labor practices are unfair labor practices affecting commerce, within the meaning of Section 2 (6) and (7) of the Act.

RECOMMENDATIONS

Upon the basis of the foregoing findings of fact and conclusions of law, the Trial Examiner recommends that the respondent, Thompson Products, Inc., and its officers, agents, successors, and assigns, shall:

1. Cease and desist from:

(a) Dominating or interfering with the administration of the Pacific Motor Parts Workers Alliance by whatever name it may be known, or with the formation or administration of any other labor organization of its employees, and from contributing financial or other support to the Pacific Motor Parts Workers Alliance or to any other labor organization of its employees;

(b) Giving effect to the agreement dated November 10, 1941, between the respondent and the Pacific Motor Parts Workers Alliance, or any extension, renewal, or modification thereof, or any other contract or agreement between the respondent and said labor organization which may now be in force;

(c) Recognizing the Pacific Motor Parts Workers Alliance as the representative of its employees for the purpose of dealing with the respondent concerning grievances, labor disputes, wages, rates of pay, hours of employment, or any other conditions of employment;

(d) In any other manner interfering with, restraining, or coercing its employees in the exercise of the right to self-organization, to form, join, or assist labor organizations, to bargain collectively through representatives of their own choosing, or to engage in concerted activities for the purposes of collective bargaining and other mutual aid or protection, as guaranteed in Section 7 of the Act.

2. Take the following affirmative action which the Trial Examiner finds will effectuate the policies of the Act:

(a) Withdraw all recognition from and completely disestablish the Pacific Motor Parts Workers Alliance, by whatever name it may be known, as the representative of any of its employees for the purpose of dealing with the respondent concerning grievances, labor disputes, rates of pay, wages, hours of employment, or other conditions of employment;

(b) Immediately post notices to its employees in conspicuous places throughout its plant in Bell, California, and maintain such notices for a period of at least sixty (60) days from the date of posting, stating (1) that the respondent will not engage in the conduct from which it is recommended that it cease and desist in paragraph 1 (a), (b), (c), and (d) of these Recommendations; and (2) that it will take the affirmative action set forth in paragraph 2 (a) of these Recommendations;

(c) Notify the Regional Director for the Twenty-first Region in writing within ten (10) days from the date of the receipt of this Intermediate Report what steps the respondent has taken to comply therewith.

It is further recommended that unless on or before ten (10) days from the receipt of this Intermediate Report the respondent notifies said Regional Director in writing that it has complied with the foregoing recommendations, the National Labor Relations Board issue an order requiring the respondent to take the action aforesaid.

As provided in Section 33 of Article II of the Rules and Regulations of the National Labor Relations Board—Series 2—as amended, effective October 14, 1942, any party may within fifteen (15) days from the date of the entry of the order transferring the case to the Board, pursuant to Section 32 of Article II of said Rules and Regulations, file with the Board, Shoreham Building, Washington, D. C., an original and four copies of a statement in writing setting forth such cxeeptions to the Intermediate Report or to any other part of the record or proceeding (including rulings upon all motions or objections) as he relies upon, together with the original and four copies of a brief in support thereof. As further provided in said Section 33, should any party desire permission to argue orally before the Board, request therefor must be made in writing to the Board within ten (10) days from the date of the order transferring the case to the Board.

C. W. WHITTEMORE,
Trial Examiner.

Dated: October 28, 1942.

[Title of Board and Cause.]

AFFIDAVIT AS TO SERVICE

District of Columbia—ss.

I, Jack McCaleb, being first duly sworn, on oath saith that I am one of the employees of the National Labor Relations Board, in the office of said Board in Washington, D. C.; that on the 31st day of December, 1942, I mailed postpaid, bearing government frank, by registered mail, a copy of the Decision and Order [and Intermediate Report] to the following named persons, addressed to them at the following addresses:

69106

United Automobile, Aircraft & Agricultural
    Implement Workers of America, C.I.O.
Att: Clarence L. Johnson, Int. Repr.
5851 Avalon Blvd.
Los Angeles, California

69107

Thompson Products, Inc.
    West Coast Plant
8354 Wilcox Avenue
Bell, California

69108

Latham & Watkins
Att: Paul R. Watkins
1112 Title Guarantee Bldg.
Los Angeles, California

69109

Pacific Motor Parks Workers Alliance
Att: Howard Baldwin
7727 Wilcox Avenue
Bell, California

JACK McCALEB.

Subscribed and sworn to before me this 31st day of December, 1942.

[Seal]   KATHRYN B. HARRELL,
                    Notary Public, D. C.

My Commission expires March 1, 1947.

[Return receipts for above Nos. attached.]

In the United States Circuit Court of Appeals
for the Ninth Circuit

No. 10383

NATIONAL LABOR RELATIONS BOARD,
Petitioner,

v.

THOMPSON PRODUCTS, INC.,
Respondent.

PETITION FOR ENFORCEMENT OF AN ORDER OF THE NATIONAL LABOR RELATIONS BOARD.

To the Honorable, the Judges of the United States Circuit Court of Appeals for the Ninth Circuit:

The National Labor Relations Board, pursuant to the National Labor Relations Act (Act of July 5, 1935, 49 Stat. 449, c. 372, 29 U.S.C. § 151 et seq.), respectfully petitions this Court for the enforcement of its order against respondent, Thompson Products, Inc., Bell, California, its officers, agents, successors, and assigns. The proceeding resulting in said order is known upon the records of the Board as "In the Matter of Thompson Products, Inc. and United Automobile, Aircraft and Agricultural Implement Workers of America, affiliated with Congress of Industrial Organizations, Case No. C-2392."

In support of this petition, the Board respectfully shows:

(1)   Respondent is an Ohio corporation, engaged in business in the State of California, within this judicial circuit, where the unfair labor practices occurred. This Court therefore has jurisdiction of this petition by virtue of Section 10 (e) of the National Labor Relations Act.

(2)   Upon all proceedings had in said matter before the Board, as more fully shown by the entire record thereof certified by the Board and filed with this Court herein, to which reference is hereby made, the Board, on December 31, 1942, duly stated its findings of fact, conclusions of law and issued an order directed to the respondent, its officers, agents, successors, and assigns. The aforesaid order provides as follows:

ORDER

Upon the entire record in the case, and pursuant to Section 10 (c) of the National Labor Relations Act, the National Labor Relations Board hereby orders that the respondent, Thompson Products, Inc., Bell, California, its officers, agents, successors, and assigns shall:

1.   Cease and desist from:
    (a) In any manner dominating or interfering with the administration of Pacific Motor Parts Workers Alliance or with the formation or administration of any other labor organization of its employees, and from contributing financial or other support to Pacific Motor Parts Workers Alliance or to any other labor organization of its employees;

(b)   Recognizing Pacific Motor Parts Workers Alliance as the representative of any of its employees for the purpose of dealing with the respondent concerning grievances, labor disputes, wages, rates of pay, hours of employment, or any other conditions of employment;

(c)   Giving effect to the agreement dated November 10, 1941, between the respondent and Pacific Motor Parts Workers Alliance, or any extension, renewal, modification or supplement thereof, or any other contract or agreement between the respondent and said labor organization which may now be in force;

(d)   In any other manner interfering with, restraining, or coercing its employees in the exercise of the right to self-organization, to form, join, or assist labor organizations, to bargain collectively through representatives of their own choosing, and to engage in concerted activities for the purposes of collective bargaining or other mutual aid or protection, as guaranteed in Section 7 of the Act.

2.   Take the following affirmative action which the Board finds will effectuate the policies of the Act:

(a)   Withdraw all recognition from and completely disestablish Pacific Motor Parts Workers Alliance as the representative of any of its employees for the purpose of dealing with the respondent concerning grievances, labor disputes, rates of pay, wages, hours of employment, or other conditions of employment;

(b)   Post immediately in conspicuous places throughout its plant in Bell, California, and maintain for a period of at least sixty (60) consecutive days from the date of posting, notices to its employees stating: (1) that the respondent will not engage in the conduct from which it is ordered to cease and desist in paragraphs 1 (a), (b), (c), and (d) of this Order; and (2) that it will take the affirmative action set forth in paragraph 2 (a) of this Order;

(c)   Notify the Regional Director for the Twenty-first Region in writing within ten (10) days from the date of the receipt of this Order what steps the respondent has taken to comply herewith.

(3)   On December 31, 1942, the Board's decision and order was served upon respondent by sending a copy thereof postpaid, bearing Government frank, by registered mail, to Messrs. Latham & Watkins, respondent's attorneys in Los Angeles, California.

(4)   Pursuant to Section 10 (e) of the National Labor Relations Act, the Board is certifying and filing with this Court a transcript of the proceedings before the Board, including the pleadings, testimony and evidence, findings of fact, conclusions of law, and order of the Board.

Wherefore, the Board prays this Honorable Court that it cause notice of the filing of this petition and transcript to be served upon respondent and that this Court take jurisdiction of the proceedings and of the questions determined therein and make and enter upon the pleadings, testimony and evidence and the proceedings set forth in the transcript, and the order made thereupon set forth in paragraph (2) hereof, a decree enforcing in whole said order of the Board and requiring respondent, its officers, agents, successors, and assigns to comply therewith.

NATIONAL LABOR RELATIONS BOARD,

By ERNEST A. GROSS,

Associate General Counsel.

Dated at Washington, D. C., this 5th day of March, 1943.

District of Columbia—ss.

Ernest A. Gross, being first duly sworn, states that he is Associate General Counsel of the National Labor Relations Board, petitioner herein, and that he is authorized to and does make this verification in behalf of said Board; that he has read the foregoing petition and has knowledge of the contents thereof; and that the statements made therein are true to the best of his knowledge, information and belief.

ERNEST A. GROSS,

Associate General Counsel.

Subscribed and sworn to before me this 5th day of March, 1943.

[Seal]   JOSEPH W. KULKIS,

Notary Public, District of Columbia.

My Commission Expires April 15, 1947.

[Endorsed]: Filed Mar. 10, 1943. Paul P. O'Brien, Clerk.

ORDER TO SHOW CAUSE

CCA #10383

United States of America—ss.

The President of the United States of America

To Thompson Products, Inc., West Coast Plant, 8354 Wilcox Ave., Bell, California; United Automobile Aircraft & Agricultural Implement Workers of America, C.I.O. Att: Clarence L. Johnson, Int. Repr., 5851 Avalon Blvd., Los Angeles, Cal., and Pacific Motor Parts Workers Alliance, Att: Howard Baldwin, 7727 Wilcox Avenue, Bell, California,

Greeting:

Pursuant to the provisions of Subdivision (e) of Section 160, U.S.C.A. Title 29 (National Labor Relations Board Act, Section 10(e)), you and each of you are hereby notified that on the 10th day of March, 1943, a petition of the National Labor Relations Board for enforcement of its order entered on December 31, 1942, in a proceeding known upon the records of the said Board as "In the matter of Thompson Products, Inc., and United Automobile Aircraft and Agricultural Implement Workers of America, affiliated with Congress of Industrial Organizations, Case No. C-2392."
and for entry of a decree by the United States Circuit Court of Appeals for the Ninth Circuit, was filed in the said United States Circuit Court of Appeals for the Ninth Circuit, copy of which said petition is attached hereto.

You are also notified to appear and move upon, answer or plead to said petition within ten days from date of the service hereof, or in default of such action the said Circuit Court of Appeals for the Ninth Circuit will enter such decree as it deems just and proper in the premises.

Witness the Honorable Harlan Fiske Stone, Chief Justice of the United States, this 10th day of March, in the year of our Lord one thousand, nine hundred and forty-three.

[Seal] PAUL P. O'BRIEN,
Clerk of the United States Circuit Court of Appeals for the Ninth Circuit.

Marshal's Civil Docket

No. 25418, Vol. 46, Page 80.

RETURN ON SERVICE OF WRIT

#25418

United States of America,
Southern District of California—ss.

I hereby certify and return that I served the annexed Order to Show Cause on the therein-named Pacific Motor Parts Workers Alliance by handing to and leaving a true and correct copy thereof with C. O. Stubblefield, Pres. of Pacific Motor Parts

Workers Alliance, personally at Bell in said District on the 15th day of March, 1943.

ROBERT E. CLARK,
U. S. Marshal.
By T. R. KEEFE,
Deputy.

Marshal's Fees	$6.00
Mileage	1.66
Total	$7.66

RETURN ON SERVICE OF WRIT

#25418

United States of America,
Southern District of California—ss.

I hereby certify and return that I served the annexed Order to Show Cause on the therein-named Clarence L. Johnson, Int. Repr. United Automobile Aircraft & Agricultural Implement Workers of America, by handing to and leaving a true and correct copy thereof with Clarence L. Johnson, Int. Repr. of United Automobile Aircraft & Agricultural Implement Workers of America, personally at Los Angeles, in said District on the 15th day of March, 1943.

ROBERT E. CLARK,
U. S. Marshal.
By T. R. KEEFE,
Deputy.

RETURN ON SERVICE OF WRIT

#25418

United States of America,
Southern District of California—ss.

I hereby certify and return that I served the annexed Order to Show Cause on the therein-named Thompson Products Inc. by handing to and leaving a true and correct copy thereof with P. D. Hieleman, General Manager, Thompson Products Inc., personally at Los Angeles, in said District on the 12th day of March, 1943.

                    ROBERT E. CLARK,
                        U. S. Marshal.
        By T. R. KEEFE,
                    Deputy.

———

[Title of Circuit Court of Appeals and Cause.]

ANSWER OF RESPONDENT THOMPSON PRODUCTS, INC. TO PETITION FOR ENFORCEMENT OF AN ORDER OF THE NATIONAL LABOR RELATIONS BOARD.

To the Honorable, the Judges of the United States Circuit Court of Appeals for the Ninth Circuit:

Thompson Products, Inc., respondent in the above-entitled proceeding, in accordance with Section 10(e) of the National Labor Relations Act (49 Stat. 453, Chap. 372, 29 U.S.C. Section 160(e), approved July 5, 1935), answers the petition presented to this Honorable Court for the enforcement of a

certain order of the National Labor Relations
Board, hereinafter referred to as the "Board".

In answer to said petition to this Honorable
Court, respondent respectfully:

> (1) Admits the allegations contained in
> paragraph (1) of said petition except that re-
> spondent denies that it committed any unfair
> labor practices as alleged in said paragraph;

> (2) Admits the allegation in paragraph (2)
> of said petition that on December 31, 1942 the
> Board entered the order quoted in said para-
> graph, but denies for lack of information or
> belief all the other allegations in said para-
> graph;

> (3) Admits the allegations contained in
> paragraph (3) of said petition;

> (4) Denies for lack of information or be-
> lief the allegations contained in paragraph (4)
> of said petition.

In further answer to said petition, respondent respectfully alleges that the findings of fact of the
Board upon which it based its conclusions of law
and order are not supported by the evidence.

In further answer to said petition, respondent respectfully alleges that the Board acted without and
in excess of its powers and contrary to law in making and entering its conclusions of law and order
in this matter by reason of the lack of evidence in
support thereof.

In further answer to said petition, respondent respectfully alleges that objection was made before
the Board as to lack of evidence to support the

Board's proposed findings, conclusions of law, and order.

Wherefore, respondent prays that this Honorable Court deny the petition of the National Labor Relations Board for the enforcement of its order, that it set aside said order of the Board in its entirety, or if such prayer be denied, that it set aside the said order of the Board in such part as the same is not supported by evidence or is improper, and insofar as set aside that the Court relieve respondent, its officers, agents, successors and assigns of any necessity to comply therewith.

Dated: March 16, 1943.

> PAUL R. WATKINS,
> RICHARD W. LUND,
> AUSTIN H. PECK, JR.,
>   Attorneys   for   Respondent
>   Thompson Products, Inc.
> 1112 Title Guarantee Building
> 411 West Fifth Street
> Los Angeles, California.

State of California,
County of Los Angeles—ss.

Richard W. Lund, being duly sworn, says that he is one of the attorneys for respondent, and that he is authorized to and does make this verification on behalf of said respondent; that he has read the foregoing Answer and has knowledge of the contents thereof; and that the statements made therein are true to the best of his knowledge, information and belief.

RICHARD W. LUND.

Subscribed and sworn to before me this 16th day of March, 1943.

[Seal]   ISOBEL V. HUGHES,
            Notary Public in and for said
            County and State.

[Endorsed]: Filed Mar. 17, 1943. Paul P. O'Brien, Clerk.

————

Before The
National Labor Relations Board
Twenty-First Region

Case No. XXI-C-2088

In the Matter of :

THOMPSON PRODUCTS, INC.

and

UNITED AUTOMOBILE, AIRCRAFT AND AGRICULTURAL IMPLEMENT WORKERS OF AMERICA (U.A.W.-C.I.O.)

Room 808, United States Post Office and
Court House Building,

Spring, Temple and Main Streets,
Los Angeles, California,

Thursday, October 1, 1942.

The above-entitled matter came on for hearing, pursuant to notice, at 10:00 o'clock a.m.

Before:

C. W. Whittemore,
Trial Examiner.

Appearances:

Robert C. Moore
and
Bartlett Breed,
Attorneys for the National Labor Relations Board.

Latham & Watkins
By Paul R. Watkins,
1112 Title Guarantee Building, Los Angeles, California, appearing on behalf of Thompson Products, Inc.

Howard Baldwin,
7727 Wilcox Avenue, Bell, California, appearing on behalf of Pacific Motor Parts Workers Alliance. [1*]

TESTIMONY

Trial Examiner Whittemore: The record shows the president is here, but as there is no motion to intervene, I thought we should have that in the record. If the notice was served upon him, that is sufficient, and his presence is noted on the record.

Mr. Baldwin: Could I explain to you why we don't have counsel here?

Trial Examiner Whittemore: I think that is un-

---

*Page numbering appearing at top of page of original Reporter's Transcript.

necessary. You either have or you haven't; I do not know that it matters. You are here. You have the right to have counsel if you wish.

Mr. Baldwin: I see.

Mr. Watkins: May I have read what took place while I was looking at this file?

Trial Examiner Whittemore: Certainly.

(The record was read.)

Mr. Watkins: The Trial Examiner has no objection to [7] Mr. Baldwin's stating his reason, does he?

Trial Examiner Whittemore: None at all, if he feels it is necessary. I don't see that it is, when he is here.

Mr. Watkins: My only thought was that so long as his statement is made, it would be well to complete it rather than to leave it incomplete, if he wants to do so.

Trial Examiner Whittemore: I have no objection. Go ahead.

Mr. Baldwin: The reason we haven't counsel, being an independent concern, we couldn't pay for it. We didn't have enough money to hire counsel for this particular hearing.

Trial Examiner Whittemore: All right. Do you think that clarifies the record, Mr. Watkins?

Mr. Watkins: Yes. I think that states his reason for it.

Trial Examiner Whittemore: All right. [8]

BOARD'S EXHIBIT No. 2

[Title of Board and Cause.]

STIPULATION

For the purposes of the above captioned case and for no other purpose Thompson Products, Inc., herein called the Company, and Robert C. Moore, Attorney, National Labor Relations Board, stipulate and agree as follows:

1. The Company is a corporation incorporated June 17, 1916, under the laws of the State of Ohio, having its principal office at 2196 Clarkwood Road, Cleveland, Ohio. The Company operates industrial plants in Cleveland, Ohio, Detroit, Michigan, and Bell, California, and through a subsidiary corporation, Thompson Products, Ltd., operates a plant in Canada.

2. The industrial plant operated by the Company in Bell, California, referred to herein as the West Coast Plant, is located at 8354 Wilcox Avenue, Bell, Los Angeles County, California. This plant was purchased as a going concern by the Company on April 8, 1937, from Jadson Motor Products Company, and thereafter was operated by the Company under the name Jadson Motor Products Company until about July 1, 1940, at which time the Comany dropped the designation Jadson Motor Products Company and continued thereafter down to the present time to operate the West Coast Plant under the name "Thompson Products, Inc., West Coast Plant."

3. The Company is engaged at its West Coast

Plant in the business of manufacturing, producing and selling aircraft engine bolts, assembly bolts and miscellaneous engine and aircraft fuselage parts. The principal material used by the Company in its manufacturing operations at said West Coast Plant is steel and during the calendar year 1941 it purchased steel valued at not less than $350,000, approximately 85% of which steel was purchased and transported from sources of supply located in States of the United States other than California.

4. During the calendar year 1941 the Company produced at its West Coast Plant and sold products valued at not less than $1,500,000. Of the sales of these products approximately 65% were made to customers located outside the State of California.

5. This stipulation may be introduced in evidence in the above captioned case as evidence of the matters herein stipulated and agreed upon. Nothing contained herein shall operate to prevent either party hereto from introducing further evidence with respect to the issues in the above captioned case.

THOMPSON PRODUCTS, INC.
By LATHAM MATTHEWS
By PAUL R. WATKINS
Its Attorney
ROBERT C. MOORE
Attorney, National Labor Relations Board, Twenty-first Region

Dated at Los Angeles, California, this 1st day of, October, 1942.

HOWARD CURTIS BALDWIN,

called as a witness by and on behalf of the National Labor Relations Board, having been first duly sworn, was examined and testified as follows:

Direct Examination

Q. (By Mr. Moore) Will you state your full name, please?

A. Howard Curtis Baldwin.

Q. Are you employed? A. Yes.

Q. Where?

A. Thompson Products, Inc., West Coast plant.

Q. How long have you been so employed?

A. Approximately two and one-half years.

Q. Are you acquainted with an organization known as Pacific Motor Parts Workers Alliance?

A. Yes.

Q. Do you hold any office in that organization?

A. Yes.

Q. Is Pacific Motor Parts Works Alliance an organization formed for the purposes of collective bargaining on behalf of those whom it represents?

A. Yes.

Q. Do you have the constitution and by-laws of the Pacific [12] Motor Parts Workers Alliance with you? A. Yes, I have.

Q. May I see them, please?

Mr. Moore: I will ask that this document be marked as Board's Exhibit 3 for identification.

(Thereupon the document referred to was marked as Board's Exhibit No. 3, for identification.)

(Testimony of Howard Curtis Baldwin.)

Q. (By Mr. Moore) Mr. Baldwin, I show you a document marked Board's Exhibit 3 for identification, consisting of four typewritten pages, three pages containing written signatures, and ask you if you know what it is.   A. Yes.

Q. What is it?

A. It's the constitution and by-laws of the Pacific Motor Parts Workers Alliance.

Mr. Moore: I offer Board's Exhibit 3 for identification in evidence.

Mr. Watkins: May I see it, Mr. Moore?

Mr. Moore: If counsel desires to stipulate that a copy may be used, I have no objection. I understand the Alliance would like to keep their original document.

Mr. Watkins: I think perhaps the photostatic copy is what you should put in the record though.

Trial Examiner Whittemore: Will you ask the witness, Mr. Moore, if this is the current constitution and by-laws [13] on which they are now operating?

Q. (By Mr. Moore) Mr. Baldwin, is the document that you have identified, the constitution and by-laws as they are now written, of the Pacific Motor Parts Workers Alliance?

A. I would have to read it over first to make sure.

Mr. Watkins: We have no objection to the introduction of the exhibit, and no objection to the replacement of the original by either a photostat,

(Testimony of Howard Curtis Baldwin.)
or copy, and I think a photostat, under the circumstances, will be best.

Mr. Moore: I agree.

Trial Examiner Whittemore: I will let the witness first examine the document so that he may answer the question still on the record.

Q. (By Mr. Moore) Will you examine the document marked Board's Exhibit 3 for identification and see whether or not the Pacific Motor Parts Workers Alliance is now operating under that constitution and by-laws?

A. I would have to examine this alongside of the present record in order to verify the exact wording of it. You know what I mean; you can't remember all of it.

Trial Examiner Whittemore: Off the record.

(There was a discussion off the record.)

Trial Examiner Whittemore: On the record.

Q. (By Mr. Moore) You have examined Board's Exhibit 3 for identification. Do you recognize it as the original [14] constitution and by-laws under which the Alliance was formed?

A. Yes, I do.

Q. Do you have your constitution and by-laws at the present time in any other form?

A. We have it in the booklet form.

Mr. Moore: Will you mark this as Board's Exhibit 4 for identification?

(Thereupon the document referred to was marked as Board's Exhibit 4, for identification.)

(Testimony of Howard Curtis Baldwin.)

Q. (By Mr. Moore) I show you a small booklet which has been marked Board's Exhibit 4 for identification and ask you if the portion of that booklet "Pacific Motor Parts Workers Alliance, Constitution and By-Laws," reflects the constitution and by-laws under which the Alliance now operates?

A. Yes, it does, except for four by-laws that have not been inserted in here.

Q. Do you have copies of these four by-laws that have been adopted since this was printed, or the four by-laws to which you refer?

A. The four by-laws were printed, the four by-laws were made when the original was made, and they were somehow or other neglected to be put in here. I don't know why they were overlooked.

Q. Do you have any document from which you can give us the [15] contents of the four by-laws which are not included in this little booklet marked Board's Exhibit 4?

A. No, I haven't that with me.

Q. Do I understand you to say that there are four by-laws in this original document that are not contained in this booklet marked Board's Exhibit 4 for identification?

A. Well, it is supposed to be in this copy here.

Trial Examiner Whittemore: When you say "copy" you are referring to Board's Exhibit 3?

The Witness: Yes, Board's Exhibit 3.

Q. (By Mr. Moore) How many sections does Board's Exhibit 3 for identification have? How many headings does it have?   A. 13.

'(Testimony of Howard Curtis Baldwin.)

Q. And what is the last section on it?

A. That's the signatures.

Q. It reads, does it not: Section **13**, "The undersigned by affixing their signatures heretofore signify their affiliation with the Alliance as regular members thereof" and after that appear the signatures?   A. Yes.

Q. It is a fact, is it not, that this booklet marked Board's Exhibit 4 for identification, with the exception of Section 13 appearing in Board's Exhibit 3 for identification, is the same as Board's Exhibit 3 for identification? [16]   A. Right.

Q. Well, now——

A. Yes, I know what you are getting at. I will tell you. The four I am referring to, evidently I am wrong in making the statement they were incorporated at the time this was done. They probably came after this was printed. What I mean is: There were by-laws passed after Board's Exhibit 3 was drawn up, there were four by-laws passed that are not incorporated in that little book.

Trial Examiner Whittemore: Can you get hold of those so that we will have a complete record?

The Witness: I could bring them here, yes. I will have to get them.

Mr. Moore: All right.

Trial Examiner Whittemore: At the next recess, is there someone you can have bring them in that you could contact by telephone, or get them here this afternoon?

(Testimony of Howard Curtis Baldwin.)

The Witness: I will try to get them here, yes, sir.

Trial Examiner Whittemore: All right.

Mr. Moore: I will offer Board's Exhibit 3 for identification in evidence.

Trial Examiner Whittemore: As I understand it there is no objection to that. Have you any, Mr. Baldwin?

The Witness: No.

Trial Examiner Whittemore: Very well. Board's Exhibit 3 [17] is received.

(Thereupon the document heretofore marked as Board's Exhibit 3 for identification was received in evidence.)

PACIFIC ~~████~~ MOTOR PARTS WORKERS ALLIANCE

CONSTITUTION & BY LAWS

I.

Pursuant to the authority granted by the National Labor Relations Act, commonly known as the Wagner Act, there is hereby organized and the undersigned do hereby associate themselves in an organization to be known as Pacific Motor Parts Workers Alliance, for the purposes and upon the conditions as set forth herein. This particular group shall be known and designated as Local No. 1.

II.

PURPOSE. The purpose of this organization shall be to bargain collectively with employers of members by means of representatives of their own choosing and to engage in concerted activities for the prupose of collective bargaining or other mutual aid or protection.

III.

MEMBERSHIP. (a) Membership shall be limited to individuals working in the automobile or airplane industries in California, Washington and Oregon.

(b) Membership in Local No. 1 shall be limited to employee of the ~~████████████████~~ *Thompson Products Inc.* who are members of the general working force and who are not in a position to employ or discharge men under them on their own initiative.

(c) The Executive Council shall act as a committee on membership and shall have the power to ~~████████████████████~~ in the organization.

IV.

EXECUTIVE COUNCIL. (a) There is hereby created an executiv council of five members. To serve as an executive councilman, an individual must be an American citizen, twenty-one years or more of age and in the employ of a firm for not less than one year.

-1-

B03-id

(b) Election for Executive Council shall be conducted annually at the regular annual meeting of the organization and shall be conducted as follows:

The members of the Alliance shall cast their ballots for Executive Councilmen. Said ballots shall be collected and counted forthwith and the names of the ten eligible individuals receiving the highest number of votes shall be again balloted upon by the members and the five eligible individuals receiving the highest number of votes shall then be declared to be elected as Executive Councilmen.

V.

OFFICERS. The officers of this organization shall consist of a President, ~~first and second~~ Vice-Presidents, Secretary ~~and~~ Treasurer. Said officers shall be elected as follows:

Immediately following the election of the representatives to the Executive Council as hereinabove set forth, said Executive Council shall meet and shall proceed to elec   t the officers *except see Trier* *be elected* herein provided, for *by ballot the* ~~~~~~~~~~~. The President, with the consent of the Executive Council, shall have the right to appoint all standing committees, representatives for the purpose of engaging in collective bargaining with employers and representatives for all other lawful activities within the scope of this organization. The term of office of Executive Councilmen shall be for one year, or until their successors are elected and qualified. The President, with the approval of the Executive Council shall have full power to carry on and manage the business of the organization in all its lawful purposes, aims, nd objectives.

VI.

MEETINGS. (a) The regular annual meeting of this organization shall be held on the 3rd day of August of each year, unless said date shall fall upon a legal holiday, in which event the said

meeting shall be held on the next regular business day. Special
meetings of this organization shall be held upon call of the
President or Executive Council.

The Executive Council shall hold a regular meeting once
each calendar month, the date thereof to be determined by the
Executive Council, for the purpose of considering the welfare of
the organization and hearing cases involving individual grievances
~~complained~~ of members of this organization.

The Executive Council shall hold such special meetings
as may from time to time appear necessary, and shall meet upon call
of the President, ~~through~~ the Vice-Presidents or the Secretary,
upon not less than six (6) hours notice to the members of the
Executive Council.

VII.

EXPULSION OF MEMBERS. Any elected or appointed officer
or member whose act or acts are detrimental to the welfare of this
organization, whether directed against an officer or member or the
organization itself, shall be subject to forfeiture of his office
or membership or any action the Executive Council may see fit to
take, after a fair trial before the Executive Council in regular
or special call session.

Where not otherwise specified herein, order of business
and rules of conduct shall be governed by Roberts Rules of Order
and such by-laws as may be adopted by the Executive Council and
approved by a majority vote of the members at any regular or
special meeting.

VIII.

VOTING. All regularly admitted members of this organizatio
shall have the right to vote in all regular or special meetings,
whether they are qualified to serve as members of the Executive
Council or not. In voting for Executive Councilmen, each member
in good standing shall have as many votes as there are Executive

-3-

Councilmen to be elected, but such votes may not be cumulated.

IX.

QUORUM. A majority of the Executive Councilmen shall constitute a quorum of the Executive Council and a majority of the members in good standing shall constitute a quorum of the Alliance.

X.

Amendments. The Constitution and By-Laws may be repealed or amended or new by-laws may be adopted by the vote of a majority of the Executive Council and the approval by vote or written consent of two-thirds of the members in good standing. The power to repeal and amend the Constitution and By-Laws and to adopt new by-laws may,,by a similar vote or written consent, be delegated to the Executive Council, and such power, when so delegated, may be revoked by a.similar vote or written consent.

XI.

POWERS AND DUTIES.

President. It shall be the duty of the President to preside at all regular and special meetings of the Executive Council and of the Alliance and he shall have such other powers and duties as are specifically set forth herein.

Vice-Presidents. It shall be the duty of the Vice-Presidents to perform the duties of the President if he shall be unable to act and to perform any other duties which may be assigned to them *HIM* by the Executive Council.

Secretary- Treasurer. It shall be the duty of the Secretary Treasurer to keep a record of the proceedings of the Executive Council and of meetings of the A lliance, to receive and keep all funds of the Alliance, to keep accurate account thereof, and to disburse such funds only upon the check of the President, oR the Vice-Presidents and the Secretary-Treasurer.

XII.

INITIATION AND MEMBERSHIP FEES. Initiation and Membership fees shall be regulated by the Executive Council, with the approval

-4-   *Type to here*

1 of a majority vote or written consent of the members in good
2 standing.

XIII.

The undersigned, by affixing their signatures hereto,
signify their affiliation with the Alliance as regular members
thereof.   Signed this 3rd day of august 193_ at maywood.

James Creel   6418 Heliotrope ave
Floyd N Plankuah   1424 Castlegate ave —
G M Fickle   6252 King ave Bell
Co Stubblefield   639 Demenie Downey
E. J. Fickle   4884 Bell ave., Bell
R. D. Hailey   6417 Otis — Bell
Waino Kangas   3522 O 56 St Maywood.
G M Ruckdachel   6423 6th ar Bell
Robert Quesenberry   3074 Southern ave South gt
Wm. L. Bright   1345 Ohio av, Long B
Chas. W. Pattetman   308 W. Raymond St. P
Otto W Guengler   1405 Cookacre Lt Comp
H F Kroeker   6705 Heliotope B gl
Bert Nodurft   6635 Otis ave. Bell
John Imboden   14 East 89 St L A.
R. A. Porter   6029 _____ H Co
Al. D. Rhine   8685 Chestnut South gate.
Joseph E. Weber   2713 Indana St South gt
Olivia A. Chandler
Mrs alta M Fickle   4884 Bell ave. Bell Calif.
Jose F. Carr   7931½ Clara Strut Bell Calif.
Harold W Barr   7931½ Clara St Bell Calif.
Dan Gardner   2814 E 58 St Maywood

George Sherlock 6517 KING ST.

Ray Ruse

Carl Homann 1331½ L a

Rudolf Kohfeld 73½ Syphon Rd. El Monte

Percy Ward 8206 S. Atlantic

Wilbur Edgell 1240 Atlantic Dr. Compton

Sam L Koop 1255 Dineore ave Compton

Orill Matthew 7317 Atlantic Blvd, Bell

William Egan 6317½ Palm ave. Bell.

Lucile Leathwood 3932 Flower St. Bell.

L. P. Leathwood 6045 Woodlawn Maywo

Ladean Gregg 6045 Woodlawn Dr., Maywood, Calif

Glenn D. Kincaid 418 W. Bailey Whittier

Byron McKinney 515 W Walnut, El Segundo Calif

Clarence B. Ackerman 7317 Atlantic Blvd, Bell

Lester Bell 6414 Walker ave, Bell.

Frank Ankers 6321 Palm ave. Bell, Cal.

Barney Banmure 3661 Virginia Lynwood

A. R. Robinson 267 Telegraph Road Rivera

El Cunningham 6018 Luber St. Bell Gardens

Warner Wood 1024 S. Maple ave. L a.

Donald J. McCuaig 8212 Atlantic, Bell

L K Cosby 6608 Imperial Downey

Mae Freitas 1918 E 84th St L A.

Emery Hicklin 8603 Compton ave. L.A.

L. J. Leathwood 6045 Woodlawn ave Maywood

James P Claburgh 2011 E Century Bvd L A

Mearl Morris 251 5 St. Downey.

Ted Lay 4251 Clara St Bell L A.

Robert Schull 312 S 6th Alhambra

113

Frank Runyan. 10258 Calif ave. So Gate

T. G. Overholser 8461 San Juan Ave So Gate

Chas. O Tompkins 10127 Pescadero ave Sp.

Stan. Edward Little 9812 San Juan South Gate

M. J. Herbert 9510 Cecelia St So (illegible)

Pauline Klein 2814 Cincinnati st La

Wm. L. Galbraith 1208-3rd Ave. Norwalk Calif.

Eddie Anderson 5142 Duncan Way So Ga

Louis White P.O. Box 214 Bell Cal.

Howard Zimmerman
7644 Atlantic Blvd.

Pearl Casson 810 E 76 Pl. Los Angeles C

S. E. Prickett 605 Atlantic ave

T. P. Hellwig 6707 King Ave Bell

Julius Harvy Glen 2624 Century B (illegible)

R. H. Royster 2617½ Somerset Drive Los An

N. A. Clifford 4500 Santa Ana Bell

(illegible) Weaver 7811½ S 5th St. (illegible)

Paul Hegl 9230 San Juan Ave So

W C Christenson 10927- Firmona ave

And Marshall 4202 Live Oak Bell Inglewood

(Testimony of Howard Curtis Baldwin.)

Mr. Watkins: I understand the Board will photostat that and give the original back, if that is the original?

Mr. Moore: Yes.

Trial Examiner Whittemore: I take it for granted counsel will do as he said he would do. If he doesn't, call it to my attention, please.

Mr. Moore: I also offer Board's Exhibit 4 in evidence.

Trial Examiner Whittemore: Any objection.

Mr. Watkins: No objection.

Trial Examiner Whittemore: Any objection, Mr. Baldwin?

The Witness: None.

Trial Examiner Whittemore: Very well. It may be received and may I suggest we reserve 4-A for the material which Mr. Baldwin is going to bring in, which will make this document complete?

> (Thereupon the document referred to, heretofore marked Board's Exhibit 4 for identification, was received in evidence.)

(Testimony of Howard Curtis Baldwin.)

BOARD'S EXHIBIT No. 4

P. M. P. W. A.

This certifies that Clyde Spencer
is a Member of
Pacific Motor Parts Workers Alliance
Local No. 1, Bell, Calif.
and is entitled while in good standing to
all its benefits

E. L. FICKLE,
President
LESTER BEBB,
Sec.-Treas.
(4 Blank)

Pacific Motor Parts Workers Alliance
Constitution & By-Laws

I.

Pursuant to the authority granted by the National Labor Relations Act, commonly known as the Wagner Act, there is hereby organized and the undersigned do hereby associate themselves in an organization to be known as Pacific Motor Parts Workers Alliance, for the purposes and upon the conditions as set forth herein. This particular group shall be known and designated as Local No. 1.

II.

Purpose. The purpose of this organization shall be to bargain collectively with employers of members by means of representatives of their own choos-

(Testimony of Howard Curtis Baldwin.)
ing and to engage in concerted activities for the purpose of collective bargaining or other mutual aid or protection.

III.

Membership. (a) Membership shall (5) be limited to individuals working in the automobile or airplane industries in California, Washington and Oregon.

(b) Membership in Local No. 1 shall be limited to employees of the Thompson Products, Inc., who are members of the general working force and who are not in a position to employ or discharge men under them on their own initiative.

(c) The Executive Council shall act as a committee on membership and shall have the power to accept or reject membership in the organization.

IV.

Executive Council. (a) There is hereby created an executive council of five members. To serve as an executive councilman, an individual must be an American citizen, twenty-one years or more of age and in the employ of a firm for not less than one year.

(b) Election for Executive Council shall be conducted annually at the regular annual meeting of the organization and shall be conducted as follows:

The members of the Alliance shall cast their ballots for Executive Councilmen. Said ballots shall be collected and count- (6) ed forthwith and the names of the ten eligible individuals receiving the highest number of votes shall be again balloted upon by the members and the five eligible individuals receiving

'(Testimony of Howard Curtis Baldwin.)
the highest number of votes shall then be declared to
be elected as Executive Councilmen.

V.

Officers. The officers of this organization shall consist of a President, Vice-President, and Secretary-
Treasurer. Said officers shall be elected as follows :

Immediately following the election of the representatives to the Executive Council as hereinabove
set forth, said Executive Council shall meet and
shall proceed to elect by ballot the officers herein
provided for except Secretary-Treasurer, who shall
be elected by ballot the same as Councilmen, Secretary and Treasurer to have no voting power in council. The President, with the consent of the Executive Council, shall have the right to appoint all
standing committees, representatives for the purpose of engaging in collective bargaining with employers and representatives for all other lawful activities within the scope of this organization. The
term of office of Executive Councilmen (7) shall be
for one year, or until their successors are elected and
qualified. The President, with the approval of a
majority of the Executive Council shall have full
power to carry on and manage the business of the
organization in all its lawful purposes, aims, and
objectives.

VI.

Meetings. (a) The regular annual meeting of
this organization shall be held on the 3rd day of
August of each year, unless said date shall fall upon

(Testimony of Howard Curtis Baldwin.)

a legal holiday, in which event the said meeting shall be held on the next regular business day. Special meetings of this organization shall be held upon call of the President or Executive Council.

The Executive Council shall hold a regular meeting once each calendar month, the date thereof to be determined by the Executive Council for the purpose of considering the welfare of the organization and hearing cases involving individual grievances of members of this organization.

The Executive Council shall hold such special meetings as may from time to time appear necessary, and shall meet upon call of the President, the Vice-President or the Secretary, upon not less than six (6) (8) hours notice to the members of the Executive Council.

VII.

Expulsion of Members. Any elected or appointed officer or member whose act or acts are detrimental to the welfare of this organization, whether directed against an officer or member or the organization itself, shall be subjected to forfeiture of his office or membership or any action the Executive Committee may see fit to take, after a fair trial before the Executive Council in regular or special call session.

Where not otherwise specified herein, order of business and rules of conduct shall be governed by Roberts Rules of Order and such by-laws as may be adopted by the Executive Council and approved by a majority vote of the members at any regular or special meeting.

(Testimony of Howard Curtis Baldwin.)

VIII.

Voting. All regularly admitted members of this organization shall have the right to vote in all regular or special meetings, whether they are qualified to serve as members of the Executive Council (9) or not. In voting for Executive Councilmen, each member in good standing shall have as many votes as there are Executive Councilmen to be elected, but such votes may not be cumulated.

IX.

Quorum. A majority of the Executive Councilmen shall constitute a quorum of the Executive Council and a majority of the members in good standing shall constitute a quorum of the Alliance.

X.

Amendments. The Constitution and By-Laws may be repealed or amended or new by-laws may be adopted by the vote of a majority of the Executive Council and the approval by vote or written consent of two-thirds of the members in good standing. The power to repeal and amend the Constitution and By-Laws and to adopt new by-laws, by a similar vote or written consent, be delegated to the Executive Council, and such power, when so delegated, may be revoked by a similar vote or written consent. (10)

XI.

Powers and Duties.

President. It shall be the duty of the President

(Testimony of Howard Curtis Baldwin.)

to preside at all regular and special meetings of the Executive Council and of the Alliance and he shall have such other powers and duties as are specifically set forth herein.

Vice-President. It shall be the duty of the Vice-President to perform the duties of the President if he shall be unable to act and to perform any other duties which may be assigned to him by the Executive Council.

Secretary-Treasurer. It shall be the duty of the Secretary-Treasurer to keep a record of the proceedings of the Executive Council and of meetings of the Alliance, to receive and keep all funds of the Alliance, to keep accurate account thereof, and to disburse such funds only upon the check of the President, or the Vice-President and the Secretary-Treasurer. (11)

XII.

Initiation and Membership Fees

Initiation and Membership fees shall be regulated by the Executive Council, with the approval of a majority vote or written consent of the members in good standing. (12)

(13 blank)

(14 blank)

1941

Date	Dues	Rec'd By
Jan.	....	....
Feb.	....	....
Mar.	25	LB
April	25	LB

(Testimony of Howard Curtis Baldwin.)

May	25	L.B.
June	25	L.B.
July	25	L.B.
Aug.	25	L.B.
Sept	25	L.B.
Oct.	25	L.B.
Nov.	25	L.B.
Dec.	25	L.B.
	(15)	

1942

Date	Dues	Rec'd By
Jan.	25	L.B.
Feb.	25	L.B.
Mar.	25	L.B.
April	25	L.B.
May	25	L.B.
June	--------	--------
July	--------	--------
Aug.	--------	--------
Sept.	--------	--------
Oct.	--------	--------
Nov.	--------	--------
Dec.	--------	--------
	(16)	

1943

Date	Dues	Rec'd By
Jan.	--------	--------
Feb.	--------	--------
Mar.	--------	--------
April	--------	--------
May	--------	--------
June	--------	--------
July	--------	--------
Aug.	--------	--------
Sept.	--------	--------
Oct.	--------	--------
Nov.	--------	--------
Dec.	--------	--------
	(17)	

(Testimony of Howard Curtis Baldwin.)

1944

Date	Dues	Rec'd By
Jan.	....	....
Feb.	....	....
Mar.	....	....
April	....	....
May	....	....
June	....	....
July	....	....
Aug.	....	....
Sept.	....	....
Oct.	....	....
Nov.	....	....
Dec.	....	....

(18)

1945

Date	Dues	Rec'd By
Jan.	....	....
Feb.	....	....
Mar.	....	....
April	....	....
May	....	....
June	....	....
July	....	....
Aug.	....	....
Sept.	....	....
Oct.	....	....
Nov.	....	....
Dec.	....	....

(19)

1946

Date	Dues	Rec'd By
Jan.	....	....
Feb.	....	....
Mar.	....	....
April	....	....
May	....	....
June	....	....
July	....	....
Aug.	....	....

'(Testimony of Howard Curtis Baldwin.)

Date	Dues	Rec'd By
Sept.	--------	--------
Oct.	--------	--------
Nov.	--------	--------
Dec.	--------	--------

(20)

Q. (By Mr. Moore)   Mr. Baldwin, is the organization of which you have testified that you are president known as Local No. 1 of Pacific Motor Parts Workers Alliance?   A.   Yes.

Q.   And membership in that, I notice by your-by-laws, is [18] limited to employees of Thompson Products, Inc.?   A.   Yes.

Q.   Have any other locals of that Alliance been formed?   A.   No.

Mr. Watkins: I wonder if it might expedite matters if we stipulate on the record that we can refer to this organization as the "Alliance"?

Mr. Moore: I think it would be well to do that.

Trial Examiner Whittemore: All right.

Mr. Moore: Will you so stipulate, Mr. Baldwin?

The Witness: Yes.

Q. (By Mr. Moore)   Has the Alliance had collective bargaining agreements with Thompson Products, Inc.?   A.   Yes.

Mr. Moore: May we go off the record a moment?

Trial Examiner Whittemore: Surely.   Off the record.

(There was a discussion off the record.)

Trial Examiner Whittemore: On the record.

(Testimony of Howard Curtis Baldwin.)

Mr. Moore: Will you mark these as Board's Exhibits 5-A to 5-E for identification?

(Thereupon the documents referred to were marked as Board's Exhibits 5-A to 5-E, both inclusive, for identification.)

Q. (By Mr. Moore) I have had the reporter mark for identification as Board's Exhibits 5-A, 5-B, 5-C, 5-D, and 5-E, five documents which purport to be agreements between Pacific [19] Motor Parts Workers Alliance and Jadson Motor Products Company, with the exception of two marked 5-D and 5-E, which appear to be agreement between Pacific Motor Parts Workers Alliance and Thompson Products, Inc.

May it be stipulated that the documents marked 5-A through 5-E are copies of contracts as they purport to be on their face, that there has been no gap in the existence of contracts between either Jadson Motor Products Company and the Alliance or Thompson Products, Inc., and the Alliance?

Mr. Watkins: So stipulated.

Trial Examiner Whittemore: Do you join in the stipulation, Mr. Baldwin?

The Witness: Yes.

Trial Examiner Whittemore: I presume the record will eventually show what the Jadson Products is.

Mr. Moore: The record does show it in Board's Exhibit 2.

Trial Examiner Whittemore: I see. [20]

Mr. Moore: The record shows that on April 8,

(Testimony of Howard Curtis Baldwin.)

1937, that Jadson was taken over by Thompson Products, Inc., and that thereafter the plant formerly operated by Jadson was operated by Thompson Products, Inc., under the name Jadson Motor Products Company until approximately July 1, 1940.

Mr. Watkins: Yes, that is correct.

Trial Examiner Whittemore: All right.

Mr. Moore: I offer Board's Exhibit 5-A through 5-E in evidence.

Mr. Watkins: No objection.

The Witness: No objection.

Trial Examiner Whittemore: The documents are received.

> (The documents referred to were marked as Board's Exhibits Nos. 5-A to 5-E, both inclusive, and were received in evidence.)

BOARD'S EXHIBIT No. 5-A

This Agreement made and executed this 12th day of August, 1937, by and between Jadson Motor Products Co., a corporation, hereinafter designated the Company and Pacific Motor Parts Workers Alliance, Local No. 1, a labor organization, hereinafter designated the Alliance;

Witnesseth:

Whereas, a majority of the employees of the Company have voluntarily associated themselves in the labor organization known as Pacific Motor Parts Workers Alliance, Local No. 1, and

(Testimony of Howard Curtis Baldwin.)

Whereas, the duly elected and appointed representatives of the Alliance have met with representatives of the Company and have agreed upon various terms and conditions of employment;

Now, Therefore, pursuant to the authority vested in the Company and in the properly constituted representatives of the Alliance and pursuant to the laws of the State of California and of the United States of America,

It Is Hereby Agreed By and Between the Alliance and the Company as follows:

1. The Company recognizes the Alliance as the exclusive representative of the employees of the Company for the purposes of collective bargaining in respect to rates of pay, wages, hours of employment and other conditions of employment in accordance with the terms of the National Labor Relations Act.

It Is Hereby Agreed that the provisions of this contract shall continue in force for thirty days from the 12th day of August, 1938.

Signed:

(JAMES CREEK
    Chairman, P.M.P.W.A.
(P. D. HILEMAN)
    Management

2. The Company adopts and makes effective as of August 16, 1937, the wage scale which is attached hereto, marked Exhibit A, and by reference is made a part of this agreement.

3. The Company agrees to pay an overtime

(Testimony of Howard Curtis Baldwin.)

premium of time and one-third for work over eight hours in one day, or forty-five hours in one week and an overtime premium of time and one-half for work performed on Sunday or on any of the following holidays: New Year's Day, Memorial Day, Independence Day, Labor Day, Thanksgiving Day and Christmas Day.

The foregoing stipulation with respect to overtime applies to all employees with the exception of maintenance men, watchmen and employees whose duties normally call for work on Sundays and holidays, these employees to be given a regular day off during the week in lieu of Sunday.

4. The Company agrees to adopt a standard work week of forty-five hours, consisting so far as practicable of five eight-hour days and five hours on Saturday morning for the day force; five nine-hour days for the evening force. When this arrangement is made effective for the night force, overtime for night workers shall not begin until after nine hours in one day or forty-five hours in one week. It is understood and agreed that this arrangement for the night force is contingent on an hourly production during nights not less than hourly production during days.

5. The Company agrees that during the life of this contract it will not employ any additional Orientals or Mexicans.

6. The Company agrees to adopt and adhere to the following system of hearing individual

(Testimony of Howard Curtis Baldwin.)

grievances and discussing matters of importance to the general working force when presented by the Alliance or its representatives.

(a) Individual Grievances:

The employee concerned or a representative of the Alliance may present the matter to be discussed to the immediate foreman of the employee concerned. Failing a satisfactory adjustment, the matter shall then be referred by the Alliance to the General Superintendent. Again failing a satisfactory adjustment, the matter shall be referred to either a regular or a special meeting between duly elected representatives of the Alliance and a representative or representatives of the Company appointed for such purpose. In the event the matter still cannot be satisfactorily adjusted, it ~~shall~~ may be submitted upon consent of both parties to arbitration by three arbitrators: The Alliance to select one, the Company one and the two arbitrators thus chosen to select the third.

(b) Matters of General Interest:

Matters of general interest to the entire working force may be presented to the Company in a regularly scheduled or special meeting between the Company and the Alliance. Regular meetings between representatives of the Alliance and of the Company shall be held once monthly at 1:30 P. M. the third Monday of each month. Special meetings may be called upon forty-eight hours' notice upon request of either party.

(Testimony of Howard Curtis Baldwin.)

7. The Company agrees to discuss and consult with representatives of the Alliance with respect to:

(a) Shop rules and regulations.

(b) Inequitable times or standards.

8. The Company agrees within thirty (30) days from the date hereof to meet and negotiate with representatives of the Alliance with respect to a seniority agreement to govern general reductions of the working force.

9. The Company agrees prior to May 1, 1938, to negotiate with representatives of the Alliance whereby, barring unexpected business reverses, a vacation plan with pay for factory workers can be made effective during the year 1938.

· 10. This agreement shall remain in force for one year from the date hereof but the Alliance reserves the right to renegotiate any wage matters which are not general in character.

11. This agreement shall not be assignable by the Alliance nor shall it inure to the benefit of any successors without the written consent of the Company.

12. It is understood and agreed that this contract may be modified or revised at any time with the consent of both parties hereto. The effects of this contract is limited to operations of the Company at its plant near Bell, California.

(Testimony of Howard Curtis Baldwin.)

In Witness Whereof the parties have caused these presents to be duly executed the day and year in this agreement first above written.

JADSON MOTOR
PRODUCTS CO.,

By ....

Its..............

The Company

PACIFIC MOTOR PARTS
WORKERS ALLIANCE,
LOCAL No. 1

By ....

The Alliance.

EXHIBIT A

FACTORY WAGE SCALE
Jadson Motor Products Company
(Division of Thompson Products, Inc.)

Effective August 16, 1937

Job	Minimum	Average	Maximum
Small Machine Operations (Hand milling, drilling, cut-off, chamfering, etc.)	.50	.55	.60
Forge Department			
Cut off	.50	.55	.60
Electric upset	.61	.66	.71
Hammers and presses	.55	.60	.65
Upsetting Ford Ends	.61	.66	.71
Flash welding	.61	.66	.71
Heat Treat Department			
Sand blast	.50	.55	....
Furnace helper	.57	.62	.67
Heat treater (Class A)	.70	.75	.80
Torch hardening	.57	.62	.67
Valve Straightening	.60	.65	.70

(Testimony of Howard Curtis Baldwin.)

Job	Minimum	Average	Maximum
Production Hand Screw Machines (Grooving, *maching* head diameter, boring and facing inserts)	.60	.65	.70
Special Screw Machines (Concave and radius lathes)	.63	.68	.73
Warner & Swasey 2A	.66	.71	.76
Valve Guide Department (Gun drilling, broaching, automatic porter cable machines)	.60	.65	.70
Grinders			
Commercial (Tip grinding, rough centerless, grinding necks, tapers, foot, reliefs, seats on valves; grinding insert faces)	.55	.65	.70
Special (Racing and aircraft valves, grinding radii, reliefs, grooves, seats, finishing stems)	.66	.71	.76
Seat Welding	.55	.70	.75
Inspection and Wrapping (Female)	.42	.45	.48
Inspectors (Male)	.50	.55	.60
Shipping Department			
Clerks	.58	.63	.68
Pickup and delivery	.50	.55	.60
Maintenance Department			
Electrician	.70	.80	.85
Machine Repair Man	.70	.80	.85
Helpers	.55	.60	.65
Tool Room			
Tool Makers (Class A)	.70	.80	.85
Tool room specialists	.60	.65	.70
Forge die makers	.66	.71	.76

(Testimony of Howard Curtis Baldwin.)

Note:

The following provisions apply to these rates:—

1. The minimum rate on a job becomes effective thirty days after the original date of employment in the event the employee has sufficient skill or ability to be retained permanently by the company.

2. The average rate becomes effective one hundred twenty days after the original employment date, unless it has been demonstrated conclusively to the employee and his representative of the Pacific Parts Workers Alliance that the employee is unable to produce the quantity or quality of work necessary to justify this rate. The average rate is for normal, standard performance on a job.

3. For better than average ability or output, an employee may be raised up to the maximum rate, in whole or in part, depending upon the judgment of the Management. The range between the average and maximum rates is reserved for better than average ability and output.

4. Employees designated as set-up men for a group or department will be paid 5¢ an hour over the maximum rate established for the job.

It Is Agreed that any maintenance man called for special work will be guaranteed two hours working time.

Signed:

(JIM CREEK)
Chairman P.M.P.W.A.

(P. D. HILEMAN)
Management

———

BOARD'S EXHIBIT No. 5-B

This Agreement made and executed this 12th day of September, 1938, by and between Jadson Motor Products Co., a corporation, hereinafter designated

(Testimony of Howard Curtis Baldwin.)

Board's Exhibit No. 5-B—(Continued)
the Company, and Pacific Motor Parts Workers Alliance, Local No. 1, a Labor organization, hereinafter designated the Alliance;

Witnesseth:

Whereas, a majority of the factory employees of the Company have voluntarily associated themselves in the labor organization known as Pacific Motor Part Workers Alliance, Local No. 1, and

Whereas, the duly elected and appointed representatives of the Alliance have met with representatives of the Company and have agreed upon various terms and conditions of employment;

Now, Therefore, pursuant to the authority vested in the Company and in the properly constituted representatives of the Alliance and pursuant to the laws of the State of California and of the United States of America,

It Is Hereby Agreed by and Between the Alliance and the Company as follows:

1. The Company recognizes the Alliance as the exclusive representative of the factory employees of the Company for the purposes of collective bargaining in respect to rates of pay, wages, hours of employment, and other conditions of employment in accordance with the terms of the National Labor Relations Act.

2. The Company adopts and makes effective as of the date of this agreement the wage scale which is attached hereto, marked Exhibit A, and by ref-

(Testimony of Howard Curtis Baldwin.)

Board's Exhibit No. 5-B—(Continued)

erence makes the same a part of this agreement.

3. All work in any one week in excess of the number of hours then constituting the company's standard work week, as herein provided, shall be considered overtime. All work on Sundays, or on any of the following legal holidays, to-wit: New Year's Day, Memorial Day, Independence Day, Labor Day, Thanksgiving Day and Christmas Day, shall be considered holiday time. The Company agrees to pay for all overtime at one and one-third the regular rates and for all holiday time at one and one-half the regular rates.

Provided, however, that from and after the date on which the Company adopts the forty-four hour standard work week, as provided in Paragraph 4 hereof, it shall pay one and one-half the regular rates for overtime.

Provided, further, however, that the foregoing provisions relating to a premium for overtime and holiday time shall not apply to maintenance men, watchmen, or employees whose duties normally call for work on Sundays and holidays. They shall receive no premium for holiday time; and they shall receive no premium for overtime except as hereinafter provided. From and after the date on which the Company adopts the forty-four hour standard work week, as provided in Paragraph 4 hereof, they shall be paid at one and one-half the regular rates for all work in excess of forty-four hours in any one week.

(Testimony of Howard Curtis Baldwin.)

Board's Exhibit No. 5-B—(Continued)

Watchmen, maintenance men and other employees whose duties normally call for work on Sundays and holidays shall be given a regular day off during the week in lieu of Sunday.

4. The Company agrees to continue its present standard work week of forty-five hours, consisting so far as practicable of five eight-hour days and five hours on Saturday morning for the day shift and five nine-hour days for the evening shift. It is understood and agreed that this arrangement for the night shift is contingent on an hourly production during nights not less than hourly production during days.

Provided, however, that on or not more than seven days prior to the effective date of Section 7 of the Fair Labor Standards Act of 1938 the Company will adopt a standard work week of forty-four hours, the reduction from a standard work week of forty-five hours to be effected for the day shift, so far as practicable, by providing for four instead of five hours of work on Saturday; and, for the evening shift, by providing for eight rather than nine hours of work on Friday evening until midnight.

5. The Company agrees that during the life of this contract it will not employ any additional Orientals or Mexicans.

6. The Company agrees to continue the following system of hearing individual grievances and discussing matters of importance to the general

(Testimony of Howard Curtis Baldwin.)

Board's Exhibit No. 5-B—(Continued)

working force when presented by the Alliance or its representatives.

(a) Individual Grievances:

The employee concerned or a representative of the Alliance may present the matter to be discussed to the immediate foreman of the employee concerned. Failing a satisfactory adjustment, the matter shall then be referred by the Alliance to the General Superintendent. Again failing a satisfactory adjustment, the matter shall be referred to either a regular or a special meeting between duly elected representatives of the Alliance and a representative or representatives of the Company appointed for such purpose. In the event the matter still cannot be satisfactorily adjusted, it may be submitted upon the consent of both parties to arbitration by three arbitrators: The Alliance to select one, the Company one and the two arbitrators thus chosen to select the third.

(b) Matters of General Interest:

Matters of general interest to the entire working force may be presented to the Company in a regularly scheduled or special meeting between the Company and the Alliance. Regular meetings between representatives of the Alliance and of the Company shall be held once monthly at 1:30 P. M. the third Monday of each month. Special meetings may be called upon forty-eight hours' notice upon request of either party.

(Testimony of Howard Curtis Baldwin.)

Board's Exhibit No. 5-B—(Continued)

7.   The Company agrees to discuss and consult with representatives of the Alliance with respect to:

(a)   Shop rules and regulations.

(b)   Inequitable times or standards.

8.   The agreement dated October 6, 1937, made and entered into between the Company and the Alliance and relating to seniority, lay-offs and promotions, a copy of which is annexed hereto, marked "Exhibit B", is by this reference incorporated herein and made a part hereof. Said agreement of October 6, 1937, shall continue in force during the life of, and shall expire at the same time as, this agreement.

9.   If and when the condition of its business warrants such a step, the Company will resume the discussions heretofore had with the Alliance regarding a vacation plan with pay for factory workers.

10.   This agreement shall remain in force for one year from the date hereof, but the Alliance reserves the right to renegotiate any wage matters which are not general in character.

11.   This agreement shall not be assignable by the Alliance, nor shall it inure to the benefit of any successor or successors of Alliance, without the written consent of the Company.

12.   It is understood and agreed that this contract is limited to the factory operations of the Company at its plant near Bell, California.

13.   It is further understood that this contract

(Testimony of Howard Curtis Baldwin.)

Board's Exhibit No. 5-B—(Continued)

may be modified or revised at any time with the consent of both parties hereto.

14. This contract supersedes the contract dated August 12, 1937, between the Company and Alliance, as the same has heretofore been amended and extended, and said agreement of August 12, 1937 is hereby terminated.

In Witness Whereof *that* parties have caused these presents to be duly executed the day and year in this agreement first above written.

JADSON MOTOR PRODUCTS
CO.

By P. D. HILEMAN

Its Genl. Mgr.

The Company.

PACIFIC MOTOR PARTS
WORKERS ALLIANCE,
LOCAL No. 1

By T. G. OVERHULSE

E. T. FICKLE

FLOYD N. PFANKUCH

L. J. LEATHERWOOD

O. P. WRIGHT

The Alliance.

G.

The name of O. P. Wright was omitted because he was on vacation at the time this contract was signed.

'(Testimony of Howard Curtis Baldwin.)
Board's Exhibit No. 5-B—(Continued)
EXHIBIT A

FACTORY WAGE SCALE
Jadson Motor Products Company
(Division of Thompson Products, Inc.)

Job	Rate per Hour Minimum	Average	Maximum
Small Machine Operations	.50	.55	.60
(Hand milling, drilling, cut-off, chamfering, etc.)			
Forge Department			
Cut off	.50	.55	.60
Electric upset	.61	.66	/71
Hammers and presses	.55	.60	.65
Upsetting Ford Ends	.61	.66	.71
Flash welding	.61	.66	.71
Special Note: Any Forge Department man transferred from his regular employment to any Forge Department operation on steel 2½" in diameter or larger shall be paid while so employed at the hourly rate for the employment from which he was transferred, plus 5¢ per hour.			
Heat Treat Department			
Sand Blast	.50	.55	xxx
Furnace helper	.57	.62	/67
Heat treater (Class A)	.70	.75	.80
Torch hardening	.57	.62	.67
Valve Straightening	.60	.65	.70
Production Hand Screw Machines	.60	.65	.70
(Grooving, machining head diameter, boring and facing inserts)			
Special Screw Machines	.63	.68	.73
(Concave and radius lathes)			
Warner & Swasey 2A	.66	.71	.80

(Testimony of Howard Curtis Baldwin.)

Board's Exhibit No. 5-B—(Continued)

Job	Rate per Hour Minimum	Average	Maximum
Valve Guide Department......................	.60	.65	.70
(Gun drilling, broaching, automatic porter cable machines)			
Grinders			
Commercial	.55	.65	.70
(Tip grinding, rough centerless, grinding necks, tapers, foot, reliefs, seats on valves; grinding insert faces			
Special	.66	.71	.80
(Racing and aircraft valves, grinding radii, reliefs, grooves, seats, finishing stems)			
Seat Welding	.55	.70	.75
Inspection and Wrapping (Female)......	.42	.45	.48
Inspectors (Male)	.50	.55	.60
Shipping Department			
Clerks	.58	.63	.68
Pick-up and delivery	.50	.55	.60
Maintenance Department			
Electrician	.70	.80	.85
Machine Rapair Man	.70	.80	.85
Helpers	.55	.60	.65
Special Note: Any maintenance man called for special work will be guaranteed two hours working time.			
Tool Room			
Tool Makers (Class A)	.70	.80	.85
Tool room syecialists ....•	.60	.65	.70
Forge die makers	.66	.71	.76
Initialed: (Watchmen	xxx		xxx
PDH (and		.55	
TGO (Janitors	xxx	xx	xxx

'(Testimony of Howard Curtis Baldwin.)

Board's Exhibit No. 5-B—(Continued)

General Notes:

The following provisions apply to these rates:

1. The minimum rate on a job becomes effective thirty days after the original date of employment in the event the employee has sufficint skill or ability to be retained permanently by the company.
2. The average rate becomes effective one hundred twenty days after the original employment date, unless it has been demonstrated conclusively to the employee and his representative of the Pacific Parts Workers Alliance that the employee is unable to produce the quantity or quality of work necessary to justify this rate. The average rate is for normal, standard performance on a job.
3. For better than average ability or output, an employee may be raised up to the maximum rate, in whole or in part, depending upon the judgment of the Management. The range between the average and maximum rates is reserved for better than average ability and output.
4. Employees designated as set-up men for a group or department will be paid 5¢ an hour over the maximum rate established for the job.

EXHIBIT B

SENIORITY AGREEMENT

Layoffs and Promotions; made between the Jadson Motor Products Company and the Pacific Motor Parts Workers Alliance

I. Layoffs will be made in accordance with seniority as hereinafter specified, provided, however, that the company shall not be required in any event to retain the services of an employee whose skill, ability and efficiency is markedly less

(Testimony of Howard Curtis Baldwin.)

Board's Exhibit No. 5-B—(Continued)

than that of another employee capable and in line for the same operation.

A. The company shall maintain adequate records of each employee's seniority by occupation, and total length of service with the company in accordance with the following rulings:

1. Only time actually worked shall be accumulated toward an employee's seniority record. (Item 4 only exception.)

2. An employee's previous seniority record shall be considered cancelled in the event he is discharged for sufficient cause, quits voluntarily, or fails to report back to work following a layoff after sufficient notification has been given.

3. In the event an employee who quits or has been discharged is subsequently offered inducement by the company to return to work, he shall be given credit for his previous employment record in the event he returns.

4. Absence due to military service or sickness of short duration will not be deducted from an employee's seniority record.

5. Leaves of absences may be obtained for sufficient cause without affecting an employee's previous seniority record. Such leaves of absences will not be counted toward the employee's total seniority record.

(Testimony of Howard Curtis Baldwin.)

Board's Exhibit No. 5-B—(Continued)

B. All records pertaining to seniority and layoffs may be reviewed by the P.M.P.W.A. Committee and action taken by the committee as provided in the contract between the P.M.P.W.A. and Jadson Motor Products Company of which this agreement is a part.

II. When a general reduction of the working force becomes necessary, the following procedure shall apply.

A. Layoffs shall be made on the basis of seniority by occupations in a department. Example—when it becomes necessary to lay off a Cincinnati finish stem grinder, the employee with the least amount of seniority on that job shall be laid off, etc.

B. An employee laid off from a skilled occupation may replace an employee engaged at a less skilled occupation in the same department provided that he is qualified and the employee thus replaced has less company seniority than the first employee.

C. An employee laid off from one department may return to a department in which he previously worked and claim a job of his own occupation, providing it is held by an employee of less company seniority.

D. Where an operation is permanently discontinued the affected employee may claim a job of the same or related craft held by another employee with less company seniority,

(Testimony of Howard Curtis Baldwin.)

Board's Exhibit No. 5-B—(Continued)

regardless of the department in which the job exists, providing he is capable of performing the job.

E. Exempt from layoffs by seniority shall be:

1. Specialists of highly developed skill whose services are considered necessary to the company's operation. These are to be listed by Management and submitted to the Alliance representatives.

2. Employees with less than six months total service with the company. (Such employees may be laid off at the discretion of Management with merit the only consideration.)

3. The following general provisions shall also apply to this agreement.

a. This agreement need not necessarily be applied in cases of temporary layoffs of one week or less.

b. Nothing in this agreement shall prevent the company laying off or discharging an employee for disciplinary reasons or failure to perform the job in a safe, workmanlike and efficient manner.

c. Employees shall be returned to work after a reduction of the working force in the reverse order of these provisions.

d. Employees shall have the right at all times to review their seniority status with the Management.

(Testimony of Howard Curtis Baldwin.)

Board's Exhibit No. 5-B—(Continued)

e. Upon being notified to return to work following a layoff, employees shall be given three days to report to the Employment Office. Failure to do so shall result in previous seniority being cancelled.

III. The company shall maintain adequate records of the work for which each employee is qualified and for which each employee has expressed a desire to obtain. When a vacancy occurs either in the factory or the factory office, these records shall be consulted and the company will endeavor to advance men within the organization in accordance with the preference expressed. Such transfers or promotions will be made solely on the basis of merit. In the event two or more employees have equal merit, then seniority will be given consideration. In the event the company is unable to fill a vacancy from its records, the job will then be posted on all bulletin boards and employees will have the opportunity to apply personally for it.

IV. The company shall advise the Committee of P.M.P.W.A. of all proposed layoffs or discharges.

V. No employee shall use his seniority to procure the job of another employee except as provided herein.

VI. This agreement shall become a part of the contract entered into between the Jadson Motor

(Testimony of Howard Curtis Baldwin.)

Board's Exhibit No. 5-B—(Continued)

Products Company and the Pacific Motor Parts Workers Alliance on October 6, 1937.

Date

P. D. HILEMAN

Management

JAMES CREEK

P.M.P.W.A. Committee

It Is Hereby Mutually Agreed That all of the provisions of the contract dated October 19, 1939, by and between the Pacific Motor Parts Workers Alliance, Local #1, a labor organization, and the Management of Jadson Motor Products Co., a corporation, (the latter now known as *t*hompson Products, Inc., West Coast Plant) shall be continued in effect for a period of thirty (30) days from October 19, 1940.

By P. D. HILEMAN

Management

E. T. FICKLE

Chairman, P.M?P.W.A.

Committee

Date: October 14, 1940

———

BOARD'S EXHIBIT No. 5-C

This Agreement made and executed this 19 day of October, 1939, by and between Jadson Motor Products Co., a corporation, hereinafter designated the Company, and Pacific Motor Parts Workers Alli-

(Testimony of Howard Curtis Baldwin.)

Board's Exhibit No. 5-C—(Continued)
ance, Local No. 1, a labor organization, hereinafter designated the Alliance;

WITNESSETH:

Whereas, a majority of the factory employees
of the Company have voluntarily associated themselves in the labor organization known as Pacific
Motor Parts Workers Alliance, Local No. 1, and

Whereas, the duly elected and appointed representatives of the Alliance have met with representatives of the Company and have agreed upon various terms and conditions of employment;

Now, Therefore, pursuant to the authority vested
in the Company and in the properly constituted representatives of the Alliance and pursuant to the
laws of the State of California and of the United
States of America,

It Is Hereby Agreed by and Between the Alliance and the Company as follows:

1. The Company recognizes the Alliance as the
exclusive representative of the factory employees
of the Company, with the exception of those employees engaged in a supervisory capacity, for the
purposes of collective bargaining in respect to rates
of pay, wages, hours of employment, and other conditions of employment in accordance with the terms
of the National Labor Relations Act.

2. The Company adopts and makes effective as
of the date of this agreement the wage scale which

(Testimony of Howard Curtis Baldwin.)

Board's Exhibit No. 5-C—(Continued)
is attached hereto, marked "Exhibit A", and by
reference makes the same a part of this agreement.

3. An overtime premium of one and one-half
times the regular hourly rate shall be paid factory
non-supervisory employees for all hours worked
in excess of 42 in one week (unless otherwise provided by law) and for all hours worked on Sundays and the following legal holidays: New Years
Day, Memorial Day, Independence Day, Labor
Day, Thanksgiving Day, and Christmas Day; provided, however, that the premium for Sunday and
holiday work shall not apply to maintenance employees or watchmen, or other employees whose
duties normally call for work on Sundays or holidays. Such employees will be paid an overtime
premium of time and one-half for hours worked
in excess of 42 during a weekly pay period, and
shall be given a regular day off during the week
in lieu of Sunday.

4. Insofar as orders, the financial condition of
the company, and efficient management of the shop
may permit, effort will be made by the Company
to provide day shift employees who are asked to
report for work on Saturday with a minimum of
four hours' work. When and as business requirements dictate the addition of a night shift, the
hours to be worked shall be mutually agreed upon
by the qualified representatives of the Alliance and
the Management of the Company. Continuance or

(Testimony of Howard Curtis Baldwin.)

Board's Exhibit No. 5-C—(Continued)
discontinuance of these arrangements rests entirely
with the judgment of the Management. The provisions set forth herewith should not under any
circumstances be construed as guaranteeing a
standard work week.

5. The Company agrees that during the life
of this contract it will not employ any additional
Orientals or Mexicans.

6. The Company agrees to continue the following system of hearing individual grievances and
discussing matters of importance to the general
working force when presented by the Alliance or
its representatives.

(a) Individual Grievances:

The employee concerned or a representative of
the Alliance may present the matter to be discussed to the immediate foreman of the employee
concerned. Failing a satisfactory adjustment, the
matter shall then be referred by the Alliance to
the General Superintendent. Again failing a satisfactory adjustment, the matter shall be referred
to either a regular or a special meeting between
duly elected representatives of the Alliance and
a representative or representatives of the Company
appointed for such purpose. In the event the
matter still cannot be satisfactorily adjusted, it
may be submitted upon the consent of both parties
to arbitration by three arbitrators: The Alliance
to select one, the Company one and the two arbitrators thus chosen to select the third.

(Testimony of Howard Curtis Baldwin.)

Board's Exhibit No. 5-C—(Continued)

(b) Matters of General Interest:

Matters of general interest to the entire working force may be presented to the Company in a regularly scheduled or special meeting between the Company and the Alliance. Regular meetings between representatives of the Alliance and of the Company shall be held once monthly at 1:30 P.M. the third Monday of each month. Special meetings may be called upon forty-eight hours' notice upon request of either party.

7. The Company agrees to discuss and consult with representatives of the Alliance with respect to:

    (a) Shop rules and regulations.

    (b) Inequitable times or standards.

8. The agreement dated October 6, 1937, made and entered into between the Company and the Alliance and relating to seniority, lay-offs and promotions, a copy of which is annexed hereto, marked "Exhibit B", is by this reference incorporated herein and made a part hereof. Said agreement of October 6, 1937, shall continue in force during the life of, and shall expire at the same time as, this agreement.

9. The Company agrees that not later than March 15, 1940 the Old Guard Association of Thompson Products will be extended to include employees of the Jadson Motor Products Plant with all the rights and benefits thereof, including a vacation plan in accordance with the agreement

(Testimony of Howard Curtis Baldwin.)

Board's Exhibit No. 5-C—(Continued)
marked "Exhibit C" attached hereto, and which
is a part of this contract, and the establishment
of a Loan and Welfare Fund from which employees may derive assistance during distressed
circumstances.

10. This contract is automatically renewable unless for specific reasons objection is raised either
by the Alliance or the Company, and written notice of such objection given thirty (30) days prior
to the renewal date.

11. This agreement shall not be assignable by
the Alliance, nor shall it inure to the benefit of
any successor or successors of Alliance, without
the written consent of the Company.

12. It is understood and agreed that this con-
tract is limited to the factory operations of the
Company, located at 8354 Wilcox Avenue, Bell,
California.

13. It is further understood that this contract
may be modified or revised at any time with the
consent of both parties hereto.

14. This contract supersedes the contract dated
September 12, 1938, between the Company and
Alliance, as the same has heretofore been amended
and extended, and said agreement of September
12, 1938 is hereby terminated.

(Testimony of Howard Curtis Baldwin.)

Board's Exhibit No. 5-C—(Continued)

In Witness Whereof *that* parties have caused these presents to be duly executed the day and year in this agreement first above written.

JADSON MOTOR PRODUCTS
CO.

By P. D. HILEMAN

Its General Manager

The Company

PACIFIC MOTOR PARTS
WORKERS ALLIANCE,
LOCAL NO. 1

By E. T. FICKLE

N. J. CLIFFORD

L. J. LEATHERWOOD

C. O. STUBBLEFIELD

GEO. McINTIRE

The Alliance

Pacific Motor Parts Workers Alliance

Local No. 1

Bell, California

April 9, 1940

Mr. P. D. Hileman

Jadson Motor Products Co.

8354 Wilcox Avenue

Bell, California

Dear Mr. Hileman:

Confirming our conversation during the meeting today, and by mutual consent, Paragraph X of

(Testimony of Howard Curtis Baldwin.)

Board's Exhibit No. 5-C—(Continued)
the agreement between the Jadson Motor Products
Co. and the Pacific Motor Parts Workers Alliance, Local No. 1, dated October 19, 1939, is hereby
amended to read as follows:

"This contract shall remain in effect until
October 19, 1940, and shall automatically renew from year to year thereafter unless either
party gives notice in writing to the other party
of its intention to terminate, said notice to be
delivered not less than thirty (30) days prior
to the end of any yearly period."

Very truly yours,

PACIFIC MOTOR PARTS
WORKERS ALLIANCE

By E. T. FICKLE
C. E. LITTLE
GEO. McINTIRE
C. O. STUBBLEFIELD
LESTER *BUBB*

EXHIBIT A

FACTORY WAGE SCALE
Jadson Motor Products Co.
(Division of Thompson Products, Inc.)

Job	Rate per Hour		
	Minimum	Average	Maximum
Small Machine Operations............................	.50	.55	.60
(Hand milling, drilling, cut-off, chamfering, etc.)			

(Testimony of Howard Curtis Baldwin.)
Board's Exhibit No. 5-C—(Continued)

Job	Rate per Hour Minimum	Average	Maximum

Forge Department

Cut off	.50	.55	.60
Electric upset	.61	.66	.71
Hammers and presses	.55	.60	.65
Upsetting Ford Ends	.61	.66	.71
Flash welding	.61	.66	.71

Special Note: Any Forge Department man transferred from his regular employment to any Forge Department operation on steel 2½" in diameter or larger shall be paid while so employed at the hourly rate for the employment from which he was transferred, plus 5¢ per hour.

Heat Treat Department

Sand blast	.50	.55	
Furnace helper	.57	.62	.67
Heat treater (Class A)	.70	.75	.80
Torch hardening	.57	.62	/67

Valve Straightening	.60	.65	.70

Production Hand Screw Machines	.60	.65	.70

(Grooving, machining head diameter, boring and facing inserts)

Special Screw Machines	.63	.68	.73

(Concave and radius lathes)

November 7, 1940

	Minimum	Average	Maximum

Tool Room

Tool Makers (Class A)		1.15

By E. T. FICKLE
P.M.P.W.A
P. D. HILEMAN
Management

(Testimony of Howard Curtis Baldwin.)
Board's Exhibit No. 5-C—(Continued)

	Minimum	Average	Maximum
Expert Welder	.85		
Cleveland Automatics	.60	.65	.70
(Turning head, radius and face)			
Thread Grinders	.60	.66	.76
Polishing	.55	.60	.65

September 3, 1940

	Minimum	Average	Maximum
Torch Harden	.60	.65	.70

By E. T. FICKLE
P.M.P.W.A
P. D. HILEMAN
Management

Maximum hourly rate changes approved in following departments:

	Maximum
Heat Treat Department	
Heat Treater (Class A)	.90
Inspection and Wrapping (Female)	.55
Tool Room	
Tool Makers (Class A))	.95
Forge Die Makers	.85

By E. T. FICKLE
P.M.P.W.A
P. D. HILEMAN
Management

	Rate per Hour		
Job	Minimum	Average	Maximum
Warner & Swasey 2A	.66	.71	.80
Valve Guide Department	.60	.65	.70
(Gun drilling, broaching, automatic porter cable machines)			

(Testimony of Howard Curtis Baldwin.)
Board's Exhibit No. 5-C—(Continued)

Job	Rate per Hour Minimum	Average	Maximum
Grinders			
Commercial	.55	.65	.70
(Tip grinding, rough centerless, grinding necks, tapers, foot, reliefs, seats on valves; grinding insert faces)			
Special	.66	.71	.80
(Racing and aircraft valves, grinding radii, reliefs, grooves, seats, finishing stems)			
Seat Welding	.55	.70	.75
Inspection and Wrapping (Female)	.42	.45	.48
Inspectors (Male)	.50	.55	.60
Shipping Department			
Clerks	.58	.63	.68
Pick-up and delivery	.50	.55	.70
Maintenance Department			
Electrician	.70	.80	.85
Machine Repair Man	.70	.80	.85
Helpers	.55	.60	.65
Special Note: Any maintenance man called for special work will be guaranteed two hours working time.			
Tool Room			
Tool Makers (Class A)	.70	.80	.85
Tool room specialists	.60	.65	.70
Forge die makers	.66	.71	.76

(Testimony of Howard Curtis Baldwin.)
Board's Exhibit No. 5-C—(Continued)

September 3, 1940

Rate per Hour
Minimum Average Maximum

3-A Warner & Swasey
    and
New Acme Turret Lathe.......................... .75   .80   .85

By E. T. FICKLE
    P.M.P.W.A
    P. D. HILEMAN
    Management

September 3, 1940
Minimum Average Maximum

Welding rates .... .80   .85   .90

By E. T. FICKLE
    P.M.P.W.A
    P. D. HILEMAN
    Management

September 3, 1940
Minimum Average Maximum

Cadmium Plating .... .70   .75   .80

By E. T. FICKLE
    P.M.P.W.A
    P. D. HILEMAN
    Management

Rate per Hour
Job   Minimum Average Maximum

Watchmen and Janitors 55

General Notes:
The following provisions apply to these rates:
1. The minimum rate on a job becomes effective thirty days
   after the original date of employment in the event the
   employee has sufficient skill or ability to be retained permanently by the Company.
2. The average rate becomes effective one hundred twenty
   days after the original employment date, unless it has
   been demonstrated conclusively to the employee and his

(Testimony of Howard Curtis Baldwin.)

Board's Exhibit No. 5-C—(Continued)

representatives of the Pacific Parts Workers Alliance that the employee is unable to produce the quantity or quality of work necessary to justify this rate. The average rate is for normal, standard performance on a job.

3. For better than average ability or output, an employee may be raised up to the maximum rate, in whole or in part, depending upon the judgment of the Management. The range between the average and maximum rates is reserved for better than average ability and output.

4. Employees designated as set-up men for a group or department will be paid 5¢ an hour over the maximum rate established for the job.

EXHIBIT B

SENIORITY AGREEMENT

Lay-offs and Promotions; made between the Jadson Motor Products Co. and the Pacific Motor Parts Workers Alliance

I. Lay-offs will be made in accordance with seniority as hereinafter specified, provided, however, that the Company shall not be required in any event to retain the services of an employee whose skill, ability and efficiency is markedly less than that of another employee capable and in line for the same operation.

A. The Company shall maintain adequate records of each employee's seniority by occupation, and total length of service with the Company in accordance with the following rulings:

(Testimony of Howard Curtis Baldwin.)

Board's Exhibit No. 5-C—(Continued)

1. Only time actually worked shall be accumulated towards an employee's occupational seniority record. In accumulating company time, an employee who works one day in a month shall be credited with a full month's company service.

2. An employee's previous seniority record shall be considered cancelled in the event he is discharged for sufficient cause, quits voluntarily, or fails to report back to work following a lay-off after sufficient notification has been given.

3. In the event an employee who quits or has been discharged is subsequently offered inducement by the Company to return to work, he shall be given credit for his previous employment record in the event he returns.

4. Employees with less than twenty years' service may be absent from work because of sickness six months in any yearly period before a deduction is made from the company service records. Employees with twenty or more years of service with the company may be absent from work indefinitely because of sickness and no deduction will be made from the company service records.

5. In case of war or national emergency, an employee who enlists or is

(Testimony of Howard Curtis Baldwin.)

Board's Exhibit No. 5-C—(Continued)

drafted into the United States governmental service and then returns to the Company immediately upon the termination of such war or emergency, shall be credited with all company seniority that would have been accumulated by him should he have continued to work.

6. Leaves of absences may be obtained for sufficient cause without affecting an employee's previous seniority record. Such leaves of absences will not be counted toward the employee's total seniority record.

7. An employee who fails to work one day in a twelve month period shall lose all previously accumulated seniority except in the cases where allowance is made by other rules.

B. All records pertaining to seniority and lay-offs may be reviewed by the P.M.P.W.A. Committee and action taken by the committee as provided in the contract between the P.M.P.W.A. and Jadson Motor Products Co. of which this agreement is a part.

II. When a general reduction of the working force becomes necessary, the following procedure shall apply:

A. Lay-offs shall be made on the basis of seniority by occupations in a department. Ex-

(Testimony of Howard Curtis Baldwin.)

Board's Exhibit No. 5-C—(Continued)

ample—when it becomes necessary to lay off a Cincinnati finish stem grinder, the employee with the least amount of seniority on that job shall be laid off, etc.

B. An employee laid off from a skilled occupation may replace an employee engaged at a less skilled occupation in the same department provided that he is qualified and the employee thus replaced has less company seniority than the first employee.

C. An employee laid off from one department may return to a department in which he previously worked and claim a job of his own occupation provided he is qualified, and providing it is held by an employee of less company seniority.

D. Where an operation is permanently discontinued the affected employee may claim a job of the same or related craft held by another employee with less company seniority, regardless of the department in which the job exists, provided he is qualified to perform the job.

E. Effort will be made to schedule working hours in such a manner that night shift employees will have a work week which will not be substantially less than that accorded the day shift.

F. Exempt from lay-offs by seniority shall be:

(Testimony of Howard Curtis Baldwin.)

Board's Exhibit No. 5-C—(Continued)

1. Specialists of highly developed skill whose services are considered necessary to the company's operation. These are to be listed by Management and submitted to the Alliance representatives.

2. Employees with less than six months total service with the company. (Such employees may be laid off at the discretion of Management with merit the only consideration.)

3. The following general provisions shall also apply to this agreement.

a. This agreement need not necessarily be applied in cases of temporary lay-offs of one week or less.

b. Nothing in this agreement shall prevent the company laying off or discharging an employee for disciplinary reasons or failure to perform the job in a safe, workmanlike and efficient manner.

c. Employees shall be returned to work after a reduction of the working force in the reverse order of these provisions.

d. Employees shall have the right at all times to review their seniority status with the Management.

e. Upon being notified to return to work following a lay-off, employees shall be given three days to report to the Employ-

'(Testimony of Howard Curtis Baldwin.)

Board's Exhibit No. 5-C—(Continued)

ment Office. Failure to do so shall result in previous seniority being cancelled.

f. In this agreement an employee shall be considered qualified if he is capable of producing standard quantity and quality of work following a reasonable adjustment period.

III. The Company shall maintain adequate records of the work for which each employee is qualified and for which each employee has expressed a desire to obtain. When a vacancy occurs either in the factory or the factory office, these records shall be consulted and the Company will endeavor to advance men within the organization in accordance with the preference expressed. Such transfers or promotions will be made solely on the basis of merit. In the event two or more employees have equal merit, then seniority will be given consideration. It shall be the responsibility of employees to officially advise the Company of the types of work desired on forms which are specially provided for this purpose.

IV. The foregoing shall apply only to non-supervisory factory workers.

V. The Company shall advise the Committee of P.M.P.W.A. of all proposed lay-offs or discharges.

VI. No employee shall use his seniority to procure the job of another employee except as provided herein.

(Testimony of Howard Curtis Baldwin.)

Board's Exhibit No. 5-C—(Continued)

VII. This agreement shall become a part of the contract entered into between the Jadson Motor Products Co. and the Pacific Motor Parts Workers Alliance on October 6, 1937.

P. D. HILEMAN

Management

E. T. FICKLE

P.M.P.W.A. Committee

EXHIBIT C

1940 VACATION PLAN

JADSON MOTOR PRODUCTS CO.

Division of Thompson Products, Inc.

(For Jadson Factory Hourly Rate Employes)

I. Purpose

The following vacation plan for 1940 is agreed upon between Jadson Motor Products Co., and the Pacific Motor Parts Workers Alliance for the purpose of recognizing continuity of service, and to provide eligible hourly rate employees with the benefits and pleasures of a period of rest from their regular employment.

II. Eligibility

To be eligible for a vacation with pay an employee must:

'(Testimony of Howard Curtis Baldwin.)

Board's Exhibit No. 5-C—(Continued)

a. Be on the Company payroll in good standing

b. Have been employeed on at *lest* 120 days during 1939. Time lost through illness of the employee will be included in the 120 days. (We do not believe this stipulation affects any Old Guard employee at the present time, but if anyone is so affected, his case may be presented to his representative for special consideration.)

c. Have an Old Guard Service Record of at least five years.

III. Length of Vacation

Employees with an Old Guard Service Record of five to nine years, inclusive, will receive one week's vacation. Employees with an Old Guard Service Record of ten years or greater will receive two weeks' vacation.

A vacation week shall be regarded as seven consecutive calendar days, including Saturday, Sunday and holidays falling within this period.

IV. Vacation Pay

a. Vacation pay will be figured on a basis of 42 hours for a one week vacation and 84 hours for a two weeks vacation.

b. An employee's vacation pay shall be based on the regular hourly rate at which he was employed the majority of his employed time during

(Testimony of Howard Curtis Baldwin.)

Board's Exhibit No. 5-C—(Continued)

the two pay periods immediately prior to April 1, 1940. In the event the employee was absent due to sickness during these two pay periods, the last thirty days employed previous to April 1, 1940, will be used as the basis of determining his vacation pay.

c. Vacation pay will be payable in advance of the vacation.

V. Vacation Season

Vacations will be granted at such times during the period of April 1, 1940 to December 1, 1940, as the Management finds most practical, considering the wishes of employees, customer requirements, and the efficient operation of the department concerned.

Vacation dates will be arranged by department heads. Every effort will be made to assign requested vacation dates. In case of conflict, employees with the greatest continuity of service will receive preference.

VI. General Regulations

a. A vacation shall be taken in one continuous period unless, because of unusual circumstances, special permission of the Management is obtained to do otherwise.

b. A vacation may not be waived by an employee and extra pay received for work during that period.

(Testimony of Howard Curtis Baldwin.)
Board's Exhibit No. 5-C—(Continued)

VII.   Termination of Service

, No vacation or vacation pay will be allowed after resignation, or discharge for cause.

VIII.   Modification or Discontinuance of Plan

, The Management reserves the right to modify or discontinue this plan at any time due to adverse business conditions or catastrophes beyond its control, provided the Management gives seven .days written notice of such action to the Pacific Motor Parts Workers Alliance and an opportunity to be heard, if the Pacific Motor Parts Workers Alliance so requests.

———

BOARD'S EXHIBIT No. 5-D

The Agreement made and executed this 19th day of November, 1940 by and between Thompson Products, Inc., West Coast Plant, a corporation hereinafter designated the Company, and Pacific Motor Parts Workers Alliance, Local No. 1, a labor organization, hereinafter designated the Alliance:

WITNESSETH

Whereas, a majority of the factory employees of the Company have voluntarily associated themselves in the labor organization known as Pacific Motor Parts Workers Alliance, Local No. 1, and

Whereas, the duly elected and appointed repre-

(Testimony of Howard Curtis Baldwin.)

Board's Exhibit No. 5-D—(Continued)
sentatives of the Alliance have met with representatives of the Company and have agreed upon various terms and conditions of employment;

Now, therefore, pursuant to the authority vested in the Company and in the properly constituted representatives of the Alliance and pursuant to the laws of the State of California and of the United States of America,

It is hereby agreed by and between the Alliance and the Company as follows:

1. The Company recognizes the Alliance as the exclusive representative of the factory employees of the Company, with the exception of those employees engaged in a supervisory capacity, for the purposes of collective bargaining in respect to rates of pay, wages, hours of employment and other conditions of employment in accordance with the terms of the National Labor Relations Act.

2. The Company adopts and makes effective as of the date of this agreement the wage scale which is attached hereto, marked "Exhibit A", and by reference makes the same a part of this agreement.

3. An overtime premium of one and one-half times the regular hourly rate shall be paid factory non-supervisory employees for all hours worked in excess of 40 in one week (unless otherwise provided by law) and for all hours worked on Sundays and the following

(Testimony of Howard Curtis Baldwin.)

Board's Exhibit No. 5-D—(Continued)

legal holidays: New Years Day, Memorial
Day, Independence Day, Labor Day, Thanksgiving Day, and Christmas Day; provided,
however that the premium for Sunday and holiday work shall not apply to maintenance employees or watchmen, or other employees whose
duties normally call for work on Sundays or
holidays. Such employees will be paid an overtime premium of time and one-half for hours
worked in excess of 40 during a weekly pay
period, and shall be given a regular day off during the week in lieu of Sunday.

4. Insofar as orders, the financial condition
of the Company, and efficient management of
the shop may permit, effort will be made by the
Company to provide day shift employees who
are asked to report for work on Saturday with
a minimum of fours hours work. When and as
business requirements dictate the addition of
a night shift, the hours to be worked shall be
mutually agreed upon by the qualified representatives of the Alliance and the Management
of the Company. Continuance or discontinuance of arrangements made rests entirely with
the judgment of the Management. The provisions set forth herewith should not under any
circumstances be construed as guaranteeing
a standard work week.

5. The Company agrees that during the life

(Testimony of Howard Curtis Baldwin.)

Board's Exhibit No. 5-D—(Continued)

of this contract it will not employ any Orientals or Mexicans.

6. The Company agrees to continue the following system of hearing individual grievances of factory non-supervisory employees and of discussing matters of importance to the general working force when presented by the Alliance or its representatives.

(a) Individual Grievances:

The employee concerned or a representative of the Alliance may present the matter to be discussed to the immediate foreman of the employee concerned. Failing a satisfactory adjustment, the matter shall then be referred by the Alliance to the General Superintendent. Again failing a satisfactory adjustment, the matter shall be referred to either a regular or a special meeting between duly elected representatives of the Alliance and a representative or representatives of the Company appointed for such purposes. In the event the matter still cannot be satisfactorily adjusted, it may be submitted, upon the consent of both parties, to arbitration by three arbitrators: the Alliance to select one, the Company one and the two arbitrators thus chosen to select the third.

(b) Matters of General Interest:

Matters of general interest to the entire working force may be presented to the Company in a regularly scheduled or special meet-

'(Testimony of Howard Curtis Baldwin.)

Board's Exhibit No. 5-D—(Continued)

ing between the Company and the Alliance. Regular meetings between representatives of the Alliance and of the Company shall be held once monthly at 1:30 P. M. the third Monday of each month. Special meetings may be called upon forty-eight hours' notice upon request of either party.

7. The Company agrees to discuss and consult with representatives of the Alliance with respect to:

(a) Shop rules and regulations.

(b) Inequitable times or standards.

8. The agreement dated October 6, 1937, made and entered into between the Company and the Alliance and relating to seniority layoffs and promotions, a copy of which is annexed hereto marked "Exhibit B," is by this reference, incorporated herein and made a part hereof. Said agreement of October 6, 1937, shall continue in force during the life of, and shall expire at the same time as, this agreement.

9. This contract shall remain in effect until November 19, 1941, and shall automatically renew from year to year thereafter unless either party gives notice in writing to the other party of its intention to terminate, said notice to be delivered not less than thirty (30) days prior to the end of any yearly period.

(Testimony of Howard Curtis Baldwin.)

Board's Exhibit No. 5-D—(Continued)

10. This agreement shall not be assignable by the Alliance, nor shall it inure to the benefit of any successor or successors of the Alliance, without the written consent of the Company.

11. It is understood and agreed that this contract is limited to the factory operations of the Company, located at 8354 Wilcox Avenue, Bell, California.

12. It is further understood that this contract may be modified or revised at any time with the consent of both parties hereto.

13. This contract supersedes the contract dated Actober 19, 1939, between the Company and the Alliance, as the same has heretofore been amended and extended, and said agreement of October 19, 1939, is hereby terminated.

In Witness Whereof that parties have caused these presents to be duly executed the day and year in this agreement first above written.

THOMPSON PRODUCTS, INC.

West Coast Plant

By /S/ P. D. HILEMAN

its Plant Mgr.

The Company

(Testimony of Howard Curtis Baldwin.)

Board's Exhibit No. 5-D—(Continued)

PACIFIC MOTOR PARTS WORKERS ALLIANCE, LOCAL NO. 1

By /S/ E. T. FICKLE

/S/ J. H. OLSEN

/S/ C. O. STUBBLEFIELD

/S/ C. E. WEISSER

/S/ R. D. HAILEY

/S/ LESTER BEBB

The Alliance

EXHIBIT A

THOMPSON PRODUCTS, Inc.
West Coast Plant

Job	Rate per Hour Minimum	Average	Maximum
Small Machine Operations	.50	.55	.70
Hand Milling, drilling, cut-off, chamfering, etc.			

Forge Department

	Minimum	Average	Maximum
Cut-off	.50	.55	.65
Electric Upset	.61	.66	.76
Hammers and Presses	.55	.60	.71
Upsetting Ford Ends	.61	.66	.76
Flash Welding	.61	.66	.76
Chambersberg Hammer			.85

Special Note:

Any Forge Department man transferred from his regular employment to any Forge Department operation on steel 2½" in diameter or larger shall be paid while so employed at the hourly rate for the employment from which he was transferred plus .05 per hour.

(Testimony of Howard Curtis Baldwin.)
Board's Exhibit No. 5-D—(Continued)

Job	Rate per Hour		
	Minimum	Average	Maximum

Heat Treat Department

Sand Blast	.50	.55	.70
Furnace Helper	.57	.62	.67
Heat Treater Class A	.70	.75	1.00
Torch Hardening	.60	.65	.75

Valve Straightening	.60	.65	.75
Production Hand Screw Machine	.60	.65	.75

Grooving, machining head diameter, boring and facing inserts.

Special Screw Machines	.63	.68	.78

Concave and radius lathes.

Cleveland Automatics	.60	.65	.70

Turning head, radius and face.

Lathes

Warner and Swasey 3A	.70	.75	.85
New Acme Turret			
Warner and Swasey 2A	.75	.80	.90
Lodge and Shipley			

September 23, 1941

Job	Rate per Hour		
	Minimum	Average	Maximum
Polishing	.65	.70	.75
Belt Polishers on Aircraft Rework	.65	.70	.80

/S/ P. D. HILEMAN
For the Company
/S/ E. T. FICKLE

(Testimony of Howard Curtis Baldwin.)

Board's Exhibit No. 5-D—(Continued)

July 25, 1941

Job	Rate per Hour Minimum	Average	Maximum
Forge Department			
Electric Upset	.66	.71	.85
Polishing			
Belt Polishers on Aircraft Rework	.60	.65	.75

/S/ P. D. HILEMAN
For the Company
/S/ E. T. FICKLE
For the Alliance

Sept. 23, 1941

Job	Rate per Hour Minimum	Average	Maximum
Forge Department			
Ajax Hammer			.85
Furnace Operator for Ajax Hammer			.75

/S/ P. D. HILEMAN
For the Company
/S/ E. T. FICKLE
For the Alliance

June 12, 1941

Job	Rate per Hour Minimum	Average	Maximum
Aircraft Stem Grinder			.95
Thread Grinders	.65	.71	.86
Commercial Grinders	.60	.70	.80
Furnace Helper	.62	.67	.77

/S/ P. D. HILEMAN
For the Company
/S/ E. T. FICKLE
For the Alliance

(Testimony of Howard Curtis Baldwin.)
Board's Exhibit No. 5-D—(Continued)

Job	Minimum	Average	Maximum
Valve Guide Department	.60	.65	.70

Gun drilling, broaching, automatic porter cable machines.

Grinders			
Commercial	.55	.65	.70

Tip grinding, rough centerless, grinding necks, tapers, foot, reliefs, seats on valves, grinding insert faces, aircraft bolts.

	Minimum	Average	Maximum
Thread Grinders	.60	.66	.76
Special	.66	.71	.85

Racing and aircraft valves, grinding radii, reliefs, grooves, seats, finishing stems, internal Cincinnati.

	Minimum	Average	Maximum
Cylindrical Grinders			.95
Welding Department	.70	.80	1.00
Inspection and Wrapping			
Female Inspectors	.42	.45	.55
Male Inspectors	.50	.55	.65
Line Inspectors	.55	.60	.75
Shipping Department			
Clerks	.58	.63	.68
Pick-up and Delivery	.50	.55	.60
Maintenance Department			
Chief Electrician			.95
Electrician	.70	.80	.85
Machine Repair Man	.70	.80	.95
Helpers	.55	.60	.70

Special Note: Any Maintenance man called for special work will be guaranteed two hours working time.

(Testimony of Howard Curtis Baldwin.)
Board's Exhibit No. 5-D—(Continued)

Job	Minimum	Average	Maximum
Tool Room			
Toolmakers Class A.	.70	.80	1.15
Tool Room specialists	.60	.65	.75
Forge Die Makers	.66	.71	.85
Polishing	.55	.60	.65
Cadmium Plating	.70	.75	.80
Watchmen & Janitors		.60	

May 13, 1941.

Rates for valve guide department are by this rider deleted, and automatic Porter cable machines are to be included with production hand screw machines.

/S/ P. D. HILEMAN
For the Company
/S/ E. T. FICKLE
For the Alliance

May 9, 1941

	Minimum	Average	Maximum
Stock Room Helper	.55	.60	.65
Electrical Department			
Chief Electrician			.95
Electrician	.70	.80	.85
Maintenance Department			
Maintenance Helpers	.55	.60	.70
Maintenance Men			.80
Machine Repair	.70	.80	.95

/S/ P. D. HILEMAN
For the Company
/S/ E. T. FICKLE
For the Alliance

(Testimony of Howard Curtis Baldwin.)
Board's Exhibit No. 5-D—(Continued)

May 13, 1941

	Minimum	Average	Maximum
Forge Department			
Chambersberg Hammer			.85
Plating Department			
Platers Helpers	.60	.65	.75
Platers	.75	.80	.90

/S/ P. D. HILEMAN
For the Company
/S/ E. T. FICKLE
For the Alliance

May 9, 1941.

Paragraph 4, Exhibit A

Exception will be made in the case of men submitting a request for transfer to the Tool and Die Department. These men will be transferred at the starting rate of the Die Department. At the end of 30 days they will automatically receive the average rate, provided Paragraph 2, General Notes, Exhibit A, has been complied with. Further increases will be made at the discretion of Management.

Men transferred at the prerogative of Management will continue at the same rate they received on their last previous machine.

/S/ P. D. HILEMAN
For the Company
/S/ E. T. FICKLE
For the Alliance

May 13, 1941.

By this rider all rates shown in Exhibit A are increased 5¢.

/S/ P. D. HILEMAN
For the Company
/S/ E. T. FICKLE
For the Alliance

(Testimony of Howard Curtis Baldwin.)
Board's Exhibit No. 5-D—(Continued)

March 28, 1941

Job	Minimum	Average	Maximum
Small Machine Operations			
Hand Milling, drilling, cut-off, chamfering, etc.	.55	.60	.70
Forge Department			
Cut-off	.55	.60	.65
Heat Treat Department			
Sand Blast	.55	.60	.70
Inspection Department			
Male Inspectors	.55	.60	.80
Line Inspectors	.55	.60	.75
Shipping Department			
Pick-up and Delivery	.55	.60	.65

/S/ P. D. HILEMAN
For the Company
/S/ E. T. FICKLE
For the Alliance

February 21, 1941

Job	Maximum
Forge Die Makers	.90

/S/ P. D. HILEMAN
For the Company
/S/ E. T. FICKLE
For the Alliance

January 23, 1941

Job	Minimum	Average	Maximum
Timekeeper	.60	.65	.70
Stockroom Helper	.50	.55	.65

/S/ P. D. HILEMAN
For the Company
/S/ E. T. FICKLE
For the Alliance

(Testimony of Howard Curtis Baldwin.)

Board's Exhibit No. 5-D—(Continued)

General Notes:

The following provisions apply to these rates:

1. The minimum rate on a job becomes effective 30 days after the original date of employment in the event the employee has sufficient skill or ability to be retained permanently by the Company.

2. The average rate becomes effective one hundred twenty days after the original employment date, unless it has been demonstrated conclusively to the employee and his representatives of the P. M. P. W. A. that the employee is unable to produce the quantity or quality of work necessary to justify this rate. The average rate is for normal, standard performance on a job.

3. For better than average ability or output, an employee may be raised up to the maximum rate, in whole or in part, depending upon the judgment of the Management. The range between the average and maximum rates is reserved for better than average ability and output.

4. The rate of any new employee when he is advanced to a different machine operation shall be the same as the minimum rate on the machine which he last operated. This rate to continue for 30 days, at which time his rate will become the average rate of the machine which he is operating. The foregoing to apply to workers who have been employed less than 120 days. Any employee of longer standing who is advanced to a different machine doing an operation with which he is not familiar shall

(Testimony of Howard Curtis Baldwin.)

Board's Exhibit No. 5-D—(Continued)
receive for the first 30 days the same rate of pay
as he received on his previous machine. At the end
of 30 days his pay will be the average rate on the
machine which he is operating.

5. Employees designated as set-up men for a
group or department will be paid .10 an hour over
the maximum rate established for the job.

May 9, 1941.

Vacation plan modified by this rider to allow ½
week vacation for employees with from one to five
years service. All other classes to remain the same.

/S/ P. D. HILEMAN
For the Company
/S/ E. T. FICKLE
For the Alliance

February 21, 1941.

The following changes are to be made to the **1941**
Vacation Plan, Exhibit C, attached to the Agree-
ment between Thompson Products, Inc., West Coast
Plant and Pacific Motor Parts Workers Alliance,
Local No. 1.

II Eligibility
c. Have an Old Guard Service Record of at
least three years.

III Length of Vacation
Employees with an Old Guard Service Record of
three to four years, inclusive, will receive one-half
week's vacation. Employees with an Old Guard

(Testimony of Howard Curtis Baldwin.)

Board's Exhibit No. 5-D—(Continued)

Service Record of five to nine years, inclusive, will receive one week's vacation, etc.

IV Vacation Pay

a. Vacation pay will be figured on a basis of 20 hours for one-half week's vacation, 40 hours for one week's vacation, and 80 hours for a two week's vacation.

/S/ P. D. HILEMAN
For the Company

/S/ E. T. FICKLE
For the Alliance

EXHIBIT C

1941 Vacation Plan
Thompson Products, Inc.
West Coast Plant
(For Factory Hourly Rate Employees)

1. Purpose

The following vacation plan for 1941 is agreed upon between Thompson Products, Inc., West Coast Plant and the Pacific Motor Parts Workers Alliance for the purpose of recognizing continuity of service, and to provide eligible hourly rate employees with the benefits and pleasures of a period of rest from their regular employment.

II. Eligibility

To be eligible for a vacation with pay an employee must:

a. Be on the Company pay roll in good standing.

(Testimony of Howard Curtis Baldwin.)

Board's Exhibit No. 5-D—(Continued)

b. Have been employed on at least 120 days during 1940. Time lost through illness of the employee will be included in the 120 days.

c. Have an Old Guard Service Record of at least five years.

III. Length of Vacation

Employees with an Old Guard Service Record of five to nine years, inclusive, will receive one week's vacation. Employees with Old Guard Service Record of ten years or greater will receive two weeks vacation. A vacation week shall be regarded as seven consecutive calendar days, including Saturday, Sunday and holidays falling within this period.

IV. Vacation Pay

a. Vacation pay will be figured on a basis of 40 hours for one week's vacation and 80 hours for a two weeks' vacation.

b. An employee's vacation pay shall be based on the regular hourly rate at which he was employed the majority of his employed time during the two pay periods immediately prior to April 1, 1941. In the event the employee was absent due to sickness during these two pay periods, the last thirty days employed previous to April 1, 1941 will be used as the basis of determining his vacation pay.

c. Vacation pay will be payable in advance of the vacation.

(Testimony of Howard Curtis Baldwin.)

Board's Exhibit No. 5-D—(Continued)

V. Vacation Season

Vacations will be granted at such times during the period of April 1, 1941 to December 1, 1941, as the Management finds most practical, considering the wishes of employees, customer requirements, and the efficient operation of the department concerned.

Vacation dates will be arranged by department heads. Every effort will be made to assign requested vacation dates. In case of conflict, employees with the greatest continuity of service will receive preference.

VI. General Regulations

a. A vacation shall be taken in one continuous period unless, because of unusual circumstances, special permission of the Management is obtained to do otherwise.

b. A vacation may not be waived by an employee and extra pay received for work during that period.

VII. Termination of Service.

No vacation or vacation pay will be allowed after resignation, or discharge for cause.

VIII. Modification or Discontinuance of Plan

The Management reserves the right to modify or discontinue this plan at any time due to adverse business conditions or catastrophes beyond its control, provided the Management given seven days written notice of such action to the P. M. P. W. A.

(Testimony of Howard Curtis Baldwin.)

Board's Exhibit No. 5-D—(Continued)
and an opportunity to be heard, if the P. M. P. W.
A. so requests.

EXHIBIT B

Seniority Agreement

Between the Thompson Products, Inc., West Coast
Plant and the Pacific Motor Parts Workers
Alliance.

1. Lay-offs will be made in accordance with
seniority as here-inafter specified, provided, however, that the Company shall not be required in any
event to retain the services of an employee whose
skill, ability and efficiency is markedly less than
that of another employee capable and warranting
consideration for the same operation.

A. The Company shall maintain adequate
records of each employee's seniority by occupation, and total length of service with the
Company in accordance with the following rulings:

1. In the accumulation of both occupational seniority and company time, an employee who works one day in a month shall
be credited with a full month's company
service.

2. An employee's previous seniority record shall be considered cancelled in the
event he is discharged for sufficient cause,
quits voluntarily, or fails to report back to
work following a lay-off after sufficient notification has been given.

(Testimony of Howard Curtis Baldwin.)

Board's Exhibit No. 5-D—(Continued)

3. In the event an employee who quits or has been discharged is subsequently offered inducement by the Company to return to work, he shall be given credit for his previous employment record in the event he returns.

4. Employees with less than twenty years' service may be absent from work because of sickness six months in any yearly period before a deduction is made from the company service records. Employees with twenty or more years of service with the Company may be absent from work indefinitely because of sickness and no deduction will be made from the company service records.

5. In case of war or national emergency, an employee who enlists or is drafted into the United States Governmental Service and then returns to the Company immediately following his honorable discharge, shall be credited with all seniority that would have been accumulated by him should he have continued to work.

6. Leaves of absences may be obtained for sufficient cause without affecting an employee's previous seniority record. Such leaves of absences will not be counted toward the employee's total seniority record.

(Testimony of Howard Curtis Baldwin.)

Board's Exhibit No. 5-D—(Continued)

7. An employee who fails to work one day in a twelve month period shall lose all previously accumulated seniority except in the cases where allowance is made by other rules.

B· All records pertaining to seniority and lay-offs may be reviewed by the P. M. P. W. A. Committee and action taken by the Committee as provided in the contract between the P. M. P. W. A. and Thompson Products, Inc., West Coast Plant, of which this agreement is a part.

II. When a general reduction of the working force becomes necessary, the following procedure shall apply:

A. Lay-offs shall be made on the basis of seniority by occupations in a department. Example—when it becomes necessary to lay off a Cincinnati finish stem grinder, the employee with the least amount of seniority on that job shall be laid off, etc.

B. An employee laid off from a skilled occupation may replace an employee engaged at a less skilled occupation in the same department provided that he is qualified and the employee thus replaced has less company seniority than the first employee.

C. An employee laid off from one department may return to a department in which he previously worked and claim a job of his own

(Testimony of Howard Curtis Baldwin.)

Board's Exhibit No. 5-D—(Continued)
occupation provided he is qualified and providing it is held by an employee of less company seniority.

D. Where an operation is permanently discontinued, effort will be made by the Company to permit the affected employee to claim a job of the same or related craft held by another employee with less company seniority, regardless of the department in which the job exists, provided he is qualified to perform the job.

E. Effort will be made to schedule working hours in such a manner that night shift employees will have a work week which will not be substantially less than that accorded the day shift.

F. Exempt from lay-offs by seniority shall be:

1. Specialists of highly developed skill whose services are considered necessary to the company's operation. These are to be listed by Management and submitted to the Alliance representatives.

2. Employees with less than six months total service with the company. (Such employees may be laid off at the discretion of Management with merit the only consideration.)

3. The following general provisions shall also apply to this agreement:

a. This agreement need not necessarily

(Testimony of Howard Curtis Baldwin.)

Board's Exhibit No. 5-D—(Continued)

be applied in cases of temporary lay-offs of one week or less.

b. Nothing in this agreement shall prevent the company laying off or discharging an employee for disciplinary reasons or failure to perform the job in a safe, workmanlike and efficient manner.

c. Employees shall be returned to work after a reduction of the working force in the reverse order of these provisions.

d. Employees shall have the right at all times to review their seniority status with the Management.

e. Upon being notified to return to work following a lay-off, employees shall be given three days to report to the Employment Office. Failure to do so shall result in previous seniority being cancelled.

f. In this agreement an employee shall be considered qualified if he is capable of producing standard quantity and quality of work following a reasonable adjustment period.

III. The Company shall maintain adequate records of the work for which each employee is qualified and for which each employee has expressed a desire to obtain. When a vacancy occurs either in the factory or the factory office, these records shall be consulted and the Company will endeavor to advance men within the organization in accord-

(Testimony of Howard Curtis Baldwin.)

Board's Exhibit No. 5-D—(Continued)
ance with the preference expressed. Such transfers or promotions will be made solely on the basis of merit. In the event two or more employees have equal merit, then seniority will be given consideration. It shall be the responsibility of employees to officially advise the Company of the types of work desired on forms which are specially provided for this purpose.

IV. The foregoing shall apply only to non-supervisory factory workers.

V. The Company shall advise the Committee of P. M. P. W. A. of all proposed lay-offs or discharges.

VI. No employee shall use his seniority to procure the job of another employee except as provided herein.

VII. This agreement shall become a part of the contract entered into between The Thompson Products, Inc., West Coast Plant, and the Pacific Motor Parts Workers Alliance on November 19, 1940.

/s/ P. D. HILEMAN,
Management.

/s/ E. T. FICKLE,
/s/ J. H. OLSEN,
/s/ C. O. STUBBLEFIELD,
/s/ C. E. WEISSER,
/s/ R. D. HAILEY,
/s/ LESTER BEBB,
Committee, Pacific Motor Parts Workers Alliance.

(Testimony of Howard Curtis Baldwin.)

BOARD'S EXHIBIT 5-E

ARTICLE I—AGREEMENT

This Agreement made and executed this 10th day of November, 1941, by and between Thompson Products, Inc., West Coast Plant, a corporation, hereinafter designated the Company, and the Pacific Motor Parts Workers Alliance, Local No. 1, a labor organization, hereinafter designated the Alliance:

ARTICLE II—REPRESENTATION

The Company recognizes the Alliance as the exclusive representative of the factory hourly employees of the Company, with the exception of those employees engaged in a supervisory capacity, for the purposes of collective bargaining in respect to rates of pay, wages, hours of employment and other conditions of employment in accordance with the terms of the National Labor Relations Act.

ARTICLE III—AGREEMENT PERIOD

This contract shall remain in effect until November 10, 1942, and shall automatically renew from year to year thereafter unless either party gives notice in writing to the other party of its intention to terminate, said notice to be delivered not less than thirty (30) days prior to the end of any yearly period.

(Testimony of Howard Curtis Baldwin.)
Board's Exhibit 5-E—(Continued)

ARTICLE IV—AMENDMENTS

This Agreement may be amended or added to at any time by the written consent of both parties hereto.

ARTICLE V.—ASSIGNABILITY

This Agreement shall not be assignable by the Alliance, nor shall it inure to the benefit of any successor or successors of the Alliance, without the written consent of the Company. It is understood and agreed that this contract is limited to the factory operations of the company, located at 8354 Wilcox Avenue, Bell, California.

ARTICLE VI—GRIEVANCES

The employee concerned or a Steward of the Alliance may present the matter to be discussed to the immediate foreman of the employee concerned. Failing a satisfactory adjustment, the matter shall then be referred by the Steward to the General Superintendent. Again failing a satisfactory adjustment, the matter shall be referred to either a regular or a special meeting between duly elected representatives of the Alliance and a representative or representatives of the Company appointed for such purposes. In the event the matter still cannot be satisfactorily adjusted, it may be submitted, upon the consent of both parties to arbitration by three arbitrators: the Alliance to select one, the Company one

(Testimony of Howard Curtis Baldwin.)

Board's Exhibit 5-E—(Continued)

and the two arbitrators thus chosen to select the third.

ARTICLE VII—HOURS AND PREMIUMS

Eight (8) hours shall constitute a day's work, to be worked within eight and one-half (8½) hours, consecutively. Except in case of the third shift. The shifts shall be known as follows:

First (1)   7:00 A. M. to 3:30 P. M.

Second (2)   3:30 P. M. to 12:00 Midnight.

Third (3)   12:00 Midnight to 7:00 A. M.

All employees working the third shift shall work seven (7) hours for eight (8) hours pay.

All employees working the second shift steady three (3) months or more shall receive five cents (.05) per hour more.

Seniority by occupation will be the rule governing the choice of shifts. If rotation is allowed on machine, no premium will be paid for second shift.

The above shift times shall be applicable to all employees except in special cases by the consent of the Company and knowledge of same by the Alliance.

Continuance or discontinuance of shift arrangements rests entirely with the judgment of the Management. The provisions set forth herewith should not under any circumstances be construed as guaranteeing a standard work week.

July 2, 1942.

(Testimony of Howard Curtis Baldwin.)

Board's Exhibit 5-E—(Continued)

ARTICLE VII—HOURS & PREMIUMS

All employees working the third shift shall work seven hours for eight hours pay. An employee who completes 30 days steady work on third shift will be paid an additional 5c premium.

Employees completing 30 days steady on second shift will be paid an additional 5c premium.

/s/ P. D. HILEMAN,

For the Company.

/s/ H. BALDWIN,

For the Alliance.

ARTICLE VIII—OVERTIME

Any time worked in excess of eight (8) hours in any one day shall be considered as overtime and shall be paid for at the rate of one and one-half times the basic hourly rate of the employee. Time worked in addition to an employee's established work week of 40 hours shall be paid for at the rate of one and one-half times the basic hourly rate of the employee, subject to any revisions or modifications of the now existing Wage and Hour Act.

ARTICLE IX—SUNDAYS AND HOLIDAYS

All hours worked by employees under this Agreement shall be paid double time for Sundays and the following legal holidays: New Years Day, Memorial Day, Independence Day, Labor Day, Thanksgiving Day, and Christmas Day; provided, however, that the premium for Sunday and holiday

(Testimony of Howard Curtis Baldwin.)

Board's Exhibit 5-E—(Continued)

work shall not apply to maintenance employees or watchmen, or other employees whose duties normally call for work on Sundays or holidays. Such employees shall be given a regular day off during the week in lieu of Sunday. In the event they work on their regular day off they shall receive double time for time worked.

May 29, 1942.

ARTICLE IX—To be added to last sentence:

"In the event they work on their regular day off they shall receive double time for the seventh consecutive day worked."

/s/ P. D. HILEMAN,
For the Company.

/s/ HOWARD BALDWIN,
For the Alliance.

ARTICLE X—REPORT TIME

An employee called to work shall receive a minimum of two hours work in the shift to which he is called.

ARTICLE XI—GENERAL MATTERS

Matters of general interest to the entire working force may be presented to the Company in a meeting between the Company and the Alliance. Special meetings may be called upon forty-eight hours notice upon request of either party.

The Company agrees to discuss and consult with representatives of the Alliance with respect to:

(Testimony of Howard Curtis Baldwin.)
Board's Exhibit 5-E—(Continued)
- (a) Shop rules and regulations.
- (b) Inequitable times or standards.
- (c) Safety Rules.
- (d) Employee training.

ARTICLE XII—SENIORITY AGREEMENT

Between Thompson Products, Inc., West Coast Plant and the Pacific Motor Parts Workers Alliance.

1. Lay-offs will be made in accordance with seniority as hereinafter specified, provided, however, that the Company shall not be required in any event to retain the services of an employee whose skill, ability and efficiency is markedly less than that of another employee capable and warranting consideration for the same operations.

A. The Company shall maintain adequate records of each employee's seniority by occupation, and total length of service with the Company in accordance with the following rulings:

1. In the accumulation of both occupational seniority and company time, an employee who works one day in a month shall be credited with a full month's company service.

2. An employee's previous seniority record shall be considered cancelled in the event he is discharged for sufficient cause, quits voluntarily, or fails to report back

(Testimony of Howard Curtis Baldwin.)

Board's Exhibit 5-E—(Continued)

to work following a lay-off after sufficient notification has been given.

3. In the event an employee who quits or has been discharged is subsequently offered inducement by the Company to return to work, he shall be given credit for his previous employment record in the event he returns.

4. Employees with less than twenty years' service may be absent from work because of sickness six months in any yearly period before a deduction is made from the company service records. Employees with twenty or more years of service with the company may be absent from work indefinitely because of sickness and no deduction will be made from the company service record.

5. In case of war or national emergency, an employee who enlists or is drafted into the United States Governmental Service and then returns to the Company immediately following his honorable discharge, shall be credited with all seniority that would have been accumulated by him should he have continued to work.

6. Leaves of absences may be obtained for sufficient cause without affecting an employee's previous seniority record. Such leaves of absences will not be counted

(Testimony of Howard Curtis Baldwin.)

Board's Exhibit 5-E—(Continued)

toward the employee's total seniority record.

7. An employee who fails to work one day in a twelve month period shall lose all previously accumulated seniority except in the cases where allowance is made by other rules.

B. All records pertaining to seniority and lay-offs may be reviewed by the P. M. P. W. A. Committee and action taken by the Committee as provided in the contract between the P. M. P. W. A. and Thompson Products, Inc., West Coast Plant, of which this agreement is a part.

II. When a general reduction of the working force becomes necessary, the following procedure shall apply:

A. Lay-offs shall be made on the basis of seniority by occupations in a department. Example—when it becomes necessary to lay off a Cincinnati finish stem grinder, the employee with the least amount of seniority on that job shall be laid off, etc.

B. An employee laid off from a skilled occupation may replace an employee engaged at a less skilled occupation in the same department provided that he is qualified and the employee thus replaced has less company seniority than the first employee.

(Testimony of Howard Curtis Baldwin.)

Board's Exhibit 5-E—(Continued)

. C. An employee laid off from one department may return to a department in which he previously worked and claim a job of his own occupation provided he is qualified and providing it is held by an employee of less company seniority.

D. Where an operation is permanently discontinued, effort will be made by the company to permit the affected employee to claim a job of the same related craft held by another employee with less company seniority, regardless of the department in which the job exists, provided he is qualified to perform the job.

E. Effort will be made to schedule working hours in such a manner that night shift employees will have a work week which will not be substantially less than that accorded the day shift.

F. Exempt from lay-offs by seniority shall be:

1. Specialists of highly developed skill whose services are considered necessary to the company's operation. These are to be listed by Management and submitted to the Alliance representatives.

2. Employees with less than six months total service with the company. (Such employees may be laid off at the discretion of Management with merit the only consideration.)

(Testimony of Howard Curtis Baldwin.)

Board's Exhibit 5-E—(Continued)

3. The following general provisions shall also apply to this agreement:

a. This agreement need not necessarily be applied in cases of temporary lay-offs of one week or less.

b. Nothing in this agreement shall prevent the company laying off or discharging an employee for disciplinary reasons or failure to perform the job in a safe, workmanlike and efficient manner.

c. Employees shall be returned to work after a reduction of the working force in the reverse order of these provisions.

d. Employees shall have the right at all times to review their seniority status with the Management.

e. Upon being notified to return to work following a lay-off, employees shall be given three days to report to the Employment Office. Failure to do so shall result in previous seniority being cancelled.

f. In this agreement an employee shall be considered qualified if he is capable of producing standard quantity and quality of work following a reasonable adjustment period.

III. The Company shall maintain adequate records of the work for which each employee is qualified and for which each employee has expressed a

(Testimony of Howard Curtis Baldwin.)

Board's Exhibit 5-E—(Continued)

desire to obtain. When a vacancy occurs either in the factory or the factory office, these records shall be consulted and the company will endeavor to advance men within the organization in accordance with the preference expressed. Such transfers or promotions will be made solely on the basis of merit, then seniority will be given consideration. It shall be the responsibility of employees to officially advise the Company of the types of work desired on forms which are specially provided for this purpose.

IV. The foregoing shall apply only to non-supervisory factory workers.

V. The Company shall advise the Committee of P. M. P. W. A. of all proposed lay-offs or discharges.

VI. No employee shall use his seniority to procure the job of another employee except as provided herein.

May 29, 1943.

ARTICLE XIII—VACATIONS

The Company agrees to the following vacation plan: Upon completion of one year's service employees will be eligible for one week's vacation, providing their anniversary date falls within the vacation period. The vacation period will be from March 1st through October 31st, but the decision as to whether or not an employee shall be permitted to take vacation time off or be paid his vacation

(Testimony of Howard Curtis Baldwin.)

Board's Exhibit 5-E—(Continued)

pay due and allowed to work shall remain solely with the Management. Vacation pay shall be based on the standard work week and will be paid at the current hourly rate of the employee at the time his vacation pay is given. No vacation or vacation pay will be allowed after resignation or discharge for cause.

/s/ P. D. HILEMAN,
For the Company.

/s/ H. BALDWIN,
For the Alliance.

April 9, 1942.

ARTICLE XIII—VACATIONS

No vacation or vacation pay will be allowed after resignation, discharge for cause.

/s/ P. D. HILEMAN,
For the Company.

/s/ H. BALDWIN,
For the Alliance.

ARTICLE XIII—VACATIONS

The Company agrees to the following vacation plan: All employees who have completed one or more years' service on January 1, 1942, will be eligible for one week's vacation. Employees who have completed ten or more years' service will be eligible for two weeks' vacation. A 31-day grace period beyond January 1, 1942 will be allowed wherein that period will permit an employee to

(Testimony of Howard Curtis Baldwin.)

Board's Exhibit 5-E—(Continued)

become eligible for a vacation or to become eligible for a longer vacation. The vacation period will be from February 1, 1942 until December 1, 1942, but the decision as to whether or not an employee shall be permitted to take vacation time off or be paid his vacation pay due and allowed to work shall be made solely by the Management. Vacation pay shall be based on the standard work week, and will be made at the current hourly rate of the employee at the time his vacation pay is given.

ARTICLE XIV—WAGES AND CLASSIFICATION

1. An employee transferred to another department or job shall not have his pay reduced without just cause and only after a hearing of the case by the Alliance.

2. An employee transferred permanently to another department or job of higher paid classification shall, after thirty (30) days of successful performance, receive the minimum rate of pay for that classification, the shop management to have final decision on successful performance.

3. The Alliance shall be notified within twenty-four (24) hours of any discharge, lay-off or demotion of any employee. The Alliance shall have the right to investigate any discharge, lay-off or demotion according to the Grievances procedure heretofor mentioned.

(a) Any discharged employe shall be per-

(Testimony of Howard Curtis Baldwin.)

Board's Exhibit 5-E—(Continued)

mitted to notify the Steward of his department before leaving the plant, of his grievance, if any.

(b) Any discharged employee must file within forty-eight (48) hours a written protest with the Alliance, if he feels aggrieved, or forfeit all right to recourse.

(c) Foregoing will not apply to employees with less than six months service.

4. An employee hired for an unskilled job will not be eligible for transfer to another job until he has served six months on the unskilled job, except at the prerogative of Management when a vacancy on a job carrying a higher rate exists and an employee has the necessary qualifications for this job.

The minimum starting rate for all male employees shall be 60c an hour and for female employees 55c an hour. During the first six months all new employees shall be considered as probationary employees. An automatic increase of 5c an hour will be given at the end of the first, second and third months of service for both male and female employees with the beginning of the first pay period following the completion of the required service. At the completion of six months' service both male and female employees shall be paid at least the minimum rate established for the work classification. Thereafter the work record of all employees shall be reviewed at least once every three months with

(Testimony of Howard Curtis Baldwin.)

Board's Exhibit 5-E—(Continued)

a view toward continually paying each employee an hourly rate which reflects as accurately as possible his worth as a workman within the wage scale. Each employee granted an increase will be so notified by his foreman.

A special review of any employee may be made at any time at the discretion of the Company or the request of the Alliance.

>   (a) Employees designated as set-up men for a group or department will be paid ten (10) cents an hour over the top maximum rate established for that job.

January 8, 1942.

RIDER TO BE ADDED TO ARTICLE XIV:

Employees hired as learners will be considered temporary employees for the duration of their training period. They will be hired at a rate of 60c per hour, and their seniority will date from the time they are transferred from the learner classification to production. Thirty days after date of this transfer they will receive their first increase to 65c per hour and an additional 5c per hour every thirty days thereafter until the minimum of 75c is reached.

>   /s/ P. D. HILEMAN,
>   For the Company.
>   /s/ IRVIN HESS,
>   For the Alliance.

(Testimony of Howard Curtis Baldwin.)
Board's Exhibit 5-E—(Continued)

ARTICLE XV
COMPANY PREROGATIVES

The Company has and will retain the unquestionable and exclusive right and power to manage the plant and direct the working forces and working hours, including the right to hire, suspend, discharge, promote, demote, or transfer its employees for just cause, subject to this Agreement and the Grievances procedure contained herein.

This agreement shall become a part of the contract entered into between the Thompson Products, Inc., West Coast Plant, and the Pacific Motor Parts Workers Alliance on Nov. 10, 1941.

/s/ P. D. HILEMAN,
Management.

/s/ IRVIN HESS,

/s/ ELMER O. SMITH,

/s/ GEO. C. OVERLANDER,

/s/ FRANK W. OSBORNE,

/s/ LESTER BEBB,

/s/ HOWARD C. BALDWIN,
Committee, Pacific Motor
Parts Workers Alliance.

By mutual consent of the Committee and the Management, this contract renders null and void and supersedes the one now in effect dated November 19, 1940.

/s/ P. D. HILEMAN,
Management.

/s/ IRVIN HESS,
Alliance.

(Testimony of Howard Curtis Baldwin.)
Board's Exhibit 5-E—(Continued)

WAGE SCALE

Job	Minimum	Maximum
Small Machine Operator	.75	.86
Forge		
Electric Upset	.75	.96
Hammers & Presses	.75	.87
Upset Ford Ends	.75	.92
Flash Weld	.75	.96
Large Hammer	.85	1.05
Large Upsetter	.85	1.05
Ajax Press	.75	1.00
Ajax Furnace	.75	.87
Heat Treat		
Heat Treater, Class A	.96	1.17
Heat Treater, Helper	.75	.88
Sand Blast	.75	.86
Torch Hardner	.75	.95
Valve Straightening	.75	.91
Production Hand Screw Machine	.75	.91
Special Screw Machine	.75	.94
Cleveland Automatic	.75	.86
Lathes		
Warner & Swasy 3-A and 4	.81	1.01
Acme		
Warner & Swasy 2-A	.86	1.06
Lodge and Shipley		
Grinders		
Commercial	.75	.91
Special	.81	1.01
Thread	.77	.97
Aircraft Stem	.86	1.06
Cylindrical	.91	1.11
Welding	1.00	1.20
Male Inspectors	.75	.96
Female Inspectors	.70	.75

(Testimony of Howard Curtis Baldwin.)
Board's Exhibit 5-E—(Continued)

Job	Minimum	Maximum
Shipping		
Clerks	.75	.84
Pick-up & Delivery	.75	.81
Maintenance Department		
Maintenance Man	.75	.96
Maintenance Helper	.75	.86
Machine Repair	.95	1.15
Steel Shed	.75	.86
Electrical Department		
Electrician	.81	1.10
Tool Room		
Tool Maker Class A	1.15	1.35
Die Makers	.86	1.06
Tool Crib Attendant	.75	.91
Polishing		
Regular Polishers	.75	.86
Belt Polishers	.75	.91
Plating Department		
Plater	.81	1.01
Plater's Helper	.75	.86
Janitors	.76	.76
Timekeepers	.75	.86
Stock Room Attendants	.75	.85

May 19, 1942

Job	Maximum
Heat Treater—Class "B"	1.05

/S/ P. D. HILEMAN
　　　For the Company
/S/ H. BALDWIN
　　　For the Alliance

(Testimony of Howard Curtis Baldwin.)
    Board's Exhibit 5-E—(Continued)

                            January 1, 1942

Job	Maximum
Boromatic Machine	.97

          /S/ P. D. HILEMAN
             For the Company
          /S/ H. BALDWIN
             For the Alliance

                          August 18, 1942

Job	Maximum
Screw Press Operators on Tubing	1.01

          /S/ P. D. HILEMAN
             For the Company
          /S/ H. BALDWIN
             For the Alliance

                          April 9, 1942

Job	Maximum
Maintenance Department Oiler	.90

          /S/ P. D. HILEMAN
             For the Company
          /S/ H. BALDWIN
             For the Alliance

                          April 9, 1942

Job	Maximum
Polishing	
Head Polisher	.98

          /S/ P. D. HILEMAN
             For the Company
          /S/ H. BALDWIN
             For the Alliance

                         March 18, 1942

    All Minimum and Maximum Rates Are Hereby Increased 7¢ Effective March 16, 1942.

          /S/ P. D. HILEMAN
             For the Company
          /S/ H. C. BALDWIN
             For the Alliance

(Testimony of Howard Curtis Baldwin.)

Board's Exhibit 5-E—(Continued)

March 5, 1942

Job	Rate per Hour Maximum
Flash Weld—Wipers	.75

/S/ P. D. HILEMAN
For the Company
/S/ HOWARD C. BALDWIN
For the Alliance

March 5, 1942

Job	Rate Per Hour Maximum
Flash Weld	1.00

/S/ P. D. HILEMAN
For the Company
/S/ H. C. BALDWIN
For the Alliance

March 5, 1942

Job	Rate per Hour Maximum
Bolt Operations on Warner and Swasy 3-A	.91

/S/ P. D. HILEMAN
For the Company
/S/ HOWARD C. BALDWIN
For the Alliance

March 5, 1942

Job	Rate per Hour Minimum	Maximum
Electric Truck Operator	.75	.90

/S/ P. D. HILEMAN
For the Company
/S/ H. C. BALDWIN
For the Alliance

(Testimony of Howard Curtis Baldwin.)
Board's Exhibit 5-E—(Continued)

January 8, 1942

	Rate per Hour
Job	Maximum
Thread Grinders	1.01

/S/ P. D. HILEMAN
For the Company
/S/ IRVIN HESS
For the Alliance

January 8, 1942

	Rate per Hour	
Job	Minimum	Maximum
Aircraft Stem Grinder	.86	1.11

/S/ P. D. HILEMAN
For the Company
/S/ IRVIN HESS
For the Alliance

January 8, 1942

	Rate per Hour	
Job	Minimum	Maximum
Tool Room Tool Maker—Class B.		1.17

/S/ P. D. HILEMAN
For the Company
/S/ IRVIN HESS
For the Alliance

———

Mr. Moore: Mr. Examiner, I anticipate that later in this hearing this witness will be necessary to identify certain of the minutes of the meetings of the Alliance and of its executive council. I am not positive at this time that I can determine just which of those minutes is material to the hearing, and, consequently, I would like to delay that now. I make this statement in order to show that I should like to recall the witness at a later time.

(Testimony of Howard Curtis Baldwin.)

Trial Examiner Whittemore: You intend to be here during the entire hearing, do you, Mr. Baldwin? [21]

The Witness: Yes.

Mr. Watkins: No objection.

Trial Examiner Whittemore: There will be no objection to your recalling him whenever you desire.

Mr. Moore: I have no further questions of this witness at the present time.

Trial Examiner Whittemore: You have no questions?

Mr. Watkins: No questions.

Trial Examiner Whittemore: All right. Then you are excused, Mr. Baldwin, temporarily.

(Witness excused temporarily.)

Mr. Moore: I will call Mr. Lewis Porter.

Trial Examiner Whittemore: Mr. Porter, take the stand, please.

LEWIS ALTENBURG PORTER

a witness called by and on behalf of the National Labor Relations Board, being first duly sworn, was examined and testified as follows:

Direct Examination

By Mr. Moore:

Q. Will you state your full name, please?

A. Lewis Altenburg Porter.

Q. How do you spell Lewis?

(Testimony of Lewis Altenburg Porter.)

A. L-e-w-i-s.

Q. Have you at any time been employed by Thompson Products, Inc.? [22]   A. Yes, sir.

Q. When were you so employed?

A. Well, I have been with them about seven years and a half up until about six weeks ago.

Q. You have worked for them only out there at their plant at 8354 Wilcox Avenue, Bell, California. Is that right?   A. Yes.

Q. The evidence in the case shows they took that plant over on October 8, 1937. You didn't work for Thompson Products, Inc., before that date, could you?

A. No, sir. No; I was working for Jadson.

Q. When you said you had worked for seven and a half or eight years, what did you mean?

A. Did I what?

Q. When you said you had worked for seven and a half or eight years, that you had worked for Thompson Products, Inc., what do you mean?

A. Well, I had worked at that plant during that time.

Q. Yes. You worked for the company they took over and continued to work after they took it over?

A. Yes.

Q. Very well. Are you now employed there?

A. No, sir.

Q. Are you acquainted with Mr. Raymond Livingston?   A. Yes, sir. [23]

Q. Who is he?

(Testimony of Lewis Altenburg Porter.)

A. As I understood it, he was personnel man in Cleveland for the Thompson Motor Parts.

Q. When did you first meet him?

A. Along in 1937.

Q. About what time of the year?

A. I guess it was along the latter part of July, the first of August, around there.

Q. And at that specific time, the time you first met him, do you know what position he then occupied with Thompson Products, Inc.?

A. As I understood it, he was personnel man at Cleveland.

Q. Where did you meet Mr. Livingston?

A. Well, as to the dates, I can't give it. It was——

Q. No, I say where.

A. Where? In the plant.

Q. And at your first meeting with him were the two of you alone, or was someone else present?

A. No, I was working by myself.

Q. Where were you?   A. In the plant.

Q. What were you doing?

A. I was running a shearing machine, as I recall it now.

Q. You say you met Mr. Livingston there?

A. Yes, he came along and spoke to me. **[24]**

Q. He came to your machine?   A. Yes.   .

Q. What was the conversation on that occasion?

A. Nothing particular.

Mr. Watkins: Wait a minute. Can we find out whether anybody else was present?

(Testimony of Lewis Altenburg Porter.)

Mr. Moore: I believe I asked him if there was anybody else present at the time.

The Witness: Just I and Mr. Livingston.

Q. (By Mr. Moore) Will you state what conversation was had at that time?

A. Well, we just talked about equipment in our plant and in their plant is about all.

Q. By "our plant" you mean the West Coast plant?   A. The one over here.

Q. And by "their plant" you mean the Cleveland plant of Thompson Products Company, Incorporated?   A. Yes.

Q. Did he introduce himself to you?

A. Yes.

Q. Who started that conversation?

A. Mr. Livingston.

Mr. Watkins: Just a minute. I move the answer be stricken. I want to object to the question on the ground it calls for a conclusion, and I move the answer be stricken; [25] and I would like to ask that the witness be examined as to the conversation which took place.

Trial Examiner Whittemore: The objection is overruled.

Q. (By Mr. Moore) Now, about how long did the conversation last, that first time you met him?

A. Oh, I would say two minutes.

Q. Do you know the date on which that was held?   A. I do not, no, sir.

Q. Can you say what day of the week it was?

A. I think it was Saturday morning; yes, sir.

(Testimony of Lewis Altenburg Porter.)

Q. What was your testimony as to the portion of the year in which the conversation occurred? When did you say it was with reference to the months that it occurred? A. What did I say?

Q. No. I say when did the conversation occur, as to what part of the month, or which month?

A. I think it was the latter part of July.

Q. Now, thereafter, did you meet Mr. Livingston again? A. Yes, sir.

Q. Where did you next meet him?

A. Down at the Jonathan Club on Figueroa.

Q. What is the Jonathan Club, and where is it?

A. Well, I don't know. It was the first time I was ever in there. I don't know just exactly what you call it.

Q. Is it a hotel? [26]

A. As to that, I don't know.

Q. When was this meeting that you had with Mr. Livingston at the Jonathan Club?

A. That evening, Saturday evening.

Q. The same evening that he had introduced himself? A. As I recall it.

Q. About what time?

A. Well, it was after 6:00 p.m. in the evening.

Q. Who was there at the time?

A. Mr. Dachtler and Mr. Livingston.

Q. Can you spell that first name for the reporter? A. No, I don't believe I can.

Mr. Moore: May it be stipulated he is referring to C. V. Dachtler, D-a-c-h-t-l-e-r?

Mr. Watkins: I don't know to whom he is re-

(Testimony of Lewis Altenburg Porter.)

ferring, but that is the way you spell that anyway.

Mr. Moore: Very well.

Trial Examiner Whittemore: How do you spell it?

Mr. Moore: D-a-c-h-t-l-e-r?

Trial Examiner Whittemore: Thank you.

Q. (By Mr. Moore) Who is Mr. Dachtler?

Mr. Watkins: Just a minute. I object to that as calling for a conclusion of the witness.

Trial Examiner Whittemore: Well, what is your understanding of who he was? I suppose he cannot very well go [27] beyond that. Who did you understand Mr. Dachtler to be?

The Witness: He was general manager of the plant.

Trial Examiner Whittemore: He was at that time?

The Witness: At that time, yes, sir.

Q. (By Mr. Moore) Where did the meeting at the Jonathan Club take place?

Trial Examiner Whittemore: Let us straighten out this matter now. Counsel can state who he was. Do you know who he is, counsel?

Mr. Watkins: I don't know.

Trial Examiner Whittemore: Is there someone from the plant who can tell us, so that we can clear it up in the record?

Mr. Watkins: Yes, we can clear up the situation.

Trial Examiner Whittemore: Very well. Suppose we go off the record while you find out.

(Discussion off the record.)

(Testimony of Lewis Altenburg Porter.)

Trial Examiner Whittemore: On the record.

Mr. Moore: May it be stipulated, Mr. Watkins and Mr. Baldwin, that Mr. C. V. Dachtler was employed by Thompson Products, Inc., as their acting general manager of their West Coast plant?

Mr. Watkins: At one time, yes.

Mr. Moore: At one time?

Mr. Watkins: Yes. [28]

Trial Examiner Whittemore: Thank you.

Mr. Moore: May I ask the last two questions on the record be read?

Trial Examiner Whittemore: Surely.

(Record read.)

Q. (By Mr. Moore) Can you answer the last question? Where in the Jonathan Club did that meeting take place?

A. It was, as I remember now, on the fourth floor of the building, in a room.

Q. In a room? A. Yes.

Q. Was there a conversation at that meeting?

A. Yes, sir.

Q. Will you state what the conversation was?

A. Well, the first that was asked me by Mr. Dachtler was if I knew what I was down there for. I told him I did.

Q. Just go ahead and give the conversation as nearly as you can, exactly as it occurred.

A. Well, then they suggested to me, Mr. Livingston and Mr. ——

Mr. Watkins: Just a minute. May I ask, Mr. Examiner, in connection with the relation of the

(Testimony of Lewis Altenburg Porter.)

conversation of this kind, whether or not the Examiner will permit us to interrupt the witness and register our objections to any conclusions and things of that kind? In testimony of this kind it is almost [29] impossible to make objections unless we do it as we go along, in lengthy conversations.

Trial Examiner Whittemore: I think I will first instruct the witness not to say "they," but say who said something to you. Try to give the conversation. You see?

Mr. Watkins: Instead of "suggesting" what the real conversation was.

Trial Examiner Whittemore: That is right. Tell us what was said, and by whom.

The Witness: Well, by both of the men. They wanted, Mr. Livingston and Mr. Dachtler, they wanted us to start——

Mr. Watkins: Just a minute; Mr. Examiner, I object to this form of testimony going in: "They wanted." That is a conclusion.

Trial Examiner Whittemore: I sustain the objection. Perhaps you do not understand me, Mr. Witness. In looking back on this you may have formed certain conclusions in your own mind. And perhaps you find it difficult to remember exact words.

The Witness: Yes.

Trial Examiner Whittemore: But do your best to recall, even if you have to think a while, and just state who said what. You see? And not form any conclusion, or state any conclusion. Try, if you

(Testimony of Lewis Altenburg Porter.)

can, to remember the exact words and who it was that said them. [30]

The Witness: Well, Mr. Livingston wanted us to start an independent union.

Trial Examiner Whittemore: What did he say?

Mr. Watkins: May I have that answer stricken?

Trial Examiner Whittemore: It may be stricken.

The Witness: What did he say?

Trial Examiner Whittemore: What did he say? How did he express this? You said, "he wanted." How do you know he wanted?

The Witness: He wanted me to go through the plant the next day——

Mr. Watkins: May I have that stricken?

Trial Examiner Whittemore: It may be stricken.

What a man wants you do not know, unless he tells you. Now, the point is, it is a conclusion on your point. That is what these lawyers are objecting to. You are quite right, from your point of view, but the lawyers have a right to be sticklers for what they feel too.

When you say "they wanted," that is something you cannot know, unless they tell you. If he said he wanted you to do that, say so; but try to confine yourself simply to repeating, as best you can, what was said.

The Witness: All right. They asked me to go to the plant the next day, or immediately, and contact some of the boys, 12 or 15 of us, come into the office and put it up to the [31] management what we wanted. We wanted to form a union of our

(Testimony of Lewis Altenburg Porter.)

own, we wanted better working conditions, and a little pay—a little more pay. Which I did.

Mr. Watkins: Before we get that, let me ask that the last statement: "Which I did," be stricken, on the ground it is a conclusion, Mr. Examiner, because the witness can relate what he did.

Trial Examiner Whittemore: Well, I will permit that to be stricken at this time, although I think a man may testify as to what he did.

Mr. Watkins: May I ask, Mr. Examiner, in connection with this witness' conversation, he just related, he started off by saying: "They asked me to do," and I would like to have the conversation so that we may know precisely who said what.

Trial Examiner Whittemore: By that, whom did you mean?

The Witness: I meant both of them.

Mr. Watkins: I would like to know who said what. I think this witness can relate a conversation of that character.

Trial Examiner Whittemore: By "both of them," you mean both Mr. Dachtler and Mr. Livingston?

The Witness: That is right.

Trial Examiner Whittemore: I think that clears that up sufficiently. You will have an opportunity to examine him more definitely on cross examination. I think it is obvious [32] that something which happened five years ago is rather difficult for a witness to recall, in exact words of exact individuals.

Mr. Watkins: That has been the basis of the

(Testimony of Lewis Altenburg Porter.)

criticism of this whole case, that it was five years ago, and we have extreme difficulty in combating what is brought up; and with respect to the complaint on file, this will appear in many instances, in this Dachtler instance. We don't know what the Board is bringing out in the complaint and that was the reason for the motion for a bill of particulars.

Trial Examiner Whittemore: I assure you you will have ample opportunity to meet whatever is brought out.

Mr. Watkins: I am sure you will give it to us, Mr. Examiner.

Q. (By Mr. Moore) Have you given the conversation that occurred there, as nearly as you can recall it?   A. Can I?

Q. Have you given it?   A. Yes, sir.

Q. Was anything else said that you recall now!
A. No.

Q. Were Mr. Livingston and Mr. Dachtler present in the room at the time you arrived?

A. Yes, sir.

Q. In what order did you leave? [33]

A. Well, I possibly was there over thirty minutes.

Q. And then did you leave?

A. Left by myself.

Q. Did you leave alone?   A. Yes, sir.

Q. Did the other two remain there at the time?
A. Yes, sir.

(Testimony of Lewis Altenburg Porter.)

Q. Have you exhausted your recollection of that conversation?   A. Have I what?

Q. Have you stated everything you can remember about that conversation? For purposes of refreshing your recollection I will ask you specifically whether or not you were offered any reward?

A. Oh, pardon me. Yes. They—Mr. Livingston offered as a lifetime job——

Mr. Watkins: Wait just a minute. Read the answer.

(The answer was read.)

Mr. Watkins: May the answer be stricken on the ground it is a conclusion, and may we get what was said? It seems to me if the witness was told he was going to have a lifetime job he would remember what was said to him.

Mr. Moore: I believe if that is a conclusion, it is a normal one.

Trial Examiner Whittemore: No, I will deny the motion to strike. **[34]**

Q. (By Mr. Moore) Continue, Mr. Porter.

A. They offered me——

Q. No. Say who, now.

A. Mr. Livingston offered me some money. I don't know just how much it was.

Mr. Watkins: Just a minute. I move this answer be stricken on the ground it is a conclusion, Mr. Examiner. How can we attack a thing of that kind? The witness says Mr. somebody offered him some money. If he stated to him: Here is some money, let us have that conversation related, in-

(Testimony of Lewis Altenburg Porter.)

stead of giving it in this manner. That is the basis of our objection.

Trial Examiner Whittemore: If you can recall exactly what he said, try to do so.

Mr. Watkins: May I have the answer stricken, Mr. Examiner?

Trial Examiner Whittemore: It may be stricken, the last answer.

Q. (By Mr. Moore) Go ahead, Mr. Porter; say what was said about that subject.

A. Well, as I say, Mr. Livingston offered me some money, and I got some money later on.

Mr. Watkins: Just a minute, Mr. Examiner. I move that this——

Trial Examiner Whittemore: It may be stricken. Try to recall exactly what he said. Did he put his hand in his pocket [35] and pull out some money?

The Witness: No.

Trial Examiner Whittemore: What did he do? What did he say?

The Witness: He said, he did say I had a lifetime job with more pay.

Trial Examiner Whittemore: That is what he said?

The Witness: More pay; yes, sir.

Trial Examiner Whittemore: All right.

The Witness: And some money, and I can't recall just how much money he offered me, but I did get the money later on.

Trial Examiner Whittemore: Does that take care of that?

Mr. Watkins: Yes, with the exception that the

(Testimony of Lewis Altenburg Porter.)

last is a conclusion. "But I did get the money later on," that is a conclusion of the witness, because if that is another instance, he can testify as to the facts.

Trial Examiner Whittemore: I will deny the motion to strike. It is a case, perhaps, where money itself talks, if he got it.

Mr. Watkins: That is what we want, the conversation, and not his conclusion about it.

Trial Examiner Whittemore: He stated he got the money; I will permit the answer to remain.

Q. (By Mr. Moore) Have you now exhausted your recollection [36] as to the conversation at that meeting, Mr. Porter?

A. Yes, sir. He—Mr. Livingston, as I say, wanted me to go into the plant and contact some of the boys and have them come in the office, which I did; I seen 12 or 15 of them.

Q. Let us leave that for a moment. I was referring to the conversation there, Mr. Porter.

Mr. Watkins: Just a minute. May I have the last answer stricken, Mr. Examiner, on the ground it is a conclusion, and repetition?

Trial Examiner Whittemore: I will grant the motion to strike.

Q. (By Mr. Moore) Have you exhausted your memory as to the conversation that took place there? You have testified to what you started to say before. Can you remember anything in addition, anything you have not yet said?

A. That was all that was offered me.

(Testimony of Lewis Altenburg Porter.)

Q. For the purpose of refreshing your recollection I will ask you if you were offered a vacation?

A. Pardon me; yes, and I got it, two weeks vacation.

Mr. Watkins: Mr. Examiner, may I have the last portion of the answer stricken: "And I got it, two weeks vacation," on the ground it is a conclusion?

Mr. Examiner, I might say that——

Mr. Moore: I will agree it may go out. [37]

Mr. Watkins: I don't mean to be captious——

Trial Examiner Whittemore: It is not necessary to continue, counsel, as Mr. Moore has agreed this may go out, and let us drop the matter there.

Mr. Watkins: I do not mean to be captious at all, or super-particular, but we have this to defend, and these are rather serious charges. We would like to know the exact details from this witness.

Trial Examiner Whittemore: All right. Go ahead, Mr. Moore.

Q. (By Mr. Moore) Will you say what was said with reference to a vacation, and by whom it was said?

A. Mr. Livingston told me he would give me the two weeks vacation, more money, and a lifetime job. I got the two weeks vacation.

Trial Examiner Whittemore: Well, now, wait just a moment. Wait until a question is put to you. That may be stricken.

Mr. Watkins: Thank you.

Q. (By Mr. Moore) After that meeting at the

(Testimony of Lewis Altenburg Porter.)
Jonathan Club about which you have been testifying, did you take any action on the basis of the instructions you had received there?

Mr. Watkins: Just a moment. I object to the question as being compound, and also calling for a conclusion of the witness, and being leading and suggestive: Did the witness take any action on the basis of instructions he received there. [38]

Mr. Moore: He has testified he was instructed to do certain things.

Mr. Watkins: May we get the facts, counsel, instead of generalities here? We have to combat these things.

Trial Examiner Whittemore: I think you can reframe the question so it will satisfy Mr. Watkins. I can assure you, counsel, however, that I pay more attention to the witness' answers than I do to counsel's questions. I am interested in what action he took. Do you mind if I rephrase the question?

Mr. Moore: Go ahead.

Trial Examiner Whittemore: What action did you take after leaving Mr. Livingstone and Mr. Dachtler?

The Witness: Well, I immediately went to work in the plant to get the boys into the office to put it up to the management what we wanted. It was, a little better working conditions, more pay, and form an independent union of their own.

Q. (By Mr. Moore) Mr. Porter, do you mean you returned to the shop after that meeting that night?

·(Testimony of Lewis Altenburg Porter.)

A.   No, that was the first Monday, I believe.   It was the first I spoke to the boys about it.

Q.   What hours were you working at that time?

A.   I was working days, 7:00 to 3:30.

Q.   Did you go to the shop Monday morning, then? [39]   A.   Yes, sir.

Q.   Did you take any action Monday morning?

A.   Yes, sir, some.

Q.   What did you do?

A.   Well, I went around to the machines where the boys was working and told them what I wanted.

Q.   Just say what you told them.

A.   Well, I told them I thought we ought to have a union in there of our own, an independent union, and we ought to have a little more money, seniority rights.

Q.   Can you name the people you talked to?

A.   Oh, I could possibly name three or four of them.

Q.   Will you do that?

A.   Well, there was Ed and George Fickel and young Kangas; then, they seen some of the boys too for me, see?

Mr. Watkins: Just a minute, Mr. Examiner, I move the answer be stricken on the ground it is a conclusion, and also hearsay.

Trial Examiner Whittemore: Well, I will grant the motion to strike.   It goes beyond your question. If you want to explore that matter, what his knowledge of it is, go ahead.

Q.   (By Mr. Moore)   Approximately how many

(Testimony of Lewis Altenburg Porter.)
men did you talk to in the shop, as you have testified
you talked to?

A. Well, I could name some more of them;
Bebb——

Q. No, the question is: about how many? [40]

A. Eight, I think probably eight of them I
talked to.

Q. Was this done during the shift?

A. Yes, sir.

Q. Did anything occur after that?

A. That evening, Monday evening, Vic Kangas
came by with his wife——

Q. Wait.   A. ——by my home.

Q. Who did you say?

A. Vic Kangas, after working hours, after 3:30,
he came by my home and picked up I and my wife,
and we drove down to a print shop on Pacific
Boulevard, south of Florence, and Vic used the
telephone. And he wrote down what was to go on
our initiation cards, you see, membership cards.
He said he was talking——

Mr. Watkins: Just a minute. I object to this
line of testimony and move it be stricken on the
ground it is hearsay testimony. Mr. Kangas is the
best one to testify to those facts.

Mr. Moore: He has not given any hearsay testimony as yet; I think he was about to.

Trial Examiner Whittemore: That is all right.
This witness can testify what Mr. Kangas told him,
who he was talking with. It may or may not establish the fact of who Kangas was talking with. Cer-

(Testimony of Lewis Altenburg Porter.)
tainly he is the best witness [41] to testify what
Kangas told him, isn't he?

The Witness: Mr. Kangas told me he was talking to Mr. Livingston on the phone; in other words,
he said Mr. Livingston is instructing him over the
phone what to put on these cards. He wrote it down
and handed it to the print man and had the cards
printed, 150 of them, as I recall it. The next——

Q. (By Mr. Moore) Who is Victor Kangas?

A. Well, he was superintendent of the shop at
that time.

Q. Are you referring to Victor Kangas?

A. Yes, sir.

Q. Do you know what his position in the shop
was at that time?

A. Well, as best I knew he was the boss. I
think he was superintendent.

Q. Your testimony is that the events you have
just related occurred Monday afternoon?

A. Monday afternoon, yes.

Mr. Watkins: Did he say the name of that print
shop? If he did, I didn't get it, it's location.

Q. (By Mr. Moore) Will you give the location
of that print shop?

A. Well, it was on Pacific Boulevard just south
of Florence two or three doors, on the east side of
the street. I can't recall the name now. I don't
think they are there any more, [42] it might be, but
I can't recall it.

Q. Is it near a theater?

(Testimony of Lewis Altenburg Porter.)

A.   As I recall it, it is the second door south of a theater there.

Q.   What theater? The Lyric Theater?

A.   I think that's it.

Q.   Did you do anything further on Monday afternoon or evening?

A.   As I recall it, the next move, I picked the cards up Tuesday, Tuesday afternoon.

Q.   Then on Monday you didn't do anything further?   A. No.

Q.   On Tuesday, did you go down to the shop and work?

A.   I went down to the shop and worked until possibly 11:00 o'clock, and then I went down and got the cards.

Q.   Say what occurred then on Tuesday, beginning at the time you went to work.

A.   Well, after I got the cards and brought them back to the shop, and they were handed out to four or five of the boys in blocks to be passed out to the employees as they went out in the evening, and as they come in, the afternoon crew.

Q.   Who passed the cards out?

A.   Well, Lester Bebb was one; Stubblefield was one; I handed out some.

Q.   When you got to the shop in the morning did you go right [43] to work?

A.   Yes, sir, I did.

Q.   Did you have any conversations with anyone between the time you went to work and the time you have testified you went for the cards?

(Testimony of Lewis Altenburg Porter.)

A. On Monday? Tuesday? Tuesday, you mean?

Q. It is Tuesday I think we are speaking of now.

A. Well, I talked to some of the boys, six or eight of them,——

Q. Can you name any of them?

A. ——about the union. Well, Stubblefield, Bebb——

Trial Examiner Whittemore: How do you spell that?

The Witness: B-e-b-b, I believe; the two Fickle boys, young Kangas.

Trial Examiner Whittemore: At that point, are there two Kangas'?

The Witness: Yes, sir; father and son.

Trial Examiner Whittemore: Let us get back to your earlier conversation. You mentioned a Kangas then. Was it young Kangas or the superintendent you talked with on Monday?

The Witness: The young Kangas.

Trial Examiner Whittemore: On Monday was it young Kangas? You mentioned several you spoke to on Monday morning.

The Witness: Yes. I spoke to him Monday morning and Tuesday again.

Q. (By Mr. Moore) Do you know the first name of young Kangas? [44]

A. No, I never did learn his first name.

Q. I believe you testified that about 11:00 o'clock you went to the print shop to get cards. Did you check out from work at that time? A. No.

(Testimony of Lewis Altenburg Porter.)

Q. Did you make any arrangement to get off work to go for them?

A. I told the personnel man that was in charge there at that time—I can't recall his name right now either. He is not there any more. I told him I was going for the cards, to get the cards.

Q. How long were gone on that occasion?

A. Oh, a half hour.

Q. You went to the print shop, did you, for the cards?   A. Yes, sir.

Q. Was it necessary to pay for the cards at that time?   A. Oh, yes.

Q. Did you pay for them?   A. Yes, sir.

Q. In paying for them did you use your own funds?   A. No, sir.

Q. Will you explain what funds you used in paying for them?   A. How much?

Q. No—how much, yes, and what money it was.

A. It was six dollars and something, as best I can recall, [45] and I never have been able to figure out who gave me that money, but somebody in the plant did, and I can't remember, and I won't say; but someone of the ups gave me the money. I can't recall who gave it to me.

Mr. Watkins: May I have the last of the answer read, please.

Trial Examiner Whittemore: Surely.

(The answer was read.)

Mr. Watkins: I would like to have stricken that part of the answer: "Someone of the ups gave me

(Testimony of Lewis Altenburg Porter.)

the money." How can we combat a statement of that kind?

Trial Examiner Whittemore: I will grant your motion to strike. If you want to, explore his recollection. I don't know what the word "ups" means.

Q. (By Mr. Moore) Can you recall who gave you money to pay for those cards?

A. No, sir, I can't.

Q. In order to refresh your recollection, I will ask you if it was Mr. Lyman Hodges?

A. It could have been possible; Hodges or Kangas.

Q. By Kangas now, will you identify him?

A. Vic Kangas, superintendent.

Q. Victor E. Kangas?

A. One of those two men gave me the money. I know at that time I was making so little I know I didn't shell any money [46] for the cards out.

Q. I will ask you if you did not receive this money before you paid for the cards?

A. I did.

Q. Are you positive of that?

A. I went over and paid for the cards.

Q. Has the Pacific Motor Parts Workers Alliance ever reimbursed you for any expenditures you have made in their behalf?   A. No.

Q. Have you ever made any expenditures on their behalf?

A. I never incurred any expense of my own, no, sir.

Q. After you went for the cards what occurred

(Testimony of Lewis Altenburg Porter.)
in the plant? After you had returned with the cards?

A. With the cards? I gave the cards to Hodges.

Q. Are you speaking of Lyman Hodges?

A. Lyman Hodges, yes, sir.

Q. Go ahead.

A. And he gave Bebb and Stubblefield, three or four of the boys, a block of the cards to hand out to the men as they came in and out to work.

Q. Were you acquainted with Lyman Hodges?

A. Yes, sir.

Q. Do you know what his duties were in the plant at that time?

Mr. Watkins: Just a minute. I object to the question as [47] to what his duties were; what he did the witness can testify to.

Trial Examiner Whittemore: I think you are probably correct. What did he do in the plant?

The Witness: Well, as I learned, he was inspector, head inspector.

Trial Examiner Whittemore: Will you concede he was head inspector there?

Mr. Watkins: I don't know that, Mr. Examiner.

Trial Examiner Whittemore: Is there anyone from the plant who knows that?

Mr. Watkins: Yes. That is correct.

Trial Examiner Whittemore: All right. That takes care of that matter.

Q. (By Mr. Moore) After you had returned with the cards from the print shop, was a meeting held in the plant?

(Testimony of Lewis Altenburg Porter.)

A.   In the office, in the manager's office, in the afternoon.

Q.   At about what time?

A.   Oh, I would say about 3:00 o'clock, as best I can recall.

Q.   And who was present at that meeting?

A.   Well, I couldn't name all the men that was in there; there was 15 or 18.

Mr. Watkins: May I interrupt just a minute? I wonder if I might have the last two answers of the witness read, please.

Trial Examiner Whittemore: Surely. [48]

(The record was read.)

Mr. Watkins: What I was trying to get was whether or not this was fixed as the same day of the morning he went in to get the cards. Am I correct?

Q.   (By Mr. Moore)   It was the same day you went to get the cards?

A.   That is the way I have got it in my memory, yes.

Q.   It was about 3:00 o'clock in the afternoon?

A.   Yes.

Q.   Name the people present at that meeting, as near as you can recall?

A.   Well, Mr. Dachtler for one was there.

Q.   Mr. C. V. Dachtler?

A.   Dachtler, yes, sir, and Mr. Livingston.

Q.   Mr. Raymond Livingston?

A.   Yes, sir.   A little later Mr. Kangas was called in.

(Testimony of Lewis Altenburg Porter.)

Q. Victor E. Kangas?

A. Victor E. Kangas. I would say it was about 15 or 18, as best I can recall, of the working men came in.

Q. Did you go in with them?   A. Yes, sir.

Q. What took place at that meeting?

A. Well, I asked the management—

Q. Who were you talking to?

A. Mr. Dachtler and Mr. Livingston, in behalf of the men and [49] with their consent, that we form a company—or independent union; better working conditions, and a little more pay. They granted us, Mr. Livingston and Mr. Dachtler granted us that permission to do so.

Q. Just say what was said.

Mr. Watkins: May I have the answer read, Mr. Examiner.

Trial Examiner Whittemore: Surely. Which one? This last one?

Mr. Watkins: This last one.

(The record was read.)

Q. (By Mr. Moore) What did Mr. Dachtler and Mr. Livingston say?

A. Well, I can't just recall the words, but I know they agreed to give us all we asked.

Q. You said Mr. Victor E. Kangas came into the meeting. Did he come into the meeting before they said this?

A. That I don't remember, whether it was before or after we asked them that. But I know he was called into the meeting.

(Testimony of Lewis Altenburg Porter.)

Q. What did you tell us was said about an independent union? You said something was said about an independent union. What was said, and by whom?   A. At that meeting?

Q. Yes.

A. Well, I asked the management if we could form a union.

Q. Was that question answered? [50]

A. Mr. Dachtler, as I recall it, and Mr. Livingston both agreed to it.

Mr. Watkins: May we go off the record just a second, Mr. Examiner?

Trial Examiner Whittemore: Surely. Off the record.

(Discussion off the record.)

Trial Examiner Whittemore: We will take a five minute recess at this time.

(A short recess.)

Trial Examiner Whittemore: All right, Mr. Moore.

Q. (By Mr. Moore) Mr. Porter, you testified that you attended a meeting with Mr. Livingston and Mr. Dachtler at the Jonathan Club?

A. Yes, sir.

Q. How did you happen to go there?

A. Victor Kangas told me to meet Mr. Livingston after 6:00 o'clock at the Jonathan Club, and when I got down there Mr. Dachtler was there too.

Mr. Watkins: May we fix this conversation with Mr. Kangas, where it was and when?

Mr. Moore: Well, I will leave that——

(Testimony of Lewis Altenburg Porter.)

Mr. Watkins: Then I will object to it as no proper foundation being laid for it.

Trial Examiner Whittemore: I see no reason why you should not fix the time; fix the time when it was Kangas told him [51] to meet him.

Q. (By Mr. Moore) Did you have a conversation with Mr. Kangas?

A. He came to my machine.

Q. When was this?

A. Saturday morning?

Q. At about what time?

A. Around 10:00 o'clock.

Q. Was anyone else present?

A. No, sir.

Q. What did he say to you and what did you say to him?

A. He told me Mr. Livingston wanted me to meet him at the Jonathan Club that evening.

Q. What did you say?

A. I told him I would go down there.

Q. Was that the entire conversation.

A. Yes, sir.

Q. Was that before or after Mr. Livingston had introduced himself and you had talked with him?

A. That was after.

Q. After the meeting in the company office to which you testified some 15 to 18 employees were present, what occurred? How long did that meeting last? Let me ask you that.

A. I would say 30 minutes.

Q. And then after that what happened, if anything, in the [52] plant?

(Testimony of Lewis Altenburg Porter.)

A. Well, as I recall now they handed out the cards.

Q. Who did that? Who handed out the cards?

A. Bebb, Stubblefield and Spurlock, I think was the third man.

Q. Did Mr. Ed Fickle help?

A. I just don't remember. I wouldn't say positive.

Q. Did you hand out any of those cards?

A. Yes, sir, a few of them.

Q. Where did you do it?

A. Out at the gate, at the entrance into the plant.

Q. Did you have any conversation with the men to whom you gave them?

A. Not in particular, no, sir.

Q. Was anything said by you concerning a meeting of employees?

A. I don't recall that we did.

Q. What happened on that day after the cards were passed out by these people and by you?

A. Well, after that I don't know, in the plant. I went right on home.

Q. You went home?　　A. Yes, sir.

Q. Did you attend any meeting on that day?

A. As I recall it now one of the boys, Ray Haley, came to the house and got me and we attended a meeting. [53]

Q. Where was that meeting held?

A. It was in Maywood on Slauson Avenue. I don't know the address; just a little place.

(Testimony of Lewis Altenburg Porter.)

Q. Who was there?

A. Well, I couldn't recall very many of them. There was, I would say 20 men there.

Q. Were they men who were employed at the shop?

A. Yes; the Fickles, Ed Fickle and his father, Bebb, Stubblefield.

Q. About what time of the evening was the meeting held?

A. Oh, 8:00 o'clock or past.

Q. And what happened at the meeting?

A. Well, I don't know hardly, I couldn't recall what did happen. In fact, I wasn't very much interested in it.

Mr. Watkins: May I have the answer read, please?

The Witness: I wasn't much interested in it, and I don't remember what went on.

Q. (By Mr. Moore) Was there a constitution and bylaws read at that meeting?

A. There was something read; I believe it was.

Q. Did you say anything at that meeting?

A. No, sir.

Q. Did you address the meeting at all?

A. No, sir.

Q. Did you tell the men what part you had played? [54]

A. No, I didn't say anything.

Q. And what you had done before this?

A. No, sir.

(Testimony of Lewis Altenburg Porter.)

Q. Did you tell them about the conversations you had had with Mr. Livingston and Mr. Dachtler?   A. No, sir.

Q. Did you hold any office?

A. No, sir.

Q. Ever, in Pacific Motor Parts Workers Alliance?   A. No, sir.

Q. At the meeting that evening was any union formed?

A. If there was, I don't remember it.

Q. Were any officers elected?

A. Possibly so; I wouldn't say. I don't remember.

Q. These membership cards you say were passed, were they at that meeting? Were they collected?

A. Well, I don't remember that, whether they taken them up or not.

Trial Examiner Whittemore: While we are on the subject of the cards, have you got a copy of a card?

Mr. Moore: No, I haven't been able to get a copy of them.

Trial Examiner Whittemore: Do you know, Mr. Baldwin, whether there is one available?

Mr. Baldwin: I beg your pardon?

Trial Examiner Whittemore: Do you know whether or not [55] there is a copy of such a card as this witness has been talking about that is available?

Mr. Baldwin: Yes, there is.

(Testimony of Lewis Altenburg Porter.)

Trial Examiner Whittemore: Could you bring one in, please?

Mr. Baldwin: I will.

Trial Examiner Whittemore: Thank you.

Q. (By Mr. Moore) Mr. Porter, do you know when the Pacific Motor Parts Workers Alliance was formed?   A. No, I don't.

Q. Do you know that such an organization was formed?   A. Yes.

Q. Did that Alliance later enter into a contract with Jadson Motor Products Company?

A. Oh, I don't know.

Q. To your knowledge?

A. I don't know whether they did or not.

Q. Did you have anything to do with any negotiations with respect to the contract?

A. No, sir.

Q. Do you know whether or not the Alliance procured the services of an attorney?

A. No, I don't.

Q. Did you understand the question?

A. Oh, yes. We did—they had a lawyer employed, an attorney—I think it was to draw up their working agreement. [56]

Q. Who was that attorney?

A. Mr. Schooling.

Q. Do you know how they happened to engage Mr. Schooling's services?   A. Yes, sir.

Q. How did that come about?

A. Mr. Livingston gave me a paper with the

(Testimony of Lewis Altenburg Porter.)
agreement written out on it and I taken it to Mr. Schooling and he didn't think much of it.

Q. Well, about when was this, now?

A. Well, I—I won't say whether it was Tuesday night or Wednesday night or what night, but it was right along in there.

Q. That Mr. Livingston gave you this document you are speaking of?   A. Yes, sir.

Q. Did you have a conversation with Mr. Livingston at the time he gave it to you?

A. Well, I was talking to Mr. Livingston and Vic Kangas both, they were both questioning me.

Q. You had a conversation with the two of them together?   A. Yes.

Q. Was anyone else present?

A. No, sir.

Mr. Watkins: Where was it? [57]

Q. (By Mr. Moore) Where was the conversation held?

A. That was in the plant, out in the plant.

Q. Was it in the office? What part of the plant?

A. Out in the operating room.

Q. What was said at that time?

Mr. Watkins: Wait a minute; what time was this? Will you get that also, please?

Q. (By Mr. Moore) About what time of the day?

A. No, I couldn't recall the time of the day.

Q. Was it during the shift while you were working?

A. I know I was on duty working.

(Testimony of Lewis Altenburg Porter.)

Q. As near as you can recall, was it after this meeting that the employees had held in Maywood?

A. I don't know whether it was before or after that.

Q. What was said at the conversation?

Mr. Watkins: May we fix the date of this meeting with a little more certainty with respect to the meeting with the management, for example, where 15 or 18 men were present?

Mr. Moore: The testimony is that it was on Tuesday just after he went for the cards, at about 3:00 o'clock.

Mr. Watkins: Well, I mean with relation to that, this present conversation.

Q. (By Mr. Moore) The conversation we are speaking of now, the one you had with Mr. Livingston and Mr. Kangas, did that occur after this delegation of employees had gone in to see [58] Mr. Livingston?   A. That was after.

Q. State, as nearly as you can, how long after?

A. Well, I couldn't state whether it was two days or three days or one day after, but I know it was along in there.

Q. Would you say it was one to three days after?   A. Well, I would say that.

Q. And it was during the time you were working in the plant?   A. Yes, sir.

Q. Only the three of you were present?

A. Yes, sir.

(Testimony of Lewis Altenburg Porter.)

Q. Would you repeat the conversation that was had on that occasion?

A. Well, one of them, I won't be positive, asked me if I knew of an attorney, or had a friend. I told him I had a very good friend who was an attorney; and then they asked me, Mr. Livingston asked me, if I would take this slip of paper. I don't believe I even read it, to this man, and have him to draw one up.

Q. Draw what up?

A. This working agreement, I would say.

Q. You are not certain whether you read that or not?   A. I know I never.

Mr. Watkins: May I get that answer, please?

(The answer was read.) [59]

Q. (By Mr. Moore) How long had you known Mr. Schooling, the attorney of whom you are speaking?   A. Oh, say six years.

Q. What is his full name?

A. Wendell Schooling.

Q. Did you go to see Mr. Wendell Schooling?

A. Yes, sir, I went to his house.

Q. Where did he live?

A. In Huntington Park. I don't know his address.

Q. At his residence?   A. Yes, sir.

Q. And at about what time?

A. Oh, I went over about 8:00 o'clock, and I had to wait at his home until after 10:00. He was out at a meeting some place.

(Testimony of Lewis Altenburg Porter.)

Q. When did the meeting with Mr. Schooling occur?   A. With me?

Q. Yes, the meeting between you and him.

A. After 10:00 o'clock that evening, he came home.

Q. You say that evening; which evening?

A. The evening I taken that paper over to have him draw it up.

Q. Was that on the same day that you received the paper?   A. Yes.

Q. What conversation did you have with Mr. Schooling? [60]

A. He read the paper, read the contents, what was on the paper. He said he didn't think much of it, and he says, "I'll tell you, Lou. You go back to the management and tell them what I said. Have them send somebody, or you come over, and I will draw them up one."

The next morning I told Kangas, Victor Kangas, about it. That was all I heard then, until in the afternoon——

Q. Let's stay there, then. After that conversation you had with Mr. Schooling did you have any further conversation with him with reference to a contract?   A. With Mr. Schooling?

Q. Yes.   A. No, sir.

Q. You never had any further contact with him?   A. No, sir.

Mr. Watkins: May I interrupt, counsel. I think it will expedite it if at this time we may

(Testimony of Lewis Altenburg Porter.)

have just the conversation the witness had with Mr. Schooling at his meeting with him.

Mr. Moore: You mean ask him to repeat that?

Mr. Watkins: Yes, just what the conversation was.

Q. (By Mr. Moore) Will you repeat the conversation between you and Mr. Schooling on the occasion you contacted him at his home?

A. I told him I was sent over by the management to have him fix up an agreement, and I gave him this paper and he read it, [61] and as I said before, he didn't think much of it, and that was about all that was said at that time.

Q. Did he say he didn't think much of it?

A. Yes, sir.

Q. And then you have already testified as to what he said after that?

A. Yes. He said, "Tell the management of the plant that they should send somebody over," he says, "You can come back, Lou, or they can send somebody, anybody they wish, and I will draw them up an agreement."

Q. Was it clear to you why he said to send someone back over there? You were already there.

A. Yes.

Q. Did you understand he meant to send someone to his office?

A. From the office, yes.

Q. After you had done that, did you have a further meeting with Mr. Livingston?

(Testimony of Lewis Altenburg Porter.)

A. No, I don't recall. That day, you mean? That day particularly?

Q. Well, did you have any other meeting with Mr. Livingston at about this time, either before or after, any meeting you haven't mentioned?

A. Yes, sir.

Q. When was that meeting? [62]

A. Well, that was, oh, I would say a day or two after that, maybe two or three days. Victor Kangas——

Q. From one to three days after you had seen Mr. Schooling?   A. Yes, sir.

Q. Yes, And where did the meeting take place?

A. At the Jonathan Club.

Q. Who was there at the time?

A. Victor Kangas, Lyman Hodges and Mr. Livingston, and myself.

Q. The four of you?   A. Yes.

Q. What time of the day was that?

A. Well, as I recall, that was after 6:00 p. m. in the evening.

Q. How did you know that a meeting was going to be held at that time and place?

A. Vic Kangas told me.

Q. Did you have a conversation with Mr. Kangas about that?   A. Yes, sir.

Q. Where was that conversation held?

A. That was in the plant.

Q. At about what time?

A. Sometime during the day. I don't know

(Testimony of Lewis Altenburg Porter.)

whether it was in the morning or evening of that particular day.

Q. Was it during your working hours? [63]

A. Yes, sir.

Q. Where did it take place?

A. Where did the conversation take place?

Q. Yes.

A. At the machine that I was working on in the plant.

Q. What did Mr. Kangas say to you?

A. Well, he says, "We are going to—Hodges and you and myself is going down tonight to have dinner with Mr. Livingston at the Jonathan Club."

Q. Did you say anything?

A. I told him I would be there.

Q. Did he say what time?

A. As I recall it now it was 6:00 o'clock or after, for dinner.

Q. What happened at this meeting at the Jonathan Club?

A. Well, we had our dinners. Mr. Livingston wanted to know from me what we would call the union, what name we would give it.

Q. Will you give the conversation that you had there, as near as you can recall?

A. How?

Q. Will you state what conversation was had there, as near as you can recall?

A. Well, I told him I didn't know what to call it. In fact, I didn't. So, as I recall, he asked me

(Testimony of Lewis Altenburg Porter.)
how would "PPWA" be. [64] And as far as I
knew it was all right.

Q. At that time the cards, the membership cards,
had already been printed, had they not?

A. Yes.

Q. What other conversation was had there?

Mr. Watkins: May I have the last question and
answer read?

(The record was read.)

The Witness: Well, I don't remember. I don't
recall of any other conversation.

Q. (By Mr. Moore) Did all four of you eat
dinner there together?

A. As I remember it rightly, Mr. Livingston
didn't eat with us. He sat at the table with us,
and we three ate, and as I remember, he was going
out to dinner later with somebody else.

Q. He said that?   A. Yes.

Q. Have you exhausted your recollection as to
what was said at that meeting?

A. How?

Q. Have you exhausted your recollection as to
what was said at that meeting?

A. I don't remember anything else right now.

Q. In other words, to refresh your recollection,
I will ask [65] you if anything was said about
the C. I. O.?

A. I can't recall whether it was said, anything
there.

Q. You have testified you were offered certain
rewards for——

(Testimony of Lewis Altenburg Porter.)

Trial Examiner Whittemore: Are you going on to another subject now?

Mr. Moore: Yes.

Trial Examiner Whittemore: Well, I think, since it is somewhat after 12:30 we will take a recess now.

Mr. Moore: That will be fine.

Trial Examiner Whittemore: We will be in recess until 1:30.

(Whereupon, a recess was taken at 12:32 p. m. until 1:30 p. m., of the same day.) [66]

Afternoon Session

Trial Examiner Whittemore: Will the witness take the stand again.

LEWIS ALTENBURG PORTER

resumed the stand, and further testified as follows:

Direct Examination (Continued)

Q. (By Mr. Moore) Mr. Porter, you testified previously that at a meeting at which you and Mr. Raymond Livingston and Mr. C. V. Dachtler were present, you were offered certain rewards for your part in assisting to set up a union among the employees?   A. Yes, sir.

Q. Did you ever receive a reward?

A. Yes, sir.

Q. When did you receive it?

A. About the first of September I got it.

Q. In what year?

A. I got a fifty dollar bill——

(Testimony of Lewis Altenburg Porter.)

Q. In what year was this you did receive it?

A. '37.

Q. 1937. From whom did you receive the reward?   A. Vic Kangas.

Q. Did you have any conversation with him at the time?   A. Yes, sir.

Q. You say it was about the first of September?

[67]

A. Around the first of September.

Q. Where was this conversation held?

A. At my home.

Q. Where was that, at the time?

A. Huntington Park.

Q. Pardon me?

A. In Huntington Park, 6029 Stafford, Huntington Park.

Q. Yes; and who was there at the time?

A. My wife, Mr. Kangas, Mrs. Victor Kangas and myself.

Q. About what time of the day?

A. Oh, it was after the dinner hour; I would say 7:00 or 8:00 o'clock.

Q. Was there a conversation at the time?

A. No more than Vic Kangas told me that Mr. Hileman sent me this fifty dollar bill.

Q. Who is Mr. Hileman of whom you are speaking?

A. Well, he is general manager of the plant.

Q. Do you know his full name?

A. Paul, I believe.

Q. Is it Paul D. Hileman?

(Testimony of Lewis Altenburg Porter.)

A. I don't know as to the middle name; Paul Hileman.

Mr. Moore: May it be stipulated Mr. Paul D. Hileman was general manager of the plant in September, 1937?

Trial Examiner Whittemore: Has the stenographer got the right spelling of that name? [68]

Mr. Watkins: H-i-l-e-m-a-n, Hileman, it is.

Q. (By Mr. Moore) Will you go ahead and repeat the conversation that was had at the time you received the reward from Mr. Kangas. What was said?

A. Well, he handed me the envelope that this fifty dollars was contained in and said that Mr. Hileman sent it to me. That's about all I remember of him saying.

Q. What did you say?

A. I thanked him for it.

Q. Did you then open it?

A. I opened it at that time, yes, sir.

Q. Did you open it in the presence of Mr. Kangas?   A. Yes, sir.

Q. Were Mrs. Kangas and your wife also present at that time?

A. They were all sitting there.

Q. Did Mr. Kangas indicate what the reward was for?

A. I don't remember of him saying anything.

Q. Did you know what it was for at the time?

A. Oh, yes, naturally I——

(Testimony of Lewis Altenburg Porter.)

Mr. Watkins: Just a minute, Mr. Examiner. I object, first of all, as calling for a conclusion of the witness' state of mind, and I move the answer be stricken, so far as it is now given.

Trial Examiner Whittemore: I will deny your motion to strike. [69]

Q. (By Mr. Moore) Had you had a conversation with Mr. Kangas previously relative to payment to you of any reward?

A. That I don't remember. No, sir.

Q. Had you had any conversation with Mr. Hileman with reference to payment to you?

A. No, sir.

Q. Are you sure that you had not?

A. No, I never said anything to Mr. Hileman.

Q. Did you receive any other reward other than this fifty dollar bill you have testified to?

A. Did I receive any other, you say?

Q. Yes.

A. No more than my two weeks vacation with pay.

Q. When did you take that vacation?

A. I don't know whether it was the first half of September or the last half. I think it was the first half of September.

Q. With whom did you make arrangements to take that vacation?   A. With whom?

Q. Yes.   A. With Kangas, Vic.

Q. Victor Kangas?   A. Yes.

Q. Did you have a conversation with him relative to the vacation? [70]

(Testimony of Lewis Altenburg Porter.)

A. No, I don't think so.

Q. Did you just stay away from the plant?

A. Oh, yes. I went on a little trip. I went up to Reno and Frisco.

Q. What I am trying to discover is: How did any official of the company know that you were going to take a vacation? Did you tell them?

A. Well, I was promised a vacation.

Q. I understand that.

A. And Vic told me to go ahead and take it at a certain time.

Q. Then you had a conversation with Mr. Victor Kangas?

A. Yes, but as to what time I don't know just when it was. But I know I——

Q. You cannot fix the date of the conversation?

A. No, I wouldn't attempt to fix a date. I couldn't do it.

Q. Can you say whether it was before or after you received the fifty dollar bill?

A. It was before I had arranged for the vacation. I had arranged for the vacation before I got the fifty dollar bill.

Q. When you spoke to Mr. Kangas with reference to the vacation were you in the plant?

A. Yes, I think I was. That was the only place I would meet him, was in the plant.

Q. Was anyone other than you and he present?

A. No. No. [71]

Q. Can you state what was said?

A. No.

(Testimony of Lewis Altenburg Porter.)

Q. More than you have already stated?

A. That is right. No, I don't remember of anything else that was said.

Q. You did take a vacation?   A. How?

Q. You did take a vacation?   A. Yes, sir.

Q. And how long did it last?

A. Two weeks.

Q. I will ask you if other employees received a vacation about that time?

A. No, sir. They wasn't giving any.

Mr. Watkins: You are talking about "that time." Can you fix that vacation, when it was, Mr. Moore?

Trial Examiner Whittemore: I think he has.

Q. (By Mr. Moore) I believe you said the vacation was in September, and you are not certain whether it was the first half or the second half.

A. I don't know whether it was the first or last half.

Q. In September of 1937, was it the policy of the company to grant to the employees a vacation?

Mr. Watkins: Just a minute. I object to that as calling for a conclusion, as to what the policy of the company was. [72]

Trial Examiner Whittemore: I am less interested in the policy than in the practice. Find out whether the practice was at that time that others were given vacations.

Q. (By Mr. Moore) Was it, to your knowledge, a practice of the company to allow employees vacation with pay during September of 1937?

(Testimony of Lewis Altenburg Porter.)

Mr. Watkins: Just a moment. I object to the question on the ground it calls for a conclusion. The witness can testify whether or not any other employees received vacations.

Trial Examiner Whittemore: That is what I am getting at, what the practice was, what was done; not what the company's policy was. The company's policy might have been one thing, and the practice something else. I think the question is correct, Mr. Watkins.

Do you know whether or not others were given vacations or took vacations?

The Witness: I don't know whether any others got a vacation.

Q. (By Mr. Moore) At the meeting you have testified to that occurred in the office at which Mr. Raymond Livingston, C. V. Dachtler and Mr. Kangas were present, and approximately 15 to 18 employees were present, was the subject of vacations discussed at all?

A. I don't remember whether that was discussed that day or not.

Q. Being spokesman for the men at that time, did you ask [73] whether or not vacations were to be had for the men?

A. Vacations with pay, and a little more money, and a union of their own.

Q. You testified previously at that time raises in pay were granted. Were vacations with pay also granted?

(Testimony of Lewis Altenburg Porter.)

A. If I remember rightly, we did get a raise, in the near future. I wouldn't say just when.

Mr. Watkins: Can we——

Mr. Moore: I am referring to the conversation he had testified concerning previously, where 15 to 18 employees had a meeting with Mr. Livingston, Mr. Dachtler, and Mr. Kangas in the office in the plant.

Mr. Watkins: Yes, I understood you, Mr. Moore. But the witness stated they did receive a raise. Find out when that was with respect to that meeting. I understood that was the basis of your question.

The Witness: I can't state just when that was.

Q. (By Mr. Moore) What I meant to ask was: Were you promised at that meeting——

A. We was promised, yes, sir, everything we asked for.

Q. ——were you promised a vacation with pay at that time?

A. I am not positive, but it appears to me we did; however, I wouldn't be positive of it.

Q. Do you know any other employees who took a vacation with pay during the year of 1937? [74]

A. No, I do not.

Q. Do you know no employee did?

A. Well, none that I know of.

Q. Referring to the period, now, prior to the time that you met Mr. Raymond Livingston, as you have testified, was any labor organization connected

(Testimony of Lewis Altenburg Porter.)

with the C. I. O. conducting an organizational campaign among the employees of the company there?

Mr. Watkins: May I interrupt to ask which meeting with Mr. Livingston? The witness has testified to more than one.

Mr. Moore: I think I said the first meeting. I should have stated that.

Mr. Watkins: Thank you.

Q. (By Mr. Moore) Prior to the time you first met Mr. Livingston.

A. I couldn't give the dates or times, but I know the C. I. O. was at that time trying to organize.

Q. You can fix the time that you first met Mr. Livingston, in your mind, even though you don't know the exact date?

A. No, I don't remember.

Q. But you can fix that point of time in your mind, and before that point of time, was the C. I. O. conducting a campaign among the employees there?

A. Yes.

Q. For about how long had that been going on?

[75]

A. Well, I don't know.

Q. Several months?

A. It was several months, yes.

Mr. Watkins: Just a minute. I should like, unless the witness will enlarge on what he means by "conducting a campaign", to ask that both of the last answers be stricken on the ground they are conclusions.

(Testimony of Lewis Altenburg Porter.)

Trial Examiner Whittemore: I think it is generally known what a campaign for membership is. But I have no objection to your exploring that matter.

Mr. Moore: I will go ahead, then, and clear that up.

Trial Examiner Whittemore: All right.

Q. (By Mr. Moore) During that period, prior to the time of your first meeting with Mr. Livingston, were organizers of the C. I. O. present outside the plant on a good many occasions?

A. I think so; yes, sir.

Q. Did they pass out literature?

Mr. Watkins: Just a minute. I object to the question now as leading and suggestive, Mr. Examiner.

Trial Examiner Whittemore: I will sustain the objection.

Q. (By Mr. Moore) What did these organizers do?

A. The best I remember, all they done was hand out pamphlets.

Q. Did you during that period of time have occasion to join the C. I. O.? [76]

A. Yes, sir.

Q. When did you join?

A. '35, the best I can remember now; 1935.

Q. Do you have any document in your possession that might refresh your memory on that point?

A. I have it at home, yes, sir; a receipt.

Q. Did you join the C. I. O. in 1937?

(Testimony of Lewis Altenburg Porter.)

A. Yes, sir.

Q. About when?

Mr. Watkins: Wait a minute. Which is correct? Was there a joining and a re-joining?

Mr. Moore: Are you asking the witness?

Mr. Watkins: I am trying to get the matter straight. The witness first testified,——

Trial Examiner Whittemore: 1935.

Mr. Watkins: That was the year it was formed?

The Witness: No, I have got the receipt at home. I should have brought it with me. It was May 15th, I think, 1937. I have the receipt at home.

Q. (By Mr. Moore) Had you ever been a member of the C. I. O. before that time?

A. No, sir.

Q. When you said a moment ago that you had joined in 1935——

A. I think that was a mistake. It was in 1937, I think it was May of '37. [77]

Q. Will you state what the circumstances were at the time you joined the C. I. O. in May of 1937?

Mr. Watkins: I would say that has no bearing on the issues. I don't care, Mr. Examiner.

Trial Examiner Whittemore: I think you had better narrow it down. We might be here a long while covering these circumstances. Just what do you mean by the "circumstances"?

Q. (By Mr. Moore) Did you have any conversation with any official of Thompson Products, Inc., at the time or shortly prior to the time you joined?

(Testimony of Lewis Altenburg Porter.)

A. Yes, sir; and I can't say truthfully what one of the management had me to join them.

Q. Who was there in a managerial capacity at that time?

Mr. Watkins: Just a minute, Mr. Examiner. May I have the previous answer read?

Trial Examiner Whittemore: Surely.

(The answer was read.)

Mr. Watkins: I would like to ask that be stricken, Mr. Examiner, on the ground it is a conclusion of the witness, and is vague and uncertain, and there is not any way we can combat that type of evidence.

Trial Examiner Whittemore: Certainly, as it stands now, there is not much there for you to combat, unless something else is brought out. He says he can't testify truthfully as to what man, apparently, if any, had him join. I would [78] like to hear more about it.

Mr. Watkins: My point, Mr. Examiner, is that it should be stricken unless some identity can be given to anybody in the management who, as he claims, had him join. There is the statement there that somebody in the management had this done. We can't combat that, unless it is more in detail.

Trial Examiner Whittemore: I will grant your motion to strike. I suggest you explore the matter further, if you wish to.

Mr. Moore: Yes. I planned to.

Q. (By Mr. Moore) Who was at the plant in

(Testimony of Lewis Altenburg Porter.)

a managerial capacity at the time you joined the C. I. O. in 1937?

A. Mr. Dachtler was the manager, Victor Kangas was under him. Lyman Hodges gave me the money to join the union.

Q. The C. I. O.? A. Yes, sir.

Q. Who was Mr. Lyman Hodges?

A. Well, he was inspector, then later he became personnel, or something like that.

Q. At the time you joined the C. I. O. what capacity did he hold in the plant?

A. I don't know whether he was still inspector or not.

Q. Did he do manual labor? A. No.

Q. Did he hire men? [79]

A. No. I think he had men working under him, yeah.

Q. Did he fire men?

A. I don't know that he did, or not.

Q. Did you have a conversation with Mr. Lyman Hodges with reference to joining the union?

A. Not in particular, only he just gave me the money and told me to use the money for the dues.

Q. You did have a conversation with him then?

A. Yeah.

Q. About when did that take place?

A. Well, I forget the dates. I couldn't give you the dates.

Q. Did it take place shortly before you joined the C. I. O.?

A. It was just before, yeah.

(Testimony of Lewis Altenburg Porter.)

Q.   Where did the conversation take place?

A.   In the plant.

Q.   At about what time?

A.   Well, as to that I wouldn't say.   It was during the day.

Q.   During your working shift?

A.   Yeah, I wouldn't say whether it was in the morning or in the afternoon.

Q.   Was anyone present other than you and Mr. Hodges?   A.   No, sir.

Q.   Will you repeat the conversation that was had, then, as nearly as you can.

A.   Well, he informed me he wanted me to join the union. [80]

Q.   Did he indicate what union?

A.   To find out what was going on, how many members they had, and all.

Mr. Watkins: Just a minute. I move the answer be stricken as a conclusion of the witness. I wish we could get the conversation in here. Here, again, we have the same type of statement made, which is a reflection on the management, and I think it should be more specific.

Trial Examiner Whittemore: I will hold it in reserve. Read the answer.

(The answer was read.)

Trial Examiner Whittemore: When you say "inform,'" did he say that to you?

A.   Join the union.

(Testimony of Lewis Altenburg Porter.)

Trial Examiner Whittemore: That's what he said?

The Witness: Yes.

Trial Examiner Whittemore: I gathered that by the word "inform" in the context, it was indicating what he said. Does that take care of the matter?

Mr. Watkins: Not very satisfactory, Mr. Examiner. I still feel that the statement is a conclusion of the witness, and that, if a conversation of some character, according to the witness, took place at this time, it seems to me the only way it should come in here was by telling what Mr. Hodges said to him and what he said to Mr. Hodges, so that we know [81] the conversation.

Trial Examiner Whittemore: As I recall, he was asking that conversation, what was said. He testified what was said, and said: "He informed me he wanted * * *" I took the word "informed" as being synonymous with "told" in this case, and that that was what was said.

Mr. Watkins: Yes. Perhaps the rest of the testimony will straighten it up.

Q. (By Mr. Moore) Go ahead. State what was said.

A. Well, I joined the union and paid dues.

Q. Just say what was said between you and Mr. Hodges.

A. Well, about all that was said was, join the C. I. O. to learn what was going on and how many members they was getting.

(Testimony of Lewis Altenburg Porter.)

Q. Did you say anything at that time?

A. I don't know that I did, no, sir.

Q. Did you say you would join?

A. I said I would join.

Q. Did you attend meetings of the C. I. O. after you did join?   A. Twice, yeah.

Q. Did you have any discussions with anyone connected with the company as to what took place at those meetings?

A. No. I didn't say much. I don't know I told them anything.

Q. Well, did you have any conversations with any of them, without reference to how much you said. [82]

A. I think I told Vic that one meeting they had that there was a dozen or so men. That was all that was said.

Q. You are referring to Mr. Victor Kangas?

A. Yeah.

Q. When did the conversation with Mr. Kangas take place, as nearly as you can recall?

A. The next day after the meeting. I don't know what date the meeting was.

Q. How long after you joined was the meeting to which you have reference?

A. Possibly a week.

Q. After that meeting you had a conversation with Mr. Kangas?   A. Yes.

Q. Where did it take place?

A. Where did it take place?

Q. Yes.

(Testimony of Lewis Altenburg Porter.)

A. It was on Otis and Florence, I believe it was, in Bell.

Q. You were standing on the street corner?

A. No, I say, that's where the meeting took place.

Q. No. I mean the meeting with Mr. Kangas. Where was it?

A. Oh, yes. It was in the plant in working hours.

Q. Who was present other than you and he?

A. Nobody.

Q. About what time of day was it?

A. Well, I don't know whether it was in the morning or [83] afternoon. I know it was during the day.

Q. What was said?

A. I just told him that there was possibly a dozen men there.

Q. Meaning men from the plant in which you were employed?   A. Uh huh.

Q. Did he say anything?

A. No, just probably laughed and walked away.

Q. Did you thereafter remain active in the C. I. O.?   A. How?

Q. Did you thereafter remain active in the C. I. O., and did you attend meetings of the C. I. O.?

A. No, sir.

Q. You attended, I think you said, a couple of meetings?

A. I think I was twice at the meetings.

(Testimony of Lewis Altenburg Porter.)

Q. After that you did not attend any further meetings? A. No, sir.

Q. Did anyone connected with the company ever ask you what happened at those meetings of the C. I. O.?

A. I don't remember that they did, no.

Q. Specifically, did Mr. Kangas ever ask you?

A. On that one occasion he asked me about how many men was there, was about all that was said.

Q. That is on the occasion you have testified to previously? A. Yeah.

Q. When, Mr. Porter, did you first appear here in the Regional [84] office of the National Labor Relations Board to give testimony in connection with this case? A. I think it was——

Q. Let me correct that: To furnish information, I should say, with reference to this case?

A. The best I can remember is May 28th of 1942, this year.

Q. Prior to coming up here did you have a conversation with anyone connected with the company?

A. Yes, sir.

Q. With whom did you have such conversation?

A. With Roy Long.

Trial Examiner Whittemore: Who is Roy Long? May I ask?

The Witness: He is shop manager of the plant.

Q. (By Mr. Moore) Are you referring to a conversation, now, that occurred before you came down here? A. How was that, please?

(Testimony of Lewis Altenburg Porter.)

Q. Are you referring to a conversation, now, that occurred before you came down to the Board?

A. No, that was after I was down here.

Q. The question I asked you was: Did you have any conversation with anyone connected with the company before coming down here.

A. Yes, sir, the day before. I told the superintendent, Billy Kerns.

Q. The conversation was had with who? [85]

A. Billy Kerns, the superintendent.

Q. Is his name William Kerns?

A. William, I guess it is.

Mr. Moore: May it be stipulated William Kerns in May of 1942 was superintendent of the plant?

Mr. Watkins: Yes, and Roy Long is a foreman.

Mr. Moore: May it be further stipulated Roy Long is general foreman?

Mr. Watkins: Yes, that is correct.

Q. (By Mr. Moore) When did you say this conversation with Mr. Kerns was held?

A. The day before I came down here.

Q. At about what time?

A. Along in the afternoon.

Q. And where was it held?

A. At the machine where I was working.

Q. In the shop?   A. Yes, sir.

Q. Was anyone present other than you and he?

A. No, sir.

Q. What was said on that occasion?

A. I told him I had come down—was coming down, I had been subpoenaed to come down and ap-

(Testimony of Lewis Altenburg Porter.)

pear before the Labor Board and make a statement.

Q. Go ahead. [86]

A. So, he says, "I suppose you know what it's for." And he said, "Well," he says, "All you can do, Lou, is to tell what you know. Tell what you know."

Q. Was anything else said?

A. I asked him not to say anything to anybody else about it, and I know I didn't.

Q. Was anything else said?

A. Not that evening. So the next morning he came to me and he says, "Lou, what's this all about?" He says, "Half a dozen in the plant already asked me about you being at the Labor Board yesterday."

Q. Mr. Kerns said that?   A. Yes.

Q. On what occasion was that? You are referring now to a later conversation you had with Mr. Kerns, are you not?   A. The next day, yes.

Q. The first conversation you testified to was the day before you came here. Is that correct?

A. Yes.

Q. Now, the conversation you have just brought in, did that occur the same day you came down here or the day after?

A. No, that was the next morning after I was down here.

Q. Then it was two days after the first conversation?

A. Yes, it was two days after I had told them.

Q. Where did the conversation take place? [87]

(Testimony of Lewis Altenburg Porter.)

A.   At the plant, at the machine.

Q.   At about what time?

A.   Along about, oh, I would say 10:00 o'clock in the morning; maybe earlier.

Q.   Was anyone there other than you and he?

A.   No.

Q.   What was said on that occasion?

A.   Well, he just wanted to know. He said he hadn't told anybody. He says, "There's a half dozen already telling me," talking to him, rather, that I was down here before the Labor Board the day before.

Q.   Did you say anything then?

A.   I told him I knew I hadn't said anything to anybody, other than him.

Q.   Was that the entire conversation?

A.   Yes.

Q.   Thereafter, did you have a further conversation with anyone connected with the company?

A.   About coming down to the Board?

Q.   Well, with reference to coming down here, yes. Or, with reference to any subject.

Trial Examiner Whittemore: Now, wait a minute. Let us hold it to this one, first.

Mr. Moore: Well, I don't know——

Trial Examiner Whittemore: The point is he may get into [88] all sorts of conversations which have no bearing on this case. So long as we stick to the issues, I have no objection. You asked the witness to testify on any subject he may have had

(Testimony of Lewis Altenburg Porter.)
a conversation about. I think you will agree we are not interested in any conversation he may have had.

Q. (By Mr. Moore) Did you ever have a conversation with Mr. C. L. Mileman with reference to talking union in the shop?   A. Yes.

Q. When did that conversation take place?

A. That was the same evening that I was talking to Kerns.

Q. The first or second time?

A. The second trip when he was talking about so many fellows in the plant knowing I had been down here that time in the afternoon. A boy by the name of Smith came to me and told me that Mr. Mileman had authorized him to come to me and tell me to cut out talking union while on duty.

Mr. Watkins: May we know what Smith's name is?

Mr. Moore: Elmer Smith.

Q. (By Mr. Moore) Did you have a conversation with Mr. C. L. Mileman?

A. Yes, I went to him.

Mr. Moore: May it be stipulated Mr. C. L. Mileman is personnel manager of this West Coast plant?

Mr. Watkins: So stipulated.

Q. (By Mr. Moore) When did you have the conversation with Mr. [89] Mileman?

A. It was after 3:30 that same evening, that he had told Smith to have me pipe down on talking union.

Mr. Watkins: Read the answer, please.

(The answer was read.)

(Testimony of Lewis Altenburg Porter.)

Q. (By Mr. Moore)   Where did your conversation with Mr. Mileman take place?

A.   At the doorway right at his office.

Q.   You said it was shortly after 3:30?

A.   Yeah.

Q.   You went off the shift when?

A.   I went off at 3:30, and I went direct to him.

Q.   Were you sent for on that occasion or did you go voluntarily?

A.   No, I went voluntarily.   I wanted to explain to Mr. Mileman that I was not talking union on duty.

Q.   Was anyone else present other than you and he at the time?   A.   No, sir.

Q.   What was the conversation?

A.   Well, I told him that I understood through Mr. Smith that he wanted me to stop talking union, and I absolutely was not talking union during working hours.

Well, Mr. Mileman I think was honest in it.   He said he didn't really know.   He said the reports had came to him that I was talking union, and I denied it. [90]

Q.   Did he indicate what union he was referring to?

A.   No, he didn't come out and call any names.

Q.   He didn't say what union he referred to?

A.   No, he didn't call any names.

Q.   Had you, prior to that time, had any conversations during working hours about any union, with any employee?   A.   Before that?

(Testimony of Lewis Altenburg Porter.)

Q. Yes.

A. Sometime before that, I would say two or three weeks, I might have said a little something about the union, but I had quieted down. I hadn't said anything to anybody.

Q. For a two or three weeks period before that conversation you had not said anything about unions?   A. No, I never said anything.

Q. Later on, did you have any conversations with any other person connected with the company on that subject?   A. Yes, sir.

Q. When?

A. The next morning after I had talked to **Mr. Mileman**; that was Saturday morning.

Q. With whom was this conversation?

A. That was with Roy Long.

Q. Where did that take place?

A. In the plant.

Q. Where in the plant? [91]

A. Well, that was at the tool crib, I was up at the tool crib when I was talking with him.

Q. Was anyone else present other than you and Mr. Long?   A. Just he and I.

Q. What was said on that occasion?

A. Well, Roy looked at me and laughed, and he says, "Yeah, Louie," he says, "We have got plenty of reports that you are talking union, talking C. I. O. during working hours."

I just kind of laughed it off with him, and he says, "Yeah," he says, "One man says you talked

(Testimony of Lewis Altenburg Porter.)
to him forty-five minutes, and another man an hour and twenty minutes.''

I asked him, I says, ''All at one period, one time?''

He says, ''Yeah.''

I says, ''Where in the h—— were all your foremen, bosses, to let me stand and talk to one man an hour and twenty minutes away from the machine?''

So he said, ''Louie,'' he says, ''That won't sound good, will it.''

I just kind of laughed and went down to the machine and went to work.

So, in the afternoon he came back to me——

Q. Well, now, in the afternoon you had a further conversation with Roy Long?

A. With Roy Long, in the following afternoon. He came back to where I was working at the machine. [92]

Q. Was anyone else present other than you and he?   A. No.

Q. What was said on that occasion?

A. Well, he says, ''Louie,'' he says, ''Let's get along.''

I says, ''Sure; I am in for that.''

''But,'' he says, ''I don't think much of that d—— C.I.O.''

Q. He used ''d'' as a swear word? Is that what you mean?   A. Yeah.

Q. All right; continue.

(Testimony of Lewis Altenburg Porter.)

A. Well, I says, "Roy," I says, "Five or six million men can't all be wrong," and I says, "I am not hanging my neck out." I says, "You don't even see me wearing a C.I.O. pin," and I wasn't wearing it at that time, but I had belonged for some time.

"Well," he says, "Louie," he says, "When you put that C.I.O. button on you are hanging out your neck," and he says, "Somebody will take a crack at it."

Q. Is that all of the conversation?

A. That was all of it.

Q. You testified previously that you joined the C.I.O. in 1937 and that you attended a couple of meetings and then dropped it. Is that right?

A. Yeah.

Q. You said just a moment ago you had been a member for [93] some time. What did you mean by that?

A. Well, I joined them in—I joined them the first of April, I think, the last time.

Q. Of what year?   A. Of 1942.

Q. You joined the C.I.O. again?

A. Yeah, but I had never put on my C.I.O. button. But I did go home that night and put on my C.I.O. button and left it on.

Q. (By Mr. Moore) You mean the night after you talked to Roy Long?

A. After Roy Long talked to me.

Mr. Watkins: Mr. Examiner, I understand that Mr. Kangas is present in the room, and I would

(Testimony of Lewis Altenburg Porter.)
like to ask that he be excluded from the cross examination of this witness.

Trial Examiner Whittemore: That is a rather
unusual [94] request.

Mr. Watkins: I beg your pardon?

Trial Examiner Whittemore: It is a rather unusual request, it seems to me. What is your reason?

Mr. Watkins: Your Honor, I have asked that a
good many times, and I have not been refused.

Trial Examiner Whittemore: Mr. Kangas, so
far, has been identified as an official of the company.

Mr. Watkins: He is no longer with the company.

Mr. Moore: I will object to that request, for
the reason that at the time this happened he was
an official of the company.

Mr. Watkins: I feel the request is entirely reasonable, Mr. Examiner, and feel that it should **be**
granted, because this witness is no longer an employee of the company, and there have been a good
many alleged conversations between the two; and
I would like to ask permission be granted. As a matter of fact, I have never had the Board refuse a request of that kind before.

Trial Examiner Whittemore: I think you will
agree—do you recall any such a situation arising
before where you had asked a witness be excluded
that would presumably be your own witness?

Mr. Watkins: He won't be our own witness.

Mr. Moore: We are attacking his credibility before he [95] ever gets on the stand, if we do that.

(Testimony of Lewis Altenburg Porter.)

There have been a good many conversations alleged to have taken place with Mr. Livingston and we assume he is going to be of the other side, so, it is all right for him to remain. I frankly oppose the request.

Trial Examiner Whittemore: I frankly do not see, by any reason you have given me so far for excluding him——

Mr. Watkins: My point is: We have here two former employees of the company, and we find a peculiar linking of the two together, in the testimony so far given. I think we should be entitled to examine this witness without Mr. Kangas being present to hear the testimony of this witness.

Trial Examiner Whittemore: There is only one witness on the stand, so far, that I know of.

Mr. Watkins: Correct

Trial Examiner Whittemore: I do not see how it links up with any other testimony.

Mr. Watkins: Because this witness has testified to many of these instances linking it to Mr. Kangas. Mr. Kangas is no longer an employee of the company. He is not our witness. He is the Board's witness.

Trial Examiner Whittemore: I do not know he is anybody's witness. I am not responsible for anyone who may be in the courtroom. I do not know he is going to be called. Do you know? [96]

Mr. Watkins: No, I don't, but I assume he is, or he wouldn't be here, and we haven't called him.

(Testimony of Lewis Altenburg Porter.)

Trial Examiner Whittemore: I will deny your request.

Q. (By Mr. Baldwin) Mr. Porter, you stated you went down to a printing office and picked up some cards. Is that right? A. Yeah.

Q. Did you pay for those cards out of your own pocket? A. No, sir.

Q. Do you know where you got the money for that?

A. As I said before, I can't remember where I got that money. But I know I didn't get it out of my own pocket.

Q. Were you ever reimbursed by the PPWA for anything at all, for any monies you might have put out? A. Not that I remember of.

Q. Do you know the name of the organization, what it was, that was on those cards?

A. It was PPWA, Pacific Parts Workers Alliance.

Q. You stated some time later, possibly it was two days later, [97] that a name had been suggested for the organization. Is that right?

A. That's the best of my remembrance, yes.

Q. In other words, a name was suggested for the organization after the cards were printed?

A. I think they were, yes, sir. I wouldn't be positive.

Q. But you don't know where you got the money to pay for the cards?

A. No, I ain't going to say, for I don't remember.

(Testimony of Lewis Altenburg Porter.)

Q. And you were never reimbursed from the PMPWA for anything you put out of your own pocket?

A. That's the best of my memory, yes.

Mr. Baldwin: That is all.

Cross Examination

Q. (By Mr. Watkins) Mr. Porter, where did you work before you worked for Jadson Products?

A. It was on the police force.

Q. Where?   A. Vernon.

Q. How many years were you on that?

A. Oh, a year or so.

Q. Where before that did you work?

A. Huntington Park.

Q. What did you do there?

A. Police force. [98]

Q. How long were you on the Huntington Park police force?   A. About two years.

Q. Where before that were you working?

A. I think I was working for myself then, cement work.

Q. Where?

A. In and around Huntington Park.

Q. Weren't you on the police force or doing some private detective work in Kansas?

A. No.

Q. Did you ever live in Kansas?

A. No, sir.

Q. Did you ever live in Missouri?

A. I have lived in Missouri.

Q. Near Kansas City?   A. Yes.

(Testimony of Lewis Altenburg Porter.)

Q. Did you do any private detective work there? You have done some private detective work, haven't you?   A. No, sir, I have not.

Q. Your work has been police work?

A. Yes.

Q. And only for the two cities you mentioned, Vernon and Huntington Park?

A. Never did any detective work in my life.

A. You know Mr. Matthews of the Bureau of Investigation, do you not? [99]   A. Yes.

Mr. Moore: What Bureau of Investigation?

Mr. Watkins: The Federal Bureau of Investigation, Mr. Moore.

Q. (By Mr. Watkins) Mr. Porter, calling your attention now to the time of your first conversation with Mr. Ray Livingston, which was at your machine, I believe you testified, sometime in the latter part of July or August of 1937, what was the condition in the plant prior to that time, so far as the men were concerned?

A. Oh, I don't know. I wasn't questioning them any. I don't know what the condition was.

Q. You didn't question them? You don't know what they were thinking or talking about?

A. No.

Q. You do not remember any conversations about better wages, better working conditions?

A. Oh, there might have been something said about that. I wouldn't say yes or no.

Q. Do you recall anything of that kind?

A. No.

(Testimony of Lewis Altenburg Porter.)

Q. Or anything about favoritism in the plant?

A. No, I don't think so.

Q. Do you recall any statements of any kind by anyone, or any conversations about Thompson Products buying out the business, [100] and perhaps going to close it?

A. I don't know that I knew that they bought it at that time.

Q. What is your answer to my question? Did you hear any conversation of that character around that period?

A. No, I don't think so. I don't remember.

Q. All right. Now, when you first saw Mr. Livingston you were working at your machine. Is that correct?   A. Yes.

Q. And he came along past your machine?

A. Yes.

Q. Had you seen him at all prior to the time he came and said something to you?

A. I don't believe I had, no. I don't think I had.

Q. Did you know who he was?

A. Not up until then, I don't think.

Q. Did he tell you who he was?   A. Yes.

Q. Had you seen him talking to any of the other men around the shop prior to the time he talked to you?   A. No.

Q. Did you see him talk to any other men around the shop after the time he talked to you, the same day?   A. No, sir.

(Testimony of Lewis Altenburg Porter.)

Q. Did you notice where he went after he left you? **[101]**

A. No, any more than just go on through the plant. I don't know where he went to; paid no attention to it.

Q. Precisely what was his conversation with you, and this is the latter part of July or the early part of August of 1937, while you were at your machine and he came up with you? Who started the conversation?   A. Mr. Livingston.

Q. What did he say?

A. He told me where he was from.

Q. What did he say to you?

A. As to that I just don't remember, how it came up.

Q. You don't recall what he said?

A. No. He said he was from the Cleveland plant.

Q. Did he say, "My name is Ray Livingston?"

A. I wouldn't say whether he did or not.

Q. You don't remember what he said to you, then, first, when he talked to you?

A. Not everything, no.

Q. What do you remember as the first thing he said to you?

A. Oh, we talked about the machinery in our plant and the machinery in their plant. It was similar, or to the effect.

Q. Who started this conversation?

A. Mr. Livingston.

Q. What did he say about it? "How is your

(Testimony of Lewis Altenburg Porter.)
machinery working? Is it satisfactory to you?"

[102]

A. I can't repeat it.

Q. You haven't any recollection as to what he said with respect to the machinery?

Mr. Moore: Objected to. He just testified he couldn't remember.

Mr. Watkins: Mr. Examiner, I submit this is cross examination.

Mr. Moore: This is argumentative.

Mr. Watkins: Mr. Examiner, this witness has very positive recollection about certain facts, and none whatever about others. I am trying to probe his memory.

Trial Examiner Whittemore: I think if you will recall his answers, you will agree he has already testified as to some matters with respect to this.

Q. (By Mr. Watkins) Do you recall anything about his conversation, that is, Mr. Livingston's conversation with you this first time, besides something about machinery back in Cleveland and machinery in the plant?

A. I do remember his saying our machinery was similar to their machinery. That is about all I can remember.

Q. Was that the entire conversation at that time?

A. Possibly some other things were said, but I can't repeat them.

Q. Was anything said on any subject besides machinery?   A. No, sir. [103]

(Testimony of Lewis Altenburg Porter.)

Q. All right. Now, then, going to the first meeting you testified to at the Jonathan Club, will you tell me, as nearly as you can recall, what date that occurred?

A. No, I can't give you the dates.

Q. When was it with respect to the time when 15 or 18 employees called on the management?

A. That was on the Tuesday following the day that I was down at the Jonathan Club, I believe.

Q. Did you testify you were down at the Jonathan Club on a Saturday?

A. That is my memory now, that I was down there Saturday.

Q. Are you certain of it?

A. No, sir. I told you in many instances I wasn't positive of the dates.

Q. All right. Let us go on to your meeting at the Jonathan Club. What was the first thing that was said when you went in? How did you get up to the room? How did you know where he was?

A. I was told what room he was in.

Q. By whom?   A. By Mr. Kangas.

Q. What did he tell you?

A. Well, I don't know the room, now; it was on the fourth floor.

Q. Did he tell you the room number you were to go to at the [104] Jonathan Club?

A. Yes.

(Testimony of Lewis Altenburg Porter.)

Q. When you went to the Jonathan Club, what did you do when you first got in there?

A. Oh, about the first thing that was said, Mr. Dachtler wanted to know if I knew what I was down there for.

Q. What was the first thing said by anybody when you·came in?

A. I think that was the first thing.

Q. Did anybody say, "Hello, Porter?"

A. Naturally they said that.

Q. Did somebody say, "Hello, Lou?" Or, "Hello, Mr. Porter?"

·A. I don't remember; possibly they would have said it.

Q. Then Mr. Dachtler was the first one that made any sentence to you of any kind? Is that correct?   A. Yes.

·Q. What did he say?

A. He wanted to know if I knew what I was down there for.

Q. What did you say?

A. I told him I thought I did.

Q. What did he say?

A. Well, that was all he had to say.

Q. All right. Did he say anything else during this entire conversation, Mr. Dachtler?

A. Well, he might have, possibly did, before the evening was over. [105]

Q. What was the next thing said by anybody?

A. Mr. Livingston wanted to know of me if I was ready to shoot.

(Testimony of Lewis Altenburg Porter.)

Q. Is that what he said?

A. Exactly the words.

Q. What did you say?

A. I told him: Yeah.

Q. You told him what?

A. I told him: Yes, sir.

Q. You didn't say anything to him about having observed him and you thought he was a man you could depend on, did you?

A. Not that I remember.

Q. Go ahead. What did he say after you said, "Yes, sir, I am ready to shoot?"

A. He then told me just exactly what I said a bit ago: He wanted me to go among the boys in the plant and get them to come into the office with me, and I would be the spokesman for them, and ask for an independent union, vacation with pay, a little more money, and better working conditions.

Q. He outlined the things you were to ask, did he?   A. He done it.

Q. That was: Vacations with pay, more wages and better working conditions?

A. Yes, sir. [106]

Q. Anything else?

A. Well, he said I was good for a lifetime job.

Q. Just a minute. Was there anything else he suggested you ask for?

A. If he did I don't recall it right now.

(Testimony of Lewis Altenburg Porter.)

Q. He might have said something about seniority in there too?   A. Could have, yeah.

Q. You don't remember?

A. I ain't going to say, for I don't remember all of them.

Q. What was the next thing he told you? I will withdraw that question, please.

When he said that to you, that is, that you were to get some of the boys and bring them in and ask for these things, what did you say?

A. What did I say?

Q. Yes.

A. I told him I would, or I would try.

Q. That was all? Did you say: "Where do I come out on this," or anything of that kind?

A. No.

Q. Then what did he say to you?

A. Well, he said I would get a lifetime job with top pay, two weeks vacation, and some money.

Q. For doing what?

A. For helping put this union in. [107]

Q. Did he ask you to do anything besides what you have already stated there, that is, to bring the men into the office and ask for certain things?

A. Oh, he might have. I ain't going to say right now. I don't remember.

Q. In other words, for having the men come into his office and request an independent union, better working conditions, and increase in pay, he was going to give you a lifetime job at top salary,

(Testimony of Lewis Altenburg Porter.)

and a vacation. Is that correct? Was that all he was going to give you?

A. I was going to get some money. I can't remember how much it was.

Q. Was that discussed, how much it was?

A. Well, I don't remember how much I was going to get, but it was spoken of, yeah.

Q. Do you remember what amount it was, or who spoke of it?

A. No, I don't remember what amount it was.

Q. And you were going to get that in addition to the lifetime job at top pay and the vacations; is that right?   A. Yes, sir.

Q. Did you ask him what top pay was?

A. No.

Q. Did you ask him if they were going to put that in writing, or anything of that kind?

A. No, sir. [108]

Q. What did you say?

A. I told him I didn't care to work all my life.

Q. Was that your answer to what they had said to you?

A. That is the way I answered them. I didn't care about a lifetime job for I didn't want to have to work all my life.

Q. Then what did they say? Any of them.

A. I don't know if they said anything or not.

Q. Was that the end of the conversation then?

A. I don't know that there was a great deal said after that.

(Testimony of Lewis Altenburg Porter.)

Q. Mr. Porter, when you left that meeting, or, when you were there at that meeting, what was your understanding of what you were supposed to do, and what was your understanding of what you were supposed to get for it?

A. What I was supposed to do?

Q. Yes.

A. I was to get around among these men, have them come into the office, tell the management what we was in there for, what we wanted; which I did.

Q. That was all you were supposed to do. Is that correct?   A. So far as I know.

Q. So far as you knew that was all you were supposed to do?   A. Yes.

Q. What were you supposed to get for doing that?

A. Vacation, lifetime job, and some money.

Q. But you didn't want the lifetime job? [109]

A. Didn't care anything about that.

Q. And you told them that?   A. Yes.

Q. So the lifetime job is out. How much vacation were you supposed to get?

A. Two weeks.

Q. Did they tell you that?   A. Yes.

Q. Did they tell you at what pay?

A. My pay was to go on, naturally, yes.

Q. The pay you were getting at that time?

A. Yes.

Q. Did they tell you at what wages you were to continue to work there?   A. No.

(Testimony of Lewis Altenburg Porter.)

Q. That wasn't even discussed?

A. I don't think so.

Q. In other words, for doing that, what you were to get was: Two weeks vacation with pay you were getting. That as the sum and substance of it, wasn't it?

A. That's the way I looked at it. I wasn't thinking much about it.

Q. What about this money you were to get some other time? When did you expect to get that?

A. That wasn't stated when I would get it.

[110]

Q. When did you expect to get it?

A. Didn't know.

Q. Did you ask them?

A. I don't think I ever asked anybody for it at all.

Q. You didn't discuss that at all. You just let that go by the board?   A. Yes.

Q. Mr. Porter, you said you first came to the National Labor Relations Board in April, I believe, of 1942, this year. Is that correct?

A. Yeah.

Q. And I think you testified it was by subpoena. Is that correct?

A. Yeah. I got a wire to come down.

Q. Oh, you got a wire to come down to the Board?   A. Yeah.

Q. And you hadn't had any discussion by telephone or otherwise with anybody from the Board

(Testimony of Lewis Altenburg Porter.)

prior to that time concerning the facts you have testified to?   A. No.

Q. When did you have your first discussion about those facts with the union, that is, the C. I. O., the charging union here?

A. I don't know just what date it was.

Q. How long before you came to the Board?

Mr. Moore: I object to that as immaterial. [111]

The Witness: That I don't remember.

Trial Examiner Whittemore: Let the answer remain.

Q. (By Mr. Watkins) How recently have you discussed the facts in this case with Mr. Victor Kangas?   A. Very very little.

Q. How recently?

A. Oh, a couple of weeks ago.

Q. About two weeks ago? Just once or more than once?   A. One time.

Mr. Moore: I will stipulate that I was present at that discussion, if you care to.

Q. (By Mr. Watkins) Mr. Porter, after this first meeting you have testified to at the Jonathan Club, what did you do to carry out your mission that you had then? What was your first step?

A. To see the boys in the plant was supposed to be about the first.

Q. When did you start doing that? The following Monday, was it?

A. Could have been the following Monday, I won't be positive in the dates; never have been; never bind myself to the dates.

(Testimony of Lewis Altenburg Porter.)

Q. As soon as you could get around to it. Right?

A. Yes.

Q. Did you think at that time that an independent union ought to be organized at the plant?

[112]

A. Oh, I hadn't given it much thought.

Q. You had belonged to the C. I. O., had you not?   A. Yeah.

Q. You got some others to belong to the C. I. O., didn't you?   A. I might have. I don't know.

Q. I mean prior to that time. You got some others to join the C. I. O. too, isn't that true?

A. I don't remember.

Q. And you discussed that with Mr. Kangas also, didn't you?

A. That I was to get new members?

Q. That you were getting members for the C. I. O. in the plant.   A. I don't think so.

Q. You don't recall?   A. No.

Q. What about the A. F. of L.? It had been organizing also there, hadn't it?

A. Never heard or seen the A. F. of L., that I know of.

Q. You didn't know that any of the men had ever belonged to the A. F. of L. in the plant **prior** to that time?   A. No.

Q. When you went to the men, carrying out your mission for Mr. Livingston, who was the first man you contacted? Do you remember?

A. No, I don't. [113]

(Testimony of Lewis Altenburg Porter.)

Q. All right. Tell me what you said to any particular individual that you contacted following that. Tell me who he was; where you talked to him; what you said to him.

A. I don't remember now. That's a good while off.

Mr. Watkins: Read the question.

(The question was read.)

The Witness: I can't remember what I said to him.

Q. (By Mr. Watkins) You have no recollection of what you said to any of the men in the plant after your meeting with Mr. Livingston, or when you were to bring them in the offiee?

A. No, I don't recall.

Q. Did you tell any of the men about your meeting with Mr. Livingston?

A. About what?

Q. About your meeting with Mr. Livingston, what he had offered you?   A. No.

Q. You didn't mention that to any men in the plant?   A. Not at that time, no.

Q. What did you say to them?

A. Well, no more than I told them we ought to have a little more money; we ought to have a vacation and a union of our own.

Q. You stated a union of your own?

A. Yes.

Q. You stated that to them, did you? [114]

A. Something to that effect.

(Testimony of Lewis Altenburg Porter.)

Q. Did you believe that? That you should have a union of your own down there?

A. I don't know. I might have at that time.

Q. Were you fostering that, then, just because Mr. Livingston had offered you this money?

A. No, I don't think so.

Q. Why were you?

A. Well, probably the plant might close.

Q. All right. What do you mean by that: Probably the plant might close?

A. It had been rumored there that the plant might close.

Q. Rumored by whom?

A. Well, I think the first man that talked to me about that was that inspector, Hodges.

Q. Mr. Hodges? A. Hodges.

Q. What did he say to you?

A. I think he said if we didn't keep it out— put the union in, that they would close and move away.

Q. If you didn't put the independent union in it would close and move away? A. Yes.

Q. When did Mr. Hodges make that statement to you? A. Oh, I can't remember the dates.

[115]

Q. When was it with respect to when you talked to Mr. Livingston? Before or after, or when?

A. I think after.

Q. How long after?

A. Probably a day or two.

Q. Was it before you had had your meeting

(Testimony of Lewis Altenburg Porter.)

with the 15 or 18 men who walked in and talked to the management?

A. I don't know whether it was before or after.

Q. Where were you when that statement was made?   A. At the plant.

Q. Where?

A. In the operating department.

Q. Who was there?

A. Just the two of us.

Q. Who started the conversation?

A. Hodges.

Q. What did he say?

A. Well, he just stated that if we didn't organize and put a union in there they would close and move to Cleveland, possibly.

Q. If you didn't organize and put a union in there, they would close and move to Cleveland, possibly? Was that the reason why you went after the organization of the independent?

A. Might have been.

Q. Was it? [116]

A. I ain't going to say. I don't know now.

Q. I notice you have lost a finger. Did you lose that working at Thompson Products or at Jadson?

 · A. No, I lost that before.

Q. Didn't you have an injury to your hand while you were working there?   A. Yeah.

Q. When did that occur?

A. Oh, a couple of years ago; a little more.

Q. Can you tell us more precisely what date that occurred?

(Testimony of Lewis Altenburg Porter.)

A. No, I think it was sometime in the spring, two years ago.

Q. Can you fix that with any more assurance than that? A. How?

Q. Can you fix it with any more certainty than that, when you lost your finger, or had it injured?

A. It has been over two years ago.

Q. Wasn't it in 1937?

A. No, that was—I think it was along in May, two years ago past.

Q. Well, now, let me ask you this: Wasn't the injury to your finger, didn't that happen very shortly before you received the two weeks vacation? A. Oh, no. This was away after.

Q. Did you receive a vacation about the time you injured your finger? [117]

A. Yes, sir. I was told, yes.

Q. Beg pardon?

A. Sure. I was told, when I got it hurt.

Q. Yes; but you were going on a vacation.

A. Wasn't out of town.

Q. And you are sure it wasn't back in 1937 when this occurred? A. No, it wasn't then.

Q. What was that?

A. I was just speaking to the lady. It was in May of 1939 or 1940. It has been about two years ago.

Q. Mr. Porter, prior to this meeting at the Jonathan Club with Mr. Livingston, did you talk to Mr. Livingston on the telephone?

(Testimony of Lewis Altenburg Porter.)

A. I don't remember of talking to him.

Q. Would you say that you did not?

A. I wouldn't say that I did or didn't. I don't remember.

Q. In the past six months have you talked to Mr. Hileman on the telephone at night from your home?   A. No, sir.

Q. Have you called him and asked him to meet with you?   A. No.

Q. Mr. Long?   A. No.

Q. Any other official down at the Thompson Products plant? [118]   A. No.

Q. You haven't called any of them during this past six months and asked them to meet with you any place?

A. Oh, I think I talked to Mr. Millman on the telephone, but not Hileman.

Q. How long ago?

A. Oh, two or three months ago.

Q. Yes. Anybody else?   A. No.

Q. You have testified previously at the present time—you understand you are under oath, don't you?   A. Yes.

Q. You understand you are testifying that previous to the present time, during the past year, you haven't called any officials of the Thompson Products and told them you had something confidential you wanted to talk to them about?

A. Not to my memory.

Q. Would you say positively you have not? I am talking about the past year.

(Testimony of Lewis Altenburg Porter.)

A. I wouldn't say positively to anything like that because I don't remember.

Q. You might have, and you might have done it more than once. Is that correct?

A. I know I did call Mr. Millman.

Q. Yes. But he is the only one you have any recollection of [119] calling?   A. Yes.

Q. Is the same answer true four, five years, that you don't remember calling anybody in the plant—

A. Don't remember.

Q. ——any of the officials of the plant and telling them you had something: "Way down under" you wanted to discuss with them, away from the plant?   A. No.

Q. During these five years you haven't had any conversation except with Mr. Millman?

A. Just had the one conversation with him.

Q. You are positive you did not have? What is your answer? You don't remember whether you did or not?

A. I don't remember ever talking to anybody else, no, sir.

Q. All right. Would your answer be the same if I asked you if you tried to reach them by telephone with a message that you had something very confidential you wanted to talk to them about?

A. I don't remember now.

Q. You don't remember anything of that kind either?   A. No.

Q. Now, I am correct, am I, Mr. Porter, in this: That when you talked to the men to try to

(Testimony of Lewis Altenburg Porter.)

get them to form this independent, as you have testified, you didn't mention to any of [120] them that Mr. Livingston had talked to you about doing it?

A. I don't think I ever talked to anybody to that effect, no.

Q. You didn't mention that to any of the men at all?   A. No.

Q. How many meetings of the Alliance did you attend?

A. Oh, I would say not over two or three altogether.

Q. Do you remember which ones those were? Were they early in the game, or late in it, or what?

A. One of them was fairly early, and then I don't remember the other.

Q. I understood you to say awhile ago, Mr. Porter, that you had tried to get the independent in for one or two reasons. One was because Mr. Hodges had made a certain statement to you that unless the independent came in the plant would be closed; the other was because Mr. Livingston had made this deal with you. Is that correct?

A. I would say that, yes.

Q. All right. Now, you attended the first meeting, I believe you testified, of the group down there at some electrical shop, wasn't it?

A. Yeah, I think so.

Q. That was their organizational meeting, the start of it?   A. Yes.

(Testimony of Lewis Altenburg Porter.)

Q. And you took no active part in it, did you?

[121]

A. No.

Q. I believe you testified awhile ago you had no interest. Is that correct? In other words, despite the fact that you had been offered a proposition by Mr. Livingston of a lifetime employment at top pay, vacation with pay, better hours, and some money on top of it, you took no interest whatever in that meeting?

A. No, I wasn't even interested in the money or vacation, to tell the truth about it.

Q. You weren't interested in that?

A. No.

Q. Let us put it this way: Despite the fact that you had been told by Mr. Hodges that if an independent wasn't formed, the plant would be closed, you didn't take any interest in the organization meeting. Is that correct?

A. I wasn't interested in it.

Q. Then the answer to my question is "Yes"?

A. Yes.

Mr. Moore: One moment. May I have the last question read.

(The question was read.)

Q. (By Mr. Watkins) Going back to a time prior to the first meeting at the Jonathan Club with Mr. Livingston, I believe you said that you had some conversation concerning that with Mr. Victor Kangas. Is that correct? [122]   A. Yes.

(Testimony of Lewis Altenburg Porter.)

Q. When did that conversation take place?

A. Well, I don't just remember when it did take place now.

Q. Was it while you were at work?

A. Yes, it was in the shop, yes, sir.

Q. During working hours?   A. Yes.

Q. And what did Mr. Kangas do? Come up and say something to you about it? How did it start?   A. Possibly did, yes.

Q. All right. How did it start? What did he say to you?

A. Well, that's a long time off. I can't remember just how it started.

Q. You remember some of the exact words, Mr. Livingston said, or that Mr. Dachtler said, didn't you? Don't you remember what Mr. Kangas said to you?   A. No, I don't, now.

Q. What did he say to you then, that indicated you were to go some place in the Jonathan Club?

A. He said Mr. Livingston wanted to see me down there.

Q. Did he say what about?

A. I believe Victor said something or other about a union.

Q. All right. Let us find out what he said.

A. I can't repeat what he said.

Q. You haven't any recollection of whether he was trying [123] to get the C. I. O. or A. F. of L. or the independent?

A. No, I don't think he said. I can't remember.

(Testimony of Lewis Altenburg Porter.)

Q. He said something about a union. That's what he wanted to see you about?   A. Yes.

Q. Do you remember anything else said to you at that time?   A. No, sir.

Q. Did he tell you they would make a deal if you helped out?   A. No.

Q. Did he tell you how long you would be down there?   A. No.

Q. Did you ask him whether or not you would be paid for going down there?   A. No, sir.

Q. Did he say anything about working conditions in the plant?   A. No.

Q. You are positive of the fact that there was no conversation except that he wanted you to go down and meet Mr. Livingston at the Jonathan Club?   A. Yes.

Q. He told you the number of·the room to get him at, did he?   A. Yes.

Q. Did he write it down on a piece of paper?

A. No, I don't think he did. [124]

Q. Did you just remember it?   A. Yes.

Q. And you went to that room that night. And that is all the knowledge you had prior to the time you stepped into the room with Mr. Livingston as to the purpose of the meeting? Is that correct? What you have just related?   A. Yes.

Q. You related an incident where Mr. Kangas had picked you up in his car and had taken you to a print shop. Do you remember that?

A. Yeah, yes, sir.

(Testimony of Lewis Altenburg Porter.)

Q. You stopped some place on the way so he could telephone. Is that correct?

A. No. He telephoned at the print shop.

Q. Oh, he telephoned from the print shop?

A. Yes.

Q. Were you alongside of him when he telephoned?   A. Yes, sir.

Q. What did he say?

A. Oh, I don't know what he said, any more than he just wrote down what somebody was giving him over the telephone.

Q. When he picked up the phone and rang somebody, did he say: I want to talk to some certain person?

A. I don't remember as he did.

Q. You don't remember anything about his end of the telephone [125] conversation?

A. No. All I know: he called somebody.

Q. Did he make any comment of any kind after his telephone conversation as to what he had talked about?   A. No, he had it wrote down.

Q. Did he tell you what it was he wrote down there?   A. It was for the cards, yes.

Q. Is that what he told you?   A. Yes.

Q. What did he say? That is Vic Kangas, isn't it?   A. How?

Q. That is Vic Kangas?   A. Yes, sir.

Q. What did he say?

A. Just said that was for the cards to be printed. I don't know where he got it and didn't ask him.

Q. You don't know where he got it?

(Testimony of Lewis Altenburg Porter.)

A. Only on the telephone.

Q. Do you know where he got it or not?

A. I know he wrote it down. I heard him talking over the telephone and seen him write it down.

Q. You heard him talking on the telephone and you haven't any recollection of anything he said on the telephone?

A. Just what was on the cards, is all.

Q. But you do not have and recollection of anything he said [126] while he was on the telephone?

A. No.

Q. Did you see him writing something while he was talking on the phone?   A. Yes, sir.

Q. Is that what he handed you, what you saw him writing there?   A. Yes.

Q. What did he say to you when he handed it to you?

A. Well, I ain't going to be right positive he handed it to me. He could have handed it to the print man.

Q. Oh, I see. He might have handed it to the print man and not you at all?

A. I won't say what hands it went through.

Q. You saw him give it to the print man, or you gave it to him?

A. I don't remember how it got to him, but I seen him write it down.

Q. You are not sure what happened to it after it was written down?   A. No.

Q. Who was it told you to go get the cards the following Tuesday?

(Testimony of Lewis Altenburg Porter.)

A. Hodges, I am positive.

Q. Is that the same Mr. Hodges you testified to awhile ago?   A. Yes, sir. [127]

Q. What did he say to you?

A. To go get them.

Q. Get what?   A. The cards.

Q. Did you know what he was talking about?

A. Did I know?

Q. Yes.   A. Yes.

Q. How did you know what he was talking about?

A. Well, he told me the cards we had printed the day before.

Q. The cards who had printed the day before?

A. Vic and I.

Q. He knew Vic and you had gone over and had the cards printed?

A. So far as I know he did.

Q. That's what he said? To go and get the cards Vic and you had had printed the day before?

A. To the best of my memory.

Q. And he gave you some money, did he?

A. No, I wouldn't say who gave me that money.

Q. Do you remember whether you said to him: Who is going to pay for this?

A. No, I didn't ask him that.

Q. You didn't ask him that?

A. No, not as I remember. [128]

Q. I believe you left at 11:00 o'clock to go over and get these cards, on Tuesday morning. Right?

A. I don't know what time.

Q. I think that is what you testified.

(Testimony of Lewis Altenburg Porter.)

A.   Sometime in the morning.

Q.   Did you have time clocks down there at that time?   A.   Yes.

Q.   Did you punch out?   A.   No.

Q.   How did you become absent without punching out your time card?

A.   It was my memory I didn't punch out or in.

Q.   Do you remember how you got excused from that?

A.   No. Could have punched out, you understand, and I could not have punched out. I don't remember.

Q.   If you punched out you would lose time for it, wouldn't you?

A.   I would if I punched out, but I don't remember.

Q.   Do you ever remember anybody reimbursing you in any way for any time you lost, if you lost time?   A.   No, I don't.

Q.   You didn't discuss your absence that morning with anybody there other than Hodges, who told you to go get them?

A.   That is my memory, no.

Q.   No discussion. Was there a personnel man there at the [129] time?   A.   No.

Q.   Was Mr. Cameron there at that time?

A.   I don't know whether he was or not.

Q.   Did they have a personnel man there at that time?   A.   I don't know that.

Q.   You didn't talk to a personnel man about your leaving, then?   A.   No.

(Testimony of Lewis Altenburg Porter.)

Q. At this meeting with the management where 15 to 18 men were present, which I believe you fixed on a Tuesday, that is the same day on which you picked up the cards, will you tell me what was the first thing that was said by anybody when you 15 or 18 men walked into that office?

A. No, I don't know just how it did start.

Q. You don't remember anything about the start of the conversation?

A. Don't know how it started now, no, sir.

Q. You had 15 or 18 men barging into the management; was anything said like: What are you fellows coming in here for? Or anything of that kind?   A. Might have been; I couldn't say.

Q. Do you have any recollection of any conversation at that meeting?   A. Oh, yes. [130]

Q. All right. What was said? Who said it, and what was said?

A. I know I asked them for a little more money and an independent union and vacations with pay, various things.

Q. Did anybody talk besides you, from your side?   A. I don't remember if they did.

Q. Would you say no one else did?

A. I wouldn't say positively, no, sir.

Q. What did the management say, anybody from the management?

A. Well, Mr. Dachtler spoke up and said he was perfectly in favor.

Q. Of what?

A. Of giving us an opportunity to put a union

(Testimony of Lewis Altenburg Porter.)

in there and they would possibly give us a little more money and maybe vacations with pay. All we asked for, they was going to consider it.

Q. They were going to consider it. They didn't say they would give it to you?

A. Later on, then, they agreed to it.

Q. Wait a minute. I mean at this meeting, did they say they would give it to you or consider it?

A. At that meeting they agreed to.

Q. At that meeting they agreed to give you these things?

A. That is the best of my memory, now, that they agreed to come to some understanding, I don't know just what. **[131]**

Q. What?

A. I don't know just how far we went into it, but——

Q. Well, you were talking about certain things. You were talking about vacations with pay. Did they say they would give you vacations with pay then?

A. I don't know whether they came right out and said they would, or whether it would be discussed, or whether they was in favor of it. As to that I can't remember.

Q. You wanted shorter working hours, didn't you, at that time? You mentioned that?

A. I don't know.

Q. Do you remember any discussion with the management of shorter working hours, or what they thought about that?

(Testimony of Lewis Altenburg Porter.)

A.   We were only working eight hours.

Q.   You had a long week, didn't you? Thirty-seven?

A.   I think we was working Saturday mornings then.

Q.   What about the increase in pay? Was there any discussion of how much increase in pay?

A.   I don't remember.

Q.   In other words, you can't say positively, Mr. Porter, what the management did say to you when you gentlemen went in there and you, as the ringleader, said to them: We want an independent union; we want higher wages; we want vacations with pay; we want better working conditions. You don't remember what they said to you? [132]

Mr. Moore: I object to that as argumentative, and also not descriptive of what the witness said.

The Witness: How?

Trial Examiner Whittemore: I will sustain the objection.

The Witness: Pardon me.

Q.   (By Mr. Watkins): You never held any office in the Alliance, did you?   A.   No, sir.

Q.   You never were on any committee?

A.   No, sir.

Mr. Watkins: I would like to take a few minutes recess, if I may.

Trial Examiner Whittemore: All right. We will take a five minute recess.

Mr. Watkins: Thank you.

        (A short recess.)

(Testimony of Lewis Altenburg Porter.)

Trial Examiner Whittemore: Will the witness take the stand, please.

Q. (By Mr. Watkins): Mr. Porter, going back to the first conversation you had with Mr. Livingston at your machine: After that conversation did any of the other men in the plant come up to you and ask you what Mr. Livingston talked to you about?

A. I don't remember of any of them, no; might have been. I wouldn't say. Don't remember. [133]

Q. Wasn't it usual when one of the head men from back East came and talked to one of the men only, for the other men to come and find out what it was all about?

Mr. Moore: I object to the question.

Trial Examiner Whittemore: If he knows.

The Witness: I don't remember.

Q. (By Mr. Watkins): You don't have any recollection of anyone asking you what it was all about? A. I don't recollect, no.

Q. As to the men you contacted to go in and meet with the management at this first meeting that had 15 or 18 men there, whom did you contact?

A. The best I remember I gave them to Hodges; Hodges gave the cards out.

Mr. Watkins: No. May I have that answer stricken as non-responsive, and ask that the question be read. I think I am responsible for the confused answer.

Trial Examiner Whittemore: The answer may be stricken. Read the question.

(Testimony of Lewis Altenburg Porter.)

(The question was read.)

The Witness: I think the cards was handed to Mr. Hodges.

Mr. Watkins: Strike the question. I will reframe it.

Q. (By Mr. Watkins): Mr. Porter, I will direct your attention to the meeting which a group of 15 or 18 men had with the management. [134]

A. Yes.

Q. Toward the end of July of 1937; prior to those 15 or 18 men going in there you testified you talked to some of the men to get them to go in there. To whom did you talk?

A. Well, I talked to George and Ed Fickle, Stubblefield, Bebb; I can't recall all of their names now.

Q. That is all you can recall at the present time?

A. Right now, yes.

Q. But you say you were responsible for getting all of the 15 or 18 men in there? Or did some of those to whom you talked bring others with them?

A. They possibly did. I didn't talk to all 15 or 18.

Q. What did you say to those men you talked to about it?

A. I told them we were going to try to get a union in there.

Q. What else?

A. To get a pay raise, and vacations.

(Testimony of Lewis Altenburg Porter.)

Q. Is that all?

A. Better working conditions.

Q. Did you tell them why you wanted to go in and talk to the management about it?

A. I don't know. I can't recall I did.

Q. Why did you want to go there and talk to the management about it?

A. Because I was told to.

Q. By whom? [135]

A. By Mr. Livingston.

Q. In other words, he told you to bring a group of men in there. Is that correct?   A. Yes.

Q. Were you one of the leaders there in the plant? I mean among the men, not a lead off man, but were you one of the popular men in the plant there at that time?

A. Oh, I wouldn't say I was so popular, no.

Q. You have had some little conflict with some of the men, haven't you, since you have been working there?   A. Not particularly, no.

Q. Don't you usually stay pretty much to yourself down at the plant, so far as your social contacts are concerned?

Mr. Moore: Objected to as not showing the time; also as being immaterial.

Trial Examiner Whittemore: I will permit the witness to answer.

Mr. Moore: I don't believe the witness understood.

Trial Examiner Whittemore: You may answer

(Testimony of Lewis Altenburg Porter.)
the question. I assume you mean at that time, don't you?

Mr. Watkins: Yes, that is correct.

The Witness: At that time?

Q. (By Mr. Watkins): Yes.

A. I done what, you say?

Q. Didn't you have some conflict? Didn't you keep pretty [136] much to yourself down at the plant around that time?

Trial Examiner Whittemore: What do you mean? Which? Both conflict, and keeping to himself?

Mr. Watkins: Strike the question.

Q. (By Mr. Watkins): Let us take the time around which you brought, or alleged you were responsible for bringing into the management some 15 or 18 men. At that time hadn't you kept very much to yourself there in the plant, socially?

A. Oh, I don't know. I may be a little distant at all times. I wouldn't say any more then than I am now.

Q. What did you do with these cards after you got them from the printers? Those application cards for the independent?

A. I gave them to Hodges.

Q. You gave them to Hodges?

A. The best I remember, I think I gave him the pack.

Q. Do you know what he did with them?

A. No, I don't know whose hands they went to from there.

(Testimony of Lewis Altenburg Porter.)

Q. Did he give any of them to you and ask you to pass them out?

A. I passed out a few, but I don't know where I got them, from him or the other boys. I know I got some.

Q. How many would you say you passed out?

A. Oh, half a dozen.

Q. Do you remember to whom you passed them out? [137]   A. No, I don't.

Q. I believe you testified to having a second meeting at the Jonathan Club. Is that correct?

A. Yes, sir.

Q. Will you tell me how you got the word to be at that meeting?

A. Vic Kangas, he told me to be down there that evening.

Q. What did he tell you?

A. I don't know just how he put it. I know we went down.

Q. Do you remember what Mr. Kangas said to you at all?   A. Word for word, no, sir.

Q. Will you state what the first conversation was that took place at that second meeting at the Jonathan Club. Who opened it?

A. I don't know that there was a great deal said there that night.

Q. Who was present at it?

A. Vic Kangas, Hodges, Livingston, and myself.

Q. Were you the last one at the meeting? Were they all there when you got there?

(Testimony of Lewis Altenburg Porter.)

A. I don't remember now whether I got up first or last.

Q. You don't remember what Kangas told you about this meeting before you went down?

A. No, I don't.

Q. What was discussed at that meeting? [138]

A. I can't remember that there was a whole lot of anything said.

Q. Just the name of the independent? I think that is what you testified to before.   A. Yes.

Q. That was all that was discussed at that meeting?   A. All I can remember now.

Q. Were you given anything that night by anybody in connection with the company?   A. No.

Q. What about this piece of paper that Mr. Livingston gave you? You testified that prior to the lawyer's office, that is, Mr. Schooling, Mr. Livingston had given you some kind of a piece of paper. Is that correct?   A. Yes.

Q. Where were you when that happened?

A. It was over at the plant.

Q. At your machine?   A. Yes.

Q. And it was during working hours, was it?

A. That's my memory, yeah.

Q. What did Mr. Livingston say to you?

. Well, wanted to know if I knew an attorney that would fix those papers up, and I did.

Q. Is that what he said to you? What did he call you? Mr. [139] Porter, or Lou, or what?

A. I don't know what he called me, no, sir.

(Testimony of Lewis Altenburg Porter.)

Q.   In other words, he said to you: Lou, or Mr. Porter, do you know an attorney who can fix some papers up? Is that what it was?

A.   Something of the kind.

Q.   Did he say what kind of papers?

A.   I don't know whether it was the working agreement or not he wanted fixed up.

Q.   You don't remember want he said about it?

A.   Yes. He wanted me to take those papers to some attorney and then have them fixed up.

Q.   But he didn't tell you just what it was?

A.   I don't think so. I don't remember.

Q.   What did you say to him?

A.   I told him I would, that I knew of an attorney.

Q.   The first thing he said to you was: Do you know of an attorney? Was that it?

A.   That's my best memory of it, yes.

Q.   He didn't say what kind of an attorney, a criminal attorney, or anything else?   A.   No.

Q.   Then he said to you: I have some papers here I want you to give to that attorney?

A.   Something to that, yes. [140]

Q.   Then you took the papers and said: Okeh? Right?   A.   Yes.

Q.   Did you know what was in the paper?

A.   I ain't sure. I don't think I even read it.

Q.   What color was the paper?

A.   I don't know that.

Q.   How big was it?

(Testimony of Lewis Altenburg Porter.)

A.   Just a sheet of paper.

Q.   What kind of a sheet of paper? A regular letter-size piece of paper?

A.   I don't remember that, now.

Q.   Was it one sheet or more than one sheet?

A.   I think just one sheet, yeah.

Q.   What did you do with it? Put it in your pocket then?   A.   Yes.

Q.   You had your working clothes on at this time?   A.   Yes, sir.

Q.   You are sure it was just one sheet of paper though?   A.   **Yes.**

Q.   How soon after that did you go over to see the lawyer? Was that the same day?

A.   I went home and I had dinner and went right over to see him.

Q.   What is the first thing you said to the lawyer?   A.   I told him what I had. **[141]**

Q.   What did you tell him you had?

A.   A sheet of paper.

Q.   What about the sheet of paper?

A.   A sheet of paper the company wanted him to fix up for them.

Q.   Fix up in what way?

A.   Type them off, I suppose, I don't know.

Q.   You took it over to have the lawyer copy it? Was that the purpose of it?

A.   Possibly, yes.

Q.   That was all you told the lawyer about it?

A.   Yes.

Q.   He took the paper and examined it?

(Testimony of Lewis Altenburg Porter.)

A. Yes, sir.

Q. Looked it over, and it was just one sheet of paper?   A. Yes.

Q. You didn't read it over his shoulder, at all?
A. No.

Q. Did he ask you any questions about any of the things contained on the piece of paper?

A. I don't think so.

Q. What did he say to you?

A. He told me he didn't think much of it.

Q. Did you know what type of paper you had there? Was it an agreement, or what was it? [142]

A. I didn't know whether it was the working agreement, or constitution, or what.

Q. You didn't know?

A. Paid no attention.

Q. And the lawyer said what?

A. He didn't think much of it, after he had read it.

Q. Did he tell you why?

A. No, he didn't.

Q. Then what did he say?

A. He said, "I'll tell you what to do, Lou," he says, "see the management; have somebody come over in the morning, and I will fix them up these papers right."

Q. Did he ask you how he was going to get paid for it?   A. No, I don't think he did.

Q. He was going to do that as a personal favor to you?   A. Oh, no.

(Testimony of Lewis Altenburg Porter.)

Q. What about paying him? Was that discussed at all?

Mr. Moore: I object to that as already answered.

The Witness: I don't remember.

Trial Examiner Whittemore: He may answer that question.

The Witness: I don't remember whether it was discussed with Schooling and I or not.

Q. (By Mr. Watkins) You don't have any recollection? A. No.

Q. You took the paper along with you when you left? [143] A. Yes.

Q. What did you do with it?

A. I had it to home.

Q. You have it at home now?

A. I say I had it home.

Q. Where is it now? A. I don't know.

Q. Do you know whether it is at home at the present time? A. No. No, it isn't now.

Q. How do you know?

A. Because I looked for it.

Q. What did you do with it?

A. I don't know.

Q. How long ago did you look for it?

A. Oh, several times here lately.

Q. How lately?

A. Oh, the last month or so.

Q. I see. You cannot find any trace of it?

A. No.

Q. Why were you looking for it?

A. Because I wanted it.

(Testimony of Lewis Altenburg Porter.)

Q. Why?

A. To read it.

Q. You didn't read it after the lawyer gave it back to you and you took it home? [144]

A. No, I didn't.

Q. What did you do? Just throw it in with some other papers? A. Yeah.

Q. You didn't give it back to Mr. Livingston or give it back to Mr. Kangas, or offer to do that?

A. No, I know I never.

Q. When this was given to you by Mr. Livingston, was it in an envelope or just a flat piece of paper?

A. Just a flat piece of paper, is my memory.

Q. Could other people around your bench there see him give it to? A. No, sir.

Q. Nobody else could have seen him give it to you? A. Not that I know of, no.

Q. Did you say anything to anybody else about his having given you this piece of paper?

A. No, I don't think so. I don't remember of it.

Q. Your machine at that time was right in the middle of the room, was it not? A. No.

Q. Where was it?

A. It was on one end of the room.

Q. Clearly visible though from the rest of the shop? A. Oh, they could see it. [145]

Q. I believe you said that Mr. Hodges had asked you to join the C. I. O. and gave you the money for your initiation fee. Correct?

(Testimony of Lewis Altenburg Porter.)

A. I think he is the man who done it, yes.

Q. You are not sure whether or not it was Mr. Hodges?

A. I ain't going to be right positive, no.

Q. What were you to get for doing that?

A. Nothing.

Q. You were going to do it for nothing?

A. Yes.

Q. Were you promised anything of any kind?

A. No.

Q. Why did you do it?

A. Oh, because I was asked to, I guess.

Q. I believe you testified after you had been up here at the Labor Board the first time that you told Mr. Long about it. Correct?

A. No, no. I told Bill Kerns.

Q. Didn't you tell Mr. Long about it?

A. No.

Q. You are sure of that?

A. Never did, no.

Q. Didn't you tell Mr. Long about it and tell him not to tell anybody else you had been up here?

A. No, sir. [146]

Q. Are you sure about that?

A. I talked to Bill Kerns, is the only man.

Q. Yes, but didn't you talk to Mr. Long and tell him that?   A. I did not.

Q. You are positive of that?   A. Yes, sir.

Q. Mr. Porter, you related an instance involving a fifty dollar bill. Do you recall that in your testimony?   A. Yeah.

(Testimony of Lewis Altenburg Porter.)

Q. Of receiving it?   A. What?

Q. About receiving a fifty dollar bill.

A. Yes, sir.

Q. That was in your home?   A. Yes, sir.

Q. And Mrs. Porter was there and Mr. Vic Kangas and his wife were there?

A. Yes, sir.

Q. And I believe you testified that was sometime around September, is my recollection, or in the fall of 1937? Is that correct?   A. Yes, sir.

Q. Had Mr. Kangas and his wife called at your home previously?

A. Yeah, they had been there.

Q. They were social callers from time to time? [147]   A. Oh——

Q. And have been subsequently?

A. Yeah, they have been over before.

Q. And have been subsequently. That is, down to the present time.   A. Yes.

Q. Do they still do it?   A. Now?

Q. Yes.

A. No, we haven't visited for, I would say, a year or more.

Q. You are still on good terms with Mr. Kangas?

A. Oh, yes.

Q. On better terms than you were with Mr. Hileman? Is that correct?

Mr. Moore: Objected to.

Trial Examiner Whittemore: I will sustain the objection.

(Testimony of Lewis Altenburg Porter.)

Q. (By Mr. Watkins) Going back to this incident about the fifty dollar bill, did Mr. Kangas, when he came to your house that evening, tell you why he was stopping by?

A. I don't remember he did, no.

Q. Do you remember any of the conversation at all?

A. Oh, no, not particularly, only he gave me the fifty dollar bill and told me where it came from.

Q. Yes. When he first came to your house, when was it? Along about 8:00 o'clock in the evening? [148]

A. 7:00 or 8:00, around there.

Q. What did he say to you when he first came in?   A. I don't remember.

Q. What did he call you? Lou? What did he do? Reach in his pocket and hand you the envelope? Is that it?   A. He gave me it.

Q. What did he say to you about it?

A. He told me Mr. Hileman gave it to him to give to me.

Q. Didn't he say what it was for, or anything else?   A. I don't remember, no.

Q. What did you figure it was for?

A. I was to get some money.

Q. This was part of the deal you made with Mr. Livingston? That's what you figured, was it?

A. Possibly it could have been that I figured that way.

Q. Is that what you did figure when you got the fifty dollar bill?   A. Yeah.

(Testimony of Lewis Altenburg Porter.)

Q. What is the answer? Yes?   A. Yeah.

Q. In other words, Mr. Victor Kangas came over to you that evening and gave you an envelope and you didn't know what was in it, and he said Mr. Hileman said to give it to you. Correct?

A. Yes. [149]

Q. And you opened it up and it had a fifty dollar bill in it? Correct?   A. Yes.

Q. And you didn't ask any questions about it of Mr. Kangas?   A. No, none that I remember.

Q. Did he ask you any questions about it?

A. I don't think so.

Q. Did your wife ask you any questions? How come you got fifty dollars from the company?

A. If she did I don't remember now.

Q. What did you do with it? Did you spend it?

A. Yeah.

Q. You saved it for a while, did you not?

A. Yes.

Q. How long did you have it in your possession?

A. I don't know; quite a while.

Q. How long?

A. I ain't going to say. I don't remember now.

Q. Would you say five days or five months?

A. Oh, yes; longer than that.

Q. Longer than five months?   A. Yes.

Q. A year and a half?   A. Possibly.

Q. Three years? [150]

A. I don't remember that far.

Q. You can't recall when you finally spent the fifty dollar bill?

(Testimony of Lewis Altenburg Porter.)

A. No, I gave it my wife. She took care of it.

Q. Do you remember when that was?

A. No.

Q. Did you make any explanation to her at the time you gave it to her?

A. She knew I got it.

Q. She knew where you got it, but she didn't know the purpose back of it, did she?

A. She might have.

Q. You don't remember telling her about it?

A. (No response.)

Q. Did you ever tell her that here was the money you were going to get?

A. Could have been.

Q. You have no recollection of that?

A. No.

Q. Did you ever ask where the rest of it was?

A. How?

Q. Did you ever ask anybody if you were going to get any more?　　A. No.

Q. Did you figure that was all you were going to get? [151]

A. That was all I got. I didn't ask for it or any more.

Q. You hadn't asked for the fifty dollars?

A. No.

Q. You didn't ask Mr. Hileman or anybody else where the rest of it was, or whether any more was coming?　　A. No.

Q. Did you ever thank Mr. Hileman for it?

A. Don't know as I did. I ain't going to say.

(Testimony of Lewis Altenburg Porter.)

Q. How long ago did you leave the employ of the company, Thompson Products, the respondent in this case? A. How?

Q. How long ago did you leave the employ of the company?

A. Oh, a couple of months ago.

Q. Had you had some little trouble, shortly before you left the company, with respect to your machine? A. Not particularly, no.

Q. Didn't you have some trouble with your machine, operating it, before you left? A. No.

Q. You had none at all? A. No, sir.

Q. Didn't you report some trouble with your machine to the Federal Bureau of Investigation?

A. I did not.

Q. Didn't the F. B. I. investigate your machine and some [152] trouble with it?

A. They might have, but I did not report to them.

Mr. Moore: I object to that and ask that the answer be stricken.

Mr. Watkins: It seems to me this is cross examination, Mr. Examiner, and it is quite pertinent in a case of this kind to test the credibility of the witness. Testimony which he has given in this case reflects greatly on the company in very many respects. If that is going to be objected to then I am going to subpoena the records of the F. B. I. and bring them in here.

Trial Examiner Whittemore: I don't know that you are going to subpoena **any** records. You may

(Testimony of Lewis Altenburg Porter.)
make application for them, of course. I don't think you mean you can bring in F. B. I. records simply by saying you are going to.

Mr. Watkins: I beg your pardon, your Honor. I understand you are the one to issue the subpoenas.

Trial Examiner Whittemore: Let us drop the matter there, then. I would like to know your purpose. I will admit you have more latitude on cross examination, but I don't see quite what credibility has to do with it.

Mr. Watkins: It is rather hard to state that without examining the witness with respect to it first.

Trial Examiner Whittemore: All right. Go ahead.

Mr. Watkins: I will be glad to let it come in subject [153] to a motion to strike, if counsel wishes.

Mr. Moore: I don't believe that is the proper way of impeaching the witness. In other words, you are not attempting to show here the man has been convicted of a crime, or has ever been charged with a crime.

Trial Examiner Whittemore: No. But on the other hand, it is conceivable this might show a certain interest in this particular case.

On the other hand, as I say, there is considerable latitude that has to be allowed on cross examination. I will permit the witness to answer.

Mr. Watkins: Thank you.

(Testimony of Lewis Altenburg Porter.)

Q. (By Mr. Watkins) Mr. Porter, first, did you report to the Federal Bureau of Investigation or any Government agency anything with respect to any foreign materials in your machine within the last six months?

A. I didn't report it to them, no, sir.

Q. Do you know whether or not any investigation was made with respect to the machine which you operated and one next to it with respect to any foreign materials in it? A. How was that?

Mr. Watkins: Read the question. If it isn't clear, I will reframe it.

(The question was read.)

Q. (By Mr. Watkins) Any emery, or anything of that kind. [154]

A. I don't remember any machine being investigated next to mine, no, sir.

Q. Was your machine investigated?

A. I heard it was.

Q. Were you investigated by the Federal Bureau of Investigation or any of its agents with respect to that matter?

Mr. Moore: Objected to, unless the word "investigated" is cleared up.

Q. (By Mr. Watkins) Were you questioned with respect to it? A. I was questioned, yeah.

Q. And that was by a Mr. Matthews? Is that correct? A. Yeah.

Q. Originally, when you were first questioned by Mr. Matthews, did you tell him that the company

(Testimony of Lewis Altenburg Porter.)
had put emery, or a foreign substance in your machine?

A.   No, sir, I did not know who done it, and didn't tell them anything of the sort.

Q.   Did you tell him someone else in the plant had done it to get even with you?

A.   I don't remember just how it was stated now.

Q.   That was the first information that you gave to Mr. Matthews, was it not?

A.   Something to that effect.

Q.   Didn't you finally tell Mr. Matthews that you yourself had put foreign materials into your machine, and the machine [155] next to it?

A.   No, sir.

Q.   Didn't you tell him you had put it into your machine?   A.   No, sir.

Q.   You didn't make any such statement?

A.   No, sir.

Mr. Watkins: That is all. I want to reserve further cross examination, because I would like to have an opportunity to ask this witness further questions after we study over the notes, because of many matters in here I was unaware of prior to this time. I do not expect to hold him here, but I would like to have him come back if we find some other matters.

Trial Examiner Whittemore: I think there was some formal understanding with counsel for the Board that he would try to get him back if he was given sufficient notice, so we could reach him.

(Testimony of Lewis Altenburg Porter.)

Mr. Watkins: Yes. I do want to ask the witness one or two other questions.

Trial Examiner Whittemore: All right.

Q. (By Mr. Watkins) Mr. Porter, did you do some investigating for the Thompson Products of the theft of some valves, kinner aircraft valves?

A. I done some, yeah; but I didn't make any headway, no.

Q. About when was this? [156]

A. Oh, that has been two or three years ago, I think.

Q. Substantially what did you do in connection with it?   A. How?

Q. What did you do in connection with it? I might say to the Board that this does not reflect on Mr. Porter in any way, shape or form.

Trial Examiner Whittemore: What is the purpose of it?

Mr. Watkins: It was some special work the witness did and I want to ask him about it.

Trial Examiner Whittemore: What bearing will it have on the issues? If you are not attacking this witness, what bearing will it have?

Mr. Watkins: No. I say this particular instance doesn't have any reflection on this witness' character. I mentioned the theft of some valves, and I didn't want the Examiner to feel there was any reflection on the witness.

Trial Examiner Whittemore: Go ahead.

Q. (By Mr. Watkins) What work did you do in that connection?

(Testimony of Lewis Altenburg Porter.)

A. Well, sir, it amounted to so little I pretty near forgot what did happen. In other words, nothing happened.

Q. Did you make some trips in your car out to Alhambra and other places to check some service stations in connection with it?

Mr. Moore: I will object to this entire line of questioning on the ground it is immaterial. [157]

Mr. Watkins: It is very material, Mr. Examiner. I as sure I wouldn't be asking for it otherwise. This is cross examination.

Trial Examiner Whittemore: All right. The witness may answer.

The Witness: No, I don't think we visited any gas stations.

Q. (By Mr. Watkins) Did you receive any— were you through with your answer?

A. Yes.

Q. Did you receive any pay for any work in connection with that investigation of that kinner valve situation?

A. Oh, nothing more, I don't think, than just my wages went on, or something like that, to the best of my memory. I don't think I received any money other than just my salary. I could have, but I don't know that I did.

Q. You don't recall anything about it?

A. If it was, it didn't amount to anything, possibly more than gasoline; but I don't remember whether I received any money at all.

Q. You wouldn't say you did not?

(Testimony of Lewis Altenburg Porter.)

A.   No, other than just my salary. [158]

Q.   (By Mr. Watkins)   Did Mr. Vic Kangas ever get you to join the C. I. O., or get some of the others to join the C. I. O., in the plant there?

A.   No, I don't remember of Vic ever talking to me about it.

Q.   You don't remember any conversation with Mr. Victor Kangas about joining the C. I. O.?

A.   I don't, no.

Q.   You don't remember any?

A.   No, sir, I do not.

Mr. Watkins: That is all.

Trial Examiner Whittemore: All right.   Mr. Baldwin, do you have any questions?

Mr. Baldwin: I would like to ask him one or two questions.

Trial Examiner Whittemore: All right.

Q.   (By Mr. Baldwin)   You stated at the time you went after [162] those cards you didn't know what the cards were, did you?   Or did you?

A.   Yes.

Q.   Do you know what was on those cards?

A.   How?

Q.   Do you know what was on the cards?

A.   Not until after I read them, no.

Q.   What was on the cards?

A.   Oh, I can't repeat it now.

Q.   Have you any idea what the heading was on the cards?   A.   My memory was: PPWA.

Q.   Well, when you got the cards they were all, probably, in a package, more than likely?

(Testimony of Lewis Altenburg Porter.)

A.   I think so, yeah.

Q.   You stated you gave the cards to Mr. Hodges on your return to the plant. Did you give him the cards without looking at them?

. A.   I don't remember whether I did or not.

Q.   You stated you didn't know what Mr. Kangas had written on the paper and you also stated you didn't know who gave it to the printer, or evidently—what I am trying to find out is if you knew what was on the cards.

A.   Possibly I did, after I read one.

Q.   You said you read one. Did you read them before you handed them to Mr. Hodges? [163]

A.   I said "possibly." I don't remember whether I did or not.

Q.   You don't know who gave you the money for those cards?

. A.   No; never been able to figure that out.

. Q..   You never put the money out of your own pocket? .   A.   I know I didn't.

Q.   Had you determined the name of the organization prior to the time you had the cards printed?

A.   I don't know whether we had or not.

Q.   You stated probably—I believe it was two days later that a name was suggested, but the cards had already been distributed. Is that right?

Trial Examiner Whittemore: Well, you are cross examining him on your own original questions there. You are going over exactly the same ground that you went over before. I don't know what your purpose is.   .

(Testimony of Lewis Altenburg Porter.)

Mr. Baldwin: I may be in error. I am sorry.

Q. (By Mr. Baldwin) You say you read the cards. You know what was on the cards, the heading? A. I think so, yes.

Q. But you don't know whether you read them after you gave them to Mr. Hodges or before you gave them to Mr. Hodges?

A. No, I don't know.

Q. You also stated you didn't pay for them out of your own pocket, that you got the money from someone, but you don't know [164] who it was?

A. Yeah.

Q. But you don't know whether the name of the organization had been determined before you had the cards printed or after?

A. I don't remember.

Q. You don't know when the name of the organization was proposed, do you?

A. Not exactly, no.

Q. Do you know if the cards that you had printed were for the same organization that is now in existence?

A. I don't know, no; don't know now.

Q. You don't know whether that was the same organization or not? In other words, there might have been some other organization? A. Yeah.

Q. Do you know what the organization is now? I mean, as to the name.

A. Yeah, I think so. I haven't paid much attention to it.

(Testimony of Lewis Altenburg Porter.)

Q.   You stated at the time the cards were printed that they had: PPWA on them. Is that right?

A.   PPWA, I believe, yeah.

Q.   Mr. Hodges told you to go get the cards. Do you know where the print office was?   A.   No.

[165]

VICTOR ELMER KANGAS

a witness called by and in behalf of the National Labor Relations Board, having been first duly sworn, was examined and testified as follows:

Direct Examination

Q.   (By Mr. Moore) Will you state your full name, please.   A.   Victor Elmer Kangas.

Q.   Mr. Kangas, have you ever been employed by Thompson Products, Inc.?   A.   Yes, sir.

Q.   When were you so employed?

A.   From 1922 until 1940.

Q.   You have worked for them only at their plant at Bell, California; is that correct?

A.   Since 1937 until 1940, yes.

Q.   When you said you worked from 1922 until 1940, did you mean that prior to the time the plant was taken over out [167] here you worked for the concern that was taken over?   A.   Yes, sir.

Q.   In what capacity did you work for Thompson Products?

(Testimony of Victor Elmer Kangas.)

A. Well, at the time that I left there I was plant superintendent.

Q. What was your position on April 8, 1937, at the time the plant was taken over by Thompson Products?

A. Assistant works manager.

Q. Are you acquainted with Mr. Raymond Livingston? A. Yes, sir.

Q. Who is he?

A. Personnel manager of all Thompson plants.

Q. Do you know whether he held that position during July of 1937, and thereafter?

A. Yes, sir, he did, to my knowledge.

Q. When did you first meet Mr. Livingston?

A. About in either April or May of 1937.

Q. Where did you meet him on that occasion?

A. I met him at the Jadson Motor Products plant, Bell, California.

Q. And did you meet him again after that?

A. Yes, sir.

Q. When was that?

A. The latter part of July, 1937.

Q. Where did that meeting take place? [168]

A. At the same place.

Q. When was that, as nearly as you can tell?

A. You mean what day of the month?

Q. Yes.

A. Well, it was, as well as I can remember, Friday, the latter part of July. I don't know what date it was, whether it was the 28th or 29th or the 30th.

(Testimony of Victor Elmer Kangas.)

Q. Who was present at the time you met Mr. Livingston on that occasion?

A. Mr. Dachtler.

Q. Mr. Livingston, you and Mr. Dachtler?

A. That is right.

Q. Was there a conversation held at that time?

A. There was.

Q. What was the conversation?

A. Mr. Livingston talked to me about labor conditions and also about working conditions, and from that it drifted into one thing or another, the equipment, and so forth.

Q. Is that all that was discussed at this meeting?

A. No. I and Mr. Livingston sat in the main office of the acting general manager's office at that time, and Mr. Livingston wanted to know about how many of the employees at that time belonged to the C. I. O.

Q. Did he ask you that?

A. Yes, sir. I told him as near as I knew, possibly around [169] 95 per cent, as near as I could gather. However, that most of them had just signed their applications, but I don't know whether they paid their dues or not.

Q. Was there some further discussion?

A. Yes. He suggested a meeting——

Q. Wait a moment now. You first said you and Mr. Livingston and Mr. Dachtler were present.

A. Yes.

(Testimony of Victor Elmer Kangas.)

Q. Did you later say that you and Mr. Livingston were in your office?   A. That is correct.

Q. Was Mr. Dachtler there during this entire
conversation?

A. Not this time, while Livingston and I were
in the office alone.

Q. Did Mr. Dachtler leave?

A. Yes, he did.

Q. After he left which part of the conversation,
you have related occurred?

A. Mr. Dachtler came into the office a little later
and sat down. I don't remember exactly what was
said during the course of this conversation other
than Mr. Livingston talked more or less about organizing a company union in the plant.

Mr. Watkins: Well, now, just a minute. I move
the answer be stricken, Mr. Examiner, as a conclusion of the witness. We should have the conversations. [170]

Trial Examiner Whittemore: It may be
stricken.

Q. (By Mr. Moore): Just state what Mr. Livingston said.

A. Mr. Livingston asked me how much unrest
there was in the plant. I told him there was quite
a bit. He wanted to know why. I told him probably due to the low rate of pay, and he asked me
what we might do about it, and I said, well, we
might possibly increase the rates of pay.

And then he asked about how the men would
feel if they had a company organization or a labor

(Testimony of Victor Elmer Kangas.)
organization of their own. I said I didn't know.
I never thought of it that way. And he thought
maybe by doing something like that, maybe he could
correct that unrest in the plant.

And the conversation drifted from that, more or
less into talking about how we might organize this,
or how we might start it——

Mr. Watkins: Just a minute. I object to that
testimony and move that it be stricken, the portion of it stating: "The conversation drifted more
or less to how we might organize this."

Trial Examiner Whittemore: That may be
stricken.

Q. (By Mr. Moore): Yes. Just say what was
said about the formation of a union there, as nearly
as you can recall.

A. Well, as near as I can remember, he wanted
to know if I could trust a few of the men, or one
in particular, and more or less get this organization,
as he called it, it was [171] new to me, something
I had never worked on, therefore, I didn't know
exactly what was going to transpire——

Mr. Watkins: Just a minute. I move that portion of the witness' answer: "It was new to me. I
didn't know what was going to transpire," be
stricken as a conclusion.

Trial Examiner Whittemore: I will permit that
to remain. Certainly he is qualified to make a conclusion as to how he felt, whether it is important
or not. I will deny your motion to strike. Try

(Testimony of Victor Elmer Kangas.)
to give the conversation without putting in other matters.

The Witness: So Mr. Dachtler told me what he wanted to do and these were the lines he talked about. He said if he organized an organization, a labor organization of their own, and could hold these men in this organization and get them to join, we can probably give them a lot of things that possibly some outside organization couldn't give them; and he suggested that maybe we could get the department heads or either the leadmen, as they call them now, and hold a meeting at Uncle Gabriel's in Downey; and he said he would let me know later on during the day, if they would do that.

And that evening I was notified there would be such a meeting at Uncle Gabriel's in Downey.

Q. Well, now, were arrangements made at this meeting you have been describing for a future meeting?

A. During this conversation in the office, that was the [172] meeting during the day; but later on that afternoon, I was notified there would be a meeting.

Q. By whom were you notified?

A. By Mr. Livingston.

Q. Where was that?

A. At the plant itself.

Q. I mean, where in the plant were you at that time he contacted you?

A. In the office. I was called in the office. That is right.

(Testimony of Victor Elmer Kangas.)

Q. Was anyone there besides him and you?

A. Mr. Dachtler.

Q. What did Mr. Livingston say with reference to this dinner?

A. He told me to be at Uncle Gabriel's place at Downey, I don't remember, 7:00 o'clock or 8:00 o'clock that evening.

Q. Did you attend a dinner at Uncle Gabriel's in Downey?   A. That's right.

Q. Who was present at that dinner?

A. Well, at that time all the department heads, all the sub-foremen or leadmen, which consisted of Roy Long, Bill Kerns, Leroy Shadrack, Eugene Drake, L. V. Corbley, Mr. Drake, myself.

Mr. Watkins: May I go over the list again? Long, Kerns, [173] Shadrack, and who else?

(Record read.)

Q. (By Mr. Moore): Who was Mr. Lyman Hodges?

A. He at that time was acting as more or less personnel manager, and also in charge of shipping, as shipping clerk.

Q. What took place at this dinner?

A. Well, we had our dinner, and after the dinner, there wasn't much discussed in the way of organizing a labor organization, other than feeling the boys out to see how the reaction was, rather. Mr. Livingston gave a talk. First of all, Mr. Dachtler suggested to me to talk, and I told him I thought it was up to Mr. Livingston to do the talk-

(Testimony of Victor Elmer Kangas.)

ing, because I didn't know what we were going to do. I didn't know what the plans were. I suggested Mr. Livingston do the talking, which he did.

Q. And what, in substance, did he say?

A. The speech was very short. In fact, he just talked to the boys and asked them what they thought of an inside organization, what they thought of it. Then all of them agreed that they thought it would be all right. However, he wanted everybody to treat it confidential, due to the fact that he did not want it out in the plant.

Q. Was anything else said that you can recall?

A. No, there wasn't, not at the dinner.

Mr. Watkins: May we fix the date of this meeting? [174]

Mr. Moore: I believe we said it was on the same day he first discussed working conditions in the plant with Mr. Livingston.

Trial Examiner Whittemore: He fixed it as the last Friday, July 28th or 29th. The exact day he couldn't recall.

Mr. Watkins: Thank you.

Q. (By Mr. Moore): Have you exhausted your recollection now as to what was said at that dinner?

A. Well, the only thing that was said at the dinner in regard to this organization was more or less to feel out the department heads to get their reaction of it, to see how they felt towards an inside labor organization, and they felt it was a very good idea.

Q. They said that at this dinner?

(Testimony of Victor Elmer Kangas.)

A.   That's right.

Q.   You testified, I believe, that only supervisors or people in a supervisory capacity attended that dinner, did you not?   A.   That is correct.

Q.   Have you now exhausted your recollection as to what was said then?

A.   At that meeting? Well, I don't know exactly; probably a lot of things were said——

Q.   You don't remember anything else?

A.   I mean in regard to this organization, that's all that [175] was discussed there.

Q.   In other words, to refresh your recollection, I will ask you if anything was said at that meeting about the C. I. O.?

A.   Yes, there was, but there wasn't very much said about it. As I remember, Mr. Livingston said that if any labor organization, outside labor organization gets in, C. I. O. or A. F. of L. either, the plant would be closed and the equipment moved back East, because of the fact that Mr. Crawford would not tolerate any outside labor organization in his organization.

Q.   Whom do you have reference to when you refer to Mr. Crawford?

A.   He was president of Thompson Products.

Q.   Do you know his full name?

A.   Fred Crawford.

Q.   Now, after that dinner, did you have further conversation with Mr. Livingston?

A.   I talked to him a little bit outside, but I don't remember exactly what was said, other than

(Testimony of Victor Elmer Kangas.)

he asked me if I had anybody in mind that I could depend on and could trust as a leadman, and get him to talk to the other men in the plant, to build this up; it must be confidential, caution him of it, to start an inside labor organization, get as many men as possible to go into the office and ask for, oh, various things, probably seniority rights, vacations with pay, and so on. **[176]**

A.   At that time I told him I couldn't think of any one right at the present time. I might. He said, "Well, you sleep on it and see what you can do tomorrow."

Q.   This conversation you are referring to now, was that after the dinner?

A.   That was after the dinner, outside.

Q.   It occurred at Downey, outside of Uncle Gabriel's place?   A.   That's right.

Q.   Was anyone present other than you and Mr. Livingston?

A.   No, sir. There wasn't. Mr. Livingston and I were the only ones present.

Q.   What action did you take thereafter?

A.   Well, after thinking over all my trusty employees in there, I thought of Lou Porter, being as he had done some police work, and I suggested him.

Q.   Did you have a conversation with Mr. Livingston at which you suggested Mr. Porter?

A.   I did later, yes, that day, Saturday, as I remember; Saturday morning.

Q.   The next day after the dinner at Downey?

(Testimony of Victor Elmer Kangas.)

A. That's right. I know it was right within a day or two, probably the next day, Saturday morning, as well as I can remember.

Q. About what time of day?

A. Oh, possibly around 11:00 o'clock, as well as I can remember. [177]

Q. Who was present at the time you talked to him on this occasion?

A. Mr. Livingston and I alone.

Q. What was said there?

Mr. Watkins: Where did it take place?

Q. (By Mr. Moore): Yes, where did it take place?   A. At the plant office.

Q. At the plant office?

A. Yeah, in Bell.

Q. What was said there?

A. He asked me if I had anybody in mind and I says, "Yes, I have got a man out in the plant by the name of Lou Porter, and I think he will fill the bill."

Q. Was that all that was said then?

A. Well, no. He questioned me on that, and I told him I would stand back of it, and I would rather trust him, rather than a lot of others, due to the fact he had done police work, and he was an older man, and I was quite sure he would treat it confidential.

Q. Is that all that was said on that occasion?

A. Yes, sir, right at that time.

Q. Did you point out to Mr. Livingston who Lou Porter was?

(Testimony of Victor Elmer Kangas.)

A. That I don't remember. I don't remember whether I took Mr. Livingston out in the plant and introduced him to him or not. That I don't know. [178]

Q. Did you have any conversation with Mr. Porter with reference to this thing at about this time?

A. After this I did, yes.

Q. When was this?

A. As well as I can remember it was that same day.

Q. At about what time?

A. Well, that I wouldn't remember. It was during the course of the day, during working hours, but when it was, whether it was immediately after lunch, or whether it was before lunch, I can't remember.

Q. But it was after you had talked with Mr. Livingston in the office?   A. Yes, sir.

Q. Who was present at the time you talked to Mr. Porter?

A. Nobody. Just Mr. Porter and myself.

Q. Where did that talk take place?

A. In the plant, at his machine.

Q. At a machine?   A. That is right.

Q. What was said there?

A. Well, I outlined it to him a little bit. But I told him that probably Mr. Livingston would give him the picture better than I can, and that Mr. Livingston would contact him, I didn't know when, either that day or maybe the following day, or whenever it was. I don't remember now. [179]

(Testimony of Victor Elmer Kangas.)

Q. Did he say anything?   A. Porter?

Q. Yes.

A. Yes. He told me he would be willing to do that.

Q. Is that all the conversation you had with him?   A. With Porter?

Q. Yes.

A. At that time it was, yes.

Q. As nearly as you can recall, I believe you have testified the day on which you contacted Mr. Porter was Saturday?

A. That is the way I remember it.

Q. Did anything else in connection with the subject we are discussing occur on Saturday afternoon?

A. Between myself and Mr. Porter?

Q. Well, between yourself and Mr. Porter, or between yourself and Mr. Livingston.

A. Not between myself and Mr. Porter. There was some discussion with Mr. Livingston as to how he could contact Mr. Porter, and wondering if Mr. Porter would go to the Jonathan Club to see him.

Q. When was it you talked to Mr. Livingston?

A. That was that day.

Q. Was it in the afternoon?

A. That Saturday; it must have been in the afternoon.

Q. After you had talked to Porter? [180]

A. Porter, that is right.

Q. Where was it you saw him?

A. Mr. Livingston?

(Testimony of Victor Elmer Kangas.)

Q.   Yes.

A.   At the plant, in the office.

Q.   In the office?   A.   That's right.

Q.   Was anyone else there besides you and he?

A.   No, sir.

Q.   What was said?

A.   Mr. Livingston asked me if I thought Mr. Porter would come up to the Jonathan Club, and I thought that he would, and I said I am quite sure he will. And as I remember, Mr. Livingston told me to give him the room number, to go up there at the Jonathan Club, and I think Mr. Livingston said he would say a few words to him that evening. Whether he did or not I don't know.

Q.   Is that all the conversation you recall?

A.   That's all I remember of it.

Q.   Now, did you have anything further—did you take any further action on Saturday?

A.   No, sir, not at that time.

Q.   What was the next thing you did?

A.   Well, on Monday morning, Mr. Livingston called me in the office, at either 10:30 or 11:00——

[181]

Q.   Were you and he alone?   A.   Yes.

Q.   It was in the plant office?

A.   That's right.

Q.   What conversation did you have there?

A.   Well, the conversation that we had, I told Mr. Livingston that I had heard that the C. I. O. was going to have a meeting Tuesday evening on the corner of Otis Avenue and Florence Avenue, at

(Testimony of Victor Elmer Kangas.)

the Veterans of Foreign Wars Home, and at that time they were going to submit a contract or agreement to the Jadson Motor Products and all of the members of the C. I. O. were to be present at that meeting, Tuesday evening.

Q. You told Mr. Livingston that?

A. I did. Mr. Livingston said: "We have got to get the ball rolling on this, because we have got to crack that meeting before Tuesday evening." Therefore, he outlined a plan to work on. There wasn't a great deal that I could do at that time.

Q. Just a minute.

Mr. Watkins: Just a minute. I would like to have that stricken.

Trial Examiner Whittemore: That last sentence may be stricken.

Q. (By Mr. Moore): Just say, as nearly as you can, what he [182] said and what you said.

A. So then he told me to be sure and work on Lou Porter and get him to contact these men out in the plant, as many of them as possible, to go in the office and ask for seniority rights, and probably higher rates of pay, or vacations with pay. He said he didn't care what they came in for, as long as they came in and asked for something.

So I told Lou, and I believe he did contact some men out in the plant.

Q. By "Lou" you mean Lou Porter?

A. Lou Porter, and Mr. Livingston told me to be somewhere——

Q. Wait. You have just said you contacted Por-

(Testimony of Victor Elmer Kangas.)

ter and told him; but we are still in this conversation now at which Mr. Livingston told you to contact Porter. Let's clear that up before we go on to what happened after.

A. After I contacted Porter and outlined the work for him to do——

Q. No. Try to give the complete conversation between yourself and Mr. Livingston before you contacted Porter.

A. Well, the conversation, as I remember, was: Mr. Livingston said that if we would get 51 per cent of the employees to organize an organization of their own, and probably get this organization started before Tuesday evening, we could probably keep them from going to this meeting, and he said that it was very imperative that we do this. [183]

Q. Will you indicate what meeting?

A. This meeting with the C. I. O.

Q. Yes.

A. So, of course, he told me to be sure and see that Mr. Porter gets started on those men out in the shop, and I did. I talked to Mr. Porter.

Q. You talked with Mr. Porter after that?

A. Well, I had talked to him after I had this conversation with Mr. Livingston in regard to the C. I. O. meeting on Tuesday, and this being Monday and these men were to go in the office Tuesday afternoon, around 2:00 o'clock.

Q. Did you have a conversation with Mr. Porter after that?   A. Yes.

Q. And where did that take place?

(Testimony of Victor Elmer Kangas.)

A.   That was in the plant.

Mr. Watkins: Was that the same day?

Q.   (By Mr. Moore):   Was that on the same day——

A.   That was on a Monday.

Q.   On a Monday?

A.   That is right.   It was Monday afternoon, rather late, though; it might have been around 3:00 o'clock.

Q.   Who was present at the time you talked with Mr. Porter?

A.   Nobody.   That was to be treated confidentially and nobody was present but Mr. Porter and myself. [184]

Mr. Watkins: I move that portion be stricken: That was to be treated confidentially, as a conclusion of the witness.

Trial Examiner Whittemore: That may be stricken.

Q.   (By Mr. Moore)   What did you say to Mr. Porter?

A.   I just asked Mr. Porter to contact as many men as he could, to get them to go into the office to ask for these seniority rights, better working conditions, probably vacations with pay.   "I don't care what you ask them," I said, "just get them in there and ask them to ask for something, because they want to organize this inside union."

Q.   Did he say anything then?

A.   He said he would do his best.

Q.   After that what happened, on Monday?

A.   Mr. Livingston later on, before he went

(Testimony of Victor Elmer Kangas.)

home—I don't remember whether he called me in the office or came to my office——

Q. You had a meeting with him?

A. Yes.

Q. Either in your office or his?

A. Yes, in the plant. I don't remember whether it was in his office or mine. I was running back and forth pretty fast, so I can't remember all these things.

Q. This was on Monday?   A. Yes. [185]

Q. Who was present?

A. I and Mr. Livingston.

Q. What happened on that occasion? What conversation took place?

A. He told me to be somewhere, and call a number. He gave me the number on a slip of paper, at 7:00 o'clock. Well, I called that number, and that number happened to be the Jonathan Club, and he asked me if I had a pencil and paper and I told him I did. He said he wanted to dictate a letter to me, or a name of a union that—or a name that he wanted to name that union. So, I wrote it down, but as well as I can remember, I can't remember too much about it, actually what it said on that. I know there was several sentences, but what it was I can't remember, word for word.

Q. At this conversation you had with him, was the thing he said there: "Call me up at this phone number"?

A. He told me he would give me more information as to the union, and he also suggested a name

(Testimony of Victor Elmer Kangas.)
they would give this organization, and he asked me
to get someone to print those cards.

Mr. Watkins: Wait a minute. Reference is
made to those cards, and there is no foundation
laid for it.

The Witness: Well, it was the name to go on
the cards, the union cards.

Q. (By Mr. Moore) Yes. At this conversation,
now, before [186] you telephone him, the conversation at which you said he gave you a telephone
number, was something said about cards at that
meeting?

A. No. He told me, he said: "I will give you
further instructions over the telephone when you
call me."

Q. Had he, before that, told you he wanted you
to get cards printed?

A. Not as I remember, about getting cards
printed.

Q. Did you contact him later?

A. Monday evening at 7:00 o'clock.

Q. You called him on the telephone?

A. I did.

Q. Did you call the number he had given you?

A. I did.

Q. Will you state what conversation you had
with him over the telephone?

A. Well, as well as I can remember, he told me
he had a letter, or had something there he wanted
to dictate to me over the telephone, and he asked

(Testimony of Victor Elmer Kangas.)

me if I had a pencil and paper. I said I did. So, exactly what the words were and what he dictated over the telephone I can't remember. He told me that he wanted to have me jot this down, this name he was putting down there, he wanted that to be the name of the organization, and he said he wanted me to get cards printed that very evening, go to some printing company and [187] get the cards printed.

I told him I was next door to a print office then.

So, after I had taken this information down, I went to the print office and gave them the slip of paper and I asked them if they could print them that evening. They said it was impossible. I asked them in regard to the morning, early, and they said not until 11:00 o'clock.

Q. Just a moment. At the time you made this telephone call to Mr. Livingston, about what time was it?

A. 7:00 o'clock in the evening, Monday evening.

Q. Did you make that call from a print shop?

A. It was next door to a print shop.

Q. What type of establishment were you in when you made the call?

A. Oh, I don't remember exactly what it was, whether it was a popcorn stand, or whether it was a machine shop, I don't know. I know I went next door to telephone there. It was next to the Lyric Theater.

Q. Was anyone with you at the time?

A. Lou Porter.

(Testimony of Victor Elmer Kangas.)

Q. Anyone else?

A. Well, my wife and his wife were outside in the car.

Q. Did Mr. Porter go to the telephone with you?

A. He did.

Q. Was there any particular purpose in you and he being [188] together at that time with your wives?

A. I don't remember whether there was or not. That I can't remember, why we were together.

Q. After calling Mr. Livingston and taking down the matter he dictated to you, what did you do then?

A. I took the sheet of paper to the printing company and asked them if they could print that for me that evening.

Q. Where was that print shop?

A. Next to the Lyric Theater in Huntington Park.

Q. Do you know the approximate address of it?

A. It was on Pacific Boulevard, but I don't know the number.

Q. Just below Florence?

A. On the corner of Florence and Pacific, south of the Lyric Theater.

Q. Did Mr. Porter go with you to the print shop?　　A. He did.

Q. Did he go in with you?　　A. He did.

Q. I think you have testified that you couldn't get them that evening?　　A. That's right.

Q. But you ordered them to be done the next day?　　A. Yes.

(Testimony of Victor Elmer Kangas.)

Q. Were they then picked up the next day?

A. Yes. I myself told Mr. Porter to go pick those up. [189]

Q. You heard him testify Mr. Hodges told him to do that?

A. He was wrong. I told himself.

Q. What time of day was that?

A. I would say probably a little before 11:00 o'clock, because I told him, "You can probably get the cards and be back by noon." I said, "Don't check out when you go."

Q. Where were you when you had this conversation?   A. At the plant, at his machine.

Q. Was anyone else with you?

A. Nobody present but us.

Q. And you told him to go pick up the cards and not to check out?   A. That's right.

Q. Did he leave the plant?   A. He did.

Q. Did he return shortly thereafter?

A. Yes, he was back, as I remember it, around noon. I don't know whether he came in before 12:00, but I know he was there during the noon hour.

Q. Do you know what he did with the cards when he came back?

A. No, I don't know what he did with them. I think he did give them to somebody in the office, but I don't remember I ever told him who to give them to.

Q. After he had returned with the cards, did a meeting occur that afternoon? [190]

(Testimony of Victor Elmer Kangas.)

A.   That afternoon, about 2:00 o'clock, the thundering herd went past my desk and almost knocked me down, and there were 22 men present.

. Mr. Watkins: Just a moment. I move to strike that as a voluntary conclusion of the witness, about the thundering herd went past my desk and almost knocked me down.

Trial Examiner Whittemore: All right.   We will strike the thundering herd.

Q.   (By Mr. Moore)   Where was the meeting held?

A.   In the general manager's office.

Q.   Who was present at that meeting?

A.   I will have to go into detail about that. I was not in the office when this group of men entered. However, it was planned by Mr. Livingston and I sometime during that day——

Mr. Watkins: Just a minute. I move the answer, "It was planned by Mr. Livingston and I sometime during this day," be stricken on the ground it is a conclusion.

Mr. Moore: I will agree to that.

Trial Examiner Whittemore: All right.

Q.   (By Mr. Moore)   Who was present at this meeting in the afternoon?

Trial Examiner Whittemore: Well, were you present?

The Witness: That's what I am trying to bring out. I got to get there somewhere. [191]

Trial Examiner Whittemore: All right.   How did you get into the meeting?

(Testimony of Victor Elmer Kangas.)

The Witness: Mr. Livingston suggested to me that he would talk to the boys and then suggest to them, ask them if they would like to have me at the meeting.

Q. (By Mr. Moore) Wait now. This is not the meeting I was inquiring about. You had a further meeting then, with Mr. Livingston on Tuesday which you have not testified about so far?

A. Before these men went into the office?

Q. Yes.

A. The only meeting I remember having with him, he asked me if everything was satisfactory and I said, so far as I knew it was.

Q. Where was that meeting held?

A. I wouldn't know whether it was in the machine shop or in the office. That is something I don't remember.

Q. It was in the plant somewhere?

A. Oh, yes; all this transpired in the plant.

Q. And at about what time?

A. Oh, I would say possibly around, maybe 1:00 o'clock or 1:30.

Q. Were you and he alone when you had this conversation?   A. Yes.

Q. What did he say with respect to this meeting that he [192] expected to occur?

A. Well, he just wanted to know if the stage was set, and I says, "So far as I know, it is." I says, "I don't know too much about it, other than what Mr. Porter has told me, and he says he has contacted quite a few men."

(Testimony of Victor Elmer Kangas.)

I asked for a few names, and he told me, but there were very few of them mentioned.

Mr. Watkins: May I have the last part of that answer?

The Witness: Very few names mentioned.

Q. (By Mr. Moore) That testimony you have just given, where you testified as to what you told Mr. Livingston—— A. What was that?

Q. In that testimony that was just given, where you were testifying to what you told Mr. Livingston—— A. That's right.

Q. ——what did Mr. Livingston say?

A. Oh, he said that was fine.

Q. Did he discuss the meeting that later occurred at all?

A. Did he discuss this meeting that occurred later?

Q. Yes.

A. After the meeting.

Q. Yes. Were any plans made for that meeting?

A. Prior to this meeting, you mean?

Q. Yes. Did he expect some men to come in? Did he say he did? [193]

A. Naturally he was the one that set the stage for it.

Mr. Watkins: I move the answer be stricken, as to: "Naturally, he set the stage for it."

Trial Examiner Whittemore: That may be stricken. Just answer the question.

The Witness: Mr. Livingston asked me if the men would be in the office at 2:00 o'clock. I said,

(Testimony of Victor Elmer Kangas.)

"So far as I know they will be. I contacted my man in the plant, and he said everything is all right, so far as he knows, and that the men will be in there around 2:00 o'clock."

And at 2:00 o'clock almost——

Q. Wait. Did he ask you to be present?

A. No, he did not ask me to be present then. He said, however, "We will let the boys come in here first," and he said, "I will talk to the boys and let the boys talk to me, and," he said, "then I will suggest or ask the boys if they would like to have me in the office."

Q. Meaning you?

A. He would ask the boys if it was all right to call me in the office, and the boys agreed it would be all right. Then they rang my telephone and called me in the office. I went in the office——

Q. Wait now. You were testifying about the plan that he was making for this meeting.

A. Yes. [194]

Q. In other words, what he told you he expected to occur there; just go up to the point where he stopped talking about that, and stop. You are speaking of a conversation now, that occurred before this meeting where the employees were.

A. That's right.

Q. What did Mr. Livingston say at that meeting?

A. Between I and him? That's all he said. He just asked me if everything was set for the boys to come in the office, and I said it was.

(Testimony of Victor Elmer Kangas.)

Q. And then he said he would talk to them and ask them if it was all right to call you?

A. That's right.

Q. Were you called into the meeting later that afternoon? A. I was.

Q. At the time you came into the meeting, who was there?

A. As well as I remember, there was Mr. Creek, Ed Fickle and George Fickle, Mr. Porter, Stubblefield, Les Bebb, and I believe Mr. McIntire.

Q. The ones you have named up to now were production employees? A. They were.

Q. Who else? Was someone there representing management?

A. Yes, Mr. Dachtler, Mr. Livingston, and then myself.

Q. Very well. What occurred at that meeting after you got into it? [195]

A. Well, Mr. Livingston told me what had transpired in there before I had entered, and I agreed with him——

Q. What did he say? What did he say had happened?

A. He told me the boys had come in there and asked for more money, seniority rights, vacations with pay, better working conditions, and I told him that was fine; and he asked me if there was anything I wanted to say to the boys, and I told him no, I didn't think there was anything I could think of.

Q. Anything further? A. No.

(Testimony of Victor Elmer Kangas.)

Q. Was there any discussion of a raise, the merits of a demand for a raise?

A. As I remember they agreed to do something in regard to those conditions, but there wasn't any rates specified, there wasn't vacations promised to them. They said they would take it into consideration and give them some answer in the near future.

Q. Was it agreed at that time that a raise should go into effect?

A. No, not as I remember. There was nothing mentioned about raising the rates.

Q. Have you stated now all that you remember of the conversation that took place there?

A. Well, that's are far as I remember, yes. [196]

Q. I will ask you if there was any talk there about the formation of a union, the recognition of a union?

A. Well, it's kind of hazy. I can't exactly remember what did transpire right during that meeting. As well as I remember, I believe that the boys were pretty well satisfied and left the office. I don't remember of anything else that transpired right then.

Q. You don't recall, then, whether there was any discussion at that time of recognizing the union, if one should be formed?

A. With those men I don't remember what the conversation was in there.

Q. All right. After that meeting, by the way, at about what time did that meeting terminate?

(Testimony of Victor Elmer Kangas.)

A.   Oh, I think that possibly terminated about 2:30. I think it was only a half hour.

Q.   Was that about the time a shift was to end?

A.   No, the shift changed at 3:30.

Q.   Did you notice any activity in the plant after that meeting by Porter or Bebb or Stubblefield?

A.   Well, as near as I can remember, these cards, union cards that been picked up by Porter, got into the hands of the men some way, and were being distributed at the gates, as they were leaving the plant, and they were trying to get their signatures on them. [197]

Now, the men that were involved in that, the ones I saw was Lester Bebb, George Spurlock, Mr. Stubblefield; that's all I can remember.

Q.   Did Ed Fickle hand any of those out in your presence?

A.   No, not in my presence he didn't.

Q.   Now, that was on Tuesday afternoon, was it not?   A.   That's right.

Q.   On that day did you have a further meeting with Mr. Livingston?

A.   After that group left, why Mr. Livingston said he was very well satisfied.

Q.   Did you remain in the office with Mr. Livingston?   A.   After the boys left I did, yes.

Q.   Was Mr. Dachtler still there?

A.   Mr. Dachtler was still there.

Q.   Was anyone else there besides the three of you?

A.   I don't remember anybody else being there.

(Testimony of Victor Elmer Kangas.)

Q. What was the conversation after the men had left?

A. Mr. Livingston said he was very well pleased with the way Lou Porter had gone ahead with it and got the men into his office, and thought probably things would roll along pretty fast, and he said that he believed from what he talked to the boys in there, there wouldn't be many boys who would go to the C. I. O. meeting that night.

Q. Anything else? [198]

A. I don't remember anything else in particular.

Q. Did you say anything then?

A. Well, I generally do, but what I said I can't remember.

Q. I will ask you specifically if the C. I. O. was mentioned in that conversation?

A. Yes, it was.

Q. Was it mentioned in any other connection?

A. At this meeting with Mr. Dachtler, myself, and Livingston, the C. I. O. was mentioned; not during the meeting with the men, as I remember.

Q. You have testified now that Mr. Livingston said something about a meeting that night. Was anything else said about the C. I. O.?

A. Well, as well as I can remember, Mr. Livingston said that if we cracked the C. I. O. and prevented the C. I. O. from getting into the plant, that I didn't have to worry much about a job the rest of my life. So, being a prune picker, I thought

(Testimony of Victor Elmer Kangas.)
that was pretty good, didn't have to worry about a job. So I thought that was swell.

Q. Did you say that?

A. Well, I don't know. Maybe I didn't say those exact words, but being a prune picker, I still thought it was pretty good.

Q. After that Tuesday, did you have a further meeting with Mr. Livingston? [199]

A. Not that evening.

Q. Did you have one at any subsequent time?

A. As I remember we had, the next morning.

Q. Where was that?

A. That was at the office in the plant.

Q. You say that was on Wednesday morning?

A. Yes.

Q. After——   A. After the meeting.

Q. ——after the conference that 15 to 18 employees attended?

A. That was Wednesday, after the meeting in the office on Tuesday.

Q. Where did this further meeting take place?

A. On Wednesday?

Q. Yes.

A. It was in the company office.

Q. Were just the two of you present?

A. I just remember the two of us, yes.

Q. What was the conversation on that occasion?

A. Well, as well as I remember, Mr. Livingston asked me if I had heard anything from the boys,

(Testimony of Victor Elmer Kangas.)
and I told him I hadn't. I didn't know what the reaction was at that time.

Q. Did you have a further meeting with Mr. Livingston after that?

A. Yes, we did. Mr. Livingston gave me further instructions [200] as to what to do with these men, or Mr. Porter, told me to contact Mr. Porter with instructions he gave me. I carried them out through Mr. Porter.

Q. You say you had another meeting after this meeting on Wednesday?

A. That was Wednesday.

Q. Are you still speaking of the same meeting on Wednesday?

A. I don't know whether it is the same meeting or not. It was sometime Wednesday, though.

Q. Only you and Mr. Livingston were present?

A. That's right.

Q. In the office of the plant?

A. That's right.

Q. What further conversation took place?

A. Mr. Livingston wanted me to carry some instructions out to Mr. Porter in regard to keeping the boys hopped up over this union, and see if we could get over 51 per cent of the employees signed up with the inside union. And Mr. Porter naturally took his orders from me, and what he did I don't know——

Mr. Watkins: May I interrupt the witness, please. If the Examiner please, in these lengthy conversations it is impossible to object to them un-

(Testimony of Victor Elmer Kangas.)

less the witness is interrupted. We have had conclusions repeatedly, and we have in this answer here. This is an illustration: Mr. Porter [201] naturally, did something.

Trial Examiner Whittemore: That may be stricken.

Q. (By Mr. Moore) Continue and relate that conversation.

A. Well, Mr. Porter was working for me, so I carried out those instructions.

Q. Now, wait.

Mr. Watkins: Just a moment. I move that be stricken as a conclusion of the witness. He is supposed to be relating a conversation.

Mr. Moore: Yes.

The Witness: The conversation between **Mr.** Livingston and myself?

Q. (By Mr. Moore): Yes. Just relate that, as nearly as you can.

A. I just stated Mr. Livingston gave me instructions.

Q. Say what he told you.

A. Yes. He gave me instructions to keep the ball rolling, to get the employees into this organization, as many as we possibly could. He wanted over 51 per cent in the organization.

Mr. Watkins: I move to strike that, Mr. Examiner. That part of the answer he gave: "He wanted more than 51 per cent in the organization," and "to keep the ball rolling," as a conclusion of the witness.

The Witness: That's what he told me.

(Testimony of Victor Elmer Kangas.)

Tried Examiner Whittemore: I will permit it to remain. [202]

Q. (By Mr. Moore) Is that what he said?

A. That's what he told me. I am just merely repeating what Mr. Livingston told me.

Q. Very well. And did you contact Mr. Porter thereafter? A. I did.

Q. Where?

A. Out at the plant.

Q. When? The same day?

A. That same day. And I told him——

Q. Were the two of you alone?

A. Yes, the two of us were alone. I told him Mr. Livingston thought he had done a very fine job, and that he asked me to tell him to continue the good work, and get as many men in that organization as he can, at least 51 per cent, as soon as possible, and Mr. Porter said he would continue to do' so, which he did. Later on, I don't remember whether it was that day or not, Mr. Livingston asked me if there was any attorney that I knew of that might handle the affair for him.

Q. Where did this conversation take place?

A. This was in the plant.

Mr. Watkins: Just a minute. Can we fix some of these conversations before we barge off into them?

Mr. Moore: It is very difficult.

Mr. Watkins: The witness is so eager to get this out. I would like to have him take time enough to get some dates [203] in.

(Testimony of Victor Ehner Kangas.)

Q. (By Mr. Moore) Did this further meeting with Mr. Livingston occur the same day, Wednesday?

A. I wouldn't say whether it was Wednesday or the next day, Thursday.

Q. Where was this?   A. At the plant.

Q. In the office?   A. Yes.

Q. Was anybody else there besides you and he?

A. Mr. Livingston? No, there wasn't.

Q. What was said on that occasion?

A. He wanted to know if I knew of any attorney, or possibly Mr. Porter knew of some attorney that might handle the agreement, or contract, for the men; and I said, "I don't know myself, but possibly Mr. Porter does," and I contacted Mr. Porter and asked him, and he suggested Mr. Schooling as attorney for the union.

Q. When did you contact Mr. Porter?

A. The same day. I don't know whether it was 9:00 o'clock or three minutes after 9:00, or 4:00 in the afternoon, but it was that same day.

Q. Where was this?   A. At the plant.

Q. At his machine? [204]   A. Yes.

Q. Only he and you were present?

A. Only I and Mr. Porter were present.

Q. What did you tell Mr. Porter?

A. I asked Mr. Porter if he knew any attorney that might handle the legal end of it, and he said he did. He knew of Mr. Schooling, that had handled such cases, as that, and he thought maybe he would

(Testimony of Victor Elmer Kangas.)

handle it. He said he was a friend of his, and I said, "That's fine."

Q. After that, did you have a further meeting with Mr. Livingston?

A. Yes, I had a lot of meetings. In fact, too many of them.

Q. Let me ask you this: Did you have a meeting with him in a room at the Jonathan Club?

A. Yes, we went to the Jonathan Club.

Q. When did you do that?

A. Golly I don't know when. It was during that week, but I don't know whether it was Thursday or Friday, or when it was.

Q. Was it after this delegation of employees had come in to see Mr. Livingston?

A. Yes. Mr. Porter, Mr. Hodges, myself, and Mr. Livingston.

Q. The four of you were present in Mr. Livingston's room?

A. Yes, we went to his room, and then we went into the dining room and had dinner. [205]

Q. You went to his room first?

A. Yes.

Q. Were the four of you in his room?

A. That's right.

Q. How long did you stay there?

A. Oh, a very few minutes, possibly five minutes.

Q. Was anything said while you were up there?

A. Why, I don't remember of anything in particular that happened in his room, no.

(Testimony of Victor Elmer Kangas.)

Q. Do you remember any conversation?

A. No, I don't, now.

Q. Then, did you later go somewhere from there?

A. To the dining room, yes.

Q. Where was that?

A. In the Jonathan Club.

Q. In the same building?   A. That's right.

Q. Did you have dinner there?   A. We did.

Q. Did the four of you have dinner together?

A. Yes, Mr. Livingston, however, didn't eat. He had an engagement with his aunt and the three of us had dinner and he waited to eat with the aunt.

Q. Did Mr. Livingston sit there with you or was he absent?   A. Yes, he did. [206]

Q. He was there during the time the three of you were eating?   A. Yes.

Q. What conversation took place on that occasion, at that dinner?

A. Mr. Livingston discussed the previous meetings in the office, and also what had transpired in the past few days, so far as organizing the union, and that we had done a very, very nice job of it.

Q. Did he say he thought you had done a very nice job?

A. He did. He said he thought we had done an excellent job.

Q. Repeat as nearly as you can the conversation.

A. It is pretty hard, because I might in some way —as well as I can remember, he said, "Well, boys, I am more than pleased," or satisfied, "with the work

(Testimony of Victor Elmer Kangas.)

you have done," and he said, "I will say you have done a bang-up job," and he said, "I think we have got this thing licked, and I think our organization will go ahead now."

Q. Do you remember any other conversation?

A. No, I don't. I don't remember exactly what was discussed at that meeting.

Q. Did you take part in the conversation at all?

A. No, sir, not this time. I done all the listening.

Q. Have you exhausted your recollection as to what was said there?　A. Well—— [207]

Q. I will ask you specifically if the C. I. O. was discussed at that time?

A. At that particular time I don't think it was, because I don't exactly remember the C. I. O. being mentioned.

Q. At that time were lifetime jobs for you and Mr. Porter discussed?

A. No, I wouldn't say that at that particular meeting they were.

Mr. Moore: I am going into a new subject now. Do you mind if we take a few minutes recess?

Tried Examiner Whittemore: How much longer will you be with this witness now?

Mr. Moore: Oh, I would judge thirty minutes.

Trial Examiner Whittemore: Do you want to stay here and cross examine him this evening?

Mr. Watkins: Well, I wouldn't want to finish up tonight, Mr. Examiner, no.

(Testimony of Victor Elmer Kangas.)

Trial Examiner Whittemore: If you are not going to finish, I don't see any reason for continuing.

Mr. Watkins: It doesn't make any difference to me.

Trial Examiner Whittemore: I am perfectly willing to.

Mr. Watkins: I would just as soon run to half past 5:00, if counsel and the Examiner and the reporter do not mind; we can get in as much time as we can.

Trial Examiner Whittemore: That is all right. We will [208] take a two or three minute recess now.

(A short recess.)

Trial Examiner Whittemore: All right, Mr. Moore.

Q. (By Mr. Moore) Mr., Kangas, prior to the time you met Mr. Livingston in July of 1937, had you noticed any organizers of the C. I. O. or any union connected with the C. I. O. in the vicinity of the Thompson Products plant?

A. No, I hadn't noticed anybody there.

Q. Did you know whether or not men were joining the C. I. O.?

A. Yes, I did know they were.

Q. How did you know that?

A. Well, from the conversations that took place in the shop, of the different employees that had told me of others that had joined the C. I. O.

Q. What employees told you who had joined the C. I. O.?

(Testimony of Victor Elmer Kangas.)

A.   Mr. Bebb asked me if——

Q.   Mr. Lester Bebb?

A.   Lester Bebb, he asked me, rather, told me he had joined the C. I. O., due to the fact that he was trying to protect his job, and that was the reason why he joined the C. I. O.

Q.   When was that?

A.   Oh, that was possibly sometime in July, the early part of July.

Q.   Prior to the time you met Mr. Livingston in the plant, in July? [209]   A.   Yes.

Q.   Did you have any conversation with Mr. Porter with reference to membership in the C. I. O.?

A.   Yes.   I asked Mr. Porter to join the C. I. O.

Q.   When was that, now?

A.   That was, oh, it could have been in June, and it could have been the first of July. I don't remember the date exactly, but I know it was sometime—it was around in June or July.

Q.   Of 1937?   A.   Of 1937.

Q.   Where did you have the conversation with Mr. Porter?

A.   Why, this particular conversation I had with Mr. Porter was on the way to work from my house.

Q.   Just you and he were present?

A.   Yes.

Q.   Were you riding in an automobile?

A.   Yes. I was riding with Mr. Porter.

Q.   In his automobile?

A.   His automobile.

(Testimony of Victor Elmer Kangas.)

Q. What conversation did you have with him on that occasion?

A. I asked him if he would join the C. I. O. if the company would pay his dues, and he wanted to know why I wanted him to do that.

Q. Did he ask you why? [210]

A. Yes.

Q. Very well, go ahead.

A. So I told him I wanted to know about how many men belonged to the C. I. O. at that time.

Q. Do you know whether or not **Mr.** Porter joined the C. I. O.?   A. He did.

Q. Do you know about when he joined?

A. Well, he either joined in the next few days, or within a week.

Q. Do you know how his initiation fee was paid?

A. I do not.

Q. After he had joined the C. I. O. did you have any conversations with him relative to activities of the C. I. O.?   A. Yes, sir.

Q. When was the first of such conversations?

A. Well, I don't remember the date. It was right after the first meeting that Mr. Porter attended, the C. I. O. meeting.

Q. Was that shortly after he had joined?

A. It might have been three or four days; it might have been a week; but it was very shortly after that.

Q. Where were you at the time this conversation took place?   A. In the plant.

(Testimony of Victor Elmer Kangas.)

Q. At his machine, or where?

A. Yes, sir.

Q. Was anyone present besides you and he? [211]

A. No, sir.

Q. What was said with reference to the C. I. O.?

A. I asked him how many employees were present at the C. I. O. meeting, and as well as I can remember, I think he said 18 people.

Q. Did you thereafter have any further conversation with him on that subject?

A. Yes, I did.

Q. When was the next one, if you recall?

A. Oh, I don't believe it was until about a month or so afterwards, but I don't remember exactly.

Q. Was it before or after your meeting with Mr. Livingston in July of 1937?

A. Mr. Porter attended a C. I. O. meeting, I think, just a very little bit—I don't remember whether it was a week or two weeks before Mr. Livingston came out. I think Mr. Porter only reported twice to me of the different ones that had attended C. I. O. meetings.

Q. Was this second conversation, now, a week or two weeks before you met Mr. Livingston for the first time in July?

A. Yes. It might have been a week before. It was in the very—I don't know whether it was very close to that or not.

Q. Where did that conversation take place?

A. As well as I can remember it was in the plant.

(Testimony of Victor Elmer Kangas.)

Q. Who was present at that time? [212]

A. Just I and Porter.

Q. What was the conversation then?

A. Well, about the same thing. I asked him how many employees were in the meeting, and he told me, but there weren't very many. I don't know; maybe 15 or so.

Q. You previously made a statement, I think, in reference to a conversation between you and Mr. Livingston, that a large percentage of the employees in the shop had joined the C. I. O.?

A. Yes.

Q. How did you know that?

A. I merely got that from the various employees in the plant that told me had joined the C. I. O. to protect their jobs.

Q. You didn't deduce that from your conversations with Mr. Porter?

A. No, I couldn't very well, because the meetings he attended, there weren't very many employees present at either one of the two meetings.

Q. And you knew for a fact that more people were members than he said had attended?

A. That's right.

Q. After the Pacific Motor Parts Workers Alliance was formed—first, let me ask you if you know what that organization is? [213]

A. The Pacific Motor Parts Workers Alliance?

Q. Yes.   A. Do I know what it is?

Q. Yes.   A. Yes, sir, I certainly do.

(Testimony of Victor Elmer Kangas.)

Q. Was it formed as a result of the activities that you testified to heretofore?

A. Yes.

Mr. Watkins: Just a minute. I object to that as calling for a conclusion of the witness, and move to strike the answer. The facts speak for themselves in the record, Mr. Examiner, not a conclusion of this witness.

Trial Examiner Whittemore: I will permit the witness' answer to stand.

Q. (By Mr. Moore) Did the Thompson Products or any representative of the company have meetings with a committee of the Alliance?

A. The general manager of the plant, once a month after this organization was originated, the PMPWA, why, they had meetings once a month with the management.

Q. Did you attend any of those meetings?

A. Yes, I did.

Q. Did you do that often?

A. Well, we were supposed to meet once a month. Sometimes it might have gone over a month. [214]

Q. Did you attend all the meetings, or practically all?

A. Oh, I attended all of them while I was employed by Thompson Products.

Q. What was discussed at those meeting generally?   A. Well——

Mr. Watkins: Just a minute. I object to that as not being the best evidence, being hearsay; the

(Testimony of Victor Elmer Kangas.)
minutes are available of those meetings. They are
official minutes kept of them.

Mr. Moore: Can you produce the official minutes
of those meetings?

Mr. Watkins: I assume we can. We have copies
of them, yes. Sure. We can produce them.

Mr. Moore: Very well.

Trial Examiner Whittemore: It seems to me there
is some justification for the objection made by counsel for the respondent, unless there is something
specific you have in mind which you believe is not
in the minutes.

Mr. Moore: I have asked him to say generally
what was discussed. It is a foundation question. I
am not going into the details of bargaining at all.

Trial Examiner Whittemore: Then, I do not see
any reason for asking the question. If the minutes
you want are available, you can put them into evidence.

Mr. Watkins: The minutes are now produced,
Mr. Examiner. [215]

Mr. Moore: The point is: Quite often there is a
discussion at a meeting which doesn't ever get into
the minutes.

Trial Examiner Whittemore: That is all right.
The minutes are here. Let the witness see them. If
there is anything else—unless you have something
specific in mind, if you have, direct the witness' attention to it. You asked him a broad question, what was
discussed at the meetings once a month over a period

(Testimony of Victor Elmer Kangas.)
of five years. It seems to me we are wasting time to get an answer to that question.

Mr. Moore: I will withdraw the question.

Q. (By Mr. Moore): At the meeting between the employees of Thompson Products, Inc., and the executive council of the Alliance, was there ever any discussion of the C. I. O.?

A. Yes, there was, sometimes in every meeting, once in a while.

Q. When was the first occasion that you recall when the subject was discussed?

Mr. Watkins: Just a minute. I object to that line of examination. I feel it is not the best evidence of what took place at this meeting. The official minutes can be had of the meetings. They were written up in detail and signed by both the Alliance and the company, an official representative of each. Those minutes are available, and I will furnish them to the Board.

Mr. Moore: I don't proposed to be downed——

[216]

Trial Examiner Whittemore: If you know all that, you apparently are anticipating this witness is going to testify to something which does not appear in the record. That is something for you to meet.

Mr. Watkins: Mr. Examiner, I am not anticipating anything. I am just trying to follow the usual procedure when we are talking about something that took place at a meeting, at which official minutes were kept. If the witness wants to examine those minutes and state dates, and say something else was

(Testimony of Victor Elmer Kangas.)
discussed besides, things that do not show up in the
minutes, that would be a different thing.

The Witness: I will be glad to look at them.

·Trial Examiner Whittemore: I will overrule your
objection.

The Witness: I might be able to answer the question very near that time. I might not hit it on the
date.

Discussions at the meetings were——

Q. (By Mr. Moore): The question was, Mr.
Kangas, about when was the first meeting that you
attended at which the C. I. O. was discussed.

Mr. Watkins: May we have our objection——

A. Possibly three months.

Mr. Watkins: Just a minute. May we have our
standing objection to this line of questioning on the
ground it is incompetent, irrelevant, and immaterial, hearsay and not [217] the best evidence?

Trial Examiner Whittemore: You may have a
standing exception. I will overrule the objection and
you may have a standing exception.

Q. (By Mr. Moore): Can you say about when
the first meeting was?

A. Possibly about three months, as well as I
remember, it was around the third meeting that
was held between the committee of the PMPWA and
the management.

Q. At about the third meeting?   A. Yes.

Q. And who was present at that meeting?

A. Mr. Hileman and Mr. Creek.

Q. You are speaking of **Mr. Paul D. Hileman?**

(Testimony of Victor Elmer Kangas.)

A. Yes, and myself.

Q. And who else?

A. And Mr. Fickle. I am not sure whether Mr. —I can't think of his name now—Mr. George McIntire, I don't remember for sure whether he was present.

Q. Where did those meetings take place?

A. In Mr. Hileman's office.

Q. About what time?

A. Oh, about 2:30 in the afternoon. [218]

Q. (By Mr. Moore): Mr. Kangas, I had asked you, at the time we closed the hearing, whether or not you attended meetings between the bargaining committee of Pacific Motor Parts Workers Alliance and management? A. Yes, sir.

Q. You attended as a representative of management? A. Yes, sir.

Q. I also asked you if at any of those meetings the C. I. O. was discussed? A. Yes, sir.

Q. I have been furnished by counsel for the respondent, copies of the minutes of meetings between management and the bargaining committee of the Alliance. I will ask you if you remember the approximate date of the first meeting at which there was any discussion of the C. I. O.?

Mr. Watkins: May I interrupt, and go off the record for [223] just a second?

Trial Examiner Whittemore: Surely. Off the record.

(Discussion off the record.)

(Testimony of Victor Elmer Kangas.)

Trial Examiner Whittemore: On the record.

Mr. Watkins: I just wanted to state to the Examiner that the minutes that are being referred to I intended to introduce as part of Respondent's case. If they could now be marked for identification, then that might make it easier for counsel for the Board to examine the witness with respect to it.

Trial Examiner Whittemore: I think that is a good idea. Would you have them marked? They be marked as Respondent's Exhibits 1-A, 1-B, 1-C, and so forth. Is that agreeable?

Mr. Watkins: Yes. That is satisfactory.

(Thereupon, the documents referred to were marked as Respondent's Exhibits Nos. 1-A to 1-GGG, both inclusive, for identification.)

Trial Examiner Whittemore: Read that former question.

(The question was read.)

Mr. Moore: I will withdraw that question for the time being.

Q.   (By Mr. Moore)   At these meetings you attended, between the bargaining committee of the Alliance and of management, were minutes kept?

A.   Yes, sir.

Q.   Who kept the minutes? [224]

A.   The secretary of the P.M.P.W.A., and also the personnel manager, or acting personnel manager, of Thompson Products

Q.   Did they keep the minutes separately, or

(Testimony of Victor Elmer Kangas.)

did they sit together and just keep one set of minutes? A. Separately.

Q. Do you know how the minutes were transcribed? Were they later typed up?

A. Yes, they were.

Q. By whom was that done?

A. That was done by somebody in the organization. It might have been a number of different people.

Q. Which organization are you referring to?

A. Thompson Products.

Q. Do you know whether or not the Alliance typed up any minutes? A. Yes, they did.

Q. What was done then? Was there a comparison of the two? A. Yes, sir.

Q. How was that done?

A. Well, there were some things that were stricken out of the minutes that were taken by the Alliance and were approved by Thompson Products, or Jadson, before they were allowed to be posted on the Board.

Mr. Watkins: I object to the line of examination unless two things are done. They are: That a better foundation be [225] laid for the knowledge of this witness for the arrangement of these minutes; second, that as to things being stricken, he must identify with more certainty the minutes he is talking about.

Trial Examiner Whittemore: He has asked in general; I suppose he will get down to the specific eventually. However, I think the witness is well

(Testimony of Victor Elmer Kangas.)

qualified. He was a member of management at these meetings. Certainly, it seems to me, he is qualified to state what his knowledge is or what was done by other members of management.

Mr. Watkins: Your Honor, my point is: A board of directors might attend a directors' meeting and know nothing about the writing up of the minutes. He hasn't so far stated what he knew about writing up minutes, how it was done; how he happened to have knowledge of that.

Mr. Moore: I do not plan to attack the contents. I was simply attempting to show how they finally got signed.

Mr. Watkins: I see.

Q. (By Mr. Moore) Did you say these minutes were posted on the bulletin board after the meetings?   A. Yes, sir.

Q. You observed them there?

Trial Examiner Whittemore: As I get the picture now, there were two sets of minutes?

The Witness: That is correct. [226]

Trial Examiner Whittemore: Which minutes are you referring to that were posted?

The Witness: After management checked the minutes taken down by the P.M.P.W.A., or P.P.W.A., at that time, the minutes that were corrected, were changed and approved by the Jadson, or Thompson Products, now, and were posted on the bulletin board.

Q. (By Mr. Moore) I will ask you if you were

(Testimony of Victor Elmer Kangas.)

ever present at any time when a comparison of two sets were made?

A. No, sir, but I saw a copy of minutes, of minutes taken by P.P.W.A. before it was transcribed and after it was revised, and there was no comparison between the two of them after.

Mr. Watkins: Just a minute, Mr. Examiner, I move the last answer be stricken, that there was no comparison between the two of them, because there is no way on God's earth we could combat testimony of that character; it is purely a conclusion of the witness.

Mr. Moore: I will agree that may go out.

Trial Examiner Whittemore: Unless you can identify the document.

Mr. Moore: I do not propose to ask him to identify it particularly.

Trial Examiner Whittemore: All right.

Q. (By Mr. Moore) What was the approximate date of the meeting between the management and the Alliance's bargaining [227] committee when you first heard the C. I. O. discussion?

A. Well, I would say possibly it might have been two or three months, but it wasn't immediately after it was organized.

Q. You mean two or three months after what time? After it was recognized?

A. After the first meeting.

Q. Do you know the date of the first meeting?

(Testimony of Victor Elmer Kangas.)

A. No, I don't. I don't remember the first meeting.

Q. Do you know the month in which it was held?

A. I think it was in September.

Q. Can you refresh your memory by referring to Respondent's Exhibits for identification 1-A to 1-GGG?   A. I think I can.

Q. My question now, Mr. Kangas, is directed toward finding out the date you started your calculation of two or three months, rather than the date at which this meeting was held.

A. Well, I would say that the organization had probably been organized for either two or three months, when this——

Mr. Watkins: May I have the answer read, and ask that the witness speak up louder?

Trial Examiner Whittemore: Will you speak up. All right.

The Witness: As well as I can remember, it was either two or three months—— [228]

Mr. Moore: After——

The Witness: ——after.

Mr. Watkins: That is all. Thank you.

Q. (By Mr. Moore) After what time?

A. After the first meeting. That, I wouldn't be certain of.

Q. Can you say in what months the first meeting was held, after having refreshed your memory by examining the minutes before?

(Testimony of Victor Elmer Kangas.)

A. The first monthly meeting was held in September, as well as I can remember, September of 1937.

Q. Is that the meeting to which you referred at which the C. I. O. was discussed, that, then, having occurred in November or December?

A. That's right.

Q. I show you Respondent's Exhibits 1-I and 1-J, which are dated, respectively, November 3, 1937, and November 22, 1937, and ask you if by examining those exhibits you can refresh your recollection and state at which meeting you heard the C. I. O. discussed?

May the record show at this time 'that Respondent's Exhibit 1-H, for identification, is dated October 20, 1937, and Respondent's 1-K, for identification, is dated February 28, 1938.

A. As near as I can remember, I believe it was 11/2/37. [229]

Q. You believe the meeting at which you heard the C. I. O. discussed——   A. That's right.

Q. ——was held on November 22, 1937. Have you read over Respondent's Exhibit 1-J, which purports to be the minutes of that meeting?

A. Yes, sir.

Q. According to your recollection, do these minutes express all that occurred at that meeting?

A. No, sir.

Q. Who was present at that meeting?

A. Mr. Hileman, Mr. Hodges, and myself, E. T.

(Testimony of Victor Elmer Kangas.)
Fickle, George Fickle, Pfankuch, and Mr. Bebb, as well as I remember.

Q. Do you remember about what time of day that meeting was held?

A. It was in the afternoon, approximately 2:00 or 2:30.

Q. Where was it held?

A. In Mr. Hileman's office, in the plant.

Q. What was said at that meeting with reference to the C. I. O.?

Mr. Watkins: Can you find out by whom, also?

Q. (By Mr. Moore) Yes. What was said, and by whom was it said?

A. Mr. Hileman talked to the committee members, asking [230] them first, how conditions were, whether or not everybody was more or less satisfied with their rates of pay, with the present management, and wanted to know what the boys thought of the union in the shop.

Q. Did he ask them those questions?

A. He did.

Q. All right.

A. And he also mentioned that he thought probably that an organization of the employees themselves would probably work out matters better with the management than they could if they had an outside organization, either the C. I. O. or A. F. of L. representing them.

Q. Is that all that was said at that meeting with reference to that subject?

A. He did ask how they felt about that, asked

(Testimony of Victor Elmer Kangas.)
the different members of the committee, and that he thought that they probably would be more satisfied with those conditions.

Q. By that do you mean the members of the committee?

A. The committee; that is right.

Q. Do you recall any other meeting between the members of the bargaining committee of the Alliance and the management at which the C. I. O. was discussed?

A. Yes. I don't know the dates. It could have happened at any time, but I couldn't—I can only remember the few words that were mentioned about the C. I. O.; but I don't remember [231] when it was.

Q. Well, was it after this date?

A. It was quite a bit after that. I would say it might have been six or seven months after that, maybe a year after, but I can't remember.

Q. Can you refresh your recollection by looking at the——

A. No, sir. I wouldn't be able to do that, due to the fact that that was brought up several times, and I don't remember at which one of those meetings. It was several months after this it was brought up again, and several times repeatedly after that, but by reading over the minutes I wouldn't know.

Q. Do you recall who was present at the next meeting?

(Testimony of Victor Elmer Kangas.)

A. It would have to be the same people, because of the fact that they was in office for that period of time, and there were several different committees there, and as far as my memory is concerned, I would not swear that any one of those were in, but I would say it was the same committee members.

Q. Where was this later meeting held?

A. In Mr. Hileman's office, at the plant.

Q. You think it was six months to a year after the meeting of November 22, 1937?

A. I would say it was somewhere in that neighborhood. I might be off on that time, but it was some time, quite awhile after that.

Q. At this next meeting, will you name the people who were [232] present?

A. To the best of my memory I will try to. Mr. Creek, George Fickle, Ed Fickle, Mr. Pfankuch, Lester Bebb, myself, and Mr. Hileman and Mr. Hodges.

Q. Where did that take place?

A. At the Jadson Motor Products' main office.

Q. What was said on that occasion about the C. I. O.?

A. Mr. Hileman told the boys that if Thompson Products, or if the C. I. O. or A. F. of L., or any outside labor organization was to come into the plant, that every man would be assured that the plant would be closed; that their equipment would be moved to Cleveland, due to the fact that their

(Testimony of Victor Elmer Kangas.)

plant is so large that in ten minutes they could do the same amount of work in their Cleveland plant as our West Coast plant could in 24 hours.

Mr. Watkins: Just a minute, Mr. Examiner; unless the witness can fix with some more certainty the matter of time when this took place, I want to ask that the answer be stricken, because there is no way we can check a statement of that kind.

Trial Examiner Whittemore: Well, can you——

The Witness: I can't definitely say when that happened, as to the day and the month, no. This was a conversation that happened in the office.

Trial Examiner Whittemore: The motion is denied. [233]

Q. (By Mr. Moore) Was anything else with reference to the C. I. O. said at this second meeting about which you testified?

A. Only repeatedly, the same conversation——

Mr. Watkins: Just a minute.

Q. (By Mr. Moore) No. I mean at this same meeting you have testified about.

A. No, sir.

Q. How did——

Mr. Watkins: Just a minute, please. I would like to move the witness' answer, something about "repeatedly——" be stricken as non-responsive, and also a conclusion.

Trial Examiner Whittemore: It may be stricken.

Q. (By Mr. Moore) How did that subject come up?

(Testimony of Victor Elmer Kangas.)

A. Well, it generally started out by their asking the boys——

Q. No. I am speaking of this specific meeting, this second time about which you have testified. How did it come up on that occasion?

A. ——asking the committee members whether or not the employees were satisfied with the company management.

Q. Who asked that?

A. Mr. Hileman. How working conditions were, how they were satisfied with their pay rates; whether or not they were satisfied.

Q. How did he get into the part about the C. I. O.?

A. And asking the committee members what the employees [234] thought of their organization, and after that was discussed Mr. Hileman always stressed the point of the C. I. O. coming in, and of the A. F. of L.——

Mr. Watkins: Just a minute. I move the answer be stricken as to that portion "Mr. Hileman always stressed the point of the C. I. O.," and so forth, as a conclusion of the witness, and not being in any way definite or certain.

Trial Examiner Whittemore: Well, that part of his answer may be stricken.

Mr. Moore: Pardon me?

Trial Examiner Whittemore: It may be stricken. You are asking him with respect to one meeting, now.

(Testimony of Victor Elmer Kangas.)

Mr. Moore: Yes. I am asking what occurred at the second meeting.

The Witness: He did mention that at this meeting.

Q. (By Mr. Moore) Referring again, Mr. Kangas, to the day on which certain cards were distributed in the plant, as you have testified heretofore, did you see any of those cards that were being distributed there?

A. Yes, sir. I just casually glanced over it.

Mr. Moore: Mr. Baldwin, may I have that original membership card which you found? May I have this marked Board's Exhibit 6, for identification?

(Thereupon, the document referred to was marked as Board's Exhibit No. 6, for identification.) [235]

Q. (By Mr. Moore): I show you a card marked Board's Exhibit 6, for identification, and ask you if the printed portion of that card is like the cards, the same as the cards that were distributed in the shop on that day?

Mr. Watkins: Just a minute. I object to the question on the ground it assumes facts not in evidence, and further, that there is no foundation laid for such identification by this witness.

Trial Examiner Whittemore: I will overrule the objection. The witness has been asked a general question to identify a document; it may not be the one. If so, you have no cause to worry.

(Testimony of Victor Elmer Kangas.)

Mr. Watkins: Unless I missed it somewhere along the line, my point is, the witness has not been asked whether or not he ever saw a similar card.

Trial Examiner Whittemore: He said he had seen the cards and looked at them. He is shown this to find out whether or not this contains the text shown on the cards. He certainly is qualified to answer that question.

The Witness: Yes, sir. I would swear that that was the card.

Q. (By Mr. Moore): You have testified that you have ordered printed certain cards?

A. Yes, sir.

Q. Can you say that the printed portion of Board's Exhibit [236] 6, for identification, contains the text that you ordered printed on the cards which you testified about?

A. Word for word I can't remember it, but the wording on there certainly is exactly the wording that was to be printed on those cards at that time.

Mr. Watkins: Just a minute. I move that answer be stricken as a conclusion of the witness: That the words on the cards mean exactly the same,—I couldn't get the rest of the answer.

Mr. Moore: Would you like to have the answer read?

Mr. Watkins: No. I don't need to have it read.

Trial Examiner Whittemore: Do you mind if I ask the witness a question at this point?

Mr. Watkins: No.

(Testimony of Victor Elmer Kangas.)

Trial Examiner Whittemore: Do you mean this, in substance, was what was on the cards you ordered printed?

The Witness: Yes, sir. That is the dictation I took over the telephone, to have the cards printed.

Trial Eaminer Whittemore: But you say you don't recall it word for word?

The Witness: No, sir.

Trial Examiner Whittemore: I think it is perfectly clear, don't you?

Mr. Watkins: Yes, I think it is. May I see the card?

Trial Examiner Whittemore: All right. You have offered [237] that, have you, in evidence?

Mr. Moore: I have not as yet.

Trial Examiner Whittemore: All right.

Q. (By Mr. Moore): For the purpose of the following question, Mr. Kangas, will you say again who you saw distribute the cards in the plant on the day after the committee, or a group of employees, went in to see the management?

A. Spurlock, Lester Bebb, Stubblefield, those are the only three I remember.

Q. You have testified that you met and discussed various subjects with a committee of the Alliance. Were any of the men you have named on the bargaining committee with whom you met?

A. Yes, sir.

Q. Which of them?

A. Mr. Bebb was on the committee, Mr. Stubblefield at one time was on the committee.

(Testimony of Victor Elmer Kangas.)

Mr. Moore: I offer Board's Exhibit 6, for identification, in evidence.

Trial Examiner Whittemore: Any objection?

Mr. Watkins: Yes. I object to the foundation laid with respect to it, but if the representative of the Alliance tells me that is the correct card, I will not object to it.

Mr. Baldwin: I can't say it is the correct card, either, because it was before my knowledge of it. I only saw a second [238] printing.

Trial Examiner Whittemore: You were asked yesterday to produce this card.

Mr. Baldwin: If I could possibly find one.

Trial Examiner Whittemore: This, to the best of your knowledge, is the card? You do not know to the contrary?

Mr. Baldwin: No.

Trial Examiner Whittemore: Well, on the basis of Mr. Baldwin's statement, do you wish to retain your objection?

Mr. Watkins: Yes. I object to it, Mr. Examiner, on the ground that there is no proper foundation laid; there isn't anything in the record that shows this was the card first distributed at the plant and to which reference has been made.

Trial Examiner Whittemore: On the contrary, all the evidence in the record so far does establish that point. The witness has testified that this contains the text, to the best of his recollection. The substance is there. He had it printed, and he saw it distributed by these three men. According to my

(Testimony of Victor Elmer Kangas.)

recollection of the testimony that is so. There may be testimony that will come in here which will attack whatever weight may be given to this testimony, but so far, the only testimony is of this witness, whose testimony is partly corroborated by my request of Mr. Baldwin to bring in the card. He brought this in, and so far as he knows, there is none other. It is the only one he has produced. Later [239] testimony here, evidence, may cast some doubt upon it, but so far, it seems to me it is established.

Mr. Watkins: Mr. Examiner, the basis of my objection on foundation was this: Yesterday this witness testified he didn't know what was on that card; he didn't know what he had taken down from Mr. Livingston, when he called him. He said, the name of the company, and two or three lines. He was asked to testify, and he couldn't. He also testified certain cards were distributed in the plant by certain individuals. He has not testified what the cards were. If he has, I haven't caught it.

Trial Examiner Whittemore: I think, on the latter point, if there is any doubt, it was my understanding he had testified these were the cards he saw distributed. But, in view of your doubt, will you inquire on that point?

Mr. Moore: I note the card is signed by the witness who has testified. I will recall the witness and identify it further.

Trial Examiner Whittemore: No. I think the point he is referring to is whether or not this wit-

(Testimony of Victor Elmer Kangas.)
ness saw that card, or one similar to it, distributed by these men you just referred to here.

Mr. Moore: I misunderstood the objection.

Trial Examiner Whittemore: Wasn't that it?

Mr. Watkins: Part of my objection is on the basis of no [240] foundation, yes.

Q. (By Mr. Moore) Mr. Kangas, did you see this card, or cards like this, distributed in the plant on the day after a delegation of employees visited the management and met, with their requests?

A. The same day.

Q. The same day?   A. Yes, sir.

Q. Did you see the cards, this card, or cards exactly like that, distributed in the plant?

A. Yes.

Q. That is the best of your recollection?

A. Yes, sir.

Trial Examiner Whittemore: Does that take care of that part of the objection?

Mr. Watkins: I think for the record, yes.

Trial Examiner Whittemore: All right.

Mr. Watkins: Subject to cross examination.

Trial Examiner Whittemore: Oh, yes, of course. Well, then the document is received in evidence. I would like to see that. All right, Mr. Moore.

(Thereupon, the document heretofore marked for identification as Board's Exhibit No. 6, was received in evidence.)

(Testimony of Victor Elmer Kangas.)

BOARD'S EXHIBIT No. 6

Porter

Pacific Parts Workers Alliance

I the undersigned employee at the Jadson Motor Products Company, do hereby apply for membership in the Pacific Parts Workers Alliance with the understanding that upon acceptance of the application for membership that the Pacific Parts Workers Alliance will be my exclusive representative in bargaining with my employer with reference to wages, hours and working conditions, and that I will abide by the constitution of the Pacific Parts Workers Alliance when drafted and approved by the elected representative.

This membership to be effective until one year from the date of signing.

L. A. PORTER

Date 7-27-37.

————

Q. (By Mr. Moore) You have testified that at the time of your first experience with the Alliance, it was called Pacific [241] Parts Workers Alliance, wasn't it? A. Yes, sir.

Q. Do you know what the name of the Alliance is now? A. Yes, sir.

Q. What is it?

A. Pacific Motor Parts Workers Alliance.

Q. Do you know how or when the change in name was effected?

(Testimony of Victor Elmer Kangas.)

A. One year from the day that it was organized, to the best of my memory, it might have been thirteen months or fourteen months, but it was in the neighborhood of one year from that date.

Q. Was the Pacific Motor Parts Workers Alliance in existence when you left the shop of the respondent? A. Yes, sir.

Q. Do you know whether or not the Alliance held meetings among its own members during the time you were employed in the shop?

A. At the plant?

Q. No. Do you know whether or not they held meeting?

A. Yes, sir, I knew they did.

Q. Do you know on what day of the week their meetings were scheduled, as a general rule?

A. No, sir.

Q. Do you know whether or not those meetings were scheduled to occur during the time when the plant was in operation? [242]   A. Yes, sir.

Q. Were the meetings so scheduled?

A. Some of the shifts were working, yes, sir.

Q. During the time you were there, how many shifts did the plant operate?

A. They were working 24 hours a day, three shifts.

Q. Was that true from April 8, 1937, until you left there?   A. Yes, sir.

Q. Three shifts every day?

A. No, not a seven-day week. We worked five days at one time and six days at another time. How-

(Testimony of Victor Elmer Kangas.)

ever, there was work going on in the plant seven days a week, but a full crew did not work seven days a week.

Q. Do you know whether or not men were sebeduled to work during the time that the Alliance held meetings?

Mr. Watkins: Isn't the answer obvious, counsel? If they were working 24 hours they couldn't help but be.

Trial Examiner Whittemore: I was going to say: How could that be, if they were working 24 hours a day.

Mr. Moore: It will withdraw that. It is obvious.

Trial Examiner Whittemore: The question is whether or not the men attended.

Mr. Moore: That is true, yes.

Q. (By Mr. Moore) Was any arrangement made by the management to permit employees scheduled to work during the time an [243] Alliance meeting was held, to attend the meetings?

Mr. Watkins: Just a minute, before the answer is given. I object to the question unless the witness first identifies the type of meeting held, of the Alliance. In other words, whether it was a general Alliance meeting, or a committee meeting, or an arrangement to meet with management, or what.

Trial Examiner Whittemore: I think you should explore the matter further.

Mr. Moore: Yes.

Q. (By Mr. Moore) I am referring, Mr. Kangas, to meetings of the membership of the Alliance.

(Testimony of Victor Elmer Kangas.)

A. That I don't remember. I can't say.

Q. Do you know whether or not men left the plant to attend those meetings?

A. No, sir; I do not know.

Q. Do you know whether or not Mr. Lewis A. Porter received any pay for—I will withdraw that.

Mr. Kangas, did you at any time receive any money from Mr. Paul D. Hileman, to be delivered to Mr. Lewis A. Porter?

A. I did not see the money. However, I delivered him an envelope.

Q. When did you receive that envelope?

A. It was in the afternoon of the—I can't tell you what day it was, or I don't remember what month it was.

Q. Well, tell us what time it was, as nearly as you can re- [244] call.

A. Well, I would say it was approximately around 2:30 or 3:00 o'clock in the afternoon, and Mr. Hileman had me come in his office, and he gave me an envelope.

Q. What I want you to do is to tell us about what time of the year, as near as you can recall.

A. It was in the fall of the year, either September, or the latter part of August, and I believe it was in 1938.

Q. 1938?

A. I think so, as well as I can remember.

Q. Do you think it was over a year after the Alliance had been formed?

A. I would say it was, yes.

(Testimony of Victor Elmer Kangas.)

Q. Were you and Mr. Hileman close at the time you received this envelope from him?

A. Yes, sir.

Q. Was a conversation held at that time?

A. Mr. Hileman told me to deliver that envelope to Mr. Porter and I went out in the plant——

Q. Was anything else said?

A. Yes. He told me that was reimbursement for his efforts in organizing the independent union, and he told me to be sure that nobody saw me give it to him. I went out in the plant and I called Mr. Porter in the washroom and I handed him the envelope. [245]

Mr. Watkins: Just a minute. I object to the anxiety of the witness to get his story in without questions being asked, and I urge he be instructed to proceed in the normal question and answer fashion.

Trial Examiner Whittemore: Well, I don't know whether any caution is necessary.

Mr. Moore: I am sure this witness knows what the normal procedure is. We can get along all right.

Trial Examiner Whittemore: Just try to confine your answer to the question, rather than tell the whole story.

Q. (By Mr. Moore) Have you repeated all the conversation between you and Mr. Hileman that you can recall?   A. Prior to this?

Q. At this meeting at which you received the envelope.

(Testimony of Victor Elmer Kangas.)

A. Did I remember the conversation that took place?

Q. Have you repeated all you could remember?

A. No, sir.

Q. Continue, and give the entire conversation at that time.

A. Well, at this time I was called in to his office and Mr. Hileman discussed with me——

Q. Just say what he said, now.

A. He told me in regards to the money that Mr. Porter was to receive as a reimbursement for his efforts in organizing the P.P.W.A., independent union, that he has some money for him in an envelope and he handed me the envelope and he told me to [246] deliver that envelope to Mr. Porter, and not to let anybody see me give it to him. I told him I would.

Q. Is that all the conversation that you recall?

A. Yes, sir.

Q. Did you thereafter——

Mr. Watkins: May I have the answer read?

Trial Examiner Whittemore: Yes. Read the answer.

(The answer was read.)

Mr. Watkins: Thank you.

Q. (By Mr. Moore) Did you thereafter deliver that envelope to Mr. Porter?   A. I did.

Q. When did you do that?

A. That same day, just right at that time. It may have been 30 seconds after, or it may have been one minute afterwards.

(Testimony of Victor Elmer Kangas.)

Q. Where did you deliver it to him?

A. In the plant.

Q. What part of the plant?

A. Where Mr. Porter was working.

Q. Well, did you deliver the envelope to him in the place where he was working?   A. No, sir.

Q. Where did you deliver the envelope to him?

A. I asked him to come into the washroom with me.

Q. You and he went into the washroom? [247]

A. Yes, sir.

Q. And did you deliver the envelope to him there?

A. Yes, sir. I gave him the envelope and I walked out.

Q. Was anyone there besides you and he?

A. No, sir.

Q. Was there a conversation at that time?

A. No, sir.

Q. Did you remain to see whether or not he would open the envelope?   A. No, sir.

Q. Did you see him open it?   A. No, sir.

Q. Did you know what was in the envelope?

A. Not at that time.

Q. You did not know at that time what was in it?   A. No, sir.

Q. Did you later learn what was in it?

A. Yes, sir.

Q. How did you learn what was in it?

A. We went to his house that evening, I and my

(Testimony of Victor Elmer Kangas.)

wife, and Mr. Porter told me what was in the envelope.

Q. Was it on the same evening that you went to his house?   A. Yes, sir.

Q. Who was present besides you and he?

A. His wife and my wife. [248]

Q. About what time in the evening was it?

A. About 8:00 o'clock.

Q. Do you recall where he lived then?

A. He lived on Stafford Avenue, at that time.

Q. Will you repeat the conversation that was held at that time?

A. Shall I say everything he said?

Q. As nearly as you can recall.

A. Mr. Porter was very much put out, due to the fact——

Q. No.

Mr. Watkins: Just a minute.

Mr. Moore: I will agree that may go out, Mr. Watkins. Just say what he said.

The Witness: Mr. Porter told me, he said, "This is what they gave me. I have got a good notion to go in and tell that Jew son of a bitch to stick that up his brown."

Q. (By Mr. Moore) What was said after that, if anything?

A. As far as that conversation, that was the end of it.

Q. If there was any other conversation, it was of a social nature?

A. He told me he would never again do any-

(Testimony of Victor Elmer Kangas.)
thing for the Alliance, to help the management in any way.

Q. Did you have any part in the conversation?

A. I beg your pardon? [249]

Q. Did you say anything at that time?

A. No, sir.

Q. Do you know whether or not Mr. Porter received any other remuneration?   A. I do not.

Q. Do you know whether or not he received a vacation?

A. I don't remember whether he did or not.

Q. Was Mr. Porter an hourly paid employee?

A. Yes, sir.

Q. In September, of 1937, did hourly paid employees receive vacations?   A. With pay?

Q. Yes.   A. No, sir.

Q. In September, of 1938, did hourly paid employees receive vacations with pay?

A. No, sir.

Mr. Moore: That is all.

Trial Examiner Whittemore: Do you want a brief recess before we resume with cross examination?

Mr. Watkins: Yes, I would like it, please.

Trial Examiner Whittemore: All right. We will take a five-minute recess at this time.

(A short recess was had.)

Trial Examiner Whittemore: I would like to set forth on [250] the record about what Mr. Porter's age is. Now, if you have it on your personnel records, so that you can stipulate to it, or get this

(Testimony of Victor Elmer Kangas.)

man's testimony, or something, that will be all right. I would like to have something on the record. You went into his past experience somewhat. I don't care who brings it out.

Mr. Watkins: We will find out, Mr. Examiner.

Mr. Moore: May it be stipulated while Mr. Lewis A. Porter was in the employ of Thompson Products, Inc., he was not employed at that time in a supervisory capacity.

Mr. Watkins: Yes. So stipulated.

Mr. Moore: Mr. Examiner, you indicated you wanted Mr. Porter's age, and I believe we are able to supply that.

Mr. Watkins: Yes. Mr. Porter's age is 62 years.

Trial Examiner Whittemore: Thank you very much.

On that point I brought up just a moment ago, the complaint says, in parenthesis, this:

"U.A.W., C.I.O." and nowhere is it stated differently that I find, in the complaint that the Aircraft & Agricultural Implement Workers are affiliated with Automobile Workers, and the Congress of Industrial Organizations.

If you will frame that in a stipulation, please, so that it may be written out in the formal report.

Mr. Moore: May it be stipulated that United Automobile, Aircraft & Agricultural Implement Workers of America, affiliat- [251] ed with the Congress of Industrial Relations, is a labor organization within the meaning of the Labor Act?

(Testimony of Victor Elmer Kangas.)

Mr. Watkins: We have already admitted that in our answer, but we have no objection——

Trial Examiner Whittemore: Yes. That isn't my point, Mr. Moore. The answer covers that.

Mr. Moore: I am afraid I do not get your point. What is it?

Trial Examiner Whittemore: In the complaint it is said in parenthesis, "U.A.W.-C.I.O.", and nowhere is it explained what the U.A.W., or what C.I.O. is, or that there is such an organization in existence.

Mr. Moore: May we go off the record, Mr. Examiner?

Trial Examiner Whittemore: Yes. Off the record.

(A discussion off the record.)

Trial Examiner Whittemore: On the record.

Mr. Moore: I will move to amend the amended complaint, in the first paragraph thereof, by striking from the complaint in the second line, the letters, "U.A.W.-C.I.O." which appear in parenthesis, and inserting instead the words: [252] "Affiliated with the Congress of Industrial Organizations."

Trial Examiner Whittemore: Do you have any objection?

Mr. Watkins: No, we have no objection to it. Of course, there will be a stipulation that our answer need not be changed, our answer and motions heretofore filed, will be deemed to comply with the complaint as amended.

Mr. Moore: So stipulated.

(Testimony of Victor Elmer Kangas.)

Trial Examiner Whittemore: Have you any objection, Mr. Baldwin?

Mr. Baldwin: No objection.

Trial Examiner Whittemore: Very well. The motion is granted. I suggest also that you move that same change be made in all the formal papers, the title of the case, as well.

Mr. Moore: Yes. I further move that the same change be made in all of the formal papers in the case, namely, in Board's Exhibit 1-A to 1-V, inclusive.

Mr. Watkins: No objection.

Trial Examiner Whittemore: Mr. Baldwin, have you?

Mr. Baldwin: No objection.

Trial Examiner Whittemore: Very well. The motion is granted.

All right, Mr. Watkins.

Mr. Watkins: Does Mr. Baldwin have any questions of the witness?

Mr. Baldwin: Yes. [253]

Q. (By Mr. Baldwin): Mr. Kangas, you stated that at one time you asked, or you received over the telephone, a message. You wrote the message down. You can't remember that message?

A. No, not word for word.

Q. You, in turn, handed it to the printer?

A. That's right.

Q. To have it printed. You later testified you sent Mr. Porter to pick up these cards?

A. Yeah.

(Testimony of Victor Elmer Kangas.)

Q. Did you give Mr. Porter the money to pay for these cards?   A. No, sir.

Q. Do you know who did give it to him?

A. No, I don't.

Q. Do you think anybody in the management gave him that money?   A. I don't know.

Q. About what time of day did he leave?

A. Oh, somewhere around 11:00 o'clock.

Q. Did he clock out at the time?   A. No.

Q. He didn't; was this on the same day that the first meeting was held—I will change that.

Was that the same day that the first group of 15 or 18 men came into your office? [254]

A. It was.

Q. You haven't any idea what that date was?

A. No. If I had a calendar I might be able to tell you.

Mr. Watkins: I think we can furnish the witness with one. I might say this isn't a calendar for the overall year, but it does contain the month of July of 1937.

Q. (By Mr. Baldwin): Will the witness take a look at that book.

A. As near as I can remember, it would be around July 30 or July 29. I couldn't swear to that, but as near as I can remember.

Mr. Moore: Pardon me just a moment. May I have the last question and answer read.

(The record was read.)

The Witness: That is not right. The day the group of men went into the office was on Tuesday.

(Testimony of Victor Elmer Kangas.)

The day Mr. Porter went to get those cards was Tuesday morning and not on a Friday or Thursday.

Mr. Moore: You want to change your testimony with regard to that date?

The Witness: That is right. I want to see that same book again. That would be on August 3rd, to the best of my memory.

Q. (By Mr. Baldwin): Then the day in which the group of 15 or 18 men came into the office would be on August 3rd, Tuesday, [255] and that is also the same day in which the cards were picked up at about 11:00 o'clock in the morning or thereabouts. Is that right?   A. That's right.

Q. You later testified you saw these cards passed out. Is that right?   A. That's right.

Q. Did you see the contents of the cards prior to the time they were passed out?

A. Not prior to the time they were passed out; I saw them after they were passed out.

Q. Did Mr. Porter give you the cards? Did he hand you the cards when he came back into the plant?   A. No.

Q. You don't know who gave them to you?

A. No, I don't.

Q. Do you know who he gave them to?

A. No, I don't know who he gave them to. I don't remember. Probably gave them to Hodges. I don't know.

Mr. Baldwin: That's all.

(Testimony of Victor Elmer Kangas.)

Cross Examination

Q. (By Mr. Watkins): Mr. Kangas, what makes you so sure it was on a Tuesday that this happened?

A. To the best of my memory it was on a Tuesday. I might not be right on the date. [256]

Q. Could it have been on a Monday?

A. No, I don't think it could.

Q. Why not?

A. Because we had some other work to do on Monday in regard to that, and it couldn't have been on a Monday.

Q. Could it have been on a Wednesday?

A. No, it wasn't on a Wednesday. It was on a Tuesday. I am quite sure of that.

Q. Going back in the early part of 1937, say the first half of the year, how many production employees were there at Jadson?

A. Oh, up until September of 1937, there was 86.

Q. What was your official job there?

A. Up to that time I was assistant works manager.

Q. Who was works manager?

A. Mr. Clark, Walter Clark.

Q. You took your directions from him, is that correct?

A. That's right. However, he left the organization sometime in June, and I was still carrying on my duties as assistant works manager.

Q. Taking this period in the first half of 1937,

(Testimony of Victor Elmer Kangas.)
what was the attitude of the employees with regard to their pay and working conditions at Jadson?   A. Well, they were dissatisfied.

Q. Well, what was said that indicated to you
that they were [257] dissatisfied? What was said
that indicated that to you?

A. Well, men would come in my office and ask
for more money.

Q. Was that on more than one occasion?

A. Oh, yes, on several occasions.

Q. Was there anything besides more money that
they were interested in?

A. Not that I know of at that time. They asked
for more money, better pay.

Q. Anything about shorter hours?

A. Not as I remember, no.

Q. Anything about vacations?   A. No.

Q. Anything about seniority?   A. No.

Q. Anything about discrimination among employees in advancement?   A. No.

Q. Anything about favoritism?

A. Well, I don't remember that there was.

Q. In other words, the only thing you can recall in the first half of the year was more pay?

A. That's right.

Q. How many different occasions would you
say there were in that six months period when
men came in and asked for more pay? [258]

A. Well, I really don't know, but I would say
practically one-third of the plant was in there
every week.

(Testimony of Victor Elmer Kangas.)

Q. Every week one-third of the plant was in there, in that first half of the year? A. Yes.

Q. Now, when it was learned that Thompson Products had bought the company, approximately when was that, incidentally?

A. As near as I can remember, in April.

Q. April of 1937? A. That's right.

Q. Was there any other disturbance around the plant there about that time? A. No.

Q. Did any of the men come to you and ask you whether or not Thompson Products was going to continue to operate the company?

A. Oh, there was some question about that.

Q. Any of the men come to you around that time and ask you what the chances were to get more money, now that Thompson Products had taken over? A. That's right.

Q. And to get some rights on seniority?

A. There was nothing said, so far as seniority was concerned, up to the first half of 1937.

Q. Nothing was ever said up through the first half of 1937? [259] A. No.

Q. Let us take the first half of 1937 again. What union activity had there been down at this plant in that first half of the year?

A. So far as union activities was concerned, I never remember of seeing an outside business agent from any labor organization around the plant.

Q. During the entire first half of 1937?

A. That's right.

(Testimony of Victor Elmer Kangas.) .

Q. Did you see any cards passed around by anybody from either the A. F. of L. or C. I. O. down at that plant?

A. Oh, I saw a few application blanks, yes.

Q. About when did you first see them?

A. Well, I would say from the first of the year on, and as far back as 1936, probably.

Q. You had a little flurry back in 1939 with the A. F. of L., didn't you?

A. I wouldn't be surprised if I did.

Q. Mr. Porter belonged to the A. F. of L. at that time?   A. I don't know.

Q. He didn't join the A. F. of L at your instruction then?   A. No, sir.

Q. Did you have an A. F. of L. flurry also, in the early part of 1937, the first half of the year?

A. That I don't remember, whether it was the C. I. O. or [260] A. F. of L.

Q. You did have some activity among the men there in the plant?   A. That's right.

Q. There weren't any outside organizers there?

A. Not that I know of.

Q. In other words, the boys within the plant were figuring that in that way they could get some more of these things for which they were asking?

A. That's right.

Q. Was there any discussion to that effect around there in the first half of 1937?

A. In the plant?

Q. Yes.   A. A little bit, probably.

(Testimony of Victor Elmer Kangas.)

Q. And they signed the boys up for C. I. O. or A. F. of L. down at the plant, didn't they?

A. No, never saw any cards signed up at the plant at any time.

Q. How did you know there was C. I. O. activity in there then?

A. Some of the boys showed me their application cards. Lester Bebb showed me his.

Q. Did he have any discussion with you about it?

A. He came and told me he wanted to be honest with me, he [261] had joined the C. I. O., due to the fact that so many of the boys were joining the C. I. O., and he wanted to protect his job.

Q. What did you say to him?

A. I told him it was entirely up to him, that it was none of my business.

Q. Did any of the other boys come to you?

A. Yes, I think a few.

Q. Who else?

A. I can't remember. I do remember Lester Bebb, due to the fact that we had a little conversation over it.

Q. Did you have any more conversation than you have now related?

A. Not with Mr. Bebb, no.

Q. Did you have a conversation with any of the other employees which you can now think of?

A. No.

Q. Were the boys wearing buttons on the job at this time?   A. No.

Q. In other words, the first conversation you

(Testimony of Victor Elmer Kangas.)

had about it was when Lester Bebb came to you and said he had joined the C. I. O., and told you why? A. Yes.

Q. You hadn't ask him whether or not he had, prior to that? [262] A. No.

Q. When was that? Can you fix the date of Lester Bebb's coming to you and telling you for the first time, the boys were joining the C. I. O.?

A. Probably around in July or August, maybe June. I don't know; it might have been June of 1937.

Q. Could it have been any earlier than that?

A. I don't think so.

Q. Could it have been as early as May?

A. No, I don't believe it was.

Q. What makes you say that?

A. As I remember, it was during the summer months, just before, probably a month or two before Mr. Hileman came out.

Q. Mr. Kangas, since you have been on the stand, have you discussed your testimony with anybody other than a representative of the Board?

A. I talked to Mr. Moore.

Q. You mean the attorney for the Board?

A. That's right.

Q. Is he the only one you have talked to?

A. Yes, sir.

Q. You didn't talk to Mr. Johnson?

A. No.

Q. Did you talk to Mr. Porter about his testimony?

(Testimony of Victor Elmer Kangas.)

A. I visited Mr. Porter one Sunday morning, but there was [263] very little said.

Q. I mean, since you have been up here?

A. That's right. I have discussed very little about anything.

Q. You have discussed very little about anything with Mr. Porter since you have been up here?

A. There might have been one or two things mentioned.

Mr. Moore: The witness obviously does not understand the question.

Mr. Watkins: I think he does too well.

Q. (By Mr. Watkins): Mr. Kangas, going on now with the union activities——

Mr. Moore: Mr. Examiner, may I have the answer to the question that was asked stricken? It is misleading as it is on the record now. The witness answered it, but I do not believe the witness understood the question.

Mr. Watkins: That is your assumption, Mr. Moore, and I don't want you to put words in the witness' mouth, on cross examination.

Trial Examiner Whittemore: Is there any doubt in your mind? He answered the question.

Mr. Moore: I will withdraw the objection and bring it out later.

Mr. Watkins: I will strike the question I started and reframe it. [264]

Q. (By Mr. Watkins): Mr. Kangas, going to the period, now, around May of 1937,—going to the period, now, around June of 1937, is my understand-

(Testimony of Victor Elmer Kangas.)
ing correct, that that was the first time in which you learned that the C. I. O. was active in the plant? A. No, sir.

Q. When was was it?

A. Oh, I would say it was probably as far back as March. I know there were members, or employees, that were members of the C. I. O., and they were increasing right along.

Q. When did they really start increasing there? About what time?

A. Oh, possibly around in June or July.

Q. Could it have been before that?

A. Well, now, I don't know. I didn't follow these boys home every night, you know, to see what they were going to do, so I don't know where they went. All I know is that some belonged to the C. I. O., and maybe some to the A. F. of L.

Q. You had Porter to join the C. I. O. to find out about it, didn't you?

A. I just asked him to do it.

Q. You did it to find out, to get a line on that, didn't you? A. Yes, sir.

Q. When was this? [265]

A. Some time in 1937.

Q. About what time in 1937?

A. Possibly in June, as I remember.

Q. You had him attend a couple of meetings and report to you, didn't you? A. That's right.

Q. Prior to the time that Mr. Livingston came out? A. That's right.

Q. You did that on your own? A. No, sir.

(Testimony of Victor Elmer Kangas.)

Q. Who instructed you to do that?

A. Mr. Dachtler, acting general manager of Jadson, at that time.

Q. When did he instruct you to do it?

A. Possibly in June, or whenever it happened; it could not have been very much before; probably that week, whenever that took place.

Q. Can you fix it with any more certainty, when that took place?

A. Can you tell me when you took a drink sometime? I can't remember dates.

Q. Sometimes you take too many, and can't remember.   A. Probably you have.

Trial Examiner Whittemore: Suppose you get down to business. [266]

Q. (By Mr. Watkins): When did Mr. Dachtler say anything about checking the C. I. O.?

A. Sometime in June, to the best of my memory.

Q. Where?   A. At the plant.

Q. Where in the plant?

A. In the office.

Q. Whose office?   A. His office.

Q. Who was present?

A. Just I and Mr. Dachtler.

Q. What did he say to you?

A. He asked me if I could get somebody to join the C. I. O., that the company would pay their dues in there, that he wanted to find out if he could possibly, the number of employees that belonged to the C. I. O.

Q. What did you say?

(Testimony of Victor Elmer Kangas.)

A. I said, "I think maybe I can do that."

Q. What did you do about it then? Is that when you got Mr. Porter to join?

A. That's right.

Q. Did you report back to Mr. Dachtler again?

A. I did.

Q. When?

A. That might have been the same day or the day after. [267]

Q. Did Mr. Dachtler promise any reward to you or Mr. Porter for getting this information?

A. The only thing he told me he would pay, the company would pay his dues.

Q. Did he suggest a man you might get to do it, or leave it up to you?

A. He left that to me.

Q. What was this man's name immediately over you at that time?

A. Walter Clark was not there at that time, he wasn't there at this period. I was in charge of manufacturing at that time.

Q. When did Mr. Clark leave?

A. Possibly in June, I think it was in June.

Q. June of 1937?   A. That's right.

Q. This date you are testifying to was prior to that, wasn't it?

A. No, I don't think so. I think it was right after Mr. Clark left.

Q. Going to Mr. Livingston's first visit out here, can you fix about the date when that was? The first time you met him.

(Testimony of Victor Elmer Kangas.)

A. Well, it was in the spring of the year, probably April or May.

Q. April or May of 1937? [268]

A. To the best of my memory, yes.

Q. Could it have been June of 1937?

A. Oh, it possibly could have. I didn't set down the dates.

Q. When did Mr. Hileman come out?

A. In August of 1937.

Q. When Mr. Livingston first came here in April or May or June of 1937, whenever it was, when you first talked to him, that was the first time you had met him, wasn't it?   A. Mr. Livingston?

Q. Yes.   A. That's right.

Q. Where did you first talk to him?

A. Well, as well as I can remember it was in Mr. Dachtler's office.

Q. Had you seen him around the plant prior to that time?

A. Yes. I saw him walking through the plant.

Q. What was he doing?

A. I don't think he was doing anything in particular, just walking around.

Q. Talking to any of the men?

A. Yes, talking to a few of the men.

Q. Did you see him talk to the men after this first meeting you had with him?   A. Oh, yes.

[269]

Q. Several of the men around the plant, while they were working?   A. That's right.

Q. Will you relate, please, this first conversa-

(Testimony of Victor Elmer Kangas.)
tion you had with Mr. Livingston. Just state what it was.

A. Well, the first conversations I had with Mr. Livingston was in regard to a case where I had discharged three employees in the shop, laid them off for lack of work.

Q. Who started the conversation?

A. Mr. Livingston.

Q. What did he say to you?

A. At that time, as well as I can remember, it was around the time the National Labor Relations Board was building up a case against the company for laying these men off

Q. The men you had laid off?

A. That's right.

Q. And the charge being that they were C. I. O., and you had laid them off, and had discriminated against them. Is that right?

A. That's right; that's the way I remember it.

Q. What did you say to him?

A. He wanted the story of how the men were laid off, and I gave it to him.

Q. What did you say?

A. Because there was not enough work at that time. One, [270] in particular, was a welder. I didn't have any welding for him at that time.

Q. What was his name?

A. Blankenship; one name was Lloyd Ackerman.

Q. Both were laid off because of lack of work?

A. Not Lloyd Ackerman.

(Testimony of Victor Elmer Kangas.)

Q. He was fired outright? What for?

A. Because he didn't do what he was told.

Q. Is that what you told Mr. Livingston?

A. As well as I remember I did, yes.

Q. One was Ackerman, and was one MacIntosh?

A. MacIntosh was the third one.

Q. There were three involved?   A. Yes.

Q. What was the matter with MacIntosh?

A. Well, he took the wrong attitude in his job, and wouldn't work, and do his job there. I don't like to be called a son of a bitch on the job. I would rather be called that outside the plant where I can take care of it.

Q. Is that what you told Mr. Livingston at the time?   A. That's right.

Q. And at that particular time Mr. MacIntosh had been calling you a son of a bitch on the job?

A. That's right. I think there are probably records on that too. [271]

Q. What was the rest of the conversation on that first meeting with Mr. Livingston?

A. It all pertained to laying off these three men.

Q. Nothing else was discussed?

A. Not as I remember, no.

Q. Did you have more than one conversation with Mr. Livingston on his first trip out here?

A. Yes, I think we had either two or three, about the same thing.

Q. That was all that was discussed?

A. That's right.

(Testimony of Victor Elmer Kangas.)

Q.   During that meeting did you tell Mr. Livingston about the C. I. O. inroads in the plant?

A.   I don't remember whether I did or not.

Q.   You have no recollection of it?   A.   No.

Q.   You have no recollection of whether or not he asked you about C. I. O. inroads in the plant?

A.   The only thing I can remember Mr. Livingston did ask me whether the boys belonged to the C. I. O., and I told him I don't believe they did, and I didn't know, and I don't know today whether they did or not.

Q.   That was all the discussion there was about the C. I. O. at that time?   A.   That's right.

[272]

Q.   Was that all the meetings you had with Mr. Livingston? Have you related everything that took place with Mr. Livingston while he was on his first trip?

A.   Yes. That's right. I can't remember anything else.

Q.   About what month did you first—about in what month did you see the greatest C. I. O. activity? During the early part or middle part of 1937? At this plant.

A.   Well, I heard more about it around July, the first of July, possibly, of 1937.

Q.   You say you heard more about it; what do you mean by that?

A.   I mean I heard from various sources that there were more and more men joining the C. I. O.,

(Testimony of Victor Elmer Kangas.)

and somebody told me that there was, possibly, or approximately about 90 per cent in the C. I. O. at that time.

Q. Do you remember who told you that?

A. No, I don't.

Q. Did the boys wear their buttons?

A. No.

Q. Did they talk freely about belonging to the C. I. O. at that time?

A. Some did; some didn't.

Q. What did you say to them about it, those that discussed it with you?

A. I didn't say anything to them. [273]

Q. Did you say it was all right as far as you were concerned, or that they shouldn't do it?

A. I told them they could belong to any association they wanted to. It was none of my business.

Q. That was what you told them?

A. Yes.

Q. Did you learn whether any of them were with the A. F. of L. there around that time?

A. Yeah. I think a couple of them were. I think I can name maybe one or two.

Q. Did any of the boys come to you and talk about the A. F. of L.?   A. No.

Q. Take the period, again, the first six months of 1937, what relatives did you have working at this plant then?

A. I had my wife working there, I had my

(Testimony of Victor Elmer Kangas.)
brother working there, and I had a cousin working there.

Q. Mr. Kangas, as I understand it, and you correct me if I am misquoting you, at the time of Mr. Livingston's first visit you didn't tell him anything about Porter's attending any union meetings?

A. No, I didn't, as far as I can remember. I don't remember telling Mr. Livingston that.

Q. Do you know whether or not Porter had attended the union meetings prior to that date? [274]

, A. Prior to Mr. Livingston's being there?

Q. His first visit.

A. I don't know. I don't remember whether he did or not. In fact, I don't know whether he ever belonged to the C. I. O. at that time or not.

Q. In other words, if Mr. Porter had belonged to the C. I. O. prior to this time and reported to you about the C. I. O. membership, you mentioned nothing of that to Mr. Livingston?

A. No, I didn't.

Q. And assuming that happened first, you didn't tell Mr. Livingston that Mr. Dachtler had had you have Mr. Porter join the C. I. O.?

A. No, not at this first visit.

Q. That is what I mean. You didn't tell him anything about it then?

A. Not as far as I can remember, I didn't.

Q. Do you have any recollection? Is there any way you can refresh your recollection so you can say whether you did or didn't?

(Testimony of Victor Elmer Kangas.)

A. I didn't have any reason to tell him about it, due to the fact I don't think Mr. Porter was in there at that time. As I remember, it was after this I asked Mr. Porter to join the C. I. O.

Q. In other words, it is your feeling at the present time if you had information on the C. I. O. prior to this time, where [275] you were involved up here at the Labor Board on charges, you would have told Mr. Livingston about it?

A. That's right.

Q. That would be particularly true, I assume, if Mr. Dachtler had given you those instructions?

A. That's right.

Q. You got along all right with Mr. Livingston at this first visit, didn't you?

A. I think we got along very nicely.

Q. You talked about machinery and conditions in the plant, and all?   A. That's right.

Q. And you didn't discuss doing something about the pay problems, and things of that kind, the first visit?   A. No.

Q. That wasn't discussed at the first visit at all?   A. No, sir.

Q. Was the condition of unrest discussed at that time?   A. I would say yes.

Q. Did you tell him about it the first visit?

A. I don't remember telling anything about it much, due to the fact I didn't talk to Mr. Livingston a great deal, other than this case where these

(Testimony of Victor Elmer Kangas.)
three men had left the employment. Two of them
were discharged and one of them was laid off. [276]

Q. You don't now recall, though, any statements by Mr. Livingston at this time, at this first
conversation, with respect to increase in pay, or
anything of this kind?

A. No, sir. I don't believe there was anything
like that discussed.

Q. Did that occur at the second conversation?
That is, on Mr. Livingston's second trip here?

A. That's right.

Q. When do you fix that?

A. Well, it might have been after Mr. Hileman
came out. I don't think Mr. Livingston at that
time took any action in that, until Mr. Hileman
came out.

Q. All right. You can't fix the time, then, of
Mr. Livingston's second visit?

A. As near as I can remember it was in the
latter part of July, when he arrived here.

Q. Mr. Kangas, going back, now, to the time
when you had Porter join the C. I. O. to find out
how many men were attending their meetings, I believe you said he reported to you some 18 attended
a particular meeting?

A. As near as I can remember.

Q. At that time how many C. I. O. members
would you say there were in the plant?

A. Just from hearsay I would say the percentage was up, possibly around 60 or 70 per cent.

[277]

(Testimony of Victor Elmer Kangas.)

Q. At that particular time? A. Yes.

Q. And that increased a little, later on?

A. That's right.

Q. Other than Mr. Porter, the incident you testified to, did you ever try to get anybody else down at this plant to join the C. I. O.?

A. No, sir.

Q. You never did? A. No, sir.

Q. And you are positive on that?

A. Absolutely.

Q. I understand Mr. Hileman came out sometime in August of 1937? A. That's right.

Q. What was the first meeting that you had with him? Do you recall that?

A. Mr. Dachtler called me in the office and introduced me to Mr. Hileman and I was probably in there, oh, three or four minutes, and I went back out in the plant.

Q. What was discussed?

A. Not much of anything; just general.

Q. Just meeting him, and that was about all there was to it? A. That's it.

Q. When did the next meeting you had with him occur? [278]

A. It might have been a day or two after that.

Q. Do you remember what was discussed at that one?

A. Yeah. I think we talked something about equipment, as to its condition, and probably that was all that was discussed at that time.

(Testimony of Victor Elmer Kangas.)

Q. Had you expressed opposition to Mr. Hileman's being sent out here to be in charge of the plant at this time?   A. I never did.

Q. You never did at any subsequent time? A. No.

Q. Going to your second meeting with Mr. Livingston, that is your meeting with Mr. Livingston at the second trip, where did you first talk to Mr. Livingston after he made the second trip out here, which was sometime, as I understand, in July of 1937?   A. In Mr. Dachtler's office.

Q. That is the first time you met with Mr. Livingston on the second trip?   A. That's right.

Q. And who was present at that meeting?

A. Mr. Dachtler and Mr. Livingston and myself.

Q. When was the next meeting you had with him?

A. Oh, possibly during that day in the afternoon.

Q. Where was that?

A. In the same place, in the office. [279]

Q. Did you see him out in the plant during any of this time?

A. I think that Mr. Livingston did go out in the plant. However, I am not quite sure of that.

Q. Did you see him talking to any of the men out there?

A. So far as I can remember, I can't remember him talking to any men.

(Testimony of Victor Elmer Kangas.)

Q. During this second visit, did he discuss with you the rates of pay that were going on there?

A. I don't believe that there was anything discussed in regard to pay rates.

Q. During the entire second visit?

A. Oh, yes, during the entire second visit there, yes.

Q. Sometime during his second visit he did discuss an increase in pay with you?

A. That was after Mr. Hileman came out, as I remember.

Q. Yes. But Mr. Livingston, during his second visit, did discuss an increase in pay rates? Correct? A. That's right.

Q. Did he discuss anything else concerning the working conditions or wages of the men in the plant?

A. Yes. He discussed organizing an idependent union.

Q. Did he discuss anything else besides that?

A. Well, he might have.

Q. Did he discuss seniority?

A. Well, seniority was discussed later, yes. [280]

Q. During this second visit?

A. That's right.

Q. Did he discuss anything about shorter hours?

A. No, I don't think there was anything said about shorter hours.

Q. Anything about vacations with pay?

A. At that time there was probably something mentioned about vacations, but they were going to

(Testimony of Victor Elmer Kangas.)
take that under consideration and see what happened.

Q. Did he say anything about any favoritism out there to you? Ask if there was any in the plant, or anything of that kind?

A. No, I don't think he said anything about that.

Q. In other words, he did make inquiry about what the complaints of the men were——

A. That's right.

Q. ——and ask you what your advice was to straighten it out, and get them happier about certain things?

A. Well, he probably did.

Q. Would you say he did, or probably did?

A. Yes, I think he did.

Q. You were in favor of that also, weren't you?

A. Yes, I was.

Q. And Mr. Livingston was too?

A. That's right. [281]

Q. Going to this meeting, I believe you said it was at Uncle Gabriel's cabin. Is that what you call it?

A. Well, it might be a cabin. They call it a cabin, but it was more or less a cafe or restaurant.

Q. All right. When was that?

A. That was, as near as I can remember, on Friday evening, the latter part of July.

Q. Of 1937? A. 1937.

Q. Are you sure it was on a Friday evening?

(Testimony of Victor Elmer Kangas.)

A. As near as I can remember, yes; it seemed like it would have to have been Friday evening, as near as I can remember.

Q. Could you fix a positive date, if you had a calendar again?

A. No, I couldn't, I can't definitely say whether it was Friday, but as near as I remember, it seems like it was Friday night.

Q. All right. Who was present at that meeting?

A. Mr. Livingston, myself, Mr. Hodges, Mr. Dachtler, Leroy Shadrack, L. V. Corbley, Eugene Drake, Roy Long and Bill Kerns.

Q. All foremen and lead off men?

A. That's right.

Q. No employee who wasn't a foreman or lead off man was there?   A. No. [282]

Q. At that meeting did Mr. Livingston tell you there about the Cleveland operations or equipment, or anything of that kind?

A. Not at this meeting.

Q. Did he say anything at this meeting about vacations for men, or anything of that character?

A. No.

Q. You are sure of that?

A Yes, I am sure of that, because we really hadn't got started to work, so I don't know where vacations would have come in.

Q. You are giving your assumption on that?

A. I know definitely no vacations were discussed at that meeting.

(Testimony of Victor Elmer Kangas.)

Q. What about higher rates of pay? Were they discussed at that meeting?   A. No, sir.

Q. Seniority; was that discussed at that meeting?

A. No, sir, nothing like seniority was discussed.

Q. Favoritism among supervisory personnel, wasn't that discussed?   A. No, sir.

Q. Was anything about the handling of grievances discussed at that meeting?

A. No, but I will tell you what was discussed.

[283]

Q. Just a minute; answer my questions. Was anything about grievances discussed at this meeting?   A. No, they weren't.

Q. Was anything about fair play towards the employees discussed there by Mr. Livingston?

A. Not as a I remember.

Q. Would you say positively there wasn't?

A. Well, I would say there wasn't.

Q. You said you wanted to tell what was discussed there?   A. Yes.

Q. Why?

A. Well, you seemed to be anxious to know what was discussed, and you went all around the question, so I thought maybe I would help you.

Q. All right. You go ahead and help. Tell me what was discussed at that meeting.

A. All right. Mr. Dachtler, after dinner, suggested I speak to the boys. I told him there wasn't anything I should talk to them about, that Mr. Livingston was sent out here to perform certain

(Testimony of Victor Elmer Kangas.)
duties, and I thought it was up to Mr. Livingston to do the talking.

Mr. Livingston got up and he did, and he asked the boys that were at this meeting what they though of an inside union in the plant.

Q. Why do you figure he asked those men there that? [284]   A. Because they were leadmen.

Q. Why did he ask the leadmen that?

A. He wanted to get their reaction on it.

Q. You mean because he contemplated they would be organizers of it?

Mr. Moore: I object to the question.

Mr. Watkins: This is cross examination, and the witness is so anxious to tell his story, to try to get all the picture——

Mr. Moore: It doesn't matter how anxious he is. I object to the question.

Trial Examiner Whittemore: The witness may answer. You asked him what was in Livingston's mind.

Mr. Moore: That is what I am objecting to.

Trial Examiner Whittemore: I have no objection. It certainly doesn't prove anything, but Mr. Watkins wants to know what he thought Mr. Livingston had in mind.

Q. (By Mr. Watkins) What was your conclusion as to why Mr. Livingston asked the leadmen what they thought about an independent union?

A. He wanted to get their reaction, see how they felt about having an inside union there.

(Testimony of Victor Elmer Kangas.)

Q. Do you think that was limited to leadmen or leadmen and foremen also?

A. Foremen and supervisors and department foremen. [285]

Q. But you think he was directing that query to just leadmen?   A. That's right.

Q. Go ahead. What else did he say?

A. He more or less outlined, in a few words, how we might go about organizing it; not in very many words.

Q. You tell me what he said?

A. Word for word what he said?

Q. As nearly as you can recall, what he said.

A. I am afraid you got me stuck, Mr.

Q. As nearly as you can recall.

A. Well, as near as I can remember, Mr. Livingston suggested we have an independent union here. He also told the men present at that meeting that he thought with an independent union there at the plant that they could probably handle labor problems and grievances better with an independent union than they could with an outside union, due to the fact that they would thrash them out right there at the plant, and if an independent union could be organized, why, they would have the committee right there, and they would meet with the management and they would discuss the problems in general, and thrash out all the grievances, and not have an outside labor organization in the plant.

Q. Then, did he say to the men assembled there, to help it all they could?   A. No, sir. [286]

(Testimony of Victor Elmer Kangas.)

Q. What did he say about it?

A. He told the men to treat that confidential, that he did not want any employees out in the plant to know the nature of that meeting. In fact, he didn't want any of them to know there was such a meeting.

Q. In other words, he didn't want any employees to learn the company ordered an independent union?

A. That's right.

Q. And told the men so? A. That's right.

Q. Anything else?

A. Well, there might be something off the record, there, that we talked about.

Q. I mean concerning the thing you wanted to tell us about.

A. Right at that time I don't remember there was anything else other than he asked the men how they felt, and they thought it was a very good idea.

Q. How many men were there there?

A. Well, I will have to count them.

Q. Then would you say, roughly?

A. Well, there was Mr. Livingston, Mr. Dachtler, myself, Hodges, Leroy Shadrock, Roy Long, Bill Kearns, Eugene Drake, and Al V. Coberly; nine there, as near as I can recollect.

Q. He told the men he didn't want them to say anything about the discussion that had taken place in this meeting? [287] A. That's right.

Q. You have given us the full story on this meeting now?

A. That's right, inside of the building.

(Testimony of Victor Elmer Kangas.)

Q. That was all that took place inside or outside, so far as the meeting is concerned? Is that correct?

A. Inside the building. Outside, Mr. Livingston said a few words to me before I——

Q. But this was not part of the meeting. Right?

A. No.

Q. At this meeting we have just been talking about was there anything said by Mr. Livingston that appeared to be to the benefit of the employees?

A. Well, the only thing, as I remember, that was mentioned in regard to that, that the employees would be able to carry their grievances to the management and thrash it out at the plant, rather than have an outside organization represent them. That's to the best of my memory. I don't think anything else was discussed in the way of doing anything outlandish for the employees.

Q. In other words, it is your conclusion that the sole purpose of that meeting was to get an independent union under way. Is that correct?

A. That's right.

Q. Now, I believe you testified on direct examination that Mr. Livingston had asked you to get some employee to get the men to come in and call on the management and ask for [288] anything, or words to that effect?

A. Yes, he mentioned that.

Q. And you chose Mr. Lou Porter who has testified here? A. That is right.

Q. That's the same Lou Porter that you had chosen to join the C.I.O.? A. It is.

(Testimony of Victor Elmer Kangas.)

Q. Was he one of the leaders there in the plant? A. Leader in the plant?

Q. I don't mean a leadman, but one of the men that the other men looked up to and respected and liked, at this time.

A. As near as I can remember at that time I think he was pretty well thought of, yes. [288-A]

Q. You don't remember any conflict at that time, with Porter?

A. No, I don't remember anything the men might have had against him, no.

Q. Was there some conflict later between Porter and the other men?

A. There probably was quite a bit after that, but not at that time.

Q. Were you on particularly close terms with Mr. Porter, socially, at this time?

A. Yes, we were very good friends.

Q. You and your wife called on him and his wife? A. That's right.

Q. Frequently?

A. Oh, possibly once every two or three weeks, or maybe once a week, sometimes. I don't know. We didn't live over there, however.

Q. Why did you pick Mr. Porter as the man? Was that because he had been a detective and knew how to keep his mouth shut?

A. That's right, because I knew I could trust him. I thought he would treat this confidential, and he was a man with a little more age to him, he was

(Testimony of Victor Elmer Kangas.)

an older man, and I thought he might be the man that would fit into the picture.

Q. What did you say to Mr. Porter when you first talked to him about this assignment? [289]

A. Well, first of all I outlined it the best I could——

Q. What did you say to him, Mr. Kangas?

A. I asked him if he would help me get an independent union organized in the plant, and he asked a few questions about it, what it would mean, and I told him what it might mean, and he said——

Q. When you said you told him what it might mean, what did you tell him?

A. I told him it might mean more money, seniority rights, might even get vacations with pay; I didn't know.

Q. For whom?

A. For everybody concerned.

Q. What else did you tell him?

A. And I believe that that covered that; and he said it sounded good to him, and he would do all he could, and he wanted to know what I wanted him to do. I told him to contact as many men as he could, but not to let any of the men know the company was trying to organize this independent union; that that was to be treated confidential; but to try to get them to swing over from C. I. O. into an independent union as soon as possible.

Q. You said that? Try to get them to swing over from the C. I. O. to an independent union?

A. That is correct.

(Testimony of Victor Elmer Kangas.)

Q. You remember those words, do you? [290]

A. Yes.

Q. Go ahead.

A. I told him it was very important to get as many members in this independent union as we can; talk it up to the men out in the plant, and get them to go into the office at a certain day, when it was going to be set.

Q. Did you talk to him about getting members into the independent, or about getting a gang to run into the office?

A. Get a group together to go into the office.

Q. Did you talk to him about getting members at that time?

A. Probably not at that same time.

Q. That is what I mean; your first conversation, where was it? At his machine?

A. Some at his machine, and some at his home.

Q. I mean, the first time when you got him started to corral the men and get them going?

A. At his machine.

Q. How long did you talk to him there?

A. Possibly ten or fifteen minutes.

Q. It was in that conversation that you told him you would get higher pay and vacations for the men and so on?

A. That was one of the things to tell the men. I said, "I don't care what you tell them; tell them anything, just so you get them in the office."

Q. You talked for ten or fifteen minutes? [291]

A. Yes.

(Testimony of Victor Elmer Kangas.)

Q.   Was his machine running?   A.   Yes.

Q.   Was it pretty noisy?   A.   Pretty noisy.

Q.   You have to holler pretty loud to hear when the machine is running, don't you?

A.   Oh, not so loud.

Q.   You can't talk with the machine running, in a normal voice?   A.   I think so.

Q.   With the machine running?   A.   Yes.

Q.   How close were other men working to where you were talking to Mr. Porter?

A.   Possibly 25 or 30 feet.

Q.   That close?

A.   As far as I can. remember.

Q.   Mr. Porter is a little deaf, isn't he?

A.   Is he?

Q.   I am asking you.

A.   I have never noticed it myself; maybe I just talked above it, I don't know.

Q.   When did you first tell Mr. Livingston that Porter was the man? [292]

A.   Oh, I think it was on a Saturday morning, as near as I can remember.   It was the next morning after this dinner at Uncle Gabriel's.   I told him that I had a man in mind that I thought was just the man to fit the bill.

Q.   That was the next morning after the meeting at Uncle Gabriel's?   A.   That's right.

Q.   You are certain of that?

A.   Oh, yes, absolutely.   I slept on it that night.

Q.   Did you make any notes at the time of any of these conversations you have related here, with Mr. Livingston or Mr. Porter?   A.   No, sir.

(Testimony of Victor Elmer Kangas.)

Q. No notes at all?   A. No.

Q. When did you first report these instances you are testifying to now, to either the Labor Board or to the union involved here?

A. I didn't report these.

Q. When did you first talk to them about it?

A. Oh, that could possibly have been about in July.

Q. July of——   A. 1942.

Q. Up here at the Board?

A. Yes, sir. [293]

Q. Is that where your first conversation was?

A. Yes, sir.

Q. You haven't told anybody anything about it prior to that time?   A. No, sir.

Q. Either in connection with the Board or in connection with the C. I. O. union?

A. No, sir.

Q. Did you find out how they had learned about your side of the story?   A. No, sir.

Mr. Moore: Objected to.

Q. (By Mr. Watkins) You don't know yet?

A. No.

Mr. Moore: Objected to.

Trial Examiner Whittemore: I will overrule the objection and let the answers remain.

Q. (By Mr. Watkins) I believe you had a further conversation with Mr. Livingston that you testified to on a Monday morning in which he told you something to the effect that you will have to get going, to get this thing moving, to beat the C. I. O. meeting?   A. That's right.

(Testimony of Victor Elmer Kangas.)

Q. You recall that?   A. That's right. [294]

Q. Do you remember where that conversation took place?

A. As near as I can remember, at the plant, Jadson Products.

Q. You mean in the office?

A. In the office, yes.

Q. You were called in by Mr. Livingston?

A. That's right. He had the girl call me; the girl called me in.

Q. Did you start the conversation or did he?

A. He did. I never have nothing to say, I always let him start it, because he was the man that was directing all this.

Q. And he said to you what?

A. He told me that he would want me to get the ball rolling, and get everything into shape just as soon as possible, so far as organizing this union, and try to have everything set for Tuesday night, or words to that effect. Now, it may not have been the same words. I don't know, but words to that effect.

Q. What did you say?

A. I told him I was doing the best I could, the thing seemed to be rolling along all right.

Q. How long had it been rolling at that time?

A. Since Saturday morning. I believe on Saturday sometime, whenever it was.

Q. It was on a Saturday around 11:00 o'clock that you first put Mr. Porter to work? [295]

A. Yes.

(Testimony of Victor Elmer Kangas.)

Q.　And this was on a Monday you talked to Mr. Livingston and he said to get it rolling, and you said they are rolling as well as they can be?

A.　Yes.

Q.　Was anything else said at that time?

A.　I wouldn't remember; I can't remember every word mentioned; there might have been something else, but not that I can remember of.

Q.　That is all of the conversation at that time that you can recall?

A.　However, he did ask me how Mr. Porter was coming along, I believe, and I said, "Well, he was doing okeh, so far as I knew." I didn't know too much about it.

Q.　Hadn't Mr. Porter reported to you as to his progress?

A.　Well, I don't believe he did up to this time.

Q.　Did you contact Mr. Porter again after that conversation you have just related with Mr. Livingston?

A.　Yes, we had several conversations during the course of the day for several days after that too, but I don't remember just exactly what transpired during all of them.

Q.　For several days after that, did you say?

A.　Yes.

Q.　How many days after that did you still have conversations with Mr. Porter about it? [296]

A.　Possibly a week or so or more.

Q.　Will you relate the first conversation you had with Mr. Porter after this meeting?

(Testimony of Victor Elmer Kangas.)

A. I went out in the plant and asked Mr. Porter what he had done, and he said he talked to two or three men, but he hadn't had much time to do much more, but he said before the day was over he would work on several more.

Q. What time of the day was that?

A. Oh, I imagine it was possibly around 11:00 o'clock, 10:30, or something like that.

Q. In the morning?   A. That is right.

Q. You are sure it was in the morning?

A. Oh, yes.

Q. It was right after you talked to Mr. Livingston?   A. Yes.

Q. Go ahead.

A. I told him to contact just as many of the men as he could, trying to get as many men as he could to go into the office and demand those seniority rights, more pay, vacations with pay, and I said it didn't make much difference what he asked for, just so he got them in there. I said the rest of it would iron itself out, I guess. He said he would.

Q. The first time you discussed this mission with Mr. Porter, did you tell him what he was going to get out of it? [297]   A. No, sir.

Q. Did he ask you what there was in it for him?

A. No, sir.

Q. Did he ask you why you picked him to do the job?   A. Yes, he did.

Q. What did you tell him?

A. I told him because he was a very good friend of mine, and I could depend on him, that is the reason I picked him.

(Testimony of Victor Elmer Kangas.)

Q. Did he say he would rather not undertake anything of that kind? Or, sure; I will be glad to do it.

A. He said he would be glad to help me.

Q. To help you?   A. Yes.

Q. Then, in this first conversation you had with Mr. Porter about this assignment, the sum and substance of it was that he was to get a bunch of the men together and go into management and ask them for everything that they could think of?

A. That's right.

Q. And he was to do the job as rapidly as possible?   A. Yes.

Q. And you told him at that time to get busy on it immediately and move along. Is that correct?

A. That's right.

Q. That is the first conversation you had with him. Is that correct? [298]

A. Yes.

Q. Now, Mr. Kangas, referring to a telephone call which you were to make to Mr. Livingston.

A. Uh huh.

Q. I believe you testified that you were supposed to call him at 7:00 o'clock on a particular night. I forget which night it was. Do you remember?

A. Yes.

Q. What night was it?

A. Well, as I can recall, it was on a Monday evening.

Q. Did you call him at 7:00 o'clock?

A. I did.

(Testimony of Victor Elmer Kangas.)

Q. Did you know what he was going to tell you before you called him?

A. I didn't know exactly what he was going to tell me, but he told me in a few words about what it was going to be, yes.

Q. When did he tell you in a few words what it was going to be?

A. That day, Monday.

Q. What time that day?

A. Oh, Monday afternoon, sometime.

Q. Then, he told you roughly what it was going to be that night, so you knew what it was?

A. That's right, I expected it.

Q. What was it supposed to be? [299]

A. Well, he dictated over the telephone——

Q. No, no. I mean when he indicated to you roughly what it was going to be. What did he say?

A. Well, he said he wanted to get some cards printed and he wanted me to call him at 7:00 o'clock, which I did, and he would have all the information, and he would give it to me over the telephone.

And I called him and he gave it to me, and I wrote it down.

Q. When he first talked to you about the call at 7:00 o'clock, he told you you were to call him at 7:00 o'clock because he wanted to have some cards printed and he was going to give you the information that went on them. Is that right?

A. Yes.

Q. And you called him at 7:00 o'clock and he gave you the information?

(Testimony of Victor Elmer Kangas.)

A. Yes.

Q. Then you went and had them printed?

A. That is right.

Q. Did you have them printed or did Mr. Porter?

A. No, sir. I turned over the information I had and asked the print shop to print some cards up with exactly the same wording I had on that paper, and I asked them if they could have them printed that night, and they said it was impossible.

Q. Did you ask them about how much it was?

[300]

A. No, sir.

Q. You didn't make any inquiry?

A. No, sir.

Q. You were the one that gave them the cards and asked them to print them?

A. I never gave them the cards. I gave them the information to print on the cards.

Q. That is right. How did you happen to have Mr. Porter and his wife with you?

A. More or less, Mr. Porter was a lieutenant to help work the thing out, and I had to have him with me.

Q. Mr. Porter was a lieutenant and you had to have him with you for other purposes?

A. No, in this particular case, because we were working on kind of a business deal, and he had to be with me.

Q. And that was the reason.

(Testimony of Victor Elmer Kangas.)

A. Uh huh.

Q. What time did you go over to his house?

A. Possibly about 6:00 or a quarter after 6:00, maybe.

Q. Had you had dinner or supper?

A. Yes.

Q. You had that?

A. Yes, I think we had.

Q. Did he know you were coming?

A. Yes, I believe I told him I would be there.

[301]

Q. What did you tell him when you told him you would be there?

A. Oh, I told him that I had to run an errand and it wouldn't take but a few minutes, probably, and asked them if they wanted to go along with us.

Q. You didn't tell him what it was?

A. Well, I didn't know myself, exactly what it was going to amount to. I told him in a few words what it might me.

Q. Oh, you told him what it might me, then?

A. Yes.

Q. In other words, when you went to the telephone, he knew what you were going to telephone about?   A. Oh, yes.   . .

Q. You are sure of that?

A. I think he did.

Q. Referring to your meeting at the Jonathan Club,. you attended more than one meeting at the Jonathan Club, didn't you, with Mr. Livingston?

(Testimony of Victor Elmer Kangas.)

A. No, I don't believe I was there only once at that time.

Q. Just once?   A. Yes, sir.

Q. All right. That was when you had dinner and the rest of them did, and Mr. Livingston didn't?

A. That's right.

Q. How long did you stay there while Mr. Livingston was [302] there?

A. Oh, it would possibly have been a half hour.

Q. Who told you to be there for that meeting?

A. Mr. Livingston.

Q. What did he tell you about it?

A. Just asked me to be up to the Jonathan Club.

Q. Didn't he tell you why he wanted you there?

A. No.

Q. When did he tell you that?

A. During that day.

Q. You don't remember what time?

A. Yes, I think it was in the afternoon, as near as I can remember. I wouldn't swear to that.

Q. But he didn't tell you why he wanted you there?   A. No.

Q. Did he tell you who else was going to be there?

A. Yes, I think he told me Mr. Porter and Mr. Hodges would be there.

Q. After you got there what was said by anybody? What was the first thing that was said?

A. Oh, we went up to Mr. Livingston's room, and was there a few minutes, possibly five or ten minutes.

(Testimony of Victor Elmer Kangas.)

Q. Was anything said up there?

A. Oh, nothing of any importance.

Q. Just passing the day? [303]

A. That's it. Then we went into the dining room and had dinner. During the dinner Mr. Livingston talked a little bit. I done all the listening.

Q. Just a minute. What did he say?

A. Well, he thought that we had done a swell job.

Q. What did he say? Did he say that? You said he thought you had done a swell job. Is that what he said?

A. Yes, he said we had done a swell job, a bang up job in organizing the union.

Q. You remember the words he used?

A. I wouldn't say he used those particular words, but——

Q. You don't know whether he said, "Bang up"?

A. Well, I believe "bang up" was used in that.

Q. Go ahead.

A. And he told us how he appreciated the cooperation he had received.

Q. Did he say anything about any reward to anybody for this bang up job that had been done?

A. I believe at that time he mentioned something about having—we would be well taken care of.

Q. Do you remember what he said in that regard?

A. Well, not word for word, meaning that we

(Testimony of Victor Elmer Kangas.)

wouldn't have to worry about a job, would be taken care of.

Q. Did any of you fellows ask him what you would get out of this business? [304]

A. No, sir.

Q. He just volunteered that you would be well taken care of? A. That's right.

Q. Did he say he would give you a lifetime job?

A. I don't think he mentioned a lifetime job. He said we would be taken care of as far as our job is concerned, and we wouldn't have to worry about work in the future. In other words, to that effect. I don't remember it word for word. He might have used "lifetime job."

Q. What did you say?

A. I told him that was pretty nice.

Q. What was your feeling about organizing this independent? Did you personally think it all right to do it?

A. It didn't make any difference to me, because I wasn't involved in it in any way. It wasn't going to help me, or anything.

Q. You didn't have any objection to doing it?

A. None.

Q. You didn't have any objection to the C. I. O. being in the plant? A. No.

Q. And you didn't have any objection to the A. F. of L. being in the plant? A. Oh, no.

Q. Can you fix the date of the Jonathan Club visit we have [305] been discussing——

A. I don't know; that might have been a week

(Testimony of Victor Elmer Kangas.)
or so or it might have been four or five days after
the first meeting with the employees in the plant
office.

Q. ——when these 15 or 18 men came in?

A. Yes.

Q. You would fix it four or five days and not
in excess of that?   A. No.

Q. About four or five days?

A. It could have been a few days either way.
I wouldn't know.

Q. That is as positive as you can fix it at the
present time?   A. Yes.

Mr. Watkins: I am going on to another point,
now.

Trial Examiner Whittemore: All right. Then
we will take our noon recess at this time until 1:30.

> (Whereupon a recess was taken at 12:30
> o'clock p. m., until 1:30 p. m., of the same
> day.) [306]

Afternoon Session

Trial Examiner Whittemore: The hearing will
please come to order.

VICTOR E. KANGAS

resumed the stand, and testified further as follows:

Cross Examination
(Continued)

Q. (By Mr. Watkins): Mr. Kangas, will you

(Testimony of Victor Elmer Kangas.)

state what time of day it was when you first contacted Mr. Lou Porter to tell him what he was to do in connection with this matter?

A. You mean during our first meeting?

Q. That is right. The first time you spoke to Mr. Porter about bringing the men into the office.

A. Oh, I would say that it was somewhere around 10:30 or 11:00 o'clock, somewhere in that neighborhood.

Q. While he was at his machine, you testified?

A. Yes.

Q. When was the next time that day you spoke to him about it?

A. Oh, I spoke to him probably several times during the day.

Q. Six or seven, would you say?

A. Several; might have been two or three times during the course of the day, in the afternoon.

Q. Do you remember when it was? Do you have any recollection now?

A. No, not exactly. I might say it might have been around [307] 1:30, it may have been 2:30; possibly could have been around 3:00.

Q. Do you remember what you said to him?

A. No, not exactly; pertaining to this same thing, I had talked to him about getting the men to go into the office, and encouraged him to go ahead with that and be sure he worked on it constantly, that he would get enough men to go into the office.

Q. Yes. This was the first day you are speaking of?   A. Yes.

(Testimony of Victor Elmer Kangas.)

Q. The first day you spoke to him at all about it, you spoke to him two or three times?

A. Yes.

Q. And along the same line, about getting the men into the offiee?   A. Yes.

Q. Have you ever belonged to either the A. F. of L. or C. I. O.?   A. No, sir.

Q. Do you belong to either of them at the present time?   A. No, sir.

Q. How far is the Porter house from your house, or was it in 1937?

A. Oh, approximately two miles.

Q. Two miles? [308]

A. Two and a half miles, maybe.

Q. What hours were you working in the plant in July of 1937?   A. From 7:00 until 3:30.

Q. You personally, were working from 7:00 to 3:30?

A. Well, I was working longer hours than that. I was working until 4:30 or 5:00.

Q. You had just one shift?

A. No, we were operating 24 hours, three shifts.

Q. In 1937?   A. Yes.

Q. Who took your place on the other shifts?

A. Well, I wasn't alternating with anybody. I was assistant works manager and then general superintendent.

Q. In other words, you were just subject to call any time anything went wrong?

A. Yes, sir.

Q. You testified that Mr. Hileman gave you an envelope to be delivered to Mr. Porter?

(Testimony of Victor Elmer Kangas.)

A. Yes, sir.

Q. I believe you testified that that was in the fall of 1938. Can you fix it more definitely than that?

A. I would say it was in either the latter part of August or the early part of September of 1938.

Q. And Mr. Hileman called you into his office with respect to that, did he? [309]

A. Yes, sir.

Q. What time of the day?

A. It was in the afternoon. I would say possibly around 2:00 o'clock, or maybe a little later, 2:30.

Q. Well, you went into his office, and what did he say to you? Do you recall?

A. Yes, somewhat.

Q. What did he say?

A. He said that he had an envelope here with some money in that to reimburse Mr. Porter for the work that he had done in respect to organizing an independent union there.

Q. Just a minute. Was that the only time you ever gave Mr. Porter any money through Mr. Hileman? A. Yes, sir.

Q. Just this one instance? A. Yes, sir.

Q. All right. And he said what it was, did he?

A. He said he had some money in that envelope, and to give that to Mr. Porter; that it was to reimburse him for his—for the work he had done in regard to organizing this union.

Q. Is that what Mr. Hileman stated to you at that time? A. Yes.

(Testimony of Victor Elmer Kangas.)

Q. Did he say anything further to you than that?

A. Well, no. He told me—he did say to be sure and not let anybody see me give it to him, be sure there was nobody [310] else present when I handed him that envelope.

Q. ' Did he tell you not to tell anybody else about it also?   A. Yes, sir, he did.

Q. Did you tell anybody else about it?

A. No, sir.

Q. How long did you carry that envelope? What did you do with it? Put it in your pocket, or what?

A. No, I carried it out to the plant in my hand. I called Mr. Porter into the washroom in the back of the plant and I handed him the envelope and I walked on out of the washroom.

Q. What did you say to him?

A. I told him "here was an envelope Mr. Hileman wanted me to deliver to you."

Q. You didn't tell him what it was?

A. No, sir.

Q. What did he say?

A. I don't remember whether he said anything. He just took the envelope and I walked out of the washroom.

Q. Did you tell him not to open it there?

A. No, I didn't.

Q. You just handed it to him?

A. That's right.

Q. You didn't see him open it then?

A. No, I did not.

(Testimony of Victor Ehmer Kangas.)

Q. When was the next time you talked to Mr. Porter about that [311] money?

A. That evening I and my wife went over to the Porter's.

Q. Did you have any particular reason for going over there?

A. No, not any particular reason.

Q. Just a social call?

A. A social call. Well, I was a little interested in knowing what was in the envelope.

Q. I see. Then, what did you say to Mr. Porter about it when you got over there?

A. I asked Mr. Porter what he found in his envelope and he told me he had $50.00 in there, and he didn't feel so well about it.

Q. Was it a check?

A. No, it was in money, he said.

Q. There wasn't any silver in it at all?

A. He didn't say anything about any silver.

Q. You didn't see the $50.00?

A. I didn't look at the $50.00.

Q. I see. What did he say to you about it?

A. He told me, he said, "I got a good notion to take this and tell that Jew son of a bitch to stick it up his brown."

Q. Then what did you say?

A. I didn't say anything that I remember of, because it wasn't up to me to make any cracks or remarks.

Q. Did you tell Mr. Hileman or anybody else in the company [312] about that?

(Testimony of Victor Elmer Kangas.)

A. No, sir.

Q. You didn't mention it at all?

A. No, sir.

Q. Why not?

A. Because I didn't think I should.

Q. Why?

A. Due to the fact that I didn't think I should take that remark to him.

Q. You didn't say to Mr. Hileman, "I delivered that envelope to Mr. Porter and he wasn't very well satisfied with it"?

A. I did, when he asked me, I told him I delivered it to him, but I did not tell him what Mr. Porter told me.

Q. In other words, so far as Mr. Hileman knew, everything was okeh on that money?

A. That's right, but Mr. Porter told me that same evening he would not go any further with the independent union, so far as helping the Thompson Products Company or Mr. Hileman with it.

Mr. Watkins: Read the answer.

(The answer was read.)

Q. (By Mr. Watkins): Did you say anything else that evening along that line?

A. Well, no, not in regard to anything like that. I think we probably talked about a lot of other things, but not shop. [313]

Q. That was all the conversation you had about the money or about the independent union that night?   A. That's right.

(Testimony of Victor Ehner Kangas.)

Q. Did Mr. Porter ever talk to you any further about it than that?

A. Oh, as I remember, he did, maybe once or twice after that, but not to any great extent. He told me at one time he thought it was rather small of them to give him only $50.00, and he said he really expected more than that, but that was after that. I don't know how long; it might have been six months or it might have been a year and a half.

Q. And Mr. Porter didn't get any more money, so far as you know?   A. So far as I know.

Q. And you are certain you yourself never gave him any money of any kind from the management except this one delivery of the envelope?

A. That is right. I never did give him any money.

Q. When did you leave the employment of Thompson Products?   A. August 8, 1940.

Q. One other thing, Mr. Kangas, do you remember an incident involving the theft of some valves, for Kinner Aircraft?   A. Yes, sir.

Q. About when was that?

A. I believe that that was in the spring of 1938, possibly [314] May, April or May.

Q. Possibly April or May, you say?

A. Yeah.

Q. It could have been later than that, could it?

A. Well, it could have been, yes; but I believe it was in the year of 1938.

Q. You are generally considered to have an extraordinary memory, are you not, Mr. Kangas?

A. That's right.

(Testimony of Victor Elmer Kangas.)

Q. You can remember numbers and dates and things like that extremely well?

A. That's right.

Q. And you have a reputation to that end?

A. I don't know whether I have gotten a reputation on that, but I think I can remember things fairly well.

Q. Yes. Now, you say this occurred sometime in the spring of 1938, April or May or June, along in there?   A. That's right.

Q. Did you have anything to do with uncovering the valve thefts?

A. Well, I engaged Mr. Porter in an investigation.

Q. You did?   A. I did.

Q. What did he do in connection with that?

A. He investigated the case, so far as the management would [315] let him go, up to a certain point, and then we was stopped because the person he thought was involved, we was afraid to get any farther into it.

Q. But Mr. Porter acted as a sort of detective or investigator on that?   A. He did.

Q. And you were responsible for putting him into that position?   A. Yes, sir.

Q. Going back to the date on which you left the company, August 8, 1940, did you quit?

A. Well, I guess I just beat them before the ink got dry. I believe that's the way it stands.

Q. What do you mean by that?

A. Well, I understand the skids were greased for me, and I quit before it happened.

(Testimony of Victor Ehmer Kangas.)

Q. Let us go back for a minute. When Mr. Livingston first came out in 1937 did you tell him you expected Mr. Dachtler to discharge you?

A. That's right.

Q. Back in 1937? A. That's right.

Q. The very first visit?

A. I don't believe it was the first visit. However, I think it was the second visit. [316]

Q. I see. All right. Now, going back to this last incident, you said something about you got out before the ink got dry. Just what do you mean by that?

A. Well, Mr. Hileman had an ad run in the paper, advertising for a plant manager for a plant that was engaged in manufacturing aircraft and automotive hardened and ground parts, and from that ad I knew exactly it was the Thompson Products, because we were the only, or Thompson Products was, at that time, the only plant engaged in manufacturing of automotive and aircraft hardened and ground parts, west of the Rockies, or west of Chicago.

Q. What did you do when you saw that ad?

A. I took it into the office and laid it on his desk and I told him to lay the cards out on the table and tell me what he wanted to do.

Q. Had you had any warnings prior to that time by Mr. Hileman that he was going to let you go? A. Yes.

Q. How many? A. Oh, two.

Q. How long before this?

(Testimony of Victor Elmer Kangas.)

A.   Possibly 60 days before.

Q.   What for?

A.   He told me to fire half of the crew and all of the foremen and he would give me 30 days to do it, and I told him I [317] absolutely refused to do it.

Q.   That was the reason he gave you for threatening you with discharge?

A.   That's what he told me.

Q.   Did he tell you any other reason than that?

A.   No, he didn't.

Q.   What was said to you at the time you came in and showed him this newspaper ad?

A.   He told me he had asked me to discharge a number of the force in the plant and some of the foremen and that I had refused to do it, hadn't carried out his instructions, and that was the only reason he had, or told me, he was leaving me go.

Q.   He didn't discuss anything about the conduct on your part?   A.   Not with me.

Q.   Or he hadn't at any previous time discussed any conduct on your part in the plant?

A.   Not with me he hadn't, because I asked him that very day in his office. He hasn't discussed it with me.

Q.   Have you got such a place as a dispensary down there?   A.   A first-aid room?

Q.   A first-aid room.   A.   Yes.

Q.   Did anybody ever find you asleep there during working hours? [318]

A.   Yes, I was asleep there during working hours one afternoon.

(Testimony of Victor Elmer Kangas.)

Q. What was said to you at that time?

A. Not a thing. He asked me what was the matter with me and I told him I didn't feel very well.

Q. What did he do about it?

A. He said, "Why don't you go down to the doctor?"

And I said, "I don't need to, I just laid down here and went to sleep."

Q. How long was this before your discharge?

A. Possibly three months.

Q. Did you go to a doctor?

A. I was under a doctor's care at that time.

Q. Somebody recommended by Mr. Hileman?

A. That's right.

Q. Am I correct in saying this, Mr. Kangas: That you now testify that at no time either at the time of your discharge or prior to it was any mention made of any improper conduct on your part, or your duties, or in connection with your duties at the plant?

A. No, sir, not to me there wasn't.

Q. How did you end your conversation—strike that, please.

What else was said in this newspaper incident that you mentioned, when you talked to Mr. Hileman?

A. You mean in the course of this conversation that Mr. [319] Hileman and I had?

Q. Yes, just about August 8th of 1940.

A. Well, I told him, I said, "If you want to

(Testimony of Victor Elmer Kangas.)

get rid of me, why don't you lay your cards on the table?''

I said, "As man to man I don't see any reason why you shouldn't." I said, "If you want me to leave, why don't you write it out?"

He said, "I will give you thirty days notice from the time I want you to leave."

I said, "That's all right, but I am going to look for new employment this afternoon."

I went out that afternoon and I got a job with Aircraft Accessories, two days later I went to work.

Q. Have you related all the conversation that took place between you and Mr. Hileman at the time you left the employment?

A. No. He told me one of the reasons was he wasn't satisfied with me, was due to the fact that I had a brother and cousin there, that they had received more overtime than any two people in the organization. I told him that was no fault of mine. "I have foremen that take care of the jobs, and they assign the work. Don't lay it on me."

Q. Was anything else said at that time?

A. Not that I remember.

Q. Have you related all the conversation that took place that afternoon? [320]

A. That was in the morning.

Q. Whenever it was; how long after that did you leave the plant?

A. Oh, I left the plant possibly about a quarter to 12:00.

Q. And you had no further conversation with Mr. Hileman about your leaving?

(Testimony of Victor Elmer Kangas.)

A. I came back the next day and the day after, when I left, I went in and shook hands with him, and told him I was leaving.

Q. You didn't ask him to take you back?

A. No, sir.

Q. Did you at any time ask him to take you back? A. No, sir.

Q. Did your wife at any time, to your knowledge, go to him and ask him to take you back?

A. Not to my knowledge.

Q. Did you make any statements after that discharge to anyone in the plant about your feelings towards Thompson Products and Mr. Hileman personally? A. Not that I remember of.

Q. You don't recall?

A. I don't recall it.

Q. You went to Aircraft Accessories after you left Thompson Products. How long were you there?

A. About two months, I guess. [321]

Q. Then where did you go?

A. I resigned there and went over to Western Aviation.

Q. How long were you there?

A. Possibly a month and a half.

Q. Then where did you go?

A. I went to Johnson and Stevenson, they were opening a new plant.

Q. How long were you there?

A. I left there three weeks ago.

Q. Then where did you go?

A. Precision Machine Works.

(Testimony of Victor Elmer Kangas.)

Q. What about the Aerial Corporation? Didn't you work for them?

A. That is the same place.

Q. As what?

A. Johnson and Stevenson.

Q. How long were you with them?

A. From November 27, 1940, until three weeks ago.

Q. Why did you quit the Aerial Corporation?

A. Because I wasn't satisfied.

Q. Over what?

A. That's my business.

Q. In other words, you would rather not state?

A. That's right.

Q. Prior to your quitting there had the American Federation [322] of Labor filed charges against you in that company for fostering C I. O. in that plant?

Mr. Moore: Objected to.

Mr. Watkins: Let me ask the witness if he knows; maybe he doesn't know.

Mr. Moore: I object to the question.

The Witness: As far as I know, they haven't.

Trial Examiner Whittemore: I will permit the witness' answer to remain, if he knows.

Mr. Watkins: The witness says so far as he knows they haven't. That is all.

Redirect Examination

Q. (By Mr. Moore): Mr. Kangas, do you know how Mr. Porter was paid for that detective work he did, if he was paid?

(Testimony of Victor Elmer Kangas.)

A. He told me, as he told me he got one fifty dollar bill.

Q. Who told you that? A. Mr. Porter.

Q. He told you he received $50.00 for it?

A. Yes.

Q. Did you give it to him?

A. I gave him the envelope, but I did not see the money.

Q. You gave him an envelope for the detective work in connection with the stolen valves, that is what I am speaking of.

A. Oh, no; so far as I know he was never paid for that work.

Q. Do you know whether or not he was paid for it? [323]

A. I don't think he was. I don't know that he was.

Q. Do you know whether or not he used his car in that investigation? A. Yes, he did.

Q. Were his expenses paid, or do you know?

A. That I don't know.

Q. Were you ever given any money to give to him in payment for that work?

A. No, sir.

Q. At the time you left Thompson Products were you and Mr. Hileman quite angry with each other?

A. Well, he didn't kiss me when I left, or anything like that, but we were on friendly terms, yes.

Q. Did you hear from him shortly after that?

(Testimony of Victor Elmer Kangas.)

A.   Yes, a telephone conversation.

Q.   Did he ever write to you?   A.   No.

Q.   Did he ever give you a written testimonial?

A.   Yeah. He gave me a note about two weeks after I left their employ.

Q.   When was that?   A.   In August.

Q.   1940?

A.   1940, possibly around, oh, the 15th or 20th of the month.

Q.   Did he hand it to you? [324]

A.   No, it was sent to me in a box of cigars.

Q.   Who sent the box of cigars to you?

A.   His secretary.

Q.   Was that done by mail?   A.   Yes, sir.

Q.   Sent by mail?   A.   Yes, sir.

Q.   A box of cigars?   A.   Yes, sir.

Q.   And inside that was a note?

A.   Yes, sir.

Q.   What did the note say?

A.   I have it in my pocket.   The note says: "V. E. Kangas——"

Mr. Watkins: Just a minute. I think if the note is here it ought to be introduced in evidence in the proper fashion, and not have the witness read it into the record.

Trial Examiner Whittemore: I agree with you.

Mr. Moore: How was that?

Trial Examiner Whittemore: I agree with Mr. Watkins.

Mr. Moore: Will you mark this as Board's 7 for identification, please?

(Testimony of Victor Elmer Kangas.)

(Whereupon the document referred to was marked Board's Exhibit No. 7 for identification.)

Mr. Watkins: May we see it, please?

Mr. Moore: I will ask him to identify it. [325]

Mr. Watkins: All right.

Q. (By Mr. Moore) I have had this piece of note paper which you produced from your pocket marked Board's Exhibit 7 for identification. Will you state what it is, if you know.

A. Shall I read this?

Q. No, just say what it is.

A. Well, it's a note from Mr. Hileman to me that I received in a box of cigars when I was employed at the Aircraft Accessories.

Q. About two weeks, I think you said, after you left?

A. Approximately, to the best of my memory. I haven't looked at the date of that.

Mr. Moore: I will offer Board's Exhibit 7 for identification in evidence.

Trial Examiner Whittemore: Any objection?

Mr. Watkins: No objection.

Mr. Baldwin: No.

Trial Examiner Whittemore: All right. The document is received.

(The document heretofore marked Board's Exhibit No. 7 for identification was received in evidence.)

(Testimony of Victor Elmer Kangas.)

BOARD'S EXHIBIT No. 7

Write It—Don't Say It!

Intercommunicating
Memorandum

To V. E. Kangas

Date August 13, 1940

From P. D. Hileman

Dear Vic:

I am sorry I didn't get in on the kitty for the shotgun the boys presented you with, but herewith a damned good box of cigars as a token of my high regard for the many good jobs you did for me while at Jadson.

With all best wishes for the new job, I am

Sincerely,

P.D.H.

PDH:G

Keep This Sheet for Future Reference

———

Q. (By Mr. Moore) On cross examination, Mr. Kangas——

Trial Examiner Whittemore: May I suggest, in view of the condition of this, that we have copies made. You do not [326] question the authenticity of this in any way, do you?

Mr. Watkins: I don't know. It is the first time I ever heard of it.

Trial Examiner Whittemore: Suppose we keep it here, in the event you do raise any question, but thereafter we have copies made so we can give it back to the witness, unless you do raise a question.

(Testimony of Victor Elmer Kangas.)

Mr. Watkins: Oh, yes. After we check on it, we have no objection to a substitution.

Trial Examiner Whittemore: Well, it will just be kept in the reporter's hands, but you have copies made, so you can substitute them in the event Mr. Watkins has no objection.

Mr. Moore: All right.

Q. (By Mr. Moore) You were asked on cross examination as to the date on which membership cards, or a card, was distributed in the plant after a delegation of employees had visited the management.   A. Yes, sir.

Q. And I think you said definitely that was August 3, 1937?

A. I said approximately on August 3rd, as well as I could remember. I think it was August 3rd.

Q. Do you recall it was a Tuesday?

A. Tuesday.

Q. Will you examine this calendar now and tell me whether or not it was exactly August 3rd, or whether it may have been [327] August 3rd or another date close to that?

A. I would say it was August 3rd.

Q. May it have been the Tuesday before August 3rd?

A. Yes, it could have been the 27th day of July.

Trial Examiner Whittemore: Do you mind if I raise a point? I think all we are interested in is determining the approximate date of this. There seems to be some confusion. I suggest you show him Mr. Porter's signature on that card, which

(Testimony of Victor Elmer Kangas.)
is produced by the Alliance here, and which bears, as I recall, the date of July 27th, and see whether or not that serves to refresh his recollection.

The Witness: As I remember now, it was the last week of August.

Trial Examiner Whittemore: I don't think after this long a period of time that one week one way or the other is going to make any difference, but it does make a difference to this trial examiner when he comes to write his report.

Mr. Watkins: I think it may make a difference in regard to whatever point——

Trial Examiner Whittemore: Whatever point you may have made in attacking the witness' credibility is already in the record. But what I am after is to establish the date. Here is the card produced by the Alliance which bears the date, and I confess I would like to have it straightened out, if I can. [328]

Mr. Watkins: All right.

Mr. Moore: I don't know whether this witness can refresh his recollection from this card. I will ask him.

Trial Examiner Whittemore: Ask him if he can.

Q. (By Mr. Moore) I will show you Board's Exhibit 6 and ask you if that refreshes your recollection as to the date on which those cards were distributed?

A. Yes, the 27th day of July, which would be Tuesday.

Q. It is your recollection now it was the 27th day of July of 1937? A. That is right.

(Testimony of Victor Elmer Kangas.)

Trial Examiner Whittemore: The point is, Mr. Watkins: I think you said either the date on the card must be wrong or his recollection, when he said August 3rd, must be wrong, because these efforts occurred the first day, as I recall it, that the cards were in existence.

Q. (By Mr. Moore) Mr. Kangas, do you know whether or not Mr. Clark was in the plant at the time you asked Mr. Porter to join the C. I. O.?

A. No, he was not, as I remember, because I very distinctly remember Mr. Dachtler asking me to have someone do it.

Q. Are you certain of that, or is that your best recollection?

A. Yes, I believe Mr. Clark was there at the time, come to think of it. I believe that was just before he left the plant, [329] as I hazily remember a conversation with Mr. Clark and myself in respect to having somebody join the C. I. O., along with Mr. Dachtler. I am quite sure now that Mr. Clark was there.

Mr. Watkins: Are we talking about two different conversations or one, or what? May we tie this down in some way.

Mr. Moore: I do not intend to inquire about the conversation. I was only trying to fix whether or not Mr. Clark was in the plant.

Mr. Watkins: Oh, I see. Then I move the witness' answer be stricken, except in answer to that question, as being not responsive to the question.

(Testimony of Victor Elmer Kangas.)

Trial Examiner Whittemore: All right, it may be stricken.

Mr. Moore: What portion of it? The explanation that he appended?

Trial Examiner Whittemore: That part in which he explains why he thought Mr. Clark was in the plant; the part containing his answer that he believed Mr. Clark was there may remain.

Mr. Moore: All right. No further questions.

Mr. Watkins: I would like to ask the witness, Mr. Examiner, if I may, to just copy in pencil the first two sentences on this Board's 7 for identification, and sign his name. Do you have a pencil?

The Witness: Yes.

Mr. Watkins: Then I would like to take a short recess, if [330] we may, for about five minutes before I determine whether or not there is anything further I would like to ask Mr. Kangas.

Trial Examiner Whittemore: All right. We will take a five minute recess at this time.

(A short recess was taken.)

Trial Examiner Whittemore: Will the witness take the stand, please?

Mr. Watkins: I had asked the witness to write a portion of Board's Exhibit 7, and print a portion of it. He did both, but I asked him to print a portion of it in capital letters, and the witness is unwilling to do that.

The Witness: Why do I have to do that? Is it necessary?

(Testimony of Victor Elmer Kangas.)

Mr. Watkins: I would like to request that he be instructed to do that.

Trial Examiner Whittemore: Is this your last request? I am not going to keep the witness all afternoon to suit your caprices on this thing. You asked him to write, and he did. Is this the last you are going to ask him to do?

Mr. Watkins: Mr. Examiner, yes; and I think, perhaps, it is unfair of the Examiner to conclude it is caprice on my part. I have a reason for asking it and it isn't caprice.

Trial Examiner Whittemore: Whatever it is, I am not going to keep the witness all afternoon to do these things. Is this the last you are going to have him do?

Mr. Watkins: I would like to have him write in capitals [331] one line, if he will do it.

The Witness: I don't see why I should have to do that.

Trial Examiner Whittemore: Go ahead then; write a line in capitals.

The Witness: Do I have to do that? I want to know why. What do you want? The first line?

Mr. Watkins: It doesn't make any difference. That is all right.

(The witness complies with request.)

Mr. Watkins: I think that's enough. Thank you.

Recross Examination

Q. (By Mr. Watkins) Mr. Kangas, in the telephone conversation that you had with Mr. Liv-

(Testimony of Victor Elmer Kangas.)
ingston with respect to the printed cards, how long
did you talk to him?

A. Oh, possibly ten or fifteen minutes.

Q. During that time you made notes of what
he had said to you over the telephone?

A. Well, I took it word for word.

Q. What did you do with that paper you had?

A. I left it with the printers.

Q. Did you ever request it back?

A. No, sir.

Q. Did you print it or write it?

A. I wrote it.

Q. On what? [332]

A. On a piece of white paper.

Q. Where, in the telephone booth?

A. Well, I don't know just exactly where it
was in the telephone booth, I wrote it as he was
talking; probably a shelf there.

Q. You don't recall?

A. Yes, I think there was a shelf I was writing on.

Q. You mentioned in your direct examination
about minutes of the meetings of the Alliance's committee and the company being changed?

A. That's right.

Q. Do you remember any instances where the
minutes were drafted by the company and were
changed by the Alliance?

A. No. I know where the company changed the
Alliance's minutes.

Q. All right, you testified to that; but do you

(Testimony of Victor Elmer Kangas.)

remember a reverse side of it, where the Alliance changed anything written by the company?

A. No, I can't say I do.

Q. You don't recall any instance of that kind?

A. No.

Q. Referring again to this card, which is Board's Exhibit 6, when was the first time that you examined one of those cards?

A. Tuesday, August—Tuesday, July 27, 1937.

Q. Where did you examine it? [333]

A. Out at the gate.

Q. Who had it?

A. I think Lester Bebb had it.

Q. How did you happen to examine it?

A. Oh, I wanted to look at it.

Q. You just asked him for one and took a look at it?   A. Yes.

Q. Since you have left the Thompson Company have you made any statements to anyone about products put out by Thompson Products being inferior, being too high priced, or anything of that kind?   A. No, sir.

Mr. Moore: Objected to as immaterial.

Trial Examiner Whittemore: I will permit the witness' answer to stand.

The Witness: I haven't anyway, so it doesn't make any difference. I haven't made any remarks like that.

Q. (By Mr. Watkins) Have you sent any telegrams of any kind to the company under assumed

(Testimony of Victor Elmer Kangas.)
names with respect to any immoral activities that
were alleged to be going on at the plant?

A. No, sir.

Mr. Watkins: I think that is all. I would like
to introduce this document in evidence as Respondent's Exhibit 2.

Trial Examiner Whittemore: For what purpose? [334]

Mr. Watkins: I will want it, Mr. Examiner, for
identification at a later time on a document.

Trial Examiner Whittemore: You can mark it,
if you wish. I certainly am not going to admit it in
evidence until I find out what the purpose is.

Mr. Watkins: The purpose now is to identify
the handwriting and printing of this witness.

Trial Examiner Whittemore: It is not material
to the issues so far. I suggest you have it marked
for identification with your next exhibit number.

Mr. Watkins: That is satisfactory, providing
that no objection will be raised at that time that no
foundation has been laid because this witness will
not be present at that time.

Trial Examiner Whittemore: Well, I don't
know about foundation. I think we all agree that's
the document you asked him to print.

Mr. Watkins: That is all I need then, Mr. Examiner. Under those circumstances I am satisfied
to have it marked now for identification.

Trial Examiner Whittemore: All right.

(Thereupon the document referred to was
marked as Company's Exhibit 2 for identification.)

(Testimony of Victor Elmer Kangas.)

Trial Examiner Whittemore: Have you any further questions?

Mr. Moore: I have no further questions. [335]

Trial Examiner Whittemore: Have you, Mr. Baldwin?

Mr. Baldwin: I would like to ask one question.

Q. (By Mr. Baldwin) You say you saw the card for the first time on Tuesday, July 27th?

A. Yes.

Q. Was that the same day in which the meeting was held, in which the group of 15 or 18 were present? A. That's right.

Mr. Baldwin: That is all.

Trial Examiner Whittemore: All right. Then the witness may be excused. Thank you.

(Witness excused.)

Mr. Moore: Will you mark this as Board's Exhibit 8 for identification?

(Thereupon the document referred to was marked as Board's Exhibit No. 8, for identification.)

Mr. Moore: I have had marked for identification as Board's Exhibit 8 a small red booklet on the cover of which appears the following: "Thompson Products, Inc., West Coast Plant Employees Hand Book."

May it be stipulated that this is a hand book published by or in behalf of Thompson Products, Inc., and that after October of 1940 up until approximately two weeks before this date, copies of this booklet were distributed to each new employee who came into the plant, and also to all old [336] employees who asked for them?

Mr. Watkins: Yes, it is so stipulated.

Mr. Moore: I offer Board's Exhibit 8 for identification in evidence.

Trial Examiner Whittemore: Well, may I inquire from you what the purpose of this booklet is?

Mr. Moore: Well, I am introducing the whole thing, but at this time I will direct your attention to the section entitled: "Labor Relations," on page 10 of the booklet.

Mr. Watkins: Do I understand counsel to say he is not introducing the whole thing?

Mr. Moore: I say I am offering the whole booklet.

Mr. Watkins: Oh.

Trial Examiner Whittemore: All right. Have you any objection, Mr. Watkins?

Mr. Watkins: No objection.

Trial Examiner Whittemore: Mr. Baldwin?

Mr. Baldwin: No objection.

Trial Examiner Whittemore: The document is received.

(Thereupon the document heretofore marked for identification as Board's Exhibit 8, was received in evidence.) [337]

United States
Circuit Court of Appeals
For the Ninth Circuit.

NATIONAL LABOR RELATIONS BOARD,

Petitioner,

vs.

THOMPSON PRODUCTS, INC., a corporation,

Respondent.

Transcript of Record
In Three Volumes
VOLUME II
Pages 485 to 979

Upon Petition for Enforcement of an Order of the National Labor Relations Board

FILED

MAY 14 1943

PAUL P. O'BRIEN
CLERK

Rotary Colorprint, 590 Folsom St., San Francisco   60-5-12-43

No. 10383

United States
Circuit Court of Appeals
For the Ninth Circuit.

NATIONAL LABOR RELATIONS BOARD,

Petitioner,

vs.

THOMPSON PRODUCTS, INC., a corporation,

Respondent.

Transcript of Record
In Three Volumes
VOLUME II
Pages 485 to 979

Upon Petition for Enforcement of an Order of the National
Labor Relations Board

Rotary Colorprint, 590 Folsom St, San Francisco   60-5-12-43

BOARD'S EXHIBIT No. 8

Thompson Products, Inc.
West Coast Plant

Employees Handbook

Index

Page

(1)

April, 1940

To Company Members:

We of Thompson Products, Inc., have always been proud of the friendly relationships enjoyed with one another, without the necessity of numer-

Board's Exhibit No. 8—(Continued)

ous restrictive regulations. Behavior of employees has never been restricted to the extent that is customary in many plants.

As our personnel increases, however, it becomes important that company members be familiar with and observe the basic rules of conduct which are necessary. It has never been the company's policy to set down hard and fast rules for behavior. But what we do expect from our members can be well expressed by the term "General Good Citizenship".

This book, therefore, is not intended to inform you of numerous rules and regulations, for which definite disciplinary (2) actions are provided. Rather, it is to give members a ready reference of company policies—an understanding of what employees may expect of management and what management expects of employees.

We take this method of giving you the fundamental information on which we have built the understanding and co-operative spirit in which we all justly take pride. From a mutual understanding of our problems comes a sound, lasting singleness of purpose, which enables us confidently to accept new business and seek constantly to provide greater job security and new opportunities for company members.

F. C. CRAWFORD,
President,
Thompson Products, Inc. (3)

Board's Exhibit No. 8—(Continued)

Company Officials
Staff Executives

F. C. Crawford—President

L. M. Clegg—Executive Vice President

A. T. Colwell—Vice President

W. M. Albaugh—Treasurer

J. D. Wright—Secretary

W. E. Close—Assistant Secretary-Treasurer

R. S. Livingstone—Director of Personnel
West Coast Plant Operating Executives

P. D. Hileman—Plant Manager

W. I. Metzger—Plant Controller

R. M. Rogers—Chief Engineer

W. H. Carhart—Sales Manager

Geo. Fary—Factory Manager

W. J. Kearns—General Superintendent

(In Thompson Products, Inc. there is no absentee management. All officers and executives are actively engaged performing the duties of their positions.) (4)

Board's Exhibit No. 8—(Continued)

DECIMAL EQUIVALENTS

Fract.	Deci.	Fract.	Deci.	Fract.	Deci.
1/64	.015625	23/64	.359375	45/64	.703125
1/32	.03125	3/8	.375	23/32	.718775
3/64	.046875	25/64	.390625	47/64	.734375
1/16	.0625	13/32	.40625	3/4	.750
5/64	.078125	27/64	.421875	49/64	.765625
3/32	.09375	7/16	.4375	25/32	.78125
7/64	.109375	29/64	.453125	51/64	.796875
1/8	.125	15/32	.46875	13/16	.8125
9/64	.140625	31/64	.484375	53/64	.828125
5/32	.15625	1/2	.500	27/32	.84375
11/64	.171875	33/64	.515625	55/64	.859375
3/16	.1875	17/32	.53125	7/8	.875
13/64	.203125	35/64	.546875	57/64	.890625
7/32	.21875	9/16	.5625	29/32	.90625
15/64	.234375	37/64	.578125	59/64	.921875
1/4	.250	19/32	.59375	15/16	.9375
17/64	.265625	39/64	.609375	61/64	.953125
9/32	.28125	5/8	.625	31/32	.96875
19/64	.296875	41/64	.640625	63/64	.984375
5/16	.3125	21/32	.65625	1	1.000
21/64	.328125	43/64	.671875		
11/32	.34375	11/16	.6875		

(5)

The Thompson Trophy

(Cut)

Sponsored by Thompson Products, Inc., the Thompson Trophy Race is the land plane speed classic of the world. America's fastest planes and most famous speed pilots compete annually during the National Air Races for the valuable trophy shown above.

(6)

Board's Exhibit No. 8—(Continued)

Employee's Handbook
To Old and New Employees

As a member of Thompson Products, Inc., you are promised fair, considerate treatment in all of your relations with the company. The company pledges its constant effort to provide conditions of work which are as enjoyable and profitable as circumstances allow.

We are glad to have you with us, and assume terms of your employment are satisfactory to you, since you have accepted them. We are unable to make any definite promises of promotion, either in wages or position, but we do closely adhere to a policy of attempting to develop our own men and advance them to higher skilled and better paying occupations as opportunities present themselves.

Prevailing spirit in this company is one of friendliness, good-fellowship and the sincere intention to do right. We ask only that you uphold your end by doing your work to the best of your ability and by dealing fairly, honestly and considerately with the company.

There are no secrets in this company. We seek to make available to company members all information we feel will be of interest to them. Perhaps you have a particular interest in some one phase of (7) the company's business. If so, we want you to feel entirely free to ask for additional information you believe will help further your knowledge.

Board's Exhibit No. 8—(Continued)

Your Company

Thompson Products, Inc., is one of the largest and most highly respected manufacturers of automotive and aircraft parts in the United States, employing over 5,000 people. In Cleveland it is one of the leading employers, having more than 3,500 people on its payrolls.

Founded in 1901, as the Cleveland Cap Screw Co., it has grown steadily in the intervening years, and has widened the scope of its manufacturing activity as the various phases of transportation have developed. From manufacturing parts for bicycles in the early days of the century, it stepped into the automotive field, grew with it, and during the World War entered the aircraft industry. Today, in Cleveland, aircraft parts production is nearly equal to production of automotive parts.

Thompson parts are manufactured for every car, truck, bus and tractor built. Thompson valves and other precision aircraft parts are used by all manufacturers of American military and commercial airplane engines, as well as in foreign engines.

The company operates plants in five cities, namely Cleveland, Detroit, Toledo, Los Angeles, and St. Catharines, Canada. (8)

Automobile parts made in Cleveland include valves, bolts, valve assembly parts, water pumps, cylinder sleeves, cast iron and aluminum pistons, and wrist pins. Principle aircraft parts are valves

Board's Exhibit No. 8—(Continued)

and numerous other important precision engine parts.

At Detroit tie rods, drag links, propellor shafts, spring seats and other tubular chassis parts are made. The Toledo plant is devoted exclusively to the manufacture of commercial valves, while in Los Angeles both automobile and aircraft valves are made as well as special aviation and marine parts. At St. Catharines the entire line of Thompson parts is made for Canadian consumption.

Rapidity with which technical changes are introduced in both the aircraft and automotive industries make the company's business a hazardous one. For this reason it is extremely difficult to predict with any accuracy the company's long term position in either field. However, management's constant efforts to diversify its manufactured products has had a strong stabilizing effect on employment, so that now the company enjoys a community wide reputation for providing steady employment.

Sales are classified in two divisions: Original Equipment and Replacement. Original equipment sales are directly to car and engine builders, while replacement sales are to jobbers and garage men. (9) More than 3,000 distributors through-out the country handle the company's products, as do agents in 86 foreign countries. Sales in the original equipment field fluctuate, being largely dependent on the rate of automobile production. Sale of replace-

Board's Exhibit No. 8—(Continued)

ment parts is more steady and has shown a constant increase from year to year.

The company's stock has been listed on the New York Stock Exchange since 1930. Its stock structure includes 28,945 shares of authorized and issued Preferred Stock, without par value, and 500,-000 shares of authorized common stock, without par value, of which only 293,290 shares are issued.

Labor Relations

Since 1937 the company has had a sole bargaining contract with the Pacific Motor Parts Workers' Alliance. Matters of wages, hours and working conditions, as well as cases concerning individuals, are discussed with regularly elected representatives of this organization at specified times each month, and special meetings are held whenever necessary. Matters concerning individuals or small groups of employees are discussed as they arise with the representative of the men concerned. It is part of the contract agreement that no basic changes in wages, hours or working conditions will be made without discussion with representatives of the P.M.P.W.A.

Wages

Thompson Products endeavors to pay each employee a fair, honest wage. In (10) determining what constitutes a fair, honest wage we take into consideration these factors: The skill required for the job; the wage paid in the community and industry for the same or similar jobs; the responsi-

Board's Exhibit No. 8—(Continued)

bility of the job and the financial condition of the company.

Wage surveys are made to determine prevailing wages in the community and industry. Representatives of the P.M.P.W.A. and management act jointly in making these determinations and negotiating an equitable wage scale for jobs at the West Coast Plant.

After a fair rate has been determined, a fair amount of work to be produced for that rate is established by means of a time study. In the time study, provision is made for the fact that the average employee requires approximately ten per cent of each hour for personal use. Allowance for this personal time is made in the standard for each job. Allowance also is made in the standard for a normal amount of tool and machine trouble.

Pay System

The Group Piece Work System is used in most departments of the West Coast Plant. In place of counting the work done by each employee, as is done under an Individual Piece Work System, the work done by a group of employees is counted together.

Rates are established for each job and a standard amount of work each employee (11) is expected to perform is determined by means of a time study. Because some employees naturally are more efficient than others, three rates are established for each job. There is the beginning rate; the 30-day rate, which is five cents higher than the beginning

Board's Exhibit No. 8—(Continued)
rate, and the base rate, which is five cents higher than the 30-day rate, and ten cents above the hiring rate.

All employees who prove satisfactory within 30 days after being hired are given the 30-day rate. Whether an employee is granted additional increases which bring him up to the base rate depends upon his ability and initiative. However, when an employee proves his ability to perform a standard amount of work consistently to the satisfaction of his foreman, he should receive the base rate.

Additional money may be earned when a group does more than the standard amount of work expected of it. For instance, in a given period the standards may call for a group to produce 10,000 pieces. If the group produces 11,000 pieces in the time allotted, it has earned a ten per cent bonus, and employees receive ten per cent on top of their regular, guaranteed pay.

Overtime

An overtime premium of time and one-half is paid after 42 hours in one week have been worked at straight time. Time and one-half is paid for any hours worked on Sunday or the six legal holidays—(12) New Years, Decoration Day, Independence Day, Labor Day, Thanksgiving and Christmas. After October 23 of this year, overtime will be paid at the rate of time and one-half after 40 hours have been worked in any one week.

Board's Exhibit No. 8—(Continued)

The working day officially begins at 7:00 A. M., including Sundays and holidays.

Seniority

A seniority agreement exists between the company and the Pacific Motor Parts Workers' Alliance, which provides a specific plan for laying off employees when a reduction of the working force is necessary.

Two types of seniority are accumulated on each employee: Old Guard Time, which is the total time worked for the West Coast Plant and Occupational Senority, which is the length of time an employee has worked on his regular operation.

When a reduction of the working force becomes necessary employees are laid-off according to Occupational Seniority on their regular job. After being laid-off from his regular job, an employee may claim a lesser skilled job, in his own department, which he is qualified to perform, providing he has more Old Guard Time than the employee replaced by such a move.

An important provision of the agreement is that employees with the most Old Guard Time are entitled to jobs on the day shift. (13)

Old Guard time is computed once annually as of Dec. 31. Employees are credited with a full month's service for each month of the year in which they have worked one day.

Employees lose all Old Guard time if they are

Board's Exhibit No. 8—(Continued)
discharged, quit or are laid-off for a continuous
period exceeding two years.

Complete, detailed provisions of the Seniority
Agreement are posted in each plant. Generally, the
agreement is designed to protect the employment of
the company members who have the greatest amount
of Old Guard Time. During their first year of employment, employees stand on merit alone. After
the first year their employment is controlled by
terms of the Seniority Agreement.

Employee Benefits

For the benefit of employees, the company offers
two insurance services, monthly premiums for which
will be deducted from employees' pay if they desire.

Life Insurance—By arrangement with the Prudential Life Insurance Company, we are able to
offer employees protection at unusually low cost.
Female employees may secure $1,000 worth of life
insurance at a cost of 60 cents a month. Male employees may secure $2,000 at a cost of $1.20 a month.

Contracts for this insurance are made out in employees' names and given to (14) them to keep. They
contain clauses providing benefits for total disabil-
ity, and for double liability in case of accidental
death. Payment of death benefits to beneficiaries
is made the same day the company is officially notified.

Employees have the privilege of naming whom
they please beneficiary in their policies, and may
change the beneficiary at any time by filling out

Board's Exhibit No. 8—(Continued)
the proper form, which is available in the Employment Office.

Hospitalization and Surgical Insurance — We have also arranged with the Prudential Insurance Company for this type of insurance at very low rates. Briefly stated the plan is as follows:

Daily Hospital Benefits—$4.00 per day for a maximum period of 70 days. (This maximum may be changed at the end of the current policy year.)

Hospital Fee Allowance—$20.00.

Maximum Surgical Benefits—$150.00.

Cost Per Month—74 cents.

As in the case of life insurance, contracts are made out in the employees' names and given them to keep. Payments of benefits are made the same day that forms, properly filled out, are presented to the company. (15)

Promotions

It is an established policy of the company to advance its own employees to better, higher paying jobs as the employees qualify and openings occur, insofar as is possible without seriously impairing plant efficiency. Selection for advancement is generally made from the Personnel Inventory, which is a record of all employees who have filed application for a specific type of work.

If at some future date you wish to file an application for a specific type of work, you may secure a Personnel Inventory form from either the Employment or Personnel Office.

Board's Exhibit No. 8—(Continued)

While management encourages employees to prepare themselves for and to seek advancements within the company, it recommends that they wait sufficiently long after they are hired to thoroughly acquaint themselves with types of work done in the plant. Employees are welcome to visit other departments in the plant after working hours, if they first arrange for this with their foreman.

Opportunities

As has been said, it is company policy to advance employees to higher skilled, better paying jobs as they qualify and as the opportunities occur. In this regard, employees who intend special study to prepare themselves for promotion, should be familiar with where the most likely chances for advancement lie. (16)

It is generally agreed that the brightest opportunities for youth in America today exist in the manufacturing end of the country's businesses. Such prominent men as William Knudsen, president of General Motors, has said if he were starting life at 21 today he would be a mechanic. It is especially true at Thompson Products that the greatest opportunities lie in the manufacturing end of the business. Few if any employees, who had worked in the manufacturing end of the company's business for as long as a year, have failed to earn at least one advancement.

Roughly, one of every 20 persons employed in manufacturing is in a supervisory capacity. That

Board's Exhibit No. 8—(Continued)

means employees have one chance in 20 of becoming supervisors, if they devote their efforts to acquiring mechanical skill and knowledge of shop practices. Opportunities for advancement occur oftener in the manufacturing end of the company's business than in any other.

The company's sales are classified according to original equipment sales and replacement sales. Original equipment sales to manufacturers of automobiles and aircraft engines, are handled by a staff of about six men. Nature of the company's business makes it possible for this small staff to contact all original equipment customers, and also requires that these men have a good engineering knowledge of products.

From time to time it is possible to (17) transfer employees with accounting backgrounds into the payroll or cost offices. These departments are comparatively small and opportunities do not present themselves with any regularity or frequency. Basic knowledge of accounting or experience in operating standard business machines are usual requirements for jobs in these departments.

The Engineering Department offers opportunity only to employees trained in the sciences. Special skills and training are required for virtually all jobs. Chemists, metallurgists, research engineers and tool and machine designers are the usual type of men sought by the engineering department. All must be highly skilled in their field.

Board's Exhibit No. 8—(Continued)

Old Guard

The Old Guard Association is an honorary organization of employees who have acquired five or more years of service with the company. Each employee who completes five years of service is awarded a service emblem, and is given a new emblem for each additional five years he serves. A bonus equivalent to 25% of an employee's annual earnings, averaged over 5 years, is paid on the 25th anniversary.

Old Guard members for the last four years have been awarded vacations with pay, the company being one of the first automotive parts concerns to adopt this practice for hourly rate employees. Each year the business outlook and the delivery situation is reviewed, and a vacation (18) plan is announced on a year to year basis as circumstances permit. Recently five year employees have been granted a one week vacation, and employees with ten or more year's service a two week's vacation.

Employee welfare is also handled by the Old Guard Association. It aids employees in time of sickness, unexpected reverses and other emergencies. Funds for this work have been raised jointly by employees and the company. Contributions are made once annually.

Social activities of the Old Guard include an annual winter banquet for members, and an annual summer picnic for all employees and members of their families.

Board's Exhibit No. 8—(Continued)

Friendly Forum—Bulletin Boards

All departments are equipped with bulletin boards, on which at frequent intervals information of interest and importance to employees is posted. In addition, once each four weeks the company publishes a paper, Friendly Forum, which contains news of the company and of employees. This is distributed free to all employees.

Employees are responsible for knowledge of information published either on bulletin boards or in Friendly Forum. Make a practice of reading the bulletin boards every day and be sure to get your copy of Friendly Forum each time it is issued. Also, employees are encouraged to contribute news items to Friendly Forum. (19)

Correct Addresses

Employees are responsible for keeping the Employment Office advised as to their correct address, telephone number (or the number of a neighbor) marital status (married or single) number of children and other dependents. This information is important and must be kept up to date.

Information

It is our desire that you be a well informed employee. If you do not get all the information you need or desire through the regularly established channels, do not hesitate to ask questions.

Your first source of information should be your immediate supervisor and beyond him the foreman of your department. Get acquainted with these men;

Board's Exhibit No. 8—(Continued)

they are your friends. If they can't immediately answer your questions themselves, they will either get the information for you or tell you where to get it for yourself.

We much prefer that you ask questions rather than go ahead without sufficient information.

Personnel Department

The services of the Personnel Department are offered all employees for assistance in any reasonable matters. This includes consultation on matters of education, vocation, company opportunities, financial matters, personal problems, etc. (20)

Your problems may be discussed with C. L. Millman or W. J. Kearns, and will be treated in strictest confidence.

Factory Regulations

These regulations have been adopted not to limit or restrain employees, but rather to guide and instruct them in the proper course to follow during their employment. Before adoption, the regulations were discussed with properly designated representatives of the employees.

Reasons for dismissal may be any of the following: Incompetency, unreliability, laziness, carelessness, insubordination, misconduct, bad habits, repeated failure to observe regulations. Rather than attempt to set forth specific instances of the above which will be considered serious enough to warrant dismissal, it is the company's policy to express its expectation of employee behavior in the broad term "good citizenship".

Board's Exhibit No. 8—(Continued)

The increased personnel of all of our plants and the large amount of work being done for the United States Government have made it necessary to supply each employee with an identification badge, which bears his picture.

These badges must be worn in a conspicuous place on the clothing at all times, so that watchmen on duty may easily see them.

A charge of seventy-five cents will be made for replacing any lost identification badges. (21)

Varying degrees of fire hazard in different departments make it impossible to establish a general policy covering smoking privileges. Smoking regulations have been formulated for each department, however, and employees will find these regulations posted on the department bulletin boards.

Sale of tickets, raffles, lotteries and solicitations within the plants are forbidden, unless permission is secured from General Superintendent Kearns.

Visitors are not permitted in the plants without passes issued by the Superintendent's Office. Employees are not permitted in plants outside of working hours, unless they have made arrangements with their foreman.

Absences due to sickness must be reported immediately to the Employment Office.

Excused absences must be arranged for ahead of time with the foreman.

Employees are held responsible for keeping the Employment Office informed as to their correct

Board's Exhibit No. 8—(Continued)
phone number, address, marital status and number of dependent children.

Employees returning to work following an absence will find their time cards in the Employment Office. (22)

Time cards must be rung in when the employee comes to work, and rung out upon leaving. They must be left in the rack. When an employee leaves the plant during the lunch hour it is not necessary to ring the card.

Employees are not permitted to leave their departments during working hours without first obtaining permission of their supervisor.

Employees should go directly to their departments on entering the factory, and are expected to be in their departments ready for work at starting time.

Time is counted from the quarter hour after the time clock is punched. (If card is punched at 7:04, time is counted from 7:15, etc.) Time cards should not be rung in more than fifteen minutes before starting time, nor rung out later than fifteen minutes after quitting time, to avoid confusion in the Payroll Department.

If an employee takes no lunch hour, a trailer card must be rung, marked "worked through" and signed by the foreman.

Pay checks are issued on the 5th and 20th of each month. The pay periods are from the 1st to the 15th and from the 16th to the 30th or 31st as the case may be. After the pay period is closed,

Board's Exhibit No. 8—(Continued)

five days are required to get the checks ready for distribution. When the regular pay day falls on a bank holiday, the company endeavors to issue checks a day in advance. (23)

If an employee is instructed to report for work he is guaranteed at least two hours working time. However, cards must be rung and approved by foremen in order that this time be paid.

Employees claiming pay check shortages must supply foremen with dates of days worked, hours worked, and money earned during the pay period in which the shortage is claimed.

All injuries incurred at work, regardless of how trivial, must be reported to the dispensary.

Female employees who marry must leave the employ of the Company. (Exception is made in the case of girls whose service dates back to Jan. 1st, 1935). Female employees who inform the Company in advance of their intention to marry may receive permission to work a period not to exceed six months following their marriage, at the discretion of the management. Under no circumstances will husband and wife be permitted to work for the Company at the same time. (24)

> Name ....
> Dept. No. ....

————

Mr. Moore: May it be stipulated Board's Exhibit 4-A for identification contains a statement of four by-laws of Pacific Motor Parts Workers Alliance, to which reference has previously been made in the record?

Mr. Watkins: We will stipulate it may be received in evidence, and that a copy may be substituted for the original.

Trial Examiner Whittemore: All right. The document is received.

(Thereupon the document heretofore marked for identification as Board's Exhibit 4-A, was received in evidence.)

BOARD'S EXHIBIT NO. 4-A

XIII

I.   The Salary of the Secretary and Treasurer shall be paid on a basis of 10c (per member) per month—Payable on the 22nd of each Month.

II.   Any elected Officer of the Alliance, excepting Secretary and Treasurer, or any member appointed by the Council who *loosed* time from work to attend to Alliance business is to be paid his or her hourly rate for the time lost.

III.   A vacancy caused by the resignation or discharge from Office of any elected or appointed officer may be filled for the remainder of the term by appointment by the Council.

IV.   The Initiantion fee into the Alliance shall be $1.00—payable in advance. Dues shall be 25c per month—payable the 22nd of the month.

Mr. Moore: I will call Mr. Crank.

JAMES WELLINGTON CRANK,

called as a witness by and on behalf of the National Labor Relations Board, having been first duly sworn, was examined and testified as follows: [338]

Direct Examination

Q. (By Mr. Moore) Will you state your full name, please?

A. James Wellington Crank.

Q. Have you been employed by Thompson Products, Inc.? A. Yes, sir.

Q. Were you employed by them at their plant in Bell, California? A. Yes, sir.

Q. During what period were you so employed?

A. From December 22, 1939 until about five weeks ago.

Q. And in what capacity were you employed?

A. I was employed there at the last as turret lathe operator.

Q. During the course of your employment with Thompson Products did you have occasion to join the Pacific Motor Parts Workers Alliance?

A. I did.

Q. About when did you join that Alliance?

A. Well, as near as I can remember it was about nine months after I—no, between six and nine months after I went to work there.

Q. What were the circumstances of your joining it?

A. Well, I was asked several times to join and finally agreed.

Q. Who asked you?

A. Well, I have been approached by the presi-

(Testimony of James Wellington Crank.)
dent there, who [339] was Ed Fickle there, at that time, and he asked me at different times.

Q. About when did he first approach you?

A. I couldn't say.

Q. Well, about when with reference to the time you went to work there, then?

A. I would say between two and three months after I went to work.

Q. Where did he contact you?

A. At my machine where I was working.

Q. In the plant?   A. Yes, sir.

Q. Was anyone else present at the time other than you and he?   A. No.

Q. What did he say to you?

A. He just asked me when I was going to join the union.

Q. Is that what he said?

A. That was all.

Q. "When are you going to join the union"?

A. Uh-huh.

Q. Did he indicate what union he meant?

A. Well, there was only one union there.

Mr. Watkins: Just a moment. I move to strike the answer as not responsive to the question.

Trial Examiner Whittemore: Oh, I will——

[340]

Mr. Watkins: I will withdraw the objection, Mr. Examiner.

Trial Examiner Whittemore: All right.

Q. (By Mr. Moore) Do you know whether or not Ed Fickle held any office in the Alliance?

(Testimony of James Wellington Crank.)

A. Yes, he was president.

Q. At the time you have testified that he contacted you did you know he held an office in the Alliance?

A. Yes, he was president of the union at the time, PMPWA.

Q. Did he contact you again after this first time?

A. Well, I have an idea I was contacted once or twice after that before I joined, maybe more.

Q. By whom?

A. By Mr. Fickle.

Q. When was the next time that you can recall?

A. Well, I would hate to say for sure.

Q. Well, according to your best recollection, Mr. Crank?

A. About a month later, then, is about as close as I can get.

Q. Who contacted you at that time?

A. Mr. Fickle.

Q. Where?   A. In the plant at my machine.

Q. Was that during your scheduled working hours?

A. Yes, sir.

Q. At about what time was it? [341]

A. Well, it seems to me like it was around 10:00 o'clock.

Q. In the morning?

A. In the morning, yes, sir.

Q. And was anyone else present at that time?

A. No.

(Testimony of James Wellington Crank.)

Q.   What did he say to you and what did you say say to him?

Mr. Watkins: Mr. Examiner, I object to the question on the ground it is incompetent, irrelevant and immaterial. I don't see it makes any difference in this proceeding what the president of the union said to this man to get him to join the union.

Mr. Moore: The time and place, maybe.

Mr. Watkins: That may be so, but you are asking him what he said.

Trial Examiner Whittemore: Is there something in particular you had in mind?

Mr. Moore: He hasn't said yet on this second occasion he was asked to join the union.

Trial Examiner Whittemore: That is what you were asking him about. He said there were two or three other occasions, and you are asking him about this second one.

Mr. Moore: I will withdraw that and ask:

Q.   (By Mr. Moore) During how many of these occasions did Mr. Fickle, during working hours, contact you on that subject?

A.   I would say three or four times. [342]

Q.   How long did your conversation with him last?

A.   Oh, never more than five minutes, if that long.

Q.   Is your machine in such a position that you can be observed from any part of the shop?

A.   Yes, it was at that time.

(Testimony of James Wellington Crank.)

Q. There were no partitions around it that would prevent you being seen clearly?

A. No. [343)

Q. Did you pay dues to the Alliance?

A. Yes, sir.

Q. To whom did you pay the dues?

A. Lester Bebb.

Q. How often did you pay dues?

A. Well, they were supposed to be paid every month. I think I paid them about every other month.

Q. You would pay for two months at one time?

A. Two, three, and maybe four months dues at a time.

Q. Where did you pay the dues?

A. Well, in the morning, whenever I would come to work I would pay it to him, I would seek him out in the shop and pay him, after we had gone to work.

Q. Were you working days during all the time you were in the Alliance?

A. No, not all of the time, no.

Q. Are you speaking of the times, now, that you were on the day shift?

A. When I was on the day shift, yes.

Q. What time would the day shift begin?

A. Seven o'clock in the morning.

Q. What time does the shift before that end?

A. Seven o'clock.

Q. There is no period between the two shifts

A. No, there wasn't at that time. [344]

Q. Did you ever pay dues anywhere besides in the shop?

(Testimony of James Wellington Crank.)

A.   I think I paid one month up at the union hall, their hall.

Q.   On the other occasions where have they been paid.   A.   Always in the shop.

Q.   During the time that you were a member of the Alliance did you ask anyone to join it?

A.   Well, I have asked several fellows to join it.

Q.   Will you name them?

A.   Well, I know of one; it was William Egkan in the inspection department. He seemed to be the hold-out.

Q.   How do you spell Egkan?

A.   E-g-k-a-n.

Q.   Where did Bill Egkan work?

A.   He was working in inspection.

Q.   How far was his place of employment from where you were working?

A.   About 75 feet to 100 feet away.

Q.   At what time of day did you contact him?

A.   About the middle of the morning, or the middle of the afternoon.

Q.   When did this occur with reference to month and day?

A.   It was shortly before the election of officers for 1941, I should judge that was about August of 1941.

Q.   Was anyone present at the time you talked to Egkan, other [345] other than you and he?

A.   No.

Q.   What did you say to him and what did he say to you?

(Testimony of James Wellington Crank.)

Mr. Watkins: Just a minute, Mr. Examiner, I don't want to object to this, it doesn't make any difference, but it is just cluttering up the record with things that are really immaterial to this case.

Trial Examiner Whittemore: I don't see that it does make any difference.

Mr. Moore: All right. That is all right.

Q. (By Mr. Moore) Did you ask him to join the Alliance?   A.   Yes.

Q.   How long did you talk to him?

A.   Two or three minutes.

Q.   Did he join the Alliance?

A.   I really don't know whether he did or not.

Q.   Was the place where he worked open so it could have been observed from any part of the shop?

A.   No, not from all parts, no.

Q.   From what part could it have been observed?

A.   From—more from the west end of the shop.

Q.   By approximately half the shop or more than half or less than half?

A.   Just about a half.

Q.   During the course of your employment with Thompson Pro- [346] ducts did you have occasion to join the C. I. O.?   A.   Yes.

Q.   When did you join the C. I. O.?

A   In April, of 1942.

Q.   Did you have any conversation with anyone connected with management of Thompson Products, Inc., with reference to your joining?

A.   Yes.

(Testimony of James Wellington Crank.)

Q. With whom did you have such a conversation?

A. Well, I talked with about three of them.

Q. Well, name one, the one with whom you had the first such conversation.

A. That was Mr. Millman.

Q. When did your conversation with him take place?

A. I should judge about two to four weeks before I joined the C. I. O.

Q. Before you joined?   A. Yes.

Q. That would be about what date?

A. Around the early part of March.

Q. Where did the conversation take place?

A. Out in front of the men's washroom.

Q. Who was present at the time?

A. Just Mr. Millman and myself.

Q. What was said at that time by you and by him? [347]

A. I just told him that I was thinking of going into a larger union, the C. I. O., and he just said he felt that I was wrong in my attitude. He didn't say much more.

Q. Is that the entire conversation?

A. Well, would all of it be necessary?

Q. Yes, yes. State the entire conversation.

A. Well, I caught him one afternoon out there—

Q. Wait. We are talking about this occasion before you joined.

A. That's right, this time. I told him before that his fair haired boys were coming there and getting

(Testimony of James Wellington Crank.)
a good mark on their name by coming to him to say
they were going to join the C. I. O., and that I was
going to tell him, to try and make a good name for
myself, and he told me then, he said he thought I
was wrong; he was sorry to hear about it, I believe
was what he said; then we drifted on and discussed
some more, the rest of it—we talked about five minutes I guess, and I have forgotten all of it.

Q. Just give the substance, as nearly as you can
recall.

A. Well, he said he felt I was wrong in my ideas
about it, that—he couldn't say much more.

Q. Did he say you could make up your own
mind. A. Yes.

Q. After that did you have a' conversation with
anyone else connected with management of the
plant? [348]

A. That was on a Friday, if I remember right.

Q. With whom was that conversation held?

A. This present time with Mr. Millman.

Q. I see.

A. Then the following Monday, the foreman out
there, Orvil Brockett——

Q. You had a conversation with Mr. Orvil
Brockett?

A. Yes, we talked a little bit there about unions.

Q. On Monday, the early part of March?

A. On Monday,—well, it was right after my talking with Mr. Millman.

Trial Examiner Whittemore: How do you spell
Brockett?

(Testimony of James Wellington Crank.)

The Witness: B-r-o-c-k-e-t-t.

Q. (By Mr. Moore) Was anyone present besides you and he?

A. No, just Orvil and I.

Q. Where were the two of you?

A. We were at the end grinding machine, is what we called it there, situated about—it was on the north side of the plant, about the middle.

Q. Is that where you worked?

A. Well, I was doing that work, because there was no work on my machine.

Q. What was the conversation on that occasion?

A. Well, I have forgotten how we went into the question about unions, but the conversation went into the union, and he [349] apparently was very strong against them——

Mr. Watkins: Just a minute. I move the answer be stricken as a conclusion, "he apparently was very strong against them."

Trial Examiner Whittemore: That may be stricken. Just state what he said and what you said.

Q. (By Mr. Moore) Are you unable to recall what he said?

A. I can't recall the exact conversation. The only thing——

Mr. Watkins: Just a minute. May I interrupt, Mr. Examiner? Before counsel refreshes his recollection by the method he has been following, we would like to have him ask the witness if he can give the substance of the conversation.

(Testimony of James Wellington Crank.)

Trial Examiner Whittemore: I assumed that was what his next question would be.

Q. (By Mr. Moore) Can you state in substance what was said there, if you do not remember the conversation in its entirety?

A. The substance of the conversation was union, and he was talking about the bigger unions, because he had at one time gotten a bad deal from one of the bigger unions.

Q. Did he say that?

A. That's what he told me.

Q. Did he indicate what he meant by the bigger unions?

A. No, he didn't say anything else.

Q. Just stated the bigger unions. After that, did you have a further conversation with anyone connected with management [350] with reference to affiliation with the C. I. O.?

A. The next day Roy Long, the general foreman, came out and worked alongside of me.

Q. You had a conversation with him?

A. Yes.

Q. Where did it take place?

A. That was in towards the east end of the shop, I was working on the drill press, drilling bolt heads, and he——

Q. Was that the day after your conversation with Mr. Brockett?

A. That was the day after.

Q. Who was present then?

A. No one was close there.

(Testimony of James Wellington Crank.)

Q. Just you and he?   A. Yes.

Q. What was said on that occasion?

A. Well, it was just the usual talk against the C. I. O. and A. F. of L.——

Mr. Watkins: Just a moment, please. I move this answer, so far given by the witness be stricken, as a conclusion: "It was just the usual talk against the C. I. O. . . . ."

Trial Examiner Whittemore: It may be stricken.

Q. (By Mr. Moore) Repeat, if you can, what he said, as nearly as you can recall.

A. As near as I can recall now to that, the exact words, he [351] asked me what the C. I. O. got for the boys out at Vultee, and he wondered why I would want to join the C. I. O. after that. [352]

Q. (By Mr. Moore) Was there any activity in the shop during working hours which appeared to you to be related to the fact that these men you talked to had joined the C. I. O.?

A. Well, yes; I guess there was.

Q. Can you say what activity there was?

A. Just more or less talk among the boys.

Q. Was there any object displayed there that caught your interest?

·A. Yes, there was, at one time.

Q. What was that?

A. They had an obscene object there, with a C. I. O. button hung on it.

Q. Who had that?

A. It was the night the electrician, I believe his name is Vincent Richards——

(Testimony of James Wellington Crank.)

Q. About when did that take place, Mr. Crank?

A. I believe I have written it down over there. I believe it was on April 20th—— [353]

Q. You have something you can refresh your recollection from?

A. I have that written down in my notebook over there.

Q. Will you get it. A. Yes.

Mr. Watkins: Just a moment. I assume the witness is going to testify from memory before he refreshes his recollection with his notes.

The Witness: That is what I had written out at that time, so I wouldn't forget. The other I didn't think important enough to remember, to write down, that is.

Q. (By Mr. Moore) Take the stand, then. Who did you say that object which you were speaking——

Mr. Watkins: Wait a minute. May I examine the notes the witness is using to refresh his recollection?

Q. (By Mr. Moore) About when, now, was this object displayed, from your own recollection?

A. Well, from my recollection, I have my own date written down here, now.

Q. Just state out of your remembrance.

A. It was on—I have it written here, now, as 5/28/42.

Q. Do you recall now that it was about May 28, 1942?

A. That's when I first saw it out there.

Q. Will you describe that object, please?

(Testimony of James Wellington Crank.)

A. About the only thing I would say is that it was an obscene [354] object made up.

Q. Just say what it was.

A. Made up as a glove, a finger of a glove.

Q. Stuffed?

A. Stuffed and made up to an obscene form.

Q. And it had a C. I. O. button pinned on it?

A. It had a C. I. O. button hanging on it.

Q. What did Mr Vincent Richards—are you sure of that name?

A. I am not sure of that; I believe Mr. Baldwin would know.

Mr. Baldwin: I will correct that; Vincent Rich.

Mr. Moore: May it be stipulated the man's name is Vincent Rich?

Mr. Watkins: I wouldn't stipulate because I don't know.

Mr. Moore: Very well. A man by the name of Vincent Richards or Vincent Rich.

The Witness: Rich, apparently is the right name; that was the graveyard electrician.

Mr. Baldwin: I don't know whether he was on the graveyard at that particular time.

The Witness: He was for awhile.

Q. (By Mr. Moore) What did he do with that object?

A. He took it around and showed it to different men working on the machines.

Q. During the time the shift was in progress?

[355]

A. Yes.

(Testimony of James Wellington Crank.)

Q. Which shift?

A. The graveyard shift.

Q. Were you at work at that time?

A. Yes, sir.

Q. And did you see him display it?

A. Yes. He brought it over and showed it to me.

Q. How long did he continue to do that?

A. Around 45 minutes.

Q. Do you know whether at any time an attempt was made to prevent him from doing it?

A. I know one of our members, after that long a time——

Q. By "one of your members," what do you mean?

A. The C. I. O. members. When he got up to him to show it to him, he says, "Now listen; you have been showing that thing around here for about 45 minutes. Don't you think it is about time for you to go to work?" and I believe he went on and went to work, then.

Q. Did Mr. Vincent Rich display that in the open where he could be seen, or did he display it to these men secretly?

A. Well, I wouldn't say secretly. Everybody around there, just about, each one saw it at different times.

Mr. Moore: That is all.

Cross Examination

Q. (By Mr. Watkins) You joined the C. I. O. in April, of [356] 1942?

(Testimony of James Wellington Crank.)

A.   April of this year, yes, sir.

Q.   Did you ever hold any office in the Alliance?

A.   No.

Q.   And it was six to nine months after you were employed by the company before you joined the Alliance?

A.   Roughly, I would say it was about that. I couldn't say for sure.

Q.   Where did you go to make your application to belong to the C. I. O.?

A.   I went over to the C. I. O. hall in Avalon.

Q.   In Avalon?

A.   Wait a minute, I am sorry. I went up on Gage Avenue in Bell, and turned in my application there.

Q.   Turned in your application?

A.   Yes.

Q.   Where did you make it out?

A.   At home.

Q.   Did you talk to anybody then about joining the C. I. O. who was favorable to joining the C. I. O.?

A.   Oh, yes. I talked to several men.

Q.   Down at the plant? Some of the men down there wanted to join the C I. O. too?

A.   Some of them, yes.

Q.   There had been some talk as to advisability of joining [357] the C. I. O.?

A.   Yes.

Q.   Had you ever discussed it with Victor Kangas?

A.   No, I hadn't seen Victor Kangas since he lost his job out at Thompson products.

(Testimony of James Wellington Crank.)

Q. All of this was subsequent to that time?

A. I beg your pardon?

Q. Mr. Kangas left there in 1940?

A. Oh, yes.

Q. Were there quite a few of you who decided to join the C. I. O. around this same time?

A. Well, I believe we more or less just drifted into it.

Q. Was there anybody—were you the leader among the boys for the C. I. O.?

A. No, I don't believe I was. I don't believe we had any leader.

Q. You had discussed it amongst each other?

A. We just discussed it amongst ourselves.

Q. You discussed a great many things down there, did you not?

A. Well, sometimes, yes.

Q. Politics, and baseball, and things like that?

A. Well, it's according to what subject usually prevails.

Q. Did you ever see anybody sign up for the C. I. O. down there at the plant? [358]

A. How was that now?

Q. Did you ever see anybody signed up for the C. I. O. down there at the plant?

A. I got their applications, but I never saw a man write it down there.

Q. What do you mean by that?

A. I got their application, they gave them to me.

Q. Have you ever been convicted of a felony?

(Testimony of James Wellington Crank.)

A.   I have.

Mr. Watkins: No further questions.

Trial Examiner Whittemore: Any further questions?

Mr. Moore: Do you intend to ask questions, Mr. Baldwin?

Mr. Baldwin: I would like to ask a few questions.

Q.   (By Mr. Baldwin) How soon, Mr. Crank, after you talked to Mr. Egkan, did he join the P. M.P.W.A.?

A.   I don't know that he joined it.

Q.   Did you ever go back there and ask him again after the first time?

A.   Oh, I talked to him several times about joining it.

Q.   At about the same time that you asked Mr. Egkan to join the P.M.P.W.A., did you ask anyone else to join any other organization?

A.   Not at that time, no.

Q.   What was your first job in the plant?

A.   Polisher. [359]

Q.   How long?

A.   I believe it was about three months.

Q.   And your second job?

A.   Heat treater.

Q.   How long?

Trial Examiner Whittemore: Well, now, what is the purpose of going into this?

Mr. Baldwin: Well, he states that he was approached at a certain time and place in the plant

(Testimony of James Wellington Crank.)

and he was talked to about joining the organization. I just want to see if he actually was or not. There seems to be a little doubt.

Trial Examiner Whittemore: What difference does it make whether he was in the polishing room or somewhere else?

Mr. Baldwin: He stated he was out in the open where everybody could observe him.

Trial Examiner Whittemore: All right. Make it brief.

Q. (By Mr. Baldwin) Were you ever approached to join the organization while you worked in the heat treatment?

A. I have been approached several times, but I don't remember just when it was.

Q. Regarding this object that was displayed, was that—were the men you referred to members of the P.M.P.W.A. at that time?

A. I wouldn't know.

Q. In what part of the plant did he display that?

[360]

A. That was back, just inside from the forge department, out towards the front end of the plant, and he went through and showed it to about every man in the plant there, in the old plant.

Q. About what time was it?

A. Right after we went to work.

Q. That would be right after when?

A. From about 12:00 to about 12:45 in the morning.

(Testimony of James Wellington Crank.)

Q. It wasn't a quarter to midnight?

A. No, I was working. I didn't go to work until 12:00 o'clock.

Q. Now, you say that some member of your organization at the time, the C. I. O., approached these men and made some remark?

A. This man approached him.

Q. I see. And as he did, a member of your organization made some remark to him?

A. Told him he had been showing it for about 45 minutes and it was time to finish and go to work.

Q. That is all you heard?

A. That is all I can recall.

Q. What part of the plant was that in?

A. That was on the old rough face grinder, if you remember the position.

Q. It wasn't in the washroom of the new section of the [361] building?

A. Not from what he told me.

Mr. Baldwin: That is all.

Mr. Watkins: Just a minute, Mr. Examiner. I thought this was information this witness had. I move all the testimony with respect to the entire incident be stricken on the ground it is hearsay. He has named individuals present, and I think they should be the ones called to testify to that.

Trial Examiner Whittemore: I will deny the motion to strike. It is a question of how much weight will be given to it.

Mr. Watkins: Yes. I would like to ask another question.

(Testimony of James Wellington Crank.)

Trial Examiner Whittemore: All right.

Q. (By Mr. Watkins) You made notes of several of these things as you went along, as you have testified to?   A. Sir?

Mr. Watkins: Read the question.

(The question was read.)

Mr. Watkins: Just strike the question.I will re-frame it.

Q. (By Mr. Watkins) You have testified to certain incidents here that happened down at the plant, and they have some bearing on the C. I. O.

A. Yes.

Q. And you made notes of the incidents at the time they [362] happened?

A. Not all of them, no.

Q. You made notes of some of them?

A. Some of them, yes.

Q. How did you happen to do that?

A. Well, I went to auxiliary police school in the early part of the year, and that was one of the first things they wanted us to do, was to take notes, and I forgot about the importance of taking notes until at this time I first started here, I believe it was in the 28th of May.

Q. In other words, the sole purpose in your making these notes was as a sort of assistance to you in your lessons in your auxiliary police work?

A. Well, no, it wasn't just as a help.

Q. All right. What was the reason for it?

A. To refresh our memories on the circumstances that had occurred out there.

(Testimony of James Wellington Crank.)

Q.   Why did you want to refresh your memory?

Let the record show the pause in the answers, please.

A.   Well, I can't remember everything. I would like to have some of that written down for my records.

Q.   Did you have any discussion with anybody at all about making these notes?

A.   No.

Q.   That was just your own idea? [363]

A.   No, not when I first started them. I talked about them two months later, but not when I first started with them.

Q.   It was just your own idea?

A.   That's right.

Q.   You started notes prior to the time you joined the C. I. O., did you not?

A.   No, it was after I joined the C. I. O.

Q.   Weren't these incidents you testified to prior to the time you joined the C I. O. in April of 1942?

A.   Some, yes; but the notes I am talking about now were after I joined the C. I. O.

Q.   In other words, all your notes contained matters after your joining the C. I. O.?

A.   These notes do, yes.

Q.   That was just your own idea, that you ought to make notes of these things?

A.   Also to refresh my memory.

Q.   Did you expect to testify at some hearing?

A.   I didn't at any time.

(Testimony of James Wellington Crank.)

Q. How did you expect to use those notes then?

A. How did I expect to?

Q. Yes. Did you expect to turn them in to the C. I. O., or what?

A. Not necessarily. I could keep them for myself, couldn't I? [364]

Q. Did you?

A. I kept them for myself, and so far there has only been one man that has seen them.

Mr. Watkins: I think that is all. [365]

———

ELMER OSCAR SMITH,

a witness called by and on behalf of the National Labor Relations Board, being first duly sworn, was examined and testified as follows:

Direct Examination

Q. (By Mr. Moore) Will you state your full name, please?

A. Ehner Oscar Smith.

Q. Have you been employed by Thompson Products, Inc.? A. Yes, sir.

Q. At their plant in Bell, California?

A. Yes, sir.

Q. When were you so employed?

A. I was first employed there in 1937. I was there only about three months, I believe, or a little less. I believe it was August, September and Octo-

(Testimony of Elmer Oscar Smith.)
ber, and then I was re-employed in October 22, 1940,
and I worked through until September 6, 1942.

Q.   In what capacity were you employed?

A.   The last time I was turret lathe operator.
First, I was [366] running gun drills.

Q.   In 1937?

A.   Yes.

Q.   You have not been employed in a supervisory
capacity?   A.   No, sir.

Q.   Had the Pacific Motor Parts Workers Alliance been formed before you were hired there the
first time?

A.   I believe it had. Yes, it had, because I joined
the union shortly after I went there, the Alliance.

Q.   In 1937 did you join the Alliance?

A.   Yes, sir.

Q.   When, with reference to the time you went
to work, did you join it?

A.   Well, I don't remember exactly the time, but
it was shortly after I started to work. I believe that
I belonged to the Alliance there two months.

Q.   Beg your pardon?

A.   I said I believe I belonged to the Alliance for
two months in 1937.

Q.   How did you come to join the Alliance?

A.   A man named Stubblefield asked me.

Q.   Where were you at the time he asked you?

A.   As I recall I was working.

Q.   You were working at the plant?

A.   Yes. [367]

(Testimony of Elmer Oscar Smith.)

Q. Did you pay an initiation fee to him?

A. Yes, I paid initiation.

Q. Did you pay that to Mr. Stubblefield.

A. Yes.

Q. Where were you when you paid that initiation fee?

A. Well, I don't recall the precise spot, but I wasn't well acquainted, and I didn't go away from my machine much, so it must have been in the vicinity of my machine.

Q. Was it in the shop?

A. Oh, yes, in the shop.

Q. And was it done during working hours?

A. Yes, sir.

Q. Were you working in a position that could be seen from other parts of the shop?

A. Yes, it was open where I was working. It could be seen pretty near all over the shop at that time.

Q. When you returned to work there in 1940, did you renew your membership in the Alliance?

A. Yes, I did.

Q. How did you go about doing that?

A. There had been a good bit of talk about joining the union, to various employees over there, so one time I approached Lester Bebb and I asked him if it was necessary for me to pay an initiation fee, or if I could continue with my membership by paying my dues, and he said he would look it up, and a few [368] days later he came back and told me I

(Testimony of Elmer Oscar Smith.),
should just carry on with dues, because I left with
good standing.

Q.   Were those conversations you had with Mr.
Bebb in the shop?

A.   Yes, in the shop.

Q.   Were they during your shift?

A.   I wouldn't state definitely. I believe they
were.

Q.   Have you paid your dues to the Association?

A.   I beg your pardon?

Q.   Have you paid dues to the Alliance?

A.   Yes, sir.

Q.   To whom have you paid them?

A.   I paid them to Lester Bebb.

Q.   Where have you made those payments?

A.   Well, Lester Bebb was a welder and he was
in the welding department, it was in one corner of
the shop, and he collected dues there. He had a tool
box in which he kept all his records, and——

Q.   Did you observe his records in the tool box?

A.   Well, I have seen him unlock the tool box
many times and get his book, and he had—he would
write a receipt, we carried a small book, and when
we paid our dues, he would write his name and the
date.

Q.   How often did you pay dues?

A.   I paid monthly. [369]

Q.   Did you always pay them to Bebb, in the
shop there?   A.   Yes, sir.

Q.   Was it always during working hours?

A.   As I recall, it was.

(Testimony of Elmer Oscar Smith.)

Q. Did you ever hold office in the Alliance?

A. Yes, sir.

Q. During what period did you hold office?

A. I was elected in the election of 1941, in September, and I held office through the latter part of 1941 and the first part of 1942, and resigned in February, I believe, in 1942.

Q. What office did you hold?

A. I was on the executive committee.

Q. Is that executive committee also referred to as the executive council? A. Yes.

Q. Have you examined the constitution and by-laws? A. Yes, sir.

Q. Were you a member of the executive council that is mentioned in the constitution and by-laws?

A. Yes, I was.

Q. Did the Alliance at that time have any other council or committee that conducted negotiations with the management? A. Yes.

Q. Was it the council of which you were a member? A. Yes, sir. [370]

Q. During the period when you were a member of that council, did you engage in any activity in the plant in behalf of the Alliance?

A. Yes. After our election, the committee had held meetings on various occasions.

Q. When you say committee, you are referring to the——

A. That is the council.

Q. Very well.

(Testimony of Elmer Oscar Smith.)

A.   The council had held meetings on various occasions and we had decided on a plan to sign up the shop 100 per cent, as near as possible, and we had a membership drive, and each one of the committee men were to take as many men as they could, getting them to join the union.

Q.   What did you do with reference to this membership campaign?

A.   Well, I contacted several men.

Q.   Can you name them?

A.   Yes. I talked with William Egkan, a good bit, in the inspection department; and I talked with J. D. Wiggs, a man named Branm; I talked with him one night for about 20 minutes.

Q.   How do you spell that?

A.   B-r-a-n-m, and another named Templeman, I believe. That's all I recall offhand.

Q.   Did you ask those men to join the Alliance?

A.   Yes, I did. [371]

Q.   Was your contact with them in the shop?

A.   Yes, it was.

Q.   Was it during working hours?

A.   Yes, sir.

Q.   In the fall of 1941 and the spring of 1942, while you were on the council, was the shop operating three shifts?   A.   Yes, sir.

Q.   Approximately how long did you talk to these men when you contacted them?

A.   Well, I remember Branm distinctly. He was running a milling machine, slightly behind the lathe

(Testimony of Elmer Oscar Smith.)
I was working on, and I talked with him for possibly 20 minutes.

Q. Is that in a position that can be observed from any part of the plant?

A. Well, it could be observed from most any-where in the shop, I would say; not every place.

Q. These other men, how long did you contact them?

A. I talked with each several minutes. I talked with Egkan on numerous occasions. He was in the inspection department. I talked with him several times. The others, possibly a few minutes, while at their machines.

Q. You have named four men you have contact-ed. Were there others also?

A. I believe I have talked to others in the shop, but I can't recall their names. [372]

Q. Can you state approximately how many you approached?

A. No, I wouldn't——

Q. Did you ever collect any dues for the Alli-ance?

A. Yes, I have.

Q. Where did you do that?

A. I collected from Templeman. I got his initia-tion fee and his dues.

Q. Where?   A. At his machine.

Q. During working hours?

A. Yes, sir. I also collected from Wiggs.

Q. The initiation fee?   A. Yes.

(Testimony of Elmer Oscar Smith.)|

Q. Did you collect dues from any of those men?

A. On various occasions as I recall, the men have given me their dues and their book, which I would take to the treasurer, Lester Bebb, and get a receipt for it.

Q. Did that occur during your working shift?

A. I took them there during my working shift. I don't recall whether the men gave them to me coming on shift or going off, or during working hours.

Q. There is no period of time between shifts, as the shop was operated at that time, was there?

A. No, no.

Q. One shift begins immediately after the other ends? [373]

A. That's right.

Q. And this collection that you did, was that in the shop?   A. Yes, sir.

Q. Who were members of the executive council at the time you were elected?

A. Well, when I was first on the council we had a meeting and it didn't end up so well, so the new council was appointed, rather than elected, and there was Irvin Hess, Frank Osborn, Howard Baldwin, and myself, and Julius Olson; Julius Olson was a member of the old committee that had resigned, and later we held an election and Julius Olson was replaced with—I can't recall the man's name.

Q. Let me ask you: Who were the members of the retiring council in the election at which you were elected?

(Testimony of Elmer Oscar Smith.)|

A. There was Julius Olson, Ray Haley, Clarence Stubblefield, Ted Weiser, and Ed Fickle. Ed Fickle wasn't—didn't retire at the time of the election, but later he was recalled.

Q. Were you acquainted with Mr. Ed Fickle?

A. Only for our acquaintance in the shop. I knew him quite well. I talked with him.

Q. What work did he do in the shop?

A. He worked in——

Q. At the time of this election?

A. Well, he was the experimental man in the tool room.

Q. Do you know how long he had been doing that work? [374]

A. No, I don't.

Q. How long, to your knowledge, had he been doing it?

A. He had been doing it ever since I had been there.

Q. Did he continue after the election of September, 1941, to do the same work?

A. Yes, so far as I know.

Q. Were you acquainted with Mr. Julius Olson?

A. Yes, I was.

Q. What was his position in the shop at the time of the election in September, of 1941?

A. He was, you might say, a shift man in the forging department. That is, he had—he directed the shift on which he worked, he was set-up man and directed the work in the forge.

(Testimony of Elmer Oscar Smith.)

Q. How long, to your knowledge, had he been doing that work?

A. I believe he had been doing work in that capacity ever since I had been in the shop too.

Q. Did he continue to do the same work after that election?   A. Yes, sir.

Q. Were you acquainted with Mr. Ted Wesser?

A. Yes, I was.

Q. What work did he do in the shop?

A. He was the head of the heat treating department.

Q. When you say "head," what do you mean?

A. Well, he was the man in charge. In fact, there were [375] several heat treaters, it must have been six or eight men working in that department, and he directed the work in that department.

Q. How long, to your knowledge, had he done that work?

A. Since I had been in the plant.

Q. Did he continue to do it after that election?

A. Yes, he did.

Q. Are you acquainted with Clarence Stubblefield?   A. Yes, I am.

Q. What did he do at the time of that election?

A. He was a welder.

Q. Was he employed in a supervisory capacity?

A. No.

Q. Are you acquainted with Ray Haley?

A. Yes.

Q. What was his work?

(Testimony of Elmer Oscar Smith.)

A. He was operating an engine lathe, working on large marine valves.

Q. Was he employed in a supervisory capacity, to your knowledge?

A. No, he wasn't.

Q. Was he related to anyone in the shop who was employed in a supervisory capacity?

A. Yes, he was a brother-in-law of Ray Long, who is now general foreman. [376]

Q. Was Ray Long general foreman at that time?

A. I believe at that time Ray Long was shift foreman.

Mr. Moore: May we go off the record a moment?

Trial Examiner Whittemore: Off the record.

(Discussion off the record.)

Trial Examiner Whittemore: On the record.

Q. (By Mr. Moore) You have described the duties of five men who were on the executive council that retired in September, of 1941. Do you know how long they had been on the executive council?

A. Well, they had all served at least a year, and I believe Mr. Fickle had been on the council since, almost, since the inception of the union. I believe there was—I will say he had been president of the union ever since the start, except for one term, and Stubblefield had served in a capacity of committeeman for two or possibly three years, and the others I don't know about.

Q. How is the executive council elected? How was it at the time you were elected?

(Testimony of Elmer Oscar Smith.)

Mr. Watkins: Just a minute. I object to that as not being the best evidence of the election. We have, as I understand it, some articles and by-laws that provide for the method of election of the executive council.

Mr. Moore: Very well.

Q. (By Mr. Moore) The evidence in this case shows the ex- [377] ecutive council is elected by the membership at large. Is that so?

A. That is true.

Q. Is that the manner in which you were elected?

A. Yes, sir.

Q. At the election of September, 1941—I will withdraw that.

The evidence in this case also shows that the executive council elect a president.

A. That is true.

Q. Was that done in September, 1941?

A. Yes, sir.

Q. In that September election who was elected president.   A. Ed Fickle.

Q. Did he thereafter serve as president?

A. He served for a short period of time, and I would say not over one month, or possibly a month and a half, at which time he was recalled, at a regular union meeting. He was——

Q. You say he was recalled. Will you state when that meeting occurred?

A. I believe it was in either the latter part of October, or in November, possibly November.

(Testimony of Elmer Oscar Smith.),

Mr. Watkins: What year is this?

Mr. Moore: This is in 1941.

The Witness: 1941, yes, sir. [378]

Q. (By Mr. Moore) Will you describe what happened at that meeting?

Mr. Watkins: Just a minute, Mr. Examiner. If there are minutes available of what happened at that meeting, then I think those should be introduced as the best evidence of what happened there.

Trial Examiner Whittemore: Will you examine the minutes and see whether or not they show what you are getting at here?

Mr. Moore: Yes, they do show it. Mr. Baldwin has brought the minutes of the Pacific Motor Parts Workers Alliance meetings, all that are available.

Trial Examiner Whittemore: Very well.

Q. (By Mr. Moore) Mr. Smith, the minutes of that meeting at which Mr. Fickle was recalled were kept?   A. Yes, sir.

Q. Will you examine these three sheets and see if they are the minutes of that meeting?

Mr. Moore: While Mr. Smith is examining the documents, will you mark this as Board's Exhibit next in order for identification?

(Thereupon, the document referred to was marked as Board's Exhibit No. 9, for identification.)

Mr. Baldwin: Mr. Examiner, would it be possible to make copies of those? Those are the original minutes and I would like to retain them. [379]

(Testimony of Elmer Oscar Smith.)

Trial Examiner Whittemore: Yes, surely; that will be all right.

Mr. Moore: I will ask the reporter to mark these documents as Board's Exhibit 10, for identification.

(Thereupon, the documents referred to were marked as Board's Exhibit No. 10, for identification.)

Mr. Moore: May the record show that the document, consisting of three typewritten pages, which has been marked Board's Exhibit 10, for identification, is the document which the witness examined immediately prior to their being marked.

May we take a short recess?

Trial Examiner Whittemore: Yes, surely. We will take a five-minute recess.

(A short recess was had.)

Trial Examiner Whittemore: The hearing will please come to order.

Q. (By Mr. Moore) Have you examined the document marked Board's Exhibit 10, for identification?   A. Yes, I have.

Q. Can you say what it is?

A. It's the minutes of the October meeting, when Ed Fickle was recalled as president of P.M.P.W.A.

Q. As councilman at the time these minutes were made, can you state these are the minutes?

A. Those are the minutes. I conducted that meeting. [380]

Mr. Moore: I offer Board's Exhibit 10, for identification in evidence.

(Testimony of Elmer Oscar Smith.)!

Mr. Watkins: No objection, and no objection to a copy being substituted.

Mr. Baldwin: No objection.

Trial Examiner Whittemore: Board's Exhibit 10 will be received. Those are the minutes of what date?

Mr. Watkins: October, of 1941.

Trial Examiner Whittemore: Thank you.

(Thereupon the document heretofore marked for identification as Board's Exhibit No. 10, was received in evidence.)

BOARD'S EXHIBIT No. 10

Meeting of P. M. P. W. A. for October, 1941.

The general meeting of the P.M.P.W.A. was held October 13, 1941 with council members Fickle, Baldwin, Hess, Osborne, Smith and Secretary Bebb present. There were 80 members at the meeting.

The minutes of the last meeting were read and approved as read.

Fickle asked Smith to take over the meeting in order that he might express his ideas in forming a new contract.

Bright suggested that Smith should have been notified before the meeting that he was going to be asked to take over so that he could have prepared for it.

Hess stated that Fickle had refused to work with the committee and that he had been accused of being a member of the C.I.O.

(Testimony of Elmer Oscar Smith.)

Baldwin gave an outline of wage scale changes to be suggested for the new contract, which had been drawn up by the committee to present to the management, also a plan for re-rating men who have been employed three months or more. The re-rating would be as follows;

> Starting rate for new employees—60 cents.
>
> At the end of three months to go to 75 cents (base rate)
>
> Machine operators to be classed as Third, Second and First Class, with a base minimum rate for each class.

In regard to the Vacation plan changes, the following was submitted;—Anyone employed for one year to be entitled to one week vacation with pay, with one day added for each additional year of employment until a maximum of two weeks was attained. Also that the paragraph stating that, "in cases of business reverses or catastrophes vacations be cancelled," be struck out.

The Council asked for full co-operation of the members to work toward getting the above.

Bright asked why proposed contract had not been written up and brought for the approval of members.

Smith stated that no statement had been made at the last meeting to that effect.

Baldwin stated that the council would take up the seniority agreement with the management. Bright said he thought the contract should be read

(Testimony of Elmer Oscar Smith.)|
as contracts of other Unions in regard to the Seniority agreement.

Olsen suggested that the council go to the management and that together they draw up a contract
which they felt would meet with the approval of all
concerned and that this proposed contract be
Brought before the members at the next meeting,
before signing.

Baldwin answered questions relating to the
changes proposed by the council. General discussion followed in regards to other union contracts
and their classifications.

George McIntyre made remark that there were
rumors that council members were being stool
pigeons but that he felt such were false, although he
knew there were stool pigeons in the shop.

Bright asked that each council member make
statement to show whether he was working in interest of men or company.

Baldwin requested that members give council men
a chance to do something for men as these council
men are all new and should be given a chance before being criticized.

Hess made charges against Fickle, that he had
said he was for himself and not the men, also, that
he opposed, suggested raise for polishers.

In reply Fickle stated that L. L. Myers who was
in the meeting with management could clarify the
above charges.

Myers said he had talked to Mr. Millman and
thait had been a misunderstanding on his part.

(Testimony of Elmer Oscar Smith.)

Fickle stated that anyone in the membership could vote him out if he did not wish him to act on the council and that if the council could do more for the members with him out, he would be glad to be voted out but that he was 100% for the **P.M. P.W.A.**

Motion was made by Hess and seconded that Fickle be re-called. Motion carried.

Ballot were cast for the re-call of Fickle as a council member. Ballots collected by Baldwin and Smith.

Three members were chosen to check the ballots;

> Olsen
> Bright
> Peterson

Results;

> Ballots cast 78 (1 ballot spoiled)
> "Yes" Ballots—54
> "No" Ballots—23

As Vice-President Osborne was asked to take over the vacancy but he asked Smith to carry on for the remainder of the meeting.

A hand vote showed that 37 members against 22, wished the council member to fill vacancy, be chosen by the council.

George Overlander was one chosen as his working in the tool-room would make council membership well divided among shop men.

Weisser made a motion that wage scale set by council be read. Motion seconded and carried.

(Testimony of Elmer Oscar Smith.)\

Wage scale rates were read by Smith.

The following rates were added;

Ajax press	$1.10
Ajax furnace	1.00
Trucker (moving stock)	.90
Change in rate of internal and centerless radius grinder from $1.00 to $1.10	
Floor inspectors	1.00

Meeting adjourned.

President ....

Secretary ....

———

Q. (By Mr. Moore) The evidence in the case shows that the membership of the Alliance voted to recall Ed Fickle as president. Was another president elected thereafter?

A. George Overlander was appointed as committeeman to take Ed Fickle's place, and then the committee met a few days later and they elected Irvin Hess as president of P.M.P.W.A.

Q. At the time Irvin Hess was elected president, did anything unusual occur at the meeting at which he was elected? Did anything unusual occur?

A. Nothing unusual occurred, except the meeting of the committeemen, where Hess was elected, was held in the welding room, in the plant of Thompson Products. I believe that's——

Q. Was anyone present other than the councilmen? A. I believe not. [381]

(Testimony of Elmer Oscar Smith.)

Q. Was Glenn Beach present?

A. No, sir.

Q. Was he present at any meeting of the council?

A. He wasn't present at any meeting of the council which I attended. He was present at a meeting of the membership.

Q. When was that?

A. That was in September of, on the day of the P.M.P.W.A. election.

Q. Was that before Ed Fickle had been recalled?   A. Yes.

Q. What part in the meeting did Glenn Beach take?

A. Glenn Beach was more or less the cause of the meeting being broken up. It was contesting the right of some of the candidates to become members of the council, and Glenn Beach took such a firm stand and caused so much argument, that finally we had to——

Mr. Baldwin: Mr. Examiner, I would like to object to that statement, because he hasn't any definite proof that he was the agitator of this thing, because there was a constant—I mean, there were calls from all sides, in every direction. In other words, he can't pin down to any one man, because there were quite a few involved, and I couldn't name all of them, myself.

Trial Examiner Whittemore: You were there, were you?

(Testimony of Elmer Oscar Smith.)

Mr. Baldwin: Yes, sir, in the room, yes. [382]

Trial Examiner Whittemore: I think if you want to give your version of what happened we will permit you to do so, but please permit this witness to give his version. I will overrule your objection.

Were you there?

The Witness: Yes, I was.

Q. (By Mr. Moore) Was there a controversy at that meeting?

A. Yes, there was a controversy.

Trial Examiner Whittemore: I do think, for my enlightenment, you might identify Mr. Beach.

Q. (By Mr. Moore) Who is Glenn Beach?

A. Beach is foreman of the maintenance department.

Q. Was he foreman of the maintenance department in September of 1941, at the time this meeting took place?

A. I don't believe he carried an official title as foreman, but he directed the maintenance department.

Trial Examiner Whittemore: First, may I ask counsel for the respondent, if he will concede Beach was at that time foreman of the maintenance department?

Mr. Watkins: No, sir; and as a matter of fact, Mr. Millman is gone, and I can't answer the question. We will have to wait until he returns.

Trial Examiner Whittemore: All right.

Q. (By Mr. Moore) Was there a controversy at that meeting?

(Testimony of Elmer Oscar Smith.)

A. Yes, there was. As I stated—some of the men contested [383] the right of some of the candidates to hold office in P.M.W.P.A. council, because of the fact that they hadn't worked in the plant long enough.

Q. Who raised those objections?

A. Well, there were several that raised the objection. I can't recall all of them off-hand, but Glenn Beach was one of them that raised them the loudest. In fact, he made quite a scene at the meeting.

Mr. Watkins: Just a minute. Mr. Examiner, I move this testimony that somebody made quite a scene be stricken as a conclusion of the witness.

Trial Examiner Whittemore: Well, that may be stricken.

Mr. Watkins: May I ask whether or not the date of this particular meeting has been fixed?

Trial Examiner Whittemore: September is the nearest I have heard it identified.

The Witness: September, yes.

Mr. Watkins: Is there any specific date in September?

Trial Examiner Whittemore: The date when the election was held, according to my understanding.

Mr. Watkins: That is correct. Thank you.

The Witness: About the 7th, I believe we have minutes on that.

Q. (By Mr. Moore) Were minutes kept of that meeting?   A. Yes. [384]

(Testimony of Elmer Oscar Smith.)|

Mr. Moore: Will you mark this document, consisting of two pages, as Board's Exhibit 11, for identification?

(Thereupon, the document referred to was marked as Board's Exhibit No. 11, for identification.)

Mr. Baldwin: Mr. Examiner, if possible, I would like to have copies made of that.

Trial Examiner Whittemore: I think that may be arranged.

Mr. Moore: Yes, easily.

Q. (By Mr. Moore) Will you examine the document marked Board's Exhibit 11, for identification, please.

Mr. Moore: While c o u n s e l are examining Board's Exhibit 11, for identification, I will show Board's Exhibit 9, for identification, to the witness.

Q. (By Mr. Moore) Have you e x a m i n e d Board's Exhibit 11, for identification?

A. Yes.

Q. Is it the minutes of the meeting at which the controversy you were referring to occurred?

A. Yes, sir.

Q. Now, on what date was that meeting held? Was it held August 24, 1941, as shown on Board's Exhibit 11, for identification?

A. It may have been August; it was either the latter part of August, or the 1st of September.

(Testimony of Elmer Oscar Smith.)

Q. It was a meeting before you were elected to the council? [385]

A. At this meeting—yes, it was a meeting before I was formally elected; that's right.

Q. Did anything occur at that meeting that is not shown in the minutes, according to your recollection?

A. Yes. It didn't occur at the time the meeting was in progress, but right after the meeting adjourned the committee as a whole resigned, except Olson, and they in turn appointed candidates receiving the highest number of ballots to fill his place until they could be elected permanently, at which Baldwin, Osborne, Hess, and myself were appointed temporary committeemen, until such time that we could have the election. Olson remained on the committee as one of the old committeemen.

Q. Was there opposition to the appointment of Mr. Hess?

A. I wasn't there at the time these officers was appointed. They informed me the next day, so as to that, I don't know.

Mr. Moore: Very well. I do not propose to offer Board's Exhibit 11 for identification at this time.

Mr. Watkins: Just a minute. It seems to me, Mr. Examiner, that this exhibit ought to be put in, out of fairness, because this witness has been asked about a great many things that took place at that particular meeting, and I think it only fair, for

(Testimony of Ehner Oscar Smith.)|
the record's sake, the official minutes should be put in.

Mr. Moore: I have no objection to offering them. It [386] was my opinion they showed nothing. I offer them in evidence.

Mr. Watkins: We have no objection, and no objection to substituting a copy.

Trial Examiner Whittemore: All right. The document will be received.

(Thereupon the document heretofore marked for identification as Board's Exhibit 11, was received in evidence.)

BOARD'S EXHIBIT No. 11

Minutes of General Meeting for the election of Executive Councilmen and Secretary-Treasurer, held Sunday, August 24, 1941, at Ebell Club.— (Council members present, Fickle, Olsen, Weisser, Stubblefield, Hailey and Secretary-Treasurer, Bebb.)

Meeting was called to order at 10:15 a. m. President Ed Fickle announced the purpose of the meeting and asked for all proxy votes to be brought forth before the election. Ed Fickle was asked to read Sec. IV of the constitution in regards to election of officers.

Ballots were posted to members for the nomination of ten for councilmen.

Ballots were collected, and counted and posted on the blackboard with the following results;—

(Testimony of Elmer Oscar Smith.)|

Ed Fickle—C. O. Stubblefield—Steve Hall—George Spurlock—Frank Osborne—Irvin Hess—Elmer Smith—Ted Parker—Johnny Ballinger—Howard Baldwin.

A general discussion as to the eligibility of the nominees followed. The President read part of the constitution relating to this subject.

Irvin Hess submitted an attorney's opinion on the constitution. A motion was made to proceed with the election of officers and carried.

Ballots were cast to elect five of the nominees for councilmen.

A motion was made and seconded that the chairman's decision on the elegibility of the candidates be abided by.

New ballots were cast. A motion was made and seconded to hold another meeting for the election of officers, but did not carry.

As a number of the *of the* members had to return to work and the members were undecided as to the eligibility of the candidates the meeting was adjourned without counting the last votes cast, at 12:30 p. m.

Signed,

. . . .

———

(Minutes written from notes given me by Lester Bebb)

Mr. Moore: May it be stipulated Board's Ex-

(Testimony of Elmer Oscar Smith.)

hibit 9 for identification is a notice posted in the plant or respondent on or about the date appearing on the exhibit?

Mr. Watkins: Yes, it will be so stipulated. That is a copy of the notice that was posted.

Mr. Moore: A copy of the notice.

Trial Examiner Whittemore: What is the date?

Mr. Moore: On October 23, 1941. Will you stipulate to that, Mr. Baldwin?

Mr. Baldwin: Yes.

Trial Examiner Whittemore: You are offering it in evidence?

Mr. Moore: I offer Board's Exhibit 9 for identification in evidence.

Mr. Watkins: No objection.

Trial Examiner Whittemore: Mr. Baldwin?

Mr. Baldwin: No objection.

Trial Examiner Whittemore: The document is received. [387]

> (Thereupon the document heretofore marked for identification as Boards Exhibit 9, was received in evidence.)

BOARD'S EXHIBIT No. 9

NOTICE

Recent National Labor Relations Board rulings hold that it is not necessary for a supervisory employee to have the power to hire and fire in order to be considered a part of the Management. An employee who supervises and directs the work of

(Testimony of Elmer Oscar Smith.)

others or exercises any of the functions of Management is considered an agent of the employer and is, therefore, according to the contract between the Management and the Pacific Motor Parts Workers Alliance, ineligible to belong to the Pacific Motor Parts Workers Alliance.

Accordingly, the following named men have been asked, or will be asked, to resign their membership in the Pacific Motor Parts Workers Alliance at once:

> G. C. Beach
>
> C. E. Weisser
>
> Julius Olsen
>
> J. E. Morse
>
> H. E. McIntire
>
> E. T. Fickle
>
> THOMPSON PRODUCTS, Inc.
> West Coast Plant
> C. L. MILLMAN
> Personnel Manager

October 23, 1941.

Q. (By Mr. Moore) Did you attend meetings of the full membership of the Alliance during the time you were a member of the Alliance?

A. You mean our regular scheduled union meetings of the membership?

Q. Meetings of the full membership?

A. Yes, I did.

(Testimony of Elmer Oscar Smith.)

Q. Were those generally scheduled on any particular day of the week?

A. They were on Sundays, always.

Q. Practically always on Sunday?

A. Yes.

Q. During the time you were a member of the Alliance, did the plant operate on Sunday?

A. Partially, not a full crew, but there were a good many of the machines and men working at the time these meetings were held.

Q. Did it occur that work was scheduled to be done in the plant at the time the meeting was scheduled? A. Yes, sir.

Trial Examiner Whittemore: Mr. Moore, do you mind if I interrupt? Have you left this meeting at which Beach was present? [388]

Mr. Moore: Yes. This witness is not familiar with what occurred there.

Mr. Watkins: At which Beach was what?

Trial Examiner Whittemore: The meeting at which Beach was present. I understand you were present.

The Witness: You mean the regular scheduled committeemen?

Trial Examiner Whittemore: At this meeting in September at which Foreman Beach was present. Weren't you present at that meeting?

The Witness: Yes, I was at the one of the membership; he referred to one of the council, and I wasn't present at one of the council where Beach was.

(Testimony of Elmer Oscar Smith.)

Trial Examiner Whittemore: Even so, I wish you would explore the matter and find out; Beach was a foreman. Find out how he happened to be present at the membership meeting.

Mr. Watkins: Mr. Examiner, I was going to raise an objection to your reference to foreman Beach, because I don't think there is any testimony in the record at this time. I think the witness testified he was not a foreman, but that he had direction over some of the men in the maintenance department.

Trial Examiner Whittemore: My notes he was foreman of the maintenance department.

Mr. Watkins: Subsequently, I believe the witness testified—— [389]

Trial Examiner Whittemore: Wasn't that your testimony?

The Witness: At the time of the election I said he didn't have the official title of foreman.

Trial Examiner Whittemore: Oh, I am sorry. I didn't hear that.

The Witness: But after the election——

Q. (By Mr. Moore) Do you know when Mr. Beach received his official title as foreman?

A. Well, I can't say as to that, but it must have been around the time this notice was posted.

Q. I see.

Mr. Watkins: "This notice" refers to Board's Exhibit 9?

The Witness: That's it, the one where the com-

(Testimony of Elmer Oscar Smith.)
pany posted the notice saying those men couldn't belong.

Mr. Moore: Yes.

The Witness: Yes, that is the one.

Q. (By Mr. Moore) Did his duties change at that time?

Mr. Watkins: Just a minute. Are you through with your question?

Mr. Moore: I will withdraw the question.

Q. (By Mr. Moore) What did he do prior to the time that notice was posted?

A. So far as I know his duties were the same. He directed the maintenance crew.

Q. What did he do after the notice was posted?

[390]

A. The same thing, so for as I know.

Q. Were you in a position to observe what he did?

A. Oh, yes. The maintenance crew worked through the shop. They were doing a lot of building, putting in power lines and sewers and such, and Mr. Beach was in charge of the work.

Q. Both before and after this notice was posted?

A. Yes, sir.

Mr. Watkins: Mr. Examiner, I presume, rather than to object to this witness' testimony, we will simply have to introduce evidence as to the official duties of this particular individual at the time. The witness has testified to conclusions here, and there has been no foundation laid for his knowledge. He

(Testimony of Elmer Oscar Smith.)
has made a statement he saw him working around occasionally.

Q. (By Mr. Moore) Did you observe Mr. Beach giving directions to men working with him?

Mr. Watkins: I object to the question as calling for a conclusion, and it is leading and suggestive. If counsel will ask him what he said Mr. Beach did, I will have no objection to it.

Trial Examiner Whittemore: I will sustain the objection.

Q. (By Mr. Moore) What did you observe Mr. Beach doing when he was working where you could observe him?

A. Well, I can't recall any specific time that I have seen [391] him do anything in particular, but it was quite obvious that he was the boss; he was giving the orders.

Mr. Watkins: Just a minute,——

The Witness: Directing the work.

Mr. Watkins: I move that portion of the witness' answer "it was quite obvious that he was the boss," be stricken as a conclusion.

Trial Examiner Whittemore: It may be stricken.

Q. (By Mr. Moore) State what you saw Mr. Beach do.　　A. Well, have seen him——

Q. What you have seen or heard.

A. I have seen him on various occasions when they were building things or moving something, possibly,——

Q. The maintenance men, you are speaking of, now?　　A. I beg your pardon?

(Testimony of Ehner Oscar Smith.)

Q. When you say he was working, are you referring to the maintenance department?

A. I have seen him directing the work, showing men what to do.

Q. He was present at that meeting of August 24, 1941? A. That's right.

Q. Now, you have testified, have you not, that the Alliance held its meetings of membership on Sundays? A. Yes, sir.

Q. Did the company make any arrangements so that the men [392] scheduled to work on Sundays could attend these meetings?

A. Yes, they let anyone off for a period of time, which was usually from 10:00 to 12:00 in the morning, to attend a meeting, if they so wished. The plant, in fact, would close down.

Q. Would they——

Mr. Watkins: May I have that answer, the question and answer read, please?

Trial Examiner Whittemore: Very well.

Mr. Watkins: Before you read it, does the record show more than one meeting here?

Mr. Moore: Yes, I am asking him about meetings.

Mr. Watkins: On Sundays?

Trial Examiner Whittemore: He has testified the majority of the membership meetings were held on Sunday.

Mr. Watkins: Read the answer.

(The record was read.)

(Testimony of Elmer Oscar Smith.)

Mr. Watkins: I move the last portion of the answer be stricken as a conclusion, "the plant, in fact, would close down."

Trial Examiner Whittemore: Well, I would like to know what the witness' basis for that is. If you will ask him what that is, I will reserve ruling on this matter.

Q. (By Mr. Moore) On occasions when an Alliance meeting was scheduled to be held on Sundays, was any work done at [393] the plant between 10:00 and 12:00 in the morning on Sundays?

A. Not to my knowledge.

Mr. Watkins: Just a minute. Before we get away from that, I don't like to interrupt Mr. Moore, but can we tie this down to a particular date?

Mr. Moore: I don't believe we can, Mr. Watkins. We are talking about general practice that extended over the time he was a member of the Alliance.

Mr. Watkins: Mr. Examiner, I don't like to interrupt counsel, but the only thing, this is something we have to refute, and we can't by records or anything else, show what the situation was on a particular Sunday unless we know what Sunday it is.

Trial Examiner Whittemore: Well, first let me ask counsel for the Board: It seems to me, so far as it goes now, it is of minor importance anyway. I would like to know just what importance counsel for the Board attaches to it.

(Testimony of Elmer Oscar Smith.)

Mr. Moore: On Sundays when meetings were not scheduled, the shift ran from 7:00 to 4:30 straight through; on Sundays when meeting were scheduled to be held, the plant operated from 6:00 to 10:00 and from 12:00 to 5:30, I believe, and closed down in the meantime, so that members could attend the meetings of the Alliance. I think that is material evidence.

Trial Examiner Whittemore: Well, it is conceivable [394] that the company might decide to run a certain shift and run all day long, and since they were working all day, they wouldn't hold a meeting. Also, it is conceivable the company might arrange another shift for another company and permit a period in there where the union could hold a meeting.

Mr. Moore: Yes, it is conceivable.

Trial Examiner Whittemore: Is there any other way you can approach this particular matter? Here is a committeeman on the stand.

Mr. Moore: I do not know any other way to approach it. This witness knows what happened. He did it himself.

Trial Examiner Whittemore: I can't very well suggest any particular method by which you can explore this matter.

Mr. Watkins: Mr. Examiner, just a thought. I don't mean to try to keep out something that is material. I frankly do not see the materiality, to start with. But assuming the Board's counsel feels it is material, I think we could find out how many

(Testimony of Elmer Oscar Smith.)

meetings he is talking about. They certainly weren't held every Sunday. If membership meetings were held, we can find out when they occurred, and whether or not any arrangement was made so far as the Alliance was concerned, with the company, with respect to it.

Trial Examiner Whittemore: I think in view of what you say the purpose is, the respondent is justified in asking for specific instances, since you will concede on one or [395] two instances it might be drawn as a general fact if proved, one which certainly could not be held against the respondent, and the one which would. In view of your concession, it may be one or the other in general, then I think you should get down to something specific so that counsel for respondent will have something specific to meet. Otherwise, he may be meeting something which you yourself will concede may not be material.

Mr. Moore: May we go off the record?

Trial Examiner Whittemore: Off the record.

(Discussion off the record.)

Trial Examiner Whittemore: Do you plan to finish with this witness tonight? If not, why don't you move on to some other subject and while you have the minutes go through them? Perhaps it will save time, by taking them over night and see which one you want to refer to and perhaps you can do it very quickly in the morning.

Mr. Moore: May we go off the record again?

Trial Examiner Whittemore: Yes, surely. Off the record.

(Testimony of Elmer Oscar Smith.)

(Discussion off the record.)

Trial Examiner Whittemore: On the record.

Q. (By Mr. Moore) During the time that you were a member of the Alliance's executive council, did you attend meetings of the council? [396]

A. Yes, sir.

Q. Where did the council hold meetings?

A. In the plant at Thompson Products.

Q. At what place or places in the plant?

A. We held them in the welding room and then at a later date we held them in the new building which was not occupied at that time by machinery, and some, in the lunch room.

Q. Were any meetings of the executive council, while you were a member of it, held elsewhere than in places you have named?

A. No, sir.

Q. Have you attended such meetings at a time during the shift when you were scheduled to work?

A. Those meetings were held in the evening after 3:30, and on——

Q. Which shift did you work?

A. Well, of course—you see, the shifts rotate out there; two weeks it would be on days, swing and graveyard.

Q. Yes.

A. And I remember distinctly on two occasions that I attended meetings of the council when I was working the swing shift during my regular working period.

Q. The swing shift began and ended when?

(Testimony of Elmer Oscar Smith.)

A.   It began at 3:30 and ended at midnight.

Q.   When was the first occasion on which you attended a council [397] meeting during the swing shift?

A.   It was directly after the first election in September, the September election.

Q.   Mr. Baldwin has furnished a file of minutes of the executive meetings of the excutive council of the Alliance.   Will you look through that file and see whether or not they are minutes there, for the meetings to which you refer?   A.   Yes.

Q.   Having examined the minutes of the executive council meetings, can you now state on what date the meeting to which you refer was held?

A.   It was August 25th.

Q.   1941?

A.   1941.   That meeting was held in the welding room at the plant.

Q.   At about what time?

A.   At 3:30 in the afternoon.

Q.   And when you came to the plant that afternoon to go to work, did you check in?

A.   Yes, I did.

Q.   At about what time?

A.   About 3:30, in time for my 3:30 shift.

Q.   And thereafter did you go to this meeting?

A.   Yes, sir.

Q.   How long did you remain at the meeting? [398]   A.   I don't know exactly.

Q.   Approximately.

(Testimony of Ehner Oscar Smith.)

A. I would say approximately 45 minutes, possibly.

Q. Was there any deduction made on your time cards for that absence? A. No, sir.

Mr. Watkins: Can we fix this specifically?

Mr. Moore: We have.

Mr. Watkins: The specific date?

Mr. Moore: Yes.

Mr. Watkins: Thank you.

Q. (By Mr. Moore) You said there were two occasions on which you attended a meeting during a swing shift when you were scheduled to work. When was the second one about?

A. Well, it was some time later than that, not very much later. I would say possibly within the following two weeks or thereabouts.

Q. Will you examine the minutes of the executive council and see if you can fix that date?

A. I believe it was the one of September 27th.

Mr. Moore: Mr. Baldwin, is it a fact that some of these minutes of these meetings are missing?

Mr. Baldwin: Yes, it is.

Q. (By Mr. Moore) After examining the file of minutes of the executive council, do you find some missing? [399]

A. Yes, I do; some are missing.

Q. You think the minutes of the meeting to which you refer are missing?

A. I attended all of these meetings, but I can't specifically state whether it was one of these which I attended at the time I was supposed to be working.

(Testimony of Elmer Oscar Smith.)

Q. Can you say that it was not the one of September—it is written September 2nd, and then it is written over, September 22nd. Do you know whether one was held on either one of those dates?

A. I don't know. I believe it was probably one on September 22nd, or the one following, on October 3rd.

Q. Do you remember what day of the week it was?   A. No, I don't.

Q. It was not on a Sunday, I take it?

A. No, it wasn't on a Sunday.

Q. Was it on a Monday?   A. I don't know.

Q. Very well. The council meetings you have testified to were meetings of the council of the Alliance, and not meetings between the Alliance and the management. Is that correct?

A. That's right.

Q. While you were a council member, did you have conversations with Mr. C. L. Millman with reference to union affiliations?

A. Yes, on several different occasions. [400]

Q. When was the first one that you recall?

A. I recall shortly after I was elected on the council, possibly October or November, maybe October, I would say, that Mr. Millman approached me?

Q. Where?

A. It was near the—it was in the plant, near the tool crib.

Q. Were you working near the tool crib?

A. No, I wasn't. I was at the tool crib window

(Testimony of Elmer Oscar Smith.)

for some tool, or something I used at my work, and he came by and asked me if he could talk with me for a few minutes.

Q. Was there anyone else present?

A. No, there wasn't.

Q. What was the conversation?

A. First he talked with me for a while in regard to an instance that came up concerning Louis Meyers misunderstanding that they had gotten straightened out and Mr. Millman——

Q. State as near as you can what he said.

A. Well, Mr. Meyers had attended one of our council meetings and he had—was representing the polishers there and he had quoted something that— I can't just recall word for word all of it—but the substance was that Meyers had also attended one of our union meetings and at both times he had made several remarks in the council meeting with management, in the union meeting, and Mr. Millman called him into the [401] office and talked to him about the meeting, that he had attended with the council. Meyers understood this to be the union meeting——

Q. Wait. Going back to the conversation between you and Mr. Millman, just repeat that if you can.

A. Well, the fore part of it I can't remember, where Meyers was involved. I can't remember word for word.

Q. Can you recall the substance of it?

(Testimony of Ehner Oscar Smith.)

A. Yes, that was the substance of where there was a misunderstanding, where Meyers had come out of the office and said it was too bad he couldn't say anything in a union meeting without being called into the office, and Mr. Millman and he got straightened out, and Mr. Millman came out and asked me if I understood that he didn't want us to think he had called Meyers into the office because of something said at our regular membership meeting.

Then he went on to tell me: "I am glad to see you have been elected on the committee." He said, "I am glad to see some of the younger men there." He said, "You are well liked by the men in the shop, and I believe you will make a good representative for them."

The conversation turned to C.I.O.

Mr. Watkins: Wait just a minute. I move that portion be stricken: "The conversation turned to C.I.O.", as a conclusion. [402]

Trial Examiner Whittemore: That may be Stricken. Go on from there. What did he say?

The Witness: Mr. Millman said he was glad to see we had a little union in there, and he said the company would be glad to give the PMPWA something it would be forced to give the C.I.O. had it gotten in. At the same time, he told me that the company had been prepared, if necessary, to go through a strike, rather than to accept the C.I.O. as a bargaining agent of the men.

(Testimony of Elmer Oscar Smith.)

Q. (By Mr. Moore) Did he refer to any date when he said that? A. I beg your pardon?

Q. Did he refer to any date when he said that?

A. Yes, at the time of the election there had been a good bit of C.I.O. agitation.

Q. First in his statement about the strike matter, did he refer to a date?

A. Yes, he said the company would have been willing, and he was referring to the time of——

Q. Did he say?

A. No. I don't believe he specified a date.

Mr. Watkins: Just a moment. May I have the portion stricken "He was referring to" something, as a conclusion?

Trial Examiner Whittemore: I don't think he finished what he was referring to. [403]

Mr. Watkins: I couldn't quite hear it.

Trial Examiner Whittemore: It may be stricken.

Q. (By Mr. Moore) Did you understand what he was referring to?

A. Yes. I understood that he was referring to the time of——

Mr. Watkins: Just a moment, Mr. Examiner. I object to that as a conclusion.

Trial Examiner Whittemore: I will permit him to testify what he himself understood Mr. Millman to mean, but I think it may be well to explore what the basis of this was. It may have been common knowledge to all there, and it may have been unnecessary to refer to an exact date.

Mr. Moore: I think that is the case.

(Testimony of Elmer Oscar Smith.)

Trial Examiner Whittemore: I don't know, but I can conceive of that being the case. I think counsel for the Board should explore it. If he doesn't, certainly he should.

Q. (By Mr. Moore) What did you understand he was referring to?

A. I understood he was referring to the time of our election of the Alliance. That was the election in September.

Mr. Watkins: Just a moment, please, if I may. I would like to move the answer be stricken as a conclusion of the witness, and request that this witness state the facts with regard to the statements made by Mr. Millman, on which he [404] based any conclusion.

Trial Examiner Whittemore: Well, it isn't necessary that this witness base a conclusion on just what Mr. Millman may have said.

Mr. Watkins: Mr. Examiner, the vice of it is, the statement is made by this witness that Mr. Millman made certain statements. Now, he has made some statements from which, so far as I could see, it would be impossible to draw the conclusion he is now doing.

Trial Examiner Whittemore: I have, frankly, lost the thread of what it is all about myself.

Mr. Watkins: We can't combat these things under the circumstances.

Trial Examiner Whittemore: I do not see anything for you to meet, so far. All you have to meet

(Testimony of Elmer Oscar Smith.)

is that this witness has testified what Mr. Millman said, and not his conclusions of it.

Mr. Watkins: All right.

Q. (By Mr. Moore) What is the basis for your understanding of Mr. Millman's remarks?

Trial Examiner Whittemore: Well, now, perhaps the witness may have lost this. What remarks are you referring to? The strike, or what? When you asked him that question referring to something about an election of the Alliance, I don't know what it has to do with the strike. [405]

Mr. Moore: I think it will appear as we go along. I think the witness was fixing the time by the election, rather than by the event.

Trial Examiner Whittemore: Go ahead and explore the matter.

Q. (By Mr. Moore) You have testified Mr. Millman said to you, in substance, the company had been willing to go through a strike rather than what?

Mr. Watkins: I object to the question as not a quotation of the witness' testimony, as to the company rather going through a strike than accept the C.I.O., as a bargaining agency for the men.

Trial Examiner Whittemore: Isn't that in substance what you are referring to, Mr. Moore?

Mr. Moore: Yes.

Q. (By Mr. Moore) Did he indicate any time that he had reference to?

A. I don't believe he specified any time.

Q. Did you know what he was referring to?

A. Yes.

(Testimony of Elmer Oscar Smith.)

Q. How did you know?

A. Well, it was understood that there had been a great deal of C.I.O. agitation in the plant at the time of the election.

Mr. Watkins: Just a moment. Are you through? [406]

The Witness: Yes.

Mr. Watkins: I would like to ask that the answer be stricken, "it was understood there was a great deal of agitation in the plant at the time of election." If we are not bound by this testimony, I don't care. But if we are expected to meet, it has to be more specific than that, or it is impossible for us to do so.

Trial Examiner Whittemore: Well, I will deny your motion to strike. I think this requires a little more clearing up though.

Q. (By Mr. Moore) How did you know what he was referring to?   A. How did I know?

Mr. Moore: May I have the last question and answer read?

(The record was read.)

Q. (By Mr. Moore) To which election are you referring?   A. To the election in September.

Q. Of 1941?   A. 1941.

Q. What occurred at the plant in September of 1941, or near that date, which caused this condition you referred to?

A. Well, there were several of the men that were in favor of C.I.O., and there was a feeling of gen-

(Testimony of Ehner Oscar Smith.)

eral unrest in the plant. The men were dissatisfied with the union, the whole committee, and they were really, a good many of them that I talked to, and others talked to, were ready to join some [407] outside union. Then, after the election, why, the men were apparently more satisfied because the committee got together and they really tried to do something for the welfare of the men. And the condition seemed to clear up a good bit after the election and a new committee had gotten in there and started to work.

Mr. Watkins: May I ask a question on voir dire?

Trial Examiner Whittemore: Go ahead.

Voir Dire Examination

Q. (By Mr. Watkins) Mr. Smith, is this date which you referred to in which the company would have been willing to have stood a strike rather than bargain with the C. I. O. some time in the fall of 1941. A. Yes, that's right.

Mr. Watkins: Thank you.

Direct Examination
(Continued)

By Mr. Moore:

Q. After that, did you have further conversation with Mr. Millman with reference to the C. I. O.?

A. I talked with Mr. Millman on various occasions about unions, C. I. O., yes.

Q. When was the next occasion that you recall?

A. Well, there were—it was shortly following that.

(Testimony of Elmer Oscar Smith.)

Mr. Watkins: Speak up just a little bit, please.

The Witness: I say, it was probably shortly after that meeting, maybe a month, maybe in November or December some time. [408]

Q. (By Mr. Moore)   What is your best recollection as to the date?

A. I would say November.

Q. Where did the conversation take place?

A. At my machine.

Mr. Watkins: May I have the answer read, please?

Trial Examiner Whittemore: Would you speak up, please?

The Witness: Yes, I will.

(The answer was read.)

Q. (By Mr. Moore)   In the shop?

A. Yes.

Q. Who was present at the time?

A. Mr. Millman and myself.

Q. What was the conversation on that occasion?

A. Well, on that occasion, I don't recall how the conversation came up, but I do recall one part of it specifically, and I told Mr. Millman that I was in favor of strong national unions, that I didn't believe in independent unions such as we had, because I didn't feel that it was the type of organization that was good for the men, and I told him that a union movement, to me, was more than a local thing. It was something that should bind workers together, nationally.

(Testimony of Elmer Oscar Smith.)

Mr.Millman agreed with me that on lots of instances, he said, in many cases, and specified one plant he worked in in Long Beach where he thought the C. I. O. was a good thing, [409] because he said they were in very bad need of a union there. But, he said in Thompson Products it wasn't so, because they had their independent union, and was getting along very well with it, and told me that the company out here was so small that their Eastern company could—well, Thompson Products could move this company back East and absorb it in their larger plant without any trouble at all, and he said rather than to accept the C. I. O., "we were prepared to do such a thing."

Q. Was that all the conversation that you recall?

A. That's all I recall.

Q. Did the Alliance, while you were a member of it, and while you were a member of the executive council, post bulletins for the information of their members?   A. Did the Alliance——

Q. Did the Alliance post bulletins for their members?

A. Yes. They have a bulletin board on which they posted minutes of meetings between management and the Alliance.

Q. Did they post any bulletins of any other character?

A. Notices of union meetings, and more recently, they posted notices of—I won't say they posted notices of union meetings; I don't know. I would

(Testimony of Elmer Oscar Smith.)

say that's about all: Alliance, and management meetings, and notices of the coming meetings.

Q. Where were those bulletins posted?

A. On a bulletin board furnished by the company.

Q. Where is the bulletin board? [410]

A. It is in the new building just on the wall, a few feet away from the personnel office; I would say 30 or 35 feet, possibly.

Q. When was that new bulletin board erected?

A. Shortly after the new building was occupied, and I don't just recall when that was, sometime during——

Q. Was it while you were a member of the executive council of the Alliance?   A. Yes.

Q. As a member of that council can you say whether or not the Alliance paid for the erection of that bulletin board?   A. I don't know.

Mr. Watkins: I never heard of any union paying for any board.

Mr. Moore: I haven't either.

Q. (By Mr. Moore) Before the new plant was opened, where were Alliance bulletins posted?

A. They were posted on a board near the tool room. It was a piece of plywood that was there, the Alliance posted their bulletins on it.

Q. And while you were employed at the Respondent's plant, did you have occasion to join the C. I. O.?   A. Yes, I did.

Q. When?

(Testimony of Elmer Oscar Smith.)

A.   In February, I believe. [411]

Q.   Of 1942?   A.   1942.

Q.   Do you know whether or not a membership campaign was being carried on at that time?

A.   It wasn't at the time I joined, no.

Q.   Was such a campaign carried on thereafter?

A.   Yes, sir.

Q.   Did you notice any activity in the shop that was related to this campaign?

A.   To the C. I. O. campaign?

Q.   Yes.

A.   No, I didn't.   Of course, at lunch times there were talks of union, but other than that very little.

Q.   Did you hear the testimony of Mr. Crank?

A.   Yes, I did.

Q.   Did you observe the obscene object about which he testified?   A.   Yes, I did.

Q.   Where did you observe it?

A.   At my machine.

Q.   Who had it at the time you observed it?

A.   A fellow named Art Smith showed it to me.

Q.   Art Smith?   A.   Art Smith, yes.

Q.   When was that? [412]

A.   I believe I was working the swing shift, and it was this spring, about May or June.   I don't recall exactly, the latter part of May or June.

Q.   What did Mr. Smith do with this object, within your observation?

A.   Well, he brought it up to me and told me he wanted me to meet a C. I. O. man and then he

(Testimony of Elmer Oscar Smith.)
showed it to me, and that was all. I don't know
where he took it.

Q. Was that done in the open shop there?

A. Yes, it was.

Q. It could have been observed from any part
of the shop?   A. Yes, it could.

Q. Do you know how long Mr. Smith had that
in his possession?   A. No, I don't.

Q. After that occurred did you have a conversation with any official in the plant with reference
to activity in behalf of the C. I. O.?

A. I talked with Mr. Hileman.

Q. When was that?

A. June, I think.

Q. Pardon me?

A. I believe it was around the first part of June.

Q. Where?   In his office.

Q. Who was present? [413]

A. There was Mr. Kerns, and Mr. Millman, Mr.
Eiseman, who was representative of the War Production Board, and Clyde Spencer.

Q. What was the occasion for that meeting, Mr.
Smith?

A. Well, the C. I. O. as a whole, had notified,
that is, our local there, at Thompson's, had notified
the War Production Board as to all the idle machines at Thompson's plant on the swing shift and
graveyard shift, and Mr. Eiseman came there as a
representative of the War Production Board to
investigate the situation.

Q. Were you called in to this meeting?

(Testimony of Elmer Oscar Smith.)

A. Yes. We were called in to the meeting in Mr. Hileman's office, Mr. Spencer and I.

Q. You said that was in June, you believe?

A. I believe it was in June, yes.

Q. Will you say what occurred at that meeting?

A. Mr. Hileman asked us to tell the——

Q. By "us" whom do you mean?

A. Clyde Spencer and I. We were the workers that were called in. I believe he directed the questioning to me. He asked me to tell Mr. Eiseman the situation that had led up to us telling the War Production Board.

So, we told him that there had been so much idle machinery, and it was the policy of the C. I. O. to speed up production as much as possible, and we thought that machinery [414] should be working; so we had notified the War Production Board.

Immediately, Mr. Hileman asked me if it ever occurred to me to investigate the matter, and I told him I had tried to find out why so much machinery was idle, on several occasions I had talked to the foreman, I told him, and one foreman in particular had told me he couldn't understand why they weren't working either, because they had more steel in the plant than they had ever had, and Mr. Hileman wanted me to tell him the foreman's name, and I told him I didn't think I should, because I hated to get the man in trouble for something that he was innocent of.

So, immediately, Mr. Hileman told me I had done that on several occasions, and he didn't like my

(Testimony of Elmer Oscar Smith.)

attitude at all for saying something, and not to tell him, who told it. I told him that I wasn't a stooge, so that was the—then, he went into quite a lengthy explanation of why the machinery wasn't working, as to the shortage of steel and skilled men, and such as that, explaining it to us.

And later in the conversation the C. I. O. was mentioned some way, and Mr. Spencer said that it was our privilege to join any union we wanted to here, as long as we didn't—as long as we didn't conduct any union activities on company time, and Mr. Hileman told him he better not, and he turned around to me and said, "That goes for you too. I will throw you out of the plant bodily." [415]

Mr. Watkins: Do what?

The Witness: Conduct any union activity on company time. He said, "And that goes for you too. I will throw you out of the plant bodily."

And he told me if I thought he couldn't do it, just to tell him so, and there the meeting ended.

Q. (By Mr. Moore) Did Mr. Hileman know you were representing the C. I. O. at that meeting.

A. Yes, he did.

Q. Both you and Mr. Spencer?

A. Yes, he did.

Q. How did he know? Did you tell him?

A. I believe I did. I won't say positively I told him, but I was called in there for that reason, because I had been representing the C. I. O. I was president of the local.

(Testimony of Elmer Oscar Smith.)

Mr. Moore: Will you mark this as Board's Exhibit 12 for identification.

(Thereupon the document was marked Board's Exhibit 12 for identification.)

Q. (By Mr. Moore) I show you a document marked Board's Exhibit 12 for identification and ask you if you can tell me what it is.

A. Yes. That was a statement issued by the company, I believe it was put in the rack with the time cards shortly after the meeting that we had been called into, Mr. Spencer [416] and I, in Mr. Hileman's office.

Q. Did you receive such a notice?

A. Yes, sir.

Q. Was the notice you received in your time card rack?   A. Yes, sir.

Q. Did you notice others in the time card racks at that time?   A. Yes.

Mr. Moore: I offer Board's Exhibit 12 for identification in evidence.

I have one other question to ask in connection with that, and I will ask it while you are examining that.

Mr. Watkins: Go ahead.

Q. (By Mr. Moore) Was it generally known by employees in the plant you had complained to the War Production Board?

A. I believe so, yes, because——

Q. What is the basis for your belief?

(Testimony of Elmer Oscar Smith.)

A.   Well, it had been discussed quite freely at lunch time and we all ate in the lunchroom.

Q.   Was it known to the employees generally that the C. I. O. had made the complaint?

A.   I believe it had, and it had been known to management, because Mr. Millman had asked me prior to this time——

Q.   I am not speaking of management: I am speaking now of the production employees generally.

A.   Yes, I believe it was generally known, because I had talked with several of them about the C. I. O. notifying the [417] War Production Board.

Mr. Watkins: You have offered this, have you?

Mr. Moore: Yes.

Mr. Watkins: We have no objection.

Trial Examiner Whittemore: The document is received.

(Thereupon, the document heretofore marked for identification as Board's Exhibit No. 12, was received in evidence.)

BOARD'S EXHIBIT No. 12

June 29, 1942

To All Employees:

A short time ago several of our factory employees indirectly notified the War Production Board that there was a great deal of machinery lying idle in our plant. The reasons for this could easily have been found out by asking either the Foremen or the General Superintendent.

(Testimony of Elmer Oscar Smith.)

The management recognizes that during the present emergency all machinery should be operated as near 24 hours per day as possible. This has been and is being done wherever and whenever possible, but other factors enter into the situation. The complexity of our product, the great number of different sizes and types of articles, most of which have varying forge time, heat treat time, grind time, etc., make it a practical impossibility to completely balance our production. Also, consider the great number of different size, though similar, parts being processed at one time.

Coupled with this have been serious shortages of material. Almost all of our steels are specially made in small quantities, subject to the strictest metallurgical inspection. Few steel companies are capable of producing our needs and these companies, like others, have a great number of orders on their books. Our needs, even though they have high priority ratings, must await their turn.

Several other things which should be considered are these:

(1)   The necessity of gearing our production to the requirements of our customers:— In some categories we are now able to outbuild their requirements, based on estimates given us a year ago of what they thought they would need.

(2)   A Forging Department "bottleneck":— This will be remedied shortly with the acquisition of a new press and tube cut off machine.

(Testimony of Elmer Oscar Smith.)

The enormous increase in demand for certain products which were developed about two years ago and which could not be foreseen, is responsible for this condition in this department.

(3) Shortage of skilled machine operators: —Shortage of skilled machine operators is well known and we do not hire a man who is already at work in a war industry. Our personnel must, therefore, be trained and upgraded in our own plant, all of which takes time and careful selection of applicants whom we think will develop some mechanical ability.

On Wednesday of last week we were visited by Mr. Wm. E. Angold and Mr. William H. Sido of the War Production Army Liaison Office. They both thoroughly inspected our plant and its products and were highly complimentary as to the way it is operating. Among other things, they said, "that our wage rate was one of the highest in this area, our working conditions are excellent, and that if all plants were operating as well, they wouldn't have much to worry about."

On Friday we were visited by Mr. Lee L. Eiseman of the War Production Board. He was shown through the plant and later the two men who had complained to the War Production Board were given an opportunity of discussing it with him. Some of our difficulties were outlined at this meeting and Mr. Eiseman's comment to the men making the complaint was that "they didn't seem to know

(Testimony of Elmer Oscar Smith.)
much about the way a plant of our type, producing the articles we do, is run.''

The foregoing is simply given to you for your information and in the interests of Company unity at a time when maximum output of good parts should be the individual goal of every one of us.

THOMPSON PRODUCTS, Inc.
WEST COAST PLANT

———

Q. (By Mr. Moore) In relating a conversation that you had with Mr. Millman you testified that there was some activity in the plant around the time of the election in September of 1941.

A. Yes, sir.

Mr. Moore: I will ask this document be marked Board's Exhibit 13 for identification.

(Thereupon, the document referred to was marked Board's Exhibit No. 13 for idenification.)

Q. (By Mr. Moore) I show you a document marked Board's Exhibit 13 for identification and ask you if you know what it is?

A. That is a bulletin issued by the Company that was put in our racks with our time cards. From time to time they issued bulletins of that sort to the employees.

Mr. Watkins: May I have that answer read? We can't hear it; it's too confidential.

(Testimony of Elmer Oscar Smith.)

Trial Examiner Whittemore: Will you speak up, so it [418] will not be confidential?

(The answer was read.)

Mr. Watkins: Thank you. Just a minute. I would like to move the last portion of it: "from time to time they issued bulletins of that sort to the employees," be stricken as a conclusion of the witness.

Trial Examiner Whittemore: Well, it may be stricken.

Mr. Moore: Very well.

Q. (By Mr. Moore) Did you receive a bulletin like this? Or did you receive this bulletin?

A. Yes, sir.

Q. How did you receive it?

A. I received it in the rack with my time card.

Q. Did you receive it on or about the date which it bears?   A. Yes, sir.

Q. Did you notice other similar documents in the time rack at the time you received it?

A. Yes, sir.

Q. Did you later give the document to me?

A. I did.

Mr. Moore: May it be stipulated it has been in my possession since he delivered it to me?

Trial Examiner Whittemore: How can he stipulate to that, Mr. Moore?

Mr. Watkins: What difference does it make?

[419]

Mr. Moore: It's just a matter of stating——

(Testimony of Elmer Oscar Smith.)

Mr. Watkins: I don't care where it has been, If you want to have it for the record of course I will stipulate to it. I don't care.

Mr. Moore: Thank you.

Mr. Watkins: We have no objection.

Mr. Moore: No further questions.

Trial Examiner Whittemore: If there is no objection this document will be received.

> (Thereupon, the document heretofore marked for identification as Board's Exhibit No. 13, was received in evidence.)

BOARD'S EXHIBIT No. 13

LET'S HAVE THE TRUTH!

Dedicated to Truth, Understanding and Real Americanism

(There is no place for hate, lies and misunderstanding in American Industry.)

Vol. 1 No. 1

November 10, 1941

Friday the C.I.O. tried to show that by diverting 1941 tax money a 25c increase could be given employees. This Is False.

HERE IS THE TRUTH

A 25¢ increase for the first six months of 1941 would have cost more than
1. All of the Profit Tax the Company paid.
2. All of the Profit
3. And $794,500 besides!

(Testimony of Elmer Oscar Smith.)

UNCLE SAM WOULD HAVE RECEIVED NO PROFIT TAX, AND THE COMPANY WOULD HAVE BEEN IN THE RED!

HERE ARE THE FIGURES
(1st 6 Mos. of 1941)

25¢ extra on actual Cleveland hours worked	$2,437,500
Additional extra compensation cost	$ 97,500
Additional payroll taxes	$ 101,400
Additional Workmen's Compensation premiums	$ 10,000
Total Cleveland cost of 25¢ increase	$2,646,400
Cost of same increase to 2000 employees in other Thompson Products plants who help make the profit	$ 882,100
Total Company cost of 25¢ increase	$3,528,500
Profits Tax was $1,811,000	
Profits were $ 923,000	
Total of Profits & Profits Tax $2,734,000	$2,734.000
If wage rates had been increased 25¢, the Company would have lost in the 1st 6 months	$ 794,500

Thompson Products is being fair to employees and Uncle Sam by paying good wages, and at the same time is carrying its load of defense costs.

In the financial report mailed to the homes of all employees last spring we said, "The Company feels it is a good bargain to pay high taxes in this emergency to help build the defenses of the country to such strength that any threats against it may be defeated. It believes that heavy taxation for defense now is an investment in the traditional

(Testimony of Elmer Oscar Smith.)
American way of life, and will make possible a
return to lower taxes in the future.''

This is an American statement!

''A Different Kind of Company!''

Voir Dire Examination:

Q. (By Mr. Watkins) Mr. Smith, referring to
Board's Exhibit 13, the document that has just been
introduced, as there any bulletin put out by the
C. I. O. which preceded Board's Exhibit 13?

A. I wouldn't say for sure; there had been
papers, the Thompson Organizer was distributed at
the gate, but whether or not there was one just
prior to that I don't know.

Q. Do you have a copy of it?

A. No, I don't.

Q. Will you get a copy from Mr. Johnson here,
the bulletin [420] to which Board's Exhibit 13
was in answer? That is Mr. Johnson, the representative of the union. [421]

Cross Examination

Q. (By Mr. Baldwin) Mr. Smith, prior to and
during your term of office with the P. & P. W. A.,
did you have any relative that was a paid organizer
for the CIO?

A. I believe not during my term of office in
the P. & P. W. A.

Q. Well, have you now a relative that is a paid
organizer of the CIO?

(Testimony of Ehner Oscar Smith.)

A. I have a brother in the east that is an officer in the CIO, yes, sir.

Q. At the time you had a conversation with Mr. Millman, you stated, I believe, a preference for a national union or large union. Were you referring to the CIO at that time?

A. Not especially.

Q. Well, is that the first time—I mean was it that day when you finally decided on that?

A. I beg your pardon? [428]

Q. Well, I will ask you it differently. Had you any inclination or any preference for the large unions prior to that time?

A. Yes, sir. I have always believed in strong international unions.

Q. You would say that you did so prior to your election as an officer of the P. & P. W. A.?

A. Yes, sir.

Q. You stated that the plant shut down to permit men to attend a P. & P. W. A. meeting, is that right?

A. To the best of my knowledge, sir. There was no work while the meeting was in progress.

Q. Did you know if all those men went to the P. & P. W. A. meeting; I mean to the best of your knowledge?

A. No, sir, I do not know that all of the men went.

Q. Could they have gone to any other organization's meeting on that day?

A. Yes, they could.

(Testimony of Elmer Oscar Smith.)

Q. Do you recollect whether or not there was any meeting of any other organization other than the P. & P. W. A. held on the same day on which the P. & P. W. A. meeting was held?

A. I do.

Q. And the men could have gone to that meeting? A. Some of them, yes.

Q. Well, is there any specific meeting that you can recall? [429]

A. I believe one meeting late—well, I won't say "late". It was during the early summer, I believe along about July.

Q. Would July 5 be about the date?

A. Well, I wouldn't recall the exact date but I believe it was about that time.

There was also a CIO meeting held at the same time that the P. & P. W. A. meeting was held.

Q. Could I ask the witness to look at this paper?

Trial Examiner Whittemore: Certainly.

(Document handed to the witness.)

Q. (By Mr. Baldwin) You say that a meeting was held on Sunday, July 5, 1942?

Mr. Moore: Objected to as being indefinite.

Q. (By Mr. Baldwin) Would you say there was a CIO meeting held on Sunday, July 5, 1942?

A. Yes, I believe there was.

Mr. Moore: I will object to that and ask the answer be stricken. There is no evidence yet that in 1942 the plant closed down at any time for the

(Testimony of Elmer Oscar Smith.)

purpose of these men to attend meetings of any kind.

Mr. Baldwin: Well, the witness has already stated that the plant shut down a number of times and I merely tied it down to this one specific date.

Mr. Moore: I don't believe his testimony was that the plant closed down on that specific day and that is the basis [430] of my objection, that the question is indefinite and the answer is meaningless.

Trial Examiner Whittemore: Well, I will permit him to answer the question. Go ahead.

Mr. Baldwin: That will be all.

Trial Examiner Whittemore: Mr. Watkins?

Q. (By Mr. Watkins) Mr. Smith, you mentioned a brother of yours who was an organizer back east. Where back east?

A. I think he is in Davenport at the present time.

Q. Davenport what?

A. Davenport, Iowa.

Q. Has he been there long?

A. He has been there, I believe, for two years. [431]

Q. Where did that take place?

A. At my machine.

Q. Did Mr. Millman come up and start talking to you?

A. Yes, sir, he did. Quite frequently we talked on numerous occasions. [434]

(Testimony of Elmer Oscar Smith.)

Q. On various occasions?

A. Yes, various occasions.

Q. What did he say on this particular occasion? Do you recall the first thing?

A. I don't recall the first part of the conversation—what opened the conversation, no.

Q. What did he say to you—what was the first thing that he said to you that you remember?

A. I can't remember the first thing that he did tell me.

Q. Do you remember what the first thing was that you said to him?

A. I remember telling Mr. Millman that I believed in strong unions and that I didn't believe in an independent union such as we had because of the fact that it wasn't strong enough; that I didn't think it had done as much for the men as a larger union, and I thought unionism was something more than a local thing and workers should be united internationally.

He told me that in some cases he did think that the CIO and the A. F. of L. were good things.

Q. Did you ask him what his viewpoint was?

A. No. We discussed it quite freely between ourselves.

Q. It was just a part of the conversation that you were both talking about?   A. Yes, sir.

Q. He might have started it or you might have started it, [435] no matter how it came up?

A. That is true. And he related to me one

(Testimony of Elmer Oscar Smith.)
incident in Long Beach where he had worked. He
said:

> "The plant surely needed a union down there
> because the condition of the workers was ter-
> rible, but" he said, "it wasn't the case at
> Thompson Products, because the Thompson
> Products treated their workers fairly."

And that he thought the little independent union
had done very well there and took care of the matters. [436]

Q. You didn't complain to him at any time
about the working conditions down there?

A. No, sir. I had always maintained that the
company treated me pretty fairly.

Q. What is your—pardon me.

A. And that was a nice place to work.

Q. You so expressed yourself and said: "It is
the best place I ever worked," did you not?

A. Well, I don't know that I said it was the
best place I [437] ever worked, but I told him
they always treated me nicely and it was a good
place to work as far as I was concerned.

Q. Don't you remember telling Mr. Millman
it was a—that it was the best place you ever
worked?

A. I may have told him that in our conversation. I do recall telling him it was a good place
to work.

Q. You joined the C. I. O. in February of
1942, is that correct?

(Testimony of Elmer Oscar Smith.)

A. I believe it was February; the last few days of February or the very first few days in March—right at that time.

Q. And that was after your talk that you have related with Mr. Millman? A. Yes.

Q. And were there a good many others who joined around that time?

A. There were several, yes.

Q. And subsequent to that?

A. After that?

Q. Yes. A. Yes.

Q. And prior to that?

A. I believe I was the first one that really carried a membership card. Well, there were other C. I. O. men in the plant but I was the first one that came out in the open and wore my button.

Q. I see. [438]

A. I told Mr. Millman and the rest of them that I joined because I didn't believe in going around and hiding behind somebody's back and doing something.

Q. And you wore your button starting about when?

A. At the time I joined the union or a few days after. I believe, maybe, I had belonged just a few days—maybe three or four days I belonged to the C. I. O. and then I started wearing my button.

Q. And you continued to wear the button until you left the employ of the company; is that correct? A. Yes.

(Testimony of Elmer Oscar Smith.)

Q. And you left of your own volition?

A. That is right.

Q. Mr. Smith, you related that you had a conversation in Mr. Hileman's office concerning the War Production Board incident?

A. Yes, sir.

Q. And you stated there that you said to Mr. Hileman that you were not a stooge. What did you mean by that?

A. Well, I meant that I didn't like to go to the management and tell things on certain men that hurt—that might hurt them in the shop, which I had heard some men did and those men in the shop had been labeled "stooges".

Q. Which was the first time that you personally noticed any shortage of use of equipment at Thompson Products? [439]

A. Well, it was after the new building was opened up and the machinery was set up there.

Q. About when was that?

A. Possibly it was May.

Q. May of 1942? A. I believe so.

Q. Not before that?

A. April—pardon me.

Q. April of 1942?

A. About April, I believe.

Q. After you joined the C. I. O.?

A. Yes, sir.

Q. All right. Then after you first noticed that, what did you do about it?

(Testimony of Elmer Oscar Smith.)

A. Well, there had been a lot of discussion among the boys at the lunch table and various places about the machinery setting idle and they wondered why it wasn't working, and on one occasion or two occasions I had talks with foremen concerning it and asked them why it hadn't been running.

Q. All right. Now, let us get to "a lot of talk about the boys at the lunch table."

Tell me when and who was present at a specific conversation of that character?

A. Well, it is hard to tell. I ate with Mr. Hess and Mr. Overlander and a fellow named Drevelo.

[440]

Q. Mr. Hess was the C. I. O. boy that you mentioned awhile ago and Mr. Overlander also?

A. I don't believe that they were active at that time.

Q. Anybody else you remember?

A. I believe Clyde Spencer—I talked with him about it.

Q. Anybody else?

A. On an occasion I talked to Mr. Baldwin about it but I don't believe that was at the lunch table. It may have been.

Q. Do you remember specifically when you talked to Mr. Baldwin about it?

A. No, I don't.

Q. Do you remember what you said to Mr. Baldwin about it?

A. No. I vaguely seem to remember I asked

(Testimony of Elmer Oscar Smith.)

him why the machinery wasn't running and he told me that they had had a meeting recently with the committee—that is the council. It was either the council or the War Production Board, that they had had a meeting with Mr. Bill Kearns and the management in the office, and there was a bulletin placed on the bulletin board explaining the reasons why the machinery wasn't running, and that was, I believe, the substance of that bulletin. It was to the effect that there was a shortage of steel and a shortage of skilled men, and that the company had or, the companies whom Thompson Products was supplying had over ordered in the previous year and subsequently some of Thompson Products machinery was idle because they had [441] ordered more machinery than they had orders at that time.

Q. This conversation you are talking about was after the meeting with the War Production Board officials, isn't that right?

A. No, I believe not.

Q. Aren't you mentioning the things that are stated in Board's Exhibit 12, which I now show you?

(Handing paper to the witness.)

A. No.

Q. Was there a bulletin posted in addition to that and prior to it, concerning this same matter?

A. I believe so.

Q. Do you know when that was posted?

(Testimony of Elmer Oscar Smith.)

A. I believe it was posted as the minutes of a— you see at the shop they had a War Production Committee. That Committee met with the management. I believe that this notice was posted on the bulletin board as the minutes of the meeting between the War Production Committee and management.

Q. Oh, I see, about some shortage of metals and some over ordering by certain companies?

A. Yes, I believe that is it.

Q. You were talking to Mr. Baldwin then about that explanation of it?

A. Yes, as I remember that is right.

Q. I believe you stated you talked to some foremen about [442] this. To whom did you talk?

A. I would rather not tell.

Q. ·What do you mean you would rather not tell? A. (No response.)

Q. Is there any secret about the foremen to whom you talked?

A. No, sir, but like I told Mr. Hileman, I didn't think I should tell who I talked to.

Mr. Watkins: Well, Mr. Examiner, that puts us in a very unusual and very difficult position if the witness refuses to tell what foremen he discussed this thing with.

Trial Examiner Whittemore: He doesn't refuse. He said he would rather not. What is the purpose of your going into that anyway?

Mr. Watkins: I will drop it for a moment and then I will come back to it.

(Testimony of Ehner Oscar Smith.)

Q. (By Mr. Watkins) Did you discuss this situation, that is the failure to use to full capacity the equipment down at Thompson Products, with more than one foreman?

A. Yes, I believe so.

Q. How many?

A. Two I remember distinctly.

Q. All right. Now, you don't recall more than one discussion or were there several discussions?

Mr. Moore: I will object to that. It is shown that there were general discussions about the plant on that subject. [443]

Trial Examiner Whittemore: I know, but he said they were general. Certainly counsel for the respondent has a right to determine whether they were general or whether they were specific.

The Witness: What is your question?

Trial Examiner Whittemore: Read the question.

(Question read.)

Q. (By Mr. Watkins): That you discussed with the foremen?

A. I recall one specific occasion that I talked with each of theese foremen—that is the foreman separately, one each time.

Q. With each?   A. No.

Q. One time each you say?

A. Yes, one time with each of the foremen.

Q. I see. When did you decide to notify the War Production Board about it?

A. It was at our—at a regular monthly meeting of the C. I. O. We discussed it as a body.

(Testimony of Elmer Oscar Smith.)

Q.   Yes?

A.   And it was decided at that time to notify the War Production Board.

Q.   That was you and Mr. Hess and Mr. Overlander, is that correct? You were the three from the company?

A.   I believe Mr. Hess was not present. **[444]**

Q.   But Mr. Overlander was?

A.   I would not say for sure. I don't know whether Overlander was at the plant at that time. I believe that Overlander had left the employment of the plant.

Q.   Yes. Was there any discussion among you as to why not take it up with Mr. Hileman, the head of the company, and talk to him about it?

A.   No.

Q.   Didn't discuss that at all?   A.   No.

Q.   Did you or anybody else say: "Well, let us talk to Mr. Millman about it?"   A.   No.

Q.   Or Mr. Kearns?   A.   No.

Q.   In other words, you concluded you would shoot it right to the War Production Board?

A.   Yes, sir.

Q.   You didn't have anything against the company at that time, did you, personally?

A.   No, sir.

Q.   Was Mr. Johnson, the C.I.O. representative who has been in this hearing, present at this meeting you speak of when you decided to do this?

A.   Yes, he was. **[445]**

(Testimony of Elmer Oscar Smith.)

Q. Who wrote the letter to the Production Board? A. Mr. Johnson.

Q. Did you sign it? A. No, sir.

Q. You gave him the information?

A. I beg your pardon.

Q. Did you give him the information?

A. I believe the information—I didn't give him the information personally, but it was discussed at the shop, the number of machines—I mean it was discussed at the meeting, the number of machines that were idle and he got his information from this meeting that we had and he notified the War Production Board.

Q. Was Mr. Porter at this meeting?

A. I believe he was.

Q. Did you have any discussion about that matter with Mr. Kangus, Victor Kangus?

A. No, sir.

Mr. Watkins: That is all. Wait a moment.

Q. (By Mr. Watkins): Mr. Smith, at this meeting with the officials of the War Production Board, I believe you said Mr. Hileman was present and pretty angry, is that right?

A. That is true.

Q. And expressed himself pretty heatedly about the entire matter? [446]

A. Yes, sir.

Q. You didn't blame him, did you, personally?

A. Well,——[447]

(Testimony of Elmer Oscar Smith.)

Recross Examination

Q. (By Mr. Baldwin): Mr. Smith, you said you talked to Mr. Baldwin about the idle machinery, is that right?   A. Yes, sir.

Q. Did Mr. Baldwin say anything to you in reference to the idle machinery?

A. Yes. I believe that you at that time told me that you had discussed it with Bill Kearns and the management, and I believe you referred to the minutes of a War Production meeting. I believe that that was the bulletin you referred to.

[448]

Q. Well, one thing, did Mr. Baldwin tell you that he made a check of all the idle machinery in the plant and had carried this or taken this to the meeting of the War Production Board in order to find out what it was all about?

A. I don't recall being told that specific thing, but I do recall that it was discussed at the meeting.

Q. Well, this was prior to the time—this happened prior to the time you took your information to the War Production Board about idle machinery?

A. I believe so, to the best of my recollection.

Mr. Baldwin: That is all.

Mr. Moore: May it be stipulated that there are now approximately four hundred employees at the West Coast plant of the Thompson Products, Incorporated?

Mr. Thompson: So stipulated.

Mr. Moore: I will call Mr. Spencer.

CLYDE J. SPENCER

a witness called by and on behalf of the National Labor Relations Board, having been first duly sworn, was examined and [449] testified as follows:

Direct Examination

By Mr. Moore:

Q. Will you state your full name, please?

A. Clyde J. Spencer.

Q. Have you been employed by the Thompson Products Company, Incorporated?   A. Yes.

Q. At their plant in Bell, California?

A. Yes, sir.

Q. When were you so employed?

A. October 18, 1940.

Q. Are you employed at the plant now?

A. Yes, sir.

Q. In what capacity?

A. Running a No. 5 turret lathe.

Q. Have you ever been employed in a supervisory capacity?   A. Never.

Q. During the course of your employment there did you have an occasion to join the Pacific Motor Parts Workers Alliance?   A. Yes.

Q. When did you join that organization?

A. March 1941.

Q. Will you state the circumstances of your joining?

A. I don't quite understand that question.

Q. Did some one ask you to join? [450]

A. Yes.

Q. Who did that?   A. Stubblefield.

(Testimony of Clyde J. Spencer.)

Q. Where did Mr. Stubblefield ask you to join —where were you at the time he asked you to join?

A. Working on my machine.

Q. In the plant? A. Yes, sir.

Q. Did he ask you once or more than once?

A. Once is all that I recall.

Q. Have you paid dues to that organization?

A. Yes.

Q. Where did you pay those dues?

A. At the plant.

Q. To whom? A. To Lester Bebb.

Q. Have you attended meetings of the Alliance?

A. Yes, sir.

Q. When were those meetings held, the ones that you attended? What day of the week, I will ask you? A. Always held on a Sunday.

Q. And during the time that you attended the meetings, did the plant operate on Sunday?

A. Some times, yes.

Q. Was any arrangement made to your knowledge, so that men [451] scheduled work on Sunday could attend those meetings?

Mr. Watkins: Just a minute. I object to the question. There has been no proper foundation laid for such a question.

Trial Examiner Whittemore: Well, I should say the best foundation possibly would be this witness' knowledge.

Mr. Watkins: As to his own case but he was on no committee or anything of that kind.

Trial Examiner Whittemore: He is asking him

(Testimony of Clyde J. Spencer.)

what his knowledge is. It may develop he has no knowledge. I don't see how he can very well approach the point without asking what his knowledge is.

You might read the question.

(Question read.)

Q. (By Mr. Moore): Just answer whether you know or not?   A. Yes.

Q. Did you ever attend one of those meetings on Sunday during a day on which you also worked at the plant?   A. Yes.

Q. When did that happen?

A. I don't recall the date.

Q. Did you do it once or more than once?

A. I done it more than once; on two occasions that I recall specifically.

Q. Can you say approximately when the meetings were held?

A. Well, I couldn't say exactly but it was prior to the [452] declaration of war, I know that.

Q. Prior to the declaration of war?

A. Yes.

Q. Do you recall what happened at those meetings that you attended?

A. Some things, yes.

Q. By referring to the minutes that were kept of those meetings, do you think you could recall the exact occasions on which they occurred?

A. I may be able to—I don't know.

Q. At the time of the meetings, who was on the executive council of the Alliance?

(Testimony of Clyde J. Spencer.)

A. Mr. Baldwin was on and——

Q. Were the meetings to which you refer held after the election in the late summer or early fall of 1941? A. Yes.

Q. Will you examine these minutes which have been furnished by Mr. Baldwin, and see if you can state the dates on which you attended such meetings?

(Handing document to the witness.)

A. This one here is one of them—September 7, and I think there was one prior to that.

Mr. Moore: Mr. Baldwin, are all of the minutes of the Alliance here?

Mr. Baldwin: Up until March. [453]

Mr. Moore: March of what year?

Mr. Baldwin: 1942.

Mr. Moore: All of the minutes up to March 1942 are here?

Mr. Baldwin: That is all there ever were.

The Witness: I don't know—I definitely recall this one but I don't recall the other one.

Q. (By Mr. Moore): On September 7, 1941, you attended a meeting? A. That is right.

Q. Of the Alliance that was held on Sunday?
A. Yes, sir.

Q. Did you also work in the plant on September 7, 1941? A. Yes.

Q. Now, during what hours on that day did you work in the plant? A. From 6:30 until 4.

Q. 6:30 a.m.?

(Testimony of Clyde J. Spencer.)

A. 6:30 to 4 with from 10 to 12 off.

Q. And did others work during the period from 10 to 12?

A. I don't know really. I was at the meeting and I couldn't say.

Q. What did you do?

A. I went to the P. & P. W. A. meeting.

Q. Did you check out first? [454]

A. No,—yes, I did too.

Q. Then when you returned, did you check in?

A. Yes, sir.

Q. And checked in again?

A. Yes, sir, checked back in; yes.

Q. How did you know, Mr. Spencer, that it would be permissible for you to check out at 10 o'clock?

A. I had received notice may be one day or two days before the hours we were to go to work on that Sunday from the foreman.

Q. From the foreman?

A. From the foreman.

Q. What foreman?

A. I remember definite that Mr. Guenzler told me.

Q. Did you have a conversation with Mr. Guenzler with reference to that?

A. No. I think he come around and asked us to work and then told us the hours that we are going to work.

Q. Where were you at the time he told you that?   A. At my machine.

(Testimony of Clyde J. Spencer.)

Q. At about what time was it?

A. That I can't recall.

Q. About what date would you say? Was it a day or two before this Sunday?

A. It would be either Friday or Saturday, and usually they would come around and tell us just maybe thirty or forty-five [455] minutes before quitting time. It would be in the afternoon to the best of my knowledge.

Q. Will you repeat what Mr. Guenzler told you as nearly as you can?

A. The exact words I wouldn't recall. He asked if I wanted to work Sunday and I know I said I would—I would always say yes, and he said:

"Well, we will start work at 6:30 and work until 4 and we will be closed from 10 to 12."

And naturally I always said: "All right;" because work was work to me.

Q. Had you worked on other Sundays?

A. Yes.

Q. And were you notified on the other Sundays what the hours would be?

A. No. I always took it as a general conclusion to work from 7 until 3:30, unless they told you that the plant would be closed for a meeting.

Q. Now, in your conversation or when Mr. Guenzler told you this, did he say why those hours would be in effect that day?

A. No. I believe he really—I don't think he said why.

Q. I beg your pardon?

(Testimony of Clyde J. Spencer.)

A. I don't think he said why. no.

Q. Did the C.I.O. notify the War Production Board of the condition existing in the plant there at any time? [456]   A. Yes.

Q. When did that happen?

A. I don't remember the exact date.

Mr. Watkins: I can't hear, Mr. Examiner.

Trial Examiner Whittemore: Speak up.

The Witness: I don't recall the exact date of that.

Q. (By Mr. Moore) Approximately when, as nearly as you can recall?

A. It was along in May, I think.

Q. Of this year?   A. Yes.

Q. What was the nature of the notice?

A. That I don't know. I just know what I have heard, is all I know.

Q. Do you know what the notice concerned?

A. It concerned idle machinery.

Q. And as a result of that notification, was a conference held in the plant?   A. Yes.

Q. When?

A. I don't remember the date of that at all.

Q. Well, approximately, as nearly as you can recall, Mr. Spencer?

A. Along in June, I imagine.

Mr. Watkins: I can't hear the witness. [457]

Trial Examiner Whittemore: Speak right up.

The Witness: It would be in June.

Q. (By Mr. Moore) And where was the conference held?

(Testimony of Clyde J. Spencer.)

A.   In Mr. Hileman's office.

Q.   Who was there at the time?

A.   Elmer Smith and Mr. Hileman, Mr. Millman and Bill Kearns and myself.

Q.   Was Mr. Eiseman there?

A.   That is right, Mr. Eiseman was there, I beg your pardon.

Q.   What occurred at that conference?

A.   There was a discussion between Mr. Hileman and Elmer Smith as to——

Mr. Watkins: Just a moment. I object to this if the Court please. I object to the form of this answer to the question. I would like to ask that the answer be stricken as a discussion and have the witness state what was said by each of the parties. This is recent, now, Mr. Examiner, so there will be no excuse for not giving a coherent answer.

Trial Examiner Whittemore: If you don't mind I will hold up the answer to the question anyway. What I would like to know is, what is the purpose of going into this whole matter? What relevancy does it have to the issues in this case?

Mr. Moore: It is a statement of the company; of the manager of the company made at this conference.

Trial Examiner Whittemore: Something that isn't yet in [458] the record, you mean?

Mr. Moore: I beg your pardon.

Trial Examiner Whittemore: Something that isn't yet in the record.

(Testimony of Clyde J. Spencer.)

Mr. Moore: It is in the record, yes, and this corroborates it.

Mr. Watkins: Mr. Examiner, if the company fired both men and we were facing charges here of discrimination because of it, I think it would be justified under the circumstances, but nothing of that kind was done.

Trial Examiner Whittemore: I don't know what particular statements there are in the record at this time that you feel bear on the issues of this case.

Mr. Moore: Mr. Hileman's statement that he would throw the C.I.O. men out bodily if they attempted to organize the plant.

Trial Examiner Whittemore: I don't recall that was his statement.

Mr. Watkins: No such statement as that was made even by Mr. Smith.

Trial Examiner Whittemore: There was a statement to the effect he would throw them out.

Mr. Moore: It may not have been in those words.

Trial Examiner Whittemore: But not if they organized .

Mr. Watkins: Organizing on company time, that is what [459] the witness stated.

Trial Examiner Whittemore: I think that is right, if they organized on company time.

Mr. Watkins: That is correct.

Trial Examiner Whittemore: It seems to me we are wasting a great deal of time on what to me now seems rather insignificant. However, if you feel it is important, go ahead.

(Testimony of Clyde J. Spencer.)

I think the issues here are far clearer than trying to determine where the merit lies in some dispute between the employees and the management.

Mr. Moore: I believe you are right.

Trial Examiner Whittmore: Quite likely they were justified in feeling the way they did about it. I don't know what bearing it has here unless there is something definitely anti-union in some remark, but if you feel that it is important, I am not going to prevent you from putting it in.

Mr. Watkins: Couldn't we short-cut it, Mr. Examiner, by letting counsel ask the witness what was said about union activities at the plant and then let him make his speech and get on?

Trial Examiner Whittemore: Is this witness for purposes of corroboration?

Mr. Moore: Yes.

Trial Examiner Whittemore: I don't think Mr. Watkins would have any objection if you asked the witness if he heard [460] the other witness' testimony as to what Mr. Hileman said.

Q. (By Mr. Moore): What did Mr. Hileman say with respect to the C.I.O., if he said anything, with respect to the C.I.O.?

A. The only thing he said, he mentioned the fact that if we mentioned C.I.O. on company time, we would most likely get fired and he made the statement that he would throw us out bodily if that occurred, with half a chance, I think he said, and that is the only thing I recall as to the C.I.O.

Mr. Moore: That is all.

(Testimony of Clyde J. Spencer.)

Cross Examination

By Mr. Watkins:

Q. You are still employed by the Thompson Products, aren't you?   A. Yes, sir.

Q. Do you belong to the C.I.O. at the present time?   A. Yes, sir.

Q. When did you join?   A. In June.

Q. June 1942?   A. Yes.

Q. Did you resign the Alliance then?

A. Yes.

Q. And did you wear your button around the plant?   A. Yes, sir.

Q. And still wear it?   A. Yes, sir. [461]

Mr. Watkins: That is all.

Trial Examiner Whittemore: Any questions, Mr. Baldwin?

Mr. Baldwin: Just one.

Q. (By Mr. Baldwin) You said Mr. Stubblefield asked you to join the Alliance, is that right?

A. Yes, sir.

Q. Do you remember whether you were on the day shift at that time?   A. Yes.

Q. You were?   A. Yes, I was on days.

Trial Examiner Whittemore: The witness is excused. Thank you, Mr. Spencer.

Mr. Watkins: May I ask one more question?

Trial Examiner Whittemore: Certainly.

Q. (By Mr. Watkins) At this meeting in Mr. Hileman's office that you testified about, Mr. Hileman was really burned up wasn't he?   A. Yes.

Mr. Watkins: That is all. [462]

ALEX FREDERICK SUNDQUIST

a witness called by and on behalf of the National Labor Relations Board, having been first duly sworn, was examined and testified as follows:

Direct Examination

Q. (By Mr. Moore) Are you now employed by Thompson Products, Incorporated?

A. That is correct?

Q. In Bell, California?

A. That is correct.

Trial Examiner Whittemore: You better ask him his name. [463]

Q. (By Mr. Moore) What is your name?

A. Alex Frederick Sundquist.

Q. How long have you been so employed?

A. Oh, approximately a year and a half.

Q. In what department of the plant are you now employed?

A. Forge Department.

Q. Who is your foreman?

A. Luther Leatherwood.

Q. Did you observe the circulation of a lewd object in the plant there at any time?

A. Yes, I did.

Q. When?   A. It was in May.

Q. Will you described the object?

A. Well, it was something resembling a large finger and it had a C. I. O. button attached to the bottom of it.

Q. At the end of it?

A. At the end of it.

(Testimony of Alex Frederick Sundquist.)

Q. In whose possession did you see that?

A. The Forge Department foreman.

Q. Who is that?　　A. Mr. Leatherwood.

Q. How long did you see him with that in his possession?

A. Well, two or three minutes, I would say.

Q. Well, what was he doing with it? [464]

A. Well, he had it strapped around his mid-section, I would say, probably showing it in its proper place; where it might have been.

Mr. Watkins: We will stipulate to that.

Q. (By Mr. Moore) Did he show it to any one?

A. Yes, a fellow working next to me saw it.

Q. Who was that?　　A. Joseph Weicken.

Q. Did Mr. Leatherwood show it to you?

A. Well, he showed it to both of us at the same time.

Mr. Moore: That is all.

The Witness: That is, we could see it.

Mr. Moore: That is all.

Cross Examination

By Mr. Watkins:

Q. Are you a member of the C. I. O.?

A. (No answer.)

Q. Do you belong to the C. I. O.?

A. Yes, sir.

Q. How long have you belonged to it?

A. Oh, since May.

Q. May of 1942?　　A. This year, yes, sir.

Q. Where did you join?

(Testimony of Alex Frederick Sundquist.)

A. I just don't quite know what you mean by that.

Q. Who first talked to you down at the plant about joining? [465]   A. (No answer.)

Mr. Watkins: I would like to have the record show the pause, Mr. Examiner.

The Witness: I joined on my own accord as far as that goes. I mean I didn't specifically speak to any one about it.

Q. (By Mr. Watkins) Nobody spoke to you at all about joining down at the plant?

A. No.

Q. You are positive of that?   A. Yes.

Q. You have never spoken to anybody down at the plant about joining the C. I. O. either, did you?

A. You mean to encourage them?

Q. Yes.

A. No, I don't believe I ever have.

Q. You never have?   A. No, sir.

Q. And you never saw anybody down there ask anybody to join the C. I. O. or talk to them about it?   A. No, sir.

Q. Do you wear your button while at work?

A. That is right.

Q. Do you still wear the button there?

A. Yes, I do.

Q. And have been wearing it since you first joined? [466]   A. That is right.

Mr. Watkins: That is all. One more question.

Q. (By Mr. Watkins) Did you ever belong to the Alliance?   A. Yes, I have.

(Testimony of Alex Frederick Sundquist.)

Q. When?

A. Well, I joined a couple of months after I began work there.

Q. And when did you resign from the Alliance?

A. It was in—I don't remember just the date but it was——

Q. Was it about the time you joined the C.I.O.?

A. Well, it was a little before that.

Q. Did you ever belong to the C. I. O. or the A. F. of L. prior to joining the C. I. O. in May of 1942?   A. No, sir.

Q. And do you mean to tell me, Mr. Sundquist, that without talking to anybody about it, you walked down to the union hall and joined the C.I.O. in May of 1942?   A. (No answer.)

Mr. Watkins: I would like to have the record show the extended pause to the answer, Mr. Examiner.

The Witness: Well, I didn't join right there, I guess—I wouldn't say.

Mr. Watkins: I think that is all.

Mr. Baldwin: One question.

Trial Examiner Whittemore: All right. [467]

Mr. Watkins: May I ask just one more question, please?

Mr. Baldwin: Surely.

Q. (By Mr. Watkins) When you were referring to this lewd object, what shift were you on?

A. Grave yard shift or third shift.

Q. What shift was Mr. Leatherwood on?

A. Day shift.

(Testimony of Alex Frederick Sundquist.)

Q. Not on the same shift? A. No, sir.

Mr. Watkins: That is all.

Q. (By Mr. Baldwin) Did Mr. Drevelo hand you a card to the C. I. O.?

A. Whose name is that again?

Q. Oscar Drevelo.

A. I don't remember of it.

Q. Do you remember who handed you the card?

A. (No answer.)

Trial Examiner Whittemore: Just a minute. There is no evidence he was handed a card.

Mr. Baldwin: I can change that.

Q. (By Mr. Baldwin) Were you handed any card?

A. Just what do you mean by "card"?

Q. Well, I will make it very clear then. Did anybody hand you a card in the plant, at the place where you were working, at any time, a C. I. O. card? [468]   A. No.

Mr. Baldwin: That is all.

Trial Examiner Whittemore: Are you through?

Mr. Moore: No, I would like to ask another question.

Redirect Examination

By Mr. Moore:

Q. What time did the grave yard shift, as you call it, end?   A. 7 o'clock in the morning.

Q. What time does the day shift begin?

A. Well, they get there about a quarter to.

Q. The men on the day shift come in at a quarter of 7?   A. That is correct.

(Testimony of Alex Frederick Sundquist.)

Q. And when did you leave the plant?

A. Well, we are supposed to punch out before quarter after.

Q. And did the circulation of this object that you described, take place between a quarter of and a quarter after?   A. That is correct.

Mr. Moore: That is all.

Trial Examiner Whittmore: You are excused. Thank you, Mr. Sundquist.

(Witness excused.)

Mr. Moore: Call Mr. Jolly.

ROY JOLLY

a witness called by and on behalf of the National Labor Relations Board, having been first duly sworn, was examined and [469] testified as follows:

Direct Examination

By Mr. Moore:

Q. Will you please state your name?

A. Roy Jolly.

Q. Are you employed by the Thompson Products Company at the Bell plant?   A. Yes, sir.

Q. How long have you been employed there?

A. Since March of last year.

Q. In what capacity are you employed?

A. As a grinder operator.

Q. Are you a member of the C. I. O.?

A. Yes, sir.

(Testimony of Roy Jolly.)

Q. Have you engaged in any activities in behalf of the C. I. O. in the plant there?

A. Well, in the lunch room I have.

Q. When did you do that?

A. It was during the lunch period on the grave yard shift.

Q. About what day?

A. Oh, it was in the last of June or the 1st of July, I think; I am not sure.

Q. Of this year?   A. Yes, sir.

Q. What did you do?

A. I handed out a couple of cards to a couple of fellows [470] in the lunch room.

Q. Do you recall their names?

A. I do not. One of the fellows 1 know his given name but I don't recall his last name—surname.

Q. Did you have a conversation with any one connected with the management after doing that?

A. Yes, the next night.

Q. With whom was what?

A. Otto, the foreman. I don't remember his last name.

Q. His first name is Otto?   A. Yes, sir.

Trial Examiner Whittemore: What department is he foreman of?

The Witness: Well, he is a foreman in the whole shop, I suppose, on the third shift, the grave yard shift.

Q. (By Mr. Moore) May we go off the record—

(Testimony of Roy Jolly.)

Trial Examiner Whittemore: Discussion off the record.

(Discussion off the record.)

Trial Examiner Whittemore: On the record.

Q. (By Mr. Moore) Was the man to whom you spoke named Otto Guenzler?

A. Yes, I believe so.

Q. Where were you at the time?

A. I was working at my machine.

Q. Was any one beside you and he present? [471]

A. No, I believe not—not there at the machine.

Q. What conversation did you have with him?

A. Well, he came and told me that the company was paying me for eight hours work on that shift and they expected me to give my time on that particular shift, and they didn't want any union organizing going on while I was working.

Q. Did he say—well, go ahead and complete the conversation.

A. Well, I told him that I hadn't been organizing any and he said that the night before in the lunch room that I had passed out a couple of cards and I told him, yes, but I thought that was my own time—that I thought the lunch period belonged to the men, and he said it wasn't—that the company was paying for it and they expected it and they wouldn't have any more of it.

Q. Did you notice any bulletin posted after that by the company?

(Testimony of Roy Jolly.)

A. Yes. The next night or two I noticed a bulletin on the bulletin board. There was a notice— I don't remember the wording of it but it was something or other to that effect.

Q. Now, about when was it posted?

A. Well, it was either the next night after that or the next one. I don't remember. It was one of the two nights I am pretty sure.

Q. And what was the substance of the notice? [472]

A. Well, it said that—I don't remember just what it was, but anyway it carried the meaning that they wanted us to give our whole time on that shift to our job and they didn't want any other private business or anything else going on while we was in the lunch room.

Mr. Moore: May I request now that that notice be produced?

Mr. Watkins: Oh, it is going to be produced, Mr. Moore, whether you request it or not.

Mr. Moore: Will you produce it?

Mr. Watkins: I can't produce it right now.

Mr. Moore: I mean at some subsequent time.

Mr. Watkins: You bet your life.

Mr. Moore: That is all.

Cross Examination

By Mr. Watkins:

Q. On the shift that you were working at the time you mentioned about the lunch room incident, your lunch time is paid for by the company, is it not?   A. Yes, sir.

(Testimony of Roy Jolly.)

Q. When did you join the C. I. O.?

A. It was, I think,—it was May probably.

Q. 1942?   A. Yes, sir.

Q. Did you ever belong to the C. I. O. before?

A. No, sir. [473]

Q. Any other union before?

A. No, sir. I belonged to the P. & P. W. A.

Q. Had you resigned from it?

A. Well, I hadn't resigned; I just quit paying dues.

Q. Did you ever resign from the P. & P. W. A.?

A. No, I never.

Q. Did you start to wear your button as soon as you joined the C. I. O.?   A. Yes, sir.

Q. And still wear it?   A. Yes, sir.

Q. Mr. Jolly, since May of 1942, you have been moved up—your job has been moved into a higher rate of pay?   A. Well, yes, it has.

Mr. Watkins: That is all.

Trial Examiner Whittemore: Mr. Baldwin, any questions?

Mr. Baldwin: Just one question.

Q. (By Mr. Baldwin) Did you at any time on a grave yard shift ask the girl in the time booth to join the C. I. O.?   A. I don't think so.

Q. Did you observe anyone else asking her to join the C. I. O.?   A. No, sir.

Mr. Baldwin: That is all.

Trial Examiner Whittemore: Mr. Moore?

Mr. Moore: Yes. [474]

(Testimony of Roy Jolly.)

Redirect Examination

By Mr. Moore:

Q. Are you required to spend your lunch hour on the grave yard shift at your machine?

A. No, sir.

Q. Where do you spend it?

A. In the lunch room.

Q. Have you observed the men engaging in discussions in the lunch room?   A. Yes.

Mr. Moore: That is all. [475]

GEORGE T. OVERLANDER

a witness called by and on behalf of the National Labor Relations Board, having been first duly sworn, was examined and testified as follows:

Direct Examination

By Mr. Moore:

Q. Will you state your full name, please?

A. George T. Overlander.

Q. Have you been employed by the Thompson Products, Incorporated, at their plant at Bell, California?   A. Yes, sir.

Q. When were you so employed?

A. From December 2, 1940 to May, I believe it was, May 23, 1942.

Q. In what capacity were you employed?

A. I was employed as a tool crib attendant.

Q. During the entire time?

(Testimony of George T. Overlander.)

A.   No.   I was for one week on inspection.

Mr. Watkins: I didn't understand when the witness left their employment.

Mr. Moore: May 23, 1942, about, he said.

Q.   (By Mr. Moore)   Did you apply for work there shortly [478] before you went to work in December 1940?   A.   Yes, sir.

Q.   By whom were you interviewed in connection with your application?

A.   Mr. Millman and Mr. Kearns.

Q.   Where did that interview take place?

A.   In the personnel office, in Mr. Kearns' office.

Q.   Were you interviewed separately by them?

A.   Yes, sir.

Q.   By whom were you interviewed first?

A.   Mr. Millman.

Q.   And where did that interview take place?

A.   In Mr. Millman's office.

Q.   And about what time was it?

A.   I believe it was around 10 o'clock in the morning.

Q.   Do you know the date of that?

A.   (No response.)

Q.   When was it with respect to the time you went to work?

A.   Well, it was—I would say it was Friday before I went to work on Monday.

Q.   And who was there?   Was any one there besides you and he?   A.   No.

Q.   What conversation did you and he have at that time?

(Testimony of George T. Overlander.)

A. Well, it all related to——

Q. Just repeat as nearly as you can the conversation you and [479] he had?

A. Well, he asked me to make out an application, which I did, and then we talked over the type of work I had been doing previously, and he asked me if I was affiliated with any union and I told him I had been a member of the Teamsters' Local. He asked me if I was still an active member and I told him, "No, sir."

He told me that they had a local in there, in their shop there that they had very friendly relations with in the past and hoped to continue, and we talked about the trouble that had been taking place out at the Vultee plant.

Q. Well, now, will you repeat what was said about that trouble?

A. Well, as near as I can remember, I think that there was something mentioned to the effect that the boys had lost a lot more than they were going to gain, or something like that.

Q. That was mentioned by whom?

A. I think that was mentioned by both of us.

Q. Continue and give us the remainder of the conversation.

A. Well, I believe at that time that I was asked then to wait and see Mr. Kearns, and I believe that was all.

Q. Was it indicated what was meant when you were discussing the trouble at Vultee, as you said?

A. Well, my impression of that was——

(Testimony of George T. Overlander.)

Mr. Watkins: Just a minute. I object to the witness [480] testifying to what his impression was, if any.

Trial Examiner Whittemore: I will overrule the objection.

Q. (By Mr. Moore) Go ahead.

A. Well, I don't know but it seems like the union activities out there was strongly against the men or something to that effect; I don't know. I got the impression that Thompson's was more or less in favor of not having an outside union in there—in the plant at that time.

Mr. Watkins: If the Examiner please, I move the answer be stricken as a conclusion of the witness and not in any way a statement of fact rebuttable by the respondent.

Trial Examiner Whittemore: Well, is your impression based upon what you have told us that Millman said to you?

The Witness: Well, yes, I gathered that, yes, sir.

Mr. Watkins: Mr. Examiner, I submit that the witness is apparently able to testify to things that were stated in that meeting. Now, what his impression was may be one thing and what was stated at the meeting may be something entirely different.

Trial Examiner Whittemore: On the contrary, I think a man's impression is quite important; what effect it had upon him. He stated what Millman said. He asked him if he belonged to a union and

(Testimony of George T. Overlander.)
the witness told him that he did not, and then' he
told him he had a union in the shop that he liked
very well, and I think he testified that he based his
impression upon [481] what Millman told him.

Now, if Millman didn't tell him that, you can
bring him in and say he didn't. [482]

Q. (By Mr. Moore) Did you terminate your connection with the Alliance?   A. Yes, sir.

Q. When? [493]

A. In February, I believe.

Q. Who was president of the Alliance at that
time?   A. Mr. Baldwin.

Q. Who had been president immediately preceding Mr. Baldwin coming into office?

A. Mr. Hess.

Q. How did Mr. Hess go out of office?

A. He resigned.

Q. Do you know whether or not his resignation
was brought to the attention of the management?

A. Yes, sir.

Q. Who brought it to their attention?

A. I did.

Q. Whom connected with management did you
tell?   A. Mr. Hileman.

Q. Did you have a conversation with him at the
time you told him that?   A. Yes, sir.

Q. When was that conversation?

A. (No answer.)

Q. Let me ask you, was it while you were still
an executive council member?   A. Yes, sir.

Q. About what date?

(Testimony of George T. Overlander.)

A. It was in February. I don't remember the exact date. [494]

Q. Of 1942?   A. Yes, sir.

Q. Where was the conversation?

A. In Mr. Hileman's office.

Q. And who was there?

A. Mr. Hileman and myself.

Q. What was said on that occasion?   ·

A. Well, I went into Mr. Hileman's office and told him that he always said if any of us had any thing on our chest, to come in and get it off. I told him that Mr. Hess had resigned from the union and felt that he should know it.

He acted surprised that Mr. Hess would do such a thing.

Mr. Watkins: What is that? Pardon me, what was the statement the witness last made?

(Answer read.)

The Witness: He acted rather surprised that Mr. Hess should——

Mr. Watkins: Well, what did he say?

The Witness: Well, he said he didn't know why Mr. Hess would want to resign; that he was doing an awfully good job and he hated to see him resign from the union; that he had recently give him quite a build up to the Society of Automotive Engineers, or some magazine that they put out or paper or something like that, and we talked on who we should put in there as president, and he wanted to know how long I had [495] been there. He said:

(Testimony of George T. Overlander.)

"You have been here about four years, haven't you?"

And I said, "No, I haven't been here two years yet."

Mr. Watkins: Just a moment. I would like to interrupt the witness long enough, Mr. Examiner, to have stricken the portion of his answer relating to "whom we should put in as president" as a conclusion of the witness, and get the conversation because I can readily see that is quite an important bit of testimony the witness has just given, and I think we should be entitled to what was stated in that regard.

Trial Examiner Whittemore: I will deny the motion to strike, but I will ask the witness to state what was said about that and by whom.

That is, did you make some statement and did Mr. Hileman make some reply or did Mr. Hileman make a statement and you make a reply?

The Witness: Mr. Hileman asked me who was present and—asked me who was president and I said that we hadn't elected a president.

Trial Examiner Whittemore: Now, will you try to do that throughout your conversation? You see that permits them to know who you are referring to when you say "we talked about it."

The Witness: Yes, sir.

Trial Examiner Whittemore: Then he knows it was Mr. [496] Hileman who made this statement.

The Witness: Yes, sir.

Trial Examiner Whittemore: If you will try in

(Testimony of George T. Overlander.)
going over these conversations to give the individuals who make the statements.

The Witness: Let me see where I was.

Mr. Moore: Will you read the answer, please?
(Answer read.)

The Witness: Mr. Hileman then said that Mr. Baldwin had only "been here a short time," and he said he thought, "we should have an older man," and he wanted to know about Mr. Osborne.

Q. (By Mr. Moore) Did he ask you that?

A. Yes. He said—and I said, "Well, Mr. Osborne, Mr. Osborne didn't want to be president of the Alliance," and then he asked me what the boys had against Mr. Fickle.

Q. Meaning whom?　　A. Mr. Ed Fickle.

Q. Did he say who he meant?

A. He said, "What did the boys in the shop have against Mr. Fickle," and I said, "I didn't know," and then he told me to let him give the matter some consideration and he would see me later.

I thanked him and left his office.

Q. Did he later call you? [497]　　A. No.

Q. You testified in that conversation that Mr. Hileman said something about you needing an older man. Did he indicate what he meant when he said, "an older man"?

A. Well, he meant a man that had been with the company for a considerable length of time—I imagine over five years.

Q. He wasn't speaking of the man's age?

(Testimony of George T. Overlander.)

A. No, he wasn't speaking of the man's age.

Trial Examiner Whittemore: Who is Osborne, if you don't mind my interrupting.

The Witness: Mr. Osborne was vice president of the Executive Council at that time.

Q. (By Mr. Moore) What was his full name?

A. Frank. I don't know his initial but it is Frank Osborne.

Mr. Moore: That is all.

Cross Examination

Q. (By Mr. Watkins) Mr. Overlander, how do you spell your name?

A. O-v-e-r-l-a-n-d-e-r.

Q. Did you work at the Aerial Corporation a short time ago?   A. I did.

Q. Were you on the C.I.O. bargaining committee there?   A. No, sir.

Q. You were on a plant committee?

A. No, sir. [498]

Q. At that plant?   A. No, sir.

Q. Did you attend some of the bargaining meetings?   A. No, sir.

Q. You quit Aerial during the bargaining, did you not, with the C.I.O.?   A. Yes, sir.

Q. Because the company wouldn't sign a closed shop agreement with the C.I.O., isn't that correct?

A. No, sir.

Q. I beg your pardon?   A. No, sir.

Q. Going back to this meeting with Mr. Hileman, when did you quit the Alliance—what day?

(Testimony of George T. Overlander.)

A. I believe I handed in my resignation on February 12.

Q. With respect to that date, when did you talk to Mr. Hileman as you related here a moment ago?

A. A few days before that.

Q. A few days before you resigned?

A. Yes, sir.

Q. All right, how did you happen to go in and see him?

A. Well, Mr. Hileman and I talked it over and I thought that I should go in and tell him that Mr. Hess had resigned from the committee.

Q. Incidentally Mr. Hess also worked down at Aerial [499] Corporation with you, didn't he?

A. Yes.

Q. And quit at the same time?   A. Yes.

Q. And also Mr. Victor Kangus?

A. Yes, sir.

Q. Kangus quit at the same time?

A. No; Kangus didn't quit at the same time.

Q. He quit the following day, isn't that correct?   A. No, sir.

Q. How many days after?

A. He quit that night.

Q. All right. Now, going back again to this meeting, how did you happen to go in and see Mr. Hileman and discuss this with him?

A. (No response.)

Q. Was it at Mr. Hess' suggestion?

A. I don't know whether it was Mr. Hess' suggestion or—I believe it was more or less just talked

(Testimony of George T. Overlander.)

over between the two of us and I went in and seen him.

Q. Then it was agreed between you and Hess to do that? A. Yes.

Q. What reason did Mr. Hess give you for suggesting that you go in and talk with him about it?

A. I don't know as he give me any reason. [500]

Q. Did you try to catch him some way?

A. Sir?

Q. Did you try to catch him in some manner?

A. I don't think there was anything to trying to catch anybody.

Q. You don't. All right. Were you delegated to go in and talk to Mr. Hileman about this matter by the union itself, about the Alliance?

A. No, sir.

Q. In other words you and Hess discussed after Hess resigned, the matter, and you decided to go in and talk to Mr. Hileman about it, is that correct?

A. I think we discussed it the day Mr. Hess resigned.

Q. All right. Then what was the first thing you said to Mr. Hileman when you talked to him about it.

A. I said: "Mr. Hileman," after he asked me in his office and offered me a cigar, I told him that any—he said that any time we had anything on our chest that we were welcome to come into his office and get it off our chest.

Q. So you had something on your chest and you wanted to get it off? A. Yes, sir.

(Testimony of George T. Overlander.)

Q. And then what did you say?

A. Well, I told him that I felt that he ought to know that Mr. Hess resigned from the union committee. [501]

Q. Did you tell him why you were telling him that?

A. I don't remember as I told him why. I didn't know there was any reason to tell him why.

Q. Did you tell him that you and Mr. Hess discussed it before you came in there and talked to him about it?   A. No, sir.

Q. Go ahead, what did he say?

A. He said he was sorry to hear that Mr. Hess resigned from the union.

Q. And then what did you say?

A. He went on further and stated that he had give Mr. Hess quite a build up with the Society of Automotive Engineers, or something to the effect, and that he thought Irve was doing a fine job.

Q. When did you join the C.I.O.?

A. I can look and see.

Q. All right, please do.

A. I joined May 1st, 1942.

Q. 1942, May 1st?   A. Yes, sir.

Q. Had you considered resigning from the Alliance some time before you actually did or did you just make up your mind in a hurry that you were going to quit?

A. Well, I had considered resigning, yes.

Q. For several days before you did resign from the Alliance? [502]

(Testimony of George T. Overlander.)

A. For several weeks before I did resign from the Alliance.

Q. I see. And you made up your mind then some time before you resigned that you were going to actually resign from the Alliance?

A. Yes, sir.

Q. But you actually resigned in February 1942?

A. I wouldn't say for sure it was in February. It might have been March or it might have been April, I don't know, but I think it was in February.

Q. And how long before that was it that you talked to Mr. Hileman; how long before that did this conversation that you have been relating occur?

A. Not more than a week.

Q. All right. Now, going back to your conversation, you got to the point where you said he had said he was sorry to see Hess resign because he had given him a good write up in the Automotive Engineers, or something of that kind. What did you say then?

A. I told him that I was sorry that he resigned too; that I thought he should have stayed on.

Q. And then what did you do? Did you say or suggest who he would have for a new president or what?

A. No. Mr. Hileman asked me what I was— something about what I wanted and I told him I would like to have a little advice. [503]

Q. Advice as to who would be the new president?

A. Yes; might have been a new president or just a little advice on the matter.

(Testimony of George T. Overlander.)

Q. That is the advice was limited to who would be the new president of the Alliance; is that correct?   A. That is right.

Q. And you had gone in there after your talk with Hess without consulting with anybody else in the Alliance?

A. I imagine that is right, yes.

Q. Well, is it right?   A. That is right.

Q. Then go ahead with your conversation. You asked for some advice about who would become president of the Alliance, and what did he say to you?

A. He asked how long I had been there. He said: "You have been here about four years, haven't you?"

I said: "No, I haven't been here two years," and he said, "How about Baldwin?" And, he said, "No," he said, "he hasn't been here very long either."

Q. Who said that about Baldwin?

A. Mr. Hileman asked about Mr. Baldwin and then he said, "He hasn't been here very long either."

Then he asked me about Mr. Osborne and I told him that Mr. Osborne said that he didn't want to be president of the committee. And then he asked me what the boys had against [504] Ed Fickle.

Q. Ed Fickle or George Fickle?

A. Ed Fickle.

Q. What did you tell him?

A. I told him that I did not know.

Q. What was next?

(Testimony of George T. Overlander.)

A. Well, he told me to let him think the matter over a day or two and he would see me later.

Q. Then he did not see you later?

A. No, he didn't see me later.

Q. And you didn't go back to him and he didn't come to you?   A. No, sir.

Q. And you resigned from the Alliance in a week after that?   A. Yes, sir.

Q. And that was after considering your resignation from the Alliance for quite some time?

A. Yes.

Q. And having made up your mind you were going to do it?   A. Yes, sir.

Q. What did you do with respect to your conversation with Mr. Hileman that you just related? Did you tell anybody in the Alliance about that?

A. I don't remember whether I did or not.

Q. Did you talk to Hess about it?

A. I think I did. [505]

Q. How soon afterwards?

A. Well, it might have been that day or the next day. I don't remember exactly.

Q. What did Hess say?

A. I don't recall what he said.

Q. You don't recall what you told Hess?

A. I imagine that I told him, Mr. Hess what happened in Mr. Hileman's office.

Q. Did either of you say that "well, don't you think we ought to go back to the Executive Committee and report this to the Executive Committee of the Allance?   A. I don't think so.

(Testimony of George T. Overlander.)

Q. You don't think so. I don't think you did either.

Now, you mentioned while you were on this Executive Committee of attending some meetings, I think, at the plant? A. Yes, sir.

Q. How were those meetings called together?

A. Now, what meetings are you talking about?

Q. Executive Committee meetings you testified to at the plant. I don't mean with management; I mean when you boys talked over matters.

A. I think it was mostly just mouth notification —verbally.

Q. Among yourselves? A. Yes, sir.

Q. And then where would you meet? Some place? [506]

A. We met in the welding room of the plant the first meeting, I think, that we had.

Q. How long did those meetings usually last?

A. Oh, from 45 minutes to an hour. Some times longer than that.

Q. You say they lasted 45 minutes to an hour?

A. I think that first meeting lasted between 45 minutes and an hour.

Q. Can you remember more than one meeting that lasted that long?

A. Oh, I think I can remember another meeting that we had out in the new building. We set there on a bunch of pipes or steel or something like that. It lasted 30 or 45 minutes.

Q. What did you discuss in those meetings?

(Testimony of George T. Overlander.)

A. We discussed what we were doing to have in our contract and what the company might say and how we would combat what they had to say and trying to get ourselves-- trying to get something for ourselves.

Q. And what did you do when you left your work to go there?

A. My work was through when I went there.

Q. Oh, I see, you were not affected that way?

A. No, sir.

Q. You don't know what the other boys did?

A. I don't know what they did.

Q. You mentioned Mr. Little making some comment to you. [507] You were Mr. Little's helper, weren't you?   A. That is right.

Q. And he worked the same kind of machinery-- he worked at the same kind of work you did except you were his helper, is that correct?

A. That is right.

Q. There were times—how many other men were there in the tool crip besides yourself and Mr. Little?   A. Two.

Q. Two in addition to yourself?   A. Yes.

Q. Four all together?

A. Yes. Do you mean on the same shift or do you mean at different times?

Q. Yes, the same shift.

A. No, there was never anyone else in there on the same shift.

Q. Just you and Mr. Little?

A. That is right.

(Testimony of George T. Overlander.)

Q. You mentioned a conversation you had with Mr. Millman prior to the time that you were employed at Thompson Products, Mr. Overlander, and I think you said you told him that you had been a member of the Teamsters' Union?

A. Yes, sir.

Q. In that conversation did you tell Mr. Millman anything about your experiences as a member of the Teamsters' Union? [508]

A. I might have. I don't know. I don't recall.

Q. Let me get it over to you in a little different way. In talking with Mr. Millman about that, did you tell him that you thought the Teamsters' Union had been a good union for you to belong to or a bad union for you to belong to?

A. I don't remember as I told him either way.

Q. You don't remember discussing that with him? A. No, sir.

Q. Now, you were employed by Thompson Products December 2, 1940; is that correct?

A. I believe that is correct.

Q. And you joined the Alliance about the following March of 1941? A. Yes, sir.

Q. Were you asked to join the Alliance by anybody in that intervening period? A. Yes, sir.

Q. Anybody besides Mr. Little?

A. I don't remember whether there was anybody besides Mr. Little or not.

Q. Had Mr. Little asked you to join the Alli-

(Testimony of George T. Overlander.)

ance on more than one occasion than this particular time that you related? A. Yes, sir.

Q. Had he? A. Yes, sir. [509]

Q. How many times prior to that?

A. Oh, I imagine once or twice.

Q. What did you tell him?

A. Well, I asked him if he could show me any reason why I should join?

Q. What did he say?

A. He said that the boys seemed to get along a little better when they belonged to the union.

Q. Did you tell him that you didn't think much of that independent union? A. No, sir.

Q. Well, why did you tell him you didn't want to belong to it? The dues were high, were they?

A. I didn't tell him I didn't want to belong to it.

Q. But you didn't join it after he mentioned it to you the first time or so?

A. I didn't join it right away.

Q. And you didn't tell him why you didn't join it right away? A. No, sir.

Q. After you joined the C.I.O., you gave the date here as, I believe, May 1st, 1942?

A. That is right.

Q. Quite a few of the boys joined at that time?

A. I don't know. There was a few, I guess.

[510]

Q. And did you wear your button at the time?

A. No, sir, I didn't have a button to wear.

Q. You didn't have any C.I.O. button?

(Testimony of George T. Overlander.)

A.   No, sir.

Q.   You never did wear your button to the plant?   A.   (No response)

Q.   Your C.I.O. button?

A.   I don't remember whether I did or not.

Q.   Did Mr. Little know that you joined the C.I.O.?

A.   I believe he did.   He wasn't working in the tool crib at that time, incidentally.

Q.   Who first talked to you about joining the C.I.O.?

A.   I believe Elmer Smith was the first man that talked to me about joining the C.I.O.

Q.   About how early or how long before this date of May 1st, 1942?

A.   Well, it was at the time when Mr. Smith resigned from the union—the Executive Council.

Q.   Where did you talk to him about that?

A.   I believe it was outside of the plant in the parking lot that evening after he resigned.   He resigned in the wash room, I believe, and we walked out of the plant together and he told me he was either going to join or had already joined the C.I.O., and wanted me to join too.

Q.   And what did you say? [511]

A.   I told him I didn't know; I would have to think it over.   I wanted to see what their policy was and what the lay out of the deal was.   I didn't want to stick my neck into anything I didn't investigate first.

Q.   How long after that did you join the C.I.O.?

(Testimony of George T. Overlander.)

A. Well, I joined the C.I.O. the first day of May 1942.

Q. How long was this after your conversation with Mr. Smith—that is Mr. Elmer Smith, isn't it?

A. Yes, sir. I don't know. It might have been a month or two months.

Q. Did he or anybody else talk to you further about it after that?

A. He or anybody else?

Q. Yes.　　A. About joining the C.I.O.?

Q. Yes.　　A. (No answer)

Q. That is before you finally joined. There were several of them talking to you about it before you finally joined?　　A. Yes, sir.

Q. Can you remember when the next conversation took place about it?

A. Yes, sir, I believe I can.

Q. About how long after this Smith conversation?

A. I don't know. It was possibly a month or month and a half. [512]

Q. Where was that?

A. It was in Mr. Hess' home.

Q. In Mr. Hess' home?　　A. Yes, sir.

Q. All right. When was the next conversation?

A. I don't know just when it was— I don't remember.

Q. Nobody ever talked to you about it down at the plant?

(Testimony of George T. Overlander.)

A. No, other than at the lunch room. Everybody talked about it there.

Q. There was quite a bit of talk about it at the lunch room?   A. Yes, sir.

Q. But never at your machine?

A. No, I don't believe there was any talk about the C.I.O. other than just—other than discussion— I don't believe there was any talk about joining any C.I.O. at the tool crib.

Mr. Watkins: I think that is all.

Trial Examiner Whittemore: Mr. Baldwin?

Mr. Baldwin: I would like to ask a few questions.

Q. (By Mr. Baldwin) At the time Mr. Hess resigned from the Alliance, did he ask you to resign also?   A. No.

Q. He didn't ask you to resign at that time?

A. No.

Q. You mentioned that Mr. Smith called the Labor Board.   Could it have been the United States Conciliator—— [513]

Trial Examiner Whittemore: Just a moment, perhaps——

Mr. Moore: Just a minute, that he been——

Trial Examiner Whittemore: Perhaps you don't understand that whole matter has been stricken out, so it is unnecessary to go into that.

Mr. Baldwin: I am sorry.

Q. (By Mr. Baldwin) At about this time did you know of any trouble between Mr. Smith and Mr. Hess?

(Testimony of George T. Overlander.)

A. I believe there was something said about it. I didn't know of anything about it. They had a little argument or something.

Q. Did Mr. Smith accuse Mr. Hess of offering to sell out to the C.I.O. for $1,000?

A. I don't know whether he did or whether he didn't. I heard he did.

Q. Mr. Hess never talked to you about it?

A. No, Mr. Hess never mentioned it.

Q. Did you repeat the conversation that you had with Mr. Hileman—did you repeat that to any of the Alliance committee afterwards?

A. I don't think so.

Mr. Watkins: May I have the question read?

(Question and answer read.)

The Witness: I don't think so.

Mr. Baldwin: That is all. [514]

———

LESTER SYLVESTER MOSES BEBB

a witness called by and on behalf of the National Labor Relations Board, having been first duly sworn, was examined and testified as follows:

Direct Examination

Q. (By Mr. Moore) Will you state your full name, please?

A. Lester Sylvester Moses Bebb.

Q. Are you employed by Thompson Products, Incorporated?   A. Yes, sir. [515]

(Testimony of Lester Sylvester Moses Bebb.)

Q. Since when?   A. Since March 1933.

Q. That is by Thompson Products, Incorporated, and the organization that it took over?

A. That is right.

Q. In what capacity are you employed?

A. Leadman in the welding department.

Q. Are you acquainted with the Pacific Motors Parts Workers Alliance?   A. Yes, sir.

Q. Are you a member of that organization?

A. Yes, sir.

Q. Do you have any part or did you have any part in organizing that Alliance?

A. In a way, yes.

Q. When was the first meeting of employees held that you remember, looking toward organization of that Alliance?

A. It was some time in the latter part of July 1937.

Q. And where was it held?

A. At the electric shop in Maywood.

Q. About how many employees were present there?

A. Well, offhand I would say there was about 45 or 50.

Q. How was that meeting announced?

A. By individual contacts. One individual would tell another and another would tell another on through the shop. [516]

Q. In the plant?   A. In the plant.

Q. At the time that meeting took place, had

(Testimony of Lester Sylvester Moses Bebb.)
you passed out—had membership cards been passed
out? A. Not to my knowledge.

Q. Did you pass out any membership cards for
the organization? A. I did.

Q. And where did you pass them out?

A. Outside of the gate of the plant.

Q. Do you recall when that was now?

A. No, I really don't remember whether it was
after our first or second meeting at the electric
shop.

Q. At that first meeting did you have a constitution and by-laws? A. No, sir.

Q. I show you Board's Exhibit 6, and will ask
you if you passed out or if that card is the same
as the ones you passed out, outside of the shop?

A. It is.

Q. You are referring to the printed portion of
the card? A. Yes, sir.

Q. Now, when was the first meeting that you
recall that was held between persons interested in
forming the Alliance and members of the management of the Thompson Products? [517]

A. It was—I don't know the exact date, but it
was a few days after our first meeting at the electric shop.

Q. And where did that meeting take place?

A. In the management's office.

Q. At what time of the day was that?

A. Between 10 and 11 in the morning?

Q. It was in the morning? A. Yes, sir.

Q. You are sure of that?

(Testimony of Lester Sylvester Moses Bebb.)

A. No, I am not sure.

Q. You think it was between 10 and 11 in the morning?   A. That is as I remember it.

Q. Who, for the management, was present?

A. Mr. Livingston, Vic. Kangus, and I am not sure but it seems to me like Mr. Doctor was there.

Q. How many employees attended that meeting?

A. Well, I would say, maybe, 20 or 25,—around 20 or 25.

Q. What was discussed at that meeting?

A. Well, I would say—I believe Mr. Lou Porter made the first statement. He told the management that a group of men—that a group of the employees wanted to ask them if they would accept or recognize an independent union if we organized it. They told us if we could show a majority of the names, why, they would make a consideration and talk it over and see whether they would recognize us. [518]

Q. Who, for the management, made that statement?   A. That I do not remember.

Q. Mr. Lewis A. Porter was spokesman for the employees?   A. Yes, sir.

Q. Do you know whether or not there had been a meeting similar to that before?

A. I do not know of any.

Q. Have you heard that there was?

A. No.

Q. Now, where did you get the cards that you distributed outside of the plant there?

(Testimony of Lester Sylvester Moses Bebb.)

A. That I do not remember. There were—I would say there was eight or ten of us outside of the gate to hand them out but who gave them to us, I don't remember at all.

Q. Who handed them out?

A. That I do not know.

Q. I mean who handed them out to the employees?

A. There was Stubblefield, Mr. Rhine.

Q. Who is that?   Mr. Rhine.

Q. How do you spell it?

A. R-h-i-n-e. And I believe Dean Gardner and myself. And I just can't recall who the others were. There were seven or eight of us that passed them out.

Q. Did Mr. Porter hand any out? [519]

A. No, sir.

Q. Did Mr. Ed Fickle?   A. No, sir.

Q. Did Mr. George Fickle?   A. No, sir.

Q. What did you tell the men at the time you gave them the card?

A. We told them that we were organizing an organization, an independent union, and if they felt they wanted to join and organize, to sign the card and bring it into us later on.

Q. Bring it in to whom, did you tell them?

A. No, we didn't tell them who.

Q. Did you also tell them there was to be a meeting that night?   A. We did.

Q. Now, you passed the cards out and you had

(Testimony of Lester Sylvester Moses Bebb.)

a meeting and then you had this meeting with management, is that correct, or——

A.   That is as I remember it, yes.

Q.   What happened after that?

A.   We had our meeting at the electric shop.

Q.   That was the second meeting?

A.   First meeting.

Q.   Well, now, as I understand your testimony up to now, you passed out the cards and then you had a meeting, is that correct? [520]

A.   Well, I don't remember whether we passed out the cards before the first meeting or after the first meeting.

Q.   And then you had the meeting with the management?   A.   That is right.

Q.   Are you sure that you had a meeting of the employees before you went in to see the management?

A.   That I couldn't recollect just what that was.

Q.   Now, after you had been in to see the management, did you hold another meeting of the employees?   A.   We did.

Q.   Where was that?

A.   At the electric shop in Maywood.

Q.   Mr. Bebb, at the first meeting that you testified about the first meeting of employees, were minutes kept?

A.   I really don't recollect whether they were or not.

Q.   I show you a group of documents here, which Mr. Baldwin says are the minutes of the Pacific

(Testimony of Lester Sylvester Moses Bebb.)
Motor Parts Workers Alliance, and ask you if you can identify the minutes of any particular meeting of which you have testified?

(Handing papers to the witness)

A. This is the minutes of the first meeting.

Q. You indicate the minutes dated July 29, 1937? A. Yes, sir.

Mr. Moore: I will ask that this be marked.

Mr. Baldwin: Mr. Examiner, may a copy be substituted? [521]

Trial Examiner Whittemore: Yes.

(The document referred to was marked as Board's Exhibit No. 14 for identification.)

Q. (By Mr. M o o r e) You have identified Board's Exhibit No. 14 for identification, as the minutes of a meeting. Was that held before the Alliance was formed? A. Yes, sir.

Q. Well, now, how do you fix the time of formation of the Alliance in your own mind?

A. You mean the organization—organizing of it?

Q. Yes.

A. After this meeting Mr. Creek, Mr. Leatherwood and Mr. Fickle and myself went to see an attorney to see about drawing up a constitution.

Q. Now, was any meeting held between July 29, 1937 and August 3, 1939?

A. Yes, I believe there was.

Q. And did you do——

(Testimony of Lester Sylvester Moses Bebb.)

Mr. Watkins: May I have the answer?

(Answer read.)

Q. By Mr. Moore) I am referring to the meeting of the membership of the Alliance?

A. Yes.

Q. If there were—there were, however, no minutes kept, is that true? [522]

A. So far as I know there wasn't.

Mr. Moore: I will offer Board's Exhibit 14 for identification in evidence. You have seen it?

Mr. Watkins: No objection, and there is no objection to a substitution of copy.

Trial Examiner Whittemore: Have you any objection, Mr. Baldwin?

Mr. Baldwin: No objection.

Trial Examiner Whittemore: The document may be received.

(The document referred to, heretofore marked as Board's Exhibit No. 14 for identification, was received in evidence.)

BOARD'S EXHIBIT No. 14

Maywood Hall   July 29, 1937
7:30 P. M.   Maywood

There were forty-two (42) Present at the first meeting. Lester Bebb read parts of the Wagner Act pertaining to forming and joining unions.

The nomination of the constitutional committee came next. The nominees were: James Creek,

(Testimony of Lester Sylvester Moses Bebb.)
Luther Leatherwood, Wayne Kangas, George Fickle and Lester Bebb.

Wayne Kangas declined the nomination, so voted on remaining five. The judges and tellers were: Sam Koop, Wayno Kangas and Ed. Fickle.

Those elected to draw up the constitution were: James Creek, G. M. Fickle, Lester Bebb and Floyd Pfankuck.

These men will get the charter and draw up the Constitution.

There can be no arrangement for payment of dues and initiation fees until the drawing up of *sied* constitution.

The committee decided to elect a chairman for their meeting.

The meeting was adjourned.

(S) DEAN GARDNER

Sec. and Treas.

Q. (By Mr. Moore) Now, after the meeting of July 29, 1937, when was the next meeting that you recall of persons interested in forming the Alliance?

A. I don't recall the exact date but I would say within the next week or seven or eight days after this first meeting.

Q. Can you refresh your recollection by referring to the minutes of meetings that are before you?

(Testimony of Lester Sylvester Moses Bebb.)

A. No. Those were taken after the second meeting.

Q. These minutes were taken after the second meeting?   A. Yes, sir.

Q. Referring to minutes dated August 3, 1937?

A. That is right.

Q. Now, Mr. Bebb——

Mr. Watkins: Just a minute, Mr. Moore. May I have the [523] answer to the last question?

(Question and answer read.)

Q. (By Mr. Moore) What did you do, Mr. Bebb, between the first meeting that you have testified to and the meeting of August 3, 1937? What did you do with reference to the formation of the Alliance?   A. I did nothing, sir.

Q. Was a constitution drawn up during that period?   A. Yes, sir, it was.

Q. Did you have any part in having that done?

A. Yes, I did.

Q. What part did you play in that?

A. Just as a matter of a committee member.

Q. I show you Board's Exhibit 3 and ask you if that is the constitution and by-laws that you assisted in drawing up as a committee member?

A. Yes, sir.

Q. Did you or did the Alliance engage the services of an attorney to assist them in drawing this up?   A. We did.

Q. What attorneys?

A. Schooling and Waytte.

(Testimony of Lester Sylvester Moses Bebb.)

Q. And which members of the firm actively assisted the committee?

A. By "firm" that is—— [524]

Q. The firm of Schooling and Waytte.

A. Mr. Schooling.

Q. What was his name; Wendell Schooling?

A. That is right.

Q. How did you happen to go to him?

A. Just through Mr. Creek said that he heard that Mr. Schooling and Waytte was competent men on labor—drawing up legal papers for the labor organizations and knowing no one else we went to them.

Q. Did he indicate where he heard that?

A. No, sir.

Q. Did Mr. Wendell Schooling draw up the constitution for you? A. He did.

Q. Now, thereafter, did the Alliance enter into collective bargaining with Thompson Products, Incorporated? A. We did.

Q. I show you an original document of which Board's Exhibit 5-A is a copy and I will ask you if the Alliance entered into that contract with Jadson Motor Products Company? A. Yes, sir.

Trial Examiner Whittemore: What is the date of the contract?

Mr. Moore: The document is dated August 12, 1937.

Q. (By Mr. Moore) Were there several meetings between the [525] Executive Council of the

(Testimony of Lester Sylvester Moses Bebb.)
Alliance and the management before that contract was entered into?   A. Into effect?

Q. Before it was signed?   A. Yes, sir.

Q. Going back now to the first meeting that you testified concerning at which employees went in to see the management, you stated that there was some discussion of the possibility of recognizing the union if the men formed one?

A. That is right.

Q. Was anything else discussed then?

A. No, sir.   .

Q. Were raises discussed?

A. Not at that time.

Q. Was seniority discussed?

A. Not at that time.

Q. Were vacations discussed?   A. No, sir.

Mr. Moore: That is all.

Cross Examination

Q. (By Mr. Baldwin) Mr. Bebb, at the time you went to Mr. Schooling, did you present him with a draft of what you wanted as a constitution, or,——

A. Not as I remember. We didn't know just exactly what to do or what to say and he said he would draw one up and let us [526] approve of it and if we wanted any changes made he would re-write it for us.

Q. Were you at one time secretary of the Alliance?   A. Yes, sir.

Q. At any time while you were secretary, do

(Testimony of Lester Sylvester Moses Bebb.)
you know if any of the documents or papers belonging to the Alliance were in the hands of Mr. Hess?   A. Yes, sir.

Q. Do you remember whether you got those papers back or not?

A. They were never returned to me.

Q. At the time of the—do you remember the date of the first meeting in which you went into the management—that is the first group went into the management—that is prior to any—prior to the time that the election of officers, and so forth, took place, when you went in—when the group of twenty or so went in. Do you remember the date of that?

A. No, I do not.

Mr. Baldwin: That is all.

Mr. Watkins: If the Examiner please, I would like to take a few minutes and go over my notes and see what questions I would like to ask Mr. Bebb. By doing that it is possible we can ask what questions we have and let him go back to his work.

Trial Examiner Whittemore: All right, we will take a five minute recess.

(Thereupon, a short recess was taken.) [527]

Q. (By Mr. Watkins) Mr. Bebb, take the period from August 1st, 1937, down to date, have there been any work stoppages of any character so far as you know down at the Thompson Products Corporation, or the Jadson Company?

A. No, sir.

Q. I believe the date on which Thompson Products took over Jadson was approximately April of

(Testimony of Lester Sylvester Moses Bebb.)

1937. Would you just briefly state what the conditions were at the plant at that time among the men—that is what the discussions were and what their attitude was?

A. Their discussions and attitude were that low rates—that their pay rates were way below the outside wages being paid in other places.

At that time rates ranged around from 35 to 55 and 60 cents an hour, and most of the fellows felt that they should be getting more and they were going to do something. They were getting to the restless point where they didn't know just what they were going to do or what they should do.

Q. Had there been some talk around that time among the men of getting an outside union in there or forming a union of their own?

A. That is right.

Q. And prior to that time?   A. Yes, sir.

Q. Have you ever belonged to either of the outside unions or [528] put in an application for them?

A. I put in an application for the A. F. of L.

Q. Was this some time prior to 1937?

A. Yes, sir.

Q. Did quite a few of the other men down there put in similar applications?   A. Yes, sir.

Q. Had there been any discussion among the men around this period that I named, around the early part of 1937, of their feeling toward the A. F. of L.?   A. Yes, sir.

Q. What was the discussion in general?

(Testimony of Lester Sylvester Moses Bebb.)

A. Generally it was they didn't feel like they should be paying such high dues and initiation fees to some one who did not know the working conditions nor the kind of work that we did in that plant.

They felt if they could organize their own union, that they would keep the money in the plant instead of going to some outside organization.

Q. And had the A. F. of L. made any move to assist the men down there who had belonged to it?

A. No, sir.

Q. Do you remember Mr. Ray Livingston first came down to the plant in the early part of 1937?

A. Yes, sir. [529]

Q. Did he talk to you down there?

A. Yes, sir.

Q. Did you see him talk to other men around the plant?   A. Yes, sir.

Q. At their machines?   A. Yes, sir.

Q. What was his conversation with you? Did you talk to him more than once during that time?

A. As I recollect it was just the one time.

Q. What was it, if you can give it as nearly as possible, what did he say to you and what did you say to him?

A. Well, he introduced himself to me and I to him, and we talked about the work and the machinery—the old machinery, and about we were going to have new machinery and just in a general conversation of the work in that plant.

(Testimony of Lester Sylvester Moses Bebb.)

Q. Was anything said by him about unions?

A. No, sir.

Q. Nothing whatsoever?   A. No, sir.

Q. Was anything said by you about unions?

A. No, sir.

Q. In any conversations you had with Mr. Livingston during that period?   A. No, sir.

Q. Or any subsequent period? [530]

A. No, sir.

Q. Now, going to this first meeting that a group of you men had with management, I believe you said there were twenty or more present. I think you said Mr. Porter spoke at that meeting. Did any one else speak besides Mr. Porter from the employees' side?

A. Yes, they did, but I don't recall who that person was.

Q. Were there several people that spoke up during that meeting?   A. Yes, sir.

Q. And as I understood it you testified that the company said they would recognize you if you obtained a majority?   A. Yes, sir.

Q. And did any one from the company say anything to you about not using coercion or not soliciting on company time?

A. I believe they did, yes, sir.

Q. Can you recall who said anything of that kind to you, and what was said?

A. I believe Mr. Livingston told us that himself.

Q. Do you remember about what he said?

(Testimony of Lester Sylvester Moses Bebb.)

A. As nearly as I can remember he stated that no union activities should take place on company property in organizing in any way of labor.

Q. Did he say anything about the men coming in through force or voluntary or anything of that kind? [531]

A. Yes, sir, he said there should be no force according to the Wagner Act, there should be no force on any man to join any organization.

Q. That was in the first meeting that you mentioned of twenty or twenty-five men?

A. Yes, sir.

Q. What did you say about the cards that you passed out at the gate? Did you state you did not recall where you got them? A. That is right.

Q. Do you know whether or not you received them from the employees—some other employee?

A. Yes, sir, I believe it was.

Q. Would you testify, Mr. Bebb, that you did or did not receive them from somebody representing the management?

A. I did not receive any from any representative of the management.

Q. You are certain of that? A. Yes, sir.

Q. Did you receive them from Mr. Porter?

A. No, sir.

Q. Am I correct in this also, Mr. Bebb, that you testified that the day that you passed out the cards you also notified the employees that there would be a meeting that same evening? A. Yes, sir.

(Testimony of Lester Sylvester Moses Bebb.)

Q. And was that the first day you passed out cards? [532]   A. That is as I remember it.

Q. Was that the first day you saw anybody else pass out cards?   A. Yes, sir.

Q. Going back again to this first meeting with the management when some twenty or more employees called on the management, did you see Mr. Lewis Porter get any employees to go into that meeting?   A. No, sir, I did not.

Q. Did he contact you with regard to it?

A. No, sir.

Q. Were you elected chairman of the first meeting that you testified to of the employees, that was held in the electric shop?   A. Yes, sir.

Q. And that was, I believe, July 29th?

A. Yes, sir.

Q. 1937?   A. Yes, sir.

Q. You were elected chairman of that meeting?   A. Yes, sir.

Q. And at that meeting were committees selected by the people there?   A. Yes, sir.

Q. How were those committees selected? [533]

A. They were selected by written ballot.

Q. And what were the committees selected for and what were they supposed to do?

A. Constitutional committee.

Q. To set up a constitution?

A. That is right.

Q. When you went over to Mister—strike that out, please.

Did this constitutional committee have a meeting

(Testimony of Lester Sylvester Moses Bebb.)
of some kind prior to the time you called on Mr.
Schooling?   A. Yes, sir.

Q. What did you do at that meeting; what did
you discuss?

A. We discussed about what articles or agreements or by-laws and so forth, that we might suggest in making up this constitution.

Q. And then when you went to Mr. Schooling,
what did you do? Did you relate to him the things
that you had discussed in that committee meeting?

A. We did.

Q. And did you take any paper or sample of a
constitution or anything of that character with you
to Mr. Schooling?   A. No, sir.

Q. Did Mr. Schooling tell you that he had had
any paper of any kind or any document from anybody else at Jadson to use as a form as a constitution?   A. No, sir. [534]

Mr. Moore: I object to the question. I believe
that the question is leading and I believe for another reason because of the testimony of the witness——

Trial Examiner Whittemore: I will sustain the
objection to the last question.

Mr. Moore: I believe the situation is clear.

Q. (By Mr. Watkins) Mr. Bebb, going back
now to the first meeting of the employees in the
electric shop, of July 29, 1937, do you know whether
or not Mr. Porter was present at that meeting?

A. He was not.

Q. He was not?   A. No, sir.

(Testimony of Lester Sylvester Moses Bebb.)

Q. Then he took no part, of course, in that meeting? A. No, sir.

Q. Do you know whether or not he was present at the second meeting? A. No, sir, he was not.

Q. Was he on any of the committees that were selected by the Alliance? A. No, sir.

Q. Did you or you and your committee make any later visit than this first one that you have mentioned to Mr. Schooling's office? A. We did.

[535]

Q. Before going into those, will you state as briefly as you can what Mr. Schooling said to you when you first came in to meet him?

A. (No response.)

Q. Or what you said to him? Just relate the conversation that took place?

A. Well, as I remember Mr. Creek acted as spokesman for us and I do not recall the conversation that started when we went in.

Q. Well, what was the substance of it?

A. The substance was we wanted him to draw up our constitution and by-laws for our organization.

Q. Did Mr. Schooling talk to you at all about the Wagner Act or the National Labor Relations Act? A. He did.

Q. Along what lines, in substance, did he talk to you?

A. If I remember he drew out a copy of the Wagner Act and read certain parts of it to us, that

(Testimony of Lester Sylvester Moses Bebb.)
would benefit us in drawing up our constitution.

Q. Do you remember what those were?

A. No, sir, I don't.

Q. I believe Mr. Victor Kangus—do you know Mr. Victor Kangus?   A. Yes, sir.

Q. When he testified here said that you at one time joined [536] the C.I.O. Did you ever belong to the C.I.O.?   A. No, sir.

Q. Did you ever tell Mr. Kangus that you belonged to the C.I.O.?   A. No, sir.

Q. That is Mr. Victor Kangus?

A. No, sir.

Q. Did you ever tell Mr. Victor Kangus that you intended to join the C.I.O.?   A. No, sir.

Q. You are positive of all of those statements?

A. Yes, sir.

Q. Have you attended substantially all of the meetings which have taken place between the Executive Committee of the Alliance and the membership?   A. Will you repeat that?

Mr. Watkins: Will you read the question?

(Question read)

The Witness: I have.

Q. (By Mr. Watkins) Do you know whether or not you have attended all of them?

A. No, sir, I have not.

Q. You have attended the major portion of them?   A. Yes, sir.

Q. Have you in any of those meetings ever heard Mr. Hileman [537] make any statements about moving this division back east?

(Testimony of Lester Sylvester Moses Bebb.)

A.   No, sir, not Mr. Hileman.

Q.   Have you heard Mr. Hileman in any of those meetings make any statement, "If the C.I.O. moved into the plant," or, "if the A. F. of L. came into the plant," that, "the plant would be moved back east?"

A.   No, sir.

Q.   Or anything to that end?   A.   No, sir.

Q.   Mr. Bebb, assuming that the company, that is either Jadson or Thompson, had wanted you to form an independent union back in 1937, what would have been your attitude with regard to that independent union?

Mr. Moore: Objected to.

Trial Examiner Whittemore: I will sustain the objection.

Mr. Watkins: Well, Mr. Examiner, I think it is quite pertinent in this connection because what we have here, is statements to the effect that some individual through the management went to these people and got them to set up the independent union, and I think it is quite important to show the attitude of these people, assuming that testimony be correct.

Trial Examiner Whittemore: Well, I ruled on the question.

Q.   (By Mr. Watkins) Did you ever have any conversation, [538] Mr. Bebb, with Mr. Porter with respect to—strike that.

Do you recall any conversation that you had with Mr. Porter with respect to the Alliance?

A.   No, sir.

(Testimony of Lester Sylvester Moses Bebb.)

Q. Did you have any conversation with Mr. Porter in which any statements were made with respect to some document of some character that he had from the company?   A. Yes, sir.

Q. Will you state when that conversation took place?

A. I can't state just when but it has been two times in the last three years.

Q. Where did it take place?

A. In the plant.

Q. At his machine or at your machine?

A. At his machine.

Q. Will you state what was said by Mr. Porter?

A. He stated that he had a letter from Mr. Livingston advising the company how to organize this union—the independent union.

Mr. Watkins: Will you read the answer?

(Answer read.)

Q. (By Mr. Watkins) Did you ask him any further questions about that?

A. No, sir, I did not.

Q. Did he say it was a letter? [539]

A. He said it was a letter.

Q. You are positive of that?   A. Yes, sir.

Q. And it was advising whom how to set up the independent union?

A. The company—Jadson Motor Products.

Q. Did he say how he had gotten hold of such a letter?   A. No, sir, he did not.

Q. Did he say what he was going to do with it?

A. No, sir.

(Testimony of Lester Sylvester Moses Bebb.)

Q. Did he tell you substantially the same story on two different occasions?   A. Yes, sir.

Q. What did you do about it?

A. I just dismissed it from my mind.

Q. Why?

A. Because I know Mr. Porter. He is very radical on any subject that you might talk to him about.

Mr. Moore: Just a moment, I will object to that answer and ask that it be stricken up to this point.

Mr. Watkins: Mr. Examiner, let me state the purpose of my question. The witness testified that this was told him by Mr. Porter, which might be of considerable interest to the witness as one of the members of the Alliance and one of the committee members, and I am asking him why he didn't do any- [540] thing about it.

Trial Examiner Whittemore: Well, I am frank to say that I don't think it means much either way. He says he dismissed it from his mind. It is quite obvious he didn't dismiss it from his mind. You know about it and are asking him questions about it.

Now, I would like to know how you know about it if he dismissed it from his mind back three years ago.

Mr. Watkins: Mr. Examiner, I don't think that is quite a fair statement of the witness' testimony or a fair conclusion to draw from it. I don't care what happens, you may dismiss a thing from your mind at the time but it may come back again at a

(Testimony of Lester Sylvester Moses Bebb.)
later time. It doesn't mean when you dismiss a thing from your mind that there is a blank spot there.

Trial Examiner Whittemore: He says he didn't do anything about it. I would like to know how you know about it.

Mr. Watkins: He told me about it.

Trial Examiner Whittemore: Very apparently he did and very apparently he didn't dismiss it from his mind.

Mr. Watkins: And that is the very point I am arguing with the Examiner on. You can dismiss a thing from your mind and still recall it and tell it to somebody at a later time.

Trial Examiner Whittemore: Go ahead, I don't think it is important anyhow.

The Witness: The reason I dismissed it from my mind is, [541] that I didn't believe Mr. Porter could get a hold of such a letter and I just didn't feel like that he was—if he did have such a letter that he would present it at some time for approval.

Q. (By Mr. Watkins) Now, Mr. Bebb,——

Mr. Watkins: I think that is all, Mr. Examiner.

Mr. Baldwin: Nothing further.

Mr. Watkins: One other question.

Q. (By Mr. Watkins) Was Lewis Porter what you would term a leader in the shop?

A. No, sir, I don't believe I could.

Q. Did he stay mostly to himself?

A. He did.

(Testimony of Lester Sylvester Moses Bebb.)

Mr. Watkins: I think that is all.

The Witness: Mr. Examiner, I would like to make one statement.

Trial Examiner Whittemore: All right.

The Witness: In bringing this case up, I feel personally very deeply that we are in vital war defense work, defending the lives of our men out on the battle field and I really feel that whoever made these charges, either managment or the union, are the largest saboteurs we have in the United States. They are drawing men away from their work, vital defense work.

Trial Examiner Whittemore: What do you mean by that?

The Witness: That all these men who are here are wasting [542] their time while away from their vital defense work. They are losing man hours in putting out our defense equipment that the men need so badly.

Trial Examiner Whittemore: Where did you get that idea?

The Witness: There is only one important thing in this world now and that is to save our country, our homes, our families and the men who are out in the field and I feel things that are of so little importance like this when life and death mean a lot. more than anything else.

Trial Examiner Whittemore: Is that your own personal feeling?

The Witness: It is.

(Testimony of Lester Sylvester Moses Bebb.)

Trial Examiner Whittemore: Did anybody suggest you make this statement when you got up here?

The Witness: No, sir.

Trial Examiner Whittemore: Why do you tell me that?

The Witness: I want it to go into the record, the way I feel about the whole thing or anything else.

Trial Examiner Whittemore: Why do you want it to go into the record? Did you say anything to counsel for the Board when he asked you to come and testify?

The Witness: No, sir, I did not.

Trial Examiner Whittemore: You waited before you got up here before you made the statement on the record?

The Witness: Yes, sir. [543]

Trial Examiner Whittemore: That is all.

Mr. Watkins: Let me say one thing, Mr. Examiner. When I talked to Mr. Bebb, Mr. Bebb told me just the same thing he has told the Examiner.

Trial Examiner Whittemore: And you suggested he put it on the record?

Mr. Watkins: Just a minute and I will make my statement precisely as it happened.

He told me substantially what he said here and wanted to state it in the hearing. I told him that nobody could ask any questions on that but if he wanted to make a statement to go ahead if he wished to do so and if the Examiner stopped him,

(Testimony of Lester Sylvester Moses Bebb.)
why, that would be all there was to it. That is
what took place.

Mr. Baldwin: May I ask the witness one question?

Mr. Watkins: And I might say I agree with
him one hundred percent.

Trial Examiner Whittemore: Well, I think the
answers show something to that effect.

Q. (By Mr. Baldwin) Mr. Bebb, when did you
resign as secretary of the Alliance?

A. In April of 1942.

Q. Why did you resign?

A. I have been studying welding—making welding my life work in order to keep up with the new
work in the welding [544] field, and I decided I
wanted to study a little harder and learn the newer
parts of welding.

Q. Did you make a statement at that time to
any one, that one of your main reasons for resigning was because you were interested in doing war
work and it was taking up too much of your time?

A. I did.

Q. Did you say at that time that the union
wasn't as important as the war going on?

A. I did.

Mr. Moore: I will object to this line of questioning. I will stipulate that he resigned because he
wanted to.

Trial Examiner Whittemore: Why all this?

Mr. Baldwin: I merely want to point out that
I know this man and I know that he is telling the

(Testimony of Lester Sylvester Moses Bebb.)
truth. I want to point out that he made these statements prior to any time he was ever here. [545]

Redirect Examination

Q. (By Mr. Moore) You stated that you were elected chairman at the first meeting. Is that strictly true now or did you just assume that position?

A. No. The majority, the unanimous verbal vote was that I carry open the meeting.

Q. That was decided on the spot by the men?

A. Yes, sir.

Q. Who chose the name of this organization, Mr. Bebb?

A. The constitutional committee.

Q. Chose the name after the cards had been printed? A. Yes, sir.

Q. Who chose the name on the cards?

A. I don't remember that.

Q. Did you know at any time—— [546]

A. I probably knew at that time but I don't remember now.

Q. On the printed cards that you have testified were distributed, was the name "Pacific Parts Workers Alliance"? A. Yes, sir.

Q. On the original constitution which is Board's Exhibit 3, what was the second word in the name that originally appeared at the top of what?

A. I do not know, sir.

Q. Was it Pacific Coast Motor Parts Workers Alliance?

A. I wouldn't say because I don't remember.

(Testimony of Lester Sylvester Moses Bebb.)

Q.   When did the Alliance assume the name that it presently uses?

A.   As I remember it was when the constitution was voted and accepted.

Q.   This word was crossed out, you think, on August 3rd, the day that it was signed?

A.   Yes, sir.

Q.   When I say, "this word" I was referring to the word in the title of Board's Exhibit 3.

Was there any discussion of the August 3rd meeting about a name for the organization?

A.   I believe there was.

Q.   And had the constitutional committee prior to that time, decided on the name "Pacific Coast Motor Parts Workers Alliance"? [547]

A.   I don't know about the "Coast" part. They decided on a name to be presented to the members.

Q.   Well, wasn't that the name that you had drawn up, that you had placed on your constitution and by-laws?   A.   Yes, sir.

Q.   And at the meeting of August 3rd, it was decided to eliminate the word "Coast"?

A.   Whatever that word was. I don't remember the word.

Q.   You stated that Mr. Lewis Porter was not at the first or second meetings that you testified about?   A.   Yes, sir.

Q.   Now, which meetings are you referring to as the first and second meetings?

A.   The first meeting that we called to deter-

(Testimony of Lester Sylvester Moses Bebb.)
mine whether we wanted to organize our independent union.

Q. Is that the one on July 29, 1937, as shown by Board's Exhibit 14?   A. Yes, sir.

Q. That is the first one?   A. Yes, sir.

Q. When was the second one?

A. Approximately, around several days afterwards. I don't know whether it was a week——

Q. Well, was the second one the August 3rd meeting?   A. No, sir. [548]

Q. At which the constitution was adopted?

A. I don't believe it was, sir.

Q. Was Mr. Porter at the meeting at which the constitution was adopted?

A. Not that I remember, sir.

Q. Do you recognize this name appearing on the first page of signatures in Board's Exhibit 3 for identification, as Mr. A. L. Porter's signature?

A. As near as I can remember that is his signature, yes, sir.

Q. You would testify then that he was at the August 3rd meeting?   A. Yes, sir.

Q. What was the substance of the portion of the Wagner Act that Mr. Schooling read to you?

A. I don't remember.

Mr. Moore: That is all.

Recross Examination

Q. (By Mr. Watkins) Mr. Bebb, referring to Board's Exhibit 3, which is the constitution of

(Testimony of Lester Sylvester Moses Bebb.)
the Pacific Motor Parts Workers Alliance, at the end thereof are a lot of signatures. Do you know whether or not all of those signatures were obtained at the meeting that you have just mentioned?   A. I believe they were, sir.

Q. In other words, you believe that they were all obtained there and not some of them written in at a later time? [549]

A. No, sir; they were at that meeting.

Q. In other words, if any one signed this he would for certain have been at that particular meeting?   A. Yes, sir.

Mr. Watkins: That is all.

Trial Examiner Whittemore: Were you a leadman in 1937?

The Witness: No, sir.

Trial Examiner Whittemore: At the time this was organized?

The Witness: No, sir.

Trial Examiner Whittemore: How long have you been a leadman?

The Witness: Since—I don't recall whether it was June or July of this year.

Trial Examiner Whittemore: Now, with respect to this: Who gave you the cards? Do you still testify that you don't know?

The Witness: Yes, sir.

Trial Examiner Whittemore: What individual gave them to you?

The Witness: I don't know.

Trial Examiner Whittemore: You have no idea?

(Testimony of Lester Sylvester Moses Bebb.)

The Witness: No, sir.

Trial Examiner Whittemore: Well, then, how do you know that it may not have been a member of management instead of an employee, as you testified to Mr. Watkins' question? [550]

The Witness: Because I did know the management well enough that if they had given them to me I would have remembered.

Trial Examiner Whittemore: All right, any further questions, Mr. Watkins?

Mr. Watkins: Nothing more.

Trial Examiner Whittemore: You are excused.

(Witness excused.)

Mr. Moore: At this time I offer in evidence a certified copy of the decision of the National Labor Relations Board in Case No. C-1848, entitled, "In the matter of Thompson Products, Incorporated, and United Automobile Workers of America, Local 300, C.I.O."

Mr. Watkins: If the Court please, we will object to the introduction of such a document into evidence in this case.

If the Board wishes to take judicial notice of its own decision, of course, that is something else and I assume that it would, but as far as evidence in this case is concerned, I don't see how it can be received.

Trial Examiner Whittemore: I would like to know the purpose of the offer.

Mr. Moore: To show that just before the Alliance was formed out here, a similar organization was formed in the Cleveland plant of the respondent and the Board made certain findings with reference to actions of the respondent and [551] through the same official who was alleged to have been active in this.

Trial Examiner Whittemore: Mr. Livingston was also involved in that case?

Mr. Moore: Yes.

Mr. Watkins: My point, Mr. Examiner, is this: That it isn't proper in this case as evidence. I see no reason why the Board as such cannot take judicial notice of its own decisions, but I don't see how the Board, a decision of the Board of this character could be received as evidence in this case and we object to it on that ground.

Trial Examiner Whittemore: Well, the objection is overruled and the document is received.

Mr. Moore: That concludes my presentation of evidence except with respect to certain documents which the respondent has produced and which the respondent received only Saturday and I believe hasn't had an opportunity to examine completely.

Trial Examiner Whittemore: Before we leave this, Mr. Moore, am I correct in saying there has been a court decision with respect to this?

Mr. Moore: There has been.

Trial Examiner Whittemore: Was the Board affirmed?

Mr. Moore: I think a general cease and desist order was taken out. [552]

Mr. Watkins: As a matter of fact one of the

statements inadvertently made by Mr. Moore was in error. He said:

> "A union of this kind was formed at the same time."

That is not the fact because there was a union there for many years. There was a reformation of a union that is true, but there had been an independent union there for years prior to that.

Mr. Moore: That is true.

Mr. Watkins: And this case has gone to the Sixth Circuit and the Sixth Circuit decision is down on it.

Trial Examiner Whittemore: Has been issued?

Mr. Watkins: Yes.

Trial Examiner Whittemore: That is what I was thinking. Did the Circuit Court decision reverse the findings of the Board?

Mr. Moore: None of the findings of fact were reversed but the order was modified.

Trial Examiner Whittemore: The order may have been modified, but I am simply questioning the matter of facts. Do you have the Circuit Court decision here?

Mr. Moore: I don't have it here and I would prefer to answer your question after the noon recess. I have read the decision but I would like to look at it again before I state definitely what it is.

Trial Examiner Whittemore: Check on that point and it [553] might be well to simply add the Circuit Court decision to this. If you are going to put one in I suppose you might have the other.

I don't know what happened to the case. Do **you** know, Mr. Watkins?

Mr. Watkins: No, I do not.

Trial Examiner Whittemore: Do you know whether the company has applied for a writ of certiorari?

Mr. Watkins: The order was complied with. Of course, I think, Mr. Examiner, the order as modified, as accepted—I think if anything is to go into this case, but for the life of me I don't see how this can be in here as an evidentiary exhibit. I think the Circuit Court decision is what should be in here rather than the Board's decision.

Trial Examiner Whittemore: I don't know, not having recently seen the Circuit Court decision. It might be that it is only a short decision. Some Circuit Court decisions are merely two or three sentences affirming the Board, in which case certain findings might be relevant, assuming Mr. Moore is correct in his statement that Mr. Livingston, who is involved in this case was also involved, let us say, involved in similar circumstances in the other case.

In that event I think it might be pertinent. Now, I don't know, but I do know that it would be well to have the Circuit Court decision here.

Mr. Watkins: Mr. Examiner, here is the difficult [554] situation this puts us in. In other words you put in here or the Board has introduced in here a copy of a Board decision in another case as evidence.

Trial Examiner Whittemore: Yes.

Mr. Watkins: Now, the position that puts us in is that we have to try to combat what is in there. In other words we would have to come in and show we have an A. F. of L. contract—we had one of the original C. I. O. contracts with this same union in Detroit. There are many facts of that kind and matters handled by Mr. Livingston that certainly should be in if a thing of this kind is in the record.

It makes it almost impossible for us to meet and we have enough of a problem, obviously, when this thing has come in in such fashion in trying to meet it.

Trial Examiner Whittemore: I think there is some justification in raising that point. Of course, if the Circuit Court case has approved the Board's findings, that is a settled matter and you couldn't question any finding of fact. If there have been modifications or a reversal of some of the Board's findings, certainly, I don't want to be put in the position of making a finding on something the Circuit Court has reversed and the Board has taken no-appeal from.

Let us say, for example, that the Board found 8(1) and the Circuit Court had reversed the Board and found it was not 8(1). If I don't have the Circuit Court opinion before me, [555] I don't want to base any finding on the basis of the Board's findings which have been reversed, and from which the Board has not appealed. That is why I would like to have the whole history here of the Board and the Court's decision, but I do think in fairness to you :that Mr. Moore should point out those sections in the Board's order as well as the Circuit Court decision, which he believes should be considered in this particular case and not just simply toss the whole business in and leave it up to the Trial Examiner to use his judgment, because in that respect the respondent's counsel doesn't know what I may do until after I have issued an intermediate report but I do feel you should go over it and point out the matters in the Board's decision, if it was affirmed and if no findings were altered by the Circuit Court, those parts which you want me to take notice of.

Mr. Moore: I will be glad to do that.

Trial Examiner Whittemore: And then counsel will know what he will have to meet, if anything.

Now, if you point out things that the Board has found the company has complied with, why, I don't see that there is much you can do to alter the findings on which they base their action.

Mr. Watkins: Mr. Examiner, my point is perhaps a ·little different than the Examiner has expressed himself.

My point is that this proffered exhibit is in there as [556] evidence in the case. Now, if it is in there as evidence, we are put in the position of having to refute or answer this. I am not talking about the ultimate findings. I am talking about facts, statements which always appear in those cases.

Now, in order to do that—in other words that was a case that occurred in Cleveland and this is a case that occurred on the West Coast.

Now, if the Board is trying to say this company has done this, that or the other thing in many other places and therefore is likely to do it here, and uses it in that respect, then we have the burden of saying here that in Seattle we have a contract with the A. F. of L., and in Detroit with the C. I. O. and in other places with other organizations.

In other words we have to go through that process to disabuse or disillusion somebody on the things that are found in this decision so far as it has bearing on this case here.

Trial Examiner Whittemore: I think you will agree, Mr. Watkins, you have had sufficient experience in these Labor Board cases to realize that even though the company had ten contracts with the C. I. O. or the A. F. of L., and if it had set up two company dominated unions, the mere fact that the percentage was ten to two, wouldn't alter the situation, that there was an unfair labor practice in setting up the two company dominated unions. [557]

The point is this: Let us assume that there was a company dominated union set up in Cleveland; that that matter has been settled, and that this particular case is with reference to the second company dominated union.

Now, it wouldn't, so far as I can see, alter the consideration of the facts in this case because you happened to have contracts with some other unions.

The Board may have brought that evidence in

in the other case and the Board still found that this case in Cleveland, under this assumption, was a company dominated union.

Mr. Watkins: But the whole point as I see it is, we are dealing with a situation out on the West Coast. All the facts occurred on the West Coast, all the actions occurred on the West Coast in this plant.

Now, what the Board is doing is seeking to introduce as evidence a Board decision involving the Cleveland plant. The purpose of that must be to say:

"Well, all right, they did something wrong in Cleveland, therefore, they must have done something wrong in Los Angeles."

My whole point, Mr. Examiner, is that if it is going in as evidence in this case, then what we will have to do to defend ourselves, will be to bring in evidence that up in Seattle we did such and such a thing and in Detroit something else. [558]

Trial Examiner Whittemore: I think I see your point on that. That is, if the inference might be drawn that because it was done in the Cleveland plant, it may have been done here and then you would have a right to show there were ten other places where you didn't have a company dominated union. I think you are correct in that respect.

Mr. Watkins: I don't see why the Board needs in this case as evidence a Board decision. The Board can take judicial notice of its own decisions and why it has to come in here, I don't understand.

Trial Examiner Whittemore: I can assure you despite the particular finding, if there is no evidence of company domination in this case, even though it was done in Cleveland, it will not alter my decision.

Mr. Watkins: Then I don't see the purpose of having it in there as evidence. I don't care if the Board takes judicial notice of its own decisions, that is something the Board is entitled to do, but when it is put in this case as evidence, then it is something we have to meet.

Trial Examiner Whittemore: Well, I think that the best way, since we do not know exactly what Mr. Moore is pointing at the present moment, perhaps both of you better forget any further discussion of it until Mr. Moore has an opportunity to let you know the points which he feels are pertinent to the issues in this case and then we can take up that matter when [559] it is finally determined.

Mr. Watkins: I might say this, Mr. Examiner, I believe I had a similar situation before and what the Board did in that case, and I don't mean, Mr. Moore, this pattern must be followed as common practice, but the Board said in those cases, "I wish to direct the Trial Examiner's attention to such and such a decision by the Board, involving such and such a company in such and such a place."

Trial Examiner Whittemore: You are quite right and that is what I am trying to get Mr. Moore to do, point out what the findings were in this particular case which are pertinent here. Now, you are right that I could take judicial notice of that decision without saying anything to you about it, but it is simply for the convenience of having it all in the record and I think perhaps in fairness to you, you should point out now before me the points that you feel are relevant to these issues here.

Mr. Watkins: Mr. Examiner, if you can tell me how I, in Los Angeles, dealing with the West Coast plant and knowing not one thing about that case, except from the Circuit Court of Appeals decision, which I read, and tell me how I can tell the Examiner what it is all about, I would like to know it.

If we expect to get through this case by Thursday we have got to move along and we certainly wouldn't do it if we have to fuss about this thing.

[560]

Trial Examiner Whittemore: Well, the document is in evidence, which is merely a formal matter, inasmuch as it is before me any way, being a Board decision, but I do feel it would be well if Mr. Moore, and not you, pointed out the parts which he feels are relevant and, also, I think if you can get a hold of an extra copy of the Circuit Court decision, you might also have that.

It would be somewhat more convenient for me to have the decision than to have to hunt it up when I get back to Washington.

Mr. Watkins: All I want to know is for the purpose of expediency. I would like to know what is ahead of us and if we are going to have to meet the various issues that are set forth in the Board's findings and the various findings that are in the decision.

If it goes in in that manner, it will entail considerable trouble for me; if we don't have to meet those, if the Board is just simply going to take judicial notice of it, all right, then I don't have to do anything about it.

Trial Examiner Whittemore: The point is you have conceded the Board has a perfect right to take judicial notice of it.

Mr. Watkins: I don't think I have conceded anything.

I said I would assume that the Board has a right to take judicial notice of its own decisions. [561]

Trial Examiner Whittemore: It is either an assumption or concession. You admit that we have a perfect right to take judicial notice of the Board's decisions?

Mr. Watkins: Don't put words in my mouth again. I still didn't admit it.

Trial Examiner Whittemore: I say it is now a question as to the difference between an assumption and a concession. [562]

BOARD'S EXHIBIT No. 15

United States of America
National Labor Relations Board

I, Beatrice M. Stern, Executive Secretary of the National Labor Relations Board, and official cus-

Board's Exhibit No. 15—(Continued)
todian of its records, do hereby certify that attached is a full, true, and complete copy of:

DECISION AND ORDER IN THE MATTER
  OF: THOMPSON PRODUCTS, INC., AND
  UNITED AUTOMOBILE WORKERS OF
  AMERICA, LOCAL 300 (CIO).

Case No. C-1848

In Witness Whereof, I have hereunto subscribed
my name and caused the seal of the National Labor
Relations Board to be affixed this 22nd day of September, A. D. 1942, at Washington, D. C.

[Seal]   BEATRICE M. STERN,
                    Executive Secretary.

———

United States of America

Before the National Labor Relations Board

Case No. C-1848

In the Matter of

THOMPSON PRODUCTS, INC.

and

UNITED   AUTOMOBILE   WORKERS   OF
  AMERICA, LOCAL 300 (CIO).

Mr. Max W. Johnstone,
    for the Board.

Board's Exhibit No. 15—(Continued)

Stanley & Smoyer,

>by Messrs Harry E. Smoyer and Frank Emerson,
>
>>of Cleveland, Ohio,
>>
>>>for the respondent.

Mr. M. A. Roemisch,

>of Cleveland, Ohio,
>
>>for the Alliance.

Mr. Sidney L. Davis,

>of counsel to the Board.

DECISION AND ORDER

Statement of the Case

Upon an amended charge duly filed on October 22, 1940, by United Automobile Workers of America, Local 300 (CIO), herein called the Union, the National Labor Relations Board, herein called the Board, by the Regional Director for the Eighth Region (Cleveland, Ohio), issued its complaint dated October 23, 1940, against Thompson Products, Inc., Cleveland, Ohio, herein called the respondent, alleging that the respondent had engaged in and was engaging in unfair labor practices affecting commerce, within the meaning of Section 8 (1) and (2) and Section 2 (6) and (7) of the National Labor Relations Act, 49 Stat. 449, herein called the Act. Copies of the complaint accompanied by notices of hearing were duly served upon the respondent, the Union, Thompson Products, Inc. Employees Association, herein called the Association, and Auto-

Board's Exhibit No. 15—(Continued)
motive and Aircraft Workers Alliance, Inc., herein
called the Alliance.

With respect to the unfair labor practices, the
complaint alleged in substance that from late in
1933 or early in 1934, the respondent fostered, encouraged, dominated, and interfered with the formation and administration of the Association, a labor organization, and furnished it active support
inter alia by (a) permitting organizational and
other meetings of the Association to be held on company property; (b) furnishing ballots and other
assistance in connection with the conduct of Association elections; (c) permitting and assisting in so-
licitation for the Association among the employees
on company time and property; (d) paying representatives of the Association for time spent on Association business; (e) dominating joint delibera-
tions of the respondent and the Association through
a Joint Council provided under the constitution of
the Association; and (f) publishing propaganda favorable to the Association in "Friendly Forum,"
the respondent's house organ.

The complaint further alleged that the Alliance
is a successor to the Association, and that in 1937
the respondent fostered, encouraged, dominated, and
interfered with the formation and administration
of the Alliance, inter alia, by (a) failing to disas-
sociate itself from the Association, and, through
its agents in the Association, encouraging and in-
viting the formation of the Alliance; (b) suggesting and securing the passage of a resolution in July

Board's Exhibit No. 15—(Continued)

1937 indicating its preference for dealing with agents who were Association officers; (c) permitting an organization meeting of the Alliance on company property; (d) using the balance in the Association treasury to defray expenses incident to the formation of the Alliance; (e) permitting and assisting active Association members to solicit membership for the Alliance on company time and property; and (f) in other specified ways participating in Alliance affairs. The complaint further alleged that in addition to the acts recited, the respondent interfered with, restrained, and coerced its employees by (a) publishing in the said Friendly Forum in April 1937 articles derogatory to the Union; (b) making a specified anti-union threat against a laid-off employee; and (c) by various other acts.

On or about November 28, 1940,[1] the respondent filed an answer admitting certain allegations with respect to its business and certain other allegations with respect to the Association but denying the alleged unfair labor practices. The respondent's answer also alleged that the Board had issued two previous complaints against it, one on May 12, 1937,[2] and the other on March 18, 1939, which was

---

(1) The date for filing an answer was twice extended by the Regional Director on the respondent's motion.

(2) See Matter of Thompson Products, Inc. and United Automobile Workers of America, 3 N. L.R.B. 332, set aside, National Labor Relations Board v. Thompson Products, Inc., 97 F. (2d) 13 (C.C.A. 6).

Board's Exhibit No. 15—(Continued)

settled after issuance of the Intermediate Report but prior to the Board decision; that both complaints involved allegations of violation of Section 8 (1) and (3) of the Act; that in the former case the proceeding was eventually dismissed by the Circuit Court and the latter case settled; that the Board was therefore barred from issuing complaints on charges based on any act of the respondent occurring prior to the date of the complaints in both earlier cases (or, in the alternative as to the second case, prior to the date of settlement) of which the Board through its agents and the Union had knowledge. The answer further alleged that the existence and operation of the Association had been common knowledge for 3 years prior to May 12, 1937, and, as to the Alliance, for nearly 2 years before March 18, 1939; that as to both, the Board and the Union were chargeable with said knowledge and barred from proceeding herein upon any matter which could have been included in the earlier complaints.

As the respondent's answer itself admits, there was no allegation of violation of Section 8 (2) of the Act in either of the earlier charges or complaints. No such findings could have been made upon the pleadings. No such allegation was in issue or litigated. The affirmative defense is based upon the theory that with knowledge of the existence and operation of the Association and the Alliance such allegation could have and should have been included earlier, and that the failure thus to

Board's Exhibit No. 15—(Continued)

include it bars its inclusion here. We are of the opinion and we find that the affirmative defenses raised by the respondent are without merit.

Pursuant to notice, a hearing was held from December 2 through December 6, 1940,[3] at Cleveland, Ohio, before Samuel H. Jaffee, the Trial Examiner duly designated by the Chief Trial Examiner. At the opening of the hearing, the Alliance filed an application for leave to intervene, which was allowed to the extent that its interests appeared. The Alliance thereupon filed an answer denying that it was company-dominated. The Board, the respondent, and the Alliance were represented by counsel and participated in the hearing. Full opportunity to be heard, to examine and cross-examine witnesses, and to introduce evidence bearing upon the issues was afforded all parties. At the conclusion of the hearing, counsel for the Board moved to conform the pleadings to the proof. There was no objection and the motion was granted by the Trial Examiner. The Trial Examiner reserved ruling on a motion of counsel for the respondent to dismiss all the allegations of the complaint which charged the respondent with violating Section 8 (1) and (2) of the Act and, on a motion of counsel for the Alliance, to dismiss all the allegations in paragraph 10 of the complaint.[4] Said motions were

---

(3) The opening of the hearing was continued by the Regional Director from November 20 to December 2 on motion by the respondent.

(4) Paragraph 10 of the complaint alleged varions acts of the respondent with respect to the formation and administration of the Alliance.

Board's Exhibit No. 15—(Continued)

denied by the Trial Examiner in his Intermediate Report. During the course of the hearing the Trial Examiner made various rulings on other motions and on objections to the admission of evidence. The Board has reviewed the rulings of the Trial Examiner and finds that no prejudicial errors were committed. Except as indicated below, the rulings are hereby affirmed.

On January 21, 1941, in accordance with a stipulation entered into between the respective counsel for the respondent, the Alliance, and the Board, the Trial Examiner issued an order directing correction of certain typographical errors in the transcript of the hearing.[5]

The Trial Examiner thereafter filed his Intermediate Report dated March 31, 1941, copies of which were duly served upon the parties. He found therein that the respondent had engaged in and was engaging in unfair labor practices affecting commerce, within the meaning of Section 8 (1) and (2) and Section 2 (6) and (7) of the Act and recommended that the respondent cease and desist therefrom and take certain specified affirmative action deemed necessary to effectuate the policies of the Act. On May 9, 1941, the respondent and the Alliance filed exceptions to the Intermediate Report, and on May 20, 1941, submitted briefs in support of such exceptions.

---

(5)   On May 29, 1941, the Board issued an order making "Additional Stipulation Correcting Errors in Transcript" a part of record.

Board's Exhibit No. 15—(Continued)

Pursuant to notice duly served upon all the parties, a hearing for the purpose of oral argument was held before the Board on May 22, 1941, in Washington, D. C. The respondent and the Alliance were represented by counsel and presented argument. The Board has considered the exceptions to the Intermediate Report and the briefs in support thereof and, save as the exceptions are consistent with the findings, conclusions, and order set forth below, finds them to be without merit.

Upon the entire record in the case, the Board makes the following:

FINDINGS OF FACT

I. The business of the respondent

Thompson Products, Inc., was incorporated in 1916 under the laws of the State of Ohio and has its principal office and place of business in Cleveland, Ohio. It is engaged in the manufacture, sale, and distribution of valves, pistons, tie rods, drag links, and other metal products used in the automobile and aviation industry. The principal raw materials used are steel, steel alloys, and aluminum alloys. It has manufacturing plants in Cleveland, Ohio, and Detroit, Michigan, and several subsidiary corporations, including one in Canada. This proceeding involves only the Cleveland plant of the respondent.

In 1936 the volume of the respondent's business amounted to $10,356,424.76. Of raw materials costing approximately $1,775,000 used by the respond-

Board's Exhibit No. 15—(Continued)

· ent at its Cleveland plant in 1936, $1,250,000 were shipped from points outside the State of Ohio. Approximately 75 per cent in value of the total products manufactured by the respondent are sold and shipped outside the State of Ohio. The respondent stipulated at the hearing that it was engaged in interstate commerce.

II.   The organizations involved

United Automobile Workers of America, Local 300, is a labor organization affiliated with the Congress of Industrial Organizations, admitting to membership employees of the respondent.

Thompson Products, Inc., Employees Association was an unaffiliated labor organization admitting to membership employees of the respondent.

Automotive and Aircraft Workers Alliance, Inc., is an unaffiliated labor organization admitting to membership employees of the respondent.

III.   The unfair labor practices

A.   Domination of, interference with, and support of labor organizations

1.   The Association

There is no evidence of the existence of any labor organization in the plant[6] prior to 1934. Early in 1934, at the request of certain of its employees, the

---

(6)   There are three plants of the respondent in Cleveland called, respectively, the Main Plant, the Piston Plant, and the Pin (or Ashland) Plant. Hereinafter, the word "plant" refers to these three plants collectively.

Board's Exhibit No. 15—(Continued)

respondent cooperated with them in the formation of the Association. At a meeting attended by some 200 or 300 employees in the respondent's dining room in January 1934, a committee was elected to draft a constitution for the Association. After the constitution was drafted, it was presented and approved at another meeting of the employees. Immediately the machinery provided in the constitution for the election of a "Committee of Employee Representatives" was put in motion, those in direct charge of handling its details being the members of the "Constitution Committee" who acted as temporary officers, assisted by an election committee the personnel of which was not disclosed in the record. Nomination notices were posted near the time clocks. Ballots were supplied by the respondent. Voting took place in the plant during and outside working hours.[7] The seven persons elected as representatives thereafter comprised the "Constitution Committee."

The constitution provided for an employee representation plan for the purpose of collective bargaining "through a Committee of Employee Representatives . . . who are vested with the power of representing each employee who participates in this plan . . . The Committee of Employee Representatives shall have the power to enter into agreements with the Company . . . binding upon the participat-

---

(7) Association elections were held each year until 1937.

ing employees." Under the plan, seven employee representatives were elected annually from specified voting districts. It was required that representatives be participants in the plan, be employed in the district from which they were elected, be over 21 years of age, and should have been continuously employed by the respondent for at least a year. The representatives elected their own chairman and secretary.

The constitution required that the respondent appoint a committee of seven management representatives; that both committees thereupon meet as a Joint Council for collective bargaining; that the Council elect its own chairman and secretary; that a majority of each constitute a quorum at Joint Council meetings; that where a quorum is present at meetings of the Joint Council and its committees, both employee representatives and management representatives shall be entitled to cast an equal number of votes; and that a two-thirds vote shall be necessary to decide a question. The constitution also barred strikes or "other independent action taken by the employees or their representatives," and any matters which had not been satisfactorily settled after appeal to the respondent's Board of Directors might be submitted to arbitration by such method as "may be determined by the Joint Council." No provision was made in the constitution or otherwise for meetings of the membership of the

Board's Exhibit No. 15—(Continued)

Association.[8] The employee representatives represented only "participants" in the plan.[9] The original Association constitution was thereafter amended in particulars not here material. The minutes of Joint Council meetings indicate that in practice the Council took it upon itself to amend the constitution.

On February 23, 1934, the respondent and "the members of Thompson Products Inc. Employees Association . . . through their elected representatives" entered into an agreement which provided *inter alia,* that the Association and, "subject to the conditions set forth in this agreement," the respondent, agreed to abide by the obligations imposed by the constitution of the Association theretofore adopted. It further provided that employees would be retained, advanced, and paid "on the basis of their individual merit and without regard to their affiliation or non-affiliation with any lawful labor or other organization." There was a further provision that minimum wages and hours "shall be in accordance with the provisions of such codes of fair competition as Employer may be operating under."

Substantially similar contracts were executed on March 4, 1935, and March 2, 1936, respectively, there

---

(8) No meetings were in fact ever so held except occasional social meetings held in the plant.

(9) Regular Joint Council meetings were held monthly, and there were occasionally additional special meetings.

Board's Exhibit No. 15—(Continued)

being in addition, however, provisions to the effect that regardless of anything in the Association's constitution to the contrary, the respondent reserved to itself "the right to take such action as, in the opinion of its President, is necessary to insure the well-being and perpetuity of Employer"; and that the respondent was not obliged to comply with any amendments to constitution or bylaws thereafter adopted unless it first consented in writing.

When new employees were hired, the respondent's personnel department sent their names to the employee representatives. Such new employees were then solicited by the representatives for the district where the new employees were hired, and in most instances their participation in the plan was secured. Copies of the constitution of the Association were printed and published by the respondent and distributed to employees who applied for membership in the Association. Employee representatives were not only paid by the respondent for time spent at meetings of the Joint Council but also for meetings of employee representatives and delegates.[10]

2. The Alliance

In March and April 1937, the Union was active in attempting to organize the respondent's em-

---

(10) Although the position of "delegate" was not provided for in the Association constitution, it appears that each employee representative appointed delegates from his department to assist him.

Board's Exhibit No. 15—(Continued)

ployees. At about this time there appeared in the respondent's factory newspaper, Friendly Forum,[11] articles which were favorable to the Association and derogatory of the Union. Thus on March 26 an article appeared which in substance stated that Association representatives "were given reason to swell their chests in pride" when Whiting Williams, "world prominent industrial relations' counsel" congratulated them and the respondent in a speech that he made the previous week "on the splendid co-operative job" they had done "in placing the Company's labor relations on a sound basis"; that employees could "do far better for themselves through representatives who are their fellow employees, than they can through strong-arm agents of outside organizations."

An article published on April 9 reported that at a

---

(11) In the 1940 edition of the "Thompson Products Inc. Employees Handbook" published by the respondent and distributed to its employees, there appears on pages 26 and 27 thereof the following concerning the Friendly Forum:

... Once each four weeks the Company publishes a paper, Friendly Forum, which contains news of the company and of employees. This is distributed free to all employees.

Employees are responsible for knowledge of information published either on bulletin boards or in Friendly Forum. Make a practice of reading the bulletin boards each day and be sure to get your copy of Friendly Forum each time it is issued. Also, employees are encouraged to contribute news items to Friendly Form.

Board's Exhibit No. 15—(Continued)
union organizational meeting a union organizer was
"embarrassed" by questions from "Thompson" employees, that he "failed to answer satisfactorily a
single question put to him," and that what happened
at the meeting was evidence that the employees "are
well satisfied with their present method of bargaining." The same issue of the Forum carried an editorial entitled "Whose Job is It?" The editorial
commented upon a speech which had been made by
Director of Personnel Livingstone a few days previously to members of a similar association at the
plant of one of the respondent's subsidiaries. During that speech Livingstone "charged the members
of the Association with the duty of preserving and
protecting their jobs against the undermining in-
fluences of young, irresponsible and easily led employees" who are "capable of great and perhaps
permanent injury to a company and its personnel";
that it was "the old employees . . . who stand to
lose most through labor disputes," and that hence
it was "to their own best interests to exert all of
their influence in helping to shape proper and sound
opinions in the minds of new employees." In commenting upon this speech the editorial stated that
"From the comments of the men who heard the
address it was obvious that most of them understood
the common sense contained in the counsel."

An "open letter" appearing in the April 9 issue
addressed to all the employees and signed by the
Association employee representatives, stated that
the Association had acted for the employees for

Board's Exhibit No. 15—(Continued)

over 4 years, that it had secured specified benefits, that "recent statements made by an outside organization . . . in an effort to invade our plants" prompt the "candid opinion that no organization can secure any concession from Management that your present Association cannot secure. And with less . . . ill will . . . to say nothing about the savings in dues or lost time"; finally, that fellow employees were more anxious to adjust employee problems "than an outsider whose only interest is in the amount of dues he can collect."

On April 12, 1937, the Supreme Court upheld the constitutionality of the Act.[12] On April 15 the respondent posted on its bulletin boards a notice stating that "due to interest in, and some misunderstanding over" the Act, it was taking the opportunity to inform employees of its "highlights." These "highlights" were summarized in five paragraphs. Paragraph 1 stated that the intention of the Act was to eliminate labor disputes. Paragraph 2 quoted the definition of a labor organization as contained in the Act but capitalized only the phrase "employee representation committee or plan." Paragraph 3 summarized the unfair labor practices defined in Section 8 of the Act. Paragraph 4 referred to "the principle of majority rule," and stated that "the collective bargaining agency selected by the majority of employees in an

(12) National Labor Relations Board v. Jones & Laughlin Steel Corp., 301 U. S. 1, and companion cases.

Board's Exhibit No. 15—(Continued)
appropriate company unit shall be the exclusive
representative of all such employees . . ." Paragraph 5 stated that the Act created the Board to
decide questions of representation and to rule on
alleged unfair labor practices, but that the Board
had no enforcement powers. Following these five
paragraphs there appeared a concluding observation emphasized in capital letters as follows:

IT SHOULD BE UNDERSTOOD THAT
THIS BILL HAS BEEN A LAW FOR
NEARLY TWO YEARS, AND THIS COM-
PANY HAS BEEN OBSERVING ITS
TERMS. THEREFORE, THE SUPREME
COURT'S RECENT DECISION CAUSES
NO CHANGE WHATSOEVER IN PRES-
ENT PLANT CONDITIONS OR RELA-
TIONSHIPS.

In spite of this assurance, there was talk among
the employee representatives concerning the effect
of the Supreme Court decisions on the Association.
As stated by William A. Hoffman, chairman of the
"employee representatives," in an affidavit submitted to the Board's agent prior to the hearing,
and supported by his testimony at the hearing, "it
became apparent to the representatives of the Association that the Association was not within the
letter and spirit of the Wagner Act. Consequently
we realized that a change would have to be made."
Accordingly, Hoffman went to see Raymond S.
Livingstone, director of personnel for the respond-

Board's Exhibit No. 15—(Continued)

ent and executive secretary of the Joint Counsel and of the "employee representatives and delegates," and suggested, as testified by Hoffman, that his opinion was that "We would have to adjust our constitution because we knew previously that it had not conformed to it, and we didn't know whether the Act would be approved by the Court or not." Hoffman testified that Livingstone "felt the same as I did; that we had to revise our constitution in order to make it conform with the Wagner Act," that "We will certainly have to do something, because previous to that we always told the representatives how to conduct themselves in their capacity as representatives . . .," and that Livingstone also said, "You better get things lined up." Hoffman said he would do so. Thereupon Livingstone said, "We would have to have quick action . . . We knew we were violating the law."

Hoffman testified under subpoena as a witness for the Board. The Trial Examiner found that Hoffman was, if not a hostile witness, at least an unfriendly one. Livingstone in his testimony did not dispute the conversations recited. We find, as did the Trial Examiner, such conversations to be substantially in accordance with Hoffman's testimony.

On April 23, 1937, an editorial appeared in the Friendly Forum entitled "At What Profit" in which "the recently announced terms of the Chrysler strike settlement" in which the Union herein was involved, was referred to as "futile" and not

Board's Exhibit No. 15—(Continued)

"exactly a smashing victory" for the Union. The same issue contained an article headed "Hoffman Calls Wagner Act Aid to Association" in which Association "Chairman Bill Hoffman" was quoted as to the effect of the Supreme Court decisions upholding the Act. Therein Hoffman stated that the Association had "always been governed by principles which" the Act "now makes a law"; that the Association "was organized spontaneously by the employees . . . and conceived by" them. He concluded that "Our relations with management at present are entirely satisfactory and at this time we see no reason to disturb them in any way."

Prior to a meeting of the representatives and delegates of the Association held on April 26, the Election Committee[13] called upon J. D. Wright, an officer of the respondent, to discuss clarification of various portions of the constitution of the Association. The Committee also asked Wright's opinion regarding the advisability of incorporating the Association. Wright replied that incorporation was unnecessary, that the Association "might be slightly improved by the election of officers and also by making certain revisions in the constitution."

The Committee reported this advice at the meeting of employee representatives and delegates on

---

(13)   Under the constitution of the Association an election committee was appointed by the chairman of the Joint Council with the consent of the Council and consisted of an equal number of employee and management representatives.

Board's Exhibit No. 15—(Continued)

April 26 held in the office of F. C. Crawford, the respondent's president, at which Livingstone was present. During the meeting Livingstone made suggestions concerning proposed revisions in the constitution. He stated that the constitution as revised "should deal only with the purpose of the Association, eligibility for membership, and rules pertaining to the election and eligibility of representatives"; that "Any provision for presentation of grievances and relationships with Management should be included in a contract . . ."[14] Pursuant to a motion made and carried, a committee was then appointed to study and recommend changes in the constitution of the Association.

Between April 29 and May 24 certain changes in the constitution of the Association were decided upon by the committee appointed at the April 26 meeting referred to above. After working hours on May 24 a meeting attended by employee representatives and delegates was held in the respondent's dining room. Hoffman, who was then and

-----

(14) The quotations are from the minutes of the meeting. Since May 7, 1934, Livingstone had not only been "executive secretary" of the Joint Council but also acted as "executive secretary" of the employee representatives and delegates at meetings held only among themselves. Livingstone prepared the minutes of the above meeting. He resigned as "executive secretary" of the Association at the conclusion of the meeting. An election was then held for a new secretary. Harry F. Stuebe, an employee delegate, was then elected secretary of the employee representatives and delegates.

Board's Exhibit No. 15—(Continued)
except for the year 1936, always had been, chairman of the employee representatives, presided at the opening of the meeting.[15]   The committee gave its report and, according to the testimony of Hoffman, it was accepted.   The record does not disclose what such revisions were except for the testimony of Hoffman that "at that meeting a revised constitution to conform to the Labor Act, as declared constitutional by the Supreme Court, was adopted."

Pursuant to acceptance of the report, Hoffman retired as chairman of the employee representatives, and thereupon, in accordance with the suggested revisions the following "temporary" officers were elected: Frank Arnold, president; Joseph Vanyo, vice president; Harry F. Stuebe, secretary; Paul Lucksinger, treasurer.[16]

During the next few days there was some discussion among the employee representatives as to the advisability of changing the name of the As-

---

(15)   The minutes of the meeting, if any were kept, are not in evidence.

(16)   It is not entirely clear whether the representatives and delegates who had hitherto been in office resigned at this meeting and whether such resignations, if any were made, were followed by new elections and appointments as such representatives and delegates.   If, however, such elections were held and appointments made, it did not materially alter the situation with reference to the identity of such persons, since in any event the same persons, with possibly two or three exceptions, continued in the same capacities after the meeting as prior to it.

Board's Exhibit No. 15—(Continued)

sociation and of incorporating it. At the suggestion of A. J. Anderson, a former delegate, Stuebe called on M. A. Roemisch, the attorney who appeared for the Alliance in this proceeding.[17] Roemisch advised against incorporating the Association and suggested the incorporation of a new organization. He indicated his willingness to handle the legal details. Stuebe returned within a day or two with the other "temporary" officers and three or four other employees, and Roemisch confirmed the advice. It was accordingly decided by this small group to proceed with the incorporation.

Roemisch advanced the necessary incorporation expenses,[18] and on June 8, Arnold, Vanyo, Stuebe, and Lucksinger signed the Articles of Organization of the Alliance, naming themselves therein as the temporary trustees. On June 11, the Articles were duly filed with the Secretary of State of Ohio.

On June 14, the four incorporators-trustees met with "the other members"[19] of the Alliance "at the

---

(17) Anderson was a personal client of Roemisch.

(18) He was reimbursed by the Alliance several months later.

(19) Quoted from the minutes of this meeting. In addition to the incorporators, "the other members" were the following employees: Lawrence Madge, Joe Strasser, Norbert Roubieu, Joseph Bosoty, Thomas McKiernan and John DeCapite. There are variations in the spelling of some of these names in the exhibits and transcript of the testimony.

Board's Exhibit No. 15—(Continued)

offices of the Corporation,[20] for the purpose of holding the first meeting, preparing and approving a
Code of Regulations for the election of the necessary
officers and committee of representatives, and trustees, and for the transaction of such other business
as may properly be brought before the meeting."
The "Code of Regulations" referred to is apparently the document in evidence entitled "Constitution and By-Laws" of the Alliance. Arnold and
Stuebe acted as temporary chairman and temporary
secretary, respectively, of the meeting. The "Code
of Regulations" which had already been prepared
was read, and adopted and signed by the 10 members. Arnold, as temporary chairman, then moved
that the "Code of Regulations" be waived, and that
officers and a committee of representatives be
elected to serve until December 31, 1937, or until
otherwise replaced by a later election. The motion
was seconded. The minutes state that "the names
of the members were placed in nomination as candidates for officers" and that balloting followed,
resulting in the following "unanimous election";
Frank Arnold, president; Joe Vanyo, vice president; Harry Stuebe, secretary; Paul Lucksinger,
treasurer. Thereupon the members proceeded to
elect "a committee or representatives," which proceeding "resulted in the unanimous election" of the
remaining six members.

------

(20) Attorney Roemisch's law office was and
continued to be the corporate offiee.

Board's Exhibit No. 15—(Continued)

On June 20 a "joint meeting of the committee of representatives and the officers of the corporation" was held, consisting of the 10 persons previously named. At this meeting election districts were defined throughout the plant and each representative was authorized to appoint four members to a "Council of Delegates." It was further voted to notify the respondent of the intent to seek a contract and further "to set up means and methods of working out a labor relations committee to perfect the various dealings, complaints and demands of this Corporation from the said company." Finally, the membership committee appointed at the June 14 meeting reported that it had received 912 applications for membership.

The constitution of the Alliance was made up of the substance of the Articles of Incorporation already described. The bylaws, so far as here material, in substance included the following: officers and a committee of eight representatives were established, all to be elected annually by ballot of the entire membership; eligibility for these positions was limited to persons over 21 years old having not less than a stated length of membership; the committee of representatives was designated as bargaining agent for the organization; all contracts and adjustments to be subject to approval by the remaining officers and the Council of Delegates; however, questions concerning general pay raises and seniority were to be further submitted to the corporate members for formal approval; elections

Board's Exhibit No. 15—(Continued)

were to be held in November, the persons elected to take office on January 1 of the following year.

The officers, representatives, and appointed delegates jointly constituted the Council of Delegates, individual delegates "being accountable" to the appointing representative, who could revoke the appointment at will. Semi-monthly meetings of the Council were provided for. It was further provided that the president should call a meeting of the entire corporation at least quarterly. However, the majority of the officers and representatives constituted a quorum.[21]

During this entire period the Union had been active, being engaged, among other things, in passing out handbills around the plant. On June 18 the following items appeared in the Friendly Forum: (1) an editorial entitled "Where Does It Lead?"; (2) articles entitled "$150,000 Added to Wages; Co. Seeks to Boost Prices"; and (3) a further article entitled "Alliance Seeks TP Membership." The editorial attacked "the labor movement" as rushing "ruthlessly along under its newly acquired power"; stated that "seemingly drunk with its power the union grows bolder and bolder in its demands";

---

(21)   It does not appear that general mass meetings of the membership were held quarterly. Roemisch testified that in addition to the meeting at the Little Theater hereinafter described, there was another such meeting in 1938. However, it was the custom upon occasion to submit to the membership by mail the question of the ratification of some important matters.

Board's Exhibit No. 15—(Continued)

and that the lot of manufacturers who had signed contracts was "no better than that of those who" had not. The opening paragraph of the article headed "$150,000 Added to Wages" etc. is sufficiently illustrative. This paragraph stated that "Gaining quick action in a series of rapid fire meetings early last week, the Employees' Association won its third substantial wage increase for hourly rate employees in less than 8 months . . ." The other article similarly headed was to the effect that the respondent's sales staff intensified a drive to secure higher prices for its products following total wage increases of $150,000 annually. The article headed "Alliance Seeks TP Membership" followed the tenor of the headline. A statement of Frank Arnold, "temporary president" of the Alliance, was quoted, stating in substance that the Alliance was "the only sane method of bargaining collectively"; that the Alliance was "not asking employees to pay high monthly dues"; and that the "small nominal dues" collected would not "go to pay salaries of officers and organizers." The article further set forth the names of the other temporary officers of the Alliance.

On June 21, in accordance with action taken at the "joint meeting of the committee of representatives and officers" the previous day, a committee consisting of the four Alliance officers (Arnold, Vanyo, Stuebe, and Lucksinger) and two representatives, accompanied by Attorney Roemisch, met with Livingstone in the office of F. C. Crawford, the

Board's Exhibit No. 15—(Continued)

respondent's president. Roemisch produced copies of the corporate charter and other incorporation papers and presented 833 signed membership cards which he said constituted a majority of the respondent's employees. He requested the respondent to negotiate an exclusive bargaining contract with the Alliance. It was arranged that Employment Manager Naff should check the signatures on the cards against the respondent's employment records.

On June 23, a letter signed by Arnold, Stuebe, and Roemisch was sent to the respondent, which stated in substance that the Alliance represented 75 per cent of the respondent's Cleveland employees, and demanded that the respondent recognize it as the sole agent for collective bargaining within 5 days, and negotiate within 30 days thereafter a contract covering specified matters. On June 25, Livingstone replied by letter that a check of the signatures on the membership cards indicated that 831 signatures were genuine;[22] that this was a decisive majority "and, in view of the terms of the Wagner Act, it leaves us no alternative but to grant your organization exclusive bargaining rights." He concluded that Crawford would be willing to meet with the Alliance for the purpose of negotiating the contract.

Sometime between June 25 and 30, the terms of the contract were tentatively agreed upon. On June 30, what was referred to by Attorney Roemisch in

---

(22)   At this time there was 1,362 employees, including supervisors.

Board's Exhibit No. 15—(Continued)

his testimony "as a regular meeting of the Alliance" was held in his law office. This so-called regular meeting was attended by only the officers and representatives, 10 in number, previously named. No minutes of this meeting were introduced in evidence, nor is it clear whether any were made. It was voted to accept the contract and to authorize its execution.

In the meantime, the activity of the Union still continued. There were also several meetings of the Joint Council of the Association during the month of June and the final meeting was held on July 1. On the latter date it was agreed that since a "new union" now represented a substantial majority of the employees, the contract of the Association should be terminated. Livingstone, who was present at this meeting, stated that it was now appropriate that a resolution be drafted "as a testimonial to the achievements of the Association." Thereupon Wright, the respondent's secretary, moved that employee representative Stuebe be requested to draft such a resolution. The motion was passed.

In accordance with the vote at the July 1 meeting of the Joint Council, an agreement was simultaneously drafted between the respondent and "the members of Thompson Products, Inc. Employees' Association" purporting to terminate the Association contract. On behalf of "the members" this agreement was signed by six Association representa-

Board's Exhibit No. 15—(Continued)

tives and one delegate.[23] The contract, *inter alia,* recited that the members represented that by reason of the fact that "another organization" now represented a majority of the employees, the Association had been dissolved on June 11, 1937.

In accordance with the vote taken at the July 1 meeting of the Joint Council concerning the testimonial referred to above, Stuebe prepared a resolution which stated that the employee representatives extended their sincere thanks to the management representatives for the consideration shown them at all times; that the representatives of management in turn complimented the employee representatives for their sincere efforts to better working conditions, and trusted that the "employees in general may appreciate the efforts put forth in their behalf and continue to select men of equal intelligence and courage to present their problems to Management for adjustment . . ." The resolution further recited that the Association had existed from "February 19, 1934 to July 1, 1937 . . ."

Livingstone testified that he received the draft of the resolution in August. He approved of it and instructed his stenographer to type it. After she typed it, she asked him "what to do with it."

---

(23) Lawrence Madge, Howard Blake, Norbert Roubieu, Joseph Bosoty, John D. DeCapite, Joseph Vanyo, and Thomas McKiernan (delegate). The record indicates that these designations were in error as Blake and Vanyo were delegates, and the others employee representatives.

Board's Exhibit No. 15—(Continued)

Livingstone replied, "Put it in the minute book, right on top." Although places were indicated on the resolution for the signatures of both the employee and management representatives, it was not signed.

On July 2, the contract between the respondent and the Alliance was signed. Under it, *inter alia,* the respondent recognized the Alliance as the exclusive representative of its Cleveland employees eligible for membership in the Alliance for the purposes of collective bargaining. The contract also provided for the creation of a Labor Relations Committee "consisting of an equal number of Alliance and Management representatives for the purpose of adjusting such grievances" arising with the employees that cannot be amicably and expeditiously adjusted by the foreman, with the individual representatives of the Alliance. The contract was signed by Arnold and Stuebe as president and secretary, respectively, on behalf of the Alliance, and by Crawford and Wright as president and secretary,-respectively, on behalf of the respondent. On July 16, a supplement to the contract was executed which clarified grievance and bargaining procedure.

At the time of the meeting of the 10 Alliance members in Roemisch's law office on June 30, above recited, it was agreed that a mass meeting of the entire membership would be held following the execution of the contract for the purpose of obtaining approval of the contract. Pursuant to this understanding, a meeting was held in the Little

Board's Exhibit No. 15—(Continued)
Theater of the Public Auditorium in Cleveland
early in August. Frank Arnold, the Alliance president, presided. Attorney Roemisch attended and
made a speech outlining the contract. There was
thereafter some discussion and finally approval was
obtained.

In October 1938 further contracts were made
between the respondent and the Alliance, which
were substantially the same as the 1937 contract.
At the time of the hearing, the Alliance was still in
existence and its structure was substantially as it
had been when created. The Friendly Forum was
still being published and distributed.

As indicated hereinabove, the 10 employees who
were the leaders in the formation of the Alliance
were Frank Arnold, Joe Vanyo, Harry F. Stuebe,
Paul Lucksinger, Lawrence Madge, Joe Strasser,
Norbert Roubieu, Joseph Bosoty, Thomas McKiernan, and John DeCapite.

Frank Arnold was an employee delegate of the
Association in 1936 and 1937, and was elected president of the Association on May 24, 1937. He became one of the four Alliance incorporators, temporary trustee, presiding officer at its early meetings, one of the signers of its contract, and first
president of the Alliance. Joe Vanyo was an employee delegate of the Association in 1935, 1936,
and 1937 and was elected vice president thereof on
May 24, 1937. He signed the July 1, 1937, agreement which terminated the existing Association contract. He was an incorporator of the Alliance, a

Board's Exhibit No. 15—(Continued)
temporary trustee, and vice president thereof in
1937 and 1938. Harry F. Stuebe was an employee
delegate of the Association from 1935-1937, and was
elected secretary on April 26, 1937. He was also
an Alliance incorporator, temporary trustee, and
one of the signers of all the Alliance contracts. He
was secretary of the organization in 1937, even
prior to its incorporation, and thereafter secretary-
treasurer in 1938-1940. Paul Lucksinger was an
employee delegate of the Association in 1937, and,
according to the testimony of Hoffman, "it may be
he (Lucksinger) was elected treasurer" at the
May 24 meeting. However, Hoffman was under
the impression that offices of secretary and treasurer were combined. Lucksinger was the remaining
incorporator of the Alliance and temporary trustee, and also treasurer of the organization in 1937.

The other six leaders in the formation of the
Alliance were equally prominent in the Association.
Lawrence Madge was an employee delegate of the
Association for part of 1935 and representative for
the remainder of the year, and served in the latter
capacity in 1936-1937. He was one of the signers
of the Association contract of March 2, 1936, and
also signed the agreement of July 1, 1937, terminating the Association contract. He was one of the
first six self-appointed Alliance employee representatives other than the officers, and acted in that
capacity for the years 1937-1939. Joe Strasser was
an employee delegate of the Association in 1934,
representative in 1935-1937, and chairman in 1936.

Board's Exhibit No. 15—(Continued)

He was one of the signers of the Association contracts of March 4, 1935, and March 2, 1936. He was one of the original representatives of the Alliance and one of its first three regular trustees. Norbert Roubieu was an employee representative of the Association in 1936-1937. He signed the Association contract of March 2, 1936. He also signed the July 1, 1937, contract of termination. He was one of the first Alliance representatives, and acted in that capacity during part of 1937 and in 1938 as well; he was also one of the three original regular trustees.

Joseph Bosoty was an employee representative of the Association in 1935-1937. He signed the Association contract of March 2, 1938; also the contract of termination. He was an Alliance representative in 1937-1939. Thomas McKiernan was either a delegate or representative of the Association during the years 1935-1937. He signed the Association contract of March 2, 1936, and the agreement of July 1, 1937, terminating it. He was an Alliance representative from the beginning of its organization and was still acting in that capacity at the time of the hearing. He was one of its first three regular trustees. John DeCapite was an employee representative of the Association in 1937. He signed the July 1, 1937, agreement terminating the Association contract. He was an Alliance representative from the beginning of the organization and was still acting in that capacity at the time of the hearing.

Board's Exhibit No. 15—(Continued)

In addition to the men above enumerated, it should be noted that Chester McMullen, who acted as the chairman of the committee for revision of the Association's constitution in April and May 1937, was an Association employee delegate in 1935-1936 and successively delegate and representative in 1937. Also on the committee for constitution revision were Stuebe, Madge, Roubieu, and De-Capite.

(3) Conclusions as to the Association and the Alliance

The respondent cooperated in the formation of the Association. Representatives of the Association were paid by the respondent for time spent in connection with affairs of the Association. The structure of the Association indicated the respondent's control through the Joint Council, its governing body. The employees were limited in their free choice of representatives. No meetings of participants were provided for or held. Association expenses were met by the respondent. This conduct, begun before the Act was passed, continued thereafter. The entire record indicates that the Association was merely an advisory agency supported by the management for adjusting differences with the employees within management limitations. It was formed, existed, and functioned only through the respondent's control, participation, financial support, and sufferance.

Despite the fact that the Supreme Court decisions

Board's Exhibit No. 15—(Continued)
of April 12, 1937, made it plain to the respondent
that the continuance of the Association was illegal,
the respondent, 3 days later, posted a notice to its
employees emphasizing that the Court's action
"causes no changes whatsoever in present plant conditions or relationships." We find that subsequent
to July 5, 1935, the respondent dominated and interfered with the administration of the Association
and contributed financial and other support thereto,
and that the respondent thereby interfered with, restrained, and coerced its employees in the exercise
of the rights guaranteed in Section 7 of the Act.[24]

The manner in which the Alliance was formed,
and the support granted to it by the respondent during the period of its formation, clearly indicated the
desire of the respondent to retain control of its employees' representatives. The leaders of the Association were the originators of the Alliance. In the
eyes of the employees, they were representatives of
the management.[25] The Association was not aban-

---

(24) See National Labor Relations Board v.
Pennsylvania Greyhound Lines, Inc., et al., 303
U. S. 261; National Labor Relations Board v. New-
port News Shipbuilding & Dry Dock Co., 308 U. S.
241; National Labor Relations Board v. H. E.
Fletcher Co., 108 F. (2d) 459 (C.C.A. 1), enf'g 5
N.L.R.B. 729, cert. den. 309 U. S. 678.

(25) For the significance of such duplication of
personnel coupled with substantial continuity of existence, see, International Association of Machinists
v. National Labor Relations Board, 110 F. (2d) 29
(App. D. C.), aff'd 311 U. S. 72; National Labor
Relations Board v. Link-Belt Co., 311 U. S. 584.

Board's Exhibit No. 15—(Continued)

doned until the Alliance was finally established.[26] Not only was there no cleavage between the Association and the Alliance, as was the respondent's duty under the circumstances,[27] but the respondent

---

(26) The respondent contends that the Association was formally dissolved on June 11, 1937. There is no evidence of a formal dissolution of the Association except for the recital in the July 1, 1937, agreement terminating the contract between the Association and the respondent that the "members represent that the Association was dissolved as of June 11, 1937." Whatever inference may be derived from this recital is rebutted by other facts such as the notation in the resolution drafted by Stuebe, secretary of the Association, and approved by Livingstone, the respondent's director of personnel, that the Association existed from February 19, 1934, to July 1, 1937, the meeting of the Joint Council on July 1, and the article in the June 18, 1937, issue of the Friendly Forum under the heading "150,000 Added to Wages." The only finding that we can make under the circumstances, as we now do, is that the Association as such ceased to function as a labor organization after July 1, 1937.

(27) As the Court said in Western Union Telegraph Co. v. National Labor Relations Board, 113 F. (2d) 992 (C.C.A. 2), an "absolute and public cleavage between the old and the new" was necessary. In Westinghouse Electric & Mfg. Co. v. National Labor Relations Board, 112 F. (2d) 657 (C.C.A. 3), aff'd 61 S. Ct. 736, the Court, commenting upon the disestablishment order in the Newport News case, supra, said:

The reason for this was that, although the new union would be lawful, if freely formed, it had in fact arisen out of the earlier organization, and the company had done nothing to mark the separation between the two and pub-

Board's Exhibit No. 15—(Continued)
also furnished direct support to the Alliance by the
Friendly Forum attacks on the Union and other outside labor organizations, and by articles extolling
the Alliance.[28] We are of the opinion and we find
that the Alliance was the successor to the Association, and that the employees were never given the
opportunity freely to choose their own representatives.

---

licly to deprive the successor of the advantage
of its apparently continued favor * * * The employees at large had not been advised that the
company was wholly indifferent whether they
joined the new union, and that, as it might, and
probably did, appear to be a successor of the
old. The separation should have been made
plain, and with it the discontinuance of any
continued countenance from the employer. The
theory is that in cases such as this, where an
unaffiliated union seems to the employees at
large to have evolved out of an earlier joint organization of employer and employees, the
Board may take it as datum, in the absence of
satisfactory evidence to the contrary, that the
employees will suppose that the company ap-
proves the new, as it did the old, and their
choice is for that reason not as free as the
statute demands.

(28) The respondent asserts that the publication
of the Friendly Forum articles was fair comment
and privileged within the first amendment to the
Federal Constitution. Viewed in their setting the
articles were not only coercive but in some instances,
such as the article in the June 18, 1937, issue under
the heading "Alliance Seeks TP Membership," constituted direct support to the Alliance. The fact
that such statements were in printed forms does not
afford the respondent any greater protection. More-

Board's Exhibit No. 15—(Continued)

The respondent and the Alliance contend that the operation of the Alliance as a bargaining agent dispels any inference or presumption of "company domination or control." While the minutes of the Labor Relations Council of the Alliance indicate that the employee representatives presented demands which were accepted by the management after discussion and submission of counterproposals, "the fact that the employees received a measure of success with the kind of organization permitted them by the employer does not forfeit their right to organize dif-

---

over, it may be noted that the Friendly Forum is the business organ of the respondent and not a publication for the general dissemination of news. "Expressions of opinion concerning labor unions by an employer, either written or merely spoken, may be of such nature that their effect is to coerce and intimidate the employees contrary to the provisions of the National Labor Relations Act. To hold that such expressions, when employer manifestly intended to give them such an effect, are not violative of the Labor Act, would be to nullify the provisions of the Act and to thwart the public policy evidenced by said Act." National Labor Relations Board v. Chicago Apparatus Company, 116 F. (2d) 753 (C.C.A. 7), enf'g 12 N.L.R.B. 1002. See also, Bethlehem Steel Company, etc., et al. v. National Labor Relations Board, May 12, 1941 (App. D.C.), enf'g 14 N.L.R.B. 539; National Labor Relations Board v. Reed & Prince Mfg. Co. (C.C.A. 1) decided April 21, 1941; National Labor Relations Board v. New Era Die Inc., 118 F. (2d) 500 (C.C.A. 3), enf'g as mod. 19 N.L.R.B. 227; Valley Mould and Iron Corporation v. National Labor Relations Board, 116 F. (2d) 760 (C.C.A. 7) enf'g 20 N.L.R.B. 211.

Board's Exhibit No. 15—(Continued)
ferently if they wish and does not legalize the obstruction by the company of such a change."[29]

We find that the respondent dominated and interfered with the formation and administration of the Alliance, and contributed support thereto, and has thereby interfered with, restrained, and coerced its employees in the exercise of the rights guaranteed in Section 7 of the Act.[30] We further find that the agreements entered into between the respondent and the Alliance and the contractual relationship existing thereunder have been, and are, a means of utilizing an employer-dominated labor organization to frustrate the exercise by the respondent's employees of the rights guaranteed in Section 7 of the Act.

The Trial Examiner found that the allegation in the complaint that the balance in the Association treasury was used by the Association to pay Alliance formation expenses was not borne out by the evidence. We concur in this finding. Accordingly such allegation will be dismissed.

B. Interference, restraint, and coercion

The complaint alleges, inter alia, that the respond-

---

(29) Corning Glass Works v. National Labor Relations Board, et al., 118 F. (2d) 625 (C.C.A. 2), enf'g as mod. 15 N.L.R.B. 598; see also, National Labor Relations Board v. Newport Shipbuilding & Dry Dock Co., 308 U. S. 741.

(30) See Link-Belt Co. v. National Labor Relations Board, 311 U. S. 584; National Labor Relations Board v. Dow Chemical Co., 117 F. (2d) 455 (C.C.A. 6) enf'g as mod. 13 N.L.R.B. 993.

Board's Exhibit No. 15—(Continued)

ent engaged in interference, restraint, and coercion contrary to the Act in that on May 8, 1940, Plant Manager McBride told a laid-off employee that if the later ever had anything to do with the Union he would never be taken back to work. This was denied by the respondent in its answer. This incident involved Earl Bennett, a former employee representative of the Association. McBride was ill at the time of the hearing and did not appear, but the parties stipulated with respect to the testimony that he would give if called. McBride's version was that on several occasions between the latter part of 1939 and July 1940 Bennett called him on the telephone and inquired about a position, and that he (McBride) referred Bennett to Naff in the employment office. However, McBride did not expressly deny Bennett's testimony that a position would be refused Bennett if he had anything to do with the Union.

Bennett testified that the alleged statement was made to him by McBride in the latter's office in a face-to-face conversation and he named several employees who had seen him in McBride's office. McBride stated that he had no recollection of any face-to-face talk with Bennett during 1940. Although the Trial Examiner found that Bennet was in some particulars not an impressive witness, he nevertheless credited Bennett's testimony since the respondent failed to call as witnesses the persons named by Bennett as having seen him in McBride's office on that date to rebut such testimony. Upon examina-

Board's Exhibit No. 15—(Continued)
tion of the record, we find that Bennett's testimony
was contradictory in many respects and that he was
thoroughly discredited as a reliable witness. We
have therefore disregarded his entire testimony. Under the circumstances we find that there is insufficient evidence to support the above allegation of
the complaint and, accordingly, it will be dismissed.

IV. The effect of the unfair labor
practices upon commerce

We find that the activities of the respondent set
forth in Section III above, occurring in connection
with the operations of the respondent described in
Section I above, have a close, intimate, and substantial relation to trade, traffic, and commerce
among the several States, and tend to lead to labor
disputes burdening and obstructing commerce and
the free flow of commerce.

V. The remedy

Having found that the respondent has engaged in
unfair labor practices, we shall order it to cease and
desist therefrom and take certain affirmative action
designed to effectuate the policies of the Act.

We have found that the respondent has dominated
and interfered with the administration of the Association and has contributed financial and other support thereto. Since the Association as such has
ceased to function and there appears no likelihood
of its reestablishment, we shall not order that it be
disestablished. We have further found that the respondent has dominated and interfered with the

Board's Exhibit No. 15—(Continued)

formation and administration of the Alliance and has contributed support thereto. The effect and consequences of the respondent's domination, in_terference with, and support of the Alliance, as well as the continued recognition of the Alliance as the bargaining representative of its employees, constitute a continuing obstacle to the free exercise by its employees of their right to self-organization and to bargain collectively through representatives of their own choosing. Because of the respondent's illegal conduct, the Alliance is incapable of serving the respondent's employees as a genuine collective bargaining agency. Moreover the continued recognition of the Alliance would be obstructive of the free exercise by the employees of the rights guaranteed them by the Act. Accordingly, we will order the respondent to disestablish and withdraw all recognition from the Alliance as the representative of any of its employees for the purpose of dealing with it concerning grievances, labor disputes, wages, rates of pay, hours of employment, or other conditions of employment.

We have also found that the contracts entered into between the respondent and the Alliance have been a means whereby the respondent has utilized an employer-dominated labor organization to frustrate self-organization and defeat collective bargaining by its employees. Under these circumstances, any continuation, renewal, or modification of such agreements would perpetuate the conditions which have deprived employees of the rights guaranteed them

Board's Exhibit No. 15—(Continued)
by the Act and would render ineffectual other portions of our remedial order. We shall therefore
order the respondent to cease giving effect to any
contracts between it and the Alliance, or to any
modification or extension thereof. Nothing in the
order, however, shall be taken to require the respondent to vary those wage, hour, and other such
substantive features of its relations with the employees themselves, which the respondent may have
established in performance of these contracts as extended, renewed, modified, supplemented or superseded.

Upon the basis of the foregoing findings of fact,
and upon the entire record in the case, the Board
makes the following:

CONCLUSIONS OF LAW

1. United Automobile Workers of America, Local
300, affiliated with the Congress of Industrial Organizations, and Automotive and Aircraft Workers
Alliance, Inc., are labor organizations, and Thompson Products, Inc., Employees Association was a
labor organization, within the meaning of Section
2 (5) of the Act.

2. By dominating and interfering with the administration of Thompson Products, Inc., Employees Association, and contributing financial and
other support thereto, and by dominating and interfering with the formation and administration of
Automotive and Aircraft Workers Alliance, Inc.,
and contributing support thereto, the respondent
has engaged in, and as to the Alliance is engaging

Board's Exhibit No. 15—(Continued)
in, unfair labor practices, within the meaning of
Section 8 (2) of the Act.

3. By interfering with, restraining, and coercing
its employees in the exercise of the rights guaranteed in Section 7 of the Act, the respondent has engaged in and is engaging in unfair labor practices,
within the meaning of Section 8 (1) of the Act.

4. The aforesaid unfair labor practices are unfair labor practices affecting commerce, within the
meaning of Section 2 (6) and (7) of the Act.

5. The respondent has not engaged in unfair
labor practices within the meaning of Section 8 (2)
of the Act in so far as the complaint alleges that the
balance in the Association treasury was used by the
Association to defray Alliance formation expenses.

6. The respondent has not engaged in unfair
labor practices within the meaning of Section 8 (1)
of the Act in so far as the complaint alleges that on
May 8, 1940, the respondent, through its plant manager, sought to discourage the union activity of a
laid-off employee.

ORDER

Upon the basis of the above findings of fact and
conclusions of law, and pursuant to Section 10 (c)
of the National Labor Relations Act, the National
Labor Relations Board hereby orders that the respondent, Thompson Products, Inc., Cleveland,
Ohio, its officers, agents, successors, and assigns,
shall:

1. Cease and desist from:

Board's Exhibit No. 15—(Continued)

(a) Dominating or interfering with the administration of Thompson Products, Inc., Employees Association, and with the formation or administration of Automotive and Aircraft Workers Alliance, Inc., or any other labor organization of its employees, and from contributing financial or other support to said labor organizations or to any labor organization of its employees;

(b) Giving effect to any and all contracts, or supplements thereto or modifications thereof, with Automotive and Aircraft Workers Alliance, Inc.;

(c) In any other manner interfering with, restraining, or coercing its employees in the exercise of the right to self-organization, to form, join, or assist labor organizations, to bargain collectively through representatives of their own choosing, and to engage in concerted activities for the purpose of collective bargaining or other mutual aid or protection as guaranteed in Section 7 of the Act.

2. Take the following affirmative action which the Board finds will effectuate the policies of the Act:

(a) Withdraw all recognition from Automotive and Aircraft Workers Alliance, Inc., as the representative of any of its employees for the purpose of dealing with the respondent concerning grievances, labor disputes, wages, rates of pay, hours of employment, or other conditions of employment, and completely disestablish Automotive and Aircraft Workers Alliance, Inc., as such representative;

Board's Exhibit No. 15—(Continued)

(b) Post immediately in conspicuous places throughout its plants at Cleveland, Ohio, and maintain for a period of at least sixty (60) consecutive days from the date of posting, notices stating: (1) that the respondent will not engage in the conduct from which it is ordered to cease and desist in paragraphs 1 (a), (b), and (c) of this Order; and (2) that it will take the affirmative action set forth in paragraph 2 (a) of this Order;

(c) Notify the Regional Director for the Eighth Region in writing within ten (10) days from the date of this Order what steps the respondent has taken to comply herewith;

And It Is Further Ordered that the complaint be, and the same hereby is dismissed, in so far as it alleges that the balance in the Association treasury was used by the Association to defray Alliance formation expenses, and in so far as it further alleges that on May 8, 1940, the respondent, through its plant manager, sought to discourage the union activity of a laid-off employee.

Signed at Washington, D. C., this 1 day of Aug., 1941.

[SEAL]   HARRY A. MILLIS
                    Chairman
              EDWIN S. SMITH
                    Member
              WM.M. LEISERSON
                    Member
              National Labor Relations
                    Board

FLORENCE LAVERNE NEAL,

called as a witness by and on behalf of the Pacific Motor Parts Workers Alliance, having been first duly sworn, was examined and testified as follows:

Direct Examination

Q. (By Mr. Baldwin): Will you state your full name?

A. Florence Laverne Neal.

Q. Do you work at Thompson Products in Bell, California?   A. I do.

Q. How long have you been there?

A. Since February 27, 1941. 1942, rather, I should say.

Q. 1942?   A. Yes.

Q. What is your position there?

A. Timekeeper in the shop.

Q. Are you now a member of the Alliance?

A. Yes, I am. [564]

Q. Were you ever approached or asked by anyone to join the C.I.O.?   A. Yes, I was.

Q. Where?

A. During working hours in the shop.

Q. Well, where at in the shop?

A. In the time booth. I was in the time booth.

Q. Did one or more ask you to join?

A. As near as I remember there were two of them. At the time I was new there. I remember one of them and the other one I don't recall who he was.

Q. Can you name the one that you know?

A. James Crank.

(Testimony of Florence Laverne Neal.)

Q.   What shift were you on at the time, do you know?

A.   It was the swing shift, from 3:30 until midnight.

Q.   Were you asked more than once by these people?

A.   Oh, yes, I was approached several times.

Q.   Could you state any of the conversations you had with Mr. Crank?

Mr. Moore: Object, if the Examiner please.   It is immaterial.

Trial Examiner Whittemore: I will sustain the objection.

Mr. Baldwin: That will be all.

Trial Examiner Whittemore: Mr. Moore, any questions? [565]

Cross Examination

Q.   (By Mr. Moore):   How long did Mr. Crank talk to you when he asked you to join?

A.   Well, he asked me several different times, but I don't recall the length of time that it took him to ask me.

Q.   Did it interfere with your work?

A.   Well, naturally it was during working hours.

Q.   Did it interfere with your work?

A.   Well, I don't know what you mean by that exactly.   I had other work to do at all times.

Q.   Well, did it interfere with your work?

Mr. Watkins: I object to the repetition of the question as being argumentative.   The witness has answered.

(Testimony of Florence Laverne Neal.)

Trial Examiner Whittemore: I will sustain the objection.

Mr. Moore: No other questions.

Mr. Watkins: I have no questions.

Trial Examiner Whittemore: Anything further?

Mr. Baldwin: No.

Q. (By Trial Examiner Whittemore): Did you report this to anyone?   A. Pardon me?

Q. Did you report this to anyone?

A. What do you mean?

Q. That Mr. Crank had talked to you during working hours and asked you to join the C.I.O.?

[566]

A. You mean did I report it to anyone at the plant?

Q. Yes.   A. Why, yes, I have.

Q. To whom?

A. Well, I don't know. To various ones.

Q. When?   A. At the time of the incident.

Q. All right.

A. It wasn't discussed—no—at length, if that is what you mean.

Q. Well, you have a foreman or forelady, or something there?

A. Yes, we have a foreman in the shop.

Q. Did you report it to the foreman?

A. No, I didn't report it to the foreman.

Q. To whom did you report it?

A. Well, I didn't exactly report it. I didn't report it.

(Testimony of Florence Laverne Neal.)

Q. Then you haven't reported it? A. No.

Q. How did Mr. Baldwin know about it?

A. Well, I have discussed it, yes, but I didn't report it to a foreman.

Q. Did you report it to Mr. Baldwin?

A. Yes, I did.

Q. When?

A. Well, I don't remember the time that I reported it to [567] Mr. Baldwin.

Q. Did he come to you and ask you if anyone had?

A. No. Mr. Baldwin didn't question me as to that.

Trial Examiner Whittemore: All right.

Mr. Baldwin: Mr. Examiner, I think I can clear it up if I ask two questions.

Trial Examiner Whittemore: Go ahead.

Redirect Examination

Q. (By Mr. Baldwin) Miss Neal, at the time that you were asked to join the C. I. O. it had happened on numerous occasions and at that time you asked me, I believe, what to do about it?

Trial Examiner Whittemore: Well, now, just a minute. If you want to take the stand, I have no objection at all.

Mr. Baldwin: All right, then I will ask her differently. I am sorry.

Trial Examiner Whittemore: All right.

Q. (By Mr. Baldwin) You mentioned the incident to me and I told you not to worry about it.

(Testimony of Florence Laverne Neal.)

Trial Examiner Whittemore: Well, now, wait a minute.

Mr. Baldwin: I am sorry.

Trial Examiner Whittemore: I am going to overlook the fact of your not being an attorney in this matter, but just ask questions, don't testify. If you want to take the stand later I have no objection that you should.

Mr. Baldwin: Yes, sir, thank you. [568]

Trial Examiner Whittemore: If you have any questions to put to the witness, why, please do so.

Q. (By Mr. Baldwin) Miss Neal, you didn't— or, rather, you told someone about the incident?

A. Yes, I have.

Q. And do you know——

Trial Examiner Whittemore: Now, wait just a minute. Off the record.

(Discussion off the record.)

The Witness: May I say something?

Trial Examiner Whittemore: Surely. On the record.

The Witness: Well, at this time I was very new there and I didn't know a thing about the C. I. O. or practically any other union because I didn't have anything to do about them, and that was what brought up my asking Mr. Baldwin about it in the first place, because I am not familiar with the C. I. O. or any other union in a case of this kind. It was the first time I had ever worked in a factory and that was the time that I asked Mr. Baldwin about it.

(Testimony of Florence Laverne Neal.)

Q. (By Trial Examiner Whittemore) When did you ask him?

A. Shortly after I was contacted. I went to work there the latter part of February and it was in March that they approached me.

Q. Did you go to Mr. Baldwin or did he go to you?

A. No, I went to Mr. Baldwin because I didn't know anything [569] about the unions.

Q. Did you go to him during working hours?

A. No, sir.

Trial Examiner Whittemore: You didn't. All right.

Mr. Baldwin: Well, I believe that will cover it.

Trial Examiner Whittemore: Does that cover that point?

Mr. Baldwin: Yes.

Trial Examiner Whittemore: All right. Then you are excused. Thank you very much.

(Witness excused.)

Mr. Baldwin: Mr. Gibbon.

WILLIAM ALBERT GIBBON,

called as a witness by and on behalf of the Pacific Motor Parts Workers Alliance, having been first duly sworn, was examined and testified as follows:

Direct Examination

Q. (By Mr. Baldwin) Will you state your full name, please?

(Testimony of William Albert Gibbon.)

A.   William Albert Gibbon.

Q.   Do you work for Thompson Products at Bell, California?   A.   Yes, sir.

Q.   How long have you worked for them?

A.   Since 1940, January 1940.

Q.   What is your position there?

A.   Thread grinder operator.

Q.   Are you a member of the Alliance? [570]

A.   Yes, sir.

Q.   Were you at any time asked to join the C. I. O.?   A.   I was.

Q.   Where?   A.   In the wash room.

Q.   Was that during working hours?

A.   Yes, sir.

Q.   Were you asked more than once?

A.   Yes, sir.

Q.   At any other place besides the wash room?

A.   Well, I work swing shift, graveyard, and at that time I am all over the shop, and many a time— I was approached at the tool crib and, well, there was quite a few places.

Q.   Can you state—

Mr. Moore: Just a moment. I will move that the latter part of the answer "a great many places" be stricken.

Trial Examiner Whittemore: I believe I will let it stand.

Q.   (By Mr. Baldwin) Can you state by whom you were approached?

A.   Elmer Smith, for one. The other fellow I

(Testimony of William Albert Gibbon.)

don't know his name. He's a new fellow in the shop.

Q. Did Mr. Smith ask you more than once?

A. Yes, sir.

Q. Did Mr. Smith ever hand you a card? **[571]**

A. Well, when the——

Q. Just say whether he did or not.

A. Yes, sir.

Q. Do you know what was on the card?

A. No, I don't.

Q. You didn't look at the card at all?

A. No, sir. The one time he gave me a card, it was a place of meeting, where they were going to hold a meeting of some kind. I don't know what it was. He asked me—it had that address and the name of a fellow's house. That was one card. But there was another card too.

Q. You couldn't state whether or not it was an application card in the C. I. O.?

A. No, I didn't pay much attention.

Mr. Baldwin: That is all.

Cross Examination

Q. (By Mr. Moore) Did you ever report to anyone that you had been asked to join the C. I. O.?

A. No, sir.

Mr. Moore: No one at all.

Mr. Watkins: Pardon me. May I have the question read?

(The question was read.)

Q. (By Mr. Moore) When did you join the Alliance?

(Testimony of William Albert Gibbon.)

A. Well, I can't state the date that I joined. I have belonged for about two and a half years.

[572]

Q. Did someone request you to join the Alliance?   A. Yes, sir.

Q. Who did that?

A. Well, fellows outside, that works there in the plant talked to me.

Q. Do you know who they were?

A. Yes, sir.

Q. Who was it?

A. One was Jimmy Clayball.

Q. Who was another?

A. Well, I can't recall their names, all who asked me to join.

Q. They always talked to you off work, is that right?   A. Yes, sir.

Mr. Moore: That is all.

Trial Examiner Whittemore: That is all.

(Witness excused.)

Mr. Baldwin: Mr. McIntire.

GEORGE EDWARD McINTIRE,

called as a witness by and on behalf of the Pacific Motor Parts Workers Alliance, having been first duly sworn, was examined and testified as follows:

Direct Examination

Q. (By Mr. Baldwin) Will you state your name, please?

(Testimony of George Edward McIntire.)

A. George Edward McIntire. [573]

Q. You work for Thompson Products in Bell?

A. Yes, sir.

Q. How long have you worked there?

A. Seven years, I believe, in January last.

Q. About 1935, the year 1935?

A. '36, I believe. Now I wouldn't say for sure.

Q. January 1936. What is your position there?

A. Flash welder.

Q. Did you know Mr. Kangas?

A. Yes, sir.

Q. Did Mr. Kangas ever ask you to join the C. I. O.? A. Yes, sir.

Mr. Watkins: What Kangas is that?

Mr. Baldwin: Victor Kangas.

Mr. Watkins: The witness' testimony, I think, should be straightened out on that, if that is who it is.

Q. (By Mr. Baldwin) Was this Victor Kangas? A. Yes, sir.

Q. Where did he ask you to join the C. I. O.? Where were you at the time?

A. In the front office, the shop, in Bell.

Q. Did Mr. Kangas tell you why he wanted you to join the C. I. O.? A. Yes, sir.

Q. Can you relate the conversation? [574]

A. I think I can relate most of it.

Q. Did he call you into the office?

A. He sent my boss out and asked me to come into the office.

Q. And did you go into the office?

(Testimony of George Edward McIntire.)

A. Yes, sir.

Q. And what did Mr. Kangas say to you?

Mr. Moore: Just a moment. I object to it until a time is established.

Trial Examiner Whittemore: Perhaps you had better establish a date.

Q. (By Mr. Baldwin) About when?

A. Well, it's approximately two months—well, I would say in May.

Q. (By Trial Examiner Whittemore) This year?

A. No, in '37. I couldn't state the exact date because I don't remember it.

Mr. Moore: May I have the answer read? I didn't quite get it.

(The answer was read.)

Q. (By Mr. Baldwin) You say it was approximately May, 1937? A. Yes, sir.

Q. What did Mr. Kangas say to you at that meeting?

A. He told me at that time that the company had changed hands and that he looked for them to send out a new shop foreman and let him go; that they were going to hire some [575] new employees in the shop and let a lot of the employees go, and he asked me to join the C. I. O. and told me that there was three or four other fellows joining and wanted us to get together and organize a C. I. O. and stand behind him and in turn he would stand behind us and see we were not discharged and we would stand behind him and see

(Testimony of George Edward McIntire.)
that they didn't discharge him; if they did, why, we'd all walk out.

Q. At that time was there any feeling of unrest in regards to Thompson taking over the plant?

Mr. Moore: Object to the question.

Trial Examiner Whittemore: No, I will permit the witness to answer.

The Witness: Well, everybody seemed more or less satisfied. There was naturally a little unrest, but not knowing who was coming in and so on and so forth, why, we didn't know anything about Thompson Products; to the extent we didn't know what to look for; but otherwise I would say no.

Q. (By Trial Examiner Whittemore) What do you mean? There was or there wasn't?

A. Well, there wasn't.

Q. And yet naturally there was. Just what is it you mean?

A. Well, you're working for one company and they sell to another one; you don't know just what this other company does, their policies. [576]

JOHN ROBERT BOWMAN,

called as a witness by and on behalf of the Pacific Motor Parts Workers Alliance, having been first duly sworn, was examined and testified as follows:

Direct Examination

Q. (By Mr. Baldwin) Will you state your full name, please?

(Testimony of John Robert Bowman.)

A.   John   Robert   Bowman.   [579]

Q.   You   work   at   Thompson   Products   in   Bell, California?   A.   Yes,   sir.

Q.   How   long   have   you   worked   there?

A.   Since   February,   1940.

Q.   What   is   your   position   there?

A.   Grinder   operator,   finish,   Cincinnati.

Q.   Are   you   a   member   of   the   Alliance?

A.   Yes,   sir.

Q.   Did   anyone   ever   approach   you   and   ask   you to   join   the   C.   I.   O.?   A.   Yes,   sir.

Q.   Can   you   state   where?

A.   Yes,   sir.   When   I   used   to   finish   grind   Douglas   Aircraft   bolts,   I   have   to   go   from   my   machine into   where   they   ground   them,   the   next   operation would   be   mine,   and   I   have   to   go   in   and   pick   them up and   then   bring   them   back   out   and   finish   them. And   Mr.   Hess   from   the   grinder   had   finished   the heads   and   then   I   finished   the   stem   and   radius; and   whenever   I   would   go   to   get   bolts   he   would talk   to   me   about   the   C.   I.   O.   and   ask   me   to   join.

Q.   This   obviously   was   during   working   hours?

A.   Yes,   sir.

Trial   Examiner   Whittemore: Well,   now,   let   us find   out,   if   you   don't   mind.

Mr.   Baldwin: Surely.   [580]

Q.   (By   Mr.   Baldwin)   Was   this   during   working   hours?

Trial   Examiner   Whittemore: Don't   let   us   pass on   whether   it   is   obvious   or   not.

The   Witness: Yes,   sir,   it   was.

(Testimony of John Robert Bowman.)

Trial Examiner Whittemore: You have to ask him when it was. Don't draw conclusions.

Mr. Baldwin: Yes, sir.

Q. (By Mr. Baldwin) Could you state about how long ago this was or when it was?

A. Oh, I would say it was probably in March or April.

Q. Of what year? A. This year.

Q. 1942. Were you ever approached by anyone else and asked to join the C. I. O.?

A. No, sir, I don't believe I was.

Mr. Baldwin: That is all.

Cross Examination

Q. (By Mr. Moore) Have you ever been a member of the C. I. O.? A. Yes, sir.

Q. When did you join?

A. I joined the day that he was talking to me about it, and then I decided it wasn't so good and so I quit.

Q. You testified, didn't you, that he would usually talk to you?

A. He would talk to me when I would go to get bolts at his [581] machine to bring to mine.

Q. Now you say you joined on the day he talked to you? A. That is right.

Q. Which time was it?

A. Just what I said.

Q. How many times did he talk to you?

A. Well, I don't know. It was several times.

(Testimony of John Robert Bowman.)

A box of bolts would last me about two hours, and I would have to go back and get some more.

Q. Did he only talk to you on one day?

A. Well, several days before that, too.

Q. When did you join the C. I. O.?

A. Well, let me see. I don't know when it was.

Q. Pardon me.

A. I don't remember the date it was.

Q. Would you say approximately?

A. No, I wouldn't, because I wouldn't be sure.

Q. You have no idea when you joined the C. I. O.?

A. Well, it was some time this year. Probably some time in March or April.

Q. And when did you drop out of the C. I. O.?

A. About a month after I joined.

Q. Why?

A. Because it wasn't no good.

Q. What was wrong with it? [582]

A. There wasn't anything I think of that wasn't wrong with it.

Q. Did you attend any meetings of the C.I.O.?

A. Yes, sir.

Q. How many?

A. I think there was two.

Q. What happened at those meetings that made you think there was nothing to it?

A. Well, heck, I don't know. It's just——

Trial Examiner Whittemore: Well, I am not interested in what this witness thinks one way or the other.

(Testimony of John Robert Bowman.)

The Witness: Could I just give my opinion?

Mr. Moore: No.

The Witness: Or reason?

Trial Examiner Whittemore: No. That has no bearing on the issues here.

Q. (By Mr. Moore) Were you a member of the Alliance before you joined the C.I.O.?

A. Yes, sir.

Q. And since you resigned from the C.I.O. did you rejoin the Alliance?

A. I never did quit the P.M.P.W.A.

Q. You never did quit it?

A. No, sir. I kept on paying my dues.

Q. You were a member of both, then, for a period? [583]

A. Yes, for one month. [584]

EDWARD FRANCIS COLLATZ

called as a witness by and on behalf of the **Pacific Motor Parts Workers Alliance**, having been first duly sworn, was examined and testified as follows:

Direct Examination

Q. (By Mr. Baldwin) Will you state your full name, please?

A. Edward Francis Collatz.

Q. Do you work for Thompson Products in Bell, California? [585]   A. I do.

Mr. Watkins: May I interrupt a minute? How do you spell this name?

(Testimony of Edward Francis Collatz.)

The Witness: C-o-l-l-a-t-z.

Q. (By Mr. Baldwin) How long have you been employed there?

A. Let's see. I believe it was in June, 1940.

Q. What is your position?　　A. Electrician.

Q. Are you a member of the Alliance?

A. I am.

Q. Did you know Mr. Elmer Smith?

A. Yes, I knew him.

Q. Did you ever have any conversation with Mr. Smith relating to unions or their activities?

A. Several.

Q. Did Mr. Smith ever state a preference for unions other than the Alliance?　　A. Yes.

Mr. Moore: I will object to that.

Trial Examiner Whittemore: Was Smith an employee there? Who was this Smith?

Mr. Moore: He was an employee but it is not shown that he was anything more than just an employee.

Trial Examiner Whittemore: Who is this Smith anyway?

The Witness: Well, at the time he was—— [586]

Mr. Baldwin: He was a lathe hand.

The Witness: He was a lathe hand down there. But at the time he was a committeeman for the P.M.P.W.A., the Alliance.

Trial Examiner Whittemore: I don't know what bearing this has, what he may have said, two employees talking to each other.

(Testimony of Edward Francis Collatz.)

Mr. Baldwin: Well, Mr. Smith has testified here and I would like to——

Trial Examiner Whittemore: Well, go ahead. Is this brief?

Mr. Baldwin: Yes, it is.

Trial Examiner Whittemore: All right.

Q. (By Mr. Baldwin) Did Mr. Smith—I asked that question before. Did Mr. Smith state a preference to you for the C.I.O.?

A. Yes, he did at the time. He stated that while he had only been a committeeman a short time, and I thought it was an odd statement, due to the fact that he was elected to the Alliance, and then tell me in his own heart he preferred the C.I.O.

Q. Will you state as closely as you can what the conversation was?

A. Well, at the time they were motorizing a machine down there that he happened to be working on, a lathe, and I [587] asked him how be liked his new job as committeeman. He said he didn't like it, it was all right, he said, but, he said, his heart was in a larger organization. And at the time, of course, naturally, he and I used to argue about it, just our own opinions, and I asked him why he thought that a larger organization, which he stated the C.I.O., was better than our little organization, and he went on and tried to explain about the power of it, and so forth.

Q. (By Trial Examiner Whittemore) Just a minute. You started this conversation, didn't you?

A. No, he did.

(Testimony of Edward Francis Collatz.)

Trial Examiner Whittemore: Read back the witness' answer, please.

The Witness: No, that is right, I started it, I guess.

Q. (By Trial Examiner Whittemore) You admit you started the conversation?

A. Yes, I started it.

Trial Examiner Whittemore: All right, then I think you should forego any further questions on this point.

Mr. Baldwin: I merely wanted to have him state the conversation exactly as it was.

Trial Examiner Whittemore: I don't think it is necessary. The witness has testified now that he started the conversation. Now whatever may have been said as a result of any questions he may have asked I don't think is material. [588]

Mr. Baldwin: I will ask one question then.

Trial Examiner Whittemore: All right.

Q. (By Mr. Baldwin) Did Mr. Smith ever tell you he had a brother as a paid organizer in the C.I.O.?

A. Yes, that's what the conversation was about.

Q. He did state that fact to you?

A. Absolutely. He said he was in the east and he was a paid organizer. And, of course, I expressed my personal opinion.

Q. Well, we won't go into your opinion.

At the time was he a committeeman with the Alliance? A. That is right.

(Testimony of Edward Francis Collatz.)

Q. Can you state the approximate date that this occurred?

Trial Examiner Whittemore: Smith himself testified to that, didn't he?

Mr. Baldwin: He merely testified to the fact he said his brother was a paid organizer in the C.I.O. after he had left the Alliance.

Trial Examiner Whittemore: Well, just what difference does it make whether he was in the Alliance or not?

Mr. Baldwin: Well, trying to show that Mr. Smith was not working for the best interests of our organization.

Trial Examiner Whittemore: Well, suppose he wasn't?

Mr. Baldwin: Well, it would have a bearing on this. It would have a bearing on this trial that has come up.

Trial Examiner Whittemore: Well, I have no objection [589] if the witness can fix the time of this conversation.

Q. (By Mr. Baldwin) Can you fix the time of that conversation?

A. Yes. It was in December, around the first part of December.

Q. (By Trial Examiner Whittemore) What year? A. 1941.

Q. (By Mr. Baldwin) 1941. Did you report that to anyone or did you talk to anyone about it?

A. No, at the time I didn't, outside of, just like the rest of the fellows working down there, why,

(Testimony of Edward Francis Collatz.)

it was just a matter of conversation. The boys elected him committeeman and he turned right around.

Q. Well, did you say this in a group at any time anywhere?

A. Several times, but I just don't recall to whom.

Mr. Baldwin: That is all.

Mr. Moore: No questions.

Cross Examination

Q. (By Mr. Watkins) Did Mr. Elmer Smith say where his brother was located back east?

A. Why, he said he was in the east and I assumed by the fact that he was back in Cleveland.

Mr. Watkins: That is all.

Trial Examiner Whittemore: That is all. You are excused. Thank you.

(Witness excused.) [590]

Mr. Baldwin: I believe that is all the witnesses I will call, Mr. Examiner. [591]

WILLIAM I. METZGER,

called as a witness by and on behalf of the respondent, having been first duly sworn, was examined and testified as follows:

Direct Examination

Q. (By Mr. Watkins) Are you employed by Thompson Products, West Coast Division?

A. Yes.

(Testimony of William I. Metzger.)

Q. In what capacity?

A. Plant comptroller.

Q. Are you familiar with the time cards used by that company, past and present?   A. Yes.

Mr. Watkins: May I please have this marked as Respondent's Exhibit 3? [595]

(Thereupon the document referred to was marked as Respondent's Exhibit No. 3, for identification.)

Q. (By Mr. Watkins) I show you, Mr. Metzger, a card marked for identification as Respondent's Exhibit 3, and will ask you to state briefly what that is.

A. It is a semi-monthly time card for the half month ended July 31, 1937 for L. A. Porter.

Q. Is that Louis A. Porter?   A. Yes.

Q. And did you have that taken out of your office records at the plant?   A. Yes.

Mr. Watkins: I will offer Respondent's 3 for identification into evidence, Mr. Examiner.

Trial Examiner Whittemore: Any objection?

Mr. Moore: No objection.

Mr. Watkins: And I should like to have permission to submit a photostatic copy in the place of it.

Mr. Moore: I have no objection to that.

Trial Examiner Whittemore: All right. The document is received in evidence.

(Thereupon the document heretofore marked for identification as Respondent's Exhibit No. 3, was received in evidence.)

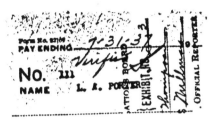

THIS SIDE

—No. 111
NAME L. R. PORTER

GROUP No.		
GROUP No.		
NON-PRODUCTIVE DAY WORK		
OVERTIME PREMIUM		
TOTAL		13
STATE U. I. TAX		74
FEDERAL O. A. B. TAX		82
BENEFIT AND GROUP INS.	1	00
OTHER DEDUCTIONS		

NET EARNINGS

TOTAL TIME 130² HRS. RATE 63
AMOUNT DUE FOR ABOVE $82.22
RECEIVED THE ABOVE AMOUNT Paid

(Testimony of William I. Metzger.)

Mr. Watkins: I want to ask the witness one question about it. [596]

Q. (By Mr. Watkins) Mr. Metzger, I will refer you to Respondent's Exhibit 3, to the date which I believe is shown on there, of July 27, 1937, and will ask you what time on that date Mr. Porter checked in and checked out?

A. He checked in in the morning at 5:58, out at noon at 12:00 o'clock, in in the afternoon at 1:22 and out in the evening at 4:31.

Q. Does that card also show what time he was paid for that day?

A. It shows he was paid for nine hours.

Q. Mr. Metzger, directing your attention to a time some time in, I believe, the year 1938, were you with the Kinner Aircraft Company about that time? A. Yes.

Q. Did you have any difficulty of any character involving valves? A. Yes.

Q. Will you explain as briefly as you can just what that was?

A. There was evidence that Kinner valves were being stolen and sold on the market. This was brought out by Mr. Herring of Airplane Parts and Supply, who was in that business, and he found them on the market being sold, as we call it, bootleg valves.

Q. Did you have some reason to believe that it might be happening through Thompson Products, or at that time, [597] Jadson Motor Parts?

(Testimony of William I. Metzger.)

A. Yes, they were readily identified as Jadson valves.

Q. Did you check with regard to it with anyone at Jadson?

A. Yes, we checked with Mr. Hileman, who was the general manager.

Q. Did you have any visit subsequent to that time from anyone from Thompson or Jadson concerning this matter?

A. Yes. Mr. Louis Porter visited us at Kinner some time about the first of June of 1938.

Q. On more than one occasion or just once?

A. Just once.

Q. And that was with respect to an investigation, was it, of these valves?

A. Yes. He was getting the information, all the information we had, in trying to run down the source of these valves.

Q. Yes. Some time after this instance did you go over as an officer or employee of Jadson?

A. Yes.

Q. About what time?   A. July 1, 1938.

Q. Then, after you went over to Jadson, did you have any discussion of any character with Mr. Hileman concerning this investigation?

A. Yes.

Q. Will you say, if you can recall, where it took place? [598]

A. It was in his office.

Q. Who was present?

(Testimony of William I. Metzger.)

A. So far as I can recall just Mr. Hileman and myself.

Q. About when was it?

A. During the first half of July, I would say.

Q. Of 1938? A. Of 1938.

Q. Yes. Will you state what was the discussion? What was said by each of you?

A. Why, Mr. Hileman said he wanted to reimburse Mr. Porter for his time and energies in connection with this valve investigation, and that the amount he wanted to pay him was $40 and he asked me what my opinion was of the way it should be paid. We decided to pay it in cash, rather than by check.

Q. Did you have a discussion as to your reasons for doing it in that fashion? A. Yes.

Q. What was your discussion in that regard?

A. It was thought that the—it might have been an inside job. That is, someone within the plant might have been taking valves out, and we did not want anyone in the office to know that this money was being paid to Mr. Porter.

Q. Why did you say that? In other words, if you had given him a check, what difference would that make?

A. Well, it would have to go through a number of hands, [599] and we didn't know who was involved at the time and we didn't care to have general knowledge that there was an investigation being made.

(Testimony of William I. Metzger.)

Q. Did you have any talk about this payment to Mr. Porter with Mr. Victor Kangas? You, yourself?   A. I don't recall I did.

Q. Did you subsequent to this discussion receive any expense voucher of any character involving this transaction?

A. Yes. I received an expense account.

Mr. Watkins: May I have this marked, please, as Respondent's next in order?

(Thereupon the document referred to was marked as Respondent's Exhibit No. 4, for identification.)

Q. (By Mr. Watkins) I show you Respondent's Exhibit 4 for identification, entitled at the top "Weekly Report of Expense, Name: L. A. Porter," and ask you if that is the document to which you refer?   A. Yes.

Q. I direct your attention to certain notations of "approved" at the top. You will note certain initials there. The top one, I will ask you if you know whose initials those are?   A. Yes.

Q. What are the initials?   A. V.E.K.

Q. And whose initials are they? [600]

A. Victor Kangas.

Q. Are you familiar with his initials and his signature, in your work down there?   A. Yes.

Q. And the initials underneath the "approved", whose are those?

A. P.D.H.; that's Paul D. Hileman.

Q. And are you familiar with his signature?

A. Yes.

(Testimony of William I. Metzger.)

Mr. Watkins: I will now offer this in evidence as Respondent's Exhibit 4.

Mr. Moore: No objection.

Mr. Watkins: I would like to also have the privilege of withdrawing it and putting in a photostatic copy.

Mr. Moore: No objection.

Trial Examiner Whittemore: The document will be received and a substitution may be made for the original.

(Thereupon the document heretofore marked for identification as Respondent's Exhibit No. 4, was received in evidence.) **[601]**

RESPONDENT'S EXHIBIT No. 4

WEEKLY REPORT OF EXPENSES

Name—L. A. Porter   Week Ending July 16, 1938
                                     Approved—V.E.K.
                                     Approved—P.D.H.

Items		Sunday	Monday	Tuesday	Wednesday
Hotel		....	....	....	....
Breakfast		....	....	....	....
Noon Meal		....	....	....	....
Evening Meal		....	....	....	....
Railroad Fare	From	....	....	....	....
	To	....	....	....	....
Baggage		....	....	....	....
Street Car and Taxi		....	....	....	....
Postage, Telegrams, Etc.		....	....	....	....
		....	....	....	....
		....	....	....	....
Mileage		....	....	....	....
Total		....	....	....	....

(Testimony of William I. Metzger.)

Items		Thursday	Friday	Saturday	Expense Summary	
Hotel		....	....	....	Sunday	....
Breakfast		....	....	....	Monday	....
Noon Meal		....	....	....	Tuesday	....
Evening Meal		....	....	....	Wednesday	....
Railroad Fare	From	....	....	....	Thursday	....
	To	....	....	....	Friday	....
Baggage		....	....	....	Saturday	....
Street Car and Taxi		....	....	....	Total	....
Postage, Telegrams, Etc.	....	....	....	Cash on Hand	....
		....	....	....	Cash from Co.	....
		....	....	....	Total	....
Mileage		....	....	....	Expenses	....
Total		....	....	$40.00	Balance	....

Jadson Motor Products Co.

LEWIS LEROY LONG,

called as a witness by and on behalf of the respondent, having been first duly sworn, was examined and testified as follows:

Direct Examination

Q. (By Mr. Watkins) Will you state your full name, please? [609]

A. Lewis Leroy Long.

Q. What is your official capacity at Thompson Products? A. General foreman.

Q. And have you been in that shop for some period of time? A. Two years.

(Testimony of Lewis Leroy Long.)

Q. What was your position for the predecessor company immediately prior to that?

A. Foreman.

Q. Mr. Long, Mr. Louis Porter, you know him, do you?   A. Yes, I do.

Q. Mr. Louis Porter testified that, I believe, at some time in 1941, I can't give you the date of it, he talked to you near the tool crib and stated, in effect, that you said to him: We have got plenty of reports of your C.I.O. talk.

Do you remember of any conversation of that character with Mr. Porter?

A. I have never had any conversation.

Q. Would you say positively you did not make that statement, or that in substance? '

A. To my knowledge, yes.

Q. To that effect? What do you mean by: to your knowledge?

A. I have never talked to Louis about any union activities.

Q. Mr. Porter further testified that this same afternoon of this date, that you came to him and said, in substance: Lou, let's get along; but I don't think much of that damned [610] C.I.O. Further than that, when you are wearing your C.I.O. button you are sticking your neck out and somebody will knock it off.

Do you recall any such conversation with Mr. Porter?

A. Never had any conversation with him like that.

(Testimony of Lewis Leroy Long.)

Q. Will you say positively you didn't say what you were supposed to have said on that, in substance?   A. That's correct.

Mr. Watkins: You may cross examine.

Cross Examination

Q. (By Mr. Moore) Mr. Long, directing your attention to the period for 1941, would your answer be the same if that period were 1942?

A. Yes, it would.

Q. Do you remember when Mr. Louis A. Porter came to the Board, here, in order to give information to the Board?

A. I know nothing about it.

Q. Did he leave the plant one day in order to come up here?

A. I know nothing about it.

Q. When was the first time you did know he had been up here?

A. I have known he has been up here? He don't tell me what he does when he leaves the plant.

Mr. Watkins: I cannot quite hear you, Mr. Long.

The Witness: He didn't tell me what he was doing when he left the plant. He told me he was sick. [611]

Q. (By Mr. Moore) Did Mr. Kearns tell you?

A. No, he didn't.

Q. You mean you have never learned, to this moment, that Mr. Porter came up here and gave evidence to the Board for use in this case?

(Testimony of Lewis Leroy Long.)

A. Well, probably after this was started.

Q. What do you mean by: after this was started?

A. When he took days off down at the shop he didn't tell me where he was going, and I didn't ask him.

Q. When did you first learn he had given information for use in this case?

A. When the case started up here.

Q. You mean after October 1, 1942?

A. That's right.

Q. You didn't learn it before October 1, 1942?

A. I wouldn't have any reason to.

Q. Well, did you?   A. No.

Q. At the time Mr. Porter quit out there you knew nothing at that time about his having given information to the Labor Board concerning the case in which the company was involved?

A. I didn't know anything about a Labor Board. I knew he had had some trouble with the F.B.I.

Q. You didn't know he had been at the Labor Board?   A. No. [612]

Q. Did you have trouble with Mr. Porter at the plant at any time?

A. No trouble at all with him.

Q. Did you ever talk to him?

A. Talked to him every day.

Q. Every day?   A. Sure, about his work.

Q. Did you give him instructions about his work?   A. Certainly.

Q. Who was his foreman?

(Testimony of Lewis Leroy Long.)

A.   Well, there was the shift foreman.

Q.   Who was that?

A.   Otto Gensler, Orville Brockett.

Q.   Do you go to every employee and give him instructions every day?

A.   If they need any instructions, I do.

Q.   How do you know whether they need instruction or not, before going to them?

A.   Well, if they are having trouble; Lou had quite a bit of trouble with his machine.

Q.   You went to him every day and talked to him?

A.   Well, in passing by I would always stop and see how he was getting along.

Q.   Did he ever talk to him about anything besides what he was working on? [613]

A.   Well, we talked about quite a bit of things.

Q.   What subjects have you discussed besides his work?

A.   Well, it was mostly his work there at the plant.

Q.   What else?   A.   That's all.

Q.   You said you had discussed other subjects. What other subjects?

A.   Well, football games and sports, and wrestling matches.   He is quite a wrestler.

Q.   Do you remember all your discussions with him, and all the subjects you discussed?

A.   What did you say?

Q.   Do you now remember all the subjects you have discussed with him?

(Testimony of Lewis Leroy Long.)

A. Well, that's all we have talked about.

Q. The subjects you have named?

A. That's right.

Q. There could have been others?

A. No.

Mr. Moore: That is all.

Mr. Watkins: No further questions.

Q. (By Trial Examiner Whittemore) Do you know that Porter was in the C.I.O.?

A. No, I didn't.

Q. Did you ever see his button? **[614]**

A. No, he never wears his button. If he was in the C.I.O. he didn't have a button on.

Trial Examiner Whittemore: That is all.

Mr. Watkins: No further questions.

Trial Examiner Whittemore: You are excused. Thank you.

––––––

FRANK HOWARD RUNYAN,

called as a witness by and on behalf of the respondent, having been first duly sworn, was examined and testified as follows:

Direct Examination

Q. (By Mr. Watkins) Were you at one time employed by Jadson Motor Parts and Thompson Products, Inc.?   A. I was.

Q. Will you state during what period?

A. Intermittently from 1929, April of that year,

(Testimony of Frank Howard Runyan.)
until May of 1933, and since that time on, continuously until August 8, 1940.

Q. Did you leave of your own volition on August 8, 1940?   A. I did.

Q. What work have you been doing since that time?

A. Police officer in the City of Southgate.

Q. That is your capacity at the present time?

A. It is.

Q. Mr. Runyan, did you join the C.I.O. in the spring of 1937? [615]   A. I did.

Q. About when, as nearly as you can recall it?

A. I believe it was in the month of May.

Q. This was before the independent union was formed down there?

A. The Pacific Motor Parts Alliance?

Q. Yes.   A. It was prior to that.

Q. Did you try to get other employees to join the C.I.O. during that period?   A. I did.

Q. What was your situation in the plant with respect to the C.I.O.? If you will, just describe it briefly.

A. I was trying to get the fellows to organize and join the C.I.O. to better working conditions.

Q. Were you one of the leaders at that time in trying to organize for the C.I.O.?

A. There was no established leadership. We merely worked under our own conscience, and the direction of the business agent.

Q. Well, did you have more intimate contact with the C.I.O. organizer in connection with the

(Testimony of Frank Howard Runyan.)
organization, than most of the other boys down there?   A. I did.

Q. Was anybody else with you in that? [616]

A. Yes, Gene Higgins was an employee of the company at that time.

Q. Did you have contact during this period with the C.I.O. organizer, as to what was going on at Thompson?   A. I did.

Q. Who was the C.I.O. organizer?

A. I don't recall the full name, his last name was Rogers.

Q. Charles Rogers, or Chuck Rogers?

A. I believe they called him "Chuck."

Q. Yes. In this period of 1937, will you state what the general situation was in the plant? That is, the early part of 1937, say, from May until July.

A. We were trying very hard to organize the men in the C.I.O.; they were very slow in coming in. I believe we had about 25 men lined up that were luke warm, or in favor of it, and there was less than ten that actually paid anything in as members.

Q. Were you familiar with the records of applicants at that time, to the C.I.O.?

A. I did go through them on one occasion I recall.

Q. What was the maximum number of applicants you had at any time during this period?

A. That is paid applicants?

Q. Paid applicants.

(Testimony of Frank Howard Runyan.)

A. I believe the exact number was seven, although I do not know [617] positively it didn't exceed ten.

Q. How many applications, maximum number of applications did you have, paid and unpaid?

A. We had 25 lined up.

Q. That is the maximum number you had at any time during the 1937 period?   A. Yes.

Q. Or, during the entire year of 1937, so far as you know?

A. So far as I know, yes.

Q. When you were attempting to get members for the C.I.O., as you testified, and, incidentally, did you do any of it on company time?

A. I did.

Q. Did you, during this period, run into any opposition so far as the employees were concerned in connection with joining the C.I.O.?

A. Yes, I did. There was a great number of reactions, but the two that were most striking, one reaction was: It was a little too radical for them and they were afraid, before we could do any good as to bettering working condtions, we would have to have a strike, and they were afraid of a strike; and another reaction was that a dollar a month was too much dues to pay a union.

Q. Were there complaints at that time about working conditions or wages or anything of that kind? [618]

A. Well, the wages were very low and the

(Testimony of Frank Howard Runyan.)
general working conditions, that is, the intangible
things, such as some of the direction of the work,
was very unsatisfactory to most of us; that is, in
relation to time put in, and overtime, and et cetera.

Q. During this period we are discussing, which
is some time around the middle of 1937 and prior
to the formation of the union down there, the independent union, was there any discussion about
the formation of an independent union?

A. There was at one time, considerably prior to
the formation of the union there, interest in the
C.I.O. when the Drake brothers were in control
of the plant. We were going to join the A. F. of
L. and we did at one time have some contacts there.

I don't recall who was trying to organize the
shop. One fellow was working in the pin department.

Q. That was along in 1935 and 1936, that activity with the A. F. of L.?

A. Yes. And at that time we had talk in regard to whether we would have a company union,
sponsored, I believe, by Lyman Hodges for the
Drake brothers, or whether we would go A. F. of
L., as sponsored by—I can't recall the fellow's
name; I believe he is still employed there; and at
that time it was obviously a company-sponsored
affair and it was emphatically voted down.

Q. And that was in 1935 or 1936? [619]

A. Somewhere during that time.

Q. Now, in 1937, around July, the month of
July of that year, was there at that time some fur-

(Testimony of Frank Howard Runyan.)

ther discussion among the men about forming an independent, or did some of the men say something to you when you were trying to organize the C.I.O., about forming an independent?

A. Yes, there was some discussion. I do recall one with Floyd Pfankuch, that we wouldn't have any outsiders handling our affairs and we had quite hot arguments as to whether we should have amateurish handling of our affairs or professional direction.

Q. And your arguments were: that you were for the outside and he was for the inside?

A. That was the situation.

Q. How do you spell his name?

A. Pfankuch? P-f-a-n-k-u-t-c-h, I believe.

Mr. Pfankuch: That is wrong. P-f-a-n-k-u-c-h.

The Witness: He is sitting back there. You had better ask him.

Q. (By Mr. Watkins) You recall, do you, the time when the Alliance was formed, the independent union, in 1937? A. Yes, I do.

Q. When the men first went in to call on the management about forming an independent union?

A. I remember that. [620]

Q. Did you, in the interests of the C.I.O. at that time, and as one of the men in the plant most interested in it, make an investigation of what was going on? A. We did the best we could.

Q. For what purpose?

A. To show a connection between the Alliance and the company.

(Testimony of Frank Howard Runyan.)

Q. After your investigation—in other words, I understand you were trying to find out whether or not that union was started by the company. Is that correct?   A. That's right.

Q. And the C.I.O., then, did make some reports with respect to it?

A. That I don't know. All the information I found I turned over to Rogers, which was practically nil.

Q. Do you know what was finally done about it, so far as [621] your union was concerned, the C.I.O.?

A. I remember the last discussion I had with Rogers about it.

Q. What was that?

A. "We may as well forget the whole thing. The men in the plant didn't want a union. There was no use trying to force it on them."

Q. About when was that? Can you fix the approximate date?

A. It must have been early in the fall, I imagine.

Q. Of what year?   A. 1937.

Q. Did you subsequently join the Alliance?

A. I did.

Q. When did you join it?

A. I believe during the month of October, 1937.

Q. Some time in the latter part of that year?

A. Yes. It may have been a little closer to the end of the year than October, but I do believe it was in October.

(Testimony of Frank Howard Runyan.)

Q. When you joined it had your feeling changed any, so far as your attitude towards the independent union as against an outside union?

Mr. Moore: I object to that.

Trial Examiner Whittemore: What bearing has that?

Mr. Watkins: I just wanted to show the attitude of this employee with respect to the matter in this particular plant, Mr. Examiner. [622]

Trial Examiner Whittemore: I don't know as I am interested or that the record is interested or that the issue is interested in what this man's attitude was.

Mr. Watkins: All right. I will stand with whatever the Examiner wishes to rule.

Trial Examiner Whittemore: Well, if you feel it has a bearing in your case I wouldn't want to prevent you putting it in. What I want to know is: What difference does it make? He joined.

Mr. Watkins: My whole point, Mr. Examiner, is that here we have a witness who has no connection with the company whatsoever, no feeling of any kind, for or against, and also, even though he belonged to the Alliance he still felt an outside union might be the better thing, but he stayed in that institution. He wasn't a fellow who went all-out for the Alliance and therefore tried to help them any way he could. That was the purpose of the question.

Trial Examiner Whittemore: Go ahead.

(Testimony of Frank Howard Runyan.)

The Witness: Repeat the question, please.

(The question was read.)

The Witness: No, it did not. I still felt the outside organizer could handle the business of the employees much better than an amateur.

Q. (By Mr. Watkins) After you joined the independent, did you continue to make any effort to find out whether or [623] not the company had any control over it? A. I did.

Q. Did you find any evidence of any character along that line?

Mr. Moore: I object to that.

Trial Examiner Whittemore: I will permit the witness to answer.

The Witness: No, although there was no serious or lasting effort to find any evidence.

Q. (By Mr. Watkins) In other words, you just didn't see anything that would indicate it. Is that it? A. That's the situation.

Q. I believe you stated that you checked the C.I.O. records regarding Thompson Products back in 1937 to determine who down there had made application for membership and who had paid dues, and so forth? A. That's right.

Q. Do you know whether or not Lou Porter ever made application or became a member of the C.I.O. at any time during 1937?

A. If he did it was without my knowledge.

Q. When you checked the records, could you testify positively at the present time he was or was not among those applicants?

(Testimony of Frank Howard Runyan.)

A. He was not among those noted.

Q. About when was it you checked these records? [624]

A. That would be just guessing. I couldn't answer that definitely. If you want me to guess, I will try.

Q. I would like for you not to guess, but tell us, as nearly as you can, with respect to the date involved here, which is the latter part of July, 1937.

A. I believe it was some time during September, as it was at the time, or within the week in which we dropped the matter.

Mr. Moore: Just a moment. May I have that question?

(The record was read.)

Q. (By Mr. Watkins) This was September of 1937?   A. I am sure it was.

Q. Who checked the records with you?

A. Rogers and myself were alone in the office at the time, I am sure. [625]

FLOYD N. PFANKUCH

a witness called by and on behalf of the Respondent, being first duly sworn, was examined and testified as follows:

Direct Examination

By Mr. Watkins:

Q. Will you state your full name, please.

(Testimony of Floyd N. Pfankuch.)

A. Floyd N. Pfankuch.

Q. Mr. Pfankuch—is that the correct pronunciation? A. Yes, sir.

Q. Will you state how long you have been with Thompson Products and its predecessor company, Jadson?

A. Approximately seven and a half years.

Q. Seven and a half years. What is your work at the present time?

A. At the present time I am set up man and supervisor.

Q. What was it in July of 1937?

A. 1937 I was machine operator.

Q. Directing your attention to a period on and shortly before [633] the month of July of 1937, what was the general situation at Jadson plant among the men, their attitude, and so forth?

A. Personally I didn't know very many of them because at the time I was employed there I didn't know anybody in the plant there. I did get acquainted with a few of the men through working with them and eating lunch with them, and so forth, and found they were a fairly good sort of bunch, and at the time, why, they were talking about getting into some union to better the working conditions and get more wages because they thought we were underpaid according to some of the other plants in the neighborhood.

Q. Yes. Had some of the men belonged to the A. F. of L. prior to that time, do you know?

(Testimony of Floyd N. Pfankuch.)

A. Well, yes, some of them had told me about joining.

Q. Had you belonged to the A. F. of L. prior to that time?   A. No, sir, I hadn't.

Q. During this latter part of July, 1937, were you among the group of men who went into management's office to ask them about an independent union?

A. No, I did not go into the office to ask them about one.

Q. Did you go into the office with a group of some 15 or 20 men to talk to management, about the latter part of 1937?

A. No, I don't believe I did.

Q. You weren't in that group?

A. No. [634]

Q. What was the first information you had about the Alliance?

A. Well, it was right after some group of men, I don't know who was in there, had been in the office and talked to somebody, I don't know who they talked to, about a union.

Q. Then what happened? What was the next thing?

A. Well, we discussed amongst ourselves during lunch hour that, about—forming a union, or joining the A. F. of L. or C. I. O.

Q. Who was in this group, do you remember?

A. I couldn't say just who we happened to be eating lunch with, or who would come into the group.

(Testimony of Floyd N. Pfankuch.)

Q. It was during the lunch period?

A. Yes.

Q. It was after the meeting, when the group went in to see management?

A. I don't know for sure if they talked to management. That's what I heard, that somebody said they were going into the office to tell them we were going into a union.

Q. This you have just related was the next thing after that, then? A. Yes.

Q. All right. What followed that discussion?

A. Well, most of the fellows seemed—some of them belonged to the A. F. of L.; some had cards that they had joined the Machinists Union, A. F. of L., and some of the fellows said [635] they were joining the C. I. O.—

Mr. Moore: Just a moment. I object to the answer as not responsive to the question. The question was, I think, what happened after that.

Mr. Watkins: Well, was there—if I may ask a question in the meantime:

Q. (By Mr. Watkins): Was there more that happened at this luncheon meeting than you have already related?

A. No, just talk amongst the men about getting into a union.

Q. Where did this talk you are just relating now take place, about the A. F. of L. and C. I. O.?

A. During lunch periods when half a dozen of us would get together and talk about getting into some union.

(Testimony of Floyd N. Pfankuch.)

Q. Was this on more than one occasion or on a particular occasion?

A. Oh, yes, it happened over a period of time. It wasn't all the same time.

Q. When was the next conversation you had about formation of an independent union down at Jadson?

A. Well, some of the boys, during the noon hour talked, and after work, talked about forming our own union instead of joining any other union.

Q. About when was this? Let me ask you with respect to the time the men went in to see the management, this large group of them. [636]

A. I couldn't say definitely.

Q. Was it before or after?

A. Well, we had talked about an independent union before anybody had ever said anything to management, or anything.

Q. Say for what period of time, if you can estimate.

A. Oh, I would say for three or four months.

Q. All right. Was there a meeting, or what was the next thing, so far as you recall, about the formation of an independent union?

A. Well, a group of us got together and decided we wanted to form a union, but we would have to do it some evening, so one of the fellows suggested he could get a place for us to meet.

Q. Who was this?

A. Raymond Hailey, and if we cared to get together some evening—so, we asked all the boys

(Testimony of Floyd N. Pfankuch.)

when they would like to meet, and they set a date, a certain night of the week, and we all went down and discussed it, or rather, had an election as to who would represent the men, conduct the forming of a union.

Q. Where was the meeting held you are referring to?

A. It was on Gage Avenue in Bell. I don't recall the exact address.

Q. At an electric shop?

A. Yes, at a radio shop. [637]

Q. How many appeared at that time?

A. Oh, I would say approximately 60.

Q. Was there a further meeting after that, so far as you know?

A. Yes, about a week or ten days later we had another meeting at the same place.

Q. At the same place?

A. At the same place.

Q. Just say briefly what was done at the second meeting.

A. At the second meeting there was read over the constitution that the men had adopted during the ten days to—forming a union, and getting the men to sign this constitution or charter, as they wanted to call it.

Q. Yes. You were elected on some committee, were you, in connection with this independent union?

A. Yes, at the first meeting I was elected to be on the committee to draw up a constitution; and

(Testimony of Floyd N. Pfankuch.)

the second meeting, when we held the election of officers, I was elected to be a representative of the union.

Q. At this first meeting when you were elected to draw up a constitution, what did you do about it?

A. After the meeting, why, oh, it was a few days after that, we went over to George Fickle's house, a machine operator's house, and we had a meeting and drew up a constitution for the operation of a union. [638]

Q. Then what did you do?

A. After we had that drawn up we suggested that we better see a lawyer, to see if it was all legal so we wouldn't get into any trouble by organizing something that wasn't legal.

Q. When you say: Draw up a constitution, this constitutional committee, what did you do? Did you sit around and talk together and discuss things which you thought should be in it? Or did you— just tell us what you discussed on that matter.

A. We discussed what we thought the union ought to consist of, and also who could be members, and that's about all.

Q. You know Mr. Lewis Porter?   A. Yes.

Q. Was he at either of these two meetings that you have mentioned, at the electric shop?

A. Well, he may have been at the second one, but I am positive he wasn't at the first.

Q. Did he take any active part in either of the meetings on any occasion?   A. Not that I recall. [639]

WAINO KANGAS

a witness called by and on behalf of the respondent, having been first duly sworn, was examined and testified as follows:

Direct Examination

By Mr. Watkins:

Q. Mr. Kangas, how long have you been employed by Thompson Products or its predecessor, Jadson?

A. Well, it's a little over 19 years.

Q. What is your position at the present time?

A. Tool maker.

Q. What was your position in 1937?

A. Well, I was either die maker or tool maker. I don't remember.

Q. Are you any relation to Victor Kangas?

A. Cousin.

Q. Going back to the period around and prior to 1937, were any of the employees down at Jadson discussing working conditions or wages or anything of that kind?

A. -Yes, there were; they were very low then, and it was hard to make what you would call a decent living, and a lot of us were figuring on joining a union or forming a union of some sort.

Q. Did you ever join or make application for any union in this period?

A. Yes. I put in an application to the A. F. of L., I think. I don't remember now whether it was just then or before that. [645] But I know

(Testimony of Waino Kangas.)

I signed one. I never paid any dues or paid my initiation fees.

Q. During this period, in the middle part of 1937, and prior to the formation of the independent union down there, had there been discussions among the men about forming some union?

A. Well, it was mostly joining a union.

Q. Well, there had been a great deal of discussion along that line. Is that correct?   A. Yes.

Q. What was the first knowledge you had of any move to form an independent union down there at the plant?

A. Well, I don't know who it was that told me that there would be a meeting at an electric shop in Maywood on Slauson Avenue.

Q. Did you go to that meeting?

A. Yes, I did.

Q. Do you remember who talked to you about it?

A. No, I don't know; somebody told me that evening after I got off work.

Q. Did you go alone or with someone else?

A. I believe I went alone. I lived quite close to there, I believe.

Q. Did you ever pass out any application cards for the independent union? [646]

A. No, I never did.

Q. You became a member of it, did you?

A. I believe I signed the card after the second meeting; quite a bit after. I wasn't so very enthused about the idea of an independent union, because I had signed an A. F. of L. card.

(Testimony of Waino Kangas.)

Q. Did you attend more than one, what we call organization meetings, when this organization was being set up?

A. Well, they had two meetings there at the electric shop, and I attended both of them.

Q. You did? A. Yes.

Q. Did you take any active part in the independent union at any time?

A. None at all.

Q. You know Mr. Ray Livingstone, do you?

A. Yes, I do.

Q. Do you remember when he came out to visit the plant sometime in 1937?

A. I believe I do.

Q. Do you remember seeing him there at the shop? A. Yes.

Q. Did he talk to you while you were working?

A. Yes, he did.

Q. More than once, did he? [647]

A. No, I believe—I couldn't remember that far back; I remember him coming out there, because I didn't recognize him and I went and asked somebody who this fellow was going around there, and they told me: Ray Livingstone from Cleveland.

Q. Do you remember what you talked about or what he talked about at this conversation?

A. No, I can't.

Q. Do you have any recollection of it at all?

A. No, I haven't.

Mr. Watkins: You may cross examine.

(Testimony of Waino Kangas.)

Cross Examination

By Mr. Moore:

Q. Why did you join the Alliance?

A. Well, it was a lot cheaper than joining the A. F. of L. then. The initiation fee for the A. F. of L. was awfully high, the dues were high, and what we were making there at the shop, why, you couldn't hardly afford them. But we did want to get something that we could get a decent living out of it.

Q. Did the Alliance already have a contract before you joined?   A. That I don't know.

Q. Do you remember about the date you joined?

A. No, I don't.

Q. Approximately how long after this meeting you attended was it?

A. Oh, I imagine a week or a couple of weeks; something like that. I wasn't so very enthusiastic about the idea at first. [648] I finally joined, though I really don't remember very much about it.

Q. Did you have any particular reason for believing that this union would be better for you than the A. F. of L.?

A. No, I did not. The only thing, I figured it would be a darn sight cheaper for us than having to pay high dues.

Q. Did you know about how many men had joined the Alliance?   A. No, I didn't.

Q. Did you know it was a recognized bargaining agency of the employees of the company?

(Testimony of Waino Kangas.)

A. Not then I didn't, no.

Q. You testified you didn't pass out any membership cards? A. No, I didn't.

Q. Did you see any being passed out?

A. I don't believe I did; I had to work overtime quite a bit then, on die making, and I never did see any of them passed out.

Mr. Moore: No questions.

Trial Examiner Whittemore: Thank you very much.

(Witness excused.)

Mr. Watkins: Mr. Wayne Kangas.

WAYNE KANGAS

a witness called by and in behalf of the respondent, having been first duly sworn, was examined and testified as follows: **[649]**

Direct Examination

By Mr. Watkins:

Q. Will you state your full name, please?

A. Wayne Kangas.

Q. How long have you been employed by Thompson Products and its predecessor, Jadson Motor Products Company?

A. Approximately 15 years.

Q. What is your position at the present time?

A. Grinder operator.

Q. What was it in the middle part of 1937?

A. Grinder operator.

(Testimony of Wayne Kangas.)

Q. What relation are you to Mr. Victor Kangas?

A. Brother.

Q. Mr. Kangas, will you state what the situation was in the plant, so far as discussion among the men was concerned, for the period on or about July of 1937?

A. Well, it seemed to be there was quite a bit of discussion about wages and conditions and lots of the boys felt that they wanted to unionize so we could get better wages, and also working conditions.

Q. Do you know whether or not any of the boys had at that time joined the A. F. of L. or the C. I. O.?

A. No, I don't know. I don't know whether there was any belonging to either one of them. There had been some talk about it.

Q. What was that? [650]

A. There had been some talk about it but I don't know whether anybody belonged at that time.

Q. Had there been any talk among the men themselves to—strike that, please.

Were you in a group which went in to call on the management about organizing an independent union, sometime in July of 1937?

A. Yes, I was.

Q. Yes; prior to that meeting with management had there been any discussion among the men about forming an independent union?

A. Yes, we had talked about it for, I don't

(Testimony of Wayne Kangas.)

know how long; it could have been several weeks time.

Q. And will you state who among the men had discussed this?

A. Well, there was quite a number. I don't know exactly. I don't recall the individuals. There was Bebb, Stubblefield, George Fickle, and Ed Fickle. Oh, there was a number of them. I can't recall exactly the names of each individual.

Q. In any of these discussions had you had in your group any foremen or sub-foremen?

A. Not that I know of.

Q. When you went in to see the management was anybody there who particularly led your group in there, so far as you know?

A. Not that I know of. I can't recall of any. It seems like we was a bunch of sheep without a shepherd; there wasn't really [651] anybody who took the lead.

Q. Had you assembled at any time prior to this in an attempt to see the management?

A. Well, there had been some talk, discussion about going in to the management.

Mr. Moore: Just a minute. I move the answer be stricken, that so far given be stricken, and the witness be directed to answer the question.

Trial Examiner Whittemore: Read the question and answer.

(The record was read.)

Trial Examiner Whittemore: Will you answer the question.

(Testimony of Wayne Kangas.)

Q. (By Mr. Watkins): Do you understand my question, Mr. Kangas?

A. Could I have the question again?

Q. I will reframe it.

Trial Examiner Whittemore: All right.

Q. (By Mr. Watkins): You testified that a group of you went in and called on the management sometime the latter part of July of 1937 about organizing an independent union.

A. That's right.

Q. Had there been any similar group assembled prior to that time to see the management?

A. Yes, there had.

Q. And on more than one occasion, or what is the situation with regard to it? [652]

A. Well, it could have been a time or two.

Q. Did you actually contact the management at that time?

Trial Examiner Whittemore: Wait a minute. We cannot make any finding on what could have been, you see. Was there, or was there not?

The Witness: Yes, there was.

Trial Examiner Whittemore: How many times?

The Witness: Well, I don't recall whether it could have been once or twice. There was at least one time that I remember of.

Q. (By Mr. Watkins): Did the group at the one time you speak of actually call on the management?

A. No, they didn't at that time.

(Testimony of Wayne Kangas.)

Q. About how long, would you say this was before the date you did call on the management?

A. As I recall it, it was three or four days later.

Q. I see. That is, three or four days after this incident that you have mentioned when you did call on the management? A. That's right.

Q. Can you state what happened that kept you from going in to see the management about it?

A. Well, it didn't seem like we could all get together; everybody was a wee bit nervous and didn't know whether they wanted to go in or not, and we didn't seem to have enough gathered there, it was only a mere handful, so those that were [653] there dropped out and went on home.

Q. Did you ever talk to your brother about the organization of this independent, or about your joining any union down here at the shop?

A. Not that I recall.

Q. Would you say positively that you did or didn't? A. I don't believe I did.

Q. Now, when you went in to see the management, as you mentioned, about how many of you were there?

A. I presume there was 15 or 20.

Q. What was said to the management? What was the substance of what the men said to the management?

A. Well, there was quite a bit of discussion. However, we felt we wanted to lay down the cards on the table. We told the management what we had in mind.

(Testimony of Wayne Kangas.)

Q. What was it? What did you tell the management?

A. We wanted to organize a union; we wanted to unionize and have an organization.

Q. What was your purpose in going in to the management and telling them that?

A. Well, we felt we wanted the management to know what we were going to do, and we felt like we wanted to know if they would recognize a union if we organized one.

Q. Was there any particular person who acted as spokesman for your group in there? [654]

A. I don't recall of any particular person.

Q. What is your best recollection? That several people talked, or what?

A. Yes, there were several different ones. I believe most all of us had a little something to say.

Q. Do you remember any statements made by management in reply to you, when you said you wanted to form a union, and wanted to know what they thought about it?

A. The management said there was nothing they could do, that according to labor law we were entitled to join any union we pleased; that they couldn't say a word about it.

Q. Did anyone in connection with management —strike that out, please.

Was Mr. Victor Kangas present at this meeting with management?

A. I don't believe he was; I don't recall seeing him.

(Testimony of Wayne Kangas.)

Q. Yes. Who talked to you from the management's standpoint?   A. Mr. Dachtler.

Q. Do you remember anything in particular he did say to you about organizing your independent?

A. No, except as I stated, that he said that there was nothing the company could say about it. We had the right to organize or join any union what we pleased to.

Q. Was there any incident occurred? About furnishing materials, or anything of that kind?

[655]

A. Yes, there was.

Q. Will you state what that was, please.

A. There was somebody there, I don't recall who it was, after we had talked it over, why, somebody asked the management if we could have a few sheets of paper so we could write down some notes and different things we wanted to keep in mind, memorize, and we got the reply that management could not do that due to the fact they didn't want to have anything to do with this union, or any union, that they didn't want to have a hand in it.

Q. That was Mr. Dachtler who made that statement?   A. That was Mr. Dachtler.

Q. Mr. Pfankuch, did you ever hear any statement made by anyone connected with the management of Thompson Products that if the C. I. O. or A. F. of L. came in, the plant would be closed up and moved back to Cleveland?

A. No, I did not.

(Testimony of Wayne Kangas.)

Q. Did you pass out any application cards for the Alliance? A. Not that I recall.

Q. Were you an officer or committeeman of any kind for it? A. No, I wasn't.

Q. What was the next thing, so far as you can recall, that took place about organizing the independent, after this meeting with management?

A. Well, there was different ones that talked it over, and [656] we decided we would have to have a meeting place, and someone got a hall there in Maywood, an electric shop or radio shop, and there was talk, also, about needing some supplies, so some of the boys got together and donated. I donated a dollar to it.

Q. What kind of supplies?

A. Well, paper, and have our application cards made, and so on, incidentals to take care of things.

Q. And you made a donation on that?

A. That's right, I did.

Q. Mr. Pfankuch, you mentioned a meeting in Maywood. Was that at an electrical shop?

A. That's right.

Q. Was that the first meeting that the employees had with regard to the formation of the union?

A. Yes, that's right.

Q. Can you state approximately how many men were present at that meeting?

A. I presume there was around about 50, could have been 60.

Q. Will you state just briefly what business was done at that particular meeting.

(Testimony of Wayne Kangas.)

A. Well, everybody got to talking and we wanted a chairman. I don't recall who took the leading part there. It seems to me it was Mr. Hailey who opened the meeting and so we put it up to have a chairman, and I believe Mr. Creek was elected as [657] chairman of that meeting.

Q. Do you recall whether there were any committees appointed at that meeting?

A. Yes, there was; there was a committee, as I remember, there was a committee elected to draw up a constitution and by-laws.

Q. Now, at the second meeting which was held, very briefly, what took place at that meeting? The second meeting held in the electrical shop in Maywood.

A. Well, we talked over conditions, and the constitution was read and put up to a vote of approval, and I believe we all were asked to sign the constitution at that time.

Q. Do you know whether or not there were any changes made in the constitution?

A. I don't remember. [658]

CLARENCE STUBBLEFIELD

called as a witness by and in behalf of the respondent, having been first duly sworn, was examined and testified as follows:

Direct Examination

Q. (By Mr. Watkins) Will you give the reporter your full name, please.

A. Clarence Stubblefield.

Q. What is your job at Thompson Products?

A. Welder.

Q. How long have you been at Thompson Products, or its predecessor, Jadson?

A. Since 1935, in March.

Q. You have been a welder ever since you have been there?

A. That's right; yes, sir.

Q. Will you direct your attention, Mr. Stubblefield, to a period in the middle and early part of 1937, and just state what the men in the plant were discussing, so far as their wages and working conditions were concerned.

A. Well, when I first went to work, in 1935, the wages were very low and I just overheard the group talking about unionizing the shop some way or the other, and, of course, I [661] was just new in there and I never thought much about it. And so, a month or so, or something like that, a certain length of time after I was there, why, I finally got interested.

I decided I thought the best thing to do would be to form a union of some kind, whether it would be an independent or whatever it might be.

(Testimony of Clarence Stubblefield.)

Q. Had you joined the A. F. of L. during this period.   A. No, sir.

Q. Had you made application to it?

A. No, sir.

Q. Going to the period around July and shortly before that, of 1937, had there been discussions then among the men about joining the A. F. of L. or C. I. O. or some union?

A. Well, I heard a few of them talking about it.

Q. You attended a meeting, did you, with the management of the company in which a certain number of men went in to call on the management to find out whether they would recognize an independent union?

A. Yes, sir.

Q. Was that sometime the latter part of July, 1937?   A. Yes, sir.

Q. Will you state how many men, approximately, were in that meeting?

A. Well, I would say around about 15, 20, something like that. [662]

Q.- Will you state what happened at that meeting?

A. Well, the men went in and told Mr. Dachtler that they wanted to organize a union, form a union, an independent. He said there was nothing he could do about it, that it was strictly up to the employees.

Q. Was anything else said, so far as you remember?

A. Well, no, not right at that time. The only thing, well, I know the suggestion was made that

(Testimony of Clarence Stubblefield.)
the men use some of the company's material, and
that was refused by the company.

Q. Now, who acted as spokesman? Did somebody act as spokesman, or did the men talk pretty
much generally at the meeting?

A. Well, the men in geenral.

Q. Now, going back to the time when you assembled to go into this meeting, how was your group
gotten together? How did you happen to get together?

A. Well, talking during lunch hours, and also
after working hours, as we went out of the plant,
there would be a group get together and talk things
over.

Q. Had there been any discussion among you
men about forming an independent union prior to
this first meeting with the management?

A. Well, the whole thing was, there just had been
talk to try to do something to get a wage increase.

Q. Had you had any discussions amongst yourselves about contacting management prior to the
time you did contact the [663] management?

A. Well, no, not right at that time.

Q. Taking this period, Mr. Stubblefield, in which
this time, in which some 15 or more of you went in
and called on the management, did you, yourself,
have any active part in getting those people together
and getting them into management?

A. Yes, I sure did.

Q. What did you do in regard to that?

(Testimony of Clarence Stubblefield.)

A. In regard, I went around to the men and told them I thought it would be a good thing for us all to get together and have a union, and go in and have a meeting with management and try to get a wage increase.

Q. When the group finally assembled there, did you have anything to do with starting them in to see the management? A. Yes, sir.

Q. What did you do?

A. Well, they was all kind of standing up in a group, so I told them, I says, "Let's get going."

Q. Did they go, with that? Was that the first time they started to move?

A. They all moved; they all went into management. [664]

Q. Did you make any donation towards getting cards or anything of that kind, for the independent?

A. Yes, sir.

Q. About when was this with respect to the meeting you have testified to, when you called on the management?

A. To the best I remember it, it was at the second meeting, I believe in Maywood, the best I remember. I wouldn't——

Q. You did make a donation?

A. I made a donation.

Q. To whom did you make it, do you recall?

A. To Mr. Creek.

Q. To Mr. Creek. How much was it?

A. It was a dollar, probably two.

(Testimony of Clarence Stubblefield.)

Q. Did you pass out any application cards for the independent?   A. Yes, sir.

Q. Where?

A. On the outside of the company property.

Q. From whom did you get the cards you passed out?.   A. Mr. Bebb.

Q. When did you pass these cards out with relation to the time that your group called on the management? [665]

A. Well, I will judge it was probably around 4:30 or after.

Q. Of the same day?

A. The same day.

Q. And after you called on the management——

A. That's right; no pardon me. It was a little later, a little later after we had seen the management; then, we had the meeting and had drawn up the cards and the constitution.

Q. I see. In other words, it was some days after you had your meeting with management?

A. That's right; that's right.

Q. Did you get any of these cards from Mr. Lewis Porter?   A. No, sir.

Q. Are you sure of that?

A. Yes, sir.

Q. Did you get any from Mr. Hodges?

A. No, sir.

Q. You are positive of that?

A. Yes, sir.

(Testimony of Clarence Stubblefield.)

Q. Now, referring to a meeting which took place at an electrical shop in Maywood, did you attend that meeting where a group of the men were present? A. Yes, sir.

Q. How many men would you say were there?

A. I would say around, possibly, oh, in the neighborhood of 50. [666]

Q. Will you state briefly what was done at that meeting?

A. Well, it was just more to organize the group, that is, to register the group, draw up a constitution and appoint a committee to go ahead.

Q. There was a second meeting at the electrical shop, was there? A. Yes, sir.

Q. Very briefly, state what was done at that.

A. Well, the committee was voted in, and then it was brought up, and then it was approved by the employees.

Q. The what was approved?

A. The constitution had been worked on and was brought up to a vote in the presence of the employees to see whether they were satisfied or not.

Q. Did you ever hear any statement made while you were working at Thompson, or Jadson, by anyone connected with management of the company, to the effect that if the C. I. O. or A. F. of L. came in the plant would be closed and moved back to Cleveland? A. No, sir.

Q. Mr. Stubblefield, with respect to the minutes of the meetings which were held between the execu-

(Testimony of Clarence Stubblefield.)

tive council and the company, how were those minutes drawn up? Will you just state briefly?

A. They were drawn up by Mr. Bebb, secretary and treasurer [667] of the PMPWA.

Q. Then what was done with them after that?

A. He taken care of them and they was posted on a bulletin board.

Q. For a definite period of time?

A. Yes, sir.

Q. What was the purpose in that?

A. Well, to let the employees and members read them to find out what was going on in the management and the committee.

Q. Were there any changes made in any of these minutes, that is, anything objected to by management or by the Alliance.   A. No, sir.

Q. You don't remember any changes made either way?   A. No, sir.

Q. Mr. Stubblefield, referring now to this meeting that you had with the management with some 15 of you, do you remember whether Mr. Victor Kangas was present as the representative of management at that meeting?

A. No, sir.

Q. Do you remember, or do you say he was not?

A. He was not present.

Mr. Watkins: I see. That is all.

Cross Examination

Q. (By Mr. Moore) Who was present at that meeting, for the management? [668]

(Testimony of Clarence Stubblefield.)

A. Oh, I couldn't recall right at the present time the names of any one individual. I believe—let's see; there was George Fickle, Ed Fickle——

Q. No. You misunderstood my question. I say: Who was present at that meeting for the management?

A. Oh, for the management.

Q. Yes.

A. Mr. Livingstone and Mr. Dachtler.

Q. Only the two of them?

A. Just the two.

Q. Did Mr. Victor Kangas come in after the meeting had begun? A. No, sir.

Q. Are you sure of that?

A. No, sir.

Q. You are not sure?

A. No, sir. He didn't come in while we were in there.

Q. At that meeting was there any discussion of low rates of pay?

A. Well, there could have been; I don't remember just now.

Q. You think possibly there was?

A. There could have been.

Q. Wasn't it discussed at that time, wasn't there some discussion at that time about a raise in the pay rate? A. Well, I don't remember.

Q. Did Mr. Livingstone know what all the rates of pay were [669] in the various classifications?

A. Well, I don't know

(Testimony of Clarence Stubblefield.)

Q. Did he ask anyone what the various rates were while you were in there?

A. I don't know.

Q. Give the conversation at that meeting, as nearly as you can recall it.

A. Well, we went in with the purpose of organizing an independent union.

Q. Yes. What was the first thing that was said, and by whom?

A. Well, there were several out of the group, we all just wanted to talk; we went in and brought the subject up to Mr. Dachtler, that we wanted an independent union, and that——

Q. Who said——

Mr. Watkins: Just a minute. I would like to ask that counsel let the witness finish his answer before he asks another question.

Mr. Moore: Very well.

The Witness: I couldn't say just who the one party was; there was several in the group discussing, expressing their opinions.

Q. (By Mr. Moore) Were they all expressing opinions on the same thing at once?

A. Well, no, not at the one time, no. [670]

Q. You don't know whether pay rates were discussed or not?

A. I couldn't remember, at that time. I know that we were wanting more money, but I couldn't say whether the management had made a discussion on it or not.

(Testimony of Clarence Stubblefield.)

Q.   When did you get a raise after that? You got one shortly after that, didn't you?

A.   Well, I had one or two, two or three since.

Q.   I mean, shortly after this meeting with management that we are talking about.

A.   Well, no. Well, yes. We got a raise a little later on. I couldn't say just in what length of time, possibly a couple or two months after we got organized and the constitution was drawn up and signed.

Q.   A couple or three months after this meeting with management?

A.   I wouldn't say just definitely that length of time, but it was a little bit after that.

Q.   Did you get a raise before you had the contract with management?

A.   Oh, about six months before.

Q.   No, no. You had a contract with management shortly after you were organized, didn't you? A collective bargaining contract.

A.   Well, yes. We got raises right after we drawn up the contract and the constitution and I got a raise about six [671] months before we drawn up the contract. The raise was very few.

Q.   You mean before the Alliance was ever formed?   A.   That's right.

Q.   Did you get a raise between the time you went in to see management and the time the collective bargaining contract was executed?

A.   No, sir.

Q.   How much was your raise as a result of that contract?

(Testimony of Clarence Stubblefield.)

A.   Oh, I would judge ten cents, seven cents; seven or ten cents.

Q.   An hour?   A.   Yes, sir.

Q.   With respect to the minutes of that executive council, and the management, in the meetings, you say Lester Bebb kept those?

A.   Yes, sir.

Q.   Did anyone else keep minutes of those meetings?

A.   No, sir. He was voted on by the members to take care of the minutes.

Q.   No. Did anyone connected with management keep minutes of the meetings?

A.   No, sir. I don't recall right at that time.

Mr. Watkins: May we go off the record just a minute, Mr. Examiner? [672]

Trial Examiner Whittemore: Off the record.

    (A discussion off the record.)

Trial Examiner Whittemore: On the record.

Q.   (By Mr. Moore) You testified that you didn't join the A. F. of L. or C. I. O. Is that right?

A.   No, sir.

Q   Did you join the C. I. O.?

A.   No, sir.

Q.   You have never been a member of the C. I. O. at any time?   A.   No, sir.

Q.   At this meeting with management were you the first one who spoke to the management with reference to what these men had come in there for?

A.   No, I wouldn't say I was the first one.

(Testimony of Clarence Stubblefield.)

Q. You were simply the one that said: "Let's get going," while they were standing around, outside the office?

A. Well, I don't know; it would just be like an ordinary word you would say, just something like— a group of men saying: What are we waiting on? Let's get going.

Q. They had not designated you in the capacity of their spokesman? A. No. [673]

WAYNE KANGAS

resumed the stand and testified further as follows:

Redirect Examination (Continued)

Q. (By Mr. Watkins) Mr. Kangas, referring now to the group which went into to see the management, the 15 or 20 men, did [677] Mr. Lewis Porter come to you and ask you to be in that group?

A. No, not that I recall. I don't know—what's that?

Q. Go ahead.

A. I don't recall Mr. Porter ever saying anything to me.

Q. About that meeting?

A. That's right. [678]

Afternoon Session

Trial Examiner Whittemore: The hearing will please come to order.

Mr. Watkins: Mr. Examiner, there has been some

(Testimony of Wayne Kangas.)

discussion as to the method of drawing the minutes of the meetings between the Alliance and the management, minutes of which are now offered for identification only, by the respondent; and it is my understanding that the Board is willing to stipulate that the method of drawing the minutes was as follows:

That the secretary of the Alliance would draw a a draft of what took place at that meeting; the secretary of the company who had been present at the meeting would draw a similar draft; that the two of them would get together and compare their drafts and from those two drafts would make a second draft; that the formal draft was then posted on the bulletin board after it was signed by the president of the company and the president of the union at that particular time, of the Alliance.

Mr. Moore: So stipulated. [679]

CLARENCE L. MILLMAN

a witness called by and on behalf of the respondent, having been first duly sworn, was examined and testified as follows:

Direct Examination

Q. (By Mr. Watkins): Mr. Millman, state your official capacity with the respondent in this case.

A. Personnel manager.

Q. Have you attended the meetings of the Alliance, executive council, and the company, since you have been with the company?

(Testimony of Clarence L. Millman.)

A. That's right.

Q. And did you, during that period, assist in the preparation of the minutes of those meetings?

A.. That's right.

Q. From the company's standpoint?

A. Correct.

Q. I will show you a group of documents marked for identification as Respondent's Exhibits 1-A through Respondent's Exhibit 1-GGG, and ask you to state if those are correct copies of all of the meetings as shown by the records, which took place between the executive council of the Alliance and the company?

A. I can't state they are all correct unless I check all the dates. But——

Q. My point in asking that question is that I wanted to make certain we did have copies of all the minutes which were [680] written up of any meetings.

A.. They were all sent up here to you.

Q. They were?   A. Yes.

Q. In other words, this is the complete set of the minutes as you copied them for me?

A. That is right.

Q. And these are all of the minutes of such meetings as were held?   A. That is right.

Mr. Watkins: I offer Respondent's Exhibits 1-A through 1-GGG into evidence.

Trial Examiner Whittemore: Any objection?

Mr. Moore: No objection.

(Testimony of Clarence L. Millman.)

Trial Examiner Whittemore: The documents will be received.

> (The documents heretofore marked Respondent's Exhibit 1-A through 1-GGG for identification were received in evidence.) [681]

RESPONDENT'S EXHIBIT No. 1-A

8-6-37

Minutes of a meeting between the Management of the Jadson Motor Products Company and a Committee representing the Pacific Motor Parts Workers Alliance held Friday, August 6, in Mr. Hileman's office. Present representing the Management were Mr. Hileman, Mr. Livingstone, and Mr. Hodges. Representing the Pacific Parts Workers Alliance were Messrs. James Creek, G. M. Fickle, E. T. Fickle, Floyd Pfankuch and Lester Bebb.

At 9:30 a. m. the Management was informed that a Committee representing the Pacific Motor Parts Workers Alliance requested a meeting. The meeting was arranged approximately fifteen minutes later. Mr. Creek introduced himself as President of the employees' Committee and stated his organization represented a majority of employees in the plant and by virtue of this majority was requesting exclusive bargaining rights and a signed contract with the company on matters pertaining to wages, hours and working conditions which he intended to present. The Management requested evidence to substantiate the claim that the Committee represented a majority of the employees in the plant. Mr. Creek submitted his evidence—signed membership

(Testimony of Clarence L. Millman.)

cards—of seventy employees. These were certified by Mr. Livingstone. Mr. Creek then submitted the Constitution of the Pacific Motor Parts Workers Alliance with ratification signatures of fifty-nine employees as evidence that the Alliance is a legal labor organization. This was read by the Management members. Mr. Livingstone then asked Mr. Creek and other members of the Committee to assure him that no coercion or intimidation had been used by the organizers of the Alliance in inducing members to join, and also that such joining was of the free will of the members. Mr. Creek and the Committee gave this assurance. Following this discussion, Mr. Livingstone stated that the company had no alternative but to grant the Pacific Motor Workers Alliance exclusive bargaining rights under terms of the Wagner Labor Relations Act.

The Committee requested that the Management enter into a Closed Shop Agreement with the Alliance. The Management replied that it would prefer not to make this concession inasmuch as the company believes that a man should be entitled to the right to work regardless of his affiliation or non-affiliation with any labor organization. The Management further pointed out that if a Closed Shop Agreement were signed and a present employee refused to join, the company might be called upon to discharge that employee, which in itself would be a violation of the Wagner Act. (The Wagner Act provides that no employee may be discriminated against in tenure of employment because of affilia-

(Testimony of Clarence L. Millman.)

tion or non-affiliation with any labor organization.)

The Committee stated it wished to negotiate with the Management a Seniority Agreement to apply when a reduction of the working force becomes necessary. The Committee was of the opinion that the Agreement should base layoffs on seniority and merit along departmental or occupational lines and that the Committee should have the right to review the reasons relative to each individual lay-off. The Management replied that it is in agreement with these general provisions and would be willing to meet with the Committee to draft the Agreement.

Mr. Creek stated that the majority of Alliance members were desirous of obtaining vacations and asked the management's position on this matter. The Management replied that this would require some investigation into the financial condition of the company and that a reply would be given at the next meeting. It was further explained that the company had lost money during the first half and that steps had to be taken against incurring any additional expense.

The Committee then requested that forty-five hours be established as the standard working week with provisions made for an overtime premium after eight hours in any one day, forty-five hours in one week and for Sunday and holiday work. In the discussion that followed, the Committee pointed out that the second-shift men would like to eliminate the necessity of Saturday afternoon work and requested whether second-shift employees could

(Testimony of Clarence L. Millman.)

work nine hours five days a week with the day men working eight hours five days a week and five hours on Saturday. The Management stated it would investigate the effect of this proposal on production and return its answer at the next meeting. The Company agreed to obtain the consensus of opinion on this arrangement from their constituents.

The Committee then proposed overtime rates of time and a half after eight hours in one day, forty-five hours in one week and for Sunday and holiday work. The Management replied that in consideration of the company's present financial condition, it would grant time and a half for Sunday and holiday work, but would prefer to pay time and a third for overtime after eight hours in one day or forty-five hours in one week. The Management pointed out that time and a half for overtime might prohibit all overtime work, whereas with a rate of time and a third, it would still be possible to give the men some overtime. After a discussion the Committee agreed that time and a third would be satisfactory and that when the Company's financial condition improved, the matter of time and a half would be brought up then. It was further agreed that maintenance employees, watchmen and other members of the working force whose duties normally must be performed on Sunday would not come under the overtime provisions, but would be given a day off during the week in lieu of Sunday.

The Committee requested that the company

(Testimony of Clarence L. Millman.)
guarantee not to hire any Mexican or oriental help. This agreement was made.

Mr. Creek stated that the Committee wished to negotiate with the Management a new wage scale for various occupations and the establishment of a minimum factory rate. The Management stated it would accumulate its figures on rates and be ready for a meeting to establish a mutually satisfactory wage structure on Monday. Mr. Creek requested that an agreement be worked out which would outline the procedure for presenting individual grievances for settlement and also for presentating matters effecting the entire working force to the Management. This agreement is also to provide for regular meetings between the Committee and Management and the calling of special meetings at the request of either party.

The meeting was adjourned at 11:00 a.m.

Agreed to:

By the Alliance

/S/   JAMES D. CREEK

By the Management

/S/   P. D. HILEMAN

———

RESPONDENT'S EXHIBIT No. 1-B

8-10-37

Minutes of a meeting between the Management of the Jadson Motor Products Company and the Representatives of the Pacific Motor Parts Workers Alliance held August 10th in Mr. Hileman's of-

(Testimony of Clarence L. Millman.)

fice. The Management was represented by Mr. Hileman, Mr. Livingstone, Mr. Kangus, and Mr. Hodges. The Alliance was represented by Messrs. James Creek, G. M. Fickle, Floyd Pfankuch, E. T. Fickle, and L. Bebb.

This was a continution of a meeting held August 6th to discuss the wage rate situation in the factory. An explanation of the parent company rates was given by Mr. Livingstone also the financial status of the company.

The question arose as to whether the method of adjustment would be by the general percentage increase or by group classifications. The meeting was open for suggestions on this matter. It was agreed to by both parties that the wage adjustment should be by the group method.

The Alliance submitted their rates and after some discussion a wage schedule acceptable to both parties was adopted. This schedule will be submitted to the members of the Pacific Motor Parts Workers Alliance at a general meeting for their approval.

At the conclusion of the meeting the Representatives of the Alliance requested that the discussions held on thse questions be sent to them as a letter.

There being no further business the meeting was adjourned.

By the Alliance

/S/   JAMES D. CREEK

By the Management

/S/   P. D. HILEMAN

(Testimony of Clarence L. Millman.)

RESPONDENT'S EXHIBIT No. 1-C

8/12/37

Minutes of a meeting between the Management of the Jadson Motor Products Company and the Committee of the Pacific Motor Parts Workers Alliance held August 12th at 11:20 a.m. The Management was represented by Mr. Hileman, Mr. Kangas, and Mr. Hodges. Representing the Pacific Motor Parts Workers Alliance were Messrs. James Creek, G. M. Fickle, E. T. Fickle, Floyd Pfankuch, and Lester Bebb.

The meeting was opened for discussion on minor changes in the contract presented to the Management by the Alliance due to a miswording in the original, but to conform with standard legal form, was considered necessary. These changes which do not effect the substance of the contract were made and approved; Mr. James Creek making the notations for the Alliance and Mr. Hileman for the Management. The wage schedule and the contract were then presented to the Management for their acceptance by the Committee and were accepted by the signature of Mr. Hileman for the Jadson Motor Products Co. Acceptance for the Pacific Motor Parts Workers Alliance was by the signatures of Messrs. James Creek, G. M. Fickle, E. T. Fickle, Floyd Pfankuch, and Lester Bebb.

The working schedule proposed by Mr. Kangas was approved by the Committee. This schedule is effective August 16th.

(Testimony of Clarence L. Millman.)

There being no further business the meeting was adjourned.

By the Alliance

/S/ JAMES D. CREEK

By the Management

/S/ P. D. HILEMAN

RESPONDENT'S EXHIBIT No. 1-D

9-1-37

Minutes of a meeting held September 1, 1937 at 3:00 P.M. in Mr. Hileman's office between the Management of Jadson Motor Products Company and the Committee representing the P. M. P. W. A. Present representing the Management were Messrs. Hileman, Kangas, and Hodges. Representing the Alliance were Messrs. Creek, Fickle, Bebb, Pfankuch, and G. Fickle.

Mr. Hileman asked the Committee if they understood the clause in the contract relating to the number of hours in one day and the number of hours in one week to be eight hours in one day and forty-five hours in one week. They agreed that that was their understanding.

It was agreed to by the Committee and the Management that if a holiday occurred during the week, the employees would work over-time that week to make up the time lost by the holiday and would not receive the payment of the over-time premium until after forty-five hours in that week.

(Testimony of Clarence L. Millman.)

Mr. Hileman reviewed the business outlook for the coming months and the prospects for a large volume of business was very good.

There being no further business the meeting was adjourned.

By the Alliance

/S/   JAMES D. CREEK

By the Management

/S/   P. D. HILEMAN

———

RESPONDENT'S EXHIBIT No. 1-E

9-13-37

Minutes of a meeting held September 13, 1937 in the company offices, between the Management of Jadson Motor Products Company represented by Messrs. Kangas and Hodges and a Committee representing the P. M. P. W. A. Representing the Alliance were Messrs. Creek, Bebb, E. Fickle, Pfankuch, and G. Fickle.

The Committee requested that thirteen of their members who were receiving the minimum or less than the average wage in their respective classification be brought up to average; also that two members who have shown exceptional ability in the commercial grinding department be given the maximum rate in that department. After discussing each employee individually in regard to his type of work, ability, and length of service, it was agreed to by the Management to grant these raises subject

(Testimony of Clarence L. Millman.)

to Mr. Hileman's approval, he being absent from this meeting.

The Alliance then presented the Seniority Agreement for approval of the Management. After some discussion, it was agreed to by the Alliance to allow the Management to further study this agreement and to make a report on September 15th.

The meeting was adjourned but will be continued on September 15th.

By the Alliance

/S/　JAMES D. CREEK

By the Management

/S/　P. D. HILEMAN

———

RESPONDENT'S EXHIBIT No. 1-F

10-6-37

Minutes of a meeting held October 6, 1937 between the Management of Jadson Motor Products Company, represented by Messrs. V. E. Kangas and L. T. Hodges and a Committee representing the P. M. P. W. A. Representing the Alliance were Messrs. Creek, Bebb, E. Fickle, Pfankuch, and G. Fickle.

This meeting was a continuation of the meeting held September 13th to further discuss the Seniority Agreement submitted by the P. M. P. W. A. After reviewing the article pertaining to the advertising of jobs for bids, it was amended as this procedure, it was agreed upon, would only result in

(Testimony of Clarence L. Millman.)

endless controversy for handling promotions, this agreement was then presented to the Management and was accepted by the signature of Mr. P. D. Hileman for the Jadson Motor Products Co. Acceptance for the P. M. P. W. A. was by the signature of Mr. James Creek.

A discussion was then held on the functioning of the group bonus system and the suggestion was made by the P. M. P. W. A. that a floor inspector and set up man was needed which they thought would eliminate some of the scrap and increase production. The Management stated that they would investigate and see if this arrangement would be advisable.

There being no further business the meeting was adjourned.

By the Alliance

/S/   JAMES D. CREEK

By the Management

/S/   P. D. HILEMAN

———

RESPONDENT'S EXHIBIT No. 1-G

10-13-37

Minutes of a meeting held October, 1937 between the Management of Jadson Motor Products Co. represented by Messrs. V. E. Kangas and L. T. Hodges and a Committee representing the P. M. P. W. A. Repreesnting the Alliance were Messrs. Creek, Bebb, E. Fickle, Pfankuch, and G. Fickle.

(Testimony of Clarence L. Millman.)

The Committee stated that eight of their members were eligible under terms of the contract to receive the average wage rate in their respective departments. After checking the efficiency of these employees, they were found to be worthy and eligible for the average rate which they will receive effective October 16, 1937. Requests were also made for two members to be given maximum rates and two to be given above maximum. The management explained that at this time business conditions being very uncertain that it would not be advisable to make these increases at this time, however, when conditions were improved and stabilized, these requests would be reviewed.

There being no further business the meeting was adjourned.

By the Alliance

/S/ JAMES D. CREEK

By the Management

/S/ P. D. HILEMAN

———

RESPONDENT'S EXHIBIT No. 1-H

10-20-37

Minutes of a meeting held October 20, 1937, between the Management of Jadson Motor Products Company represented by Messrs. V. E. Kangas and L. T. Hodges and a Committee representing the P. M. P. W. A. Representing the Alliance were Messrs. Creek, Bebb, E. Fickle, Pfankuch, and G. Fickle.

This was a special meeting called by the Man-

(Testimony of Clarence L. Millman.)

agement to inform the Committee of an intended layoff. The Management explained that the reason for this layoff was due to the rapid decline in the stock market which had effected business conditions to such an extent as to cause cancellation and postponement of delivery dates on our orders.

The names of all employees to be laid off were given the Alliance and after checking their seniority and ability, the Alliance gave their approval of the men to be laid off.

There being no further business the meeting was adjourned.

By the Alliance

/S/   JAMES D. CREEK

By the Management

/S/   P. D. HILEMAN

RESPONDENT'S EXHIBIT No. 1-I

11-3-37

Minutes of a meeting held November 3, 1937 between the Management of the Jadson Motor Products Company and the Committee representing the Pacific Motor Parts Workers Alliance. Present representing the Management was Mr. L. T. Hodges. The Alliance was represented by Messrs. James Creek, E. Fickle, L. Bebb, F. Pfankuch, and G. Fickle.

The purpose of this meeting was to inform the P. M. P. W. A. that due to the lack of orders and the present decline in business it was necessary for

(Testimony of Clarence L. Millman.)

the Management to reduce the number of working hours from forty-five hours to forty hours per week, also that a reduction of factory personnel must be made.

The Management stated that rather than layoff a number of men for an indefinite period, which they were reluctant to do, they proposed that each employee be given a week's layoff. This layoff to be made by a group of five or six men each week. By this method the temporary layoffs would cover a twenty weeks period, and by that time, if business conditions were improved, no further layoffs would be necessary.

The Management also stated that due to lack of work in some departments employees in those departments would either have to be transferred to a department in which there was work or be laid off until the work resumed in their own departments. Employees thus transferred would receive the average rate of the department to which they were transferred.

- After discussing these proposed changes, the Alliance stated that due to the circumstances which necessitated these changes, this procedure met with their approval.

There being no further business the meeting was adjourned.

By the Management

/S/ P. D. HILEMAN

By the Alliance

/S/ JAMES D. CREEK

(Testimony of Clarence L. Millman.)

RESPONDENT'S EXHIBIT No. 1-J

11-22-37

Minutes of a meeting held November 22, 1937 between the Management of the Jadson Motor Products Company and a Committee representing the Pacific Motor Parts Workers Alliance. Present representing the Management were Messrs. Hileman, Kangas, and Hodges. Representing the Alliance were Messrs. James Creek, E. T. Fickle, Floyd Pfankuch, and Lester Bebb.

The purpose of this meeting was to discuss the procedure to be followed in the changing of rates when a workman changed from his own department, in which he is regularly employed, to another department. It was mutually agreed that when these changes were made the following provisions shall apply :

(a) No change in rate shall be made when the transfer to another department is for less than two hours.

(b) When the difference in rate is three cents an hour or less, no change shall be made.

(c) When work from one department is brought into another department, the prevailing rate of the department into which the work is transferred shall be maintained.

(d) A list of operations and machines shall be compiled showing the transfer rate for these machines and operations. This list to be available to any employee at any time.

(Testimony of Clarence L. Millman.)

(e)   When a workman is transferred from his own department on request of the foreman to work on a special or rush job and not because of lack of work in his own department, his base rate shall not be changed.

It was also agreed that when men in the Forge department designated as set-up men, were not working in that classification, their rate would be reduced to the maximum rate in that department.

There being no further business the meeting was adjourned.

By the Management

. . . .

By the Alliance

/S/ JAMES D. CREEK

––––––

RESPONDENT'S EXHIBIT No. 1-K

2-28-38

Minutes of a meeting held February 28th between the Management of Jadson Motor Products Company and a Committee representing the Pacific Motor Parts Workers Alliance. Present representing the Management were Messrs. Hileman, Kangas, and Hodges. Representing the Alliance were Messrs. James Creek, E. T. Fickle, Lester Bebb, Floyd Pfankuch, G. E. Fickle, and Secretary, Joe Walker.

Mr. James Creek informed the Management that a number of complaints had been registered by

(Testimony of Clarence L. Millman.)

Alliance members regarding the placing of female employees of the inspection department on machine operations in the plant. The Management replied that this was done in lieu of sending the employees in question home because of lack of work in the department in which they were regularly employed.

The Management also stated that the higher rate now being paid on these simple machine operations had so affected the manufacturing costs that in a number of cases the cost of manufacture exceeded the selling price, and that some adjustment would have to be made if the company was to retain this service division business, as this plant was on a competitive basis with other divisions.

In the opinion of the Management the only method of reducing the cost on these simple machine operations would be the employing of female help, as, under terms of the contract now in effect with the P. M. P. W. A., the average rate for these operations is .55c per hour, while the maximum rate for female employees is .48c per hour. The Alliance then stated that they did not favor the employment of female help on machine operations, and that they would prefer male employees in the actual production work.

It was then proposed to classify the machine operations and to establish a new rate schedule of a maximum of .50c per hour which would only apply to the operations so listed. This was to be in the form of an addenda to the now existing rate schedule. It was further stated by the Manage-

(Testimony of Clarence L. Millman.)

ment that, as a "gentleman's agreement.", no female help would be used on machine operations for the present time.

There being no further business the meeting was adjourned.

By the Management

/S/ P. D. HILEMAN

By the Alliance

. . . .

RESPONDENT'S EXHIBIT No. 1-L

4-28-38

Minutes of the meeting held April 28, 1938 at 1:30 P. M. in Mr. Hileman's office between Jadson Motor Products Co. Management and the Committee representing the Pacific Motor Parts Workers Alliance. Present representing the Management were Mr. Hileman, Mr. Kangas, and Mr. Hodges. Representing the Alliance were Messrs. Creek, G. M. Fickle, E. T. Fickle, Floyd Pfankuch, and L. Bebb.

The purpose of this meeting was to inform the Alliance that, plant equipment having been put in good condition which has made it possible to increase production on these machines, it is necessary that a revision of the production standards be made. This change in the production rate will only effect four machines at the present time. A discussion was held and in reviewing the new standards it was agreed that it would be possible to meet

(Testimony of Clarence L. Millman.)

them and also for the employees to obtain a bonus.

It was also agreed by the Management that an equitable distribution of overtime would be made.

There being no further business, the meeting was adjourned.

By the Management

....

By the Alliance

....

————

RESPONDENT'S EXHIBIT No. 1-M

7-26-38

Minutes of a meeting held July 26th 1938 between the Management of Jadson Motor Products Company and a Committee representing the Pacific Motor Parts Workers Alliance. Those present representing the Management were Messrs. Hileman, Kangas and Hodges; representing the Alliance were Messrs. James Creek, E. T. Fickle, Floyd Pfankuch, George M. Fickle and Lester Bebb.

The Alliance requested an extension of thirty days be given to the present contract between the P. M. P. W. A. and Jadson Motor Products Company, which expires August 12th, 1938, stating that an election of new officers would take place prior to the expiration of the contract and that there would not be sufficient time for the new Committee to familiarize themselves with the procedure

(Testimony of Clarence L. Millman.)

to follow in negotiating a new contract. This extension was granted.

The Alliance also asked if it would be *posible* to enlarge the men's wash room, located in the West side of the plant, as it was in a very crowded condition at noon and at the end of the working day. The Management replied that a lack of floor space in this area made it impossible to do this; however, it was proposed that the rear wash room be enlarged and a survey made to see if there was a sufficient number of employees desiring additional showers, if so they would be installed.

It was also proposed to install one large locker in each Department, as lack of space made individual lockers impractical.

A general round table discussion on business conditions was had, after which the meeting was adjourned.

By the Management

. . . .

By the Alliance

. . . .

————

RESPONDENT'S EXHIBIT No. 1-N

8-25-38

Minutes of a meeting between the Management of the Jadson Motor Products Co. and the Committee representing the Pacific Motor Parts Workers Alliance held August 25, 1938 at 2:30 P. M.

(Testimony of Clarence L. Millman.)

The Management was represented by Messrs. Hileman, Kangas and Brooks. Representing the Alliance was the recently elected Committee: Messrs. T. G. Overhulse, President: E. T. Fickle; Floyd Pfankuch: Luther Leatherwood; and O. P. Wright.

The Alliance requested a raise of five to ten cents per hour on the present maximum wage rate and also a ten cent per hour raise for work done on the very large size valves. The Management replied that the financial condition of the Company was such that it would be impossible to grant a blanket raise on maximum rates as requested, but that a raise of five cents per hour had been considered for work done on the large valves. The Committee also brought up the subject of paying a bonus for work on the large valves, the Management pointing out the impracticability of attempting to arrive at any fair and equitable bonus system on parts which were of a highly specialized and individual nature, such as seats and the afore-mentioned large valves.

The Management reviewed in detail the provisions of the Fair Labor Act which becomes effective October 26, 1938, laying special emphasis on the maximum of forty-four hours in any one week. The question was asked by the Management if the old contract had proved satisfactory and if the Alliance wished to make any changes. The Alliance agreed that the contract had been satisfactory and no changes were desired except to incorporate those in compliance with the Fair

(Testimony of Clarence L. Millman.)

Labor Act. Mr. Hileman mentioned the fact that the regular meetings between the Alliance and the Management had not been held the first Monday of each month as specified in the contract due to the fact that there have not been enough subjects of discussion to warrant meetings of this frequency. It was decided that in the future the Alliance would notify the Management at least twenty-four hours in advance when a meeting was desired.

The Alliance discussed a bonus to be paid to die makers. They explained that the cooperation given the Forge Department enabled this last named group to speed up production and earn a bonus. The Management explained that no bonus could be paid on this type of work, but the die makers after having been on the job at least four months could be raised to the maximum wage, if, in the opinion of the Superintendent, the men were deserving of the maximum.

The Alliance brought up the fact that they felt that 50% of the men were receiving minimum wages and that very few have reached maximum. The Management then produced figures showing that almost the reverse was true; over 40% received maximum wages, less than 5% were receiving the minimum ,the balance falling in the average group. The question was brought up as to whether the group bonus system was satisfactory, and it was found that the majority of the Alliance was in

(Testimony of Clarence L. Millman.)

favor of continuing with the arrangement without making any change. Complaint was registered concerning the transfer of two men, watchman and janitor, from an hourly wage to monthly salary without consulting the Alliance. Mr. Hileman agreed that the move had been made without discussion, but it was done in this case as it is the usual practice of janitors and watchmen to be paid on a salary basis in other Thompson Divisions.

The Management agreed to have a new contract drawn up and presented to the Committee for consideration as soon as possible.

There being no further business, the meeting was adjourned.

By the Management

/S/ P. D. HILEMAN

By the Alliance

The Management said it was not their intention to make a general practice of transferring men from hourly rate to salary.

RESPONDENT'S EXHIBIT No. 1-O

9-12-38

Minutes of a meeting between the Management of the Jadson Motor Products Company and a Committee representing the Pacific Motor Parts Workers Alliance held September 12, 1938. Present representing the Management were Messrs. Paul Hileman, Vic Kangas, and Arthur Brooks. Representing the Alliance were Messrs. T. G. Overhulse, Ed

(Testimony of Clarence L. Millman.)

Fickle, Floyd Pfankuch, and Luther Leatherwood. O. P. Wright not being present.

The meeting was opened with discussion on the wage hour rates resulting in adjustments being made in some cases. It was brought up by the Management that due to the Fair Labor Standard Acts of 1938 a change of hours of the janitor and watchman would have to be made, and it was agreed to have two men work six hours and fifteen minutes a day, seven days a week. This would give them their regular forty-four hours a week, and their work would be divided so that each man would have his share, and that they would be classified as janitor and watchmen.

The subject was brought up to install a second wash basin in the men's lavatory as the men have to wait their turn at the lunch hour, and it is very inconvenient. This Mr. Hileman agreed to have done. It was also decided to install five large lockers in the shop so that the men could change their clothes at the shop if they wished and have a proper place to keep their belongings.

The new contract combining Seniority Agreement and Wage Agreement was then signed by both parties covering the period to September 12, 1939.

There being no further business the meeting was adjourned.

By the Management

/S/ P. D. HILEMAN

By the Alliance

/S/ T. G. OVERHULSE

(Testimony of Clarence L. Millman.)

RESPONDENT'S EXHIBIT No. 1-P

1-5-39

Minutes of a meeting between the Management of the Jadson Motor Products Company and a Committee representing the Pacific Motor Parts Workers Alliance held January 5, 1939. Present representing the Management were Mr. Paul Hileman, Mr. Vic Kangas, and Mr. Arthur Brooks. Representing the Alliance were Messrs. Ed Fickle, Floyd Pfankuch, Luther Leatherwood, and O. P. Wright.

One of the main topics brought up was the bonus problem as to whether or not the bonus would be left to accumulate for a period of one year to be paid in a lump sum at Christmas or paid each pay period as in the past. After a short discussion, it was decided to have a petition passed to each employee to sign whether in favor of or to the contrary.

Mr. Hileman discussed the possibility of transferring the Jadson service stock to one of the Eastern warehouses, where, by making this change, it would mean quite a saving in handling our merchandise in this manner.

He also outlined a plan of installing Oil and Gas Pumps and a Grease Rack at the plant, explaining how the employees would benefit by this plan by being able to purchase gasoline and oil at a figure considerably lower than service station prices.

(Testimony of Clarence L. Millman.)

New jobs that are opening in the Sales department and various other departments were discussed. Mr. Hileman explained that men would be selected from the plant to fill these positions wherever it was possible to do so.

There being no further business the meeting was adjourned.

By the Management

/S/ P. D. HILEMAN

By the Alliance

/S/ E. T. FICKLE

RESPONDENT'S EXHIBIT No. 1-Q

3-28-39

A special meeting between the Management of the Jadson Motor Products Company and a Committee representing the Pacific Motor Parts Workers Alliance was held March 28, 1939.

Present representing the Management were Mr. P. D. Hileman, Vic Kangas and A. R. Brooks, representing the Alliance were Mr. E. T. Fickle, L. J. Leatherwood, O. P. Wright and N. J. Clifford.

The open subject for discussion was the Group Bonus. Ed Fickle explained that although some of the men in the group were producing a high average, it was pulled down by a very few in the group that were below the bonus rates. He also suggested dividing the large group into several

(Testimony of Clarence L. Millman.)

groups, thereby, giving the higher producers the benefit of his earned bonus. After a short discussion, Mr. Hileman suggested this be set aside to see the outcome of the bonus figures for the past pay period.

The subject of the handling of tires and batteries by the Company Station was mentioned, and it was agreed that these two items would not be stocked at the Station, but Mr. Brooks would order tires and batteries for any employee wishing to purchase same at Service Station discount.

One of the P. M. P. W. A. Committeemen complained about the gasoline being mixed and causing him trouble in starting his car. Mr. Brooks explained that on the original purchase of gasoline 300 gallons of Flash had been purchased, but due to the slight difference of only one-half cent per gallon between the Flash and Hi-Octane, that the Station was unable to sell the Flash. After two weeks trial, it was then decided to transfer the Flash into the Hi-Octane tanks to rid the Station of this Flash in order to leave the Flash pump open for the handling of Ethyl, which the Station had demands for. It was explained that at the time this mixture was made the gasoline pump man explained to the employee buying the Hi-Octane gasoline that it had been mixed. A letter also was posted on the bulletin board explaining the above reason for mixing this gasoline. It was further explained that all gasoline at the present time and

(Testimony of Clarence L. Millman.)

in the future would be 100% Hi-Octane and Ethyl.

The subject of a soda pop dispenser being installed for the summer months was discussed, and it was agreed by all that should the Benefit Fund wish to install a pop dispenser this year that the electric type should be used to eliminate the handling of ice, and that the Benefit Fund would be approached on this matter.

With no further business the meeting was adjourned.

By the Management

/S/ P. D. HILEMAN

By the Alliance

/S/ E. T. FICKLE

RESPONDENT'S EXHIBIT No. 1-R

7-25-39

Minutes of a meeting held in Mr. Hileman's office July 25, 1939 between Committee members E. T. Fickle, L. J. Leatherwood, Ladean Gregg, and N. J. Clifford, representing the P. M. P. W. Alliance, and P. D. Hileman, V. E. Kangas, and D. M. Cameron, representing the Company.

The meeting was opened by Mr. Hileman who outlined a plan recently discussed with Cleveland Management and purchasing whereby a blanket order covering the more popular service parts might be issued to Jadson with a six month delivery period specified. This in turn might be used to

(Testimony of Clarence L. Millman.)

our advantage in eliminating production peaks and valleys, and assuring our men of steadier employment, as well as tending to reduce costs through larger quantities.

Mr. Hileman also discussed and explained various angles of the completion of recent orders from Douglas Aircraft for hardened and ground precision aircraft bolts, and the prospects for the standardization of the aircraft industry on our development, which we hope will result in quantities of five to eight thousand pieces per month beginning September 1. Thus far, Jadson has produced the only satisfactory part of this type which Douglas has used and other aircraft manufacturers are much interested in standardizing their own requirements.

Several questions were asked by the Committee concerning the recent refinancing program through the selling of 20,000 shares of Prior Preference Stock. Considerable publicity had been given this move in local newspapers. Mr. Hileman explained the reasons for needing additional working capital in order to liquidate our present short-term bank notes and also supply ready capital for expansion of machinery, primarily for aircraft business. He also explained that the increase of our business in five years had amounted to approximately $6,000,-000.00, which in turn necessitated larger raw material inventories and greater float of money between the time we had paid for raw material and invested labor for its manufacture into the finished

(Testimony of Clarence L. Millman.)

product, delivered it to the ultimate consumer, and the time check for payment from our customer reached us.

Satisfaction was expressed by members of the Committee as to working conditions, hours, etc., with no complaints from any member.

The subject of the renewal of the contract which comes up next month was then brought up, and the promise of a year ago to discuss a vacation plan with pay for hourly rate employees was commented upon. Mr. Hileman asked the Committee to formulate their ideas on the subject and present them for discussion and consideration before the end of next week.

The Committee expressed satisfaction and pleasure concerning the arrival and installation of various new pieces of machinery recently purchased. The feeling generally was that the outlook for Jadson was better today than at any time in the past five or six years.

There being no further business to discuss, the meeting adjourned.

/S/ P. D. HILEMAN
By the Management
/S/ E. T. FICKLE
By the Alliance

(Testimony of Clarence L. Millman.)

RESPONDENT'S EXHIBIT No. 1-S

8-8-39

Minutes of a meeting held in Mr. Hileman's office on August 8, 1939 between Committee members, E. T. Fickle, C. O. Stubblefield, L. J. Leatherwood, N. J. Clifford, G. E. McIntyre and Secretary, J. J. Walker representing the Pacific Motor Parts Workers Alliance and P. D. Hileman, V. E. Kangas and D. M. Cameron representing the Company.

The meeting was opened by Mr. Hileman, who asked what was new and interesting and if any vacation plans had been formulated by the Pacific Motor Parts Workers Alliance which they would like to discuss at this time. Three plans were submitted, which are as follows—

Plan No. 1—Any workman employed under one year—no vacation. If employed from one to five years—one week vacation. If employed from five to ten years—one week plus one day for each year over five. At the end of ten years—two weeks vacation. Mr. Hileman asked whether or not the Pacific Motor Parts Workers Alliance thought an employe of, for example; 15 years standing on the payroll should have special vacation recognition. Mr. Fickle replied that two weeks vacation was considered maximum.

Plan No. 2—Workmen employed from one to five years should have one day vacation for each completed work year. If employed over five years he would receive the maximum vacation of two weeks.

Plan No. 3—Workmen employed under three

(Testimony of Clarence L. Millman.)

years—no vacation. From three to five years—one week. From five years on—two weeks.

Mr. Hileman then asked if any plans for pay rates during vacations had been formulated. Mr. Fickle replied that this had not as yet been discussed. Mr. Hileman stated that everyone's rate was being averaged with the view of setting up their vacation rate, provided a vacation plan for next year was adopted.

Mr. Hileman asked for opinions on the plans submitted. Mr. Kangas stated that he did not think plan No. 1 to be fair; his reason being that a five year man would have no better vacation standing than a one year man. This brought up the question as to the percentage of five to ten year men employed, which was judged to be 30%. For employees of ten years or more, 25%.

The general opinion was that plan No. 2 was the most acceptable of those submitted.

Mr. Hileman asked if any Pacific Motor Parts Workers Alliance member had suggested working during his vacation and get double pay during that time. None had. Mr. Hileman stated that the suggestion was made frequently, but was definitely out. He further stated that vacation plans would have to be made carefully due to the fact that at times the absence of four or five men in specialized jobs would handicap us to a great extent, and also suggested that we think the various vacation plans over carefully for comment during a meeting to be called at some later date.

(Testimony of Clarence L. Millman.)

Upon being asked by Mr. Hileman if there were any complaints regarding working conditions or any other matters which should be discussed at this meeting, Mr. Fickle replied that the Pacific Motor Parts Workers Alliance would like to have the Group Bonus plan rates written into the new contract, which should be presented for signature on or before September 12, 1939.

Mr. Hileman replied that the Company liked the Bonus plan and intended the retention of same. Mr. Clifford asked if the Bonus rates would be changed should production increase. Mr. Kangas replied that they would if new machinery, which might be purchased, were the cause of the increased production. Mr. Hileman and Mr. Kangas were both against incorporating Bonus rates into the new contract.

There followed another complaint from an employee who considered himself due a more advantageous rate of pay. The matter was referred to Mr. Kangas by Mr. Hileman for settlement.

Another employee thought his pay rate should be increased due to the higher efficiency on his particular job since the installation of a new machine. This matter was also referred to Mr. Kangas but there is some question as to whether the man's efficiency has increased or whether the increased rate of production is entirely due to the new machine.

Mr. Hileman pointed out the fact that two years ago the average wage for the shop was 57c per

(Testimony of Clarence L. Millman.)
hour and for the first six months of this year it was
68c per hour, which is an increase of 19%.

Mr. Fickle stated that there had been some dissatisfaction expressed by members of the Pacific
Motor Parts Workers Alliance because of the Company's hiring outside labor for Tool Room Work,
and that said members thought men in the shop
should be promoted to those jobs. Mr. Kangas explained that there were no men in the shop who were
competent to do the work and that the Company
could not afford to break in a man, at his regular
wages, to learn the work required. He further stated that the job in question was of short duration
and that it was not the Company's policy to go
outside for skilled help except in special cases.

Since the new contract was not ready for presentation to the Company, Mr. Hileman asked that
the present contract be extended for thirty days, to
which Mr. Fickle and Committee members gave
their assent. An extension of the present contract
was drawn up and duly signed.

Mr. Hileman then brought up the subject of the
Jadson Annual Picnic. Everyone seemed in accord
as to its being held during the first week in October. There followed a round table discussion regarding the event. Mr. Clifford agreed to investigate
a proposed new location for this year's outing, although much satisfaction was expressed with the
beauty and facilities of Banning Park, where the
picnic was held last year.

(Testimony of Clarence L. Millman.)

There being no further business to discuss, the meeting adjourned.

By the Management

/S/ P. D. HILEMAN

By the Alliance

/S/ E. T. FICKLE

. RESPONDENT'S EXHIBIT No. 1-T

Minutes of a meeting held in Mr. Hileman's office on October 19, 1939 between Committee members E. T. Fickle, L. J. Leatherwood, C. O. Stubblefield, N. J. Clifford and Secretary L. S. Bebb representing the Pacific Motor Parts Workers Alliance, and P. D. Hileman, V. E. Kangas, and D. M. Cameron representing the company.

The meeting was opened by Mr. Hileman who asked all of those present if they had a good time at the company picnic, which was held at Banning Park October 14, and also what the consensus of opinion of the shop was. Everyone agreed that the picnic was the best of all three which have been held since 1937.

The discussion then shifted over to our present production schedules and the lack of inter-plant orders for Thompson and Toledo Service Divisions. The committee was much interested as approximately twenty-five (25) of their members have been recently laid off. Mr. Hileman explained that this was due in a measure to a too optimistic outlook on replacement sales for the last quarter of

(Testimony of Clarence L. Millman.)

this year; that because so many valves had already been manufactured and were still in Cleveland inventory, we could not expect additional orders until the first part of 1940. It was also pointed out that total production of all valves for the year of 1938, including old Jadson Service, inter-plant business and original equipment, was about 700,000 and that this year for the first nine months inter-plant transfers alone were over 800,000 pieces.

A new product which we are to make for the aircraft industry was displayed by Mr. Hileman. It is part of a heat regulator to be used by various aircraft companies building transport planes.

The Old Guard Emblems which were received recently were displayed to the Committee and it was unanimously agreed that the design was excellent. Management explained the aims of the Old Guard Association and all those present were very enthusiastic regarding Jadson's becoming a part of the organization.

The subject of the new P. M. P. W. A. contract for 1940 was discussed at great length—numerous questions being asked concerning the vacation plan and the wording changes from last year's contract. All questions being answered to the satisfaction of the committee, the contract was then duly signed, and the meeting adjourned.

> By the Management
> /S/ P. D. HILEMAN
> By the Alliance
> /S/ E. T. FICKLE

(Testimony of Clarence L. Millman.)

RESPONDENT'S EXHIBIT No. 1-U

Minutes of a meeting held in Mr. Hileman's office on December 8, 1939 between Committee members E. T. Fickle, L. J. Leatherwood, C. O. Stubblefield, G. E. McIntire, C. E. Little, N. J. Clifford, and Secretary L. S. Bebb representing the P.M.P.W.A. and P. D. Hileman, V. E. Kangas and D. M. Cameron representing the company.

The meeting, a special one requested by the P.M.P.W.A. to settle a few questions which had arisen since our last meeting on October 19, was called to order by Mr. Hileman who asked that the problems be presented.

The first request was made by Mr. Fickle who asked that men working the night shift be paid 3c more per hour, that they be assigned a definite shift (either day or night instead of alternating every two weeks) and that the choice of shifts be given the men according to their seniority. The 3c per hour increase *who* asked as compensation for working a steady night shift.

Mr. Hileman expressed his opinion that such a plan might be worked out since it would eliminate much of the timekeeping which is now necessary under the present alternating system. Mr. Kangas stated that a steady night or day shift had been tried once but did not work out because those on the night shift grew tired of it after two or three months, however, with an additional 3c per hour to be gained on night work, it might work out by alternating shifts every six months.

(Testimony of Clarence L. Millman.)

To Mr. Hileman's question as to whether or not a vote among the P.M.P.W.A members had been taken, Mr. Fickle replied that it had and that a majority desired a steady shift, their reason being that they would be on one shift barely long enough to get used to it and then would have to do the same thing over, thus upsetting their sleeping and eating habits.

Mr. Hileman asked that another meeting be held within ten days, at which time he would have formed a definite decision, and that he would consider the proposed increase for night work after an opportunity to study its effect on material costs.

The second question was a complaint on the part of the die makers that they were not being advanced to tool making, but instead outside help was being brought in. To this Mr. Kangas replied that this had been done because the die makers were not capable of doing the work necessary. Mr. Fickle then asked that the die makers be advanced to the making of collets and other jobs at which tool makers are usually broken in. Mr. Kangas replied that the job of making collets was not steady enough to warrant doing this and that it would necessitate breaking new men in on die making. Mr. Hileman pointed out the fact that since our advent into the airplane parts field our delivery requirements were oftentimes very limited and that jobs had to be finished as quickly as possible, and that for this reason he would be unwilling to break in die men on tool making.

(Testimony of Clarence L. Millman.)

The next topic under discussion was the bonus system. Forge workers had complained that they lost money when they were transferred temporarily from their department to another job which paid no bonus. Mr. Kangas agreed to think the matter over and see what could be done.

Mr. Fickle then brought up the question of having an absolutely closed shop, stating that there was some grumbling among members of the P.M.P.W.A. because others who would not pay their dues, but still reaped the benefits derived from belonging to the organization and that there was still one worker who would not join the union. Mr. Hileman replied that an absolutely closed shop could not be granted nor could the non-union worker be forced to join, since this would be interfering with the rights of a citizen and would be contrary to the Wagner Labor Law.

There being no further business to discuss, the meeting adjourned.

By the Management
/S/ P. D. HILEMAN
By the Alliance
/S/ E. T. FICKLE

RESPONDENT'S EXHIBIT No. 1-V

Minutes of a meeting held in Mr. Hileman's office on December 29, 1939 between Committee members E. T. Fickle, C. O. Stubblefield, G. E. McIntire, C. E. Little, N. J. Clifford and Secretary

(Testimony of Clarence L. Millman.)

L. S. Bebb representing the P.M.P.W.A. and P. D. Hileman, V. E. Kangas and D. M. Cameron representing the Company.

The meeting was opened by Mr. Hileman. The first topic under discussion was the proposed 3c increase per hour for men working the night shift. He stated that, after giving the matter serious thought, he was not in favor of granting this increase but instead he submitted the following plan which would be more beneficial to the employee as well as the Company:—That the employees on the night shift should be given a minimum of two hours overtime per week at the time and one-half rate. This would, in effect, increase the employees earnings from 8 to 10% and at the same time benefit the Company through increased production which is badly needed. This proposal was considered a good one by the P.M.P.W.A. Committee members who agreed to put the proposition up to their fellow members; if accepted, the plan to go into effect as soon as necessary arrangements could be made, Mr. Kangas to be notified as to rejection or acceptance of the plan.

The next topic dealt with the length of time to be worked by the night shift at a single stretch. Mr. Clifford thought that a three months period was regarded by the majority as more acceptable than the original six month plan. Mr. Hileman agreed to accept this proposal but expressed a preference for a six months steady night shift. Mr. Fickle promised to present the plan to the Union

(Testimony of Clarence L. Millman.)

members and to advise the management as to the outcome; if accepted, the workers now on night shirt to continue on same until April 1, 1940.

Mr. Fickle then brought up the subject, which had been discussed in previous meetings, of advancing men now engaged in die making to tool making. Mr. Hileman stated that the Management would be unwilling to do this, again pointing out the time factor and stressing the Company's need for production and accuracy especially in aircraft work. He then suggested a plan the substance of which is as follows:—That if there were enough men interested, the Company would stand the expense of hiring an instructor in tool making to come to the plant and teach them on specified nights of each week. Mr. Fickle agreed to investigate the matter and report his finding to the Management.

There being no further business to discuss, the meeting adjourned.

By the Management
/S/ P. D. HILEMAN
By the Alliance
/S/ E. T. FICKLE

RESPONDENT'S EXHIBIT No. 1-W

Minutes of a meeting held in Mr. Hileman's office on January 30, 1940, between committee members E. T. Fickle, G. E. McIntire, C. O. Stubblefield, C. E. Little, N. J. Clifford, and Secretary L. S.

(Testimony of Clarence L. Millman.)

Bebb representing the P.M.P.W.A., and P. D. Hileman, V. E. Kangas, and D. M. Cameron representing the Company.

The meeting was opened by Mr. Hileman, who asked how the proposed plan for a steady, night shift with overtime had been received by the Union members. Mr. Fickle replied that the plan had not been accepted; the only objection being that of working a steady three months night shift. Mr. Hileman then asked if there would, be any objection to continuing as at present with overtime being worked by men doing operations which were necessary to step up production. It was the opinion of all committee members that this would be satisfactory.

The next topic under discussion dealt with rates of pay on polishers, thread grinders and on automatic machines. Mr. Fickle expressed an opinion that 50c per hour should be the minimum rate for polishing. Mr. Kangas stated that, in his opinion, a minimum rate of 45c and a maximum rate of 55c should apply on this job. Mr. Clifford pointed out the fact that this particular job was quite injurious to the operator's lungs. Mr. Hileman requested that Mr. Kangas look into the matter and to install a fixture to remove this dust hazard. Mr. Kangas agreed to do this at once. In regard to thread grinders' rates, Mr. Kangas expressed his opinion that this operation should not pay more than 70c per hour. It was generally agreed by all present that this would be a fair rate. Mr. Hileman then asked

(Testimony of Clarence L. Millman.)

for opinions regarding the rates to be paid on the automatic machines. Since no one was very familiar with this particular operation, opinions were slow in forthcoming. Mr. Kangas wrote his on a slip of paper and asked that all those present do likewise. Suggested rates ranged from 45c per hour for a beginner to 75c per hour for a man capable of making his own set-ups. Mr. Hileman asked that the rate question be left open for two or three weeks, at the end of which time a definite rate would be decided upon and written into the agreement. The committee members expressed their willingness to do this.

A difference of opinion between Mr. Kangas and Mr. Fickle regarding an employees senority standing upon resuming work after his being fired or after quitting the company employ was settled satisfactorily to all concerned. Mr. Livingstone interpreted the senority clause as follows:—If an employee quite his job or is fired and is, after a period, asked to return to work his senority rating resumes.

The subject of a soft ball team was introduced by Mr. Clifford who had agreed at our last meeting to determine if there were enough persons interested to warrant the forming of a club. Mr. Hileman expressed a desire for having a team this year and offered to get particulars regarding our entering a local league. This information he would turn over to Mr. Clifford or Wayne Kangas.

(Testimony of Clarence L. Millman.)

Only one complaint was entered at this meeting, the plaintiff being George E. McIntire, who asked that his rate per hour be increased in order that the amount of his pay check equal that of the operators on electric up-setters who were doing more of the type of work which paid a higher bonus. Mr. Kangas stated that he could not do this without making a general increase throughout the plant.

There being no further business to discuss, the meeting adjourned.

By the Management
/S/ P. D. HILEMAN
By the Alliance
/S/ E. T. FICKLE

RESPONDENT'S EXHIBIT No. 1-X

Minutes of a meeting held in Mr. Hileman's office on March 26, 1940 between committee members E. T. Fickle, G. E. McIntire, C. O. Stubblefield, C. E. Little, N. J. Clifford, and Secretary L. S. Bebb, representing the P. M. P. W. A., and P. D. Hileman, V. E. Kangas and D. M. Cameron representing the Company.

Mr. Hileman opened the meeting by asking what had developed for discussion. Mr. Fickle replied that many complaints had been received from union members that they were not receiving the correct wage rate for their particular job. Mr. Hileman re-

(Testimony of Clarence L. Millman.)

quested that a list of the men not receiving the correct rate be typed and delivered to him immediately, further stating that if this condition were existent, it would immediately be corrected and that if any back pay was due the men in question, it would be paid.

The next complaint made by Mr. Fickle was that a man recently assigned to a set-up job was not receiving set-up pay. Mr. Kangas replied that the man in question was not yet familiar enough with the work to be regarded as a full set-up man, drawing set-up rate. There followed a general discussion as to when a man became fully capable and Mr. Fickle suggested that this decision be left up to the foreman under whom the man in question might be working.

Mr. Hileman called for a copy of the Articles of Agreement and Wage Scale between the P. M. P. W. A. and the Company. After reading the clause dealing with set-up men, he stated that in his opinion any man designated as a set-up man should receive set-up pay. He further stated that any back pay due the man under discussion would be paid.

Mr. McIntire brought up the question as to whether or not a new employee should receive a bonus during the first thirty days of his employment. Mr. Kangas replied that under the terms of the agreement no bonus would be paid any employee with less than thirty days standing as he was not eligible to participate with the group.

(Testimony of Clarence L. Millman.)

The next topic was presented by Mr. Fickle who stated that the committee would like to set the rates of pay on the automatic machines, the thread grinder and the polishing machine. Mr. Hileman stated that he and Mr. Kangas had recently discussed this problem and asked Mr. Fickle what he considered a fair rate for automatic machine operators. Mr. Fickle replied that he considered a minimum rate of 60c, average of 65c, and maximum of 70c per hour as reasonable and fair. Mr. Kangas agreed that this would be fair enough after a man was capable of making their own set-ups. This rate was agreed as fair and was accepted by both Management and the P. M. P. W. A. Committee.

Mr. Hileman inquired of Mr. Fickle his opinion of a fair rate for thread grinder operators. To this he replied that a maximum rate of 75c per hour would be about right. Mr. Clifford expressed an opinion that the same rate should apply on the thread grinder as that now applying on finishing stem grinders, which is 76c per hour maximum. Mr. Kangas contended that the operator on automaties had a tougher job than the thread grinder operator and that thread grinding should not pay more than work on the automatics. Mr. Hileman pointed out to Mr. Kangas the added responsibility of the thread grinder operator because of the very close tolerance to which the threads must be held and also the fact that thread grinding is the final operation on these expensive parts having a ground thread. Mr. Kangas held to his opinion that thread

(Testimony of Clarence L. Millman.)

grinding should not pay over 70c per hour. The Committee almost unanimously maintained that thread grinding should be paid a maximum of 76c, average of 66c and minimum of 60c per hour. Mr. Hileman sided with the Committee and this scale was accepted by all present.

Mr. Hileman asked for opinions of rates to be paid on polishing machines. Mr. Kangas replied that he believed a higher rate than the tentative one of 55c an hour maximum, which was decided upon at the last meeting, should be paid, stating as his reasons the fact that this is a tedious and ticklish job and should pay somewhat more. The new rate he proposed was 55c minimum, 60c average, and 65c maximum per hour. This rate finally accepted after discussion.

Mr. Hileman inquired if there were any more questions or problems to be presented, to which Mr. Fickle replied that the most important one had been saved until last—that being that the P. M. P. W. A. was requesting a 10% increase in wages for all union members. Mr. Hileman inquired if a general increase was asked for all brackets, or whether the increase of 10% was for those receiving maximum pay. Mr. Clifford stated that the request covered an increase of 10% for those now at the maximum rate. Mr. Hileman stated that such a raise would substantially increase the company's costs, in that aircraft parts or specials had a greater number of man hours per piece and also, for the most part, had operators earning the top

(Testimony of Clarence L. Millman.)

rate. This also would reflect an increase not only in direct labor, but it would result in a reduction of the profit which could be earned if an increase in sale prices could not be obtained—which, at this time, seems doubtful due to a prolonged price raising campaign which had met with considerable success over the previous two year period. Mr. Clifford replied that the request for pay raise was occasioned by the increased cost of living, which was up at least 10% since the first of January.

Considerable additional discussion of the pay raise problem was had. Mr. Hileman finally asked for at least a two weeks period of grace in which he might confer with department heads and study the effect on our costs or granting such a proposal.

There being no further business, the meeting was adjourned.

By the Management

/S/ P. D. HILEMAN

By the Alliance

/S/ E. T. FICKLE

RESPONDENT'S EXHIBIT No. 1-Y

Minutes of a meeting held in Mr. Hileman's office April 9, 1940 between Committee members E. T. Fickle, G. E. McIntire, C. O. Stubblefield, C. E. Little and Secretary L. S. Bebb representing

(Testimony of Clarence L. Millman.)

the P. M. P. W. A., and P. D. Hileman, V. E. Kangas and D. M. Cameron representing the Company. Committee member N. J. Clifford was absent.

The meeting was opened by Mr. Hileman who gave to each person present a copy of the Annual Report To Employees of Thompson Products, stating that a copy of this report had been mailed to each employee the previous day. Various items contained in the report were commented on by Mr. Hileman, among which were the cost of plant operations, the large percentage of the Company's total cash receipts paid to employees in wages and the huge amount spent to modernize plant equipment and machinery; stressing the importance of the last item because of keen competition from other manufacturers.

Mr. Hileman then brought up the subject of a 10% increase in wages for all employees now receiving maximum pay, stating that *we* wished to express what it would mean to the company in the event that such an increase were granted. (This proposed increase was requested at the previous meeting.) His statements were as follows: The proposed increase would cost the Company at least $7,200 per year. On vacations alone, which are to be granted this year for the first time, the cost will be $1,300; and a 10% increase would increase this cost to $1,397. The vacation plan itself actually effected about a 4% increase in wages for everyone entitled to vacations inasmuch as they receive 52 weeks pay for 50 weeks work. The bonus plan

(Testimony of Clarence L. Millman.)

which was put into effect shortly after the absorption of Jadson by Thompson Products has in effect averaged a 9% increase for those working on group bonus in the Forge Department, and an average of 3% increase for those working Group 3, or the finishing operations of valves which are made by group bonus men. He further stated that wages paid by Jadson were equal to or better than any shop in Southern California manufacturing similar precision articles.

In summing this all up, he emphatically stated that, while he was not against increased pay rates when justified by Company earnings, such an increase if granted now would be disastrous to the program which has been so carefully laid out, as it would mean that no new equipment could be purchased this year which is sorely needed in order for us to compete with other manufacturers. It would also mean a distinct possibility of having to cancel some of the interplant commitments as additional price increases cannot be obtained from Cleveland. This in effect might mean continuing to produce the merchandise at higher costs and obsorb the loss through Original Equipment or cancelling the commitments with Cleveland and Toledo and laying off approximately fifty men.

He also emphasized the fact that numerous orders have been lost in the past year and a half through our drastic policy of increasing prices. In substantiation of this, he asked Mr. Carhart, Sales Manager, to tell the Committee of some of his ex-

(Testimony of Clarence L. Millman.)

periences and show them letters from our various customers complaining of our high prices, and in a number of instances dating back over a period of a year, letters to the effect that we had lost business due to being considerably above our competition. The Committee read a number of letters which were obtained by Carhart from his Sales Department files.

Mr. Hileman then asked the Committee how many old hands were dissatisfied with their jobs, and, if there were any, the cause of their dissatisfaction. Mr. Fickle answered this quite fully by stating that two old hands had expressed to him dissatisfaction with their wage rate but that working conditions and personnel relations were entirely satisfactory throughout the shop. The same opinion was expressed by all members of the Committee. Mr. Hileman asked what the Union members had to say regarding the list of new employees who had claimed not to have received the correct wage rate as set forth in the Union agreement, the investigation of this complaint had proved that they had received more pay than they were entitled to had the Union agreement been strictly adhered to. Mr. Fickle replied that a meeting had not been held yet. Mr. Hileman stated that the only possible way to increase wages would be to increase the sale price of our product to the consumer and to reduce the Company's losses by scrap.

Mr. Hileman stated that he planned a campaign

(Testimony of Clarence L. Millman.)

against losses by scrap, stating that for every $100 worth of material produced, about $5 was lost by the scrap route. He stated that most of the scrap was on aircraft parts and cited one instance where 13 bolts were made at a cost of $6 each and that not one of the bolts passed inspection, making a total loss to the Company of $78 plus valuable time. This, of course, he stated, was an extreme case but served to illustrate the seriousness of the scrap problem. Mr. Kangas, who on his recent visit to the Cleveland plant had inspected various plants in and about Cleveland and Detroit, stated that a majority of the shops were equipped with modern automatic machines and that one such shop had automatics which turned out bolts with the precision tolerance of .002″ on the pitch diameter of the threads. He stressed the great importance of the Company's purchasing new machinery, stating that many pieces of Jadson's machinery was obsolete and not productive.

The merits of a steady job against higher wages and short terms of employment were the next topic under discussion. The Committee expressed unanimously that they were decidedly in favor of the former. Mr. Hileman asked if there were any new complaints. Mr. Fickle replied that the Committee would like to have set a wage rate for welders capable of doing all types of welding. Mr. Hileman asked Mr. Fickle his opinion as to a fair rate, to which Mr. Fickle replied that 85 or 90c per hour would not be out of line. Mr. Stubblefield replied

(Testimony of Clarence L. Millman.)

that in his opinion 85c per hour would not be any too much. Mr. Kangas held to his opinion that 85c was a fair maximum rate. This rate was agreed upon by all members of the Committee.

The subject of vacations was brought up by Mr. Fickle. Mr. Kangas stated that inquiries as to vacation periods had already been made by some employees and that some dates had been tentatively set. The question arose as to when the general vacation period started and when it ended. Mr. Hileman replied that April 1st was the starting date and that due to the exceptionally fine weather conditions prevailing in California, the period did not end until December 1st. This, he added, gave Jadson employees a better break than those of Thompson Products proper, since their vacation period ended October 1st. He pointed out that it also gave an employee two months more to become eligible for vacation and that no quibbling would be done should an employee be lacking a few weeks or a month on his total employment time to make him eligible for a vacation. Mr. Hileman gave Mr. Fickle a copy of statistics substantiating his statements in the foregoing regarding wage increases since 1937, vacation plan costs, wage increases effected by adoption of the bonus system, etc. for the edification of any or all Union members.

(Testimony of Clarence L. Millman.)

There being no further business to discuss, the meeting was adjourned.

By the Management

/S/ P. D. HILEMAN

By the Alliance

/S/ E. T. FICKLE

RESPONDENT'S EXHIBIT No. 1-Z

Minutes of a meeting held in Mr. Hileman's office on June 25, 1940 between committee members; E. T. Fickle, C. O. Stubblefield, N. J. Clifford, C. E. Little, and Secretary L. S. Bebb, representing the P. M. P. W. A. and P. D. Hileman, V. E. Kangas, and D. M. Cameron, representing the Company.

The meeting was opened by Mr Hileman who gave a short discussion regarding the new identification badges which have recently been received and the reasons for requiring each employee to wear his own badge in the future. He explained that this form of identification is being adopted by almost every plant in the United States which is now engaged in the Government's Rearmament Program.

Mr. Hileman next asked for an opinion with reward to shutting down the plant from July 3 until July 8, with the provision that the employees should work as much overtime as possible on the first, second, and third days of July to make up for the loss of production during the Fourth of

(Testimony of Clarence L. Millman.)

July holidays. Everyone present received the suggestion with enthusiasm, and it was agreed that this should be done.

Mr. Hileman next read a program of National Defense measures which proved very interesting and enlightening. He also read several items of proposed new tax legislation, among which is a ten per cent price increase on new automobiles. From his point of view, he explained this tax measure is not being adopted so much to increase National Revenue as to discourage the purchase of new automobiles, thus freeing skilled workers from their regular task of making new jigs and dies for the production of new cars and making them available for work on the National Defense Program. He pointed out that this particular tax will probably affect our business, inasmuch as there will be a greater demand for parts with which to repair older model cars.

Mr. Hileman then asked if any one had any complaints to make or suggestions to offer. Mr. Bebb replied that the flash from the arc welder bothered the men working on the power saws close by. Mr. Kangas stated that steps had already been taken to remedy this and that within the next few days the condition would be taken care of.

A suggested rate by Mr. Kangas, of 95c per hour maximum for heat treaters, was discussed. Mr. Hileman asked that he be given a week to consider the proposed rate, as he believed for our type of heat treating the rate was somewhat high. The

(Testimony of Clarence L. Millman.)

Committee agreed to this request. The rates for female workers were raised from a maximum of 48c per hour to 55c per hour.

A request was made by Mr. Kangas who asked that the article in the P. M. P. W. A. agreement dealing with progressive rates of pay for new workers be changed to read as follows:

"The rate of any new employee when he is advanced to a different machine operation shall be the same as the minimum rate on the machine which he last operated. This rate to continue for 30 days, at which time his rate will become the average rate of the machine which he is operating."

The foregoing to apply to workers who have been employed less than 120 days. Any employee of longer standing who is advanced to a different machine doing an operation with which he is not familiar shall receive for the first 30 days, the same rate of pay as he received on his previous machine. At the end of 30 days, his pay will be the average rate on the machine which he is operating.

It was agreed by the members of the P. M. P. W. A. Committee that **Mr.** Kangas' request be **granted.**

Mr. Hileman then touched upon the subject of scrap, which subject had been discussed quite fully at our last meeting. He stated that the amount of money lost by the Company through scrap parts and material was very large. He asked that Mr. Fickle discuss the scrap situation with the employees at their next meeting, and that he try to

(Testimony of Clarence L. Millman.)
impress upon them the gravity of the Company's losses via the scrap route. Mr. Fickle replied that he would discuss the matter with them.

There being no further business to discuss, the meeting adjourned.

By the Management
/S/ P. D. HILEMAN

By the Alliance
/S/ E. T. FICKLE

RESPONDENT'S EXHIBIT 1-AA

Minutes of a meeting held in Mr. Hileman's office on August 9, between committee members: N. J. Clifford, G. F. Bywater, C. E. Little, E. T. Fickle, and Secretary L. S. Bebb, representing the P. M. P. W. A.; and P. D. Hileman, W. J. Kearns, and D. M. Cameron, representing the company.

The meeting was opened by Mr. Hileman who said that the meeting had been called because of rumors which he had heard were circulating throughout the plant regarding the imminent discharging of certain employees. He stated that the rumors were entirely false and that the management is contemplating no radical changes in personnel. He then asked if there were any questions in the minds of the Committee which they would like to have answered.

Mr. Bywater replied that the Committee would be expected to give some explanation as to why Mr.

(Testimony of Clarence L. Millman.)

Kangas left so suddenly. Mr. Hileman replied that for some time past he and Mr. Kangas had not been in perfect accord on matters which had to do with company policy, and that he had decided that Mr. Kangas' resignation would be best for all concerned. He further stated that he had this morning talked to Mr. Kangas and that he wished him the best of luck in his new position.

Mr. Fickle said that it was chiefly the employes of longer standing who were apprehensive of being fired, to which Mr. Hileman replied that the rumor was preposterous, and that all of the men now working were to be retained, provided that they continued to do their jobs as they should be done.

Next, Mr. Hileman brought up the subject of a change in the company name which is to take place in about two weeks. The company will be known as Thompson Products, Inc., and will have a plant name such as West Coast Plant, or something on that order. He explained that the change in name was being effected chiefly because of the fact that Thompson Products, Inc., is a much larger and better known company than Jadson Motor Products Company, and that its manufactured products are much more numerous than those of Jadson, this being especially true of the aircraft industry which has become so important to this division.

The views expressed by Mr. Hileman in the foregoing were unanimously approved by the Committee.

(Testimony of Clarence L. Millman.)

A short discussion regarding new equipment followed.

Mr. Hileman stated that the duties of Superintendent of the Plant would be carried on by Mr. Kearns, which statement was heartily received and approved by all present.

There being no further business to discuss, the meeting was adjourned.

For the Company
　　/S/ P. D. HILEMAN
For the Alliance
　　/S/ N. J. CLIFFORD

––––––––

RESPONDENT'S EXHIBIT NO. 1-BB

Minutes of a meeting held in Mr. Hileman's office on August 19, between Committee Members: N. J. Clifford, C. E. Little, G. F. Bywater, C. O. Stubblefield, and Secretary, L. S. Bebb, representing the P. M. P. W. A.; and P. D. Hileman, W. J. Kearns, and D. M. Cameron representing the Company

The meeting was opened by Mr Hileman who stated that vicious rumors had been circulated throughout the shop regarding the circumstances surrounding the dismissal of Mr. Kangas. Rumor had it, he said, that underhand methods had been employed to effect the dismissal. This, he stated, was entirely false, and that Mr. Kangas had been discharged outright.

(Testimony of Clarence L. Millman.)

Mr. Hileman then gave the Committee a better understanding of the things which finally led him to decide that the best thing for all concerned was to ask for Mr. Kangas' resignation. Both the Committee and the Management do not feel that it is fitting or proper that these things appear as a permanent record in our Minute Book. Suffice to say, reasons for Mr. Kangas' leaving had included violation of conduct and inefficiency extending over a period of more than a year.

Mr. Hileman next touched on the subject of men leaving our employ to go to work for Aircraft Accessories Corporation, with which Mr. Kangas is now affiliated. In order that those who considered leaving Jadson's employ to go to work for the above named company be better informed as to the size and financial condition of that company, Mr. Hileman expressed a desire to give further information which he had at hand. Mr. Metzger was called in to give a report on the financial condition and business outlook of the concern, which report had been compiled by Dunn and Bradstreet and was a very thorough one.

Mr. Little next brought up the subject of incorporating into the Old Guard Association a Sick Benefit plan to be financed by regular monthly dues from each member. The possibility of a Personal Loan plan was also touched upon. Mr. Hileman thought the Sick Benefit plan a good one and also agreed that such a plan be put into effect provided a ma-

(Testimony of Clarence L. Millman.)
jority of members were in favor. He voiced doubts as to the advisability of the Loan plan.

A request was made by Mr. Bebb for a ten cent per hour raise for all welders capable of doing commercial and general welding. Mr. Hileman requested that he be given a few days to consider the matter. His request was granted.

There being no further business to discuss, the meeting was adjourned.

For the Company
    /S/ P. D. HILEMAN
For the Alliance
    /S/ N. J. CLIFFORD

RESPONDENT'S EXHIBIT NO. 1-CC

Minutes of a meeting held in **Mr. Hileman's** office August 22, between Committee Members, N. J. Clifford, C. O. Stubblefield, C. E. Little, and Secretary L. S. Bebb, representing the P. M. P. W. A. and P. D. Hileman, W. J. Kearns, R. S. Livingstone, and D. M. Cameron representing the Company.

The meeting was opened by Mr. Hileman, who stated that the meeting had been called so that **Mr.** Livingstone, might familiarize the Jadson personnel with various pieces of Federal legislation dealing with the employment of aliens, and to explain the necessary steps to be taken for the procurement of birth certificates or other papers to establish proof of an employee's citizenship.

(Testimony of Clarence L. Millman.)

He explained that in recent years several laws had been passed, each succeeding law becoming more rigid, until at this time it has become imperative that each employee establish definite proof of his citizenship; or that he has expressed a desire for citizenship by applying for citizenship papers.

The above mentioned laws, which are too lengthy to be explained herein, are to be found printed on Page One of the August 23rd issue of Friendly Forum; also on Page three of the same issue will be found instructions as to ways of proving citizenship.

Mr. Hileman stated that some person in this Plant in the very near future will be designated to assist any employees who might have difficulty in proving their Citizenship or eligibility for such.

There followed a Round Table discussion, during which Mr. Livingstone outlined the prospects for future aviation business, which, according to his lights, are excellent inasmuch as this country's facilities for producing airplane parts are only about one-tenth of what they should be in order to complete on schedule the Government's plans for mass airplane production.

There being no further business to discuss, the meeting was adjourned.

For the Company

/S/ P. D. HILEMAN

For the Alliance

/S/ N. J. CLIFFORD

(Testimony of Clarence L. Millman.)

RESPONDENT'S EXHIBIT No. 1-DD

Minutes of a meeting held in Mr. Hileman's office August 26, 1940, at 2:00 P. M. between Committee Members: E. T. Fickle, N. J. Clifford, C. O. Stubblefield, C. E. Little, G. F. Bywater, and Secretary, L. S. Bebb, representing the P. M. P. W. A., and P. D. Hileman, W. J. Kearns and D. M. Cameron, representing the Company.

The meeting was opened by Mr. Hileman who stated that he had some pleasant news to impart. He outlined a Profit-sharing plan which is to be adopted by Thompson Products, Inc. West Coast Plant. This plan will be retroactive to August 15, 1940. The plan is as follows: Each hourly rate employee on the factory pay roll will receive on September 5th, in addition to his regular wages, a bonus check totaling six per cent of his gross wages for the preceding month. Each month thereafter on the same date he will receive a bonus check figured on the above basis. This plan is to remain in force as long the Company's profits for the current month are in excess of ten per cent to warrant the payment of the new bonus.

Mr. Hileman next touched upon the subject of the 40-hour work week, which is to go into effect on October 23. He stated that the Company planned on working all men possible 42 hours per week, as at present. This would mean that those working a 42-hour week would receive pay for 43 hours, since the two extra hours would be worked at over-time rates.

(Testimony of Clarence L. Millman.)

He pointed out that the bonus check mentioned in the foregoing plus the two extra hours at overtime rates would effect an approximate increase of 8.5 per cent in each employee's earnings. Mr. Hileman's statements were heartily received and approved by all present.

A proposal was made by Mr. Clifford that an American flag be purchased by the employees, and the funds for which would be gained by popular subscription throughout the plant. The proposal was approved by everyone present. Mr. Hileman expressed his opinion that the idea was excellent and stated that the Company would have an all-steel flag pole erected immediately.

Mr. Hileman next suggested that a ten-minute rest period be put into effect during both the morning and afternoon hours, in order that employes who wish to smoke or purchase soft drinks or relax might do so during this interval. He explained that the present system of purchasing soft drinks during working hours decreased production to quite an extent, and that employees applying to the tool room window for change worked a hardship on the tool room attendant. It was agreed by the Committee that Mr. Hileman's suggestion held merit and that they would approach their fellow employees on the matter.

Mr. Hileman next touched upon the subject of scrap. He stated that much progress had been made to reduce the scrap condition, but that as yet the problem still presented itself.

(Testimony of Clarence L. Millman.)

It was agreed by the Committee that they should talk the matter over with their fellow Union members at their next regular meeting.

There being no further business to discuss, the meeting was adjourned.

For the Company

/s/ P. D. HILEMAN

For the Alliance

/s/ E. T. FICKLE

RESPONDENT'S EXHIBIT No. 1-EE

Minutes of a meeting held in Mr. Hileman's office Friday, September 13, 1940 between Committee Members N. J. Clifford, C. F. Bywater, C. O. Stubblefield, C. E. Little, E. T. Fickle and Secretary, L. S. Bebb representing the P. M. P. W. A. and P. D. Hileman, George Fary, W. J. Kearns and D. M. Cameron representing the Company.

The meeting was opened by Mr. Hileman who inquired of Mr. Fickle why the meeting had been called. Mr. Fickle replied that there were a few questions of rates on different machines which the Committee would like to get settled before their regular meeting to be held on Sept. 14. There followed a discussion of the rate questions. These were settled tentatively pending Mr. Hileman's decision which was to be given on Saturday morning, Sept. 14.

The next subject for discussion dealt with the

(Testimony of Clarence L. Millman.)

present bonus system and was introduced by Mr. Fickle. He stated that there were several men in the shop who were actually doing 120 per cent on their jobs and yet the bulletin board notices showed their department to be doing only 96 per cent. Mr. Hileman replied that this condition would be investigated at once to find out who the men are who are causing the deficiency and that as soon as they are located, they will be replaced by men who really want to work on a bonus paying job.

Mr. Hileman stated that there were evidently some men who were not putting their quota of work out since no bonus had been paid recently. He pointed out that the bonus rates had not been changed; that the company had spent, during the past two years, $140,000.00 for the purchase of new, and for the overhauling of old machinery and equipment. He further stated that allowances had been made for the breaking in of new men on bonus-paying jobs, and that with the improvements already mentioned taken into consideration, he was at a loss to understand why a bonus was not being paid except for the reasons stated in the preceding paragraph.

Another complaint made by Mr. Fickle was that no raise in pay had been given to any employee who had been employed a sufficient length of time to justify the increase. Mr. Kearns stated that he would investigate the matter at once and that he would have proper adjustments made.

Mr. Hileman next opened the subject of the Com-

(Testimony of Clarence L. Millman.)

pany Picnic by asking the Committee Members their ideas concerning the best day to hold the festivities. A definite date of October 12 was agreed upon unanimously.

There being no further business to discuss, the meeting was adjourned.

For the Company

/s/ P. D. HILEMAN

For the Alliance

/s/ E. T. FICKLE

———

RESPONDENT'S EXHIBIT No. 1-FF

Minutes of a meeting held in Mr. Hileman's office Monday, November 18, 1940 between Committee Members E. T. Fickle, C. O. Stubblefield, R. D. Hailey, J. H. Olsen, C. E. Weisser and Secretary L. S. Bebb, representing the P. M. P. W. A. and P. D. Hileman, George Fary, W. J. Kearns and C. L. Millman, representing the Company.

The meeting was opened by Mr. Hileman who stated that the meeting had been called to discuss the new contract between the Company and the P. M. P. W. A., that a few changes had been made in the Seniority Agreement and the Vacation Plan in an effort to more nearly conform to the Parent Company policy; but the basic contract had not been changed. These changes were reviewed and found satisfactory.

Mr. Hileman then asked Mr. Fickle what the

(Testimony of Clarence L. Millman.)

first question was that he wished to discuss. Mr. Fickle replied that the Committee believed that the maximum rates in the Forge Department should be raised .05 per hour. Mr. Hileman reminded the Committee that the Forge Department had been receiving a Group Bonus steadily for the past several months to which Mr. Olsen replied that this was true but although the department was working more hours, the hours of work on bonus paying jobs had been decreased. Mr. Hileman agreed that this was no doubt correct and that he would check on the matter.

Mr. Weisser then stated that he felt that the maximum rate for Heat Treater Class A. should be increased from .90 per hour to $1.00 per hour. Mr. Hileman remarked that this seemed to be a rather large increase and inquired of Mr. Weisser his reasons for desiring such a large increase. Mr. Weisser replied that he did not wish it for himself— he was perfectly satisfied—but felt that it would give the men in his department something to look forward to. The Management agreed pending further consideration.

Mr. Olsen suggested that the rate for set-up men be increased from .05 per hour extra to .10 per hour extra because of the great responsibility resting with the set-up men and the fact that the work was done at night. After some discussion, this was agreed to by the Management.

Mr. Stubblefield then requested that the maximum rate for welders be increased to $1.00 per hour. Mr.

(Testimony of Clarence L. Millman.)

Hileman referred to a survey made by a manufacturers' association in Southern California covering about fifteen plants, which showed the welding range from .65 to $1.25 with but five plants having a maximum of $1.00 or more and an average of the fifteen of .91 per hour. The Management also pointed out that our rates are now better than average and that an increase was not justified. However, at the insistence of Mr. Stubblefield and several of the Committee, the increase was agreed upon.

There followed a general discussion of the pay rates of the balance of the plant and it was requested by the committee that the maximum rates of several jobs be increased from .05 to .10 per hour. The Management agreed to take the entire matter under consideration.

There being no further business at the moment, the meeting was adjourned until 2:30 p. m. Tuesday, November 19, 1940.

For the Company
　　/s/ P. D. HILEMAN
For the Alliance
　　/s/ E. T. FICKLE

———

RESPONDENT'S EXHIBIT No. 1-GG

Minutes of a meeting held in Mr. Hileman's office at 2:30 p. m. Tuesday, November 19, 1940, between Committee Members E. T. Fickle, C. O. Stubblefield, R. D. Hailey, J. H. Olsen, C. E. Weisser and

(Testimony of Clarence L. Millman.)

Secretary L. S. Bebb, representing the P. M. P. W. A. and P. D. Hileman, George Fary, W. J. Kearns and C. L. Millman, representing the Company.

The meeting was opened by Mr. Hileman who stated that the raises in rates requested by the Committee in the meeting of November 18 had been discussed with Mr. Kearns and Mr. Millman and that a majority of them had been agreed upon, but there were a few that the Management felt were not justified. He again referred to the survey made by a Manufacturers' association and said that in almost every case our present rates were substantially above average for a like job in the plants studied, which included most of the large manufacturing plants of the state. He further emphasized to the Committee that the continuance of the 6 per cent extra compensation depended entirely upon the company's realization of a ten per cent net profit on business done, and if the payroll was increased too greatly or too rapidly, the net profit would naturally decrease with the resulting loss of bonus.

In the case of the Heat Treaters, the Management felt that a $1.00 maximum was somewhat high and suggested that it be set at .95 which would be .05 higher than the present maximum. He asked Mr. Weisser how many men in his department were receiving the maximum to which Mr. Weisser replied he was the only one but that he was not thinking of himself, but wanted it for the men under him in order that they might have a goal to work toward.

(Testimony of Clarence L. Millman.)

The Company records were consulted which showed that the two highest paid men in the department, excluding Mr. Weisser, were now receiving .85 which was .05 under the present maximum and would be .10 under the proposed new maximum of .95. As long as Mr. Weisser himself was satisfied with his present rate, the Management failed to see the reason for wishing the maximum raised to $1.00. There followed considerable discussion on the subject and the new rate of $1.00 was finally agreed upon by all.

Mr. Hileman next addressed Mr. Stubblefield with the remark that he would prefer to set the maximum rate on the Welders at .95 instead of the proposed $1.00. Mr. Stubblefield replied that he still believed the job should pay $1.00 and felt that the Company should make that the rate. The Management pointed out that the average for the locality was .91 and that the proposed .95 rate would still be above average. However, at the insistence of Mr. Stubblefield and Mr. Bebb, the rate was finally set at $1.00.

Mr. Olsen next inquired of Mr. Hileman why the words "when warranted" had been added to the paragraph regarding the .10 per hour extra pay for the set-up men. Mr. Hileman stated that the Management was of the opinion that a good deal of the monthly scrap was due to faulty set-up and that he felt that if the Company reserved the right to withhold part of the set-up rate until the man in question was deserving of the full amount, it would re-

(Testimony of Clarence L. Millman.)

sult in more care being taken by the set-up men in performing their duties. Mr. Olsen replied that the majority of the scrap from the Forge Department was due to faulty machinery and that he felt that inasmuch as the set-up work was done at night, the full amount of the raise was justified. Mr. Hileman replied that he realized that the machinery in the Forge Department needed repairs and that steps were being taken to this end. Mr. Olsen declined an offer of a day time job if he no longer desired to work a straight night shift, and after much discussion, the full amount of the set-up rate was agreed upon.

Mr. Fickle then introduced a request that the pay checks of the factory employees be placed in envelopes in order that no one except the man himself would see them. He said that there had been complaints from the men that too many people had the opportunity of seeing the checks during the distribution. Mr. Hileman replied that the cost of placing the checks in envelopes with the individual's name typed thereon would be prohibitive, but some other method of distribution would be found. It was suggested by Mr. Millman that a small wooden box with partitions for the arrangement of the checks either alphabetically or by number be furnished which would enable no one but the person distributing the checks to see them.

(Testimony of Clarence L. Millman.)

There being no further questions, the meeting was adjourned until 11:30 a. m. November 20.

For the Company

/s/ P. D. HILEMAN

For the Alliance

/s/ E. T. FICKLE

RESPONDENT'S EXHIBIT No. 1-HH

Minutes of a meeting held in Mr. Hileman's office at 11:30 a. m. Wednesday, November 20, 1940 between Committee Members E. T. Fickle, C. O. Stubblefield, R. D. Hailey, J. H. Olsen, C. E. Weisser and Secretary L. S. Bebb, representing the P. M. P. W. A. and P. D. Hileman, George Fary, W. J. Kearns and C. L. Millman representing the Company.

Mr. Hileman opened the meeting by informing the Committee that the contract had been completed and was ready for signing pending final approval of all concerned. He suggested that Mr. Millman read aloud the contract in its entirety which was done. It was suggested by Mr. Fickle that the Valve Straightening be increased to .75 and the Special Screw Machine to .78 since the Production Hand Screw Machine had been already increased to .75 and the former job had always been considered worth .05 per hour more. It was also suggested that the Warner and Swasey 3A and the New Acme Turret Lathe rates be changed to read

(Testimony of Clarence L. Millman.)

.70-.75-.85 instead of .75-.80-.85 in order to increase the spread between the average and the maximum, and that a minimum and average rate of .75 and .80 be set on the Warner and Swasey 2A and the Lodge and Shipley lathe.

These changes were approved and made and the contract was signed by the Committee Members and the Management.

Mr. Fickle raised the question as to the date on which a man's Old Guard Service, in regard to vacation eligibility, began and whether or not a definite line was drawn on men who had started to work for the company shortly after January 31 of any year, for instance, in February, Mr. Hileman replied that no definite decision had ever been made on the subject and that he would give it some serious thought.

The Committee also inquired whether or not a man eligible for vacation could waive the vacation and add it to the one he would receive the following year. The Management stated that such a procedure could not be agreed to inasmuch as it might permit a valuable man to be absent from his work for too long a period at one time.

There being no further business to discuss, the meeting was adjourned.

For the Company

/s/ P. D. HILEMAN

For the Alliance

/s/ E. T. FICKLE

(Testimony of Clarence L. Millman.)

RESPONDENT'S EXHIBIT No. 1-II

Minutes of a meeting held in Mr. Hileman's office Thursday, Jannary 23, 1941, between Committee Members E. T. Fickle, C. O. Stubblefield, R. D. Hailey, J. H. Olsen, C. E. Weisser and Secretary L. S. Bebb representing the P. M. P. W. A. and P. D. Hileman, George Fay, W. J. Kearns and C. L. Millman representing the Company.

Mr. Fickle opened the meeting by inquiring of Mr. Millman if he had received any information regarding the pay policies of the parent company for several questions had arisen regarding the rumor that the other plants of the company paid every Friday. Upon Mr. Millman's affirmative answer, Mr. Hileman remarked that the Cleveland plant paid every two weeks but due to the greatly increased amount of clerical work involved in such a method of paying, the Management would prefer to leave our pay days as they are unless too much agitation was made on the subject. The Committee suggested that they discuss the subject with the members at the next meeting of the P. M. P. W. A.

The next question of the Committee concerned the vacation plan of the eastern plants of the company. Mr. Hileman replied that the plan in the Cleveland and Detroit plants was three days vacation for from three to five years service and one weeks vacation for from five to ten years service and two weeks vacation for ten years or more service.

(Testimony of Clarence L. Millman.)

He also informed the Committee that the Management had been considering conforming with the Cleveland Office plan and that he would like to have time to determine the number of men eligible for three days vacation and the approximate cost to the Company. The Committee was assured that if it were at all possible to do so, the Company would allow three days vacation for the three year men.

Mr. Fickle then asked the reason for cutting the Toolroom work week to forty hours and then sending work out to other shops to be done. Mr. Fary replied that he was not aware that the work week had been cut but that the only work being sent out was the parts for the new upsetter and only those parts which could not be made rapidly or economically in our plant were being sent out. Mr. Hileman referred to the recent orders for the Solar tubing and stressed the need of speed in completing the new upsetter. Both Mr. Fary and Mr. Kearns stated that they would investigate the reason for cutting the work week in the Toolroom to forty hours.

The next question dealt with the possibility of raises being due to E. P. Frech and J. H. Holder, and the seniority status of C. Moretz and C. B. Ackerman. Mr. Millman promised to check on these matters at once and to make any adjustments that were necessary.

The Committee then brought up the subject of Oscar Drevlo, who, they stated, was dissatisfied as an oiler and wished to be transferred back to the

(Testimony of Clarence L. Millman.)

Maintenance Department. Mr. Kearns remarked that Mr. Drevlo was an excellent oiler and Mr. Hileman suggested that if this were the case, his rate should be increased or else he should be returned to maintenance work. Mr. Kearns promised to investigate and take some action.

Mr. Fickle then remarked that the men on the Centerless Grinders felt that they should have the maximum rate established for the job but the Management pointed out that considerable rework was caused by rough stems and when this item had been reduced to a minimum, the grinder operators would be increased. Mr. Weisser called attention to the fumes being given off by the Radiac Cut-off machine and suggested that a blower or suction be installed and that additional protection be given to the operator of the Flash Welding machine to protect him from the sparks.

Mr. Millman brought up the subject of two new jobs that had been created in the plant, those of Timekeeper and Stockroom Helper, and suggested that rates be established for these jobs. After some discussion it was decided that a rate of .60-.65-.70 be placed on the Timekeeper job and .50-.55-.65 be placed on the Stock-room Helper job.

Mr. Hailey again brought up the subject of the men who started to work shortly after January 31 of any year and was it necessary for them to wait until January 1 of the following year before their Old Guard and Vacation time service began. The Management decided that a dead-line must be placed

(Testimony of Clarence L. Millman.)

on the subject and decided that January 1, with 30 days grace period, must be observed.

Mr. Hileman told the Committee that the questions brought up at the meeting would be discussed and a definite answer would be given at the next meeting.

There being no further business, the meeting was adjourned.

/S/ P. D. HILEMAN,
For the Company.
/S/ E. T. FICKLE,
For the Alliance.

RESPONDENT'S EXHIBIT No. 1-JJ

Minutes of a meeting held Friday, February 21, 1941 in Mr. Hileman's office between Committee Members E. T. Fickle, C. E. Weisser, R. D. Hailey, C. O. Stubblefield, J. H. Olsen and Secretary L. S. Bebb, representing the P. M. P. W. A. and P. D. Hileman, George Fary, W. J. Kearns and C. L. Millman, representing the Management.

The meeting opened with a general discussion by Mr. Hileman of the current shortage of bolt steel and of other specialized types of steel now in use in the manufacture of our various products, and the possibility of using substitutes. Mr. Hileman gave the Committee a clear picture of the business at this time, pointing out that it was practically impossible to anticipate orders far enough

(Testimony of Clarence L. Millman.)

ahead to have enough steel on hand since it is now necessary to order from six to eight months in advance. He emphasized the fact that orders have, in almost every case, doubled their size for the same period of 1940. The question was raised by Mr. Hailey of the men who are working on bolts and it was decided by the Management that if there was no work in other departments for these men, they would have to be laid off until steel arrived.

It was suggested by the Committee that the maximum rate for Forge Diemakers be increased from .85 to .90 which change was approved by the Management.

Mr. Millman brought up the question of the Old Guard status of several employees discussed at the last meeting. Mr. L. E. Drake, President of the West Coast Plant Old Guard Association, was called in the meeting at this point, and after some discussion, it was decided that the subject was a matter for the Old Guard Committee and one member of the P. M. P. W. A. to decide and was referred to them for action.

The Management next commented on the recent tampering with the soft drink vending machines in the plant and warned the Committee that if this happened again, it would be necessary to remove the machines permanently from the plant. The Committee was reminded that the machines were purchased by the Company for the convenience of the employees and that the Management would not like to penalize all employees for the misdemeanors

(Testimony of Clarence L. Millman.)

of a few but that there was no other alternative. The Committee was asked to inform their members of this decision.

It was suggested by Mr. Weisser that a plank walk be placed in the parking lot to enable the men to walk from their cars to the plant without stepping in mud. Mr. Fary promised that something would be done about the parking lot in the near future.

Mr. Hileman announced that the Vacation Plan had been changed to allow a vacation of one-half week, or 20 hours, for all men who have an Old Guard Service record of from three to four years. The vacation plan for five to ten year men will remain the same. The vacation week is to be based on the regular work week of 40 hours. This announcement was enthusiastically received by the Committee and Mr. Millman remarked that the vacation preference lists would be made up immediately and the vacation period would start on April 1.

There being no further business to discuss, the meeting was adjourned.

/S/ P. D. HILEMAN,

For the Company.

/S/ E. T. FICKLE,

For the Alliance.

(Testimony of Clarence L. Millman.)

RESPONDENT'S EXHIBIT No. 1-KK

Minutes of a meeting held Friday, March 28, 1941 in Mr. Hileman's office between Committee Members E. T. Fickle, C. E. Weisser, R. D. Hailey, C. O. Stubblefield, J. H. Olsen and Secretary L. S. Bebb, representing the P M. P. W. A., and P. D. Hileman, George Fary, W. J. Kearns and C. L. Millman representing the Management.

The meeting was opened by Mr. Millman who stated that it had been called to acquaint the committee with several new policies adopted by the company and to discuss some phases of the new factory building addition.

He informed the committee that management had decided to set a minimum starting rate for male employees at 50c per hour to conform with the prevailing rate in the community and to make it a little easier for the first thirty days of a new man's employment. A general discussion of the jobs which now hold a 50c minimum followed and the necessary adjustments were made. All men who now receive the old starting rate will automatically be increased to the 50c rate.

The Committee was told that the Prudential Insurance Company, handling our group insurance, had permitted the company to carry life insurance of draftees for one year, or until the expiration of the master contract in July, 1941. It was pointed out that the insurance company reserves the right to terminate this privilege whenever the contract

(Testimony of Clarence L. Millman.)

comes up for renewal, but that no difficulty is presently anticipated. Mr. Millman also stated that any man called in the draft was eligible for vacation would be given his vacation pay upon departure.

Mr. Hileman then discussed the plans for the locker and shower rooms in the new factory building and asked the committee for their suggestions regarding a cafeteria or a room where employees might eat their lunches. It was pointed out that to include this room in the plant proper would cost the company about $12,000 for space, whereas an outside shelter could be built adjacent to the plant for a much more moderate expenditure. The committee was in favor of this latter plan inasmuch as eight to nine months of the year are warm and the men seem to prefer the outside eating stand. Any such arrangement, Mr. Hileman said, would be well screened in and have ice water available.

Mr. Millman reported that the soft drink vending machines had again been broken into and reminded the committee that management had in the past promised to remove them from the plant if this problem continued. There followed a discussion of the subject with the theory being advanced that if the machines were out in full view of the employees at all times, it would prevent further tampering. Management stated that it did not wish to penalize the entire personnel for the acts of one or two individuals whose sense of responsibility seemed lacking, but that something must be done at once as the cost of repairs and delays was a nuisance.

(Testimony of Clarence L. Millman.)

Mr. Hileman again suggested the ten minute rest period twice on each shift at which time drinks could be sold from the stock room. The committee promised to discuss the idea with their members and it was tentatively decided to try to place the vending machines in a central location, possibly near the time booth. Mr. Fary and Mr. Kearns agreed to make a survey and find a suitable place in a final attempt to have these machines operate to the benefit of both employees and management.

Mr. Hailey remarked that the current rumor in the plant was to the effect that the 6% extra compensation was to be discontinued as such and would be added to the employees' hourly rate. Management assured the committee that the bonus would be continued as a separate pay item so long as operation costs permitted the company to realize a 10% net profit.

The committee also suggested that when a new job was created or a current job open in the plant, notice to that effect would be placed on the bulletin boards so that present employees would be informed and if they desired to try out for the new job, would be given the opportunity to do so.

There being no further business to discuss, the meeting was adjourned.

/S/ P. D. HILEMAN,
For the Company.

/S/ E. T. FICKLE,
For the Alliance.

(Testimony of Clarence L. Millman.)

RESPONDENT'S EXHIBIT No. 1-LL

Minutes of a meeting held Friday, April 18, 1941 in Mr. Hileman's office between Committee Members E. T. Fickle, C. E. Weisser, R. D. Hailey, C. O. Stubblefield, J. H. Olsen and Secretary L. S. Bebb, representing the P. M. P. W. A., and P. D. Hileman, George Fary, W. J. Kearns and C. L. Millman representing the Management.

The meeting was opened by Mr. Hileman who inquired of Mr. Fickle his reason for calling the meeting. Mr. Fickle stated the Committee felt there was some unfairness in our present method of transferring men to better paying jobs as required in Exhibit A, Page 3, Paragraph 4 of the contract between the P. M. P. W. A. and Thompson Products, Inc. West Coast Plant, which states that a man transferred to another job shall continue for 30 days at the rate he was earning on his previous job; after which time he would be increased to the average rate on the new job.

The committee suggested if a man requested a transfer to another job that he be hired on the new job at the minimum rate, but if he is transferred by the Company that he continue at his present rate.

Mr. Hileman remarked that he felt 30 days was sufficient time for the average man to become proficient on a different machine, and suggested that in special cases a man's breaking in period be extended to 60 days. Mr. Millman pointed out that the Die Department was the only department in

(Testimony of Clarence L. Millman.)

which a man might not be qualified for the average rate in 30 days. After a general discussion of the subject it was decided that a man transferred to the Die Department would work at the minimum rate for that department for 30 days, at the end of which time he would be increased to the average rate; further progress in rates of pay to be decided upon by the Management judged by the type and quality of work being produced.

Mr. Millman suggested that a re-wording of Paragraph 4, Exhibit A. be made and discussed at a later meeting.

The Committee next brought up the question of seniority versus ability in making transfers to better paying jobs and express the belief that seniority should take preference. Management replied that this had always been the policy of the company and would continue to be so, except in isolated cases where it was obvious that an employee with less seniority was the best qualified.

The next subject brought up by the Committee was the possibility of increasing the rate on the new centerless grinder to correspond with that of the cylindrical grinder. Management expressed the opinion, which was affirmed by several members of the Committee, that the cylindrical grinders should carry higher rates since their work was more varied and the responsibility somewhat greater owing to the higher cost of the valves run on the cylindrical grinders. However, this subject was referred to Mr. Kearns and Mr. Fickle for a decision.

(Testimony of Clarence L. Millman.)

Committee suggested that since a new parking lot was to be constructed for the employees, it might be a good idea to build a few shelters or sheds in which parking space would be rented to employees desiring same for a suggested rate of $1.00 per month. Management replied that this could and would be done providing there was assurance of a sufficient number desiring this space to make it worth while. The Committee was asked to bring the subject up at their next meeting to determine the approximate number of employees interested.

Mr. Stubblefield requested that electric fans or some sort of ventilating system be installed in the welding heat treating and forge departments before summer, to which the management agreed, and **Mr.** Fary was asked to make an investigation as to approximate costs and methods and give his findings at the next meeting.

There being no further business to discuss, the meeting was adjourned.

/S/ P. D. HILEMAN,
For the Company.
/S/ E. T. FICKLE,
For the Alliance.

RESPONDENT'S EXHIBIT No. 1-MM

Minutes of a meeting held Friday, May 9th, 1941, in Mr. Hileman's office between Committee Members E. T. Fickle, C. E. Weisser, R. D. Hailey, C. O.

(Testimony of Clarence L. Millman.)

Stubblefield, J. H. Olsen and Secretary L. S. Bebb, representing the P. M. P. W. A., and P. D. Hileman, George Fary, W. J. Kearns and C. L. Millman representing the Management.

Mr. J. H. Waddell and Mr. Milton Bracy were introduced as guests of the Committee.

The meeting was opened by Mr. Hileman who inquired of Mr. Fickle why the meeting was called. Mr. Fickle stated he had several subjects to bring up, the first being the Maintenance Department which now contained Maintenance Helpers but no provision for Maintenance Men. The Committee believed it advisable, in view of possible future additions to this department, to set up a Maintenance Department and an Electrical Department, with a man in charge with the status of Foreman of both departments. Mr. Fary inquired the reason for desiring separate departments, and Mr. Fickle stated that this would insure Electricians doing electrical work and Maintenance men and helpers doing maintenance work instead of both classes doing all kinds of work as at present. A suggested maximum rate of 80c for Maintenance men and 70c for Maintenance helpers was made and agreed upon. Mr. Millman was requested to make a rider to the contract to this effect.

The Committee then stated that they felt the commercial grinders should· be on a par with the production hand screw machines and should carry a top rate of 75c. It was also felt that the polishing rate was rather low and suggested that it be in-

(Testimony of Clarence L. Millman.)

creased. Management requested a few days to check these rates to see the effect on direct hourly production rate and overhead in the plant.

Mr. Fickle then stated he believed the large hammer in the Forge Department should carry a better rate than the small hammers inasmuch as this operator took care of the reheat on large valves and wasn't eligible for the group bonus. Management called on Mr. Stewart to learn the average bonus in the Forge Department in the past year, which was found to be 7%. It was agreed that the rate on the large hammer machine should be increased 7%.

The Committee then suggested that our present system of shift changes be changed as follows:

Day shift: 7:00 A.M. to 3:30 P.M. with ½ hour for lunch.

Afternoon shift: 3:30 P.M. to 12:00 midnight, with ½ hour for lunch.

Graveyard shift: 12:00 midnight to 7:00 A.M. with no lunch period, the men on this shift to eat their lunch on the job and to receive 8 hours pay for 7 hours work.

Management expressed its willingness to give this method a trial, believing that production on the graveyard shift would not drop appreciably due to the increased morale occasioned by receiving 8 hours pay for 7 hours work. However, if the drop in production was too great it would be necessary to go back to the present system of shift changes. It

(Testimony of Clarence L. Millman.)
was agreed to start the new system on the first Monday after the beginning of the next pay period, at which time a regular shift change was due.

Mr. Millman brought up the subject of the Old Guard Party to be held on Thursday night, May 22, and it was agreed that the plant would be closed at 3:30 P.M. on Thursday and would reopen at 7:00 A.M. Friday. The Committee was informed that Mr. Crawford would definitely be present at this party and would address the group. All employees are to be invited for this reason.

Mr. Stubblefield remarked that the night watchmen were working 12½ hours now and only collecting pay for 12 hours. They were formerly instructed to punch out before the lunch period, and inasmuch as their lunch period came at the change of shift time they were forced to tend the gate while eating lunch. Mr. Fary and Mr. Kearns expressed surprise at this condition and agreed to notify the watchmen to check out when their work was finished.

Mr. Hileman informed the Committee that an investigation had been made by Mr. Anderson on the cost of shelters for employee cars in the new parking lot. Mr. Anderson's report was read, which stated that the county regulations required each building hold not more than five cars with fire walls between each car, and that the approximate cost would be $30,000 for the building alone. Management did not feel that such an outlay was justified, to which the Committee agreed.

(Testimony of Clarence L. Millman.)

Mr. Fickle stated that the Committee, after much discussion and investigation, and in view of the rising cost of living in the locality, believed that a general raise of 5c per hour for all employees was in line. Management pointed out that our rates were being increased steadily, and requested that some time be allowed for a study of this subject. It was also asked that several days be allowed for investigation. Mr. Millman was instructed to call another meeting on May 13 or 14.

Mr. Hileman announced the vacation plan for hourly employees was to again be modified to grant one-half week vacation for all men with from one to five years Old Guard Service.

Mr. Weisser said he felt Mr. A. C. Baker, now operating a centerless grinder, was entitled to the top rates, to which Mr. Kearns agreed. Mr. Millman and Mr. Kearns promised to take care of this.

Mr. Olsen stated that G. E. McIntire, who formerly worked in the Forge Department, but was now under the machine shop classification, would like to return to the Forge Department. Management requested his reason for wishing this transfer, and Mr. Olson replied he believed that Mr. McIntire had received a Forge bonus while connected with the Forge Department. It was pointed out to Mr. Olsen that this bonus was paid on upsetting Ford ends in the Forge Department and that this was no longer done; whereas a rate for flash welding has been established and it would be necessary to keep Mr. McIntire on this rate.

(Testimony of Clarence L. Millman.)

Mr. Fickle pointed out that the rate in the stock room had not been increased at the time the starting rate was increased. Mr. Millman promised to take care of this and to see that Mr. Buntrock received whatever increases were due him.

There being no further business, the meeting was adjourned.

/S/   P. D. HILEMAN
        For the Company
/S/   E. T. FICKLE
        For the Alliance

RESPONDENT'S EXHIBIT No. 1-NN

Minutes of a meeting held Tuesday, May 13, 1941, in Mr. Hileman's office between Committee Members E. T. Fickle, C. E. Weisser, R. D. Hailey, C. O. Stubblefield, J. H. Olsen and Secretary L. S. Bebb, representing the P. M. P. W. A. and P. D. Hileman, George Fary, W. J. Kearns and C. L. Millman representing the Management.

Mr. R. P. Gindra was introduced as a guest of the Committee.

Mr. Millman opened the meeting by stating that he had been investigating the grinder rates for the community and found that the average rates for first class grinders or cylindrical grinders, was 90c compared to our 95c; second class grinders, or special grinders, was 75c compared to our 85c; and rough grinders, or commercial grinders, was 68½c

(Testimony of Clarence L. Millman.)

as compared to our 70c. Management believed that since our rates were already above average, no adjustment was necessary.

Mr. Hileman informed the Committee that Management had decided to grant their request for a 5c blanket raise, effective May 16, 1941, because he felt it was justified and because the employees were producing a satisfactory amount of work. This blanket raise to include all employees who have been with this company longer than the probationary period, and employees who are due to receive automatic increases on May 15, 1941.

Mr. Hileman reviewed some figures taken from an analysis of the April payroll which showed the average base rate in the plant as 70c and the average overtime rate at $1.06, which means that the average amount of overtime earned per man for the month of April was $32.61. The overtime premium brings the average hourly rate in the plant up to 88c per hour, an increase of 25.75% over the base rate.

Mr. Hileman also cautioned the Committee on the importance of keeping the scrap percentage as low as possible. The scrap is now much better than a few months ago and looks high because of the high content of aircraft parts being manufactured since the scrap value of one aircraft part may be around $2.00 as compared to possibly 15c for a Ford valve. The Committee was asked to bring the subject up at their next meeting in order to keep this problem before the employees at all times.

(Testimony of Clarence L. Millman.)

Mr. Millman referred to the minutes of the last meeting regarding the large hammer and upsetter operator in the forge department. He pointed out that this operator was already receiving the upsetter rate, which was the highest in the forge department, and suggested that the large hammer and upsetter be rated separately. After some discussion it was decided that a top rate of 85c would be satisfactory on these machines. The Committee suggested that the Solar Tubing be placed on the same basis, but Management requested a little more time on this subject inasmuch as this operation is still new in the plant and the proper time studies have not been made.

Mr. Millman reminded the Committee that arrangements had been made with the National Defense Training Office for Southern California to set up a Blueprint and Mathematics Class for Thompson employees at the Bell High School. A guarantee of at least 15 employees must be made and to date but 13 had responded. The Committee was asked to remind their members that many new jobs would be available in the next few months and that the men who were chosen would be the men who were best qualified.

Mr. Fickle raised the question of the heat treaters helpers which carry a *low* rate than the sand blasters, and suggested the rate be increased. Mr. Millman requested a little time to check on these rates in the community and if it was found that heat treaters helpers should be paid more than sand

(Testimony of Clarence L. Millman.)

blasters or as much, proper adjustment would be made with Mr. Fickle, Mr. Fary and Mr. Kearns.

The Committee then brought up the subject of the plating department which now carries a top rate of 80c, and stated they believed this rate should be raised 5c, or to 90c, including the general 5c raise. Mr. Millman reported that 90c was the average for the community, and that this rate did not include a bonus. He also suggested that a rate for platers' helpers be created inasmuch as it is anticipated that the personnel of the plating department may be doubled when the new plant is in operation. After some discussion Management agreed to increase the plating rate to 90c and to set a rate of 60c, 65c and 75c for platers' helpers.

Mr. Weisser remarked that Mr. G. M. Fickle would like to have a job as line inspector because it would give him a chance to keep moving around instead of standing on his feet all day. Mr. Kearns said he had discussed this with Mr. Fickle at one time and Mr. Fickle had decided that due to the night work in this job he would prefer not to take it. Mr. Hailey remarked that in his talks with Mr. Fickle he had indicated that the night work would be acceptable. It was pointed out by the Committee that Mr. Fickle was one of the oldest men in the employ of the company and that he should have some consideration, to which Management agreed. Mr. Kearns stated that it might be necessary to have two inspectors on the day shift and in that event Mr. Fickle, because of his senior-

(Testimony of Clarence L. Millman.)

ity, might be given a steady day shift. Mr. Kearns and Mr. Fary agreed to discuss this further with Mr. Fickle.

Mr. Ed Fickle suggested that the rate for valve guides be abolished since these guides were no longer being produced here, and the Porter Cable machines be included with the Production Hand Screw machines, which was acceptable to Management. The Committee then suggested that the Thread Grinders be classified with the Special Grinders, and Mr. Kearns remarked that only bolts were threaded on the Thread Grinding Machines, while Special Grinders do a varied type of work and should require more skill. Management requested a few days to thoroughly check these two jobs as to the relative skill required on each.

The work being done by Mr. McCracken was next brought before the meeting and it was stated that his machine will now be doing grinding for the Toolroom; therefore, it was felt he should have a higher rate. After some discussion and statements by Mr. Kearns that he would be doing this Toolroom grinding indefinitely, it was suggested by Mr. Millman that he should be classed under the Toolroom Diemakers, which was agreeable to both the Management and the Committee.

Mr. Fickle said he felt Mr. Wright should have a higher rate inasmuch as he wasn't eligible for a bonus and was doing straight aircraft work. Management asked if the Committee felt Mr. Wright's job required more skill than the Special Grinders,

(Testimony of Clarence L. Millman.)

to which Mr. Fickle replied that it did not if the work was the same, but since it was straight aircraft work the scrap content would be much higher in the case of any spoilage. Management requested a few days to investigate.

Mr. Fickle said the members were asking for the company's policy regarding draft deferments, and Mr. Hileman replied that deferments were made only on the basis of the value of the individual to the company, and that only necessary men are being deferred. Deferments are only good for six months and the company feels it isn't advisable to request blanket deferments on the majority of the jobs in the plant since the Draft Boards make investigations and are familiar with all of the operations, realizing that there are a few jobs in our plant for which a man could not be trained within six months. The Committee stated there was a current rumor to the effect that only men with five or more years of service would be deferred, in answer to which Mr. Millman stated that deferment for one man had been asked who had been here but six weeks, and that the length of service with the company wasn't considered. The Commitee was again reminded it was very important that each man communicate with the Personnel Offiee immediately upon receipt of his questionnaire, and also to report his classification as soon as it is received by him.

Mr. Weisser asked what had been done about the donation of two hours time from each employee for

(Testimony of Clarence L. Millman.)

Defense Work, and Mr. Hileman replied that this was agreeable to Management at any time the Committee requested it, but that the Cleveland Office had encountered several difficulties in their plan inasmuch as the Army has no set method for accepting gifts. Mr. Millman agreed to investigate and attempt to learn what could be purchased with the money made available and under what plan it could be donated to the Army.

There being no further business the meeting was adjourned.

> /S/   P. D. HILEMAN
>   For the Company
> /S/   E. T. FICKLE
>   For the Alliance.

RESPONDENT'S EXHIBIT No. 1-OO

Minutes of a meeting held Tuesday, June 12, 1941, in Mr. Hileman's office between Committee Members E. T. Fickle, C. E. Weisser, R. D. Hailey, C. O. Stubblefield, J. H. Olsen and Secretary L. S. Bebb, representing the P. M. P. W. A. and P. D. Hileman, George Fary, W. J. Kearns and C. L. Millman, representing the Management.

The meeting was opened by Mr. Millman who called it to discuss several questions which had arisen at previous meetings and upon which Management had requested more time for decisions.

The first item was the classification of the ma-

(Testimony of Clarence L. Millman.)

chine operated by O. P. Wright, and whether or not this machine should carry the same rate as the Cylindrical Grinders. A general discussion of the subject revealed that the concensus of opinion was that while the machine performed more intricate work than the usual aircraft grinding, it wasn't as highly skilled as the Cylindrical Grinders. Mr. Millman suggested a new job be created called Aircraft Stem Grinding to carry a top rate of 95c. The suggestion was agreeable and a rider is to be made for the contract.

The next item to be discussed was the Thread Grinder and whether that should carry the same rate as the Special Grinder. Management took the stand that the Thread Grinder Work was repetitive and should not pay as much as the more diversified work on the special Grinder. However, Management did feel that a higher rate was in line, and suggested 86c, which was agreed upon.

Mr. Weisser asked if additional items would be added to the Thread Grinder work in the future, to which Mr. Hileman replied that three or four items were being studied and that if the operations of the Thread Grinder proved to be more varied or to closer tolerances, Management would then be willing to set a new rate. Mr. Fickle remarked that he understood Vultee Aircraft now operated the Excello Thread Grinder with a rate of slightly more than $1.00, but he did not know what parts were ground on it. Mr. Millman promised to contact the Vultee Company and find whether their work was

(Testimony of Clarence L. Millman.)

production or precision work. Mr. Fickle said he knew the Wiley Machine Company and the Axelson Manufacturing Company used Thread Grinders at a higher rate but he realized their work was on gauges only and the nature of this work would necessarily require a higher rate.

The next question concerned the Commercial Grinders—should they carry the same rate as the Production Hand Screw Machines. Management agreed that they should, and it was decided to set the top rate on the Commercial Grinders at 80c.

Mr. Millman then referred to a previous meeting where the question had been raised concerning the Furnace Helpers and the Sand Blasters and what relation there should be between those two rates. He reported that a survey had been made over six companies employing Furnace Helpers and that their rates ranged from 69c to 85c, with an average of 75c. Our rate, plus the 6% bonus, is 76c. Rates in four companies listing Sand Blasters ran from 65c to 80c with an average of 72c. Our rates plus 6% is 80c. It being apparent that Furnace Helpers should have a slightly higher rate than Sand Blasters, a rate of 77c for Furnace Helpers was suggested and approved.

The next question concerned the possibility of allowing third shift men to work from midnight to 7:00 a.m. Friday, July 4, at their regular hourly rate and dispense with the third shift on Saturday, July 5; thereby allowing third shift employees Friday, Saturday and until Sunday midnight off. Man-

(Testimony of Clarence L. Millman.)

agement reported that according to the labor agreement overtime must be paid to all men working on holidays, but that if the Committee could get the written consent of all employees who would work the third shift on July 4, Management would be agreeable to allowing this procedure. Mr. Fickle reported that all the employees he had so far contacted were in favor of the plan and that he would attempt to see each man.

Mr. Millman then informed the Committee that Management was seriously considering requesting all employees to give up their vacations and accept pay instead. It was pointed out that the Defense program must go on and that hours lost by expert operators could not be made up. Mr. Hileman, in impressing the Committee with what lies ahead in the way of production, reviewed some figures from the Office of Emergency Management which showed that the production of airplanes since May, 1940, has been tripled but must be again doubled before the end of 1941. Tanks have had a 600% increase since May, 1940, and must be quadrupled before the end of 1941. Powder has had a 1000% increase and must still be tripled; and so on down the line of Defense products. This means that every man-hour available must be used and that while Management has not definitely made a decision on vacations, it is very likely that such a plan may become necessary.

(Testimony of Clarence L. Millman.)

Mr. Millman reported that the machinery had now been set up for making voluntary deductions from the payroll for the purchase of Defense bonds and stamps. Forms are being prepared which employees will sign to authorize the company to deduct a definite amount each month, and when the deductions total $18.75 this money will be forwarded to the Federal Reserve Bank in San Francisco where a Defense Bond will be issued to the employee. These bonds are purchased at $18.75 each and mature in ten years with a face value of $25.00, or can be cashed in at any time after sixty days from date of issue.

Mr. Millman reported that the recent election on the Benefit. Fund showed the results of 81 in favor of having the fund handled by the **P. M. P. W. A.** and 86 in favor of the Old Guard Association, making a total of but 167 ballots being cast. The ballot box is to be held for a few more days in hopes of getting a larger percentage of employees to vote, and if the results are still in favor of the Old Guard Association, it will be turned over to the Old Guard Executive Committee for their action.

Mr. Fickle remarked that two men on the Grooving Lathe understood that the Sunday work was to be divided evenly among all three operators but that so far one man had worked four Sundays. Mr. Kearns stated that he had not understood any such agreement was made. Mr. Hileman stated that it was not the intention of Management to favor any one person and asked Mr. Kearns to thoroughly

(Testimony of Clarence L. Millman.)

check into the situation to see that this overtime was more evenly divided.

Mr. Fickle remarked that no decision had been made regarding Mr. George Fickle as a floor inspector. Mr. Kearns stated that since Mr. George Fickle had been ill for over a week and intended to take the rest of the month of June off, he had not considered the problem yet.

The question was asked if Management intended to have two inspectors on the day shift, and Mr. Hileman replied that we definitely would, that he was convinced the floor inspectors had shown their worth since our scrap content for the first eleven days of June was but 3% as compared to approximately 10% for the same period last year.

Mr. Weisser remarked that two of the men most recently hired were going ahead of the polishers on machines, to which Mr. Millman replied that these men were hired as learners and had a general knowledge of Machine shops before coming to Thompson Products.

Men who are hired as polishers are comparatively inexperienced and may, if they wish, be transferred to the learner class at the learner rate for the general training; which remark brought up a general discussion of the observer training now in effect. Mr. Millman stated that every man in the plant was eligible for observer training and that in making advancements, ability for the particular job in question would definitely be given strong considera-

(Testimony of Clarence L. Millman.)

tion, and men who have profited by observer training are, naturally, better qualified.

Mr. Millman also mentioned that several questions had arisen regarding the men to operate the new machinery which will be received shortly, and stated that whenever transfers were made to a better paying job on a new machine the older operators would be given preference, but if the machine carried the same rate as the operator now earned, more than likely a new man would be trained for the job. It was pointed out that an old operator would of necessity have to go through a training period on the new machine and a new man would have to go through a training period on the old machine, thereby causing the company the expense of two breaking in periods; whereas if the new man was trained directly for the new machine there would be but one breaking in period required.

Mr. Millman stressed the fact that wherever possible the older men would be given preference, as in the past.

There being no further business, the meeting was adjourned.

/S/ P. D. HILEMAN
For the Company
/S/ E. T. FICKLE
For the Alliance

(Testimony of Clarence L. Millman.)

RESPONDENT'S EXHIBIT No. 1-PP

Minutes of a meeting held Friday, July 25, 1941, in Mr. Hileman's office between Committee Members E. T. Fickle, C. E. Weisser, R. D. Hailey, C. O. Stubblefield, J. H. Olsen, and Secretary L. S. Bebb, representing the P. M. P. W. A., and P. D. Hileman, George Fary, W. J. Kearns, and C. L. Millman representing the Management.

Mr. Hileman opened the meeting by remarking that Management had called this meeting, not for any special reason, but merely to acquaint the Committee and its members with what the company was doing and to bring them up to date on recent activities. He remarked that orders had been recently placed for 90 machines with a total cost of $187,000. These machines are in part: Six Warner and Swasey Lathes; a Heald Boromatic machines for terminal ends; two Lodge & Shipley tool room lathes; two Centerless grinders four plain Landis grinders; one Universal Grinder; one Blanchard surface grinder; two milling machines, one for tool room and one for shop; one Doal Contour machine; two Thread Grinders; two Landis face grinders; one large air compressor; seven new furnaces for the heat treating department; complete new plating equipment; and miscellaneous inspection parts, such as gauges, snap gauges, micrometers, etc.

Mr. Hilesman made reference to a recent order from the Boeing Aircraft plant in Seattle for taper pins and Douglas bolts, an order from the Northrup

(Testimony of Clarence L. Millman.)

Aircraft Company for bolts on which Thompson Products, Inc., West Coast Plant, has been specified as the manufacturer, recent Vultee orders for bolts and engine mounts, and the possibility of the Lockheed-Vega plants using our bolts. This new business was mentioned to acquaint the Committee with the amount and kind of work needed within the next year, and to emphasize how urgent is the need for as much production as possible with a minimum of rejects.

Mr. Hileman then remarked that the plans for the new lunch room had been completed and construction had already started. Copies of the plans were shown the Committee, who gave their unanimous approval. It was explained that the lunch room was being placed at the far end of the property to allow for possible future building of two more bays on the plant.

Management then asked the Committee if there were any points which they should like to bring up. Mr. Fickle replied that the electric upsetter operators felt there should be a larger differential between their jobs and the hammer operators, due to the knowledge and skill required and the fact that one upsetter operator handles three machines at one time. After some discussion, Management agreed that this request was fair and reasonable and suggested a rate of 85c, to which the Committee was agreeable. It was decided that a rider to this effect would be attached to the contract.

(Testimony of Clarence L. Millman.)

Mr. Olsen stated the flash welders felt they should carry the same rate as the upsetters. Mr. Millman replied that this seemed to be a case of deciding whether the flash welders were on a par with the upsetters in skill and knowledge. He requested a little time to check with flash welding rates in the community.

Mr. Weisser mentioned that the platers' helpers thought they should have a higher classification than helpers. Management replied that it did not feel the helpers would be qualified at this time to handle the job without supervision, but that after the new plating room was set up it would probably be necessary to operate three shifts in the plating department, and if these men were then qualified to supervise a complete shift their ratings would be changed to that of platers.

Mr. Hailey then brought up the subject of the polishers, who felt that the 70c top on their machines was not sufficient. Mr. Weisser spoke up to include the belt polishers. Mr. Kearns remarked that belt polishers on aircraft work should be rated higher than ordinary machine polishers because they do the rework on aircraft valves, and without sufficient skill a polisher might very easily make a stem undersize. Management was agreeable to increasing the belt polisher rate on aircraft rework to 75c, but found that the machine polishing rate was comparable to the rates in other plants and was not due for an increase.

Mr. Fickle brought up the subject of employees

(Testimony of Clarence L. Millman.)

not punching out for the noon lunch period, but Management was not agreeable. The Committee claimed that it took too long for employees to punch out at noon, and stated that at least five minutes were spent by the average employee in standing in line. Mr. Millman remarked that the present plan was for two time clocks, which would relieve this congestion, and promised to make a check of the time required for all employees to complete checking out for the lunch period.

Mr. Stubblefield remarked that Mr. Cunningham and Mr. Spurlock felt they should have the maximum rate. Mr. Kearns replied that they were not yet ready for this rate and should acquire more skill.

Mr. Millman reminded the Committee that requests for rate increases should first be referred to Management and then to the Committee if satisfaction is not received.

There being no further business the meeting was adjourned.

/S/ P. D. HILEMAN
For the Company

/S/ E. T. FICKLE
For the Alliance

———

RESPONDENT'S EXHIBIT No. 1-QQ

Minutes of a meeting held Tuesday, September 23, 1941, in the Conference Room between Com-

(Testimony of Clarence L. Millman.)

mittee Members E. T. Fickle, I. W. Hess, E. O. Smith, H. C. Baldwin, F. W. Osborne, and Secretary L. S. Bebb, representing the P. M. P. W. A. and P. D. Hileman, George Fary, W. J. Kearns, and C. L. Millman, representing the Management. The 1940 Committee members were guests at the meeting; also L. L. Myers and R. W. Pearce, who were guests of the new Committee.

The meeting was opened by Mr. Millman who gave a resume of the plans for the company picnic to be held on October 18, at Banning Park in Wilmington. Mr. Millman explained that he had taken the liberty of setting a date without discussing it with the employees, due to the fact that since the park is very popular for picnics of this type, reservations must be made from 30 to 60 days in advance. The Committee was asked their opinion as to the kind of door prizes to be given, and Mr. Olsen suggested a $50.00 Defense Savings Bond. Mr. Stubblefield felt that a radio such as was given last year would be preferable. A vote taken among the members present indicated a majority in favor of two $25.00 Defense Savings Bonds, with a small radio as a prize for children.

Mr. Millman next told the Committee of the plans for the DeLuxe Box Lunch Company to furnish hot lunches to employees, and submitted for inspection the proposed cartons in which the lunches will be served. Mr. Stubblefield suggested that arrangements be made for the DeLuxe Box Lunch

(Testimony of Clarence L. Millman.)

Company to issue meal tickets which could be purchased by employees, instead of paying cash each time. Mr. Hileman remarked that the tables and benches for the lunch room were on order and delivery was expected within three weeks.

Mr. Millman then informed the Committee that plans were being made for larger Coca-Cola dispensing machines and that the Coca-Cola Company wished to install a new machine on a trial basis, which could be purchased by the Old Guard Association less a substantial trade-in allowance for the old machine. It is also planned that a trial will be given the cup dispensing machines for Coca-Cola, one to be placed in the shop and one in the lunch room—their continuance depending upon approval or disapproval of the employees.

Mr. Millman then gave a brief resume of the new tax law which takes effect October 1st, and warned the Committee that since exemptions have been lowered many more people will be paying income taxes this year; for instance, a single employee who has earned $1500. will now pay $69 taxes instead of $24.20 under the present law. A single employee earning $2500 will pay $165 taxes as compared to $63.80, and the married employee will pay $90 as compared to the present $11. It was also pointed out that many hidden taxes would be imposed on practically everything purchased and that these taxes would be included in the price of the article and under no circumstances should an employee pay a 10% tax on top of the retail price.

(Testimony of Clarence L. Millman.)

These taxes, in most cases, amount to 10% of the present retail price and cover all wines and liquors, telephone, telegraph and cable messages, all electric, gas and oil cooking, heating or cooling appliances.

Mr. Hileman then asked Mr. Fickle what items he had to discuss, and Mr. Fickle replied that he felt the seniority status in the plant should be checked into a little further, especially concerning polishers who felt that they were not being moved fast enough; also that the recent hiring of an experienced man was creating considerable dissension inasmuch as this filled a vacancy at the top, thereby preventing men all along the line from moving up.

Mr. Smith remarked that it was generally felt among the polishers that they should be moved up instead of learners being hired for the better jobs. Mr. Millman and Mr. Kearns both stated that polishers were being moved at a fairly rapid rate and would be moved faster in the near future because of increasing requirements for machine operators. Mr. Millman said that he would prepare a report of the polishers who had been moved to machines during the past year, to present to the Committee at the next meeting. Mr. Millman explained that the trade questions on the back of the application blanks were used as a basis for determining whether a man would be classed as a learner or as a polisher, and that if a man satisfactorily

(Testimony of Clarence L. Millman.)

answered these questions he was considered as learner material because of his apparent knowledge of machine shop practice, whether or not he had formerly worked in a shop.

It was pointed out that learners start at the beginning rate of 50c an hour and continue at this rate for 60 days before being increased; whereas polishers who are hired with absolutely no knowledge of machines, work for 30 days at 50c and then are increased to 60c. It was shown that two men coming to work at the same time, one as a polisher and one as a learner, at the end of 120 days the polisher would be receiving a higher rate than the learner. Mr. Smith stated that the polisher felt because of their observer training they were well qualified to step onto a machine and operate it satisfactorily. Mr. Millman remarked that this was possibly true but that the men still would require from 30 to 60 days breaking-in training on the machine and that it was considerable expense to the company to transfer a polisher at 70c an hour onto another machine and still have to spend time in training him; whereas a learner is willing and eager to come into the shop at the beginning rate of 50c and to take his training at that rate.

Mr. Smith remarked that one polisher in particular had told him he was willing to start at the learner rate, at which Mr. Millman and Mr. Kearns expressed great surprise, because neither could remember any instance of a polisher offering to step down to the learner rate in order to take ad-

(Testimony of Clarence L. Millman.)

vantage of the training. Mr. Myers stated that Mr. J. E. Chorley, a polisher, had completed some 80 hours observer training and felt he was well qualified to operate the machine which he had been observing. Mr. Hess remarked that Mr. Chorley had actually operated the machine for 40 hours of his 80 hours observer training, to which Mr. Millman and Mr. Kearns replied that they had known nothing of this, and if such were the case they would see that this practice .was stopped at once since observers are not allowed to operate machines on production work while taking training. Mr. Millman remarked that the observer training was instigated to give employees an opportunity to better themselves and that polishers taking this training would be given an opportunity to become a machine operator. He stated that the company made no promises of better job but that if a man proved himself qualified he would be advanced. Mr. Millman also pointed out that if the company chose they could hire learners exclusively and leave the polishers where they are, but that it was the earnest desire of Management to advance men whenever possible and that for this reason the openings which come up from time to time were being distributed between the learners and polishers.

Mr. Smith remarked that some of the polishers stated they had been told at the time of hiring that polishing was a temporary job and advancement was promised to them. Mr. Millman replied that this was very unlikely since it was his policy to tell

(Testimony of Clarence L. Millman.)

the men who were being hired that the polishing job was an opportunity for them to enter the shop and that if they were employees it was possible for them to receive training which would qualify them for better positions. Under no circumstances were they promised advancement.

Mr. Fickle asked if the Ajax Hammer had been operating long enough to set a rate on it. Mr. Kearns and Mr. Fary replied that they believed it had, and Mr. Millman asked what rate Mr. Fickle thought was advisable. Mr. Olsen said he believed it should be the same as the up-setter rate for the Ajax operator but less for the furnace man. Mr. Olsen suggested that the furnace man be given the same rate as the hammers, 76c, but Mr. Fickle said he felt the polishers should be worth more than the furnace operators. Mr. Millman asked if the jobs were considered equal, to which Mr. Fickle replied that they were, so Mr. Millman suggested 75c on both jobs.

Mr. Weisser stated that the heat treating department furnace helpers' rate of 70c should be more than the rate of the furnace operators in the forge department. Mr. Millman replied that the furnace helpers in the heat treating department had the opportunity of progressing to the heat treaters' rate, but suggested 75c for polishing and 70c for furnace operators. Mr. Kearns said the men now operating the furnace were making more than 70c.

Mr. Meyers remarked at this point that the *publishers'* rate should be higher, or at least the head

(Testimony of Clarence L. Millman.)

polisher should have a higher rate because of his responsibility and the fact that he attended to the rework. Mr. Millman agreed, and suggested a higher rate of 75c for head polisher and rework man, but Mr. Kearns felt that the original work was just as important as rework and would prefer to see a rate of 75c set for all polishers. Mr. Fickle inquired if this would be a blanket raise for polishers, to which Mr. Millman replied no, that the maximum would be raised and the men now at the maximum would be increased to the new maximum. However, Mr. Hileman said he would prefer a blanket raise for all polishers at the beginning of the next pay period, or October 1st, which was acceptable to the Committee.

Mr. Hileman then remarked that the discussion had got off the subject of the Ajax hammer, and it was finally agreed by the Committee and Management that a rate of 85c would be set on the Ajax hammer. Mr. Millman referred to the furnace operator and suggested a rate of 75c, which, after considerable discussion, was agreed to by all present.

Mr. Fickle then stated that Mr. Pearce felt he should be entitled to the rating of Plater instead of Plater's Helper. Mr. Hileman asked Mr. Kearns what his opinion was, and Mr. Kearns replied that he felt Mr. Pearce was now qualified for this job. Mr. Hileman asked if Mr. Pearce could do the same work as Mr. Starkey and Mr. Pearce answered that he could and on various occasions when the

(Testimony of Clarence L. Millman.)

Pacific Motor Parts Workers Alliance and the West Coast Plant of Thompson Products, Inc., to replace the present contract which was scheduled to expire on November 19, 1941. He suggested that Mr. Hess take over the meeting and present the requests of the Committee.

Mr. Hess stated that before a discussion of the contract was made, it was the desire of the Committee to ask for a blanket 10c increase at once since it was possible that contract negotiations might continue for several weeks before a satisfactory agreement was reached. Mr. Millman stated that Management could not agree to any increase at present until there was an opportunity to see the new contract, and suggested that Mr. Hess read the contract in its entirety, which he did.

At the conclusion of the reading of the contract, Mr. Hess remarked that the man now doing the torch hardening would like to be classed as a welder because of the fact that a torch was used on this job. Mr. Kearns replied that if this individual was capable of doing the same work with the torch that the welding department does, this would be agreeable, but he did not believe that such was the case.

Mr. Millman referred to the minimum rates as suggested by the Committee and asked if it was still contemplated having three rates on each job, to which Mr. Baldwin replied that the rates listed were minimum rates and that no top had been set.

Mr. Hileman asked for a clarification of the term "learner" after the 75c beginning rate had been

(Testimony of Clarence L. Millman.)

reached at the end of three months. Mr. Baldwin replied that after the third month an employee is considered a learner for three more months, and at that time should receive the minimum as listed in the contract.

Mr. Hileman asked to have the point of the 10c increase clarified, since the Committee had asked for an immediate 10c increase and the contract also called for a 10c increase at the time of signing. Mr. Hess assured the Management that one 10c in-crease was all that was asked, and if an increase was granted at once this provision would be stricken from the contract.

Mr. Millman asked if it was desired that vaca-tions be granted a year from starting date of the employee or if any definite time was to be set to determine the year's service. Mr. Hess replied that the vacation should start a year from the time the employee began working for the Company.

Mr. Hileman remarked that Management had been studying wage structures for some time with a view of making adjustments, but that it was also necessary to consider the possibility of increasing the sales prices of our products in order to bring in more revenue. He stated that the raising of prices was a delicate subject which must be handled with great care in order to guard against losing business. He recalled that about 1½ years ago the Company had attempted to raise prices on some of its products, and asked Mr. Bebb if he remembered what happened at that time. Mr. Bebb replied that

(Testimony of Clarence L. Millman.)

we lost several large orders, one of which we were just beginning to win back, and several of which we have not yet been able to again enjoy.

Mr. Hileman pointed out, for instance, that if our sales department informed the Douglas Aircraft Company it was necessary to ask more money for our Douglas bolts, they would be very likely to design around a large number of these bolts, thus relieving the cost increase on this part, and substituting a cheaper bolt, which has been done by several aircraft companies already. Management requested at least a week to consider these new demands in order to obtain complete figures on the effect of increased labor costs on our selling prices, and suggested another meeting on October 29th, which was agreed to by the Committee.

Mr. Kearns asked Mr. Hess their reason for desiring time and one-half over eight hours per day, and Mr. Hess replied that some men, particularly in the Maintenance Department, had worked 50 hours in a period of three days and then had been laid off for the balance of the week. Management questioned this, and learned that this had happened some eighteen months ago, to which Mr. Hileman remarked that it must have been due to some special circumstance of the moment, but that an attempt would be made to check to see why this had happened.

Mr. Hileman called attention to the provision calling for a guarantee of four hours work for any employee called to the plant at any time other than

(Testimony of Clarence L. Millman.)

his regular shift, and stated that this had been abused several years ago. He pointed out that if a Maintenance Department man was called to install a fuse this would make us liable to pay him four hours wages for possib*ility* ten minutes work. The Committee agreed that a special provision could be made for Maintenance Department employees.

Mr. Hileman remarked that since the Committee was making all of these requests they should be willing to give something to Management in return, and suggested that we instigate ten minute rest periods, two on each shift, and abolish the present privilege of smoking, drinking, soft drinks or purchasing from the lunch man at all other times during the shift. Mr. Hess believed that no argument would be offered except on the no smoking clause and he felt that considerable opposition would be given by the membership of the Pacific Motor Parts Workers Alliance to such a ruling.

Mr. Hileman stated that the Federal Bureau of Investigation is planning a survey of this plant to consider our plant protection and the provisions to be made for guarding against sabotage, and they would probably ask that all employees be finger printed and insist on a no smoking rule.

Mr. Baldwin remarked that on the line of plant protection, he noticed that the guards had recently been making a note of the badge numbers of the employees as they entered the gates, and suggested that guards take these numbers actually from the badges rather than asking the employee his number.

(Testimony of Clarence L. Millman.)

Mr. Millman stated that guards had been instructed to see all badges of the men who came in and to compare the pictures of each individual, but that it was possible they had become a little lax on this subject inasmuch as they knew by sight the majority of employees.

Mr. Millman remarked that he believed some misunderstanding existed in the plant regarding the financing of the recent additions, and that the general impression was that all expansions have been made with Government money. He then asked Mr. Hileman to review the financing of our buildings and equipment. Mr. Hileman stated when he realized a year ago that more production would be needed, Management wanted to protect the jobs of all employees against the inevitable let-down of the defense program, which, incidently was his reason for keeping inter-plant valves going through the plant at the rate of 160,000 a month. He pointed out, with the increased shortage of new car production, it would be increasingly necessary for individuals to repair their present cars and run them a few more years. He noted that the Office of Production Management had notified the automobile industry that automobile production for January, 1942, would be but 49% of their production a year ago if they could get material, which meant that the Cleveland plant, for instance, would be able to make less than half of their original equipment parts for the coming year.

(Testimony of Clarence L. Millman.)

This let-down of the defense program was considered when the question of "should company money be used for the expansion or should the Defense Plant Corporation be asked to build it." (The Defense Plant Corporation is a subsidiary of the Reconstruction Finance Corporation, which was created in 1932 by Herbert Hoover for making loans to small businesses.) It was finally decided that company money would be used to build the plant, the lunch room, parking lot and all improvements on the old factory building, but that a loan of $250,000 would be made from the Defense Plant Corporation for machinery and equipment. By doing this the company would own all of its property and buildings, and Mr. Hileman pointed out that we had not built a new plant which would be too large to take care of our decreased production after the defense program stopped. However, the company is required to pay back to the Government 22% per year as payments on the $250,000 loan. It is, therefore, not only necessary to make enough profit to pay stockholders a dividend, but also enough to make these yearly payments to the Defense Plant Corporation. It was pointed out that if the war should end at once and the defense program stop, the company is not over-burdened by debt but can return the new machinery to the Defense Plant Corporation, move our old machinery into the new building and continue to operate. The attention of the Committee was drawn to the metal tag which appears on each piece of equipment belonging to

(Testimony of Clarence L. Millman.)

the Defense Plant Corporation, which says "Property of the Defense Plant Corporation, an instrumentality of the United States Government, T. P. W. C. Serial No..........."

Mr. Baldwin remarked that he would like to go back to our discussion of increasing our selling price, and stated that if sub-contractors were required to increase their wage scales, is it not logical to pass this increased cost on to the prime contractors. Mr. Hileman replied that if we asked Douglas more money, they will shop around to try to find someone to make the bolt more cheaply. Mr. Baldwin remarked that with everyone busy on defense work it would probably be difficult to find another manufacturer who could make these bolts, and Mr. Hileman said in that case Douglas would probably design around this particular bolt, as he had explained previously.

Mr. Hess said he believed no definite answer had been given to the request for an immediate 10c increase, but Management declined to give an answer at once, saying it would be necessary that such a move be carefully considered.

Mr. Smith asked if men transferred to this plant from Cleveland retained their seniority or if they started as new employees. Mr. Millman replied that this was governed by individual cases and that the men who had been transferred had retained their seniority because, after considerable correspondence between the Personnel Department of the West Coast Plant and that of Cleveland, it was

(Testimony of Clarence L. Millman.)

felt these men were valuable enough to the organization as a whole to consider it wise to keep them rather than let them quit their jobs in Cleveland and come to California, thereby causing the company to lose the benefit of years of training. It was pointed out that transfers were not agreed to between plants of the company except in extreme cases, and in both cases referred to, the wives of these employees were advised to come to the West Coast in the interests of their own health. Any man who voluntarily quits his job at another plant and applies to this plant for work starts as a new employee if his application is accepted.

Mr. Kent asked if a man is now getting the top top rate set on the job and a new rate is established, does this man automatically receive the new rate. Mr. Hileman replied that in most cases it has been the policy of the Management to give the new rate, but Mr. Kearns stated the man's ability was also considered, and it was not agreed that the new rate would be automatically given at the time it was established.

Mr. Hess suggested it would be a good idea to hold a mass meeting once a month and that Mr. Hileman address the employees and bring them up to date on company business, etc., and answer questions that individuals might raise. Management felt this would be advisable and suggested that a public address system be installed in the lunch room and that such meetings be held regularly, possibly at intervals of two or three months.

(Testimony of Clarence L. Millman.)

There being no further business, the meeting was adjourned until Wednesday, October 29, 1941.

/s/ P. D. HILEMAN
For the Company

/s/ IRVIN HESS
For the Alliance.

————

RESPONDENT'S EXHIBIT No. 1-SS

Minutes of a meeting held on October 29, 1941, in the Conference Room between Committee Members I. W. Hess, F. W. Osborne, H. C. Baldwin, E. O. Smith, and G. C. Overlander, representing the Pacific Motor Parts Workers Alliance, and P. D. Hileman, George Fary, W. J. Kearns and C. L. Millman, representing the Management. Guests of the Committee were M. J. Sterbens and T. L. Parker.

Mr. Millman opened the meeting by saying some changes had necessarily been made in the contract as submitted at the last meeting by the Pacific Motor Parts Workers Alliance, and suggested that he be allowed to read the contract through and the Committee make notes on their questions to be discussed at the conclusion of the reading, which was done.

At the conclusion of the reading of the contract, Mr. Hileman stated it was the desire of the management to abolish the present 6% extra compensation plan and replace it with a 6c increase to the

(Testimony of Clarence L. Millman.)

Respondent's Exhibit No. 1-SS—(Continued) hourly rates. He explained the 6% extra compensation plan was entirely dependent upon the condition that the company earn a 10% net profit and the possibility was always present that the net profit would be under 10%, thus making it impossible to pay the 6% extra compensation. If the 6c is added to the hourly rate, this amount is assured and could not be taken away in the event the company experienced a bad month in sales. It was pointed out that this was a good arrangement for the men earning less than $1.00 an hour since 6% on their hourly rates did not amount to 6c; for instance, an 80c man gets. 048c per hour as his 6% extra compensation, where as if 6c is added to his 80c rate he receives a straight 86c rate per hour. Mr. Hileman further stated the Management wanted to grant a 5c increase on top of the 6c, making a total blanket raise for all employees of 11c.

Mr. Hileman remarked that in the few cases of individual jobs now carrying a rate of $1.00 or more, satisfactory adjustments would be made in the maximum rates on these jobs to insure a fair deal for these men. He stated that the wage scale presented by the Alliance was considerably out of line in some cases and pointed out that should such a large increase be granted, it would be impossible for the company to continue to operate on a 49 hour basis as at present. He showed the Committee that the average work week for the past six months had been 48.8 hours per man. This means that over 20%

(Testimony of Clarence L. Millman.)

Respondent's Exhibit No. 1-SS—(Continued)
of the 49 hours are worked at time and one-half;
whereas it might be necessary to cut the working
week to 40 hours by the installation of four rotating
shifts.

If the Alliance requests for wage increases were
granted it would mean an increase in our direct
labor costs of 25.8%, which might mean that at least
an increase in sales price from our customers of an
equal amount would have to be asked, and it is
obvious that this could not be done without running
serious risk of losing desirable customers. **Mr.
Hileman** further stated the rate increase as suggested by the Management represented a 13% increase in direct hourly rates which he felt was ex-
ceedingly fair to the men in the shop.

Mr. Smith asked why the 6% extra compensation
plan had been instigated and did it cover all plants
of the company. Mr. Hileman answered that about
a year ago all Plant Managers assembled in Cleveland to discuss wage increases. It was decided at
that time, inasmuch as our business was particularly
hazardous in that development in engines **and** motive equipment is rapid and present methods are
continually being replaced by more efficient ones, it
was possible at any time that certain parts might
be replaced by other parts which the company could
not or would not be given a chance to manufacture,
and it was suggested that a 6% extra compensation
plan be adopted in lieu of a wage increase on the
hourly rate, dependent upon whether or not the in-

(Testimony of Clarence L. Millman.)

Respondent's Exhibit No. 1-SS—(Continued) dividual companies earned a 10% net profit. This plan was adopted as being the best at the time, and in the event a certain plant was unable to realize a 10% net profit, the extra compensation would be financed by the Cleveland Plant.

The West Coast Plant was felt to be fairly stable as long as from 60 to 70% of our total output was aircraft parts. The Company, however, retained the right to cancel the 6% extra compensation plan at any time a 10% profit was not realized.

Mr. Hileman remarked, with the rising costs of labor, material and overhead, it was possible a 10% net profit could not be realized, but the Management was willing to take a chance and add the 6c to the hourly rate, plus a 5c general increase. Mr. Hess said he believed this would be acceptable to the Committee, but, of course, the Committee would have to discuss it with the members of the Alliance, and would like to have a general meeting before an answer was given.

Mr. Hess noted Management had agreed to pay double time for Sundays and holidays and asked if Sunday work would be continued when necessary —to which Mr. Hileman replied as long as the demands of our business warrant it there will be Sunday work.

Mr. Hess remarked that a 5c bonus on the second shift had been granted by Management for men working that shift steady for six months, as requested by the Committee, but would this be appli-

(Testimony of Clarence L. Millman.)

Respondent's Exhibit No. 1-SS—(Continued)
cable to employees who have been working this
shift for six months or more at the present time.
Management stated the second shift bonus would
be granted to all employees who have been steadily
working this shift for six months or more upon the
signing of the contract.

As for the third shift bonus, Management offered
the Committee the alternative of continuing the
present shift plan of eight hours pay for seven
hours work, or seven hours pay for seven hours
work plus a 5c hourly bonus. It was pointed out
that the present set-up provided a substantial
hourly increase for third shift employees and it
would be impossible for the company to grant an
additional premium on this shift.

Management suggested seniority would rule in
the delegation of shifts in that the man on the machine with the most seniority would have his choice
of the three shifts. Mr. Hess remarked the Committee had failed to include a seniority clause in the
new contract but would like to have the present
seniority clause from the old contract incorporated
in the new contract, which was agreeable to Management.   :

Mr. Baldwin pointed out that the chief **electrician** and maintenance foreman was now considered
a supervisory employee and, therefore, not under
the Pacific Motor Parts Workers Alliance and this
rate should be removed from the contract, to which
Management agreed.

(Testimony of Clarence L. Millman.)

Respondent's Exhibit No. 1-SS—(Continued)

Mr. Hess referred to the minimum and maximum rates as suggested by Management and asked if the maximum rate would be assured an employee after one year's service. Mr. Millman said Management would prefer the present methods of granting the difference between minimum and maximum rates since it was believed a man's ability should be considered in giving him a maximum rate.

Mr. Hess remarked that Management had asked that the vacation plan be left open for the present time in order to conform with other vacation plans of the company, but wanted to know what assurance the Committee would have that the company would decide a vacation plan before March 31, 1942. Mr. Hileman replied the Committee had the company's word that a vacation plan would be decided upon by that time. He pointed out that all plants are influenced by what one plant does and a plan which was satisfactory for our comparatively small number of employees might present very serious difficulties in the Cleveland plant where 12,000 employees would be affected by a changed vacation plan, and for this reason Management would prefer to delay discussions on this subject until a decision could be reached with other Plant Managers.

Mr. Smith pointed out that actually, 6c was the average increase if the 6% extra compensation was removed, to which Management replied that this was true, but the 6c was assured, and stated the company could grant a blanket 10c increase at

(Testimony of Clarence L. Millman.)

Respondent's Exhibit No. 1-SS—(Continued)
this time and discontinue the 6% extra compensation, but the employees would actually have gained much less than they will under the present plan.

Mr. Hess asked if the 11c blanket raise would bring present employees to the maximum, to which Management replied it would for the employees getting the maximum now, since the maximum rate set on the job was 11c more than the present maximum. The minimum rate is approximately 20c less than the maximum but in no case is under 75c except for female employees, on which the minimum is 70c.

Mr. Hess asked why the inspection department had received no Saturday work. Mr. Millman replied that not enough work was going through the plant to warrant Saturday work in the inspection department, and remarked it was obvious that less time was required to check a bolt in inspection than to machine it in the shop. If Saturday work was performed in this department, it would necessitate the laying off of some member of the force.

Mr. Smith remarked if women are doing the same work as men, should they not get the same wages. At this point Chief Inspector Carl Cummings was asked to join the meeting and this question was put to him. He stated the girls did not do the same work as the men since the men do all the precision inspection and the girls in the bolt department *to* visual inspection, check the plating and threads. In aircraft inspection the girls do visual

(Testimony of Clarence L. Millman.)

Respondent's Exhibit No. 1-SS—(Continued) checking and gauges and dial indicators are set for them. The men in the inspection department set their own gauges and do their own inspection work without supervision. Mr. Smith remarked that the girl now checking bolts says bolts pile up on Monday and Tuesday forcing her to work faster in order to catch up; to which Mr. Cummings replied his idea of work is to do what is necessary, and remarked that while she may be working faster on Monday and Tuesday, she is able to slow down toward the end of the week because of the lesser amount of work coming through. He remarked if the plating department worked on Sunday, bolts would sometimes pile up. Mr. Osborne stated this situation was found in the heat treating department when the forge department worked week-ends.

Mr. Smith reported the male inspectors in the inspection department felt there was some unfairness in the distribution of Overtime. Mr. Cummings replied that the requirements of the work dictated the man who would be asked to work overtime, but he believed it was pretty evenly distributed. Mr. Millman asked the Committee to allow him time enough to make a check on the average overtime per man for the past six months, in the inspection department, and submit this report at the next meeting, which was agreeable to the Committee. The Committee thanked Mr. Cummings for his information and agreed these questions had been satisfactorily answered.

(Testimony of Clarence L. Millman.)

Respondent's Exhibit No. 1-SS—(Continued)

Mr. Hess stated he had asked Mr. Sterbens to be a guest in order that he might present his problem to the Management. Mr. Sterbens said he believed the torch hardening work required as much or more skill than welders. He said he had learned torch hardening in this plant and had made it an important job. He had seen men go from this work to other machines but had felt if he stayed on this job and made it a good one, the company would take care of him. He stated that he had worked hard and had increased his production from 600 to 1000 pieces per hour. Mr. Hileman asked who had gone ahead of Mr. Sterbens, and Mr. Sterbens said that several men had gone from behind him to lathe and grinders and were now earning more money. Mr. Millman remarked that this was not the same type of work and that machine operations required a little more skill than torch hardening. He asked if Mr. Sterbens had requested to be moved up, to which Mr. Sterbens answered no, but he believed he could be worth more to the company by staying on this job, and feels his rate should be equal to the welders. Mr. Hileman called Mr. Sterben's attention to his overtime, which had in some cases amounted to 25 hours per week, and remarked that the company could put more men on the job and work them all less hours. However, Management agreed to consider this situation and make an answer at the next meeting.

(Testimony of Clarence L. Millman.)

Respondent's Exhibit No. 1-SS—(Continued)

Mr. Smith asked why a maximum rate had been placed, to which Mr. Hileman replied that the Management set a top on wages in order that there could be some basis for figuring costs. He cited an example of certain orders which were bid upon six months before but by the time the orders were actually placed with the company, labor costs had changed considerably, and that if the company had no top on labor costs by which to make their estimates, it would be impossible to make a reasonable bid on a job. The Committee was again reminded that our business was conducted on a competitive business basis and that labor costs must be more or less controlled if the company was to survive. He explained that the company must pay a dividend to its stockholders and that if a person who has worked for twenty years and saved his money decides to invest his money in Thompson Products stock, he does so with the expectation of receiving a certain income from it to take care of him when he is no longer able to work. If dividend time comes around and this person receives no money from the company, he calls on the Board of Directors and says "now, look, I have invested my savings in this company and have given you a certain amount of my money to use. In return I have expected that you will pay me a fair rate of interest in the form of an annual or semi-annual dividend payment." If Mr. Crawford says "Well, it

(Testimony of Clarence L. Millman.)

Respondent's Exhibit No. 1-SS—(Continued) seems that our Plant Managers have not been making a profit," the stockholder then replies that the thing to do is "get a new Plant Manager." Therefore, it behooves Mr. Hileman to see that the West Coast Plant does make a profit.

He remarked, incidentally, that if anyone believes the story being circulated that Thompson Products stock is worth $520.00 per share, he should go to a brokerage house and try to sell it. Reference to the financial page of any newspaper will show that this stock now sells for approximately $28.00 per share, and the seller would also be required to pay the brokerage house a commission.

Mr. Baldwin remarked that men getting maximum rates had not been granted new maximums when increases had been made—to which the Management replied this seemed unlikely because, why would a new maximum be set on a job if it was not because these men were worth more money. Mr. Hileman drew attention to the approximately 30 increases in the maximum rate which has been granted since the signing of the current contract on November 19, 1940, as examples of the willingness of Management to listen to reasonable requests for wage increases. Mr. Millman remarked he believed a large percent of employees were now making the maximum rate and that the maximums were being granted within twelve months after date of hire. He, however, would like to check to see how many men

(Testimony of Clarence L. Millman.)

Respondent's Exhibit No. 1-SS—(Continued) were receiving the top rate before October 1st, at which time several employees were increased.

Mr. Baldwin was asked to base his comment on facts and to give Management the names of the men who did not receive maximum rates when the present contract was signed last November and maximum rates increased.

Mr. Hileman summarized the meeting by saying the company had agreed to nearly all points suggested by the Committee; allowing a 5c bonus for employees working second shift steady six months or more; giving a choice of two alternatives for third shift bonus; agreed to pay overtime in excess of eight hours per day; to pay double time for Sundays and holidays as noted in the contract; to discuss a vacation plan before March 31, 1942; to make the starting rate 60c with 65c after 30 days, 70c after 60 days and 75c after 90 days; female employees starting rate of 55c, with 60c after 30 days, 65c after 60 days and 70c after 90 days; and offered a blanket 11c increase in place of the present 6% extra compensation plan—and suggested that the Committee take the contract to their members and give Management a reply at the next meeting which was set for 2:00 p.m. Tuesday, November 4th. He further stated that if the Management and the Committee could come to an agreement on that date the wage increases would be effective as of November 1st.

(Testimony of Clarence L. Millman.)

Respondent's Exhibit No. 1-SS—(Continued)

Mr. Sterbens brought up the subject of the discontinuance of the company purchase of gloves and remarked it would cost him $2.00 per week to buy his gloves since he used one or more pairs per day. Mr. Hileman remarked it was found the company was spending over $140.00 per month for gloves and the gloves were being wasted by employees who had no consideration of this privilege, and it was felt the best thing to do would be to discontinue this service. He remarked that it was now impossible to buy gloves in large quantities, and the only way to get them was by one or two pairs at a time.

Mr. Smith asked what machines were classified under Production Hand Screw Machines, and Mr. Kearns referred him to the wage scale in the current contract. Mr. Smith then remarked Porter Cable Machines should carry the same rate as the rough grinders, to which Mr. Kearns replied that they both carried a rate of 80c, to be increased to 91c.

Mr. Smith asked why the seat lathe could not be classed with the Warner and Swasy lathes, and Mr. Kearns replied that the tolerances on the seat lathes were not as close as those held on Warner and Swasy lathes. Mr. Smith said the seat lathe operators do not get a group bonus and that Mr. Long said it took considerable time to break a man in on this job, and he felt it should pay a

(Testimony of Clarence L. Millman.)

Respondent's Exhibit No. 1-SS—(Continued)
higher rate. Management asked time to consider
this matter until the next meeting.

Mr. Smith noticed that the company had changed
the assignability clause of the contract as submitted by the Pacific Motor Parts Workers Alliance,
and Mr. Hileman replied that it would be impossible for any company to sign a contract containing
such a clause, because if Thompson Products was
purchased by some other organization—which was
extremely unlikely—the purchaser would require a
new contract in any event.

Mr. Baldwin again brought up the subject of
maximums on the job and cited the case of ·Mr.
Davis who had been receiving slightly more than
the maximum set by the Committee on the Ajax
furnace, and who had been reduced 1c per hour.
He felt if no maximum was set on a job this reduction would not have been necessary. Management
replied that it was still considered highly desirable
to set a maximum on the rates, but that the past
record of the Management's dealings with the Pacific Motor Parts Workers Alliance should be sufficient proof that Management was willing to bargain on any subject of wage increases.

There being no further business, the meeting was
adjourned.

/S/ P. D. HILEMAN,
For the Company.
/S/ IRVIN HESS,
For the Alliance.

(Testimony of Clarence L. Millman.)

RESPONDENT'S EXHIBIT No. 1-TT

Minutes of a meeting held November 4, 1941, in the Conference Room between Committee Members, I. W. Hess, F. W. Osborne, H. C. Baldwin, E. O. Smith, and G. C. Overlander, representing the Pacific Motor Parts Workers Alliance and P. D. Hileman, George Fary, W. J. Kearns and C. L. Millman, representing the Management. Guests of the Committee were F. N. Pfankuch and H. W. McCracken.

Mr. Millman opened the meeting with the statement that Management had considered some of the rates discussed at the previous meeting and had decided to increase the torch hardening rate to 95c, electrician rate to $1.05, and the tool makers to $1.35. He then asked Mr. Hess what the general opinion of the membership had been regarding the new contract. Mr. Hess stated that the contract as submitted to the P. M. P. W. A. by the Company after revision had been rejected because of certain objectionable clauses and because of the wage scale as offered by Management. The membership at the meeting gave their Committee a vote of confidence and asked them to proceed in further negotiations with Management. It was suggested by Mr. Millman that the contract be reviewed by articles, which was done.

Article I concerning the agreement was accepted. Article II regarding representation was accepted. Article III, the agreement period, was accepted. Ar-

(Testimony of Clarence L. Millman.)

Respondent's Exhibit No. 1-TT—(Continued)

tiele IV, amendments, was accepted. Article V, assignability, was accepted. Article VI, grievances, was accepted.

When Article VII was brought up, Mr. Baldwin suggested that there be included in the contract a specification of the regular work week. Management pointed out that sometime ago a bulletin had been posted establishing the work week to start at 12:01 a. m. Monday and ending at 12:00 midnight Friday, and was agreeable to having this included in the contract, provided it applied to our present three-shift basis.

Mr. Millman asked the opinion of the employees regarding the bonus on third shift. Mr. Smith said the members felt there should be a cash bonus on the third shift as well as eight hours pay for several hours work. He stated that several of the aircraft companies had such a practice; whereupon Mr. Millman again called his attention to the fact that what the aircraft companies did could not be compared with parts manufacturers who are in an entirely different category as regards obtaining their business, and a review of the aircraft parts manufacturers shows a standard practice such as the one offered by Management of eight hours pay for seven hours work. He again reminded the Committee that this already amounted to an average of 13c per hour bonus and if it was insisted a cash bonus be paid also, it would be necessary to revert

(Testimony of Clarence L. Millman.)

Respondent's Exhibit No. 1-TT—(Continued)

to three 7½ hour shifts which would mean but 45 hours per week per man.

Mr. Overlander stated that the men do not like the six months period on second shift before receiving the 5c bonus. Management pointed out this was inserted in the contract by the Committee themselves and it was believed this period was too long. Mr. Overlander asked if this period could be changed to 3 months, which was agreeable to the Management.

At this point Management called in Mr. Geo. Stewart, Plant Auditor, who asked what extra work would be entailed by paying this extra bonus for second shift. Mr. Stewart replied if a man was on the second shift steadily there would be practically no extra work involved, but if the men were allowed to move from one shift to another the extra bookkeeping would be very considerable.

Mr. Smith asked who would be eligible to work these night shifts, and Mr. Kearns replied it seemed logical the employee with the most seniority in the department would be the man to have first choice. Mr. Hileman remarked that questions such as Mr. Smith brought up could be answered at our contemplated open forums, plans for which are now being made. It is expected a first class public address system will be installed in the lunch room and about every two months a meeting will be called for 3:15 with some member of the Management group giving a short talk on the work of his de-

(Testimony of Clarence L. Millman.)

Respondent's Exhibit No. 1-TT—(Continued)
partment and certain other members of Management would be on hand to answer any questions on company policy, rules, etc., which might be brought up at that time.

Mr. Baldwin asked how long a new machine should be in operation before a rate could be set, if the machine was performing a definite kind of job such as the Boromatic. Mr. Hileman replied this was entirely dependent upon the machine, the type of work it was doing and the difficulties that might be encountered in getting the machine set up.

The Committee went on to Article VIII concerning overtime in excess of eight hours in any one day, which was agreeable. Article IX concerned double time payments for Sundays and holidays as listed, which was agreeable to both parties.

Article X concerning report time, guarantees an employee two hours work if he is called to work unexpectedly. Mr. Baldwin asked the company's reason for cutting this time from four to two hours, and Mr. Hileman replied that the four hour period could not be agreed to because at present no instance could be called to mind where a man would be called to work and would work less than a full shift, except the maintenance crew which might be called to make sudden repairs taking possibly a half or three-quarters of an hour, and under the proposed agreement the company would be forced to pay for four hours work. It was further pointed out to the Committee that such an arrangement

(Testimony of Clarence L. Millman.)

Respondent's Exhibit No. 1-TT—(Continued)
would undoubtedly result in nobody being called
and the repair job or machine job of necessity
would be held over until the next day. This would
detract from efficiency and production of the company. After a vote of the Committee this article
was agreed to.

Mr. Overlander brought up the question of the
man who has completed his shift but who must
stay on the job until his relief comes. He wondered
if this man would be eligible for two hours pay,
but management pointed out that the man had
already completed eight hours, he would be receiving overtime and that he had not been called from
his home for any special work.

Article XI concerning general matters was agreed
to by both parties, but Article XII regarding vacations was not. Mr. Hess stated the members
wanted a definite vacation plan included in the contract. Mr. Hileman asked Mr. Hess just what the
members wanted and Mr. Hess replied they wanted
one week for one year's service with date of hire
as the determining factor of eligibility. Management offered the Committee one week vacation for
one year's service, with January 1st plus 30 days'
grace to be the eligibility date; one week vacation
to apply through nine years and two weeks for
10 years or more. Management asked that the determining factor remain as is and hereinabove set
forth.

(Testimony of Clarence L. Millman.)

Respondent's Exhibit No. 1-TT—(Continued)

Mr. Smith said some of the older men were getting less pay per hour than the newer men and should have a little better deal. Management pointed out that plenty of opportunity had been offered in our plant for advancement and it was not Management's responsibility if a man did not progress to a higher paying job. It was pointed out to the Committee the older men had been getting vacations for two years now, and the vacation plan had been a voluntary· one on the part of *the and* had been granted in recognition of the work done by the employees since the purchase of the company by Thompson Products, Inc., five years ago.

Mr. Hileman stated it might be Government orders by next year that no vacations could be granted to any defense employee but that employers would be requested to pay cash in lieu of the vacations. After a vote by the Committee it was decided to accept the vacation plan as suggested by Management.

Article XIII was next considered by paragraphs, and paragraphs 1, 2 and 3 were agreeable to both parties.

Mr. Hess said the members had taken exception to paragraph 4 because they felt Management had inserted this paragraph in order to keep them from advancing. Management denied this completely, and informed the Committee the intention had been to stop the shifting of employees at any time they

(Testimony of Clarence L. Millman.)

Respondent's Exhibit No. 1-TT—(Continued)
grew tired of their present work. A case was cited
of an employee who was very dissatisfied with his
work and asked to be transferred to another department. In an attempt to satisfy him this transfer was made, and a few months later, upon seeing
some of his former fellow workers advanced to
higher paying jobs than the one he had requested,
he asked to be transferred again. Management had
already spent two breaking in periods on this individual and would have had to suffer another one
had his request been granted. Mr. Millman offered
to rewrite this paragraph to read "except at the
prerogative of the General Superintendent when a
vacancy exists on higher paid machine and an employee had the necessary qualifications" which was
agreeable to the Committee, but Mr. Hess said it
was the older men who were complaining because
of the 12 months stipulation on a skilled machine.
Management then suggested that the 12 months
clause be stricken from this paragraph, and the
paragraph was accepted.

Mr. Hess continued to the paragraph regarding
female employees and asked permission of the Management to bring in two of the girls from the Inspection Department. Mrs. Jenkins was the first
to speak and she stated her work was visual inspection of bolts, plating and stamping, but that she
worked along side of the male employees in the bolt
department. She admitted she did not perform
set-up operations of the gauges, but that she could

(Testimony of Clarence L. Millman.)

Respondent's Exhibit No. 1-TT—(Continued)
and felt she did as much work as the male employees. Mr. Cummings stated she undoubtedly did as much work as the male employees but the male employees were required to alternate on night shifts and were capable of performing any of the jobs in the Inspection Department, including the Magnaflux machine, and it was further pointed out that the male employees perform their own set-up work on the gauges and for the most part are capable of performing either aircraft or commercial inspection. Mr. Hess asked if the girls did their own lifting of boxes containing valves and other parts, to which Mr. Cummings replied no, but Mrs. Jenkins said she had been lifting her own pans of valves from the inspection bench since the first of the week. Mr. Cummings replied if Mrs. Jenkins had been doing the work as stated for three days he had not been aware of it.

Mr. Hess then asked Miss Fought if she did the same work on valves as the men, to which she replied she did not but she did inspect all equipment valves and set up her own indicators. Mr. Cummings remarked the setting up of an indicator was a very simple job and required no skill.

Mr. Hess asked if it wasn't true that the girls remained on the job more steadily than the men; to which Mr. Cummings replied he did not believe this could be true because the men now helped the girls in moving parts which had been inspected and were of necessity away from their jobs a little more

(Testimony of Clarence L. Millman.)

Respondent's Exhibit No. 1-TT—(Continued)
than the girls. Mr. Hileman stated it appeared the
girls did approximately the same work as the men
on certain jobs, but did not possess the versatility
to do all jobs in the Inspection Department. It
was pointed out by the Management if the girls received the same rate of pay as the men it was only
logical to expect them to do the same work, including alternating on night shifts and the operation
of the Magnaflux machine.

Mr. Hileman asked for a little time to consider
this question and Mr. Hess suggested the Committee accept this paragraph pending further decision.

Mr. Baldwin suggested that the spread between
minimum and maximum rates be divided into thirds
and that whenever a man's rate was changed he be
given the amount equal to one-third the difference
between the minimum and maximum. Managment
replied there seemed to be no objection to this procedure but would like a little more time to consider
it. Article XIII was then decided acceptable to
both parties except for the notations made above. ˙

Article XIV concerning the company prerogative; Mr. Hess requested the following clause be
added "subject to this agreement and the griev-
anecs procedure contained herein" which was acceptable to Management.

Mr. Hess then turned to the wage scale and said
it was the desire of the Committee to add approximately 4c to most of these rates. He suggested the
electric up-sets carry the same rate as the large

(Testimony of Clarence L. Millman.)

Respondent's Exhibit No. 1-TT—(Continued)
hammer and the large up-setter but Management declined his request on the grounds that the large hammer and large up-setter are not bonus earning machines and, because of the higher cost of the articles handled on the large up-setter, a higher rate was felt justified. Mr. Hileman reviewed the Forge Department bonus for the past year and found the average to be a little over 7%, and noted that while in some months there was no bonus, in the other months it ran from 10 to 13%.

The Committee requested a rate of $1.05 on the large hammer and the large up-setter, which was agreeable to Management. $1.00 on the small electric up-sets, and 90c on the hammers and presses was requested by the Committee but was not agreed to by Management at that time. It was suggested a rate of $1.00 be set on the flash welding machine, and Mr. Millman remarked, in his surveys the only flash welding machine he was able to find was at Douglas Aircraft, which carried a rate of 90c top. He commented that since our Flash welders do their own set-up work he felt 96c was a fair price.

A rate of $1.00 was asked for the Ajax Press, but Management did not consent.

Mr. Osborne stated the heat treater's helpers felt their rate should carry 91c, or 25c less than the first class heat treater. Management commented there was considerable difference in skill and ability between a heat treater's helper and a first class heat treater, and did not feel a higher rate was justified

(Testimony of Clarence L. Millman.)

Respondent's Exhibit No. 1-TT—(Continued)
since a helper, when qualified, would move on to
the heat treater classification.

Mr. Hess asked that a rate of 95c be set on the
valve straightening machine, but Management informed the Committee while we could find no comparable work in this locality, our Cleveland Plant,
from which this machine was obtained, had a number of valve straightening machines and the work
is classed as unskilled. It was believed 91c was a
fair rate on this machine and a higher rate could
not be considered.

Mr. Smith said the production hand screw machine rate was satisfactory except for the grooving
lathe, whose operators wanted $1.00. He suggested
a rate of 95c. Management did not agree because it
was felt these jobs were very well paid for the skill
required.

Mr. Smith asked that 98c be set on the special
screw machines since these operators felt their work
was very nearly as skilled as the large lathes and
should carry a rate not less than 5c under the Warner and Swasy #3 and #4. At this point it was
again asked that seat lathe #167 be classed with the
special screw machines, to which Management
agreed.

Mr. Pfankuch believed the Warner and Swasy
2-A and Lodge and Shipley machines should have
a larger spread over the Warner and Swasy #3 and
#4 machines because of the fact they were work-
ing on large valves and that a greater percentage of
profit was realized on this work. Mr. Hileman in-

(Testimony of Clarence L. Millman.)

Respondent's Exhibit No. 1-TT—(Continued)
terrupted at this point to state that Marine valves
carried the lowest rate of profit of any in the plant
and that abandonment of our sales effort on this
material had seriously been considered.

Mr. Pfankuch stated he believed it required a
higher skill to run two machines as these operators
did, but it was pointed out by Management the operator would be standing idle while waiting for a
long cut to be taken on the Lodge and Shipley and
that he should be expected to perform eight hours
work for eight hours pay.

Mr. Pfankuch remarked he did work for the Tool
Room when Tool Room machines were busy, and
felt these jobs should carry a rate comparable with
the Tool Room machinists, but management
doubted that these operators would have the skill
and versatility required to operate the Tool Room
machines. It was finally proposed by the Committee that the Warner and Swasy #3 and #4 machines carry a rate of $1.05 and the 2-A Lodge &
Shipley carry a rate of $1.10. Mr. Pfankuch stated
he wanted $1.15 on this job and would just as soon
run a 3-A machine at $1.01 as the 2-A at $1.06.
Management replied, if this were the case, it might
be well to transfer Mr. Pfankuch to a Warner and
Swasy 3-A machine.

Mr. Hileman asked a little more time to consider
these requests, and Mr. Millman agreed to check
with other aircraft parts manufacturers to deter-

(Testimony of Clarence L. Millman.)

Respondent's Exhibit No. 1-TT—(Continued)
mine if a man running more than one machine was
paid a higher rate.

Mr. Hess asked that the commercial grinder rate
be increased to 95c, special grinder to $1.05 and
thread grinder to $1.00. Mr. Millman replied he
had pretty thoroughly checked these rates through
the community and found it extremely difficult to
classify each machine other than as first class or
second class grinders. Management considers the
aircraft stem grinders and cylindrical grinders as
first class; the special grinders as second class and
rough grinders, or commercial, as third class. The
average rate for first class grinders is $1.09, sec-
ond class grinders 89c. In view of this, it was felt
our grinding rates were well in line with other
rates, but these jobs would also be considered before the next meeting. Thread grinding rates carry
a 95c average for production. Gauge grinders, naturally, carry a slightly higher rate, running up to
$1.10, but it was pointed out that our work does
not compare in any way with the precision skill required to grind gauges.

Mr. Baker remarked he was now doing Tool
Room grinding and believed he should have a
higher rate. Mr. Kearns answered knowledge Mr.
Baker was doing a comparatively small amount of
Tool Room grinding, but if it was found the majority of his work was Tool Room grinding he
would receive a higher classification.

The subject of one man running two machines

(Testimony of Clarence L. Millman.)

Respondent's Exhibit No. 1-TT—(Continued)
was again raised in connection with the thread
grinders, and Mr. Millman agreed to check further
to learn if it was standard practice for one operator to run two machines.

Mr. Baldwin suggested the maintenance rate be
increased to $1.00, and Mr. Millman answered it
had been difficult to compare our maintenance rates
with those of other companies since most companies
class their maintenance men as janitors, sweepers,
carpenters, painters, etc., with rates averaging between 75c and 80c, but he had found two companies
with a top of 85c. Management felt our rate of
96c was very reasonable, but this rate, too, would
be taken under consideration.

Mr. Baldwin remarked that the steel shed employees seemed to be fairly well satisfied with their
rate of 86c, but stressed the point that while these
shearing machines required no special skill, the
work was strenuous and if Management would consider a slightly higher rate he believed it justified.
He further stated that the electrician rate had been
found to average $1.15, whereupon Mr. Millman re-
plied, in his survey he found the average rates between $1.00 and $1.15, with some electrical foremen
as high as $1.40. Management agreed to further
check these rates.

Mr. Overlander stated the Tool Room die makers
believed their work should carry a rate of at least
$1.10 instead of the proposed $1.06, but Management replied that our die work was a comparatively

(Testimony of Clarence L. Millman.)

Respondent's Exhibit No. 1-TT—(Continued)
easy type of die making. However, Management
was willing to reconsider this rate.

Mr. Overlander suggested the Tool Crib attendant's rate be increased to 95c, but Mr. Millman
stated his surveys showed this job in every case
was considered as a minor clerks job, carrying a
high rate of 75c. Mr. Overlander remarked that
for the past several months he had been grinding
shear dies and contacts for up-setting tubing, blades
for the valve straightener, and doing tool grinding.
Mr. Millman asked Mr. Overlander what the job
would consist of if not this work.

Mr. Hess said he believed the timekeeper rate
should be increased to 90c instead of the present
86c because of the fact that these men were doing
considerable production control work and the need
for accuracy was paramount, also that the men
were working under the handicap of the continual
noise both from adjacent machines and the Forge
Department. Mr. Millman referred to previous discussions on this subject, saying he had talked to Mr.
Benham and Mr. Stewart about this work but it
seemed the work consisted primarily of accurate
copy work. Mr. Fary stated it was the intention of
the Management to build sound proof booths for
timekeeping which would, to a great extent, eliminate the noise.

Mr. Smith asked the status of the young man
now acting as stock mover. He remarked this man
did not know what classification he was in, and sug-

(Testimony of Clarence L. Millman.)

Respondent's Exhibit No. 1-TT—(Continued)
gested setting a rate for stock mover. Mr. Hileman
informed the Committee that an electric hand truck
had been ordered; this man would be placed in complete charge of this truck and it was preferred to
wait until the truck was received before attempting
to set a rate on the job. Mr. Millman remarked
that when this person was hired he was told he
would be classified for the time being under the
polishers and that he was receiving the polishers
rate.

Mr. Hileman stated if an agreement was reached
on Monday, the blanket 11c increase would become
effective November 1st, but if it was necessary to
carry over into the next week it would be impossible
to make the raises effective before November 15th.

There being no further business the meeting was
adjourned.

/S/ P. D. HILEMAN
        For the Company

/S/ IRVIN HESS
        For the Alliance

RESPONDENT'S EXHIBIT No. 1-UU

Minutes of a meeting held Monday, November
10, 1941, in the Conference Room between Committee Members I. W. Hess, F. W. Osborne, H. C.
Baldwin, E. O. Smith, and G. C. Overlander, representing the Pacific Motor Parts Workers Alliance,

(Testimony of Clarence L. Millman.)

Respondent's Exhibit No. 1-UU—(Continued)
and P. D. Hileman, George Fary, W. J. Kearns
and C. L. Millman, representing the Management.

Mr. Millman opened the meeting by saying that
the contract was now ready for final approval and
suggested that he read it in its entirety; which
was done.

At the conclusion of the reading, Mr. Baldwin
remarked he noted the company had not agreed
to give an employee an answer if he had been refused a raise after being considered at the end of
three months. Mr. Millman replied that after
some consideration on this point, it was believed
such a procedure would entail so much work that
it could not be done. He pointed out that there
are now 212 employees and since these periodic
reviews would be coming up every three months,
it was definitely not practicable to notify every
man in the shop whether or not he received an increase. Under the present system, the foreman notifies the employee of his increase. If an employee
is not notified it should be taken for granted that
an increase was not made in his rate at that time.
If he wishes to question it he can ask his foreman
for the reason.

Mr. Smith referred to Article XIV, Wages and
Classification, and asked what there was to protect
a man from getting a cut in wages if the company
chose to transfer him. Mr. Millman replied that
paragraph 1, of this article, which states "an employee transferred to another department or job
shall not have his pay reduced without just cause

(Testimony of Clarence L. Millman.)

Respondent's Exhibit No. 1-UU—(Continued)
and only after a hearing of the case by the Alliance" would protect a man against taking a cut in pay without a thorough hearing.

Mr. Smith stated it was the general opinion of the employees that the maximum rate on a new job would be granted 30 days after transfer. Mr. Millman replied that this paragraph was the same as the one submitted by the Committee, and asked their reasons for questioning it now. Mr. Baldwin stated the Committee had interpreted this paragraph differently, believing that the rate now considered the maximum would be considered a minimum rate which would be given automatically. Mr. Millman pointed out it was obvious a new man was not worth the maximum on any machine within thirty days. He agreed that in some cases a man transferred to another job would be worth the maximum in thirty days, but in most cases, such as learners or employees who have taken observer training, this would not be true. He informed the Committee a survey had been made of the rates in the plant, and it was found that prior to October 1st, at which time a number of maximum increases were given, 75% of the employees of the shop who had been here for one year or more, were receiving the maximum rate.

Mr. Baldwin answered that he had been referring to the time the last contract was signed, in November 1940, and that practically no one received the new maximum set on the jobs at that time.

(Testimony of Clarence L. Millman.)

Respondent's Exhibit No. 1-UU—(Continued)

Mr. Hileman again pointed out the fact that a new maximum would not have been set had it not been for the purpose of granting the men more money, and said he believed the men who had been getting the old maximum did receive the new maximum when it was granted. If this were not the case, he wanted to know the names of the men who did not receive this rate.

·The question was again raised by the Committee of the men who are getting the maximum rate now and whether or not they would receive the new maximum. Mr. Millman referred to the minutes of the last meeting, in which it was stated by the Management that employees receiving the maximum now would be in receipt of a new maximum on November 15th. He informed the Committee that due to the large amount of paper involved, it would be necessary that the Management be allowed a few days in which to prepare the change of rate slips for men who were in a different classification under the new contract. The blanket 11c increase for all employees except those still on the starting rate or learner rate would be effective November 1st, if the contract was agreed upon during this meeting.

Mr. Hess referred to Article VIII regarding overtime and asked why the words has been added at the end of the paragraph "subject to any revision or modification of the now existing Wage and Hour Act." Mr. Hileman replied that

(Testimony of Clarence L. Millman.)

Respondent's Exhibit No. 1-UU—(Continued)
this was placed there to take care of any Government action in increasing the standard work week.

Mr. Smith asked if a man was required to work shifts steady whether or not he wanted to. The Management replied if he desired the premium for second shift, it would be necessary that he work this shift steady, but that if all three men on the machine were agreeable they could continue to rotate as they now do. The Committee suggested that some such wording be placed in the contract, and it was decided to include this sentence: "If rotation is desired on a machine, no premium for second shift will be paid".

There being no further questions on the main body of the contract, the wage scale was next considered. Mr. Millman then reviewed the concessions that had been granted by the Management and gave approximate figured on what these new procedures would do to our costs. He listed the Management's agreement for time and one-half over eight hours and double time on Sundays and Holidays, and stated it was impossible to make any estimate on cost of these two concessions, but it was obvious that the labor costs would be greatly increased. He referred to the new hiring rate and remarked it was impossible to make an accurate estimate on the increased cost, but showed that 200 men starting at 50c an hour and working a 40 hour week would cost the company $4000; whereas, 200 men starting at 60c an hour and working a 40 hour

(Testimony of Clarence L. Millman.)

Respondent's Exhibit No. 1-UU—(Continued) week would cost the company $4800. 200 men is a rough estimate of the number of new men required within the next year.

The vacation plan as granted under the new contract will cost the company $2424.00 for next year. The 5c bonus for the second shift will cost $168.00 a week. Mr. Millman informed the Committee that Management had considered these costs when viewing the wage increase asked at the last meeting over and *over* the 11c blanket increase, and found that it was impossible for the company to make any further concessions. Various surveys made through the community and through the other aircraft parts manufacturers had shown that our rates were comparable, and in many cases, above the rates being paid for like jobs, and that further adjustments could not be made at this time. He agreed that the rate for electricians according to the surveys made, was a little low, and the Management had suggested a $1.10 rate as per the request of the Committee.

Mr. Hess replied that there undoubtedly would be many complaints from the employees in the shop, and that Mr. Decker on the Ajax Press had said that he neded 50c a day for gloves. The Management was unable to see how a man could use one pair of gloves per day on this machine since he does not handle any valves but handles only the tongs.

(Testimony of Clarence L. Millman.)

Respondent's Exhibit No. 1-UU—(Continued)

The Management stated this was the best offer that could be made now, and if the men were not satisfied and could get more money at other plants it was suggested that they do so.

Mr. Hileman cited a case of an employee who owns his home in Downey, Bell or South Gate, and who accepted employment with Lockheed or Vega in Burbank. While this man may be making 10 or 15c an hour more, it was obvious that his increased transportation cost would more than make up this difference.

Also, if the man chose to move to Burbank the increase in his living expenses would be so great that he would be losing money rather than making more. Mr. Hileman asked Mr. Hess how many men were not satisfied. Mr. Hess replied that he would judge about thirty. Mr. Smith stated that practically everyone on his side of the shop was dissatisfied with the wage scale as submitted by the Management, and he had been informed he was not to sign the contract unless the Management agreed to the higher rates as requested. Mr. Hess remarked if the company would agree to furnish gloves for the employees, the present wage scale might be satisfactory.

At this point Mr. Cameron, buyer for the company, was called into the meeting and asked what the glove situation was. Mr. Cameron stated gloves were very scarce and that he could not get the usual gloves he had been buying because they

(Testimony of Clarence L. Millman.)

Respondent's Exhibit No. 1-UU—(Continued) were not available. Prices were 25% higher, and that the company had been paying $2.75 and $3.30 a dozen for the two types of gloves furnished; one for welders and Forge Department and a leather palm glove for use in the shop. He remarked it was impossible to buy these gloves in larger quantities than one or two dozen. Mr. Hess remarked there would only be ten or twelve in the shop who actually needed gloves and that the company might do well to furnish these. **Mr.** Hileman asked **Mr.** Overlander to list the jobs he felt needed gloves and **Mr.** Overlander listed the steel storage men, the platers, and sand blasters, the Forge Department, the heat treaters, the welders, snagging wheel operators, valve straightener, torch *hardner,* maintenance crew and a few on the lathes. **Mr.** Millman pointed out this was roughly 56 men, which was 25% of the shop.

Mr. Baldwin remarked the platers, sand blasters and Magnaflux machine operators required a special type of glove, and Management replied it was its intention to furnish special gloves for these operators. Mr. Bebb suggested the company buy what gloves they could secure and allow the employees to purchase them through the small stores stock room, allowing the employees the advantage of whatever discount the company could obtain. Management replied this was entirely agreeable and would be done when and if the gloves could be purchased.

(Testimony of Clarence L. Millman.)

Respondent's Exhibit No. 1-UU—(Continued)

Mr. Millman suggested the meeting adjourn for ten minutes to allow the Committee to discuss Management's proposition and take a vote. The adjournment was made at 3:45.

Upon resuming discussions at 4:30, Mr. Smith remarked that Mr. Pfankuch still felt men operating two machines were deserving of more money. Mr. Hileman replied that Mr. Pfankuch had stated at the previous meeting he would prefer working on a #3 lathe at $1.01 an hour to working the #2 Warner-Swasy and Lodge and Shipley at $1.06, and that the Management was perfectly agreeable to transferring Mr. Pfankuch. He stated that Management expects eight hours work for eight hours pay, and if necessary for a man to wait while his machine performed a job, it was only fair that the employee be expected to turn around and start another machine. He stressed the fact that it was the intention of the company to see that every man received a square deal, and if there was any man in the factory who felt he was not receiving a square deal, he, Mr. Hileman, would like to have this man come to his office and discuss the situation.

Mr. Hess referred to the last meeting at which Mr. Baker was a guest, and asked if anything had been done about the work Mr. Baker was supposed to have been doing for the Tool Room. Mr. Kearns replied a check was being made on this work and an answer would be given to the Committee at a later date. Mr. Hess asked if Mr. Ackerman, who is

(Testimony of Clarence L. Millman.)

Respondent's Exhibit No. 1-UU—(Continued)
acting as set up man in the shop, was supposed to
be getting 10c more than the highest rate in the
machineshop; to which Management replied that
this was true. Mr. Hess pointed out Mr. Ackerman had been receiving but $1.00 an hour and the
highest machine shop rate was 95c, so he should
have been getting $1.05. Mr. Millman promised
he would check into this matter and if this were
the case a check would be issued to Mr. Ackerman.

Mr. Hess then told Management that the Committee was willing to accept the contract as offered
by Management if a clause would be included guaranteeing any raises to be at least one-third of the
difference between the minimum and the maximum
rates. Mr. Millman · asked the Committee what
their reason was for insisting on this clause, and
showed them that this could work both ways, in
that if the Management wished to follow the contract to the letter, they could, in the case of a spread
of 11c or less, grant but one-third of that amount,
which would be approximately 4c. Mr. Baldwin
replied that the primary reason had been to insure
the employees that the spread between the minimum
and maximum would not be dragged out by granting 2 or 3c increases. Mr. Millman asked Mr.
Baldwin if he thought it was a common practice
of Management to grant increases for less than 5c,
to which Mr. Baldwin replied he was not aware
of this being done except in a few cases where a
2 or 3c raise was required to bring a man to the

(Testimony of Clarence L. Millman.)

Respondent's Exhibit No. 1-UU—(Continued) average maximum rate. Management was unable to see a logical reason for making this inclusion in the contract, but would agree if the Committee insisted; or would agree to attach a rider to the contract if too much protest is raised by the members of the P. M. P. W. A.

The Committee voted to leave the contract as it was for the present and to make a rider if necessary.

The subject of the Ajax Hammer was again brought up it being the opinion of the Committee that this job should pay considerably more than the other jobs in the Forge Department. After much discussion, Management agreed to set this rate at $1.00.

Mr. Hess inquired if the rate for all of the girls was to go to 75c, to which Mr. Millman replied, everyone in the shop, with the exception of the men on learner basis, would receive the 11c blanket raise effective November 1st, but all individual rate adjustments would be made November 15th. He pointed out that all of the girls who had been employed three months or more on November 15th, would receive the minimum rate of 70c, and such girls as Mr. Rogers, Mr. Cummings and Mr. Shadrach felt were deserving of the maximum rate would receive that rate on November 15th.

The Management and the Committee being in perfect accord then signed the contract with the traditional yellow and gold fountain pen which has

(Testimony of Clarence L. Millman.)

Respondent's Exhibit No. 1-UU—(Continued)
been reserved for this ceremony since the signing
of the first contract with the Pacific Motor Parts
Workers Alliance.

There being no further business the meeting was
adjourned at 5:45 p. m.

/S/ P. D. HILEMAN

For the Company

/S/ IRVING HESS

For the Alliance

RESPONDENT'S EXHIBIT No. 1-VV

Minutes of a special meeting held Tuesday, December 31, 1941, at 11:00 a. m. between the Management and the Executive Committee of The Pacific Motor Parts Workers Alliance. All members
of both groups were present with the exception of
Mr. Smith for the Alliance.

Mr. Hileman opened the meeting by reading a
letter from the War Department which had been
received that morning, in which they notified the
Management that New Year's Day was not to be
considered as a holiday and they would expect full
production for that day. Mr. Hileman telephoned
the War Department upon receipt of this letter to
ascertain if this was authentic or whether the letter had been sent in a moment of hysteria by some
person with little authority. However, Mr. Trib-
bett informed Mr. Hileman that the letter was
authentic and meant just what it said.

(Testimony of Clarence L. Millman.)

Mr. Hileman told the Committee that Mr. Millman had checked with other plants and found in almost every case the parts manufacturers were working on New Year's Day, and the ones who were not were unable to because of a shortage of material and if they worked on New Year's Day they would have to shut down just one day sooner.

Mr. Hileman suggested that the day shift continue until 3:30 p. m. and that Mr. Millman contact the DeLuxe Box Lunch Company to have them bring a lunch wagon out at one o'clock.

The afternoon shift which had been told to report at 12:30 p. m. would be asked to return home and come back at 3:30 and waive the two hours pay which the contract guaranteed them inasmuch as this was an emergency and something beyond the control of the Management. Mr. Hileman pointed out that we were desperately trying to produce war materials and that it seemed only fair that the afternoon shift agree to this.

The Committee was unanimous in their approval of this procedure and Mr. Hess suggested that Mr. Hileman call both shifts together at 12:30 and explain the situation, which was agreed upon.

There being no further business, the meeting was adjourned.

/S/ P. D. HILEMAN
For the Company
/S/ IRVIN HESS
For the Alliance.

Lightning Source UK Ltd.
Milton Keynes UK
UKHW041153150219
337249UK00016B/483/P

9 781527 984899